PENGUIN BOOKS

THE RISE AND FALL OF THE BRITISH NATION

'Every so often a book comes out that the entire political class needs to read . . . Edgerton is Britain's most exciting and arresting late-modern historian . . . this rich and compelling book . . . challenges many of the fundamental preconceptions of Brexiters and Remainers alike' Colin Kidd, *New Statesman*

'Beautifully written and can be read with pleasure by the general reader as well as the trained historian' Vernon Bogdanor, *Daily Telegraph*

'Myth-busting, stimulating and bracing . . . He demonstrates that the story the British tell about themselves is bogus' Iain Martin, *The Times*

'An unsentimental and rigorous rewriting of British history . . . It looks beyond the froth of political debate, takes business seriously and analyses government as much from Whitehall and administration as Westminster and politics' A. W. Purdue, *Times Higher Education*

'By exposing exceptionalism, Edgerton offers a timely jolt to a deluded "Bullshit Britain". David Edgerton fillets the national delusion and historical amnesia . . . of a country that knows so little of its own history' Christopher Kissane, *Irish Times*

'Brilliant' Neil Ascherson, *London Review of Books*

'Marks the apotheosis of England's foremost revisionist historian . . . Edgerton is a mixture of forensic accountant, crime-buster and naysayer who doesn't do group think. He provides the history of the gradual escalation of self-serving dishonesty. *The Rise and Fall of the British Nation* is exhaustive in its coverage and invaluable for its pitiless shredding of myths. Richard Davenport-Hines, *The Times Literary Supplement*

'One of the must-read non-fiction books of this year' Tyler Cowen, *Marginal Revolution*

'Barely a page goes by without a surprising detail or bold
challenge to received wisdom. . . . Edgerton will make you
reconsider what you thought you knew about the last hundred
years. Labour founded the welfare state in 1945? Wrong. The
Second World War as the people's war? Not quite. The British
elite were aloof and hostile to new ideas and science? Couldn't
be further from the truth' Oliver Wiseman, CapX

'A sweepingly, and ambitiously, revisionist account of
20th century British history . . . full of striking lines . . . and a
very important challenge to much of the existing historiography'
Duncan Weldon, *Progressive Review*

'Edgerton is an extraordinary historian . . . Written with
bracing élan, *Rise and Fall* generates insights at every turn.
Edgerton set out to rattle "the cage of clichés which imprison our
historical and political imaginations", and succeeds magnificently . . .
a rich and arresting account that is likely to be the central reference
for historiographical debates on 20th century Britain for a long
time to come' Nick Pearce, OpenDemocracy

ABOUT THE AUTHOR

David Edgerton is Hans Rausing Professor of the History of Science and
Technology and Professor of Modern British History at King's College
London. He is the author of a sequence of ground-breaking books in
twentieth-century British history: *Science, Technology and the British
Industrial 'Decline', 1870–1970*; *Warfare State: Britain, 1920–1970*; as well
as *Britain's War Machine*, and *England and the Aeroplane*, both published
by Penguin. He is also the author of the iconoclastic and brilliant *The
Shock of the Old: Technology and Global History Since 1900*.

DAVID EDGERTON

The Rise and Fall of the British Nation

A *Twentieth-century History*

PENGUIN BOOKS

PENGUIN BOOKS

UK | USA | Canada | Ireland | Australia
India | New Zealand | South Africa

Penguin Books is part of the Penguin Random House group of companies
whose addresses can be found at global.penguinrandomhouse.com.

First published by Allen Lane 2018
Published in Penguin Books 2019

008

Copyright © David Edgerton, 2018

The moral right of the author has been asserted

Set in 9.35/12.40 pt Sabon LT Std
Typeset by Jouve (UK), Milton Keynes
Printed and bound in Great Britain by Clays Ltd, Elcograf S.p.A.

A CIP catalogue record for this book is available from the British Library

ISBN: 978-0-141-97597-9

www.greenpenguin.co.uk

MIX
Paper from
responsible sources
FSC® C018179

Penguin Random House is committed to a
sustainable future for our business, our readers
and our planet. This book is made from Forest
Stewardship Council® certified paper.

In memory of Alicia Edgerton (1927–2019)

Contents

List of Maps

List of Tables

List of Figures

List of Illustrations

List of Abbreviations

AEU Amalgamated Engineering Union
AGR Advanced gas-cooled reactor (a nuclear reactor)
ASTMS Association of Scientific, Technical and Managerial Staffs
AUEW Amalgamated Union of Engineering Workers
AV Alternative Vote
BAT British American Tobacco
BBC British Broadcasting Corporation
BMC British Motor Corporation
BNOC British National Oil Corporation
BP British Petroleum Company, previously Anglo-Iranian
BUF British Union of Fascists
CEGB Central Electricity Generating Board
EFTA European Free Trade Association
EMB Empire Marketing Board
GDP Gross Domestic Product
GEC General Electric Company
GLC Greater London Council
GRT Gross Register Tonnage
ICI Imperial Chemical Industries
ILP Independent Labour Party
INLA Irish National Liberation Army
IRA Irish Republican Army
LRC Labour Representation Committee
LSE London School of Economics
NACODS National Association of Colliery Overmen, Deputies and
    Shotfirers
NATO North Atlantic Treaty Organization
NDLP National Democratic and Labour Party
NEDC National Economic Development Council
NHS National Health Service
NUM National Union of Mineworkers

NUR National Union of Railwaymen
PFI Private Finance Initiative
PIRA Provisional IRA
PPP Public-Private Partnership
PWR Pressurized water reactor (a nuclear reactor)
RAF Royal Air Force
SDLP Social Democratic and Labour Party (Northern Ireland)
SNP Scottish National Party
STV Single Transferable Vote
TUC Trades Union Congress
WMD Weapons of mass destruction

N

FIFE
COALFIELD
LANARKSHIRE
COALFIELD
• Kircaldy
• Edinburgh
• Glasgow
LOTHIAN
COALFIELD
Ayr •
AYRSHIRE
COALFIELD

North Channel

NORTHUMBERLAND
AND DURHAM
COALFIELD

NORTH
SEA

Newcastle •

CUMBERLAND
COALFIELD

Bradford • • Leeds • Hull
LANCASHIRE COALFIELD
Manchester •
Liverpool •
• Sheffield
YORKSHIRE
COALFIELD

IRISH SEA

N. WALES
COALFIELD
• Chester
N. STAFFS
COALFIELD
Stafford •
LEICESTERSHIRE
COALFIELD

Shrewsbury •
Wolverhampton •
SHROPSHIRE
COALFIELD
• Birmingham
WARWICKSHIRE
COALFIELD

S. STAFFS
COALFIELD

SOUTH WALES
COALFIELD
Milford •
• Swansea
Bristol • • Bath
GLOUCESTER AND
SOMERSET COALFIELDS

• London

Bristol Channel

ENGLISH CHANNEL

Coalfields of Great Britain, 1910

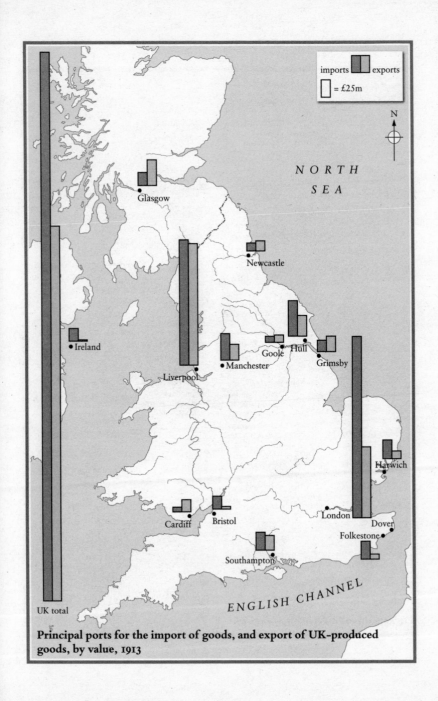

Principal ports for the import of goods, and export of UK-produced goods, by value, 1913

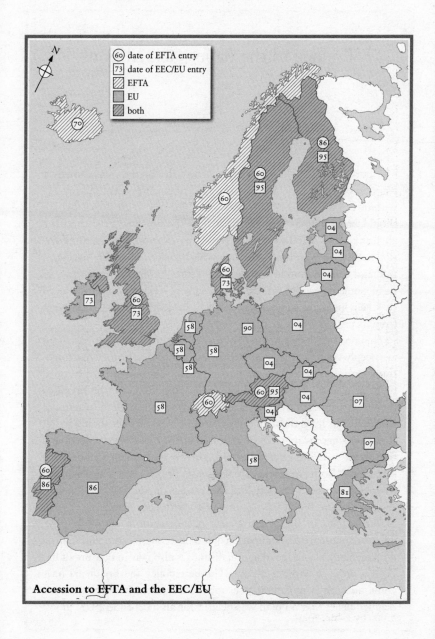

Accession to EFTA and the EEC/EU

Preface to the Paperback edition

The bulk of the book was written before the Brexit vote, though it was completed after it. I write now as Parliament rejects the May-EU withdrawal agreement. The book does not deal with Brexit (which should be known as UKexit) or indeed the financial crisis and the austerity which it followed. It ends its story in 2000, with some extension to the Iraq War. But as the topics this book deals with are so central to Brexit debates, and indeed because history has been so important in them, some reflections on this thorny subject seem appropriate. Indeed they help highlight some ways in which this British history is different from its predecessors.

This book endorses neither Remainer nor Brexiteer histories. Both are deeply wanting, not least in their insistence that history has something profound to tell us about the present because we are trapped by it, or waiting to be guided by it. We shouldn't grant the Brexiters their own argument that they are somehow in tune with the essence of Britishness as lived through centuries of history. Neither should we let Remainers get away with the repeated claim that the Brexiteers and the Brexit vote are expressing old, ghostly and deluded imperialist sentiments. Both arguments are nonsense. Brexit a is recent phenomenon, with causes in the here and now, and is opposed by roughly half the population. Brexit has nothing to do with deep history.

The politics of Brexit are a new phenomenon, a distinctly post-Thatcher one, a fresh combination of radical economic internationalism with ideological and racial nationalism. It is also new in that Brexit has been a promise without a plan. The best policy the Brexiteers have come up with is unilateral free trade. More often it seems simply a deluded belief that no plan was needed for an independent UK to just slot into its supposedly pre-ordained place as global champion of free trade. In fact, unilateral free trade would make the exciting trade deals they want impossible to negotiate, and mean the UK would be a rule-taker in every market in the world. Such indifference to the realities of global capitalism contrasts sharply with other restructuring movements of the past – in the Edwardian years Joe Chamberlain looked at future policy for tariffs in detail and with experts; in the 1940s Labour's nationalisers had a plan, of what to do and how to do it; in the 1960s and 1970s those who argued for going in to the EEC had to think long and hard as to what it meant for the UK and its allies. The Thatcherites of the 1970s also had a programme, as did the Labour Left of the time. At no time during the twentieth century could one find an influential section of the British elite so obviously deluded about how the global economy works or so keen to recreate a place for the UK it can no longer have as has been displayed by Brexiteer politicians.

How are we to explain this difference, this discontinuity in political realism? The first point to make is that Brexit was not mostly about the EU at all, but a protest about domestic politics. The second is that no serious political party or government had Brexit as its policy, indeed it was never expected to succeed. It is only after the Brexit vote that the Conservative party has become Brexiter and official organs now scream out a delusional revivalism in which Britain was now, again, an innovation nation, ready to lead the world into the fourth industrial revolution as it led it into the first, and a, for some, the, global champion of free trade. There is a cynical disregard for evidence here, but it is worth noting that the delusions are framed not in the language of empire but of British liberal exceptionalism already in use in more moderate forms by New Labour as well as the Conservatives since the beginning of this century.

Between the Brexiteers and the voters for Brexit there was an extraordinary mix of irreconcilable and inchoate nostalgias. Voters for Brexit were not voting for the radical economic cosmopolitanism of the Brexiteers. They were voting it seems for controls on immigration, at least as much from outside the EU as from within it, and for taking back national control. In the blaming of the voters there was much talk of there being poorly educated, left behinds, as well as being carriers of an imperialist virus. That missed two crucial points – that the

Brexiteers were overwhelmingly old Tories, and as Anthony Barnett points out very powerfully, were English living outside the big cities. The result of the vote was itself a discontinuity not just historically but biographically. The over-65 Brexit voters (who as one would expect would, however rich, have had fewer years of education than younger voters) would have voted in the 1975 referendum, when they voted Yes. If they were motivated by imperialism, and imperialism correlates with being hostile to European integration, what needs to be explained is why they were anti-imperialist in 1975 and imperialist in 2016.

What most struck me was the expressed desire to take back internal control, not control of others, and the sense of losing a country, by people of whom many were well-off. The book helps make sense of this. Since the 1970s, this book argues, there has been (for good and ill) a loss of national control (though not mainly to the EU). That suggests that the Brexit vote, far from being imperialist or free trading, was a cry of nationalist rage from inner England, largely from those who grew up in a national age when there was national industry making national goods. It also helps explain the old working class vote from areas which once had national industries, not least coal mines. But such has been the catastrophic and sudden decline in quality of public ratiocination in what is supposed to be a 'knowledge economy' in an 'information age' that they voted not for national renewal but for self-harm.

My account of British history is, like my account of Brexit above, a story of discontinuities rather than of invented continuities either celebratory or condemnatory. This book shows there have been extraordinary changes in the nature of the economy, its connections to empire and the rest of the world over time, and in the politics of those relations. Over time parties reversed their historical positions on these matters, from free trade to protection; from anti-marketeers to pro-Europeans. Things changed, profoundly so, even though much national discourse insists, as it perhaps must, on continuity.

What writers think they have written and what readers read are not always the same thing. A preface to a new edition gives an author a chance, having learnt a little about how a book is read, to make clearer what was intended, and to extend the argument in fresh ways in the light of those readings.

Inevitably perhaps the title of this book has been taken by some to suggest that at least in part it is a story of growth and decline, with the decline transplanted in time to the years after 1970s rather than after 1870, or 1945. But that is not so. British people got richer over the whole twentieth century, though the proportion of the world's income they controlled decreased as other peoples also became richer. As it happens that national period from the late 1940s into the early 1970s was one of high and still unsurpassed rates of economic growth, though also of rapid relative decline. Since the Thatcher years, growth was no better overall, and the global relative decline continued. For me, however, this rise and fall is nothing to do with relative economic power over time, or relative to the rest of the world. It is about the making and unmaking of the particular kind of formation I call the British nation, one which came into being through economic controls at its borders, whether of goods, or finance, or people, and through a self-understanding of itself as a distinct political and ideological unit with a certain internal homogeneity. But this is also the story of the non-national – of the openness to the world of the British economy at times, and also of Empire. It could have been entitled 'The Strange Death and Rebirth of Liberal England' or 'How the British Nation freed itself from the British Empire'.

There are some elements of the story which I have not made enough of. The first is that of course all sorts of local affiliations mattered before 1945, and some had a national character. Equally, that is true of the period since the 1980s. For the latter it is important to note that a national UK-wide welfare state is a greater presence in the economy than ever before. There are also many industries and services which are necessarily local (like transport) which may, or may not, be locally owned and run, but are of their nature local. I have made some minor changes to bring this 'foundational economy' out more. I am grateful to Jim Tomlinson for making me make this clear. I hope then that the book will not be read to say there was no national organisation before 1945 or after say 1990. But it should certainly be read to say that the balance of what is national and what is not changed very radically. A related point is that different policy and politics and were always in tension, it was just that some were stronger than others at particular times. For example, the imperial project was not dead in 1945, nor a liberal one, but a national one, weak before then, was now dominant though not hegemonic. History is complicated! More than that it is full, British history too, of ironic reversals.

Readers have been drawn most to my argument that a new nation arose from 1945, and what happened to it. Perhaps it attracts attention because this part of the story is a new story of a nation, a form with which we are very familiar. Indeed I make the point that it was in this national era that peculiarly national histories of this nation which still dominate our understanding of modern British history were written. Extending this point Adam Tooze has noted rather felicitously that right across Europe historians writing after the second world war created a short and narrow twentieth century, writing out empire and the global economic relations of Europe, and taking the story from say 1914 or 1917, or even later, as a story of nations. My book is an attempt to break out of those confines, to write both a longer and broader history, by going back to 1900 and forward to 2000 to tell non-national stories too.

However, much less attention has been given to my account of the period to 1945, perhaps because it is just too different from the national story mode to be easily assimilated, though personally I found these sections the most challenging and interesting to get to grips with. It is a story of a remarkable non-national, free trading, capitalist formation. It is a story of a powerful global enterprise, which relied on this very globality to emerge victorious in two world wars. For the more recent non-national period I make clear that this was a return to openness, but with very different consequences: the bringing of foreign capitalism into what had been the nation, rather than extending the reach of British capital. Indeed I have been surprised how little reaction there has been to my emphasis on the story of British capitalism, its economics and its politics.

In this light some words on the assumptions this book makes and the way it tells its story might be helpful. This book is not to be thought of, say, as a refutation of some deluded declinist, or a daring revision of conventional wisdom. Instead it suggests we need to understand the peculiar ways in which British history has been constructed, and that once that is clear, a new history can emerge. The book thus contains within it a thoroughgoing *critique* of the hidden and practically unknown assumptions that have been foundational to understanding modern British history. For example, it rejects the assumptions and arguments of what I take to be richest formulation of modern British history there has been – that created by the New Left of the 1960s. It is a critique too of what I see as the pioneering national histories of the 1960s, which remain central to shaping the (limited) imaginarium of twentieth century British history. They have in common hidden elements of nationalist critique of globalism and of imperialism. In these histories, and others, are many claims to historical continuity, which are in reality the repetition of a particular thesis about British history. There is indeed a long tradition of criticisms of an enduring British imperialism, using it to explain everything from economic decline to delusions of grandeur, making it not surprising at all that readers of histories, particularly of the centre and left, should blame Brexit on the empire. Nor is it a surprise that Brexiteers should come up with fanciful notions of what happened during the second world war as a key part of how they appear to think about Brexit. Such ideas were central to national and nationalist histories of the war for years, including those of the left. But the brutal reality is that there are other very different ways of telling the story of the second world war, and the politics of accession to the EEC, as this book will show.

One of the deep ways in which British history has been structured is through the welfarist assumption that New Liberalism, Labour and New Labour have been the main creative forces in British history. Thus, my brief treatment of New Labour has been criticised precisely for failing to highlight its progressive social democratic welfare measures. Yet my point was that what was most interesting about New Labour was not its welfarism but its rejection of national productivism. As far as its welfarism is concerned what is most interesting is that it did not follow from the social democratic welfarism of the 1960s and 1970s, but from the previous Tory focus on the extension of means testing. In welfare New Labour really was very different from Old Labour, just as Old Labour was very different from New Liberalism. Indeed one of the key arguments of the earlier part of the book is precisely that the 1945 Labour welfare state was an (important) reworking of a Tory welfare state for the working class dating mainly to the 1920s.

Welfare has been too visible in histories. The book also seeks to understand and overcome the ways in which many crucial elements of

British history were hidden in plain sight. For example the dominance of a certain kind of abstract political economy as the language of enquiry and debate, meant the realities of capitalism and militarism proved difficult to understand. I try to bring to light these histories, not least telling very material stories of both, to challenge highly partial ways the material is usually addressed in modernity. Pig-iron and power stations are not very visible in histories, but the politics of the past knew about them, and at times were about them.

As a result of these multiple reworkings of how we understand British history this book has an unfamiliar structure. This is obviously not a so-called political history – in fact a term for one-administration-after-another histories – but nor is it a thematic history which goes from chapters on politics, to the economy to society and culture, with each interpreted through the schemes developed by modern economists, sociologists of welfare, and literary critics. Instead each chapter develops elements of an argument, layering on the previous ones, and within them interleave different aspects of history each understood in much more historical and critical ways. All this makes for a complex read at times, but adds a depth that could not otherwise be achieved at all compactly.

For this paperback edition, as well as making some clarifications as noted above, I have corrected an error on public spending in the Thatcher era and given more details on welfare under New Labour, as well as correcting a few other detailed points, thanks to some observant and knowledgeable readers, among them Catharine Elliott who spotted a subtle error in my rendering of the Romans in Britain trial over which her father presided. Peter Mandler by chance told me that he had discovered that the biography of a post-war writer I had included in the first edition was in fact invented by its subject. Alas the book was already in press, but I have excised it from this edition, and look forward to Peter telling the whole real story, which is even more interesting than the invented one. I have also taken the opportunity to straighten out many convoluted sentences and paragraphs.

London, January 2019

Introduction

*Objectivity is not the same thing as conventional judicious-
ness. A celebration of the virtues of our own society which
leaves out its ugly and cruel features, which fails to face the
question of a connection between its attractive and cruel
features, remains an apologia even if it is spoken in the most
measured academic terms.*

Barrington Moore Jnr, The Social Origins
of Dictatorship and Democracy *(1966)*

The past, it has been said, is another country, but twentieth-century
British history is a familiar place. We know how it looked, how it
changed, how it thought. We know its heroes, its villains and its story-
lines. This book offers an unfamiliar when, why and who of British
history, reflecting transformative historical research of recent years.
This research, in social and cultural history, but also in economic,
political, imperial and military history, has not only widened the
scope of recent British history, but perhaps most significantly also
refreshed and revised accounts of core themes. We can now write our
history not just as observers of the theatre of government but as ana-
lysts peering behind the scenes in Westminster and Whitehall, and
indeed beyond. We can distance ourselves from national sentimentalities about people, politics and parliament. We need not follow the
politicians and pundits of the past or present in focusing on the welfare state, or the empire, or economic decline or more recent revival.
We can address ideas from the outside rather than writing from
within them, and can discuss national stories we do not take at face

value. Above all we can engage with the question of power in its many dimensions, both power within the United Kingdom, and the power of the United Kingdom. In other words, we can study the history of the United Kingdom as we might study that of Germany or the Soviet Union. As well as making the past foreign we need to take account of foreigners in our national history. While this point would be obvious in the historiographies of Germany and Russia, it bears making for the UK.[1] The United Kingdom did not just forge itself – it was made as other nations were, and other nations had a great impact on its making. If the United Kingdom was distinctive in 1900, and it was in astonishing ways, it was transformed over the century into a nation much like other rich nations. In making the United Kingdom's national past different, at times unsettlingly so, I hope to render it less suitable for the political purposes it currently serves.

This book tells the history of the United Kingdom around a core theme of the twentieth-century rise, as well as the fall, of something I call the British nation. The United Kingdom, just like Ireland and India, Canada and Australia, had its own post-imperial, indeed anti-imperial, nationalism, though one which could not speak its name. This nationalism, which flourished from 1945 to the 1970s, manifested itself in, for example, the internal rebuilding of the nation. A British nation was created, by which I mean a distinctive economic, political, and social unit within the borders of the United Kingdom. This new British nation was then unmade. The many barriers between the British nation and other nations were pulled down from the 1970s, a process which in part meant a return to the situation existing at the beginning of the century. Rise and fall refer to these processes and not to the rise and decline of British power, or the rise and fall of the British Empire, or the British economy, which concerned an entity different from the British nation in my sense. Indeed, as I show, it is a mistake to conflate nation, empire, power and economy: each had different dynamics. Untangling them is a central concern of the book, and it does so by highlighting the rise and fall of a very distinct object. This British nation is something a history of the United Kingdom should necessarily be centrally concerned with, but it has been curiously invisible, for reasons to be discussed.

The British nation, as I define it, was not a natural state of affairs.

The British nation was created: it emerged out of the British Empire, and out of a cosmopolitan economy, *after* the Second World War. Leaving behind empire entailed the rejection of imperial citizenship and imperialism and the development of a peculiar kind of nationalism. Leaving behind economic liberalism meant creating not just an economic border but increasingly a culture of national self-supply. None of this was the product of a choice by the British elites, who favoured free-trading and/or imperialist projects, but they were thwarted by many brute realities. Taking serious note of this British nation, and in that light, what came before and after, provides richer explanations for many well-known elements of the story of the United Kingdom, from its politics, to its economics and foreign relations, to the evolution of its welfare state and more, than conventional histories do. It also allows previously marginalized aspects such as the warfare state and the history of its capitalism into the picture in fresh ways.

The term 'British nation' requires some more explanation. It was used in the early nineteenth century, meaning the political nation within the United Kingdom, and less so in the early twentieth century, when its meaning often extended to encompass a broader empire.[2] For the remainder of the twentieth century it was barely used, even as a term of art. In my account, 'British nation' refers unambiguously to the United Kingdom as a whole rather than to a larger entity such as the British Empire, or a smaller one, such as England and Wales. It is important to note that 'United Kingdom' was itself a term barely used in political and historical discourse through most of the century. It was the preserve of statisticians, diplomats and the military. But its use is now required in historical work in recognition of legal and economic realities. I don't use the term 'Britain' except when actors did, which was often. After 1945, especially, 'Britain' was the standard usage in politics, and in histories, apparently shifting its meaning between Great Britain and the United Kingdom without warning.

The national moment was the time of what might be called a developmental state, one of many features of the nation which have been supposed not to exist (among the others in older accounts are militarism and technocracy). This was the time (and not the nineteenth century) when the United Kingdom was at its most industrial. It was also the moment when it was refashioned by the state to look much more like its continental neighbours, with conscription and development of national agriculture, and protected industry. Ideologically it generated national rather than imperial histories, a nationalist critique of cosmopolitan capitalism and a powerfully nationalist declinism. Thinking of this period in this way is a more explanatory alternative than the common references to Keynesianism, the welfare state, decline, social democracy and consensus. It allows us to rethink the politics of the Labour Party, which I see as much more national productionist than welfarist after 1945. It also allows us to rethink the story of racism and immigration, and of emigration. It also points to the need to think of foreign policy in new ways, from the Suez invasion to going into the Common Market. I see the former as a national not an imperial war, and entry to the EEC not as moving from liberalism and empire to protectionism and subsidy, but from economic nationalism to a European economic liberalism.

Making the national element explicit allows us to notice the vital non-national features of earlier and later periods. Recognizing its temporary nature allows us to also write what might seem paradoxical – a non-national national history. For while nationalism has not been overt in histories of the United Kingdom, a certain methodological nationalism which assumes away the nation and nationalism overtly, but covertly makes both central, has been.[3] Taking seriously the nationalism of the national period allows us to see that in the first decades of the twentieth century cosmopolitanism, and imperialism, were central. This allows a reasoned account of the very great differences then existing in its economic structure and military posture compared with the nations and empires of continental Europe. These differences are of vital importance in understanding British power in two world wars – it was based on its position as a great trading enterprise, as well as an imperial one. British power at its peak was not national power, but rather a form of global and imperial power.

Turning to the end of the twentieth century, I suggest we can only understand the move to economic liberalism from the 1970s, and especially the 1980s, if we recognize the significance of previous nation-building. Thatcherism relied on the earlier successes of national development to make it workable, whether self-sufficiency in food or the expanding welfare state. The great transformation of the economy from the 1980s followed from its reintegration with the external world to such an extent that it no longer made sense to talk of a national economy. In addition, the United Kingdom ceased to have a distinctly national capitalism and became instead a major financial centre, now largely for the capital of others. The re-emergence of subnational nationalist parties from the 1970s made a specifically British nationalism politically ever more incoherent as well. New Labour more than the Conservatives embodied this new non-nationalist politics and economics.

The central concern of this book, the British nation and what came before and after it, is supplemented by considering three main subthemes: the stories of British capitalism, of militarism and the state, and of political economic ideas. These are not there to provide colour or context, but are central to the story itself. My aim especially in telling very material stories of capitalism and militarism is to suggest fresh ways of thinking about British history more generally, rather than to provide material examples to supplement existing stories. British capitalism, to be understood not just as the market system, or the political doctrine of liberalism, but as the private ownership of capital, was at the core of the economy through the century. This capitalism was never merely abstractedly financial, though it has often been treated as such. The story of British capitalism was one of particular metals and textiles, of factories and farms, of managers and workers, of plants and of animals, from pit ponies to continental cattle breeds, both in the United Kingdom and overseas. British capitalism, as well as geology, made the United Kingdom the largest exporter of energy in the world down to 1939, as well as the largest exporter of manufactures. British multinational enterprises operating overseas supplied the United Kingdom, the largest importer in the world at the beginning of the century. Ships of many types, and ports, docks and warehouses were as central to it as factories. British capitalism, its global, and especially European reach, was a source of strength, not weakness. Although it became relatively less important, it was at least into the 1960s one of the three great capitalisms of the world, and far more successful than its many critics contended. But in the recent past it is hardly possible to speak of British capitalism, and to the extent it exists, it is hardly confined to or even dominant within the United Kingdom.

The success or otherwise of British capitalism was the central issue in British politics through the century. More than this, throughout, but especially before 1945, British capitalist families supplied many members of the political class including prime ministers. The two main political parties into the 1920s were parties of capitalists, as was the dominant political party of the rest of the century. The Conservative Party was in office for nearly seventy of the 100 years of the century, and at least thirty years in each half of the century. The politics of capital – whether of free trade versus protection or national versus global – were the central political fights of the twentieth century. There was a politics of returns on investments, not mainly of investments in the empire, but in the British national debt. Capitalism was also, of course, a matter of class, and this book discusses business, politics and the politics of labour very much within this context. The Labour Party was a party which, while it wanted to do away with class distinction, was created and maintained by the organized employees of a class-divided society and needs to be understood as such. Its relationship to power was structurally different from that of the other main parties.

The second theme is not so much war as the warfare state. The United Kingdom was long distinctive in its approach to warfighting, opting for machines over men. Its distinctive liberal militarism was a thoroughly modern way of war, one which, like British capitalism, needs to be understood in its material manifestations, not least great battleships and long-range bombing aircraft and atomic bombs. Only from 1945 did the United Kingdom conform to the European pattern of conscription in peacetime. The warfare state was always strong, and at the core of the state, and shaped the United Kingdom, the rest of the empire and much of the world so as to emerge victorious, with allies, in two world wars. The Dunkirk/Blitz Churchillian national moment of 1940 and 1941 was, in my account, the last moment of the British Empire, and the global United Kingdom, as a great power, a period which ended with the Japanese conquest of Malaya. The warfare state was also central to the internal story of the colonial empire – it was kept by force, kept going in part to preserve military bases and lost by an inability to use enough force to keep it. British imperial power flowed out of the barrel of a British gun, not the Anglican Bible or textbooks of liberal political economy. The empire was not lost or given up; it was taken away. In matters military the national moment was brief, its life that of the short-lived independent national nuclear bomb. It gave way to a policy of dependence on the USA, from as early as the late 1950s, though the fiction of an independent bomb and defence policy was maintained. Yet the post-national period saw the creation of a new expeditionary force and new claims for the need for a global military capacity – bizarrely and tragically British arms returned East of Suez from the 1990s. The warfare state, like the story of British capitalism, makes clear that empire needs to be kept in proportion. The empire was far from the only foreign entanglement – Europe was generally more important.

The third theme is ideas. We need to recover the nature and power of the key animating ideas, not least the powerful assumptions that undergird national histories – the idea of the centrality of governments, rather than the state, of Westminster rather than Whitehall, of 'political' ideas rather than economic or scientific ones. The key set of ideas discussed in this book are summed up by the term 'political economy', which I take to be the central language and conceptual scheme for understanding and acting in the twentieth-century United Kingdom. It is an abstract, universalist language which hid as much as it illuminated, yet was the language not only of politics, but of thinking about international relations, and indeed of thinking about the nation. The most important form was liberalism, with its cosmopolitanism, its economism and its internationalism. It was hugely influential in shaping even British militarism, whose central ideas owe more to British liberalism than to jingo Tories or US imperialists. Liberal political economy was the language of the key public intellectuals from Beveridge to Hayek and beyond. It is also important because of what it made difficult to think about or describe. One cannot get a full enough picture of the economy from within the conventions of liberal political economy, Keynesianism included. Political economy even rendered the empirical manifestations of a capitalist economy invisible – its abstractions had no need for the discussion of particular capitalists or particular firms. The British left, steeped in political economy, itself notably failed to write an account of actual British capitalism, of British militarism, of the British state, and instead, in nationalist mode, criticized British capitalism for not being British enough and the nation for being subservient to the militarism of others. Social democratic political economy was weakly developed, at least until the 1970s, as was Marxist political economy. The language of class has been important, but not class analysis.[4]

British nationalist political economy is much less familiar not least because it had little overt presence. I associate it mainly but far from exclusively with Labour, though only after 1945. This is in contrast to the more common view in which Labour is seen as a weak carrier of social democracy, which is itself seen as the main alternative to liberalism. But nationalism too was a great challenge to both liberal and imperial orthodoxies and was, I suggest, at least as important as weak forms of socialism in the British case. I think, for example, that the actual post-Second World War United Kingdom was in some ways better prefigured in the programme of the Tories and the British Union of Fascists (BUF) than that of the Liberals or the Labour Party. Although explicit nationalist political economy was a rarity, it was to become implicit in much economic commentary, concerning everything from the balance of payments to research policy. As economic practice it was very important.

Nationalism was also important in history-writing. Like historians in other post-imperial formations, whether Hungary or Australia, or Ireland, British historians from the 1960s especially created national histories of the twentieth century, which downplayed and/or criticized the imperial and global context in which the proto-nation existed. Many national histories tended to criticize the United Kingdom for not being national enough, and were both national-celebratory and declinist. They also downplayed the fact that the United Kingdom was and is a country of countries, a nation of nations – England, Wales, Scotland and Ireland. These national histories, mostly written by the centre-left, especially those from the 1960s, tended to tell the story of the nation in terms of the rise of the welfare state. Other key concepts deployed in national histories were such notions as appeasement, consensus, Keynesianism, post-war settlement, people's war, decline, welfare state, affluence, permissiveness, reconstruction and indeed neo-liberalism. Such ideas have powerfully constrained the writing of histories, much more so than they constrained or explained the actions of historical actors. We no longer need to think with such clichés, but rather with new principles which help us understand the power they once had.

This book has a much greater focus than most on the right rather than the left, on capitalists rather than workers, on liberals, imperialists and nationalists rather than socialists, on warfare rather than welfare, on the material rather than particular assumptions about the material. The consequence is not to ignore the welfare state, the Labour Party and social democracy, and the empire – all staples of histories – but rather to put in a new light. For example, Lloyd George's people's budget, so called, funded the building of battleships and not only the emergent welfare state. The Great War led, in the 1920s, to the creation, by Conservatives, of a comprehensive, specifically working-class welfare state. This was extended by Labour in the 1940s, as a national welfare state, and transformed in the 1960s and 1970s. In the 1940s welfare had a lower priority, for the Labour government, than warfare and production, understood very nationally. Peak welfare in terms of generosity arrived in the 1970s, and in many respects very much later, and came into its own only with the decline of the warfare state, and indeed of the weight of industrial production. The empire was an alternative to globalism, a controversial one, desired by a fraction of capital and the Conservative Party in particular. Empire was an economic, political and racial project, which very largely failed. The British economy was in fact at its most imperial in the 1940s and 1950s, long after the ideological or military heyday of empire.

Much recent historical work on the United Kingdom has stressed the significance of imperialist ideas, seeing nationalism as indivisible from imperialism. In fact nationalism needs distinguishing from imperialism. If we do so we can see the significance of nationalist critiques of imperialism, from both the right and the left. Many on the left have for a long time attacked British imperialism and its domestic consequences long and short term from a national perspective. They have blamed militarism, economic decline, racism, global pretensions and more on it. Some external force, it seemed, had corrupted the true beneficent nature of the British, whose mission to, say, rid the world of nuclear weapons was being thwarted. Even on the left, there has been a deep reluctance to criticize close to home. Over-playing the significance – economic, ideological and political – of empire has been at the expense of understanding non-imperial, indeed national, sources of inequality, racism, economic problems and militarism too. Blaming empire and imperialism has let the guilty get away scot free!

In histories of the twentieth-century United Kingdom we have to take into account what I call anti-histories. Anti-history is a history of opposition to things which the commentator values, leading to the dis-appearance from history of what such histories intended to promote. Thus the national project was invisible partly because the nation was not nationalist enough in that it was always too imperial and too lib-eral for nationalist critics, especially of the left. Promoters of military power wrote the military out of British history, putting in its place a peculiarly powerful liberal pacifism and/or imperialist illusions. Declinism rendered positive economic growth and change invisible and emphasized backwardness and immobile continuity from the nine-teenth century. Successful British capitalism was buried in mountains of evidence of what supposedly thwarted it, like aristocratic culture, cosmopolitan finance and empire. It is said, by those who wanted the United Kingdom to join the Common Market, that it damagingly resisted European integration because of the strength of imperial, global and US orientations, such that it was not possible to explain why it in fact applied as early as 1961. C. P. Snow and many followers insist on the patently delusive thesis that science was smothered by the condescension of an elite of novelists and poets. We need to take account of this particular form of historiography from below, in which the realms of elite practice – of soldiers, scientists, politicians, and economists and politics – generated their own sets of historical stories. They have been very influential in telling stories now so tangled that they could be described as things that never happened being routinely explained by imaginary argument and evidence. Instead of being a his-tory of absences, this book makes power present.

Although it is rightly observed that most history is the history of elites, for twentieth-century British history this is perhaps not the case. Paradoxical as it might seem, British labour is better known than British capital, the working class than the ruling class, trade unions than businesses. The reason is clear – histories reflect visibility in the public sphere. Welfare, trade unions, and labour had to operate publicly, in a way which British capitalism, given its power, never did. Thus the welfare state has been much more visible than the warfare state, the welfare sociologist more visible than the defence intellectuals. Many men operated in the public sphere while most women were confined to a separate private world. Private British capitalism was less visible than public nationalized industries. Socialists have been more present than reactionaries, Labour figures more than Conservative ones. Liberalism as ideology is much more visible than capitalism as practice. The state has been more visible than the private sector, the state pension more than the occupational pension, the ordinary old-age pension more than the military pension. The imperial, extra-European orientation has been more visible than the orientation towards Europe. Immigration by non-white people has been more visible than that by white people, or the very important white emigration. Indeed, one of the threads running through the book is a concern with what was public and what was private, what was open and what was closed, visible and obscured. The mere visibility of ideas and of things is no guide to their significance; the visibility of arguments no guarantee of their plausibility.

This, then, is a history in many dimensions – cultural, political, economic and military – which is sceptical of the standard analytical apparatus used to understand British history. The very ideas which structure historical accounts, how they conceptualize the nation, the economy, war, knowledge, need to be challenged, it suggests. It is sceptical, too, when it comes to many key claims. It is a history full of paradox and contradiction, of ideas often out of kilter with reality. However, the main point is to tell a coherent story at a time when the old apparent certainties have crumbled, one which is more consonant with what we now know and what we now need. That includes more description of what for earlier generations would have been obvious, and a stronger analytical grip than older narrative histories allowed. I hope that by the end of this book the reader will find it obvious that just as no British historian would dream of writing a history of the Soviet Union or Germany without ideology, militarism, nationalism,

I. G. Farben, the Wehrmacht, Magnitogorsk and the Dnieper dam, no British historian of the United Kingdom should ignore British militarism and nationalism, Imperial Chemical Industries and the Royal Air Force. If there was a German iron cage of modernity there was assuredly a British one too. But I also hope the reader will reflect on how and why histories without one should have made so much sense to generations of readers.

History has played and continues to play a powerful role in British public life. The past is appealed too as explanation of the present, as legitimation for this or that policy, the place where a true national essence is revealed. The issue is not that historical perspective is lacking in policy and politics, it is very obviously present. The issue is the kind of history that is in play. I hope that for those in public life, for those concerned with politics and policy, this book will help liberate us from the conventional framings of British history and all they imply for political action. For I show again and again that history was not destiny: things changed, radically so, over time. Not only are there many pasts, there are also many histories. The histories of this or that episode, the national as a whole, are not the same in every book. History, like politics and policy, is, or rather should be, a contended matter. In any case the time is long overdue for a good rattling of the cage of clichés which imprison our historical and political imaginations.

PART I

1900–1950

The first half of the book covers the period 1900 to 1950. This is an unusual periodization – starts in 1914 or 1918 and breaks in 1939/40 or 1945 are more common. Beginning in 1900 allows analysis of much that was novel around 1900, in politics, economics, ideology and industry, and to explore fully the extraordinary global liberal economy the United Kingdom was central to. 1950 has the convenient arbitrariness of being halfway through the century, but there are other points in its favour. While the 1940s as a whole are usually taken as the most important beginning in twentieth-century British history, they were more of an ending than might be obvious. The 1940s welfare state was in many ways the fixing of that of the 1920s. In military terms 1941/2 saw the ending of the British Empire as a great power. Economically force of circumstance kept the United Kingdom tied to the past: the years 1945 to 1950 saw the rebuilding of the Edwardian economy, while rationing from 1940 into the 1950s froze the interwar diet in time. While many historians have taken the period 1939–51 as a whole, I emphasize the importance of changes from 1945, a dramatic rupture with the internationalism of the war, the emergence of a workers' party with power for the first time and a distinctly nationalist programme.

This part consists of nine thematic chapters. Each can be read independently, but they build on each other, developing common threads of argument. The first chapter introduces the themes of nationalization through the analysis of the politics of free trade and empire, and the history of the party and political systems. We then proceed through chapters on war and militarism, the transformations in energy and food supply, the nature of the British ruling class and

3

its relation to politics, and on to the industrial economy. The story then shifts to ideas, focusing on those most relevant to statecraft, war, economics and politics, with a chapter on ideas and another on plans for the future. Only then do we get to two chapters on workers, the rise of the Labour Party and the creation of the welfare state, once the central themes of histories of this period, including the wars. Here they are seen in a new light, and in new contexts.

Parliaments, governments and prime ministers, 1900–1950

Parliament	Government	Prime Minister
1900	Conservative / Liberal Unionist	Marquess of Salisbury
		1902 Arthur Balfour
	Liberal minority	1905 Henry Campbell-Bannerman
1906	Liberal	Henry Campbell-Bannerman
		1908 Herbert Asquith
January 1910	Liberal minority	
December 1910		
	1915 Coalition	
		1916 David Lloyd George
1918	Conservative / Lloyd George Liberal	
1922	Conservative	Andrew Bonar Law (prime minister for a week before as well)
		1923 Stanley Baldwin
January 1924	Labour minority	Ramsay MacDonald
November 1924	Conservative	Stanley Baldwin

1929	Labour minority	Ramsay MacDonald
	1931 National	
1931		
		June 1935 Stanley Baldwin
1935 November		1937 Neville Chamberlain
	1940 National / Labour / Liberal Coalition and brief 'Caretaker' National Government	Winston Churchill
1945	Labour	Clement Attlee

NB: detailed election results are available online. Note that summary results for the Conservatives usually include those for Liberal Unionists and Ulster Unionists and for 1945 the various Liberal Nationals and National Labour. In the interwar years there were various Liberal parties.

I

The Country with No Name

The Englishman has long been used to living in a certain haze as to what his country is – whether England, or England-and-Wales, or Great Britain or the United Kingdom of Great Britain and Northern Ireland or the United Kingdom plus its dependent territories or that larger unit which he used to call the British Empire ...

Sir Dennis Robertson, speaking to a US audience, 1953[1]

The inhabitant of London could order by telephone, sipping his morning tea in bed, the various products of the whole earth, in such quantity as he might see fit, and reasonably expect their early delivery upon his doorstep; he could at the same moment and by the same means adventure his wealth in the natural resources and new enterprises of any quarter of the world, and share, without exertion or even trouble, in their prospective fruits and advantages ... The projects and politics of militarism and imperialism, of racial and cultural rivalries, of monopolies, restrictions, and exclusion, which were to play the serpent to this paradise, were little more than the amusements of his daily newspaper, and appeared to exercise almost no influence at all on the ordinary course of social and economic life, the internationalization of which was nearly complete in practice.

John Maynard Keynes, The Economic Consequences of the Peace *(London, 1919)*

Side by side, unaided except by their kith and kin in the great Dominions and by the wide Empires which rest beneath their shield, the British and French peoples have advanced to rescue not only Europe, but mankind from the foulest and most soul-destroying tyranny which has ever darkened and stained the pages of history. Behind them – behind us – behind the armies and fleets of Britain and France – gather a group of shattered States and bludgeoned races: the Czechs, the Poles, the Norwegians, the Danes, the Dutch, the Belgians – upon all of whom the long night of barbarism will descend, unbroken even by a star of hope, unless we conquer, as conquer we must; as conquer we shall.

Winston Churchill, 'Be Ye Men of Valour',
broadcast 19 May 1940[2]

I was very glad that Mr Attlee described my speeches in the war as expressing the will not only of Parliament but of the whole nation. Their will was resolute and remorseless and, as it proved, unconquerable. It fell to me to express it . . . It was a nation and race dwelling all round the globe that had the lion heart. I had the luck to be called upon to give the roar.

Sir Winston Churchill on his eightieth birthday, 1954[3]

'You can't understand Great Britain when all you know is the island itself'. This resonant banality came from the lips of the German industrialist and philosopher of industry Walter Rathenau addressing the Austrian novelist Stefan Zweig.[4] It was hardly original. It half plagiarizes the British writer Rudyard Kipling, who asked: 'what should they know of England who only England know?' The line comes from his poem 'The English Flag, 1891', an attack on the street-bred English, who did not know what the British did abroad, especially in the empire, where Kipling was born. The expression, which became a cliché, has a lot going for it. To understand the United Kingdom (and not just Great Britain, or England) one needs to know its peculiar relations with the rest of the world. This was not, as fans of Kipling might imagine, primarily a question of empire.

The United Kingdom's relations, economic, military and political, with foreigners, mostly Europeans, like Rathenau, were almost always more significant. The United Kingdom's economy was quite exceptionally open. Its people, ships and factories were spread all over the world; its largest wheat fields and its abattoirs were abroad, and its coal fuelled a whole hemisphere. It was not, in short, self-contained. The story of the United Kingdom was not, for the first half of the twentieth century, a domestic, insular story, nor a merely imperial one, even in two great wars.

In 1900 the United Kingdom was (comparatively speaking) cosmopolitan, liberal, free-trading with the rest of Europe and the world, and part of a much larger British empire. It was the world's greatest importer and the empire the world's richest and most populous. By 1950 the force of foreign events and the evolution of domestic politics created a novel situation which satisfied neither internationalists nor imperialists. By 1950 the United Kingdom had national borders impermeable in ways they were not in 1900. While the United Kingdom had been part of an empire, it now *had* an empire, but a much reduced colonial one. It was part of a Commonwealth of Nations, but one which was no longer British. It had been changed, by what happened abroad, more than by the desires of its people.

The new British nation increasingly knew only itself. The character of its politics was different from what had gone before. Now the nation was at the centre of politics, and for the first time one-person-one-vote was achieved. The Labour Party, which transformed the character of the House of Commons in 1945, saw itself as a new sort of national party whose politics were those of the collective, national interest. Politics was now national politics, based on the politics of class, of production and of national social services. Whereas once politicians addressed 'the nation' – a term of unclear geographical scope, and in any case referring to a notion of a political community, not all the people – they now spoke of 'Britain'.

To understand the history of the period 1900–1950 we need to think our way out of national assumptions and enter a world in which the nation as it existed in the third quarter of the century was not yet in existence, nor yet even much argued for. The political story of the United Kingdom can usefully be framed as a contest between two programmes or projects: the liberal, internationalist, free-trading one and the imperial-protectionist one. Imperialism was probably more visible than liberalism. But the third option, nationalism, is practically invisible, and insofar as it is seen, it is as a feature of the Second World War. This trio of positions may be compared with the standard implicit story which is that liberalism, perhaps liberal-imperialism, was superseded by a weak socialism or social democracy in the war or after 1945. Events, foreigners, elevated nation over Empire or the world economy, after 1945.

FREE TRADE

Whether measured by stocks or flows, the United Kingdom in 1900 was a place of plenty. The great fluxes of modernity – materials, people, information – passed through it as nowhere else, in unprecedented density. The United Kingdom was the largest importer as well as the largest exporter in the world. Trade followed the potentials of capitalist production, not empire. Telegraphic traffic with the United States was much greater than that to British Africa; tremendous tonnages of British coal flowed into the Baltic, but not the Caribbean.

It was the only major free-trading economy on earth, the most exposed and integrated into the trade of the world. Anything could be imported into the United Kingdom free of duty, excepting those applied on such things as tobacco, alcohol, sugar, tea, hydrocarbon oils, for the purpose of raising revenue and which were applied (many only in principle) to domestic production too. Indeed, indirect taxes, including the internal excise and the external custom duties, accounted for nearly half of state revenue before the Great War. All other countries of any size were defined by economic borders which protected domestic industrial and agricultural producers. In the first half of the twentieth century the United Kingdom imported about half its food and, as a consequence, had the lowest agricultural population of any major nation. It was easily the most urbanized and industrial, which it could not have been had it needed to grow its own food. There was nowhere else like it. Much of the success and wealth of the United Kingdom was attributed to the policy of free imports.

The United Kingdom was rich, and in a poor world stood out as such. The territory of the United Kingdom had the highest average income per head of any European national area. It was exceeded only by that of the United States, and was comparable to that of the main white British dominions, Canada, Australia and New Zealand. Germany and France, while rich by the standards of most of Europe, were poorer. That comparative wealth was central to understanding its politics, the nature of its armed forces, the power of its business class and much else. Indeed, contrary to what might be inferred from a generation of declinist histories, the United Kingdom would stay without question the richest large economic area of Europe into the 1960s.

Free traders pointed out repeatedly that most of the United Kingdom's trade was with countries outside the empire, not least in Europe. Most imports of meat, wheat, sugar, fruit, came from 'foreign countries' rather than 'British countries'. For most raw materials, the empire was not very important at all – cotton came largely from the southern USA, while bulky imports, such as iron ore and timber, came mainly from Europe and its immediate environs.

Free trade was a major ideological and moral cause, not merely because it argued for laissez-faire economics. It was often anti-imperialist and anti-militaristic, and called for a genuine internationalism, and was most certainly hostile to nationalism.[5] For the free trader, nation did not compete with nation. It made no sense to talk of British trade – only individuals and firms traded with each other. In this scheme of things there was no reason to favour one trader over another – the exporter over the importer, or the producer over the consumer, and in a significant gendering of this argument, of the male producer over the female housewife consumer. The 'English', said H. G. Wells, were a 'world people'.[6]

Free traders objected to their very core to the new Conservative imperial/national project. From the beginning of the century this called for a new Great Policy, as it was known, for protection of the national economy and preferential trade within the empire, following the lead of some dominions. It meant differentiating between British and non-British territories, including the 'informal empire' (fully foreign countries such as Argentina, where British capital and political influence were important), to create an imperial economic block. It was meant to effect a change in direction of trade, to loosen economic bonds with the people of the world and to promote both the national and the imperial economy. These protectionist-imperialists promoted the view, influentially so, that the United Kingdom depended on empire for raw materials and food, when their argument was that it should, not that it did. The free traders responded by arguing that where states tried to make political borders correspond to economic borders they impoverished and degraded themselves. Imperial Germany, which did so, was seen by free traders not only as nationalistic and militaristic, but as a place where wages were low, bread was brown, and meat came from horses and dogs.[7] The Conservative campaign failed. The free-trading Liberal Party won the election of 1906, fought on this issue, with a huge majority. The 1910 elections, thought of as being about the welfare state and the House of Lords, were at heart about whether the state should be funded by taxes or tariffs. Free trade won again, just.

The 1906 and 1910 elections were not the end of the matter with respect to free trade. The Great War led to measures which free-trading liberals regarded with distaste. The wartime coalition, formed in 1915, when Conservatives joined the existing Liberal government, introduced what some liberals regarded as Prussian measures: conscription and some economic nationalism. In September 1915, the Liberal chancellor of the exchequer, Reginald McKenna, introduced a $33\frac{1}{3}$ per cent levy on luxury imports in order to fund the war effort. It fell on such things as motor cars (but not commercial vehicles), musical instruments and gramophone records. When the wartime coalition went to the polls in 1918, it noted that 'One of the lessons which has been most clearly taught us by the war is the danger to the nation of being dependent upon other countries for vital supplies on which the life of the nation may depend.' Thus they proposed that 'key industries' should be supported, and dumping controlled. Imperial preferences would be given.[8] The non-coalition Liberals, and the new Labour Party, in its first outing as a major party, remained loyal to free trade: 'Labour is firm against tariffs and for Free Trade,' they said, and looked to new international labour legislation to make 'sweating impossible'.[9]

The coalition won the election and introduced many protectionist measures with imperial preferences. It continued the McKenna duties and introduced the Safeguarding of Industry Act, 1921. The duties on manufactured goods under the act did not affect empire, which did not export such goods. Where imperial preference mattered was in a 1919 measure which granted imperial preference on revenue duties on sugar, dried fruit and tobacco.

Table 1.1: The United Kingdom's most important suppliers and export markets, 1928

Imports from £m		Exports to £m	
USA	188	India and Burma	83
Argentina	76	Australia	55
Germany	64	USA	46
India and Burma	64	Germany	40
France	61	Eire	35
Canada	57	Canada	34
Australia	54	Argentina	31
Denmark	53	South Africa	31
New Zealand	47	France	25
Eire	45	Netherlands	21
Belgium	43	New Zealand	19
Netherlands	43	Belgium	17
Egypt	26	China	16
Sweden	22	Brazil	16
USSR	22	Japan	15

Source: Board of Trade (in conjunction with the Ministry of Labour and the Registrars-general), *Statistical Abstract for the United Kingdom for Each of the Fifteen Years 1924 to 1938. Eighty-third Number*, 1939–40, Cmd. 6232, pp. 370–75, 378–81.

The story of interwar politics can also usefully be understood as, in part, the politics of free trade versus protection. David Lloyd George was deposed in 1922, to be succeeded by Andrew Bonar Law of the

Conservatives. He was succeeded by another Conservative, Stanley Baldwin, who called an election in an attempt to get a popular endorsement for protection. He failed to get a majority, and the result was the short-lived first minority Labour government under Ramsay MacDonald. It phased out McKenna duties and cut the revenue duties. It also wanted in principle to abolish all customs and excise duties, all the indirect taxes. The Labour Party, which from 1922 had around 30 per cent of the popular vote, was deeply committed to free trade, as openly and proudly so as the Liberals. The Labour government did not last long, and Baldwin was returned with a majority in the 1924 general election, following moderately protectionist policies. In 1929 the Conservatives stood on a more limited protectionist programme and again failed to get a majority. The new minority Labour Party which came into office that year was as committed to free trade as it was to financial orthodoxy and the continued search for a new international order. Their policy to deal with the Great Depression which enveloped the world from 1929 was to maintain the pound fixed to the value of gold, to retain free trade and to stimulate world trade and reduce British prices to increase British exports. The government collapsed with MacDonald deserting Labour to form a National government with the Conservatives in 1931, which went to the country within a few months and got a huge mandate for protection. The National government, with strong public support, would continue in office alone to 1940. Its three prime ministers, Ramsay MacDonald (1931–5), Stanley Baldwin (1935–7) and Neville Chamberlain (1937–40) would all later acquire reputations for inaction in the face of poverty and unemployment at home and the rise of the dictators abroad. Yet they did pursue what the Tories saw as a very positive new approach – protection.

The transition to protection was ideologically dramatic. Liberals were, of course, deeply opposed, but so was Labour. The left was almost universally free trading and internationalist. Even mildly protectionist voices, such as the leader of the largest trade union, Ernest Bevin, found their propositions rejected. In a speech to the Trades Union Congress (TUC) in 1930 he stated: 'The object of the world federation would be, from our point of view, to create an easy access to the raw materials of this planet.' But Bevin went on to say that it might be necessary and useful to create a 'Commonwealth bloc', given that either an Atlantic or a European bloc was not practical, and empire development was a good thing even if he was not an imperialist. There was opposition from within the TUC on the grounds that tariffs were a capitalist policy; that an empire bloc was artificial since there was no such economic unit; what it really meant was greater colonial exploitation. Others worried about dividing the world into antagonistic blocs – that led to war. Miners worried it would bring ruin to the export of coal, practically none of which went to the empire. Ernest Bevin could only say in response that he was not endorsing empire free trade but wanted a licence to face realities. The TUC left Bevin's option open.[10]

Perhaps the most important Labour protectionist was an MP who had crossed the floor of the House of Commons from the Conservatives. The dashing Sir Oswald Mosley, a hereditary knight and a former Royal Flying Corps pilot, resigned from the government in 1930 over the issue. In the short term he wanted to deal with unemployment, then rising very fast, with early retirement, later school-leaving and public works. But, what was most interesting was his plan for a much more national economy (see also pp. 165–7). He claimed that it was no longer possible to export as much as before, and that the country should export only enough to get essential food and raw materials. He was against exporting in order to invest abroad on a huge scale, as was the case before 1914, or to import luxuries.[11] In his view imports needed controlling. Tariffs were not enough: import control boards were needed to promote domestic agriculture and other industries.[12] He quickly moved from this nationalist position to a more imperialist version. But the Labour left, while keen on the planned trade he called for, could not stomach the imperialism, so he dropped it.[13] Mosley's 'New Labour Group' opposed the expenditure cuts the government made in 1931 and six members resigned to form the protectionist New Party. It failed miserably in the 1931 general election and would turn into the radically nationalist British Union of Fascists. The party articulated the thesis that the City of London had, as its main business, investment overseas, which brought a return in the form of imports into the United Kingdom and which therefore undermined the economic nation.[14] This was to become the standard thesis of economic nationalists of the left, too, but only later, as we shall see in Chapter 6. For the moment it is important to note that the nationalism of Mosley's position is insufficiently recognized, just as the significance of protection was not sufficiently recognized by historians writing after the economy became supposedly Keynesian.

Protection versus free trade was a central element in the 1931 general election. This is not very obvious because the usual framing of the election is as a contest between something like Keynesian reflation and financial orthodoxy, with Labour and Lloyd George on one side, and the recently created National government on the other. But the challenge to orthodoxy came not from Keynesian reflationists but from protection. And that challenge came not from outsiders, but from the Conservative Party itself.

The National government was formed in the summer of 1931 under the prime minister, Ramsay MacDonald, to effect the policy of cuts in expenditure. It was a coalition which the Conservative Party dominated, but also had a handful of MPs elected for Labour, and Liberals. This government was forced to take sterling off the gold standard, allowing it to devalue. The various parties in the National government stood in a general election soon after, but each on their own manifesto. The dominant Conservatives called for 'Empire Economic Unity', which meant tariffs, and quotas for cereals. Indeed, the need for protection was practically the only point their manifesto made. Their minor partners, MacDonald's National Labour and the Liberal Nationals, were confused on this key issue. The free-trading Liberals also supported the National government. The main opposition – the Labour Party and the Lloyd George Independent Liberals – were, however, firmly in favour of free trade. Labour was categorical:

> The Labour Party has no confidence in any attempt to bolster up a bankrupt Capitalism by a system of tariffs. Tariffs would artificially increase the cost of living. They would enrich private interests at the expense of the Nation. They would prejudice the prospect of international co-operation . . . In the face of the millions unemployed in high-tariff America and Germany, they are clearly no cure for unemployment. They would permanently injure our shipping and export trades and conceal our need for greater efficiency in industrial organisation.[15]

The winners were the Conservatives and protection.[16] In November 1931 the newly elected government pushed through immediate tariffs on the pretext of preventing dumping. In February 1932 the Import Duties Act was passed (over which members of the cabinet were allowed to differ in public, an innovation not to be repeated until the 1975 Common Market referendum). The act was the work of the protectionist chancellor of the exchequer, Neville Chamberlain, son of the original Edwardian advocate of the measure. Conservatism, imperialism and nationalism had, after a long fight, won.[17] National Labour's Philip Snowden, who had been the ultra-orthodox Labour chancellor 1929–31 now resigned from the government with two Liberals (the home secretary, Sir Herbert Samuel, and Archibald Sinclair), and a couple of junior ministers, because they still believed in free trade, and did not like the imperialist Ottawa agreement. The government now had only three National Labour ministers, and the only Liberals in the coalition were Sir John Simon's Liberal Nationals, who for decades would be stronger in parliament than the Liberals who stayed out of or left the National government.[18]

Opinion quickly shifted in favour of protection. The liberal economist Maynard Keynes now waxed lyrical about the benefits of national self-sufficiency.[19] Amongst his heretical thoughts were that tariffs on cars had created a British car industry; that steel could be modernized behind tariffs; that domestic agriculture was a good thing; that tariffs could indeed save jobs; and that the quality of jobs mattered. As he put it: 'Free traders, fortified into presumption by the essential truths – one might say truisms – of their cause, have greatly overvalued the social advantage of mere market cheapness, and have attributed excellences which do not exist to the mere operation of the methods of *laissez-faire*.'[20] The Labour Party too shifted its position in favour of protection, slowly and silently. Thus it was that by the late 1940s both major parties, which now dominated politics, were in practice protectionist, a change of great significance, but usually invisible precisely because it ceased to be a matter of contention. If the politics of free trade was very visible and public, the politics of protection became private and complicated, but no less important for that.

At first the British tariff was restricted to 10 per cent on manufactures, from which empire producers (of which there were few) were entirely exempted. Following the 1932 Ottawa conference on imperial trade, tariffs were raised and extended, granting further imperial preference.[21] However, the unwillingness of British imperial territories to open their own markets to national British production meant that empire free trade remained a pipe dream. For the policy of the protectionists, in all parts of the British empire, was nation first, empire second, foreigners third. And that was the rub – it was never empire first. Nationalism trumped imperialism, all over the empire.

Within the empire there were struggles over tariffs *against* British goods. The case of India is especially revealing and important. A minimal amount of self-government was granted to India in 1919 over the objections of 'die-hard' imperialists. India could now set its own tariff; in 1931 it raised it, for *British* goods, from 11 per cent to 25 per cent. A higher still Indian tariff applied to non-British goods. The British cotton industry launched a campaign to get the British government to intervene to lower Indian tariffs, which it would not, and to stop the process of giving even greater powers to Indians through the Government of India Bill, proposed in 1934. This became a highly sensitive issue in Lancashire, which voted Conservative, where the cotton industry was concentrated. In late 1934 and early 1935 Sir Oswald Mosley (whose family had been lords of the manor in Manchester), now at the head of the British Union of Fascists, campaigned on the policy of removing the Indian tariff against British cottons, claiming that, with other restrictions, this would create 65,000 jobs in Lancashire.[22] His was a policy of making India an open market, but only to British goods.

In this case the wider politics of British India trumped the interests of Tory voters in Lancashire. The Conservatives were able to manage not only the die-hard opposition to the Government of India Bill, among whose partisans was Winston Churchill, but also the industrial interests of Lancashire.[23] In fact the British government intervened secretly to sustain the interest of Lancashire, at least marginally. The Japanese had pressured the government of India to reduce tariffs, with a threat to reduce Japanese purchases of Indian raw cotton. London promised to buy any cotton the Japanese would not, stiffening the resolve of the Indian government.[24] Furthermore, the Indian tariff came down a bit for British goods, from 25 to 20 per cent in 1936. The direction of travel was clear, however. British textiles, for which the Indian market had been pre-eminent before 1914, would lose out, and the government of India would become ever more Indian.

The idea of the imperial economy was also challenged from outside the empire. During the Second World War the heavily protected United States of America re-entered the world economy through its own overseas military operations. As part of the price for lend-lease of arms and materials to the United Kingdom the United States exacted a promise from the British government that it would give up imperial preference in the future. But it lived on.

In the 1940s and 1950s British trade was more imperial than it had ever been. This was not primarily a matter of choice. Imperial trade was a necessity, as the war broke what were central trading relations with Europe, and they took time to restore, not least given the poverty of the war-racked economies of the continent. The Labour Party, which came into office in 1945, presided over a protectionist, state-controlled economy, with a strong imperial focus. Even in 1950 the Conservative Party was calling for an Imperial Economic Conference.[25] Furthermore, imperial preference was supported by both the imperialist right and the left as a shield against the USA.[26] Economic imperialism affected even the Communist Party. Its leader called for mutual economic assistance at the level of the old empire; like an interwar imperialist he demanded: 'Our locomotives for wool; our coal for cotton; our textiles for wheat . . .' He claimed, unconvincingly, that these policies were quite unlike those of Lord Beaverbrook.[27]

EMPIRE

Thinking about imperialism from the perspective of the economy has important benefits. First it highlights the significance of opposition to imperialism in the United Kingdom. Secondly it makes clear that the British economy was at its most imperially oriented (though trade was overwhelmingly between the by then independent dominions and the UK) in the 1940s and 1950s, and not in the Edwardian years, as can too easily be assumed. Thirdly it helps underscore the point that imperialism was in a crucial respect not an orthodoxy but a

THE RISE AND FALL OF THE BRITISH NATION

challenge to it. It was also always a plan, a project, more than a reality.[28] It was the political project of the Conservatives. Empire was central to party education, and to the writing and thinking of ideologues like the popular historian Arthur Bryant. The term 'empire' figured repeatedly in the party manifestos of the interwar years – imperial preference, imperial defence, imperial unity, imperial development being constant themes (Labour ignored empire, and stressed national development and national ownership and in the 1930s national planning). Whether or not empire was important to the public is an open and debated question, whether it was important to the political elite is not.

British imperialism and the empire were complex and multi-faceted, making them difficult to describe. Thus, while the British empire was regarded by much of the British elite as a good thing, imperialism was not. The British empire was not imperialistic in the way other empires were or had been, for example the Spanish empire. Even the king-emperor denied the empire was imperialist. Speaking by radio on Empire Day 1940 to his people at home and overseas, he noted: 'There is a word our enemies use against us – Imperialism. By it they mean the spirit of domination and the lust of conquest. We free peoples of the Empire cast that word back in their teeth. It is they who have these evil aspirations.' This was not an idiosyncratic royal opinion, but the official view. Pro-imperial propaganda insisted on the benign and different nature of British imperialism, and was conscious of anti-imperial sentiment.

The fact that an Empire Day existed might suggest that there was an official imperialism. Yet the story of Empire Day itself points to its limits. It came about through private initiative from 1904. Some schools began to celebrate it, and it gained the support of local authorities and worthies, though its supporters lamented that it was more enthusiastically taken up overseas than at home. During 1916 Lords Milner and Meath got some official recognition for it, in that government buildings would fly the flag on the day, but they had to insist that Empire Day was not a manifestation of militarism and jingoism, or even imperialism. They claimed it stood for one king, one flag, one fleet, one empire; that it was non-party, non-sectarian, non-aggressive, non-racial. While this was hardly a frank account of

British imperialism in which systematic racial exclusiveness and segregation was routine, it was significant that this is what was claimed.

The British empire was unique in scale and nature, even if having an empire was not uniquely British. It is not well described by its most common representation – the map covered in pink. For it was not the land mass of the empire that mattered, or that the sun never set on it, but its great wealth and vast population. The wealth was concentrated in the temperate territories of white British settlement, Canada, Australia and New Zealand, which were as rich per head as the United Kingdom. These territories came to be known, from the Edwardian years, with South Africa, as the dominions, and later collectively with the United Kingdom, as the British Commonwealth of Nations. They were intimately connected to the United Kingdom as suppliers of certain foods. If the wealth and trade was concentrated in the dominions, the population of the empire was concentrated in desperately poor India, which had a population of 300 and more million souls, far more than any colonial territory of any other power (the closest was the Dutch East Indies with around 40 million). Every other territory was below 10 million in population. India accounted for four-fifths of the British empire. Only China had a larger population.

Just as there was never one empire economically, so there was never one administratively. The United Kingdom was governed by a complex set of departments of state, some of which covered the whole empire, others the United Kingdom only, and others only parts, like Ireland, or England and Wales. Outside the United Kingdom parts of the empire were administered by different Whitehall departments. There was an India Office and a Colonial Office and from 1925 a separate Dominions Office (dealing with Canada, Australia, New Zealand, South Africa), encapsulating the different relations with white dominions, India, and the colonies. The colonies were of differing types. There were also a whole series of protectorates, mandated territories (for example Palestine), as well as places clearly in the British sphere of influence such as Egypt, Iraq and Persia. There were at least four civil services manned by UK officials – the Home, Diplomatic, Indian and Colonial services; and two big armies, the British, and the Indian. The dominions, the economic core of empire, did not

THE RISE AND FALL OF THE BRITISH NATION

have London-recruited or directed civil services or armed forces. The empire was never one thing.

Yet there was, in the Edwardian years and later, a tendency to think of the empire (defined in different ways) as one body politic, with its capital in London, its second city in Glasgow. In this picture, the United Kingdom was part of the empire, not something which had an external empire. Thus the Committee of Imperial Defence, an Edwardian development, was the key British defence policy committee, while the chief of the imperial general staff was the professional head of the British army. The monarch was notionally at the head of one united empire. The parliament at Westminster was also known informally as the 'imperial parliament' (usually in a nineteenth-century usage, as the parliament which covered the whole United Kingdom, as it did from 1801). It was imperial in the sense that it passed legislation covering subordinate governments and legislatures, among them the Commonwealth of Australia Constitution Act, 1900, the Government of Ireland Acts, of 1914 and 1920, the Irish Free State (Constitution) Act, 1922, and the Government of India Acts of 1919 and 1935. The powers over the dominions (that is Canada, Australia, New Zealand and South Africa) were effectively abolished in 1926, and in statute in 1931, with the creation of the British Commonwealth of Nations, of independent dominions, represented to each other by high commissioners (ambassadors in all but name). It is telling that Scottish nationalists of the interwar years argued not for independence from the United Kingdom or the empire, but rather that the whole empire be recognized as Anglo-Scottish: it had the union of two nations at its heart – Britain was Anglo-Scotland, not England writ large (as the histories nearly always had it).[29]

Furthermore, in some respects the empire did act as one body, and was certainly presented as doing so. The whole British empire went to war in 1914. The war was presented as one fought by the empire as a whole, with for example the numbers enlisted given as those for the whole empire, sometimes divided into white (7 million) and other races (1.5 million). An imperial war cabinet was formed, with representatives from the dominions. The burial places of service personnel were in the custody of the Imperial War Graves Commission, created in 1917 by Fabian Ware, a pre-war pro-conscription imperialist, editor of the Tory *Morning Post*. An Imperial War Museum was created also in 1917 and also as a memorial to the Great War. The Tomb of the Unknown Warrior in Westminster Abbey, commemorated the 'many multitudes' who gave 'life itself for God, for King and Country, for Loved Ones, Home and Empire, for the Sacred Cause of Justice and the Freedom of the World'.

The identification with empire was far from complete. Only in Great Britain and some dominions (but not in Ireland or the rest of the empire), was conscription successfully imposed. British soldiers did not, to judge from most war memorials, die for 'King and Empire'. They died, in most cases, for 'King and Country', in which there is a studied and necessary ambiguity in 'country'. They died for a country with no name. Many memorials invoked, like the Westminster Abbey one, notions of fighting for freedom, and for honour.[30] All these complexities are encapsulated in the prominent monument erected next to the National Portrait Gallery to commemorate the execution of Edith Cavell, the Florence Nightingale of Belgian nursing, who had long lived in Brussels. She was shot by the Germans in 1915 for aiding the escape of Allied soldiers from occupied Belgium. The biggest letters are reserved for the word 'HUMANITY', but above them we find 'King and Country'. Added later after pressure from women's organizations supported by the Labour prime minister Ramsay MacDonald were the words 'Patriotism is not enough'.

The Second World War was at its beginning also a war presented as one in which the empire fought as a whole. After the fall of France in June 1940 if anything was alone it was the entire empire, not the 'island nation'. No one in authority could or would have said 'Britain stood alone' – that was a phrase from post-war nationalist history books. Indeed, 'alone' was a rarely used term – the standard image was that of a fortress or citadel, a forward base of an empire, and/or the forces of freedom. The empire had allies, even in 1940–41. The mood was more internationalist than imperialist and would become more so. There would be no imperial war cabinet this time. From early 1942 the war was fought by the 'United Nations'. There was still, however, a measure of imperial accounting, as when the United Kingdom government noted that four-fifths of the arms in use by the 'British Commonwealth and Empire' came from within, and only one-fifth from the USA.[31] Furthermore, across many battlefields the world over, the empire had fought as one, and been presented as doing this.

Hardly surprisingly, then, there was imperial feeling after the war, not least in connection to the recent war. When Princess Elizabeth addressed the nations of the empire from South Africa on her twenty-first birthday in 1947, she spoke in terms of empire not nation. It was the 'British family of nations', she said, which had the 'high honour of standing alone, seven years ago, in defence of the liberty of the world'; the 'British Empire has saved the world first, and has now to save itself after the battle is won'. There the future queen, still on the throne today, declared: 'My whole life whether it be long or short shall be devoted to your service and the service of our great imperial family to which we all belong.'[32] As we shall see, by the time she was crowned in 1953, the implied unitary empire had already gone.

Subjects of the British crown were in principle equally free and could move freely from one imperial territory to another. This was certainly true of white ('European') subjects, but not in general. Systematic racial discrimination was central to the British empire and it was codified in the border controls of, for example, 'White Australia', which in its essentially racist policies did not discriminate between empire and non-empire. For many official positions throughout the empire one had to be 'of European descent' as well as being a British subject. In different forms there were essentially racial administrative distinctions made. The empire, in so far as it was a project, was also a racial project, with white rule over subordinate and carefully segregated peoples. A strict racial ordering determined everything from voting rights to housing to job segregation. The Indian railway colony, African mines and Caribbean plantations operated not merely with whites at the top and locals at the bottom, but with intermediate racial and economic groupings, like the Anglo-Indians in India, or the Indians in the Caribbean and Africa.

Quite overt discrimination applied to local 'natives' all over the empire, not just South Africa. Even when in the United Kingdom itself subjects of the crown faced different treatment based on colour. There were small but well-known non-white communities within the United

Kingdom. They were concentrated in port cities and associated with seafaring. Around 120–170,000 British seamen were employed on British ships, along with 10–20,000 foreigners and 50,000 lascars.[33] The Indian lascars were the main group of non-white mariners but they were joined by Chinese or African ship-board workers. They lived in specific areas close to the docks, like the communities in Limehouse, and Bute town in Cardiff. Their position was precarious. They could be and were thrown out of the country, irrespective of marriage to locals. The Second World War saw more arrive, notably from the West Indies, to serve in the forces, and in industry.[34]

When the troopship *Empire Windrush* (a requisitioned German passenger ship, hence the prefix *Empire* which was given to all government-owned vessels) landed in Tilbury in 1948, carrying black British subjects from the Caribbean, it attracted negative attention, and has become a symbolic starting point for immigration. Yet the *Empire Windrush* was far from the first ship to bring West Indians to the United Kingdom, as is clear from the fact that many of the men on it were returning to it. Indeed, one-third were either in the Royal Air Force or returning to re-enlist (many had served as mechanics during the war, and some as aircrew). For many West Indians arriving in the United Kingdom in the 1940s and 1950s the shock was not the imperialism of the British, but the lack of it – these British failed to recognize the West Indians as fellow, equal, subjects of the empire, as the official version of empire required. They found that race and nation trumped empire. The West Indians, the Chinese and the Africans were in fact outnumbered by new immigrants from Europe.

THE EMERGENCE OF THE NATION

As we have seen there was a powerful imperial dimension to the British war effort in the Second World War, though it receded rather quickly. The empire which entered into the Second World War suffered a great defeat in the east in 1942. The consequent ramping up of the liberation struggle in India led to India following Ireland (a case to be discussed later) out of the empire in 1947. The dominions became in effect independent members of the 'United Nations' rather than being fully constituent parts of the British empire. They developed a more national and a more US-focused orientation. This happened to the United Kingdom also. The United Kingdom of Great Britain and Northern Ireland of the late 1940s can usefully be seen as one of the new nations which arose from the dissolution of the one empire. For when the war was accounted at its end, the statistical tables, the listing of the dead, were not, as they had been after the Great War, tabulated for a British empire, but rather for the United Kingdom alone. The official histories, too, would focus on the United Kingdom, rather than the units which actually organized and fought the war.

The war came to be written about in national terms, as a nation that looked inwards, and changed itself internally. From 1945 it was said that 'Britain' had been alone during 1940–41, and it would soon be said that a new nation had been forged in the Battle of Britain and the Blitz. From the 1960s, 'alone' was regularly used in histories to describe 'Britain' in 1940–41. The national 'alone' was not a myth of 1940, but a post-war creation, part of a general process of nationalizing the history of the war. Churchill deployed the 'island nation' rhetoric in 1945 not in 1940. It was indeed the central national myth, laden with possibilities and meaning well beyond its immediate reach. It came to be linked, again, long after the war, with the idea that a new nation, and a new politics, was born, in what became, from 1940, a 'people's war'. In this later account, the war saw many social and economic advances. Churchill ran the war front, but Labour ran the home front, and set in motion what would become the post-war welfare state. In this national framing the story of empire is the story of the loss of imperial territory, through a process of decolonization. What is missing is the sense of parallel emergence out of empire – for the United Kingdom too was, in important ideological and constitutional senses, a part of empire, not merely the owner of an empire. This was a process invisible in standard historical accounts.

A national United Kingdom arose after 1945. To be sure, it was still multi-national and indeed this was a period in which Northern Ireland had Home Rule, and a prime minister of its own. Still, it is notable that Northern Ireland, Unionist dominated, enacted its own legislation over vast areas of concern, but generally followed

Westminster, even in the case of the socialist National Health Service, because the Union came first. Most importantly, the whole United Kingdom formed a self-consciously national economy, which was directed and controlled, forced and exhorted to export, and to restrict imports, irrespective of where they went to or whether they came from 'British countries'. Economic propaganda did not distinguish between exports to empire and foreign markets, though sterling imports were much preferred over dollar imports. That the Labour Party was elected with a distinctly nationalist but non-imperial orientation was important. Labour promised in 1945 to create a 'Socialist Commonwealth of Great Britain' (thus excluding Northern Ireland) and did not bring itself to use the term 'empire', and made only the most cursory mention of the 'British Commonwealth' and 'Colonial Dependencies'; on the question of India, it advocated only the 'advancement of India to responsible self-government'. It was not accidental that its main policy was called 'nationalization'.

The United Kingdom also became a separate body from the empire in that it got its own nationality. Under the British Nationality Act 1948, a new national-imperial person was created, the Citizen of the United Kingdom and Colonies. This was a 'common citizenship', as propaganda insisted.[35] The colonies, looked after by the Colonial Office, were in the Caribbean, Africa and the Far East (numbering around 60 million people). These imperial citizens were now distinguished from another new and much larger category: the Citizens of the Independent Commonwealth (dealt with by the Commonwealth Relations Office, formed in 1947). The need for the act arose because Canadians wanted to have their own nationality, and through it British nationality (rather than the other way around). The United Kingdom, too, had to define its nationality in an analogous way. The act gave citizens of the United Kingdom and colonies the same rights of entry as the Citizens of the Independent Commonwealth. Indeed, the main concern was to give free access to citizens of the white dominions, whose ranks were once again being filled by encouraged emigration from the United Kingdom. Yet it created a distinctively different nationality for the members of the Commonwealth, distinct from that of the United Kingdom.

This new British nation was much more welcoming to aliens than it was to its own non-white overseas citizens. In this it reflected a long history of openness to Europe. Edwardian London was not as cosmopolitan as New York, but it was cosmopolitan rather than imperial in its composition. Although from 1905 the United Kingdom restricted the immigration of aliens, they could and did come in, and they were often naturalized too. The Irish, even after full independence, were never treated as aliens. But there were many aliens. There were Germans and Italians, working at many levels and in many industries; there were 'Russians', usually Jews from Poland (until 1916 in the Russian empire), concentrated in the east end of London. In the Great War there were thousands of Belgian refugees. During the Second World War the country had large numbers of Poles and Czechs, Norwegians and Dutchmen, soldiers, sailors, airmen and civilians. After the war more than 100,000 Poles were allowed to remain.[36] A recruitment drive among refugees in Europe brought in over 345,000 workers, mainly men.[37] By 1950 the United Kingdom had a population of European migrants of well over a million, including the Irish. The Pole, Irish, Ukrainian or Balt, was a more common sight than the non-white imperial citizen; white aliens alone (excluding the Irish) were more numerous and welcome than British blacks.

A new national monarchy appeared, though this was well hidden behind imperial and Commonwealth imagery. When Queen Victoria died on 22 January 1901, her son, King Edward VII, was proclaimed 'By the Grace of God, of the United Kingdom of Great Britain and Ireland and of the British Dominions beyond the Seas King, Defender of the Faith, Emperor of India'. His son, King George V, was crowned with the same title, but in 1927 the 'United Kingdom' disappeared from it. He was now 'King of Great Britain, Ireland, and the British Dominions beyond the Seas'. His son, George VI, retained this style but had to give up the title of emperor of India (though he was briefly king of India and, for a little longer, king of Pakistan), though the Irish no longer recognized him as king from 1937. From 1949 the Commonwealth of Nations, at Indian insistence, was no longer British. Queen Elizabeth II, who came to the throne in 1952, was to be Queen of the United Kingdom, and separately and distinctly of specific other places too. She was a post-imperial monarch.

This new national United Kingdom did not declare itself a new formation. Indeed there was much left over from the past – from liberalism and internationalism to imperialism – which allowed a story of continuity to be told, as indeed it should be. But the break was real enough even if not advertised in the sort of language that made clear what was going on. One reason was that the very notion of nationalism was very problematic at the heart of the empire.

Yet the signs were there. In 1951 a great national exhibition was opened, called 'The Festival of Britain', labelled a 'Tonic for the Nation'. In the past exhibitions of a comparable scale and scope had been imperial and not national. 1938 saw a vast Empire Exhibition in Glasgow. In 1924–5 there was a British Empire Exhibition at Wembley in London, which included a new Empire Stadium. This stadium was known as such at least into the 1960s, though it is now remembered as the old Wembley Stadium.[38] But just as for the British there could never be any such thing as British imperialism (as opposed to the British empire), so there could be no such notion as British nationalism (as opposed to the nation). Nationalism was in British understanding an ideology which threatened the empire, and indeed the nation, not something a British nation could itself have.

IRELAND

Ireland was the first nation to emerge out of the British empire in the twentieth century. Into the early twentieth century the majority of the Irish people were represented at Westminster by the Nationalist Party. Indeed, 'nationalism' and the 'national' were from this moment terms particularly associated with the opponents of empire, with anti-British sentiment. Among them were the Indian National Congress (1885 – better known as the Congress Party), the African National Congress (originally 1912) and many more. This was the context in which British nationalism would make little sense to most British people, though Irish, Scottish, Indian and African did. Nationalism in British parlance was the doctrine which encapsulated the dubious claims of natives, whether Indian, African, Irish, Scottish, Welsh (and only sometimes of allies). Indeed British imperialism paraded itself as anti-nationalist. As Jawaharlal Nehru, leader of the

Indian nationalists, put it in the 1930s: '[British] Liberals and pacifists and even so-called socialists ... chide us for our narrow
nationalism, and incidentally suggest to us that the way to a fuller
national life is through the "British Commonwealth of Nations".'[39] In
this view the empire prefigured an interdependent liberal association
of nations; its enemy was the nationalism of others, and the nationalisms within it. On top of this, nationalism was what dangerous
continental enemies espoused. Nationalism was, in the official British
liberal view, what brought disaster to Europe twice over. Prussians
and Nazis were nationalists; to be British was to be anti-nationalist.
It was a matter of pride that the British did not go in for the displays
of nationalism or imperialism newer, vulgar, nations needed. British
stamps and coins had the figure of the sovereign but needed no further identification. British schoolchildren did not salute a flag, or
recite patriotic poems.

The Irish Nationalist Party, for decades the third party in the
House of Commons, wanted what was called Home Rule for the
whole of Ireland, within the United Kingdom. In this they were supported by Liberal governments, who passed Home Rule bills which
were rejected by the House of Lords, and a sizeable majority of the
political class. 'One Law, one Land, one Throne' was, as in Rudyard
Kipling's notorious anti-papist and anti-Irish poem of 1912, a slogan
of the Unionism which resisted the very idea of Home Rule. It was
not until 1914, after the powers of the House of Lords had been
trimmed, and when the Liberal Party was dependent on the support
of the Nationalists in the House of Commons, that the Home Rule
Act was passed. The leader of the Conservative Party and senior army
officers openly stated they would not accept the verdict of the imperial parliament. This was the other great issue of Edwardian
politics – the constitution – meaning the place of Ireland in the United
Kingdom, the House of Lords in parliament and the established
churches. This was, according to the brilliant young journalist George
Dangerfield (writing in the 1930s), one of the three extra-parliamentary rebellions which destroyed British liberalism. This ruling-class
rebellion is much less remembered than those by workers and women.

The war intervened to delay the act, and the Unionist rebellion,
together with those of women and workers. Instead there was a

doomed small nationalist uprising in Dublin in 1916. By 1918 things had changed. An attempt to impose conscription on Ireland in 1918 (a policy earlier controversial even in Great Britain) led to a transformation of the situation. Conscription and nationhood went together – to impose it on Ireland was a powerful Unionist statement. The result was an electoral victory in the 1918 general election by a new party, Sinn Féin, which in one jump became the third-largest party in the parliament at Westminster. The MPs refused to take their seats. They declared independence and there followed a brutal war of repression by the British government. It ended with the creation of the Irish Free State, which remained technically within the empire. It rejected in time all the features even of association with the empire – dominion status and the role of the king. 'Republicanism', like nationalism, thus became a concept which was for many anti-British. Ireland imposed tariffs in 1932 and there was a damaging trade war with the United Kingdom between 1932 and 1938, where tariffs were applied to food and to coal. Even so close to home, Commonwealth free trade was a non-starter.

One part of Ireland, named Northern Ireland, remained within the United Kingdom, though paradoxically it got Home Rule, even though the Protestants of the North were the great opponents of the idea. The first devolution went to those who did not want it. A new parliament, and a new state, was set up, under the control of the Unionists, close allies of the Conservative and Unionist Party and the Scottish Unionists.

Ireland points to the importance not just of territory and empire in the politics of the early twentieth century but also, of course, of religion. The United Kingdom was uniquely divided in terms of its Christian religious convictions, rituals and beliefs. Its religious make-up was more complex than straightforwardly bi-confessional Germany, let alone obviously Catholic or Protestant nations.

The British empire organized its affairs as a self-consciously Christian body, with a Protestant monarch at its head. There were a number of official, established churches. The status of these churches was central to politics. The Church of Ireland (Anglican) was disestablished by an act of 1869, hardly surprisingly, since it was not the church of he majority. The Church in Wales was Anglican but was disestablished by an act of 1914 as the result of objections to a national Anglican church, when so many Welsh people were non-conformists. It was a significant constitutional issue for the Tory Party. There was a non-established Anglican church in Scotland, the Scottish Episcopal Church, alongside the official Church of Scotland, which was not Anglican. Then there was the Roman Catholic Church, dominant in Ireland, and important wherever the Irish settled. Thus it was that Liverpool and Glasgow had distinctly Catholic football teams, Everton and Celtic, and a Labour vote which was strongly Catholic too.

The relations of politics and religion were complex – Unionists were closely associated with the Protestant established church. Much of the Tory working-class vote was a Protestant vote, in many places a more specifically Anglican one. On the other hand the more non-conformist Liberal Party attracted Catholics because of its position on Ireland, as did Labour. British socialism was suffused with Christianity (for example in the case of Stafford Cripps) to an extent unthinkable in Catholic Europe. British anti-clericalism has usually been Christian. Catholicism was associated not with order and authority but with rebellion and subversion. The supposed threat of Papism and indeed sometimes mere Anglicanism affected politics. For example, religious issues were central to the politics of education in the Edwardian years – the key issue around the 1902 Education Act was 'Rome on the rates', 'rates' being local property taxes. The Liberals opposed it, forced by its non-conformist grass roots. The last significant religious confrontation in the House of Commons came when it rejected revisions to the Anglican *Book of Common Prayer* in 1927 and 1928 in a notable revolt by non-conformists and evangelical Anglicans against what they saw as papist modifications. Generally speaking, the dominant Anglicanism was moderate and there were no legal bars to divorce or contraception, for example. Religious division relaxed, if not religious feeling. Particularly notable in this respect was the public persona of the Conservative leader and prime minister Stanley Baldwin. Baldwin was clearly Protestant, indeed Anglican, but obviously open to the non-conformist churches – there was in Baldwin a clear notion of a united Christian, though Protestant, front against atheistic ideologies, socialism and more generally against 'materialism'. For Baldwin, divine providence was at work in the United Kingdom and in the empire.[40] Neville Chamberlain retained his family's Unitarianism.

Indeed, it was not only religious controversy which waned. By the 1930s the great polemics around free trade and protection, empire, the House of Lords and Ireland had also all moderated very considerably, and were certainly no longer directly linked to party conflict. Protection and imperial preference were now accepted, and religious toleration was established in what was and remained a clearly Christian nation. Yet there was to be an important though hidden transformation, as class became the central divide in politics, politics which was now national rather than imperial. The politics of free trade, empire, protection, the constitution, religion were the politics of elites, elites which controlled state and society. The shift to a politics of the nation coincided with a dramatic change in political life – the emergence of a class-based party designed to put workers into parliament. Politics and political structure changed together. Just as the subject matter of politics was different from what it would become, so too was the political system.

DEMOCRACY?

The United Kingdom and the empire were governed by an abstraction few had heard of – the crown-in-parliament, an extraordinary combined legislative, judicial and executive power. Much policy and administrative practice went on without much intrusion from the electorate. His Majesty's government ruled; the servants of the crown worked on His Majesty's service, as the marking on official letters and telegrams had it. Although the House of Commons proclaimed its sovereignty over all others including the House of Lords, it was not a creative, policy-making force in its own right. It expressed party power, and approved proposals put forward by the state (whose highest officers were drawn from parliament, but the high civil servants were not under parliamentary control). Ministers of the crown proposed; parliament passed.[41] Power passed through Westminster, and might get blocked there, but it originated elsewhere. It is telling that the House of Commons was always deeply respectful of the crown and the state. It routinely showed particular respect to members who were also members of the Bar (lawyers) and officers of the armed services. They were not merely 'Honourable Gentlemen', or 'Honourable Ladies', but were addressed as Honourable and Learned in the case of barristers, and Honourable and Gallant in the case of officers. State culture and political culture were intertwined.

Parliament included the House of Lords, which was easily the least democratic upper house of all the major empires of the world. While there were many upper houses where nobles and noble voters were overrepresented, before 1914 only Austria, Prussia and Japan had legislative Houses of Lords. Not even the Russian empire, or imperial Germany, had one. After 1918 only the United Kingdom and imperial Japan (until 1947) had such a hereditary legislature.

One entered the Lords by birth, by appointment, by election by fellow old Irish or Scottish peers or by virtue of reaching the very highest ranks of the established English and Welsh Churches or the judiciary (including the Scottish). Welsh bishops disappeared with the disestablishment of their Church in 1920, Irish peer representatives in 1920, and all Scottish peers would sit from 1963. Peerages of the United Kingdom (as they were known – all the other types having been abandoned) were routinely created and they were all hereditary until 1958. Two Parliament acts, those of 1911 and 1949, would limit the powers of the Lords, but they remained real. The Lords had vetoed Irish Home Rule in the 1890s, and would have again had it not been for the 1911 act, which meant that the Lords could only delay legislation, which they did in the case of the 1914 Government of Ireland Act. In 1900 the prime minister sat in the Lords, but he would be the last. The Marquess of Salisbury, of the Cecil family, was to cede the position to his nephew, Arthur Balfour, who sat in the House of Commons.

The House of Commons was what mattered and it determined the shape of the government. Here too the high politics of the elite were what counted. The Commons was not a place for or of the common people. It was a place where elite members of parties of the elite deliberated. Most people, when they had a vote, voted not only for parties of the elite, but for members of parliament drawn from the upper reaches of society. Furthermore, politics was fundamentally about what happened in parliament and the elite public sphere, rather than a matter for the electorate. Only rarely did the electorate and electoral system give unambiguous instructions. In 1906 the electorate returned a free trade Liberal government. In 1918 the electorate endorsed a coalition, as it was to do in 1931, with protection the likely result. The 1945 general election brought a Labour majority government, with a distinct programme and parliamentary candidates.

The politics of party and the politics of parliament were usually more important than the votes of the electorate. Politicians decided on governments. Indeed, minority and coalition governments predominated. There was a brief 1905–6 Liberal minority government under Sir Henry Campbell-Bannerman before the 1906 election, won by the Liberals through their support for free trade, and from 1910 to 1915 (led by Herbert Asquith from 1908) the Liberal minority government relied on Irish Nationalist and Labour votes. There was a minority Labour government (January to November 1924) and another 1929–31. In fact, coalition was the commonest form of government. Coalitions were in office for some twenty-one years of the forty-five years to 1945; twenty-six if one includes the 1900–1905 Conservative-Liberal Unionist administration. Single-party majority administrations were confined to the Liberal governments of 1906–10 and the Conservative government of 1924–9.

By definition minority governments were formed by agreement, not by parliamentary necessity. Surprisingly, that was also true of most coalitions. The largest party could have governed alone in all the main coalitions: the 1900–1905 government, the Great War coalition (1915–18), the National government (1931–40), and the Second World War coalition (1940–45). Only the Lloyd George coalition of 1918–22 was an exception, but that was the result of a pre-election pact. The Labour Party was a member of both wartime coalitions, and in neither case because of parliamentary arithmetic. The aim was to include the wider labour movement, not the small number of Labour MPs.

Nor did the electorate often decide the fate of governments of any type. A Liberal government took office in 1905, without an election, but in anticipation of one. The 1915 coalition under Herbert Asquith between the ruling Liberals and the Conservatives involved no election, nor did Lloyd George's accession to the premiership in 1916, a matter of the highest politics of the state. It resulted in a split in the Liberal Party from 1916, between the followers of Asquith and those of Lloyd George, which the electors had no say in until 1918. Lloyd George was ejected from the premiership by Conservative MPs in 1922, which was followed by a general election. The creation of the minority Labour government of 1924 under Ramsay MacDonald was entirely a matter for MPs, indeed uniquely the government was formed by the second, not the first, party in parliament: the leader of the opposition had more MPs backing him than did the prime minister. It was terminated by MPs also. The formation of the National government coalition of 1931 involved no electors, nor did its transformation into the Churchill coalition including the Labour Party in 1940.

The centrality of parliamentary rather than electoral politics is also evident in the importance of breakaways and shifts of MPs between parties. The Liberal Unionists had split from the Liberals, over Ireland; among them was Joseph Chamberlain. As prime minister Lloyd George created his own party, the National Liberals, to stand alongside the Conservatives in the election of 1918. Labour lost MPs to this Liberal-Conservative coalition as well. The 1924 Labour government was well staffed with former Liberals and Conservatives, including a former viceroy of India, Lord Chelmsford, at the Admiralty (see chapter 8). More important figures also changed party affiliation, notably Winston Churchill, who started as a Conservative MP, became a Liberal, and then a Conservative again. The New Party and the Independent Labour Party (ILP) split from Labour in 1931 and 1932. A small National Labour Party existed as part of the National coalition, 1931–45, and the new Liberal Nationals, also formed in 1931, were more successful than the original Liberals for many years.

The nature of politics was determined by the elite, but also by the electoral system. At the beginning of the century the first-past-the-post electoral system operated differently from its later incarnations. This was because not all seats were contested by all the big parties. Before 1918 many candidates were unopposed, notably but not only in Ireland. Candidates did not stand where there was no hope of winning.

Liberals abstaining in favour of Labour allowed the Labour Party to exist before 1918 as the fourth party in parliament. Some constituencies returned more than one MP and some of these constituencies still existed until 1950 (for example Blackburn and Derby). Overall, the number of MPs elected by party had only a loose relationship to total votes received for parties. Although the total voting for each party did not have the meaning it would later have, it is worth noting that the Conservative and allied parties won a greater share of the vote than any other party in *every* general election between 1900 and 1935 with the exception only of 1906. In another example of the lack of correlation of votes and government formation, the Labour vote went up very considerably between the 1923 election, which led to it becoming a minority government, and the election in 1924, after which a Conservative government took over. What the election revealed was the falling popularity of the Liberals, not of Labour. In 1935 Labour got roughly the same vote as 1929, but in the former case it was able to form a minority government as the largest party (though with fewer votes than the Tories), in the latter it remained very firmly in opposition, with only about one-quarter of all MPs. Thus the temptation to read changes of national mood from the number of parliamentary seats won by each party needs to be resisted.

The electoral system was not entrenched by tradition. New systems were not only proposed but implemented. The general election in 1918 was expected to be on the basis of a more proportional system. The House of Commons wanted the Alternative Vote for parliamentary elections, while the Lords wanted Proportional Representation; the result was the status quo, except for the university seats (mostly multi-member), which were in future to be elected by Single Transferable Vote (STV). These university seats were voted for by graduates of individual or groups of universities. In 1918 fifteen members were elected for nine constituencies, two each for Oxford and Cambridge, one for London, three for Combined English Universities, and so on. A new Northern Ireland parliament created in 1920 (with a House of Commons and a Senate) was formed at Stormont, leading to a reduction in the number of MPs sent to Westminster. The Northern Ireland House of Commons was elected by STV up to 1929 (though STV was retained for its four-member university seat for Queen's University

Belfast, which was represented in Westminster by one MP). In 1931 the fall of the Labour government prevented the implementation of the bill that would have introduced the Alternative Vote system in large constituencies. There was no lack of ideas and support for the reform, indeed for the abolition, of the House of Lords either. The problem was not conservatism, but politics. The 1945 Labour government, though committed to the abolition of the hereditary, conservative and inefficient House of Lords, merely reduced its delaying power to one year in the 1949 Parliament Act. This was a backing-down from a clear position.[42] The problem was what to put in its place.

If the electoral system did not change much between 1900 and 1950, the nature of the electorate changed in multiple ways. Changes were slower, more complicated and more dependent on unfamiliar arguments than might be supposed. For example, it was not until 1950 that it could be said that all adults were equally entitled to cast a vote. Before 1918 the right to vote rested mainly (but not exclusively) with resident heads of households (when British subjects – from anywhere in the empire), except where they were women. Some 60 per cent of men over twenty-one had the vote. This was in marked contrast to the universal male suffrage for, say, the French national assembly and the German Reichstag. British women, when ratepayers, voted in local, but not parliamentary elections.

Women's suffrage did not, as we might suppose today, necessarily mean votes for all women (as had been introduced in Finland and New Zealand). Many of the suffragettes who campaigned for it wanted votes for women on the existing basis for men as heads of households, etc., which would have given few women the vote. Thus the first so-called Conciliation Bill supported by the suffrage campaigners proposed allowing women the household suffrage, but not the property, university and other suffrages, giving an estimated 1 million women voters compared to an existing electorate of around 7 million male voters. It was claimed that most of these women were working-class householders, thus meeting the objection that a vote for female householders would mean extra votes for higher classes.[43] The failure of these parliamentary moves led radical suffragettes to turn to violence. Many went on hunger strike in prison, demanding that their actions be recognized as political rather than merely criminal. By brutal force-feeding, and then by release and rearrest, the government prevented death in state custody, though some women did die outside prison as a consequence. They suffered not for all women, but for some women, for the removal of the 'sex disability' rather than votes for all women. The decidedly non-militant suffragist Mrs Millicent Fawcett turned to support the small Labour Party, the only one committed to votes for all women, and all men. Votes for all men was as objectionable to much of the political class as votes for some women.

The objections to male suffrage dissolved during the Great War. It would become intolerable that conscripted young men who had fought, but were not yet householders, should not have the vote. Servicemen would get a vote at nineteen, below the usual twenty-one years. The second change was an age-restricted (over thirty) suffrage for women, though only if they were householders or married to one (it was this last criterion which made the greatest difference). The electorate went up from roughly 30 per cent of adults to 75 per cent. In the case of the additional university franchise, women who had passed the necessary exams, even if the university barred them from degrees, though not university education (Oxford to 1920, Cambridge to 1948), could vote. The result of these twin changes was that the overall franchise for the 1918 election was three times greater than for that of 1910.

It was left to a Conservative government, that of 1924–9, to make the franchises equal, which added greatly to the electorate for the 1929 election. Yet the system was still not one-person-one-vote. Additional votes could be got by both men and women owning property in a second constituency, and university graduates voted also in university seats (where votes in effect counted for more than in most constituencies). Both were abolished by the 1949 Representation of the People Act, passed by the Labour government in time for the 1950 election.

The extension of suffrage made little difference to the nature of political representatives until 1945. The people generally voted for members of the elite to represent them, rather than people like them, at least until 1945. This is very evident from the small numbers of women elected. The few women elected after 1918 tended to be elite women. The first woman elected never sat in Westminster as she was elected for Sinn Féin in its 1918 landslide. She was the daughter of a baronet, and by marriage a Polish countess. The second was an American-born viscountess, who stood for the Conservatives for her husband's old seat after he was elevated to the Lords as the 2nd Viscount Astor. The number of women MPs remained tiny. Labour had a female minister of labour in 1929–31, and a female minister of education, 1945–7, but that was the sum total of women in the cabinet before 1951.

The case of workers shows more change. The Liberal Party put up a few workers as candidates, and later agreed not to oppose a small number of working-class candidates from the Labour Representation Committee, which became the Labour Party in 1906. These workers were in public life not as full members but there to represent special sectional concerns only, even though these concerns affected a majority of the population. They focused on working-class and trade union concerns just as the very small numbers of women in parliament often, but certainly not always, focused on women's issues.[44] The parliamentary Labour Party of the interwar years was dominated by workers, though it was increasingly fortified with MPs drawn from the elite. Yet the whole parliamentary Labour Party was not strong in parliament before 1945. They made up a rough average of 25 per cent of all MPs between 1922 and 1945, significantly less than the share of the Labour vote. The exceptions were 1929–31, when Labour had 47 per cent of MPs, much more than the vote share, and 1931–5, when Labour MPs were only 7 per cent of the House of Commons.

The Conservative and Unionist Party, and the Liberal Parties, which dominated politics up to 1945, were both parties of elites. They represented each of the two programmes we have discussed – the liberal, internationalist and free-trading tendency and the imperialist protectionist one – as well as differing attitudes to the Irish, constitutional and religious questions. There were additional dimensions which will figure later in the book. Broadly the Conservative Party was the party of the constitution. It was the party of the landed elite and the House of Lords, of the Anglican Churches, of the Union with Ireland, of empire, of armaments and, at many times, of protection and of alcoholic refreshment. The Liberal Party was the party of trade and industry, of free trade, of peace not war, of trade not empire (though led by liberal imperialists, that is free traders who supported empire), of non-conformity (though its greatest nineteenth-century leader, William Gladstone, was an Anglican), of Home Rule for Ireland, of temperance (though its long-serving leader Herbert Asquith was for good reason known as 'Squiffy'). Of the two the Conservative Party was the closer to established authority, the Liberal Party to reform, to liberty and to internationalism.

The parties were in some ways too easily distinguished from each other. Both relied on working-class votes and both were anti-socialist.[45] They were often allies. Thus the Conservative Party was in alliance with the large Liberal Unionist Party until 1912, when the two merged to form the Conservative and Unionist Party. From 1918 to 1922 the Lloyd George Liberals were in electoral alliance with the Conservatives, and not merely in coalition. The coming-together of Conservatives and Liberals can be seen in that most remarkable political phenomenon, the Liberal Nationals. What was defeated in 1945 was not merely the Conservative Party, but the National coalition. The remaining National Labour MPs were all defeated but the Liberal Nationals got 3 per cent of the vote. Renamed the National Liberals, they were effectively part of the Conservative Party into the 1960s, when they disappeared.

Both parties changed. In a remarkable transformation, the Conservative Party of the ultras and diehards of 1914 became the party that marginalized these diehards, as in the case of the Government of India Act. It supported extending the franchise in 1918 and extended it to all women in 1928. It transformed the social services in the 1920s. Under industrial leadership, it would become increasingly open to business of all kinds, to the British people as a whole, to all religions. As an electoral machine it showed concern with the social sciences, the use of cinema and other media, the control of image and indeed the press.[46] It never, until 1945, scored less than 38 per cent of the vote, and scored more than 50 per cent in 1900 (if one includes Liberal Unionists) and 1931.

In political terms 1945 represented a major shift. It was not until 1945 that a majority of the British working class, making up 70–80 per cent of the population, voted for the Labour Party. A new party emerged which now rejected to a significant degree the programmes of other parties (though it claimed to be continuing the programme of the wartime coalition in some important respects). It was neither imperialist nor now free-trading. More importantly, it was a very different kind of party from those that had previously dominated. From 1945 Labour now had more than 60 per cent of the House of Commons. The Parliamentary Labour Party had many more graduates and public school boys than the population as a whole, yet was radically more representative than the Conservatives or the Liberals. The Labour leader Clement Attlee was quite explicit in saying that while the Tory and Liberal candidates in 1945 were all essentially rich, only Labour candidates reflected all of society. He denounced the Tories for calling themselves National, when their MPs came only from those born rich or who became rich.[47] If the working class were under-represented they were nevertheless strongly present. Over half of the 393 Labour MPs had education no higher than a secondary school, just under half (43 per cent) had elementary school education only.[48] Though the numbers differ, it seems clear that the absolute number of working-class Labour MPs was higher after 1945 than the 1922–35 average, at about the level of the temporary 1929 peak, a period of fewer Labour MPs, but a higher proportion of workers among them.[49] The difference now was that they were in a majority governing party, and installed for the long term. These working-class members of parliament, as well as the teachers and other middle-class occupations, were not part of elite or state culture. Most Labour MPs were not familiar, through quotidian contact, with power or the secrets of the state, its experts, its ways and its means. Political culture and state culture were now separate spheres. Indeed, there were now not even senior trade unionists in parliament.

The orthodox view is that the Labour Party inherited the role of the largely defunct Liberal Party as the party of reform. The Liberal Party in this account was a proto-social-democratic party of so-called

'New Liberals' who started a wave of welfare reforms before 1914, which would be taken up again by Labour in 1945. In the left version of this view Labour is seen as trapped within the confines of Liberal thinking, about welfare and much else, its social democracy limited to advanced liberalism.[50] While there is something in both these views they miss the essentials. First the Liberals were, well past 1914, a party of business, and a party which always allied with Conservatives over Labour. The Liberals of all stripes were anti-socialists, and for them Labour was, after 1918, socialist (it had stood aside for Labour in some seats before then, when Labour was nearly exclusively a trade union party). Furthermore, as we have noted and shall also see in detail in later chapters, the great innovations in welfare were made not by Liberal governments before 1914, but by Conservatives in the 1920s. In matters of social services Labour opposed, though it would later accept, the main tenets of the New Liberal and Conservative welfare state. Where Labour was liberal was in its dedicated support to the old liberal doctrines of free trade. However, even if Labour inherited liberal policies, old and new, it was a party of a very different character and by 1945 had left free trade far behind it. Free trade (as opposed to free enterprise) was supported only by the now tiny Liberal Party from the 1930s. Indeed, as we see in detail in chapter 8, the Labour Party presented itself to the post-war electorate in a remarkably national way. It was a nationalist as well as a social democratic party.

After 1945 there was a class-aligned politics which was national in new ways. The direction of the nation, the definition of the national interest were the object of politics, and there was a national economy, and a national society, to direct. The Labour Party and the Conservative and Unionist parties were national in that they were contesting nearly all seats all over the country (with the exception of Labour in Northern Ireland). Each party presented itself as a national party, but in different ways: the Conservatives as the party of established authority, with an imperial bias still; the Labour Party as the party which represented all classes, the true nation, one which was clearly non-imperial. This is not to say that Labour did not inherit a large measure of liberal internationalist thinking, or that the Conservative Party was not in some measure still extremely imperialist. But the basic concerns and political debates had shifted. But on balance the Labour Party was now, and was long to be, the party of the national project, and the Conservative Party an uneasy mix of the party of empire, nation, free enterprise and, in the future, free trade.

In the following eight chapters we will see how in many fields, from food control to energy, from ideas to inventions, there was this same basic shift to nation over the period 1900–1950, and most markedly after 1945. As we shall see, this new national focus was expressed in many different forms – in the existence for the first time in peace of a conscript army, with high military spending, and of the creation of national industries owned by the national state. The creation of a ruling economic elite connected the nation as never before, with much of its wealth tied up in national debt, was also a novel feature. Its industry was bent, for the first time, to a national purpose, that of exporting. Its inventive effort was directed as never before to national aims. And it created social services, what would later be called a welfare state, for the whole nation rather than for just the working class. The corollary is that one can only understand what was happening in all these fields before 1950, or 1945, by taking a non-national approach which allows one to capture both the liberal and the imperial dimensions of British life. What made the United Kingdom different before then was its openness to the world, its wealth and its distinctive modes of sustenance and indeed of exertion of power.

2

Mightier Yet!

All that is moulded of iron
Has lent to destruction and blood
Herbert Palmer, 'Woodworkers' Ballad'[1]

Land of Hope and Glory, Mother of the Free,
How shall we extol thee, who are born of thee?
Wider still and wider shall thy bounds be set;
God, who made thee mighty, make thee mightier yet,
God, who made thee mighty, make thee mightier yet.
'Land of Hope and Glory', lyrics
by A. C. Benson (1902)

How can I live among this gentle
Obsolescent breed of heroes and not weep?
Unicorns, almost,
for they are falling into two legends
in which their stupidity and chivalry
are celebrated. Each, fool and hero, will be an immortal.
Keith Douglas, 'Aristocrats' (1943)

The warfare state was very evident on Whitehall, the London street where government offices were and are concentrated. It runs between Parliament Square and Trafalgar Square. In the Edwardian years three great new buildings were completed on or near it. The War Office building and the Admiralty Extension, together with the Admiralty Arch, were the giant new headquarters of the army and the navy. The third building, the New Public Offices, was shared by

45

the Board of Education, the Local Government Board and the Ministry of Works. The Foreign Office, the India Office, the Colonial Office and the Home Office shared a Victorian building. As the size of their headquarters implied, the armed services carried weight in the state. The Royal Navy alone consumed around one-fifth of all central government expenditure before 1914, more than all expenditure by local and central government on education, and even more than was paid in poor relief.

Over the first fifty years of the century, a whole decade was spent in total war. On average over the period, up to around 15 per cent of national output was devoted to the waging of war. Even in the interwar years, the single largest budget item, very much larger than welfare spending, was servicing of the war debts. Between 1900 and 1950 war and not welfare is what mattered when it came to state expenditure.

Armed force shaped the state, and the state shaped armed force. Many liberal Britons prided themselves on the smallness of British government, and of the British armed forces. Being British was being part of a polity which was pacific, and not nationalist or militarist, or even imperialist. Naval and military spending was seen as something akin to an insurance policy, a necessary business expense. Liberals took pride in the Royal Navy as an institution which kept the seas open not just for British vessels, but for all the shipping of the world.

The structure and nature of British armed force was notable in that it was made up of professionals and focused on the navy. In this the United Kingdom was quite distinct from the major European powers, who all conscripted young men to varying degrees for peacetime military training and duties, turning peasants into citizens. For British liberals, such a notion was abhorrent – military service was not seen as a civic duty but an unjust impost on youth, and a danger to freedom. In any case, the United Kingdom did not have the vast reserves of young agricultural labourers conscript armies wanted. Opposition to conscription ran deep: for many patriotic Britons, to adopt continental militarism was unthinkable. Indeed, the British armed forces were regarded with some suspicion and regarded as a left-over from a more militaristic age. Despite the professionalism of the forces there was a long-standing image of the British officer as chivalrous, brave but decidedly backward both intellectually and indeed in the arts of modern war, particularly in the case of the army.[2]

Hatred of conscription did not imply opposition to the maintenance or use of armed force. The Royal Navy, the senior service, was without question the largest and most modern naval force in the world. While there to defend vital British trade, it was also a weapon to fight enemies. These were not natives to be put down by gunboats, but rather other European great powers, with larger armies, to be subdued by depriving them of the means to live. British liberal militarism was very different from the national Prussian model which came to define the concept. It was by choice an asymmetric militarism. It did not replicate the armed forces of potential enemies, it planned to defeat them using its own chosen means, great floating machines rather than men. It was a thoroughly modern militarism, predicated on high relative income per head and a strong industrial base.

The British warfare state was able to unleash great violence on the world. It did this primarily in Europe rather than in the empire, in what was called the Great European War, and in the Second World War. The bodies of the empire's fallen in the twentieth century rest mainly in France (580,000) and Belgium (200,000), with 55,000 in Tanzania, 50,000 each in Egypt and Italy, 40,000 in Turkey, 35,000 in Burma, 30,000 each in Germany, Singapore and Iraq, 20,000 in the Netherlands.[3] In Europe, as in the empire, it inflicted far more violence on its enemies than it was itself forced to endure.

Yet the two wars were, in part, the exceptions that proved the rule about the nature of British militarism. The wars had logics and contingencies of their own, which led to the creation of mass British and imperial armies and the militarization of British society, something liberal militarism was designed to avoid. Yet success in both world wars depended on the international, modern and capital-intensive orientations of British armed force and British ability to harness the resources not only of the nation and empire but of much of the rest of the world. It did not depend anything like as much as in other countries on the quantity of its national population, or its ability to exploit national resources. The British empire was victorious in two world wars because it was rich and it could and did use its unique position in the world to fight wars of steel and gold. It also succeeded because it maintained, in peacetime, strong armed forces, armament industries and creators of new weapons.

The brute realities of the British warfare state, in both peace and war, were hardly visible in British political discourse and later historical writing and social theory. This was partly because its liberal nature did not square with what was taken to be the pacifist implications of liberalism. Political and wider ideological culture, it was suggested, militated against the development of any sort of militarism, and especially a modern militarism. It was assumed that modern militarism implied the rejection of liberalism, and the adoption of a thoroughgoing political and economic nationalism. What counted in this view, were large armies. Furthermore, in many accounts written from the 1960s onwards the story of the wartime state and its success was told, oddly, in terms of the rise of the welfare state. Histories of the home front became histories of a welfare state, rather than the history of a radically expanded imperial warfare state.

WE WANT EIGHT AND WE WON'T WAIT

In 1900 the United Kingdom was at war in South Africa, fighting white opponents, in the South African Republic and the Orange Free State. It was a politically divisive issue. There were 'Jingos' on one side and so-called pro-Boer anti-imperialists on the other.[4] This was the great era of British theorizing on imperialism and its relationship to capitalism. It was also a time of debate about the nature of British armed force. Field Marshal Earl Roberts, who led the British army to eventual victory in the war, became the figurehead for the National Service League. 'National Service' was and would remain a euphemism for conscription. Support for an at least partially conscript army typically went along with support for tariffs, for imperialism and hostility to Home Rule for Ireland. One of its intellectuals was F. S. Oliver, a businessman who ran the Debenhams department store. He was to be the author of the militaristic *Ordeal by Battle* (1915). Concessions were made to this new militarism. Concern about the physique of recruits led to government support for maternity services, and for children, including medical inspections and school meals.

Maternalism and militarism marched together. There were moves to increase military training, through a new Territorial Army (created under the Liberal government), but there was no conscription, even in the first years of the Great War. Overall, free trade and liberal militarism won out.

Financing increased naval expenditure was a central aspect of the so-called 'People's Budget' of 1909, presented by the Liberal chancellor of the exchequer, David Lloyd George. This has an important place in British history, because it is seen as a key measure on the way to developing the welfare state, and because it led to a confrontation which changed the nature of parliament. Yet this picture can mislead. Additional revenue, it would become clear, was as much needed for new large warships as for the new old-age pension for the aged, mostly female, poor.[5] The budget was rejected by the House of Lords, which led to a constitutional crisis and, following two elections, the permanent diminution of the power of the Lords. The central political issue was not the raising of taxes in itself, or whether they were used for welfare or warfare – it was the form of taxation that mattered. The Conservative opposition wanted tariffs to fund both the armed forces and the social services while the Liberals wanted income taxes and excise duties instead. The budget went through, ignoring these views and entrenching taxes rather than tariffs as sources of state income. The best-known increases in taxes were those on very high incomes, a proposed land value tax and death duties, which affected only the very rich. In fact, the increase in these was roughly matched by increases in excise duties, paid largely by the working class.

The People's Budget financed the controversial 1909 naval programme. The Liberal government had first proposed starting four battleships in the 1909–10 financial year. In March 1909 the government said it *might* add *another* four as a result of immense pressure from the Conservative opposition and public agitation, with its chant of 'we want eight and we won't wait'. The navalist ultras won. In July 1909, the government said it would in fact add four, to be finished by March 1912, but not started in 1909–10 but at the very beginning of 1910–11. So it turned out that within a very slightly expanded 1909–10 financial year, eight warships were laid down, which were built over the next two years or so, but with a slight 'wait' that the Conservatives still complained of. The costs were immense. Each battleship cost more than the *Titanic* or the *Olympic* (some £2 million). The total annual building cost, since they took around two years to complete, was £8 million, the entire annual cost of the new old-age pension. For these were not mere gunboats for the patrolling of empire but the heaviest and most powerful warships ever built. Two were *Colossus*-class dreadnought battleships (with 12-inch guns), four were *Orion*-class battleships (the first superdread-noughts) with 13.5-inch guns, and two *Lion*-class battlecruisers, also with 13.5-inch guns.[6] One of the *Orions* was the last and largest warship built on the Thames. When she was completed, the shipbuilder, Thames Iron Works, went out of business, leaving behind the West Ham Football Club. Arsenal Football Club, the gunners, had been the team of the Woolwich Arsenal, the gun works on the Thames.

The campaign for eight battleships in one financial year involved Herbert Mulliner, the managing director of a new heavy armaments firm called Coventry Ordnance Works. He claimed (falsely) that the Germans had been preparing to build more than they had announced. His firm, recently formed by four large warship-builders, had got contracts from 1909 for heavy mountings (the complex machinery to aim the heavy guns) and was very busy (though unprofitable) all the way to the war.[7] These were boom years for the British armament giants, Armstrong-Whitworth and Vickers, and for new ventures, not only Coventry Ordnance Works, but also a new Beardmore naval shipyard and gun works at Dalmuir on the Clyde, and new shipyards on the Tyne. They were also the years of building new repair facilities. Devonport got an extension with dry docks for four dreadnoughts (costing £4 million), and Portsmouth another two. Rosyth Dockyard was completed in the Great War, with three dreadnought-scale dry docks. Gibraltar was given three new dry docks (named for King Edward, Queen Alexandra and the Prince and Princess of Wales).

The Royal Navy quite deliberately used this expanding industrial and infrastructural capacity to out-build the Germans both quantitatively and qualitatively. The *Queen Elizabeth*-class super-dreadnoughts of 1913 were twice the size of the last pre-dreadnoughts, and cost roughly double; their 15-inch guns were bigger than anything the Germans had.

The combination of more and bigger guns and ships gave the Royal Navy a huge advantage over the Kriegsmarine by 1914.[8] The British empire went into the Great War with brand-new warships operated by a competent and modernizing Royal Navy.[9] These were the products of a navy where the director of naval education was Sir Alfred Ewing, FRS, former professor of engineering at Cambridge, and where the command of the navy in 1915–16 was in the hands of Admiral Sir Henry Jackson, FRS (elected 1901), a co-inventor of the radio.

THE GREAT EUROPEAN WAR

The British empire was not compelled to enter the European war which broke out in August 1914. It ostensibly went to war, in alliance initially with France, Russia and Serbia, to defend Belgium from the barbarous Hun. Ideologically it became a liberal's war, one against Prussianism and militarism, in the name of freedom and civilization. Yet the British empire, not the German Reich, was allied to the world's most despotic, backward and anti-Semitic power – Russia – against the most philo-Semitic, scientific and well-educated – Germany. The Reich, not the empire, had universal male suffrage; the Reich, not the empire, had the greatest socialist and anti-militarist party in the world. The Belgians had at least as bad a reputation as the Germans for colonial atrocities. But there were, from the British state's point of view, very good reasons to go to war – a victorious Germany controlling one side of the Channel and North Sea was regarded as a very great danger indeed.

The British empire was a rich global power; the United Kingdom alone was as populous as France. Yet in August 1914 it sent into battle a British Expeditionary Force of only six divisions, organized in three corps, about the same size as the entire Belgian army. By contrast, the French army mobilized twenty-one corps. The poverty-stricken Russian empire, too, mobilized a much larger army than the British one. There was no mystery here – the British contribution was to be primarily naval: its navy would blockade the Central Powers. The naval war, though not very visible, was important. The German navy was not able to operate freely, and the German merchant navy was rapidly driven from the seas. The British naval blockade of Germany cost hundreds of thousands of German lives. At the battle of Jutland in 1916 the Kriegsmarine escaped destruction by the Royal Navy but it was never to put to sea again, with the important exception of its submarines. They sank British and allied shipping to the extent of causing significant problems, a threat not properly countered until the introduction of convoys in 1917, but which was contained.

British naval power, significant as it was, was not enough. New armies had to be made to fight alongside the French, on the Western Front, and elsewhere. At first volunteers were recruited on an enormous scale. By 1916 there were four volunteer British armies in France. The 4th Army, for example, went into action on the first day of the Somme offensive in July 1916. In that same year conscription was introduced in Great Britain, though not in Ireland, or most of the rest of empire. Surprising as it now seems, this was a contested and controversial decision, one which seriously discomfited liberals. From now on the British armies would be like those of the other belligerents. It was, however, the most tank-, air- and artillery-intensive army of the Great War, deploying violence of unprecedented and unusual intensity.

The new armies, volunteer or conscript, required arms and equipment on a vast scale. To meet this demand, the great Edwardian armament firms expanded. Before the war, Vickers, the leading armourer, was already making not just guns, machine guns and dreadnoughts, but submarines, aeroplanes and airships. They, like Armstrong-Whitworth, Beardmore and Coventry Ordnance Works, and the specialist warship yards, grew into enterprises employing tens of thousands of workers. On top of this, new government factories were built for explosives and propellants, and for filling munitions.

The mobilization of women into the war factories was unprecedented, and much remarked on. It should not be thought of as the product of a general replacement of men by women. While this occurred in some sectors, for example in transport and in office work, generally speaking women went into new women-only plants and factories designed specifically to employ them to make armaments. An example of such a factory was indeed the largest new one – the cordite factory at Gretna, of 20–30,000 workers, some housed in the new settlement of Gretna, built next to the tiny Scottish village of Gretna Green, close to Carlisle, just over the border.[10] With the end of the war those factories were closed down, and the women's jobs disappeared.

An extraordinary feat of arms and industrial mobilization saw British troops victorious on the Western Front in 1918, and the world over. The German empire was forced into an armistice in November 1918, and to surrender to the terms of the Allies in June 1919, the blockade still holding. For this reason, some, but not all, war memorials note the Great War ended in 1919. Its armed forces were reduced, its territory cut back, its colonies taken away. The entire German navy was interned, mostly in Orkney, from November 1918 (it was scuttled as a last act of resistance in June 1919). Its merchant marine was handed over to the victorious powers. The United Kingdom got three ocean liners; two, the former *Bismarck* and *Imperator*, were in fact the largest ships in British service into the 1930s, as the White Star Line *Majestic* and the Cunarder *Berengaria*. The only somewhat smaller *Columbus* became the White Star *Homeric*. The Germans seemed finished as global players.

There were other armistices, and other peace treaties, and continuing wars. In 1918 British imperial troops were in Baku and Basra, Istanbul and Irbil, Mosul and Murmansk, Sebastopol and Salonika, the Veneto and Vladivostok. British forces remained deployed around the world in large numbers. They continued to fight in Russia until the end of 1919, supporting the counter-revolutionary white forces in the Arctic and the Black Sea. There were continuing operations against the remnants of the Ottoman empire. The army had moved into the Dardanelles and Constantinople in 1918, but in 1922 the new Turkish nation fought back and threatened the British and French positions in Chanak (near Gallipoli). The British government, without the support of the rest of the empire, threatened war against Turkey. The Conservatives, less rash in their foreign policy, deposed the prime minister, Lloyd George, as a result, fearful for the impact on the empire, and on relations with France. The Turks would get everything they wanted.

Lloyd George was the 'man who won the war'. He was a politician of supreme talent; brought up speaking Welsh, he attended no university, but entered politics as a solicitor, the minor branch of the legal profession. He was known as an anti-imperialist, a radical liberal opposed to armaments, a scourge of the aristocracy and its powers, though a man close to plutocrats. He went into the war as chancellor of the exchequer, becoming minister of munitions in 1915, creating that vital ministry which took over supply responsibilities from the War Office, and then became secretary of state for war (that is, army minister). Lloyd George, the Welsh Wizard, transformed the capacity of the British government to wage war, leading the empire to victory in 1918. He argued for conscription, anathema to most Liberals, and ousted his fellow Liberal Herbert Asquith, prime minister since 1908, in December 1916. Like Asquith since 1915, he presided over a coalition with the Conservatives, but a deeper one, which also included a greater representation of labour. It was Lloyd George's coalition government which greatly extended the franchise for the 1918 election, in which it won a great victory. The Conservatives were the major beneficiaries and established themselves as the dominant party for the next generation. The United Kingdom, then, went into the war with a Liberal government and came out of it with a Conservative-dominated coalition.

A long, stalemated war required profound changes in the British state, economy and society. This should not be understood simply or even primarily as making the nation more democratic and extending the scope of welfare. For example, the new war cabinet, and cabinets thereafter, would be minuted and served by a new secretariat. The first cabinet secretary was the secretary of the Committee of Imperial Defence (founded 1902), where such practices were routine. War, and the involvement of the Conservatives, pointed in the direction of militarism, empire and protection. Indeed, the militaristic, nationalistic and imperial mood of the Tories hardened. Some Tory MPs and peers during the war defected to form a hard-right National Party, committed to empire protection, a stronger war effort, the bombing of German towns, and a vigorous anti-alien policy. They failed to win any fresh seats. At least one hard-right figure did win a seat. Noel Pemberton Billing, a Royal Navy pilot, was elected as an independent MP in

1916. He had founded a seaplane firm called Supermarine, which would later be famous for its Spitfire. He stood as the anti-alien, homophobic, bomb-Berlin candidate. In an extraordinary 1918 libel trial, which was at once comical yet deadly serious, he threw allegations of a German homosexual plot to undermine British strength, from seducing soldiers to blackmailing the elite. Asquith and his wife were particular targets. In this extraordinary caper, the state was deeply involved behind the scenes.[11] In another example of a shift to the right, Emmeline Pankhurst's Women's Political and Social Union turned into the Women's Party, a vehemently pro-war, pro-conscription and imperialist party, for which Christabel Pankhurst stood in the 1918 general election (with coalition support).

The war did not in itself promote progressive politics. Socialist internationalism was an early casualty. Pre-war socialists, far stronger in Germany, Austria and France than in the United Kingdom, had hoped to avert a war by an international general strike. It was not to be. The murder of Jean Jaurès, the French socialist leader, and the German Social Democratic Party's vote for war credits were great blows. The European left would be divided between pro-war and anti-war sections, a difference which would solidify into competing, antagonistic socialist and communist parties. The British anti-war left did exist but was tiny, certainly by comparison to that which had emerged in Germany and Russia towards the end of the conflict. It was nothing to do with the Labour Party, which in contrast to European socialist parties produced a right not a left splinter group (see chapter 8). The former Labour Party leader Keir Hardie MP died in 1915, in poverty and rejected by most of his party for his anti-war stance. His seat was won by a pro-war, working-class independent, standing against the official Labour candidate. The anti-war left centred on new and old small parties, and figures like the Irish nationalist and socialist James Connolly, executed in 1916, and the 'British Lenin', John MacLean. Sylvia Pankhurst, sister of Christabel, created the Workers' Socialist Federation, and was among the founders of the revolutionary, internationalist and anti-imperialist Communist Party of Great Britain (formed in 1920), allied through the Third International to other parties of the anti-war left. Yet in contrast to much of the rest of Europe, the state remained in control, and no serious repression by the state or ruling class was needed. It was a time of tension, but there was no British fascism or Freikorps, the German post-war counter-revolutionary militia, in Great Britain.

KEEPING THE EMPIRE

There was, however, one extremely important exception to this generalization within the United Kingdom, and that is what happened in Ireland. The attempt to impose conscription in Ireland in 1918 re-ignited and transformed nationalist politics. The Easter Rising of 1916 failed, but in 1918 Ireland voted for intransigent nationalist politicians who refused to sit in Westminster (where they would have formed the third party). The army, and new paramilitary forces recruited for the purpose, not least from the ranks of ex-soldiers, unleashed the violence states keep in reserve, to a degree which revolted even the king-emperor. This was the worst state violence in the United Kingdom that there had been for over a century. Ireland was lost to the United Kingdom by an agreement of 1921, and the Irish Free State (the name echoing the Orange Free State destroyed by the empire in the Boer war) would step by step leave the orbit of British power. Although the British empire was not dissolved, as were the great German, Russian and Austro-Hungarian empires, it had also lost European territory and some prestige. If there was a British Freikorps it was the auxiliary police forces serving in Ireland.

The Irish revolt was not the only one. In Egypt, though not formally a colony, nationalist riots in 1919 against British rule led to formal independence, though under British tutelage. There was revolt in India. The Montagu-Chelmsford (Edwin Montagu was the Liberal secretary of state for India, Lord Chelmsford was the viceroy of India) reforms of 1919 creating a new kind of semi-democratic government of India were one side of the coin, the massacre at Amritsar the other. Reform and repression would be recurring common features of a revitalized empire, the product of an attempt to reorder a new progressive world.[12]

Force was, and remained, central to the government of empire.

One view was that the administration of empire provided outdoor relief for the aristocracy, giving them public roles, propping up their status. They used old methods of administration and rule, of show and of exemplary violence with rude tools. Imperialism was, in this view, an old impulse, like militarism, out of which nothing good or modern would come. Another view has arisen in which a colonial modernity laid bare the true inner meaning of a totalizing modernity – exercising control through knowledge, machines and myriad forms of imposed self-control. Both views mislead in that the aims of colonial repression were limited to maintaining such control as was necessary to maintain empire and key industries, and because modern means were inevitably used to do so.[13]

Colonial policing protocols stipulated that arms be used early and decisively. They should not be used to fire warning shots, but rather be fired at 'ringleaders' in the crowd. This practice was indeed followed across India and the colonial empire. What stood out in some cases was not the fact of killing unarmed civilians, but the numbers involved. In 1906 the Natal government put down a Zulu rebellion against a poll-tax – thousands were killed. In the Amritsar massacre of 1919 hundreds were killed.

New methods came into use. From 1919 British air power was in action in Sudan, Afghanistan, Palestine, the North West Frontier and Mesopotamia as a cheap means of maintaining order in these territories. 'Air control' by bombing and aerial ferrying of hit squads was an important aspect of the work of the RAF, from new British air bases from Basra and Hinaidi in Iraq to Peshawar and Quetta in British India. Gunboats too still had their place. In 1926 British warships bombarded the town of Wanhsien on the Yangtze, killing between hundreds and thousands, for interfering with British trade; the result was a long-running boycott. In 1927 a full army division was sent to Shanghai as the Shanghai Defence Force.

The 1930s were also hardly peaceful either in the empire or the mandated territories acquired from the defeated powers. In Palestine in the 1930s the British authorities, together with Jewish settlers, fought and eventually crushed a Palestinian uprising against the British policy of allowing large-scale Jewish immigration. While succeeding as a counter-insurgency, it was a political failure, as in 1939 the British government was forced to change direction, recognizing the claims of the Palestinians.

Labour unrest was a serious issue in the empire, especially in the 1930s. It was a concern at the giant Singapore naval base (which acquired its own police force) and in the Caribbean. Here there were serious strikes on sugar plantations in Jamaica, for example in April and May 1938. Police shot four strikers at the new Frome sugar factory (owned by the Tate & Lyle subsidiary, the West Indies Sugar Company). In June 1937 Trinidad had disturbances in its oil fields and refineries. The modern cruisers HMS *Ajax* and HMS *Exeter*, serving with the Americas and West Indies Station, were sent in, and their marines and sailors were used to help put down the protests and guard the refineries and their management. These two ships would become better known two years later, when they drove the German heavy cruiser the *Graf Spee* into Montevideo in December 1939. The rebellions, strikes and repression in the Caribbean led to the growth of trade unions and labour parties in the region. They engaged the attention of the British Labour Party and trade unionists, and in some places, notably in Trinidad, by far the main fully imperial source of oil, made order and progress seem important to the British state. The response came, slowly but definitely, with the passage of the Colonial Development and Welfare Act of 1940 and in effect a decision that the empire would not engage, at least not in Trinidad, in repression. An accommodation with local workers would be sought, bypassing the declared interests of the local whites who dominated local politics.[14]

The imperial police forces outside Great Britain were quite different from our image of the domestic British police force. They were like the Royal Irish Constabulary, an armed gendarmerie with a distinct officer corps. In Asia and Africa they had white officers at the head, and local, or non-local, usually non-white, constables and other lower ranks. Officers were a distinct cadre, recruited after public school, trained in special schools and put into positions of command. Eric Blair, an Etonian, served seven years in the imperial Indian Police, stationed in Burma – he returned to Britain and became the writer George Orwell. It would have been unthinkable for him to have joined a domestic police force, though had he stayed in the

Indian Police he might have returned home to become a chief constable. The chief constables of the largest forces were recruited from imperial police officers, or the armed forces. London's Metropolitan Police was headed by very senior former officers including General (later Field Marshal) Viscount Julian 'Bungo' Byng and Marshal of the Air Force Baron (later Viscount) Hugh 'Boom' Trenchard. In the early 1930s Trenchard created a police college at Hendon modelled on the imperial police and service officer training colleges to produce a senior officer corps for the national police services, and the imperial ones as well. The college was marked by a particular commitment to scientific policing and produced a remarkable generation of chief constables who took over from imperial policemen and soldiers from the 1940s, including the first British policeman to head the Metropolitan Police, appointed in 1958, in succession to a former member of the Indian Police.[15]

THE BRITISH EMPIRE AS A GREAT POWER

The war had created new nations and nationalisms; it also created a new internationalism and revitalized imperial projects.[16] The British and French were the core of the League of Nations, a body created by the victors of the Great War to keep the world in order. British intellectuals, and French and American too, fantasized about a global military force which could maintain discipline everywhere. Such a force was never created, but national forces retained global roles.

The British armed services once more abjured the use of mass armies and relied on the navy and the newly independent Royal Air Force (created in 1918). The Royal Navy would no longer be clearly the most potent sea-going force in the world. In 1922 the Washington Treaty gave the United Kingdom naval parity with the USA and a clear margin against Japan, followed by the other signatories, France and Italy, now the only others with navies of consequence. This balance was essentially maintained by the London treaty of 1930. In the air the RAF was for many years the only independent air force, and into the 1930s could claim to be the strongest in the world.

From the early 1930s, with the hoped-for global economic order collapsing into depression and economic nationalism, the outlook would change dramatically and quickly. As liberals had feared, the nations and empires of the world rearmed, waged wars of conquest and eventually engaged in an extraordinarily brutal conflict. A global arms race got underway.[17] Italy and Japan invaded parts of Africa and Asia, provoking only limited action from the League of Nations. Germany and the USSR rearmed to secure the influence they had before 1914 and to pursue new ideological and economic projects. All these developments were of grave import to the British empire. It was still the greatest global trading nation, still in the early 1930s, though by a small margin, the greatest power on earth. The USSR was over the horizon from India; Japan was in increasing control of China and threatened the empire in the east; Italy was increasing its influence in the Mediterranean, a vital British route. A nationalist and militarizing Nazi Germany threatened in Europe. In 1935 the United Kingdom started to rearm seriously. It was no secret. The 1935 general election was in part fought on it – with the National government supporting it, opposed by Labour – and by Lloyd George, on classic liberal anti-militarist lines.[18]

To be sure, although British arms spending in the years 1935–9 was rising, it was below that of Germany, and this gave Germany greater stocks of some weapons in 1940 (though aside from infantry weapons the margin was not large). But the depth of British rearmament and its orientation to future production was remarkable. In 1940 the United Kingdom had the highest proportion of GDP devoted to war (higher than Germany); the highest aircraft production, and warship production, and tank production approaching Germany's thanks to the rearmament programme begun in 1935 rather than to the circumstances of 1940. The Royal Navy went into the war as clearly the leading navy in the world, strong in all the key weapons, not least aircraft carriers, and as a force of global reach. In 1937 two of the Gibraltar dry docks were extended to take the largest aircraft carriers and battleships. A large new one was built in Durban, South Africa. In 1938 it completed what was by some measures the largest dry dock in the world in Singapore (named for George VI); it was second in length only to the King George V in Southampton, built for the gigantic Cunard-White Star liners *Queen Mary* and *Queen Elizabeth* and opened in 1933.[19] In the biggest engineering project in Australian history to that date the Captain Cook Graving Dock was built from 1940. It remains the largest in the whole southern hemisphere, with the Sturrock Dry Dock in Cape Town, built between 1942 and 1945. The contrast with the Germans becomes clear when we note that the Normandie (built for the liner of that name) Dry Dock at St Nazaire was the furthest from Germany they controlled. It was put out of action by a daring but costly British naval and commando raid in 1942. Germany remained a merely regional power.

In the air also there was a huge programme of base construction. New airfields appeared across the United Kingdom and overseas. Among them was RAF Habbiniyah, a huge base in Iraq with a 7-mile perimeter, an adjacent airfield and on Lake Habbiniyah, a seaplane base. The late 1930s saw the building of huge new aircraft and aero-engine factories. It was very clear that capacity was being built up for future production. It was thus that many great new aircraft factories came into production in 1940. For land armaments the scale of rearmament was lower, but even so enormous plants for munitions were constructed from 1935.

If rearmament was hardly a surprising response to a generalized arms race, neither was appeasement. The British government was not looking for war, but for order and stability. It was bound to seek agreement with those who wished to disrupt the existing order as long as it thought this possible. Furthermore warmongering could be disastrous, even if it led to victory in war. The winners could be communism, and the Americans, and the losers could be the British empire and the British elite. In any case, acting against the Nazis required forming alliances which might not be palatable. Thus it was that appeasement and rearmament were two sides of the same coin.

The politics of both rearmament and appeasement were complex. Those most alert to the ideological and military threat posed by the Nazis were the liberal internationalists and the socialist internationalists. They would later be misleadingly denounced for naivety and pacifism. Only the hard-bitten conservatives, it would be suggested, had understood the real dangers in the world, while the liberals and the left opposed rearmament. If they had themselves appeased, it was, they would claim, because they needed to gain time to rearm. In fact, the self-consciously realistic geo-politicians were more inclined to accept realities and cynically accommodate, and indeed appease. In short, the long-established contrast between rearmers who supported vigorous anti-Nazi measures and the disarmers who appeased is doubly false: the rearmers were generally appeasers; anti-appeasers were anti-rearmament, at least while it was not clear (not least because of appeasement) against whom the rearmament was directed. In the United Kingdom the keenest anti-Nazis were communists, socialists and liberals appalled by economic nationalism, militarism and racialism, and maverick conservatives, most notably Winston Churchill.

The Spanish Civil War (1936–9) was a portent: it was not just a war between Spaniards, or Spanish regions and nations, but also an international ideological war. France and the United Kingdom pursued a policy of non-intervention in part because intervening on either side (the British elite favoured Franco's rebels) would generate political conflict at home. The first Britons to fight fascism were not conservatives, but the volunteers who fought in the British battalion of the International Brigades in Spain. The British Communist Party claimed, turning an internationalist campaign into a nationalist argument, that 'The real Britain is represented by the heroes in Spain – the immortal British Battalion. They carry forward the traditions of the past, they, and they alone, have redeemed the honour of the British people.'[20] Thus was ideology, internationalism and nationalism conflated and confused.

The coming of the Second World War in Europe was heralded by, perhaps required, a dramatic ideological shift. The Nazi-Soviet pact of August 1939 shattered the central divide of the 1930s, that between communism and fascism, leaving many conceptually and emotionally numbed. It broke an ideological log-jam and was militarily and politically consequential in ways which it is difficult to think back to. It obviously not only made possible the destruction of Poland from west and east in September 1939, but it also created new conditions which eased the declarations of war by the United Kingdom and France. A war against, even to varying degrees, both Germany and the USSR, against both red fascism and brown bolshevism, united the bulk of left and right and marginalized both communists and fascists. In the words of Evelyn Waugh's character, the Catholic gentry soldier Guy Crouchback, the pact brought an end to a decade of shame, as now 'the Enemy was plain in view, huge and hateful, all disguise cast off; the modern age in arms'.[21] In France, though not in the United Kingdom, the Communist Party was banned, though the party newspaper was shut down only in early 1941. It is notable that some of the first planned attacks by the British and the French were to be directed not at Nazi Germany, but at the Soviet Union. In 1939–40 the war was presented in terms of good versus evil, democracy versus tyranny and barbarism. It was a liberal's war against a totalitarian enemy.

A RICH PEOPLE'S WAR

The British and French governments declared war on Germany in September 1939 confident of victory. Between them they were far more militarily powerful than Germany, and especially industrially and economically. They had access to the world – Germany, even with access to the resources of the Soviet Union, was, by contrast, severely constrained. Except with respect to army weapons the United Kingdom was or soon would be producing more than Germany, not counting the contribution of France. France was no minnow. It had one of the world's largest economies, and the French empire was second only to the British in its global reach. This is not to say that there were not problems – from late 1938 sterling fell, especially on the eve of war, though held up by sales of foreign reserves. It was fixed at the outbreak of war at $4.03, much lower than its typical rate in the 1930s, which reached $5.00.[22]

The key to the confidence of British economists was that they understood that the capacity to produce weapons was not simply a product of the absolute size of belligerent economies. While this was important, a critical factor was the wealth of the population – the higher the income per head the greater the proportion of the economy which could be turned over to arms production after meeting the basic needs of the people. The relative wealth of the United Kingdom, and the dominions also, compared with Germany was a decisive advantage, compensating for the sheer scale of the German population and economy.[23]

The Germans, having defeated Poland in September 1939, gambled and won by launching attacks in Western Europe in face of the superior might of the British and French empires. Norway was vanquished in the van of an Anglo-French attack on that country to block Swedish iron ore exports to Germany. Germany attacked further south on 10 May 1940, quickly subduing the Netherlands and Belgium. The British Expeditionary Force, with some French forces, had to be evacuated from the port of Dunkirk in late May and early June. Casualties were light and indeed many of the French forces returned to fight elsewhere in France. British forces remained in other parts of France and were evacuated later. France surrendered only at the end of June 1940.

While the implications of the fall of France were immense for the British Empire, it should not in itself be taken as being the consequence of British failure or weakness. It resulted from a highly contingent defeat of the French Army, part of an Anglo-French alliance which had, with very good reason, been confident of their overall superiority in military force in 1939 and early 1940. Even after the fall of France, the British empire fought on, and not without a well-founded confidence in eventual victory.

Neither 'Britain' nor the British empire, was ever alone. It was allied with many governments in exile, which brought with them small armed forces, sometimes large merchant marines and rich imperial territories, such as the Belgian Congo and the Dutch East Indies. Nor was the empire always on the back foot. There were small but significant victories – the Battle of Britain in the air in the summer of 1940 bested the Luftwaffe, though it did not stop the bombing of British cities which followed. The Royal Navy inflicted a defeat from the air on the Italian fleet at Taranto in 1940. There was a successful offensive in Africa in 1941 against the Italians. The greater part of the war effort was a steady general blockade of Germany from 1939 and of continental Europe from 1940, and the building of massive forces for later use. Germany and Italy were confined to a corner of a world which the British empire could draw on freely.

The United Kingdom was, however, ejected from continental

Europe and from important sources of supply. Just how important these were is not evident in historical accounts which assume, it seems, that the United Kingdom imported only from the empire and other faraway places. Yet it relied on Swedish and Mediterranean iron ore, Baltic timber and paper pulp, and Dutch eggs and Danish bacon, and much else. Extraordinarily, with ships, some acquired from European allies, and with money, it could and did get all the food and raw materials it needed from elsewhere and now also imported manufactures on a large scale. During the war British imports in value stayed at pre-war levels, with munitions becoming very important. The United Kingdom did not turn in on itself to fight the war but rather connected to the world in new ways. It was not national effort which characterized the British war effort, but the fact that it was global and allied. It was in many respects, and from the British point of view, an international and internationalist war. To be sure, some elements of the economy became more national, notably the growing of wheat and vegetables and the supply of timber, but these were specific cases rather than instances of a general trend.

The British state had the ability to acquire, and transport, food, fuel and materiel from around the world and to do so without having to export in return. This was made possible not just by US Lend-Lease, but by in effect forcing suppliers to lend to the United Kingdom, including the poor of the empire. As the only important market for food exporters it could demand to be supplied in return for deferred payment. In the case of the colonies, control of the economies deepened and the rate of exploitation increased. It also meant that it could afford machine-intensive forms of warfare that kept the majority of British forces out of the front line for most of the war.

1941 saw two transformative developments. First Germany and its allies attacked the Soviet Union. This was of immense benefit to the British empire, and Winston Churchill, the British prime minister since May 1940, immediately sought to help its new ally with armaments and other supplies. They would go to the Soviet Union's Arctic ports, and via Iran. The second event was the December 1941 Japanese attack on the British empire in the East. This opened a new and unwanted front for imperial forces. In its war in the East the empire performed disastrously. From December 1941 to February 1942

Malaya was lost to a small Japanese expeditionary force, a defeat which led to the loss of the allied Dutch East Indies and British Burma and threatened India. In ignominious retreat, the empire applied scorched-earth policies not just to the great oil refineries in the Indies and Burma, but also to the boats which allowed the transport of food for the poor. British planters, officials and soldiers acted to save themselves, ignoring the plight of the non-white, not least the very vulnerable Indian minority in Burma.[24] The war in the East decisively weakened the British empire in many ways – 1942 should indeed be more widely recognized as a key year in the dissolution of the empire.

India was mobilized and impoverished. Far from adopting a policy of national unity, the government of India dissolved provincial govern-ments, imprisoned the leaders of Indian nationalism, and in the words of one of them, returned the Raj to the worst of nineteenth-century autocracy.[25] The Raj regressed and repressed. Repression strong enough to hold on was applied, but it was more than enough to turn key elements of the Indian elite into determined opponents of British rule. Furthermore, millions died in a famine in Bengal, caused by multiple factors, including rising prices and the loss of the rice of Burma. Elsewhere, territory also had to be held by force. British and imperial troops garrisoned, operated from and controlled important subject territories, notably in the Middle East, where it extended its informal control in its great base, Egypt, and also in Iraq and Persia. It would prove damaging for British power in the medium term.

The war in the East affected not only the integrity of the empire, but also its power. All the great British armies were, to varying degrees, imperial forces. In mid-1944 British Commonwealth and empire forces numbered 8,713,000, of which 4,542,000 were in the forces of the United Kingdom.[26] Even the 21st Army group, the force which went from Normandy into Germany, was composed of a United Kingdom and a Canadian Army. The 8th Army had elements from the Indian, South African, Australian and New Zealand armies. The 14th Army was largely Indian, with African troops also: that this huge army of nearly 1 million men had to fight to regain imperial territories meant it could not be used in Europe. Furthermore, more Australian and New Zealand forces would have been available in

Europe than the relatively small number that could be spared from the defence of Oceania.

The war in the East weakened the British empire yet massively strengthened the overall Allied war effort by bringing in the full weight of the United States. The US naval base in Pearl Harbor and its empire in the Philippines were attacked at the same time as Malaya.

THE CHALLENGE OF THE USA

The relative military and economic strengths of the USA and UK changed dramatically, not because the United Kingdom was clapped out (as many historians writing from the 1970s onwards would insist), but because the USA became so strong, so quickly. In 1940–41 the British empire was the world's superpower, but in the blink of an eye the USA was to have easily the largest air force and navy in the world, the largest merchant fleet. US forces would deploy all over the world, including the United Kingdom itself, where they established bomber bases of similar scale to the British ones.

Winston Churchill (who had an American mother) would later celebrate the rise of the English-speaking peoples as a factor in world history. While there were many interconnections, mainly economic ones, there were also tensions and rivalries, not least in the inter-war years, when they were the two great global economic centres. British imperialists lamented that instead of emigrating to populate the empire, Britons flocked in their millions to the USA, before 1914 especially, out of reach of British influence. The English-speaking USA was always very much larger in population than the dominions. It was a large country growing very fast in wealth and population, with productivity levels in the farm, the factory and the mine which no one else could match. It was to become, unlike the dominions, a major exporter of manufactures in many important areas and a distinct economic threat to European nations. Yet its presence in world markets was a poor measure of its productive capacity or potential. For all its reputation for economic liberalism, the USA was heavily protectionist, and in proportion to its size its imports and exports were low by the standards of the United Kingdom and the British dominions too.

The relative strengths of the US and the British empire had already changed rapidly during the Great War. The USA entered the conflict in 1917 alongside the British empire and France as an associated power, not a full co-belligerent. Its main contribution was economic. Its bankers financed the shipping of quantities of materiel to the European allies. The United Kingdom borrowed huge sums from them, though it lent more to its allies, who themselves owed money to the USA. This was business: lending money to buy weapons and supplies, rather than supplying materiel for a common struggle. US financial muscle was such that Europe would be forced to agree to pay back its loans. In the end that did not fully happen. In the British case, the debts owed to it became unpayable, and in turn the British defaulted on part of the US loan. The United Kingdom, once the central source of foreign investment, yielded that place to Wall Street.

The rise of US economic power was very notable in the 1920s, both financial and industrial. It was very visible across the world, not least in the United Kingdom, and indeed the empire as a whole, where US firms set up branches and where, the UK excepted, US motor cars became common. In the 1930s the story was rather different. The US economy crashed much more severely than the European economies and retreated behind very high tariffs. There was a move to open up trade between the British bloc and the USA in the Anglo-American trade agreement of November 1938, which reduced tariffs on US wheat, and on fruit and the like, and on British manufactures such as woollens. But it was a limited agreement between two heavily protectionist economic systems.

It was the rearmament of the 1930s and the war which followed which would transform Anglo-American relations. The United Kingdom, and France, began importing large quantities of aircraft and machine tools for rearmament, starting in 1938. These orders had a major impact on US industry. After the fall of continental Europe to the Nazis the United Kingdom replaced its European sources of food and raw materials with US sources, and added more and more orders for manufactures, from weapons to ships. To the end of 1941 the United Kingdom paid in cash for these imports, running down its reserves. With the passing of the Lend-Lease Act in March 1941, which started having an effect only later, the US would donate to the United Kingdom, to the British empire and to other belligerents, much of the wherewithal to wage war. This time there was no serious question of loans. The United Kingdom got a loan from the USA only after the war, to pay for imports from the USA which had been coming in free under Lend-Lease during the war itself.

Leaving aside the crucial Eastern Front and the Sino-Japanese War, the war became an Anglo-American one, directed by a combined command structure based not in London but in Washington. Under the Combined Chiefs came supreme allied commanders in various theatres. They were American in Europe and the Pacific; the British got only Southeast Asia. A combined bomber offensive would pummel Germany from British bases.

The United Kingdom and the empire, fought an international and internationalist war. From January 1942 the title of the 'United Nations' was given to those who pledged to fight the Axis and subscribed to the Atlantic Charter: the original signatories were the big four, the USA, the USSR, China and the United Kingdom; the four dominions, Australia, Canada, New Zealand and South Africa; India; eight European governments-in-exile; and nine Caribbean/ Central American states. Henceforth the war was, in much propaganda, a war of the United Nations. Thus a British newsreel described the Lancaster bomber as the 'Finest heavy bomber operated by the United Nations'.[27] The plans of the 'United Nations for their war effort,' claimed Stafford Cripps, the minister for aircraft production, involved 'nothing less than the subordination of private and national interests to the public and international good'.[28] It was telling that United Nations Day, 14 June, celebrated from 1942 with Allied military parades, was on the National Flag Day of the United States.[29] The United States had clearly taken over as the great global power.

Far from wanting to leave the war in the Pacific to the USA, the British were desperate to grab a share of the action. After the defeat of Germany in May 1945 they were willing to devote extraordinary resources to the war against Japan. It amassed a huge fleet in Sydney. The British Pacific Fleet had all four of the surviving new wartime battleships (had the *Prince of Wales* not been lost to the Japanese in

1941 there could have been five), together with no fewer than ten air-craft carriers plus supporting escort carriers, cruisers, destroyers and submarines. By the end of the war, which came before the force was at planned peak strength, there were 142 warships in the fleet, which had about 125,000 officers and men.[30]

MACHINES AND MYTHS

In the Second World War in particular, the army was where male workers in non-essential occupations ended up – bank clerks, drivers, shop assistants, estate agents.[31] The state's priorities were elsewhere, in the air force and navy, and in transportation and production.

Much of the British war effort involved moving stuff around the world. For example, convoys carrying equipment and troops went to Egypt from the United Kingdom, India and Australasia. Ships crossed the Atlantic with food, fuel, raw materials, arms and troops. There were convoys through to Murmansk and Archangel, starting in 1941 and continuing to 1945, two to three convoys per month in the dark Arctic winter (with a longer route around Iceland for the few summer voyages). Of some 811 loaded merchant ships, 104 were lost, a rate of 13 per cent. The 24 out of 35 merchant ships lost in the July 1942 PQ17 convoy was altogether exceptional, not least as it was one of the few summer convoys. The losses in the Atlantic were lower.

Another critical issue was production. This depended on the Anglo-American dominance of much of the world. Matters were arranged so that the United Kingdom could maximize its forces and its arms production at the expense of its exports and domestic food produc-tion. The 'combined war effort'[32] made this possible, not, as it was later to be suggested, a national mobilization which marked the beginning of a new nation. It simply could not have happened had the British empire run its own war effort, much less had the United King-dom done so.

The aeroplane, British and German, remains central to the national myths of wartime Britain, in a way that warships, or merchant ships, let alone tanks and artillery do not. National memories of the war centre on the aeroplane and its effects, in particular on the Battle of

Britain and the Blitz, stories of defence by fighters and endurance by the civil population. There was a very different story of the United Kingdom and the aeroplane to be told – one centred on British, not German, bombers. The RAF was committed, long before the war, to a strategy of strategic bombing. It launched its bombers on Germany, unsuccessfully, in May 1940, before the Blitz of late 1940 and early 1941, even before the Battle of Britain of the summer. The bomber continued to be central to British strategy, with a huge bomber production and airfield-building programme central to the war production effort. The large-scale bombing of Germany started in 1942, after a disastrous debut in 1940 and 1941. The combined bomber offensive mounted year by year such that, by 1945, the Allies had the capacity to destroy whole cities at will. The US bomber force in the United Kingdom was itself about as large as Bomber Command and both depended on US resources. The aviation spirit came largely from the USA or via the USA. Many of the engines on British bombers, and the bombsights, were made to British designs in the USA. Here was the apotheosis of British global and capital-intensive warfare.

From the 1960s the British war effort came to be described, though this description only became at all common in the 1980s, as a 'people's war'. The term carried the sense not merely of a total war, but of a kind of war in which the left came into its own and in which social reform, and the extension of the rights of workers, was a central and visible part of the war effort. It was clearly a national conception, since no such policies applied in the crucial case of India. It was suggested that in the United Kingdom equality of sacrifice engendered a new consensus, which drove the essential reformist politics of the war. This is far too sanguine a picture. Death from bombing was far from indiscriminate – it hit East Enders and people living in other ports, much more than those in the West End or market towns. Merchant seamen were much more vulnerable to enemy fire than other civilians. In the armed services death was more likely to visit front-line soldiers, and bomber crews, than the majority in the ranks. While war increased equality in some dimensions it introduced huge new inequalities. British troops, and munitions workers, were fed off the civilian ration, and generously. Provision for the elderly – indeed for nearly everyone except service personnel and arms workers – got worse. The reality was that the war was essentially fought with the interwar welfare system (see chapter 9).

The 'people's war' image also suggests the mobilization of the whole population and of existing industrial resources and work-forces. One particularly resonant example was the mobilization of women, which was assumed to have gone further in the United King-dom than in Germany. Yet in reality the proportion of women employed remained lower than in Germany, where not only were they critical in agriculture, but men were needed and were lost in hugely greater numbers in the army. What happened in the United Kingdom was very similar to what happened in the Great War. Young women were mobilized into new specialized arms-making factories rather than replacing men in the economy as a whole. The young women who went to work on the land were very largely an additional labour force to meet the increased labour needs of domestic food production, rather than a replacement for men. New forms of segre-gated work were also created in the new women's branches of the army, navy and air force, the ATS, the WRENS and the WRAF. The essential point is this: the war saw the expansion of a warfare state with its distinctive needs and procedures, rather than the take-over of the state and nation by a mobilized people.

The wartime warfare state was the creation of the existing elite, not the left: it was the work of businessmen, not of socialist planners, of soldiers rather than public health physicians. Yet so powerful has been the idea of a civilian and civilizing war driven from the left, that a generation of history books claimed that while Winston Churchill ran the military side of the war, Labour ministers ran the 'home front' and the war economy. Historians claimed that Ernest Bevin, the minister of labour, was the real deputy prime minister, that Clement Attlee (the actual deputy prime minister from 1942) was crucial to the home front and that the Trades Union Congress was virtually a department of state.[33] In reality Churchill and his right-wing ministers, many from business, ran the home front, the war economy and the military oper-ations of the war. Lord Beaverbrook, of Express Newspapers, was minister of aircraft production and of supply. Oliver Lyttelton, from British Metals Corporation, was to become minister of production and, like Beaverbrook before him, a member of the war cabinet. Perhaps most important of all was Sir John Anderson, a former civil servant, who was lord president and then chancellor of the exchequer. Among the others were Lord Leathers, an expert in the transport of coal who became minister of war transport (1941); Lord Woolton, from the department store John Lewis in 1939, who became minister of food; and Lord Reith, of Beardmore, the BBC and Imperial Airways who served briefly as minister of information. The Labour contribution was significant, but not because Labour supposedly understood how to run a war economy.

Although wartime politics saw a shift to the left, that was not the only move. A new right emerged, though not as successfully as in the Great War. One of the most successful challengers of the party truce in 1941 was none other than Noel Pemberton Billing again, who stood in three by-elections as a 'research engineer', and once again as the Bomb Berlin candidate. His politics were unmistakably of the right. The first independent candidate to be elected was a production engineer who ran the Hispano-Suiza machine gun factory in Grantham. Denis Kendall, elected for Grantham and Sleaford in 1942, was a figure secretly connected to the hard right.[34] Only in 1943 did the first of three Common Wealth Party candidates (which argued that the war was not, but should *become*, a 'People's War') get elected. This was a party of the left, but hardly revolutionary. Two of its victorious candidates were in the RAF, the other was a Royal Engineer.

The dominant figure of war, covering all aspects of the war effort, was Winston Churchill. He was brought into office in May 1940 in the wake of the failure of the Norway campaign he had promoted as first lord of the Admiralty. He was prime minister because of his anti-Nazi record and because he was acceptable to the Labour Party, whose entry into a coalition seemed necessary to all. Churchill also brought in the small Liberal Party, in semi-opposition from 1933. Today Winston Churchill overshadows Lloyd George, but both men and their achievements are usefully compared. Lloyd George was the senior only by a decade; both had served in the Edwardian and Great War Liberal governments, Churchill as home secretary, first lord of the admiralty and minister of munitions. As prime minister Churchill inherited a conscript army and a warfare state already out-producing Germany in many critical weapons. By contrast, Lloyd George had to create the modern fully mobilized warfare state and, furthermore, faced a divided kingdom, serious labour unrest and a toxic political atmosphere. There was another great difference: the victorious leaders of 1918 – Lloyd George, Georges Clemenceau and Woodrow Wilson – each stood at the head of a very great power. By contrast, Churchill inherited a global empire and presided, through no fault of his, over a relative British decline of extraordinary speed. While Lloyd George, as he put it, led the empire, Churchill emerged as the leader of a nation, and one which was not a superpower. Lloyd George won his war; of Churchill it was to be said that he was 'the saviour of his country'.[35]

THE POWER OF THE NATION

The 'people's war' historiography focused on supposed transformations internal to the nation, often exaggerating their significance. In fact, the greatest changes the war brought about were in the United Kingdom's external position.[36] These changes were central to the emergence of a distinct British nation after 1945.

The wartime internationalist spirit of combination disappeared with victory. Lend-Lease was suddenly ended after August 1945. That meant that the United Kingdom would have to start buying imports from the USA again, before it had the chance to build up its export trade. The British view of matters was very different to that of the USA or its allies. They insisted they were first into the war and ought to be recompensed for this. The British wanted the Americans to pay for British orders and investments in arms in the USA before 1942, when Lend-Lease kicked in. They also wanted the supplies and services rendered in return for deferred payment (in effect loans), especially in India and Egypt, to be turned in part into gifts. But neither the Americans nor those territories which had in effect lent the United Kingdom vast sums were having this. The British were forced to take out a loan from the USA, of around £1 billion, in order to continue to import necessities which could only come from the USA, and which they could not pay for because of the wartime mobilization, which had prioritized British arms production over exports. Furthermore, the loan came with controversial conditions. The British side was forced to agree to make sterling convertible by 1947. The US also wanted to dismantle imperial preference, to open to its own producers a global market. As it happened, the priorities of the Cold War intervened, and imperial preference continued, and, apart from a very brief spell in 1947, sterling was not convertible till 1958. The US loan of 1945 was supplemented by Marshall Aid from the USA from 1947, which allowed the purchase of dollar raw materials, food and tobacco, and machinery.[37]

The British nation was an active participant in the Cold War. For the left, then and since, this was a measure of subservience to the USA. For Harry Pollitt of the Communist Party, writing in 1946, British economic weakness presented the very real danger that the British people would become 'the slaves and cannon-fodder of the United States of America', its 'aircraft carrier, its rocket and flying-bomb base'.[38] Yet the British contribution to the Cold War had its own internal dynamic.

From 1945 the United Kingdom no longer commanded the seas of the world as it had once done. Nor did it command the air, as it had aspired to. Nor did it command the electronic ether, or the atomic realm, though it would make great play of its contributions in radar and atomic physics. Yet the British state did not shrink from devoting very scarce resources of labour, research and development and foreign exchange to fight communism globally. Even in the face of labour shortages, conscription was maintained. British exports to a significant degree paid for the maintenance of British troops abroad, rather than for desperately needed imports. While there was no money for new hospitals, there was finance in abundance for new weapons laboratories and a comprehensive weapons development programme which some senior advisers, like Sir Henry Tizard, thought over-ambitious. It built, as we shall see in a later chapter, a distinctly national atomic bomb.

The post-war Labour government not only maintained but developed the warfare state, giving it support unprecedented in peacetime. Comparing public expenditure of the late 1940s with that of the

1930s, the great difference was not in the rise of welfare spending, but the much greater rise in warfare spending. Fighting, and especially preparing to fight, communism in the 1940s and beyond drove warlike expenditure to above 10 per cent of GDP in peacetime. These were levels of military expenditure once associated with continental powers.

After 1945 British conscripts were a feature of peacetime armed forces for the first time, another way the United Kingdom became European in peacetime. The British state needed this conscription because the empire was in greater turmoil than before the war and because it no longer had the Indian army, which during the war had provided troops for all the major operations in Asia and Africa. With the Indian army gone, these bases and operations would have to be taken over by British conscripts, with the remnants of the Indian army, the Gurkhas, and, as ever, local forces. As during the war, young men were released from education at the age of fourteen and then fifteen to enter the workforce, and then recalled by the state at age eighteen for 'National Service' in national forces.

Nearly everywhere that British national troops were stationed in large numbers during the war saw British influence and presence ejected – Egypt, Palestine, Iraq, Iran, India, Burma, Ceylon are all examples. Once the war was over, it was clear that taking full control of India in the face of mounting opposition would not be worthwhile. The die-hards might talk of 'scuttle' but they had no alternative. Control over India was given to the Congress Party led by Jawaharlal Nehru in the summer of 1946; he was de facto prime minister by September 1946.[39] Independence, intended for 1948, was brought forward to 1947. Within two years of the end of the war in the East, British India was no more. The United Kingdom also walked away, quickly and decisively, from its mandated territory of Palestine. Here, in the 1940s, it was now fighting a Jewish rather than an Arab insurgency. It withdrew at the end of 1947; the mandate ended in 1948.

However, within the state the Labour prime minister Clement Attlee did have to face down those, like the foreign secretary, Ernest Bevin, who did not fully understand the imperial game was up. Attlee was hostile to Middle East bases because he thought they were dangerously redundant in an age of nuclear weapons and aircraft;

defensible lines were to be found in Africa instead. He lost the argument, and the army and air force numbered 80,000 in the Canal Zone in 1951. By 1954 they had been kicked out by Egypt. But he stopped the plan of his second foreign secretary, a former conscientious objector, and the advocate of the public board form of nationalization Labour had adopted, Herbert Morrison, to use force against Persia in 1951 after the nationalization of the Anglo-Iranian oil company.[40] Iraq lasted longest in the British sphere; despite rebellions in 1948 and 1952, it was not till 1958 that the pro-British monarchy was ejected.

Only further east was the empire re-established, and then in territory that had been lost. Malaya was taken back into the colonial empire after the defeat of Japan. There was, however, opposition from the local communists, who had been at the heart of the resistance against the Japanese occupation, to which the British empire had surrendered Malaya in 1942. Some 50,000 British troops were sent to fight them and to defend a rubber industry which alone exported more to the USA than the UK economy. The Malayan emergency, as it was called, was the first imperial war in which conscripts from Great Britain were engaged.

3

Globalization to Nationalization

Oh, where are you going to, all you Big Steamers,
With England's own coal, up and down the salt seas?
We are going to fetch you your bread and your butter,
Your beef, pork, and mutton, eggs, apples, and cheese.
                  Rudyard Kipling, 'Big Steamers' (1911)[1]

In the metabolism of the Western world the coal-miner is
second in importance only to the man who ploughs the soil.
                  George Orwell, The Road to Wigan Pier (1936)

Justice for the miner has meant fuel and power for the nation.
                  Let Us Win Through Together, *Labour*
                  Party manifesto, 1950

In 1900 the United Kingdom was a very different entity from most other great nations. As we have seen, it had no conscription but a large navy, and it was free-trading and had a small state. It was rich and globally oriented as well as imperial. This was the period when these islands depended on what have evocatively been called 'ghost acres': instead of vast forests, underground seams of compacted ancient vegetation in the form of coal; instead of fields of wheat at home, vast tracts of land farmed by Europeans living thousands of miles away.[2] Britons depended not on the careful husbandry of their fertile lands, but on artifice. They were kept alive by triple expansion engines and refrigeration chambers, all powered by British mineral energy.

In the first half of the twentieth century the United Kingdom had as many colliers as farm workers. Of no other country was this remotely true. About 1 million tilled the land and husbanded animals, and another million dug the coal that lay beneath it in extraordinary quantities. Far more coal than wheat came out of the lands of the British Isles, about 100 times more.[3] By head of population it produced less food, and more energy, than any major country. It was easily the largest importer of food in the world. It was also the largest exporter of energy. It was the Saudi Arabia of 1900. Nearly every home in the land had white bread made from wheat imported from far away and in effect locally dug black coal. British coal was much cheaper than wheat, which was around ten times more expensive by weight. In the 1920s, very roughly, the 50 million tons of coal exported paid for the 5 million tons of wheat imported.[4] The United Kingdom's coal was generally exported to poorer countries, while food came from countries at least as wealthy.

Rich comparisons were made between coal mining and agriculture. The importance of coal was highlighted by arguing that it was as fundamentally important as food, at a time when food accounted for 30 per cent of consumer expenditure (alcohol was another 20 per cent in 1900, down to 10 per cent in the 1920s, and lower still in the 1930s).[5] The varying productivity of mines by analogy was compared with the different productivity of farms set on land of different sorts.[6] Much land was owned by a class of landowners who rented it out to 'tenant farmers'.[7] Landowners owned the coal too and charged a 'royalty' to the colliery companies who exploited these mineral rights. The fruit of the land profited not those who worked it, but those who owned it, and owned it not by virtue of their own industry, but through inheritance. Mining was very largely, though not exclusively, a rural rather than an urban industry (though this runs against the standard equation of coal with other industries, and with the urban). It is not for nothing people spoke of 'pit villages' – for many miners lived in small, isolated communities built around mines. Indeed, like agriculture, mining was horse-powered. Before 1914 there were some 70,000 pit ponies, about one-tenth of the number of agricultural horses. Lastly, British land was remarkably productive above as well as below ground: yields per acre of grains were among the highest in the world, and the United Kingdom produced more coal even than physically very much larger countries such as Germany or Russia. In terms of the productivity of *labour* the story was different – here the farmers and colliers of the New World were way ahead.[8]

These were the fundamentals of the United Kingdom's material balance with the rest of the globe, and its political economy more generally. They defined the United Kingdom as industrial rather than agricultural, as maritime rather than land bound, as free trading rather than protectionist, as internationalist rather than nationalist.

But things would change. Coal output would peak in 1913 and it would be on a nearly uninterrupted downward path thereafter. Food production would jump during the wars, and after the Second World War the state became committed to ever-increasing domestic production. There was a shift from coal to food production, a fall in coal exports and a fall in time in food imports. By the 1950s the United Kingdom was a net importer of energy (imports being mainly oil) and, while still a very significant food importer, was on a path to self-sufficiency. From being quite exceptional in this and many other regards, it was now very much closer to the European norm.

COAL

Sheer abundance of cheap coal was a crucial feature of British life. Coal was overwhelmingly the most important material (other than water) being used in the economy. Each miner produced around 300 tons per annum, roughly 5 tons of coal per head of population, the highest per capita coal production in the world. In the 1920s coal supported one-twelfth of the population, earned £250 million, 10 per cent of exports by value, 75 per cent by volume.[9] In 1913 287 million tons were dug, and 98 million tons left British ports, in bunkers of ships going abroad, as coal and as coke. Taken as a whole, the British coalfield (a good description) was comparable in output to the combined Ruhr, Belgian and Northern French coalfields, and very much larger than the other two big European fields in Silesia and the Ukraine. The sheer quantity of coal below the ground was a source of wonder – there were hundreds of years of production left; only a tiny fraction had been extracted.[10]

Consumption within the United Kingdom was about the same in 1913 as in 1950 (at roughly 200 million tons), with a trough in the early 1930s (-20 per cent), and peak consumption to be reached in 1956 (+10 per cent). Between 1900 and 1950 coal drove both the main means of transport – ships and railways – and it produced nearly all the electricity and arrived in 1-hundredweight (50 kg roughly) bags to nearly every home in the land. Coal produced nearly all the gas, made the coke for the steel industry, powered nearly every steam engine and was the source of heat for most industrial processes. Although many industries and cities were sited close to mines, it was moved about in vast quantities. Much was carried by sea, as in the case of the proverbial coals to Newcastle, and the shipments of steam coal from South Wales. The railway system was an intricate coal pipeline network, taking coal to every town and city in the country, whence it went to nearly every factory and every home. Coal, coke and patent fuel provided one-third of the freight revenue of the railways.[11]

The majority of coal was burned raw, causing fogs to the extent that wash days *were* rainier. Urban areas got 20 per cent less sunlight than the countryside.[12] Acrid soot blackened buildings of every British city. It was from the 1970s that buildings were cleaned to reveal the colours which lay behind the corrosive blackness which had covered them. 'Smogs', the terrible mixture of smoke and fog, disoriented pedestrians and motorists alike, but killed thousands of aged and infirm. The bronchitic catarrh was as common a sound as that of the clanking and whooshing of steam engines of railway locomotives, which for good measure also covered their surroundings in grime.

The coal industry was not a left-over from the past, nor was it seen as such. Before 1914 it was expanding, though less than elsewhere. The number of British miners went up by hundreds of thousands between 1900 and 1913 to over a million; new mines and new coalfields were opened up. Nineteen new pits were sunk in South Yorkshire and Nottinghamshire, a major new field in the first quarter of the century, as well as new fields in Kent. During 1924 the twentieth-century pits produced around 10 million tons.[13] It was a changing industry. Looking back from 1934 to the 1880s, Sir Richard Redmayne, a noted mining engineer and adviser to government, claimed to see a transformed industry, one in which coal was cut by machine and hauled electrically through whitewashed mines as brightly lit as the London underground, where mechanical appliances replaced manual labour, and steel had replaced wooden pit props. It was safer than mining abroad, he claimed, and a healthy industry. Yet he had to admit that in fact less than half the mines cut coal by machine or were electrically powered.[14]

It was also an industry thought to have a long future. In 1915 Herbert Stanley Jevons, professor of economics in the University of Allahabad (in the United Provinces), published *The British Coal Trade*, a mammoth work of description and analysis. He was the son of another academic economist, William Stanley Jevons, author of *The Coal Question* (1865) and the founder of marginal economics. Jevons Junior saw domestic coal consumption increasing with population, remaining at under 5 tons per capita; he predicted consumption at 266 million tons in 1951. He foresaw more and more coal being exported, such that the nearly 100 million tons of exports of 1913 (including bunkers) would increase to 272 million tons in 1951, more than domestic consumption.[15] He was not far off on domestic consumption, but wholly wrong on exports, which dwindled to practically nothing.

British coal was, until the Second World War, the single most important internationally traded form of energy. Before the Great War, it represented 70 per cent of the global sea trade in coal. France, Scandinavia, Italy and Germany each took around or more than 10 million tonnes each. One could find British coal not just in coastal Germany but in Berlin. British coal made Lisbon's town gas and drove Egyptian railways, Swedish ironworks and Argentine abattoirs, grain elevators and railways. The key was not just cheap production, but closeness to the sea: no one else could get coal on board ship so easily; and, once on board, it could go vast distances very cheaply. So, even after the USA took over as the world's leading producer around 1900, British coal continued to dominate the export market.

Coal was shipped from specialist docks but in standard ships. In 1913 the combined Cardiff, Barry and Penarth Docks exported some 20 million tons; the Tyne 14 million (excluding a large coastal trade),

Grimsby and Hull shipped 7 million tons, Newport 5 million, Blyth 4.5 million, the ports around Kirkcaldy on the Firth another 4.5 million.[16] Coal was exported by freighters of 4–7,000 'tons' (the volume of merchant ships was measured in 'tons', a particular measure of volume not mass), powered by coal, and a small triple-expansion reciprocating steam engine. These ships steamed slowly, at around 10 knots, were cheap to operate and very basic. A characteristic long journey would involve taking coal from Cardiff to the River Plate and returning with wheat, recalling that ten times more coal went out than wheat came in. These tramps, for such they usually were, made up half the British fleet and were run by firms concentrated in the Northeast, Scotland and Cardiff. The liberty ships of the Second World War, from a British design, were of this type and were still to be found in the 1960s (though the US liberty ships had boilers fired by oil, not coal).[17]

By far the most important determinant of the fate of the coal industry was what happened abroad. The international coal market changed in the interwar years – Germany lost one-third of its mines to the new Polish state including the Silesian coalfield, which produced hard coal. Poland subsidized its transport to the sea, with less going to Germany than before the war. Post-revolutionary Russia imported less, as did Germany, where lignite substituted for imported coal.[18] Trade depression depressed coal markets. That was not immediately felt because of strikes in the USA in 1922, and the occupation of the Ruhr by the French in 1923, but British exports would never again reach the levels of exports of 1913 (nearly 100 million tons). Exports had dropped to about 50 million tons per annum through the 1930s. It was this loss of exports and fall in price which shaped the fate of the British coal industry, and its million miners.

The politics of mining was the politics of hours and wages and even in the Edwardian years involved the government. In 1908 the miners had secured an eight-hour underground day, by legislation; and a seven-hour underground day in 1919. The wages of coal miners depended in many cases on the price of coal. The first national miners' strike, which brought out nearly a million miners in 1912, led to legislation which instituted regional minimum wages. During the war the mines and coal prices were controlled, which lasted until

March 1921. The miners refused the new conditions proposed for their future, which included wage cuts, and were locked out. The fellow members of the 'triple alliance', the railwaymen and the dockers, had been called out on strike in their support, but the order was rescinded on what came to be known as Black Friday, 15 April 1921. The lockout continued into July 1921.

From 1921 to 1924 the British industry was on an even keel as exports were buoyed by the lack of production from various foreign coalfields. But by mid-1925 all the British coalfields were making losses. The coal owners wanted a further reduction of wages and an increase in the hours of work. The TUC supported the Miners' Federation in their rejection of the terms, and on Red Friday, 31 July 1925, the government averted a strike by instituting an inquiry, subsidizing the industry to maintain existing wages and hours. The inquiry, into the 'economic position of the Coal Industry', was headed by a senior Liberal politician, Sir Herbert Samuel, along with a general, a textile magnate and Sir William Beveridge, an expert on labour. In preparation for the expected showdown, the government arrested twelve leaders of the Communist Party in October 1925. They were all imprisoned for between six and twelve months, to keep them out of the political fray, 'the chief instance of a purely political trial in the interwar years'.[19] For the future the mine owners wanted the end of national negotiations, longer working hours and, in some areas, huge falls in wages: down from 78s to 45s 10d per week for the hewers of South Wales.[20] The miners, of course, said no, insisting on 'not a penny off the pay, not a minute on the day'.

The Samuel Commission reported in 1925; its recommendations for the short term, the ones that mattered, a reduction in wages, were unacceptable to the miners. The owners, backed by the government, locked out the miners, and they would stay out for six months. Half a year of coal production was lost, no trivial matter, including 28 million tons of exports. Coal was imported. The government passed two crucial acts during the lockout – the first allowed an eight-hour day (repealing the 1919 provisions of seven hours). A second allowed but did not compel rationalization and put a levy on coal royalties for miners' welfare (which were often to be used to create basic facilities like pithead baths, many of which were built in the 1930s. More than half of miners (but not mines) had them by nationalization. The mine owners were intransigent, and, with government support, by December 1926 they were utterly victorious. 'Neither Baldwin nor his senior Cabinet colleagues withdrew their sympathies from the owners,' says the official historian.[21] This defeat damaged the union structurally, when the Spencer union in Nottingham broke away from the national federation. In most districts, the mines went on to eight hours, and on lower pay per shift. In 1927 the government passed the Trade Disputes Act, which severely constrained the right to strike, and made it much more difficult for unions to fund the Labour Party.

The labour movement proved very weak in its defence of the locked-out miners. At the beginning the TUC had called a national strike.[22] During the so-called 'general strike' the TUC did not call out all workers but only those in the railways, docks, road transport, printing, iron and steel, metals, building, electricity and gas. They called off the action only nine days later, one day after calling out the engineers and shipbuilders, claiming in public that they had achieved an understanding by which serious negotiations would begin; they had in fact just called off the strike in return for nothing.[23] Employers victimized returning workers, which led to a second semi-official national strike, which lasted a few days. But the victimization continued: nearly a quarter of the National Union of Railwaymen's membership were refused a return to work.[24]

In the 1930s the position of the coal mines and the miners was even worse than in the late 1920s. Bunkers and exports were down to 50 million tons. Domestic consumption fell too. The result was hundreds of thousands of unemployed miners. One consolation was that the 7.5-hour day was brought in, as promised, in 1930, where it remained. The 1930s saw slow recovery in output of the mines under price-control schemes, but at a low level. Exports remained low despite bilateral trade agreements which gave British coal huge market shares in the Nordic and Baltic countries, and Argentina.[25] British coal was becoming distinctly less hemispheric, and a tad more national.

OIL

The early twentieth century saw the emergence of a new universal fuel – oil. With it came a new vision of modernity – the petrol-powered world of the private mass-produced motor car. In this world the United Kingdom was not first, but it was second to the USA, by far the greatest petroleum producer and car maker in the world. The United Kingdom was the world's largest importer of oil and had the most motorized economy after the USA. Its oil companies were second only to the US giants, and at least as important as these outside the USA itself.

British capital was very quick to get into oil, and did not discriminate between imperial and other territories. British and Anglo-Dutch enterprises were to remain the only competitors to the American companies as they too looked to oil fields outside the USA. The British oil industry had origins in the firm created in the late 1880s by the brothers Marcus and Samuel Samuel to transport oil from Baku, in the Russian Empire, called Shell Transport and Trading. It merged with the Royal Dutch company (producing in the Dutch East Indies) in 1907 and expanded rapidly thereafter as an Anglo-Dutch enterprise producing in Russia, Romania, Venezuela, Mexico and the United States. The first major fully British oil producer was Burmah Oil (operating in Rangoon), followed by the Anglo-Persian Oil Company, operating in Persia, and soon controlled by Burmah. The huge refinery at Abadan started production in 1914. The British government took a controlling share in order to secure supply for the navy, now rather remarkably beginning to be oil fired. The oil fields were in the British sphere of influence in southern Persia, agreed with the Russians in 1907. A third British oil company was created by Sir Weatman Pearson, a civil engineering contractor who found oil in Mexico in 1910 and created a fleet to transport it. His Eagle Oil Company was bought by Shell in 1919, making Shell the key producer in Mexico – it had 60 per cent of the second-largest production area in the world.[26]

The interwar years brought mixed fortunes. The new Soviet Union nationalized the Baku oil fields and refineries. In 1938 Mexico nationalized its oil industry, including the very significant Shell operations.

The British capture of former Ottoman territories in the Great War opened up important new fields to British oil companies. In Iraq the partly Anglo-Persian-owned Iraq Petroleum Company found oil, which was to be shipped by pipeline to a new refinery built on the Mediterranean, in Haifa, Palestine in the 1930s.

In the interwar years there were three major British oil companies operating globally – Shell, Anglo-Persian and Burmah. They had very little capital invested in the United Kingdom itself except in selling operations. In the home market they competed with Standard Oil of New Jersey (Esso), and overseas with the small numbers of US companies that at this point operated outside the USA, which included Standard Oil.[27] The reason for the small amount of domestic investment was that all the very large refineries were close to the oil fields. The Anglo-Iranian company employed 50,000 workers in Iran and produced 10 million tons per annum of refined products in the late 1930s, comparable to the coal output of a similar number of British coal miners.[28] The United Kingdom thus imported refined petroleum products – a manufacture, rather than a raw material.

The transport by sea of petrol and other refined products was central to British thinking about oil supplies. Dating from the 1880s, the oil tanker was at least partly British in conception. From before the Great War to 1939, the British tanker fleet was the largest in the world, as befitted the greatest importer of oil products, its only significant competitor the US fleet (which was largely domestic). Command of the seas meant it was worthwhile to import not only crude oil, but rather refined oils. Oil companies and the government pointed out that investing in tankers gave access to oil at a low price. With command of the sea, also needed for all other supplies, there was no need to go to the huge and inefficient expense of making oil products locally or from coal.[29] There were, however, as we shall see in more detail in a later chapter, nationalists who wanted to make oil from British coal. They had limited success. An oil-from-coal plant was built by Imperial Chemical Industries at Billingham, and the technique was used in a second large plant built during the war at Heysham, where Imperial Chemical Industries collaborated with Shell and Trinidad Leaseholds, the oil company which operated in Trinidad, the only significant imperial producer of oil other than Burma.

FOOD

The import of food on a gigantic scale had great consequences for the economic and social structure of the United Kingdom. Its farming population was radically smaller than that of France, Germany or the United States. The British housewife was typically only a consumer of food, and a cook, not a producer. She was connected as a matter of quotidian experience to the far corners of the earth. Like petroleum products supplies, British food was not national, nor imperial. By 1900 and into the 1950s, the United Kingdom was a huge importer of food from near and far, the hub of an extraordinary gastro-cosmopolitanism.[30] Even the full English breakfast was typically made from Danish bacon, Dutch eggs and the bread from Canadian or Argentine wheat. Fish and chips were made from British potatoes but with fish caught in the waters off Newfoundland or Iceland. Butter might come from Denmark or New Zealand. Margarine, an industrial butter substitute, was made primarily by the Anglo-Dutch firm Unilever, created in the 1920s. A large margarine factory at Purfleet on the Thames (from 1930 part of Unilever, and still in operation) had its own jetty for the import of whale oil.[31] There was a similar large facility, also with its own dock at Port Sunlight, the main Unilever factory. British and Norwegian whalers dominated whale oil supply. The whaling industry was based in the cold waters of the southern Atlantic, consisting of British and Norwegian whale oil factories on South Georgia as well as floating factory ships. It was to South Georgia's whaling stations that Ernest Shackleton made his epic 800-mile journey from Antarctica in an open boat, following the failure of his Imperial Trans-Antarctic Expedition in 1915.

So important was food from far away that it set prices. Thus it was that reference pricing of food in the United Kingdom included 'No 2 northern Manitoba wheat', 'Canadian Western' barley, 'Argentine chilled, fores and hinds' of beef and 'Australian frozen, hinds and crops', as well as 'Lamb New Zealand' and 'Bacon Danish green sides'.[32] As these cases suggest much food came from vast expanses of land worked by few workers and many horses – the arable farms, cattle ranges and sheep stations of the Americas and Oceania.[33] It is important to note that most did not come from empire – the exceptions being (by the 1930s) – dairy products, fruit, tea and sugar.

Food made up the bulk of imports by value. Meat alone accounted for 20 per cent. The London docks were a gigantic complex for the importation of food. Appropriately enough the grocer Hudson Kearley (Lord Davenport), of the International Tea Co. Stores chain, was the first chairman of the Port of London Authority, created in 1908. The authority was to control what was from the 1920s the largest dock in the world, formed by the interconnected Royal Victoria, the Royal Albert and the King George V Docks.[34] The Royal Victoria Dock had special berths for the meat boats of among others the Royal Mail and Blue Star Lines, which supplied Smithfield, the greatest dead-meat market in the world. There were cold stores for meat on the Royal Albert Dock. Sugar was imported for the two Tate & Lyle cane sugar refineries between the docks and the Thames (one remains at the time of writing). The Royal Victoria Dock was also a centre for flour-milling. Mills were built around 1900 and rebuilt or extended in the 1930s, such as the Cooperative Wholesale Society Mill, the Rank Empire Mill, the William Vernon Millennium Mill (whose structure also still stands at the time of writing), later part of Spillers, and the Rank Premier Mill. On a smaller scale, similar facilities were found in other docks. For example, there were many new mills and granaries built in the 1930s in Cardiff, Newcastle and Avonmouth.[35]

Wheat was the most important corn (the old term for cereals) consumed in the United Kingdom; most was imported. Although the Corn Laws were long repealed, allowing free entry of cereals, it was only in recent decades that the growth of production in the Americas and Australasia, and its cheap transport by steamer, had made foreign corn dominant. Cheap bread for the British worker was a central theme of politics – a key to the Liberal landslide of 1906, a dramatic reaffirmation of free trade. But what Tories could not do, German U-Boats could. In 1917 a new corn law was passed – the Corn Production Act, guaranteeing minimum prices for wheat and oats, and a minimum wage for farm workers, to encourage domestic production.

The manifesto of the coalition which stood for election in 1918 was clear on the meaning of this momentous change: 'The war has given fresh impetus to agriculture. This must not be allowed to expire. Scientific farming must be promoted.'[36] The Labour Party also wanted to expand agriculture and nationalize the land but was against protection: 'The land is the people's and must be developed so as to afford a high standard of life to a growing rural population not by subsidies or tariffs, but by scientific methods, and the freeing of the soil from landlordism and reaction.'[37]

The new corn law of 1917 was extended in 1920. But in 1921 the Corn Production Acts (Repeal) Bill was passed, 'the great betrayal', as it was called, which meant agriculture was fully back in the world market, once more among the great 'unsheltered' trades. Less land was ploughed, and it became a space where dairy cattle were fed with imported fodder. In the 1930s livestock accounted for 70 per cent of the value of British farm production. They ate in calories twice the amount of the human population of the United Kingdom.[38] The other expanding sector was orchards and market gardens.

The Great Depression meant there was very cheap wheat on the world market, a boon for most of the British people, but not for British or foreign farmers. Support for domestic arable production would return in the 1930s. Nationalists were especially keen to make use of the full productive potential of British land. Many published on the special virtues of the British earth.[39] There were moves to increase domestic production, to the detriment of both foreign and imperial producers, through state support for wheat production. The threat of war prompted further intervention. The 1937 Land Fertility Scheme, under the Agriculture Act of the same year, gave large subsidies to farmers to apply British lime and British basic slag (a waste product of iron production containing phosphate) to grasslands, to increase their fertility in anticipation of the need to plough them up for grain.

The story of sugar supply shows more dramatic shifts to national and imperial supply. The British people had a notoriously sweet tooth. By 1900 the British consumed three times as much sugar per person as continentals.[40] Surprisingly, 80 per cent of this sugar came from beet grown in continental Europe itself. Germany and Austria paid export subsidies to stimulate exports. For some this was dumping to be controlled, for others a situation which the British consumer should take advantage of.[41] The tariff reformers wanted sugar to come from British colonies in the Caribbean, as it had in the past. But others wanted the United Kingdom to copy the continentals and start growing sugar beet. The imperialists and nationalists were to win out in this case more than any other. The National Sugar Beet Association was founded in 1909, the first beet sugar factory in 1912. But this vegetable symbol of economic nationalism came to the United Kingdom on a large scale only in the 1920s, with subsidies and protection. In 1936 the British Sugar Corporation was created by the Sugar Industry (Reorganisation) Act to take the entire crop. With protection came imperial preference, and by the 1930s the market was divided between national and imperial suppliers. Sugar now came from factories in the English countryside, and via refineries in ports, from redeveloped plantations and sugar factories in the colonies, such as the new Tate & Lyle ones in Jamaica.

MEAT

Meat provides a case of global-national supply which endured through peace and war. The British people were the great meat-eaters of Europe, and proud of it, but something like half of all British meat came from abroad. Pork and bacon came from Denmark and the Netherlands mainly, and beef, lamb and mutton from the River Plate and Australasia, in a remarkable trans-equatorial trade in refrigerated and preserved meat.

Around 1900 London had two enormous cattle markets, with small slaughterhouses nearby. One was in Islington, where British cattle were sold, having been brought in by train. This had replaced Smithfield as a market for live animals. The second one was at Deptford, which was used for imported cattle. It was to very quickly lose its significance as live imports were restricted, and as frozen and chilled meat imports soared. The Royal Docks were soon bringing far more meat to London than both markets combined; London's slaughterhouses had in effect moved to Buenos Aires, Montevideo and Wellington. These distant abattoirs and the farms which fed them were quite unlike anything found at home. The UK exported pedigree breeding stock and imported its dead offspring. Cattle, typically from British breeds, refined by breeders working in the United Kingdom to suit both the land, the processing and the British palate, were raised on vast *estancias* or stations. For example the Bovril company from 1908 owned 1.5 million acres of the Argentine province of Entre Rios – three English counties' worth – in Santa Elena on the river Parana. There it had a company town and meat works – which produced corned beef and meat extract and from the 1930s chilled and frozen meat. The Liebig Extract of Meat Company owned *estancias* on both sides of the river Uruguay and had company towns and slaughterhouses on either side – at Pueblo Liebig and Fray Bentos. Just as New York got its meat from Chicago by rail so London got its fill from the River Plate, and beyond, by ship.

In the interwar years one British group owned by the Vestey family created an integrated global food operation supplying the United Kingdom, the only British rival to the US meat trusts, which themselves also supplied the British market from South America and Australasia. For example, Vestey took over the Fray Bentos farms and works in the early 1920s and transformed them into a chilled meat plant. The meat was shipped to the even larger Vestey plant on Dock Sud in Buenos Aires, there loaded onto a Vestey-owned Blue Star Line ship, a veritable floating cold-store, and taken to Vestey-owned Union Cold Storage cold stores in London and elsewhere, and then onto Dewhurst butchers – also owned by Vestey. Vestey's main competitors in the British market were the Chicago meat trusts, Swift and Armour, but they had nothing like this integrated operation, relying on others to ship and sell their meat.

The meat ships were expensive, fast, often motor-powered ships which carried other refrigerated food and often passengers over the vast distances from Australasia and the River Plate. They were operated as liners, by visible companies with plush offices in London and elsewhere, and they sailed mainly to London and Liverpool. They were quite unlike the slow tramps which shipped wheat. They were indeed a distinctively British kind of ship – no other country had need of anything like so many.[42]

The novelty of the years before the Great War was the import of premium chilled beef from the River Plate, of much higher quality than frozen (all lamb and mutton was frozen and came from Australia and New Zealand as well as the River Plate). Chilled beef was a central item of the Roca-Runciman agreement between the United Kingdom and Argentina of the 1930s – it guaranteed 1920s levels of chilled beef imports in return for the payment of interest and profits on British investments and tariff-free entry for many British goods, including coal.[43]

COAL, OIL AND FOOD IN THE SECOND WORLD WAR

On the eve of the Second World War, therefore, the United Kingdom was still in the unique position of importing around half its food, and it remained the largest exporter of energy, and the largest importer of oil products. According to the nationalists who had called for more national self-sufficiency in both food and oil, this left the United Kingdom appallingly vulnerable to blockade. But for economic liberals overseas supply was seen as a source of strength – having to grow its own food and produce its own oil would make the United Kingdom poorer, and indeed much less able to mobilize troops and produce armaments.

The received image of the Second World War economy is one in which economic nationalism triumphed. The new nation turned inward and found strength there. It cut food imports by half and grew its own food; it eliminated private motoring and by implication cut oil imports. Yet when we look in detail at energy and food, a rather different picture emerges. It retained and reconfigured a remarkably global supply of food and oil. The story of coal in wartime for different reasons also points to a history of the war rather different from that suggested by the phrase the 'people's war'.

Throughout the war the number of miners, the output of coal and the productivity of work would all decrease.[44] The shortage of mining labour was so acute that from 1943, one in ten conscripts was sent into the mines, a total of 21,800 young men; more than 8,000 appealed, overwhelmingly unsuccessfully, against this, showing just how unpopular the mines were, even at normal mining wages, higher than the pay of soldiers.[45] There was no patriotic Stakhanovism, no new proto-welfare state for miners. Wages went up but were still comparatively low. The British economy could survive these falls in output because during the Second World War coal lost most of its export markets. At first more exports were needed, to support France, which had lost its Polish and German suppliers in 1939. But from 1940 supplies ceased not only to France and Italy, but to Egypt and the Mediterranean also. Coal became a national industry.

The story of oil was very different. While petrol consumption was cut quite radically for civilians, petrol and other oil imports into the British Isles surged during the war. The British armed services consumed oil on a lavish scale, at sea, in the air and on land. Imports reached 20 million tons, double pre-war and nearly three times peak German output. This figure does not include the huge quantities which went direct to British forces overseas, or to the British empire as a whole. For example, some 5 million tons went to northwest Europe from D-Day to the end of the war. Well over 90 per cent went to Normandy by tanker, and most of that never touched the United Kingdom and was not accounted for in British imports. The PLUTO pipelines built by the British were important in propaganda but not in petrol supply.

The ability to procure gigantic quantities of oil was central to the British machine-based war effort; without oil the bombers, the tanks, the warships with which British forces were lavishly equipped could not have been sustained. Oil products supply was arranged on a global scale. From 1940–41 the British Isles were themselves now supplied mainly from the USA, essentially to save on shipping, both because the Mediterranean was closed, cutting the short route to the Middle East (as it became known during the war), and because the USA was closer than Curaçao (Shell) or Aruba (Standard Oil), which refined Venezuelan crude, or Point-à-Pierre (Trinidad Leaseholds). Oil products would be shipped from east-coast ports of the USA. British-controlled production in the Caribbean would in turn go to the USA. The mainly British facilities in the Middle East supplied not the United Kingdom, but British imperial forces in the Middle East, India and points east. Abadan was expanded to supply 100-octane aviation spirit to the USSR by pipeline and railway, with US finance and US-made equipment. In 1942 the British reckoned Abadan strategically more important than Egypt.[46] So great was the supply that the losses of great oil fields and refineries in the Dutch East Indies and Burma in 1942 barely registered in the ledgers of Anglo-American oil supply. Globalism trumped nationalism, the tanker the oil-from-coal plant.

The case of food is a case of both national and global supply. On the one hand there was a very large expansion and modernization of domestic food production. Tractors, once made for export, and consuming imported fuel, now tilled vastly increased arable acreage. Taking one tractor as the equivalent of four horses, there was an increase of 68 per cent from before the war to 1948 in total horsepower, with a decrease in the number of horses of one-third.[47] If grain supply became more national, the supply of meat was further internationalized. Domestic production (with the exception of meat from dairy cattle) was driven down to save on imports of animal food, while meat imports actually went up. The policy was straightforward – import more expensive, highly concentrated food like meat and cheese and restrict the import of bulky animal feed. Meat now came frozen and, more often than before, canned. During the war government added, at the cost of £7 million, 47 cold stores, which would amount to one-third of cold storage capacity. One of the largest was in Cardiff docks, of 10,000 tons capacity. Meat continued to come from the southern hemisphere, but Danish and Dutch pork and bacon were replaced by pork products from North America.

Rationing was restricted to foods which were largely imported. Food was bought abroad by the state, through its agents, usually consortia of pre-war private importers. Meat, fats, butter, cheese, tea and sugar, all imported, were also relatively expensive, dense foods. Wheat/flour was the only significant imported food not rationed, but here imports were very much lower than before the war. The aim of rationing was partly to stop imports increasing, as well as to distribute these rich foods fairly. This is why rationing continued into the 1950s, long after the war was over. Bread rationing came in for the first time in 1946. Rationing did not imply going short, at least not by much. Meat consumption was only 25 per cent down. Sugar was one of the very few areas where consumption was pushed down drastically, whether as sugar, sweets or chocolate. The story of wartime food supply is radically different from that on the continent, a place of shortage, and of often drastic rationing of the most basic foodstuffs.

NATIONALIZATION

After the war energy and food were in different senses of the term, and to different degrees, nationalized. They were either taken into public ownership, relocated to national territory or more controlled by the state for national purposes.

The first and best-known sense was that of taking into public ownership, sometimes known as 'socialization'. There had been some municipal gas and electricity undertakings from before 1914; some would grow to be quite extensive. Furthermore, the government had taken a controlling shareholding in the Anglo-Persian oil company in 1914 and kept it. Coal-mining royalties were nationalized by the Conservative-dominated National government in 1938, in a costly exercise; owners were compensated with £76.45 million in Coal Commission stock.[48] The great wave of nationalizations of 1945–51 had the nationalization of coal mining at its core. This had been the aim of the miners and the Labour Party since the Great War. The mines were bought by the state in 1946 with the creation of the National Coal Board (costing over £310 million, paid in government stock).[49] The state did not underpay.[50] The vesting day, 1 January 1947, then a working day, saw the creation of the largest civil employer in the capitalist world. Apart from domestic heating and general industrial use, all the main users of coal were nationalized by the Labour government. They were the railways, the gas and electricity utilities and the steel industry. Much of the gas and electricity supply industry was private, along with the railways and steel mills. Thus by 1950 the main elements of what was in effect the coal economy were now in the public sector and accounted for the great bulk of the industries nationaliszed.[51] Manufacturing industry and exporting industry, with the exception of steel, were barely even considered for nationalization, which was firmly directed inwards and towards utilities.

'We cannot afford to lose a coal export trade,' said the Conservative manifesto of 1945; for the Communist Party, if the country could get back to exporting 30–40 million tons of coal, 'we could be independent of the American millionaires and blackmailers'.[52] It was not to be. The post-war peak in exports, in 1949, was at a mere 20 million tons. Coal became a national industry. For deep-mined coal 1955 was a post-war peak year, but output was no higher than the worst non-strike years of the interwar years.[53] Expansion of coal production could only come in the short term from expanding the workforce. This did happen with interesting national limits. The communist leader of the South Wales miners, and soon to lead the new National Union of Mineworkers, Arthur Horner, rejected the use of prisoners of war, or the 'importation of foreign – Polish, Italian or even Irish labour to stifle the demand of the British people to have decent conditions in British mines'. The mining industry, he said, 'must be so improved as to attract the voluntary labour of British boys in British mines'.[54] The government wanted Poles and later European volunteer workers in the mines, but local branches resisted strongly. Only about 8,500 foreigners went into the mines in 1948 (against a government target of 30,000) and that was the end of serious recruiting.[55] By 1951 there were 10,000 foreign miners, and later attempts to get Italians, and after 1957 Hungarians, failed.[56] In this sense, too, the industry remained firmly national.

In the cases of oil and food, nationalization in the sense of national production was something which was now a key policy aim. In a reversal of previous practice large oil refineries were to be built at home rather than in the oil fields. This was an expensive commitment: by 1950, 2.2 per cent of all investment in the United Kingdom was in petroleum.[57] This went largely into refineries in Shell Haven (Shell), Stanlow (Shell), Grangemouth (BP), Fawley (Esso), Coryton (Vacuum Oil) and the Isle of Grain (BP), all completed in the early 1950s. Another huge project started in the 1940s was the Imperial Chemical Industries Wilton works, which would produce chemicals and new fibres from petroleum, on the other side of the Tees from

Table 3.1: Imports of food and animal feeding stuffs to the United Kingdom, 1934–44 (thousands of tons), excluding imports from Eire

	1934–8 average	1940	1941	1942	1943	1944 Jan.–June
Wheat and flour	5,451	6,331	6,099	3,864	3,975	1,747
Rice, other grains and pulses	1,524	1,095	514	164	258	60
Maize and maize meal	3,395	2,192	702	135	66	24
Other animal feeding stuffs	1,719	1,058	325	74	12	12
Meat (including bacon)	1,423	1,298	1,203	1,301	1,358	848
Canned meat	63	116	230	282	300	107
Oilseeds, oils and fats	1,783	1,974	1,948	1,905	2,154	1,001
Sugar	2,168	1,526	1,658	773	1,458	497
Dairy produce	889	606	665	789	655	289
Fruit and vegetables	2,604	1,484	462	457	327	368
Beverages and other foods	1,007	1,154	847	862	963	441
Total	22,026	18,834	14,654	10,606	11,525	5,394

Source: *Statistics Relating to the War Effort of the United Kingdom*, Cmd. 6564, table 19.

ICI's coal-based Billingham works created from the end of the Great War to make fertilizer and which later made synthetic oil from coal.

In the case of food the post-Second World War years saw a drive to increase domestic production, one which would be sustained for decades. Reducing imports of food was a high aim of the state. The industry

Figure 3.1: UK coal production, inland consumption and exports (including bunkers)

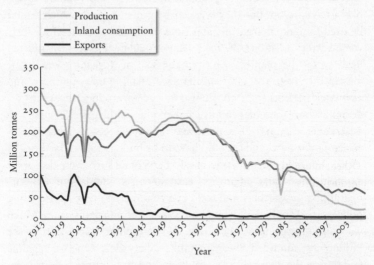

Source: ONS, *Historical Coal Data: Coal Production, Availability and Consumption 1853 to 2016.*

remained private, and in contrast to the mines, some 250,000 prisoners of war worked the land *after* the war. Germans and Italians were helping make the United Kingdom to be more like their own countries. The Agriculture Act 1947 had as its aim a permanent increase in self-sufficiency. It would take decades to achieve, but the path was mapped out. Agriculture was taking around 5 per cent of total investment in the years to 1951, about the same as the railways, and more than the coal mines.[58] Between 1937 and 1951 the proportion of the economy represented by agriculture, and the proportion of employment, increased, with the proportion of output then remaining constant from 1951 by one measure into the 1970s at 4.4 to 4.5 per cent.[59]

The post-war years saw state-led food production schemes in the empire. They were for the benefit of the UK and went along with the high levels of exploitation of the colonial empire in both war and post-war periods, where the United Kingdom was able to keep down prices of commodities produced in the colonies, for its benefit, and at the expense of the producers.[60] The most ambitious scheme, thought up by a Unilever subsidiary and a colonial agricultural officer, was one to grow groundnuts (peanuts) in Tanganyika. Peanuts sound like a trivial crop, but they were to be grown for oil, which would be used to make margarine, at a time when oils and fats of all sorts were scarce. Millions of acres of unpopulated, tsetse-fly-infected bush would be planted. An area the size of Yorkshire was to be managed in over 100 large mechanized farming units (with around 300 African workers each). It was hoped to produce (by 1950–51) 600–800,000 tons of peanuts, at half the world price, saving £10 million per annum.[61] New ports and railway lines, and living accommodation for thousands, would have to be built as well as facilities to service hundreds of large tractors. Experts of all sorts were deployed: agriculturalists and engineers, entomologists and labour experts, operational researchers and soil experts and even an up-and-coming policeman, Tom Fallon, who had invented the 999 call system. Much war surplus was used, including US Caterpillar tractors from the Philippines, modified Sherman tanks (Shervicks), a petrol pipeline laid during the war in Burma, tank landing craft, military tents, telephones, jeeps and aeroplanes. Many of the personnel from the local director to the maintenance crew were ex-army technical staff; clearing operations were run by a team that had built and repaired airfields during the war. The key engineering contracting firm was run by Sir John Gibson, the builder of the Jebel Aulia dam on the White Nile, and the designer of part of the Mulberry Harbour. It was rushed, there were problems with maintenance and an inadequate understanding of local rainfall and of the soil, which wrecked machines. The scheme was cancelled in 1951, having spent nearly £50 million and produced fewer peanuts than had been bought as seed. The government, which ran the scheme through a new Overseas Food Corporation under the Ministry of Food, was much criticized, and for decades Labour was taunted with cries of 'groundnuts' whenever it proposed a large state-led project Tories did not like. It was a fiasco, but a heroic mechanical and modern one.[62]

Labour, in its 1950 manifesto, called itself 'the true party of the nation'. It claimed 'Big Business did not believe in Britain – it believed only in profit. So money went into cinemas, not coal; into luxury flats, not looms for Lancashire; into land speculation, not into agri-culture.' By contrast, Labour 'Put the nation first'.[63] It is telling that among the industries Labour now thought of nationalizing were elements of the food industry. The proposal to nationalize beet sugar manufacture and sugar refining prompted Leonard Lyle (Harrow and Cambridge), director and chairman of Tate & Lyle, as Lord Lyle, to launch the Mr Cube campaign. Labour also proposed that, for meat, 'The present system of distribution should become a permanent public service' and that the 'development of cold storage, an essential service in food distribution, will be effected through public owner-ship'. These were the only ones on the list apart from cement, and possibly parts of chemicals.[64] By 1951 all these commitments had been dropped.

Nationalization was the most controversial policy of the 1945 Labour government. It meant buying entire industries from their owners, the great capitalists of the United Kingdom. Their removal from the management of some of the greatest industries in the realm was of key political importance, and it is a story which needs to be told not just in terms of the politics and policies of the Labour Party, but in terms of the history of British capitalists and the British ruling class. Although elements in Labour, and the Liberal Party, and even some Conservatives, presented public ownership as merely a tech-nical matter, to most Conservatives it could never be just that.

4

Kingdom of Capital

*The most interesting study for an intelligent worker to take
up and make his own is, in our opinion, the natural history
of the ruling class.*

James Connolly, 1915[1]

*If the English proletarian is entitled to an equal share of the
income now derived from England's capital resources, and
of the control of their use, because they are the result of
exploitation, so on the same principle all the Indians would
be entitled not only to the income from but also to the use of
a proportional share of the British capital. But what socialists seriously contemplate the equal division of existing
capital resources among the people of the world? They all
regard the capital as belonging not to humanity but to the
nation.*

F. A. Hayek, The Road to Serfdom (1944)[2]

The British ruling class of the first third of the twentieth century was
rich, confident and distinct. It bestrode the world, not merely the
empire. It was spectacularly successful, doing far better than any
excepting that of the United States. It gave the world a model for elite
behaviour, whether in education or in the playing of sports, indoor
and outdoor. The dress of the British gentleman became the uniform
of the elites of the world; British ladies were, however, fashion-takers.
This is not to say the British elite did not suffer major defeats – it did
so, but nothing on the scale of say the German or the Russian elites
ruined in war and revolution. Yet it has come in for a lot of ill-informed

criticism, much of which suggests that it was, by implicit comparisons with other ruling classes, backward. Its many supposed
failures – to be tough or business-like enough – have sometimes produced a fantastical picture of stupidity, decay and ineptitude. Indeed,
this very picture has in part been produced by the ruling classes
themselves. They carefully played dead, and many foolishly danced
on an empty grave. Any realistic assessment needs, however, to note
the strength and accomplishments of the haute bourgeoisie and
aristocracy.

Nationalist political economy criticized the ruling class for having
interests different from those of the nation. This thesis arose as a
nationalist explanation of economic failure and of what was taken to
be an imperial, global and financial orientation of British capitalism.
As the declinism of the 1960s took hold the image of a decadent capitalist class also took root – it was a mish-mash of assumptions – of
aristocracy as backward, of finance capital distant from industry,
and both unconcerned with national economic development. For
some the emergent capitalist industrial ruling class was robbed of its
virility by a decadent aristocratic embrace. For others, finance linked
up with aristocracy at the expense of industry. Indeed, the story is
told as a series of moralizing oppositions: north versus south, finance
versus industry, aristocracy versus bourgeoisie, cosmopolitan versus
national, imperial versus national, or science versus arts. These divisions appeared, it was typically suggested, in the late nineteenth and
early twentieth centuries and were then, it seems, set in stone in the
context of a liberal economy. These clichéd images endure and are
granted inordinate explanatory power. In fact, our knowledge of the
ruling class is remarkably limited, but the cases this chapter will present will make clear that most of these arguments are misleading.
What stands out are the close connections between all elements of the
ruling elite – whether manufacturing and finance, commerce and
aristocracy, business and politics, the national and the international,
as well as change over time.

Capital was not visible for much of the twentieth century, for many
thought it irrelevant – what mattered in analysis of class and stratifi-
cation was occupation and qualification. Strikingly the *Dictionary of
Labour Biography* is very much more complete than the *Dictionary*

of Business Biography. The business life of people in the *Dictionary of National Biography* is seriously played down, and business people are under-represented. Capitalists were invisible in literature and film. During the Second World War, for all the emphasis in propaganda on production, the story in documentaries and movies is one of factories and workers, not firms and capitalists. This is made very visible by its very invisibility in *I Know Where I'm Going!* (1945), a notable wartime film by Michael Powell and Emeric Pressburger. An attractive go-getting twenty-five-year-old from Manchester is to marry the older Sir Robert Bellinger, who runs Consolidated Chemical Industries. He clearly has power as well as wealth, but is heard (briefly) but not seen in the whole film. He has, in wartime, leased a Hebridean island for pleasure, from a laird who is serving in the navy. He is to marry his young bride there, but she is prevented by a storm from reaching him. Waiting on the next island for the weather to clear, she falls in love with the laird, who is on leave, and joins the society of earthy Hebrideans, the old down-at-heel gentry, and a very blimpish colonel. It is the most complete critique of capitalism in wartime British film.[3] But these are very rare indeed in other periods.[4] On to a blank screen all sorts of images of the British capitalist came to be projected.

LANDOWNERS AND RENTIERS

The most visible, and for long the most contentious, form of wealth was the ownership of land. The British landed estates were not latifundia worked by armies of landless peasants. Landowners typically rented land in large parcels to 'tenant farmers', who employed agricultural labourers. Farmers were generally not landowners, though after a long struggle that was largely the case in Ireland by 1914, where half the land had in effect been bought out by the state and sold to tenants. In the rest of the UK, much land was sold to tenants in 1919–21, who from the mid-1920s farmed one-third of the land in England and Wales.[5] The idea of sudden, massive land sales after the Great War is a myth. They were no greater than in the years before the war, especially in real terms.[6] At the end of the twentieth century much land was still in the hands of the same rich families as in 1900.

IF BOLSHEVISM CAME TO ENGLAND.   Nº I.– CAPITAL LEAVES THE COUNTRY.

Illustration 4.1: Kingdom of Capital 1928. The British Capitalists singled out by Low were from left to right: Sir J. Ellerman, Lord Ashton, Lord Derby, the Duke of Portland, Lord Iveagh, Sir Solly Joel, Mr J. B. Joel, Lord Vestey, Lord Woolavington, Lord Dewar, and the Duke of Westminster. Low's caption in a book of his cartoons reads: 'The very essence of patriotism, the sine qua non, is securely packed in their bags. They are so to speak, merely removing the seat of British national life to somewhere else.' He has them choosing to go to either Crusoe's Island or Fiji. (Low, *The Best of Low* (London, 1930), p. 67). What all have in common is public visibility, mostly through interests in horseracing, and in most cases peerages. Three were major landowners – Derby, Westminster and Portland. Ashton was in textiles, Iveagh in beer, Woolavington and Dewar in whisky, Vestey in meat, and the Joel brothers in diamonds, gold and railways. (British Cartoon Archive LSE0435, Associated Newspapers Ltd)

Half of the great once-landowning families had no land; the rest had, on average, half the acreage they once held. Edwardian landowning families ceased to function as a distinct class but had most certainly not been expropriated by taxes or land reform at any time in the twentieth century.[7] The seeming decline of the aristocracy illustrated by the tearing-down of country houses in the interwar years – a much echoed theme – was grossly overstated.

Even Edwardian aristocratic landowners did not rely on farming rents for their income. Hence the otherwise seeming paradox that the House of Lords, largely a landowners' assembly, could support free trade in food. Many owned urban land and urban buildings – a fact still evident today in parts of London, for example the Grosvenor Estate of the Dukes of Westminster in Mayfair and Belgravia, the [Earls of] Cadogan Estate in Chelsea and Knightsbridge; the [Dukes of] Bedford Estate in Bloomsbury; the [Viscounts] Portman Estate in Marylebone. Some aristocratic landowners had the immense good fortune to find themselves owners of millions of tons of coal. This made the fortunes of the Marquesses of Londonderry (in Ireland) from an estate in County Durham, and the Marquesses of Bute (in Scotland) from estates in South Wales. Some aristocrats mined their coal themselves, as will be shown below; others had colliery companies exploit their coal. Great aristocrats might even go into industry directly. The Dukes of Devonshire (whose seat was in Derbyshire) created the Naval Construction and Armaments Co. of Barrow-in-Furness, which they sold to Vickers, in which they acquired a large shareholding, among many others. The British aristocrat had become a plutocrat, a rentier, an owner of capital in the abstract, a passive beneficiary of the labour of both workers and managers, on a grand scale. There was no more cosmopolitan capitalism than that of red-blooded British peers of ancient lineage.[8]

The income that came from investment was central to the income of the ruling classes. Oscar Wilde's *The Importance of Being Earnest* (1895) is a pointed commentary on this. What Wilde subtitled *A Trivial Comedy for Serious People* has as its central character a very fortunate and very idle twenty-nine-year-old, John Worthing, JP. He is forced to reveal to his intended's mother, Lady Bracknell, that he is a Liberal Unionist, with an income between £7,000 and £8,000 per annum from investments, and has a country house with 1,500 acres and a house in Belgravia.[9] Whether the money comes from 'the purple of commerce' or aristocracy is left unanswered, for it is revealed that he had been found as a baby in a handbag left in Victoria station. The pure luck of being found and brought up by a man of means, not even birth, and certainly not talent, gave 'Jack' Worthing an income larger than the very best-paid employees of his time – £5,000 per annum was the sum commanded by general managers of the greatest banks and railway companies, the prime minister and the chancellor of the exchequer, then paid twice as much as the most senior civil servants.[10] £5,000 was the level at which the supertax would start under the 1909 budget. A real Jack Worthing would have been one of around 10,000 income-tax payers who would be subject to supertax when it was introduced.[11]

Those in the top tax bracket derived most of their taxable income from ownership of assets, not employment. They lived off what came to be called 'unearned income', income from property in all its forms. Sidney and Beatrice Webb denounced these 'functionless rich', their 'futile occupations', their 'licentious pleasures and inherently insolent manners', all of which 'undermined the intellectual and moral standards of the community'.[12] Beatrice was not one of those who, according to Lady Bracknell, spoke ill of Society because she could not get in, as she had a large private income herself.[13]

Criticizing such figures and their supposed influence has been central to British radicalism since the nineteenth century, down to the declinist theses of the 1960s and beyond. Aristocratic landowners have borne the brunt of the attention and criticism. Even socialist critics had very great difficulties in establishing the ownership of capital, as opposed to land, and also of discerning the links between ownership of capital other than land and political power, except abstractly. Even in critical literature the British capitalist, rentier apart, has been invisible.

What is rather astonishingly missing, in both celebratory and critical commentary, is what might be called the productive capitalist. The income of the productive capitalist would itself be largely from property but from property that was managed, a shipping line, for example, or a coal mine.

MEN OF BUSINESS

The United Kingdom was a land of business magnates, rich men who owned and operated vast enterprises. A few of these men were well known, usually because they made themselves visible, often through the sports pages. Sailing was a plutocratic sport, which made Sir Thomas Lipton famous. Lipton ran a grocery chain and moved into tea plantations. Horseracing was another. J. Arthur Rank, a giant among flour millers, became so famous for his film-making and film-showing activities he figures in Cockney rhyming slang. But the very richest of the era was the reclusive Sir John Ellerman, a company promoter and manager, an accountant by background, who set up the large Ellerman Line, which owned about 1 million tons of cargo-passenger liners in 1939. He died in 1934, leaving £37 million, more than the previous record of Lord Iveagh, owner of Guinness.

The case of coal is particularly instructive because, while the industry has been very visible indeed, its capitalists have been singularly obscure. The coal-mine owners are as invisible as miners' leaders are visible.[14] The discourse on coal owners, not least in the histories, has condemned them namelessly as small-time backward operators clinging on to an old industry. Even when some large-scale organization is noted in the history, the story is told without histories of businesses or owners or managers. Yet once we look we see that, by the standards of most enterprises anywhere, a single coal mine was a large employer, and a grouping of just a few mines produced enterprises amongst the biggest in the land. There were many men who directed enterprises which employed thousands of miners and mined millions of tons of coal.

Many of them were significant figures in British politics, as one might expect in a country so coal intensive. They were more often than not educated in public school and Oxbridge. Two were hereditary peers. The Earl of Crawford and Balcarres ran the Wigan Coal and Iron Company, had his country house in that area and represented nearby Chorley as a Unionist MP before succeeding to the title. He was a senior figure in Conservative politics and in cultural administration and a notable political diarist. The 7th Marquess of Londonderry was chairman of Londonderry Collieries (5–7,000 workers). Londonderry (Eton and Sandhurst) was first elected as a Unionist MP in 1906 and rose to be air minister between 1931 and 1935. As a pro-Nazi he was known as the 'Londonderry Herr', a play on the tune the 'Londonderry Air'. Many other major coal owners were MPs and rose to be peers. David Davies (King's Cambridge) was elected as a Liberal MP in 1906, unopposed, and would be repeatedly until 1929, when he stood down. He was inactive politically. He was, unusually in a Liberal, a tariff reformer and a unionist. His big cause was the League of Nations and the international air police. He endowed a chair in international relations in Aberystwyth University, filled to his dismay by the hammer of utopians like himself, E. H. Carr, an appeaser. He endowed the Temple of Peace and Health in Cardiff, providing offices for organizations promoting health and peace; this massive building opened in 1938. David Thomas (Lord Rhondda) (who had studied mathematics at Cambridge) abandoned a Liberal political career in 1906 and returned to the mining industry. He built up the huge Cambrian Combine. He was minister of food during the Great War. He died in 1918 and was very unusually succeeded by his daughter in the title, though she could not sit in the Lords. Lady Rhondda was unquestionably the leading businesswoman of the interwar years, and a leading feminist; she paid for and ran the journal *Time and Tide*. It is a telling case of the bias towards public rather than business life of biographical sources that the *Dictionary of National Biography* fails to give anything like an adequate account of the business lives of the above.[15] As the table below shows, they were not the only peers; of the others nearly all also served in the House of Commons, mostly as Liberals.

Table 4.1: The top eighteen colliery companies by size of labour force in 1935, with senior figure if peer

1. Manchester Collieries Ltd 14,193 (formed 1929)
2. Lambton, Hetton & Joicey Collieries (Northeast) 13,636 (Lord Joicey, chairman, Liberal)
3. Powell Duffryn Steam Coal Co. (merged with Welsh Associated, 1935) 13,512 (Lord Hyndley, one of the managing directors, 1931–46; Lord Buckland, deputy chairman from 1935). Hyndley was the

controller-general of the new Ministry of Fuel and Power and first
chairman of the National Coal Board

4. Wigan Coal Corporation 12,697 (Earl of Crawford and Balcarres, chairman, Unionist)
5. Amalgamated Anthracite Collieries Ltd (Wales) 12,558 (Lord Melchett, deputy chairman, Liberal, then Conservative)
6. Ashington Coal Co. Ltd 10,550 (Newcastle) (connected earlier to Milburn line and Milburn House)
7. Yorkshire Amalgamated Collieries Ltd 10,000 (Lord Aberconway, chairman)
8. Horden Collieries Ltd (Northeast) 8,762
9. Pease & Partners, Ltd (Northeast) 8,512 (Lord Gainford, chairman, Liberal)
10. Bolsover Colliery Co. Ltd 8,292
11. Welsh Associated Collieries Ltd 8,090 (formed 1929 from Cambrian and others; merged with Powell Duffryn 1935) (successor to Lord Rhondda (Liberal) enterprises) (Lord Buckland, chairman)
12. Ocean Coal Co. (Wales) 7,490 (Lord Davies, chairman, Liberal)
13. Bairds & Dalmellington Ltd 7,368 (formed 1931, dominated Ayrshire coalfield)
14. Butterley Co. Ltd (Derby) 7,332
15. Barber Walker & Co. Ltd (Notts) 7,272
16. Consett Iron Co. Ltd (Durham) 6,921
17. Ebbw Vale Steel, Iron & Coal Co. Ltd 6,710
18. Fife Coal Co. Ltd 6,568 (Sir Charles Reid, general manager, wrote the wartime Reid Report, a technical argument for nationalization)

Location given where not obvious.

Not ranked: Londonderry Collieries Ltd (Northeast) 5,244 (Marquess of Londonderry, chairman, Unionist) and Cory's (Wales) c.5,000.

There were further mergers. On the eve of nationalization the large firms were Doncaster Amalgamated Collieries (formed 1937), over 16,000; Bolsover, Ashington and Amalgamated Denaby (formed 1936), around 9,000 each; Manchester Collieries, over 14,000; Wigan, over 12,000; Bairds, 9,500; Fife, 8,000; and Powell Duffryn, 27,000, and 32,000 if Cory's included; Amalgamated Anthracite; 8,500; and Partridge Jones and John Paton (expanded late 1930s), over 12,000.[16]

Sources: Largest employers coal mining 1935, from David J. Jeremy, 'The Hundred Largest Employers in the United Kingdom, in Manufacturing and Non-Manufacturing Industries, in 1907, 1935 and 1955', *Business History* 33 (1991), pp. 93–111, and Peter Wardley, 'The Emergence of Big Business: The Largest Corporate Employers of Labour in the United Kingdom, Germany and the United States *c*.1907', *Business History* 41 (1999), pp. 88–116. Londonderry and Cory from Durham Mining Museum database at dmm.org.uk.

Notes: 'Cambrian Combine' was the unofficial name given to the grouping of mines, including Cambrian Collieries, formed by the future Lord Rhondda before the Great War, including also the Glamorgan, Naval and Britannic Merthyr Companies. In 1929, the Cambrian Colliery and other Combine mines merged with other coalmining companies to form Welsh Associated Collieries Ltd. This company was itself amalgamated with the Powell Duffryn Company in 1935, creating Powell Duffryn Associated Collieries Ltd, by far the largest coal-mining company ever seen in the UK. The 'United Collieries', formed by the merger of twenty-four Scottish collieries before the war, would have been very high on the list had it kept its pre-war employment. It shrank to well below 5,000 by 1933.

GENTLEMAN INDUSTRIALISTS

Many of the new plutocrats bought country houses, and surrounding land, as a leisure pursuit. The brewer Edward Cecil Guinness, 1st Earl of Iveagh (1918), bought Elveden Hall in Suffolk in 1894. In 1907 the coal owner and newly created Baron Joicey bought the ancient Ford Castle in Northumberland, and the neighbouring estate in 1908 (both remain with the family).[17] Lord Pirrie bought Witley Park near Godalming.[18] Lionel de Rothschild, banker and Tory MP, built a neo-Georgian house and created the famous gardens in Exbury from 1919. In 1927 the 2nd Viscount Bearsted, chairman of Shell, as his father had been, bought and expanded Upton Park in Warwickshire and filled it with Old Master paintings. Charles Gunther, chairman of the Liebig Extract of Meat Company, bought the Tongswood Estate (*c*.3,500 acres) in Kent in 1903. The chief of Bovril, George Johnstone

(Lord Luke), bought the Odell Castle estate in Bedfordshire in 1934. Lord Vestey bought a peerage and the Stowell Park estate in the early 1920s. William Beardmore (Lord Invernairn) bought a sporting estate in Scotland. Sir Hugo Hirst, Lord Hirst of GEC, bought Foxhill House in Wiltshire, now part of the University of Reading. Joseph Watson (Repton, Cambridge), later Lord Manton, took his grandfather's soap business, Joseph Watson & Sons Ltd, to new heights, making it a rival to Lever, to which he sold out. He bought Compton Verney and a 5,000-acre estate, becoming before his early death Baron Manton of Compton Verney. Some built new houses. Two examples illustrate the range of industrial and commercial taste: Sir Hugo Cunliffe-Owen of British American Tobacco had a neo-Georgian pile built in 1931, Northcote House, which was to pass to the government as Sunningdale after the war. Not far away, Frank Parkinson of Crompton Parkinson, electrical engineers, built an art deco masterpiece, later owned by another Leeds industrialist, Sir Montague Burton, the pioneer of made-to-measure suits. This was an unusual though not unique case of modern taste among the haute bourgeoisie. These capitalists, mostly gentlemen, many with important operations overseas, were primarily producers, not financiers.[19]

While the country house is well known, as is its decline, the story of the London house is not. Aristocratic London residences were at their peak in the Edwardian years.[20] By the 1930s only Londonderry House, Park Lane (demolished 1965), remained both an aristocratic and political house – it was here that the first Labour prime minister, Ramsay MacDonald, succumbed to the aristocratic embrace. But the new plutocrats bought and built grand houses in London. Aristocratic Belgrave Square became the home of Lord Pirrie the shipbuilder and Sir Otto Biet the Rand lord (the name for men who made their wealth in South Africa). The Hill on Hampstead Heath was bought in 1904 by Lord Leverhulme, the soap and margarine magnate, who extended it; what was now a sixty-room mansion was bought on his death by Andrew Weir, Lord Inverforth, a shipowner who lived there to the 1950s. Witanhurst in Highgate (1913–20) the largest house in London apart from Buckingham Palace, was built by Sir Arthur Crosfield on the proceeds of the sale of his soap and margarine business, based in Warrington, to Brunner, Mond. Sir Francis Cory-Wright, a coal shipper, owned Caen Wood Towers (now Athlone House) in Highgate. In 1919 it was bought by Sir Robert Waley Cohen of Shell, who lived there to his death in 1942. Heath Hall, Bishops Avenue, Hampstead, was built in 1910 for William Lyle. Edward Cecil Guinness, first Earl of Iveagh (1918), bought Kenwood House and estate in 1925 but bequeathed it to the nation 1927. Gordon Selfridge bought Lansdowne House. The last great private house to be built in London was Aberconway House in Mayfair (1920–22) for the 2nd Lord Aberconway, who chaired John Brown and other companies, including the Yorkshire Amalgamated Collieries.

British capitalists, at least into the interwar years, were rather like capitalists in the USA, and Germany to a lesser extent, in endowing creative institutions. Capitalists endowed research stations, museums and libraries, and supported expeditions and had bits of the world named after them (Beardmore and Coats are immortalized in Antarctica). In Liverpool, 'tropical medicine' and associated disciplines were funded by local ship owners.[21] There was an Iveagh Lister Institute and Radium Institute and a Milford (one of the Philipps brothers) Institute for Animal Health. The tobacco kings of Bristol, the Wills family (members of parliament many of them, and peers), endowed the University of Bristol. The ammonia king, Edward Brotherton (who made ammonia products from gas works' waste products), gave his money and his name to the University of Leeds library. Lord Nuffield, the car maker William Morris, endowed the sciences in Oxford. Jesse Boot endowed what became the University of Nottingham. It seems very likely indeed that most medical research in the United Kingdom in 1900 and beyond was private – in voluntary medical schools, in charitable research centres (the Lister for example or Imperial Cancer Research) and the pharmaceutical firms (Wellcome Physiological Laboratories).

BUSINESS IN POLITICS

Not only was much of politics about business, but both Liberal and Conservative politics were dependent on business and property. The standard British member of parliament was a man of means and with sufficient leisure to take part in public life and to sit in the House. He came from the few per cent of families who sent their boys to public schools, who supplied officers to the British forces and were gentle. In fact they tended to come from a much smaller group, less than 1 per cent, who were not merely gentle, but in 'society': those not just with private education, but education at elite public schools, who became the high officers of the armed forces, the civil service, the clergy, the judiciary, the directors of businesses, the top scientists, engineers and doctors. A member of parliament was most likely a graduate of an ancient university, and if entering parliament young after the Great War was likely to have served as an officer. Many were also business-men, who were often also graduates of ancient universities and soldiers or barristers. Although from 1912 MPs were paid sufficiently well to support the small number of Labour MPs, the pay was not enough to support the standard of life expected by and of most MPs. Politi-cians, like members of the diplomatic service and the officers of elite regiments, were expected to sustain the mutual prestige of position and person with privately funded, expensive lifestyles.

Furthermore, the very business of party politics relied on private money. Fighting seats cost money, and candidates were often the ones who paid their constituency election agent and more besides. Where parties took over funding elections they themselves relied on private money, which they recognized with the granting of knighthoods and peerages to the donors. There was a shift from the rich funding local activity to funding a party nationally, especially across the Great War. The practice was already well established in both parties before the war – that was how plutocratic politics worked. Edwardian and interwar Liberalism was particularly associated with the selling of honours to businessmen.[22] But Lloyd George simply went too far after the war, selling too many peerages and far too many baronet-cies, making Cardiff, for example, the City of Dreadful Knights. The ennoblement of Lord Vestey was particularly scandalous, offending the king because Vestey avoided UK tax.

The imperial parliament was remarkably open to wealth, even not wholly British wealth. Take the case of the North Paddington seat. In 1906 the leading contenders were the liberal economist and journalist Leo Chiozza (who added Money to his surname in 1905), the author of a famous study of wealth, and the Unionist Arthur Strauss, a very rich non-ferrous-metals trader and founder of the London Metal Exchange. One was born in Italy, the other in Germany; the latter, although naturalized, spoke English with an accent. This was noticed, and a fully British candidate was put up by outraged patriots – the result was that Chiozza won. In the 1910 elections there was no patriotic candidate, and Strauss was returned. Strauss had sat for Camborne 1895 to 1900, the first naturalized Briton in the House.[23] Darlington was won in the first 1910 election by an extraordinary con-man, the recently naturalized Hungarian Ignatius Trebitsch Lincoln, with the support of his wealthy employer, Seebowm Rowntree.[24] The wealthy Parsee cotton trader Dadabhai Naoroji sat for a London seat as a Liberal in the 1890s; and his fellow Bombay-born Parsee, Mancherjee Bhownagree, sat for the Unionists for another London seat until 1906. A third wealthy Bombay-born Parsee, Shapurji Saklatvala, sat for another London seat in the 1920s as a Communist. Money and class could trump race and nationality. Money could trump class in the Labour Party too. Sir Oswald Mosley MP, who defected from the Tories in the 1920s, was able to finance election campaigns in the Midlands not only for himself (Smethwick) and his wife (Lady Cynthia, daughter of the Marquess of Curzon, Stoke on Trent), but for others too. George Strauss, son of Arthur, was welcome to stand for Labour in North Lambeth as a very young man as he could contribute to party funds. Hugh Gaitskell, on being selected for a Leeds seat in 1937, promised to give the local party £300 (the annual salary of a university lecturer).[25] Private and public power overlapped in crucial ways.

One might be tempted, following Churchill (himself from an aristocratic family), to believe that aristocratic rule was over once the son of the Duke of Devonshire failed to take the family seat in Derbyshire in a by-election in 1944. Certainly aristocrats were now exceptional, but they did not go away – after all Churchill returned as prime minister in 1951, and there would be Marquesses of Salisbury in cabinet into the 1950s. In 1963 the 14th Earl of Home (pronounced Hume) gave up his peerage to become prime minister. The men who displaced the aristocrats and their sons and relations were the businessmen. But in fact seriously aristocratic leadership was really over with Arthur Balfour before 1914, with Churchill as an exceptional intruder.

The Edwardian parliament, Commons and Lords, was full of businessmen, and this remained true into 1945. More than half of both Conservative and Liberal MPs already before 1918 were from 'commerce and industry'.[26] Nearly half the new peers of the interwar years came from business, many having already served as MPs.[27] There were about 1,000 peers, roughly one in 20,000 men; it is perhaps not entirely surprising that men who might command 10,000 workers would be peers. Many have already appeared in our story. Such was the number that there were cases of brothers and other close relatives separately ennobled (three Berry brothers, three Philipps, two Weirs, two Dewars, two Wills, and two Harmsworths). No businessman ever reached the heights of a dukedom, a title reserved for royals or the rare marquesses. A very few businessmen became earls, including Edward Guinness (Iveagh) and James MacKay of the Peninsular and Oriental Shipping Company, who was made Earl of Inchcape. As well as creating Eagle Oil, Weatman Pearson was a Liberal MP (but because he never turned up he was called the 'member for Mexico'). He was (as Viscount Cowdray) chairman of the Air Board, a predecessor to the Air Ministry. Hudson Ewbanke Kearley was also a Liberal MP, before, as Viscount Davenport, he became the first chairman of the Port of London Authority (1908), and minister of food under the Lloyd George coalition. New viscounts included a good number of businessmen; among those not already mentioned were the newspaper barons, not just Rothermere and Northcliffe, but Burnham and others, including Viscount Camrose, who owned, by the late 1930s, *The Sunday Times*, *Financial Times*, *Daily Telegraph* and *Morning Post*. Among the others were Viscount Bearsted, Marcus Samuel of Shell; Viscount Leverhulme, William Lever of Lever Brothers; Viscount Nuffield, William Morris of Morris Motors; Viscount Weir, William Weir of W. G. Weir; Viscount Wakefield, Charles Wakefield of Castrol lubricating oils; Viscount St Davids, one of the Philipps brothers, of the Buenos Ayres and Pacific Railway; Viscount Furness, Marmaduke Furness, of the shipping line Furness Withy; and Viscount Runciman, Walter Runciman, the 2nd Baron Runciman, owner of a Newcastle tramp shipping line, as well as president

of the Board of Trade. Put another way, there was hardly a major businessman not ennobled.[28]

Roughly half the Conservatives in the House of Commons from 1918
were from business. We have already come across some, including the
many coal owners who sat on both the Liberal and Conservative
benches. Leonard Lyle (Harrow and Cambridge) director and chairman of Tate & Lyle, was elected for an east London seat in 1918.
There were many, many more. The ammonia king, Edward Brotherton, was Tory MP for Wakefield, the site of his main factory. Sir Frank
Hornby invented Meccano, and from factories in Liverpool, and soon
from new foreign factories, supplied the world with Meccano kits,
Hornby train sets (early 1920s), and Dinky dye-cast models (1934).
These were the most popular toys for boys the world had seen and
made Meccano the largest British toy maker in the interwar years,
and Hornby a Unionist MP for Liverpool Everton, from 1931 to his
death in 1936. Sir Isidore Salmon, managing director and chairman
of Joseph Lyons (a huge food and catering firm) was a long-serving
Tory MP for Harrow. Garfield Weston, a Canadian who set up the
huge Allied Bakeries in the 1930s (baking Canadian wheat), was a
Tory MP 1939–45. John Colville, of the giant Scottish steel firm Colville's, left the Commons in 1943 to become governor of Bombay and
served as acting viceroy of India at times.[29] Sir Robert Houston, an
immensely rich Liverpool ship owner (the Houston Line specialized in
the River Plate meat trade), sat for a Liverpool seat as a Conservative
(his widow Lady Lucy Houston used her wealth to support many
ultra-right causes). Colonel Sir Robert Ropner, a major Hartlepool
tramp steamer owner, sat for the Conservatives for Sedgefield, and
then a Yorkshire seat into the 1950s. The Scottish businessman Sir
Robert Horne, director and chairman of rail and steel companies, was
MP for Glasgow Hillhead and served as minister of labour, president
of the Board of Trade and chancellor in the 1920s.

The clinching bit of evidence is that business provided most of the
prime ministers of the era. Henry Campbell-Bannerman, Liberal
leader (1899–1908) and prime minister 1905–8, and Andrew Bonar
Law, the Conservative leader (1911–21) and prime minister (1922–3),
had both come from business. Stanley Baldwin, prime minister
1923–4, 1925–9 and 1935–7, had been managing director of a

gigantic enterprise of some 6,000 workers before 1914, including the Port Talbot steel company (fully taken over by Baldwins in 1915). Son of an ironmaster, he went to Harrow and Cambridge (History) and briefly studied at Mason College, Birmingham before joining the family firm; in 1908 he succeeded his father as MP for Bewdley, his home town, close to the family works. He would be ennobled as Earl of Bewdley. Baldwin was also the director of a major bank, and of the Great Western Railway. He lived in London, moving into Eaton Square in 1912. He was not a mere provincial industrialist, but one of many who contradict the image of industry versus finance, because like many he was a senior figure in both worlds.[30] Despite being associated with the image of county squire, the embodiment of an eternal England, he was a grand capitalist and an imperialist.[31] Neville Chamberlain, prime minister 1937–40, also came from a business and political family: his father had been a partner in Nettlefold and Chamberlain, later part of Guest, Keen and Nettlefold. Neville Chamberlain (who also briefly studied at Mason College) worked in other companies; he was for seventeen years managing director of Hoskins & Co., makers of ship's berths. He entered parliament for a Birmingham seat in 1918.[32]

Although this was not for public consumption, bourgeois prime ministers lorded it over the British monarchy when it was important. The mighty British and Japanese monarchs were the only two emperors left in the world by 1936. In that year political power deposed Edward VIII easily and speedily. He had succeeded to the throne in January 1936 and was forced to abdicate before the year was out, because British and imperial politicians, led by Stanley Baldwin, would not tolerate a king marrying a divorced woman. His abdication was no personal matter – he abdicated officially on three different days because of political imperatives.[33] Furthermore, it was the parliament of the United Kingdom, not his own action, which stripped him or future issue of any right of succession whatever. He was forced into exile. Even king-emperors of the most ancient lineage, of the most successful royal house on earth, did as they were told.

Churchill, a supporter of Edward VIII who fawned on royalty, and set a different tone, was the great exception to the run of bourgeois prime ministers. He had no business interests except his own profitable journalism and history writing. Yet his government, formed in May 1940, was in significant measure one of businessmen. It differed from previous ones in that most were not members of the Commons or the Lords, but rather newcomers, and many were cronies of the prime minister. These men, with others, mostly from Conservative ranks, included Lord Beaverbrook and Oliver Lyttelton. Many would return to office with Churchill in 1951 – among them Lyttelton and Lord Woolton.

The defeat of the Conservatives in 1945 inaugurated a new parliament in which workers were prominent and businessmen far less so. The Labour cabinet had no one from business. Knowledge of industry came from acting in patent law cases for Cripps, and for others, working in industrial ministries during the war, and a background in academic economics (which applies to Hugh Dalton, Hugh Gaitskell and Harold Wilson). The closest to a minister with business experience was George Strauss, minister of supply. The bourgeois, perhaps more than the aristocratic elite, had lost its full legitimacy by the 1940s. The crisis of capitalism of the 1930s, the want of investment in the national economy, the sense the elite had appeased Hitler, all undercut their authority. The focus was now much more national, technical and administrative than on the celebration of capitalist or financial values. Perhaps partly for this reason, the previous importance of businessmen in high politics has tended to be ignored by historians.

THE NATIONALIZATION OF CAPITAL

The concentration of wealth was extraordinary. One estimate for the Edwardian years is that 1 per cent of the population owned 69 per cent of the wealth, and 10 per cent fully 92 per cent, making it perhaps more unequal than before or since, and more unequal than most European countries.[34] Another estimate for 1914 has 0.25 per cent of the occupied population owning a third of the wealth (and 2.5 per cent had two-thirds).[35] The issue was not simply a matter of distribution – the quantity of wealth needs to be recognized for its scale. Total wealth amounted to three or four times the annual incomes of the whole population.

Such skewed ownership of wealth made a very large difference to the distribution of income. Income from wealth accounted for fully 45 per cent of the national income in 1911, down to 32 per cent in 1924 and 30–35 per cent in the early 1930s.[36] It fell to a quarter of all incomes in the late 1940s.[37] That income went to a very small proportion of all the population, the owners of land, houses, factories, infrastructure and public debt. The rich lived not on incomes from employment, but from property. These incomes, not high salaries, ensured that 1 per cent of receivers of all incomes got 30 per cent of the national income in 1910.[38] Income taxes were to a large extent taxes on income from property rather than employment.

Wealth was not taxed, except through estate duties, death duties, which were low. Taxing wealth was a radical cause. The taxing of increments in land values was introduced on a small scale under the People's Budget. In 1909 the Liberal chancellor of the exchequer, David Lloyd George, increased death duties. There was no specific wealth tax, which was strongly resisted. Nor was the Labour policy of the 'capital levy', a one-off wealth tax to bring down the wartime debt, ever put into practice. However, wealth was taxed through the income it generated. At the beginning of the century income tax was largely a tax on incomes from property, and from 1907 there was a lower rate of tax for earned income under £2,000, higher rates of tax on high incomes (the sur-tax) and death duties. In 1948 there was a charge on especially high non-earned incomes. In principle and on average, taxes on the income from investments and death duties should have reduced the scale of great fortunes – whether they did or not is another matter.[39]

As befitted a capitalist class the rich held their wealth in shares. From the limited data we have, which is derived from estate duties (which taxed the declared assets of the dead above a certain limit – in this case some 100,000 estates) – it is clear that the single largest item was shares (over 30 per cent before 1914). This was followed by a house or houses (around 10 per cent before 1914) and government securities. This last was low before 1914 with less held in British government (c.3 per cent) than municipal, foreign and dominion loans. In the interwar years, shares were about the same level as before the war, but British government securities jumped to 13–15 per cent and approached 20 per cent in the late 1940s, with houses increasing slightly to 12–15 per cent.[40] The national debt became a vitally important form of private wealth.

It was a commonplace of literature of the nineteenth century that some character had money 'invested in the Funds'. In fact there was relatively little in the funds until the Great War; thereafter the sums invested were huge, though then invisible to novelists. Up to 1914 the stock of foreign investment (around £4 billion) was very considerably greater than the levels of holdings of British government debt. The small pre-war central government debt swelled to over £7 billion at the end of the Great War when foreign investment was still around £4 billion. And there it remained. For comparison, one heroic estimate of the fixed capital stock at depreciated values suggests that in 1930 all UK buildings and civil engineering works were worth £7 billion; and plant, ships and vehicles £1.7 billion. The total for residential buildings was £2.7 billion, which dwarfed the total of all fixed assets in manufacturing, £1.5 billion.[41] After the Second World War the national debt was perhaps seven times larger. The national debt was an investment, just as much as investment in government debt overseas. What the increase tells us is that, assuming most of the national debt was nationally owned, a reasonable assumption, then there was a huge shift to ownership of national, rather than imperial or global, wealth.

How this national wealth was treated changed very dramatically over time, reflecting the changing strength of the debt-owning classes. It gives us a very important insight into the nature of politics. Historians have generally missed these crucial politics, especially those of the 1920s. The standard story goes like this. There were great hopes for post-war reconstruction – for homes for heroes – destroyed by a recession and cuts in government expenditure. In terms of price changes, they are seen as a matter of a gentle deflation which benefitted the middle classes, a position which downplays its import for the rich, and the speed, brutality and costs it entailed.[42] Usually only one tiny aspect is treated, in a different context: the return to the gold standard in 1925 at the pre-war parity of £1=$4.86, taken to be a 10 per cent overvaluation which damaged exports. Yet that was merely the very last stage of a much more radical revaluation, not only of sterling but of the entire national debt.

Most of the Great War debt was bought at high interest rates at times of rising prices. £2 billion of the 1917 war loan bought at 5 per cent cost the taxpayer £100 million per annum. The total debt of over £7 billion, cost nearly £300 million per annum to service. More than 8 per cent of GDP was spent on debt interest in the 1920s, some 40 per cent of the state budget, and three times the defence budget. The British taxpayer therefore owed the British rentier a living. This generosity to the rentiers was the result of choice and dramatic economic actions. Rather than inflate that debt away (as for example the Germans did, though with terrible consequences) from 1920, the British government took active measures to drive down the level of prices, to match the pre-1914 level of relative prices with the USA (where prices rose much less) and thus return to the pre-war sterling-dollar parity. [43] This reduced the cost of loans owed to the USA, taken out during the war at the gold standard rate, but increased the value of the much larger domestic loans and the income from them. (The United Kingdom had no net overseas debt – in the war it had lent more (to Europe) than it had borrowed (from the USA), and the payments roughly balanced out in the 1920s; however, much debt was cancelled in 1931, resulting in a (technical) loss to the United Kingdom). The pound was revalued from around $3.70 in 1920 to $4.86, while prices roughly halved, achieved by raising interest rates to unprecedented peacetime levels. By 1922 most of the revaluation, and the price fall, had been achieved, at terrible cost to industrial output and employment. [44]

The state would pay out, to the rich, much more than the poor received in benefits, often as a result of unemployment caused by the deflation itself. The great gainers were investors who bought debt in 1917, 1918 and into 1919, when prices were high. We don't, alas, have figures for the distribution of the debt – while many millions doubtless had some, most was surely in the hands of the wealthy. We need, however, to put in a counter-argument. It is that income tax rates were dramatically raised, and these were taxes that hit the income from wealth, if not the wealth itself. Indeed, income tax receipts were somewhat higher than debt interest payments. That is another way of saying that out of income tax there was little left over after paying the interest on the debt, largely, we must assume, to income tax payers.[45] This is not to say the rich were better off than before. Their incomes were indeed squeezed by high income taxes and death duties. The distribution of income became more equal after tax.

Nineteenth-century radicals denounced government for taxing the poor to pay interest on government debt to the rich. Radicals did so again in the 1920s. Maynard Keynes argued against the policy of deflation, and for keeping prices level, which would certainly have reduced the burden of debt and increased economic activity.[46] He was brutally clear:

> To restore the value of pre-war holdings by Deflation means enhancing at the same time the value of war and post-war holdings, and thereby raising the total claims of the rentier class not only beyond what they are entitled to, but to an intolerable proportion of the total income of the community.[47]

Keynes was far from alone. Oswald Mosley criticized the bounty that went to bondholders, in the 1920s and into 1931.[48] So did the Labour Party, but its solution, the Capital Levy, a wealth tax, was never to be implemented.[49]

It was not radicals who would put an end to this extraordinary state of affairs, but the Great Depression. The pound came off gold in 1931 and was devalued. Interest rates came right down ('cheap money'), and much of the national debt was converted to lower interest bonds by the new chancellor of the exchequer, Neville Chamberlain. This war debt conversion was saving £100 million per annum by 1935, about the same as the entire defence budget; interest payments were down to around 4 per cent of GDP. These policy changes of the 1930s put into sharp relief the policies of the 1920s – policies which benefited the rich at the expense of the workers in very direct ways.

After the Second World War things would be very different compared with the aftermath of the Great War. As in the Great War, internal borrowing was central to financing the Second World War, though this time taxes were as important, with each accounting for equal shares of government income. This time government borrowed at low rates – 3 per cent generally – and forced savings in government debt by all sorts of controls. There was essentially nowhere else to invest or spend, and as a result some £14 billion entered state coffers, much more than came in (free) via Lend-Lease, or by accumulated sterling balances. The British wealthy owned much more British government debt (£21 billion) than overseas assets (at most still £4 billion) or the value of overseas liabilities (around £3 billion). The debt trebled over the pre-war level and was more than twice GDP. After the war Labour again refused a capital levy to reduce that debt, but it would not countenance a policy of dear money. The result was a policy of low interest rates and relatively low interest payments. Debt payment temporarily reached up to 6 per cent of GDP; it generally remained around 4 per cent. The rich were not allowed to profit; rates were kept low, and the debt was gently inflated away.

The British wealthy added to their ownership of national debt in the late 1940s through the nationalization of coal and related industries. After the war, under the Labour government, capitalists were forced to swap shares in certain industries for government debt. This was the process of nationalization, by which a total of around £2.6 billion of fixed-interest securities were issued in return for the coal and railway industry firms, and those parts of the electricity and gas industries not already in public ownership. The financial compensation was generous – the stream of income from government at least what one might expect from private operation of the industries concerned, but without the former owners taking any risks or doing any work. Nationalization removed the power of shareholders in the economy, not their income. Of course nationalization had an ideological impact, both nationally and locally. A ruling class which claimed the monopoly of effort, ingenuity and enterprise – entrepreneurship we might say today – was told, at some expense, that they were not fit to run the infrastructural industries of the nation, that they had put their private interests ahead of those of the nation and had in any case not invested properly in the industries in their care. That marked an extraordinary transformation in the status of the capitalist, one not visible if British capital is seen as financial, commercial and cosmopolitan.[50] The rule of capital was by this measure also much reduced after 1945.

CAPITAL OVERSEAS NATIONALIZED

The British rich were not rich simply by owning the United Kingdom, but over time their wealth became increasingly national as overseas holdings were lost. In the Edwardian years some one-third of all the capital stock of British capitalists was abroad; about 40 per cent of all capital owned abroad was British capital; about half of British invest- ment went overseas.[51] Put another way (as it was put at the time), British capital built not only the British railway system, but the Argentine one too (although by mileage similar to the British, it was by all sensible measures perhaps one-tenth the size). In the 1950s and 1960s some were to complain about the delusion that the United Kingdom was owed a living. It was no delusion for the rich. The flow of investment income into the United Kingdom before 1914 was stag- gering. The income was worth about a third of all exports, and about the same as income from shipping and the like.[52] British capital exports (that is overseas investment flow) may not have deprived Brit- ish industry of capital (long a standard nationalist view); high income from investments required capital exports and high imports.[53] What the overall effect was, in either the short term or the long term, is dif- ficult to estimate. But it certainly helped maintain a capitalist class who were fortunate that much of the world owed them a living.

Some of what British capitalists owned abroad was the public debt of imperial and foreign countries and municipalities. But much was fixed capital owned by British firms, many of which operated only or mainly overseas. They were enterprises like oil fields and oil refiner- ies, agricultural land and meatpacking works, telephone, gas and electric utilities, plantations for rubber, tea and coffee, and mines of all kinds. And of course there were railways, like the Buenos Ayres Great Southern Railway. By 1930 the company was perhaps the larg- est private enterprise in South America with 30,000 employees, 8,000 kilometres of tracks, 504 stations, 857 steam locomotives, 955 car- riages and 16,602 coaches.[54] A director and sometime chairman of the Buenos Ayres Southern Railway was Sir Herbert Gibson, Bt, an Anglo-Argentine, owner of vast *estancias* in Argentina, member of the board of the cattle farmers and meatpackers Liebig (LEMCO) in Buenos Aires. Gibson moved between Argentina and the United Kingdom, becoming, for example, a wheat commissioner during the Great War, which bought millions of tons of wheat on behalf of the state, including from Argentina.[55] There were also important manufacturing enterprises. Some were associated with other activities – as was the case of oil refineries and meatpacking works – others were free-standing manufacturing enterprises. Some operated on a vast scale. An example is British American Tobacco (BAT), originally a joint enterprise of British and US tobacco enterprises outside their home markets, but soon a British company operating outside the UK. It made cigarettes in Venezuela, Chile, Mexico, Central America and the USA, as well as in China. By 1927 it had 120 subsidiaries and more than 75,000 employees worldwide.[56]

British investors, the British rich, would continue to own many foreign assets. They did, however, slow the investment in new ones after 1914. But the stock of investment and the income from it remained huge. British capitalists were fortunate in where they had invested. French and German capitalists were, compared to British, major losers from the Russian revolution. Furthermore, Germany lost most of its foreign investments during the war when they were seized as enemy property. It is notable that Germany had no significant presence in the world oil industry. British capitalists did lose some assets. Some were sold in the USA in the Great War, and there were losses in Soviet Russia during the revolution and in Mexico in the 1930s (in 1947 Mexico paid Shell $130 million compensation). However, in 1939 the world still owed British capitalists a living.

In the Second World War there were some significant losses of British overseas capital. In some cases, British nationals had to swap ownership of certain assets abroad, mostly in the USA, for sterling; the assets were sold to foreigners for dollars. The forced sale of Courtauld's subsidiary American Viscose raised £17 million; they thought it worth £30 million; the British government ended up paying a total of £27 million to Courtaulds. BAT did a deal by which it retained control of its US subsidiary but got paid $25 million in sterling.[57] There were also physical losses in the East, for example the destruction of the Burmah oil facilities in Burma and those of Shell in the Dutch East Indies. The

Japanese, more than the Germans, changed the distribution of British capital around the World.

The British government was keen to present a picture in which a desperate United Kingdom had basically liquidated all its foreign investments. It did this by publishing a net figure – the difference between its assets and liabilities overseas. They made much play of 'external disinvestment', though most of this was due to the rise of liabilities owed to the empire and sterling area (£3.35 billion), rather than actual losses or sales of overseas investments (£1 billion).[58] British liabilities were largely in the form of increased sterling balances (in effect foreign loans to the United Kingdom, largely from India, Egypt and South America). It was these liabilities which supported much of the claim that 'national wealth' fell by over a quarter as a result of the war, some £7 billion. This was made up of 'external disinvestment' of £4.2 billion, estimated physical destruction on land of £1.5 billion (almost certainly an overestimate) and losses at sea of £700 million.[59] These private losses, overwhelmingly of property, machines, factories and ships, were not borne by the owners, but by the state.

However, accounting tricks could not hide that the United Kingdom was far from bankrupt on the overseas capital account. The sterling liabilities added to less than the remaining value of overseas assets. Furthermore, there was still a positive net flow of investment income in that the United Kingdom still earned more from abroad in interest and dividends than it sent abroad in interest and dividends. The big returns to foreign investments was no longer in rails but in rubber, coming back into production, in tea and coffee, in mining, and above all in oil. At huge expense forces were sent to Malaya to defend rubber plantations and tin mines from 1948.

After the war there were some swaps between the sterling balances and overseas invesments. British investors sold their Argentine railways to the Argentine state for part of the Argentine sterling balances, which reduced both investment and debt. For the 24,000 kilometres of British-owned railway around £150 million was paid (compared to around £1 billion for the railways nationalized in the United Kingdom by the British government). These were very run-down and unprofitable railways, more so than the British ones, so this was probably an inflated price. Along with the Great Western Railway, the LNER, LMS and Southern Railways, British capitalists sold the Buenos Ayres Great Southern, Central Argentine, Buenos Ayres and Pacific, Buenos Aires Western Railway, Entre Ríos and Argentine North Eastern, and the Buenos Aires Midland Railway.

The 1940s and 1950s saw some further losses. The Chinese revolution of 1949 meant the loss of interests in textiles, tobacco and much else (though it led to the British colony of Hong Kong becoming a manufacturing centre). However, the greatest losses came from destruction by the enemy. BAT had lost plants with the expansion of the Japanese empire and subsequently to the revolutionary government in China and, as a result of nationalizations by governments across the world, in Egypt and Indonesia. BP was nationalized by the Iranian government in 1951 (to outrage from the British Labour government). This was easily the single most important British asset anywhere in the world. The Suez Canal Company, another partly British government enterprise, was nationalized in 1956 by the Egyptian government.

GENTLEMANLY FINANCIAL CAPITALISTS?

In the 1960s it became a common critique from the left that the British elite persisted with Edwardian aristocratic values. One variant of the thesis was the gentlemanly capitalist thesis – suggesting that a dominant group of elite financiers were mainly interested in reaping easy profits from investments abroad and controlling the British state to help them do so. There is some force in the argument that policy for empire and informal empire was driven by the financial interests of overseas investors. They, and the British government, were very concerned with what were called invisible earnings – that remitted profits on investments, and shipping insurance, etc., should remain high. In the 1930s this often meant doing deals with countries so that British profits would continue to flow home, which meant granting access to the British market so that they could acquire the sterling to pay their debts. Thus Argentina was given continued access to the UK, against the interests of empire producers, because gentlemanly capitalists wanted a return from their Argentine investments. Similarly Australia got continued preferential access to the UK, but the British government was unconcerned about Australian manufacturing protection against the UK. In other words, under gentlemanly capitalist rule the UK was in the business of collecting debts rather than maximizing domestic production, or exports.[60] British industry, the argument suggests, was sacrificed in favour of the bond-holding City and other investors overseas.

This thesis, while partly true, in the end gives a distorted account of British capitalism, even that of British rentiers and finance. While overseas investment (including in the rest of the empire, and in overseas government and municipal stocks) was large before 1914, after

Figure 4.1: Share of total personal wealth by percentile, 1895–2015

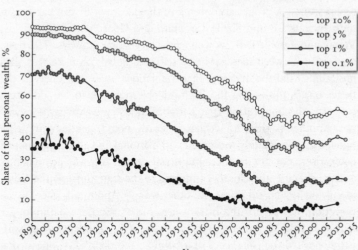

Source: Facundo Alvaredo, Anthony B. Atkinson and Salvatore Morelli, 'Top Wealth Shares in the UK Over More Than a Century', Working Papers. Department of Economics, Ca' Foscari University of Venice, No. 01/WP/201 7.

1914 the UK national debt was far larger than overseas investments of all kinds. The politics of rentiers' income was the politics of the valuation of the national debt, not that of empire. The rentiers won a great victory in the 1920s, achieving a big shake-down of taxpayers by the British rich, not those of the dominions or colonies.[61]

A second objection concerns the nature of British overseas economic activity. The thesis overplays the role of pure finance. British overseas interests were not merely those of financiers and rentiers: British capital was international, but also commercial and industrial. The City was as much about commodities as money, as much about shipping as stocks and shares. One image to keep in mind is that of the London Royal Docks, just east of the City, where the trade, controlled from the City, was in goods, not money, and industry processed imported raw materials. British capital was as much about mining abroad as government debt. British capital was producing oil, chilled and frozen meat, textiles, tea, tobacco and sugar in fields and factories overseas. It was also operating railways and utilities from telephones to gas works. A proper accounting of the nature of British capitalism must include BP and Shell, Rio Tinto and Consolidated Goldfields, Vestey and Tate & Lyle, as well as the Argentine railways. The basic opposition between national-industrial and global-commercial is thus misleading, and the inference that the national-industrial one was the better one is misleading too. A third objection, yet to be addressed, concerns the implication that national industry was weak – it was not. Another is that, as we have already noted, gentlemanly, elite figures were intimately concerned with national and global productive enterprises, not just finance. Industrial capital too was gentlemanly and aristocratic and closely connected to the state through the Commons and Lords and in myriad other ways.[62] And finally there is the objection that even if the thesis were true of 1900, it was no longer true of 1950. The main thrust of the thesis is that gentlemanly capitalism prevented the emergence of a politics, and the reality, of a strong national-industrial economy and that this was the central feature of the economic history of the United Kingdom. That, as we shall see, did not indeed exist in 1900. It was, however, a feature central to British economic history and politics after 1945.

5
British Capitalism?

When we were a rich country and, as a result of our overseas investments, were able to buy everything we wished to buy abroad, and indeed had to buy if we were to get a return from our foreign investments, it was only natural that the financial and accounting sides of industry should assume a very prominent part in the control and development of industry . . . Now that conditions have changed, and we have to rely on what we can produce ourselves, and sell to others to keep the nation solvent, we must again turn to our technical men and to our scientists and rely on them to take the lead as they did when this country's industrial wealth was first built up . . . In the battle before us our mechanical engineers are our armoured divisions.

Herbert Morrison, June 1947[1]

At the beginning of the twentieth century an iron works at Blaenavon in South Wales closed down. Much is still there, a treasured bit of Welsh industrial patrimony. It stands for, as do many other sites, the pioneering industrial revolution of the early nineteenth century, telling a story of the rise and decline of British industry. Yet the reason it closed was that much larger and more efficient iron and steel works were being built in Wales, for example by Stanley Baldwin's firm at Port Talbot on the coast, where an iron and steel plant still operates.

Around 1900 the United Kingdom was still industrializing. It was a new as well as an old industrial country. Not only were new coal mines sunk and coal docks dug, but new warship yards, engineering works, cotton mills, electrical engineering works, power stations and steel works went up. It was more industrial in 1900 than in 1850, when it was 'the workshop of the world'. It was even more industrial in 1950, when its highest ever, to that time, proportion of the workforce was in industrial occupations. It remained in 1950 the most industrial country in the world.

British industry as a matter almost of routine could pride itself on having the biggest firms and the biggest factories and the biggest products of any in the world. Belfast alone could claim Harland & Wolff, which was said to be the largest shipyard in the world; Belfast Harbour built the largest dry dock in the world, the Thompson Graving Dock, for the completion and maintenance of the *Titanic* and her sisters, themselves briefly the largest ships in the world. It had, in the Sirocco Works, the world's largest tea-drying machinery maker; and in the Belfast Ropeworks Co., which employed 3,600 in 1913, the largest maker of rope in the world, and in the York Street Flax Spinning and Weaving Company, the greatest maker of linen. We need to enter a world where British industry was described and understood in superlatives, as will be noted further in passing for many other cases.

We should not think of British industry too nationally, as it operated on a world stage, just like British banking and British shipping and the coal industry. Nor was all industry in the United Kingdom British-owned. But if we were to think in national terms, we would note that before 1913 firms in the United Kingdom were the world's leading exporter of manufactures, ahead of those in Germany, and a very long way ahead of the USA. From the late 1920s the UK and the USA exported comparable quantities of manufactures, both ahead of Germany.[2] This was rather remarkable in that the United Kingdom had a considerably smaller population than the USA or Germany – even Germany had nearly twice the population. To put the point another way: while the USA and Germany manufactured primarily for internal consumption, with some notable exceptions, British-made manufactures were much more oriented towards exports. Industrial capital was doubly global – open to and oriented towards world markets from British factories, as well as producing in many parts of the world. British capital was not just concerned with exporting, it also produced globally, from food to textiles to oil, some for import into the United Kingdom. Foreign direct investment took a number of forms. In some cases an enterprise with a strong domestic base also operated abroad, the classical multinational, but much more important in the British case were companies headquartered in London, with directors who met in London, but whose business was mostly abroad. There were thus British companies hardly operating in the United Kingdom itself. British capitalists owned half the world's foreign direct investment (that is assets managed from abroad, not all of course in industry). The United Kingdom was still way ahead in 1938, but the USA had emerged very strongly into second place.[3]

There was, especially to 1939, a large deficit in the balance of trade – imports were consistently larger than exports. The United Kingdom in its pomp did not export in order to pay for all its imports. A large proportion was paid for, as we have seen, by what were called 'invisible earnings' – mostly the return from investments, as well as shipping services and insurance and so on. The world did indeed owe some British people a living, and what they owed in effect came in as imports not paid for by exports. It was not until after the Second World War that manufacturing exports had to make an attempt to pay for all imports of goods. Only then was it a matter of 'export or die', but the idea that exports paid for all imports was pushed to the past.

TEXTILES AND COTTON

The British textiles industry was an enormous, truly global affair. As in the case of coal, its share of world exports was much greater than that of world production. The United Kingdom produced far more cotton goods than it could ever absorb, and it had a monopoly of the home market before the 1950s. Before 1914 some two-thirds of cotton textiles (the term for cloth and yarn) went abroad, to the clothing industries of the world, not least to India, its main market; they accounted for about one-third of value of all British exports. They were the largest single export down to 1939, by value, accounting for well over 20 per cent of the total. Employment in the industry, one which employed men and women, peaked at 1.4 million in 1913, with a secondary peak after the Second World War at 1 million. It was the only significant exporting industry to employ many women. The cotton industry (the larger of the two main ones) was concentrated in Lancashire – radiating out from the warehouses and head offices in Manchester. There was a Scottish cotton industry around Paisley. Yorkshire was the seat of the woollen and worsted (that is yarns made from wool for suitings, carpets, etc.) industry.

British textiles were of high quality and were produced extremely efficiently by its skilled workforce. Women wove, men and women spun, though in the case of spinning in different mills using different machines (in pre-industrial textiles, women spun, while men often wove). The British spinning and weaving industries came to be distinctive in their equipment – they used labour-intensive techniques, since they had skilled labour which was cheap, and the machines were suited to quality production. The United Kingdom was also the centre of the textile machinery industry, itself a very major exporter, which made equipment of all types.

From the 1930s it became a cliché to distinguish between new and old industries, the first modern in all respects, the latter stuck in the industrial past with cotton textiles a prime case. That is to ignore the huge growth of this industry, as of coal mining, or shipbuilding, in Germany and the USA. The contrast between new and old is in any case fictional, nicely illustrated by the electricity-powered 'New Old Mill', later the 'Royal Mill', built in Ancoats, Manchester, in 1910–12 for the spinning of cotton. It was built by Fine Spinners and Doublers, a new multi-plant conglomerate, and one of the largest employers of the time with 30,000 workers. Indeed, to judge modernity by size of plant would lead one to conclude that the industry was in the van of progress. The Calico Printers' Association, with 20,000 workers, dominated the market in printed cloth; the Bleachers' Association had 10,000 workers. Another huge firm was the Lancashire Cotton Corporation, of 15,000 workers, formed in 1929.[4] Indeed, Edwardian Manchester was a centre for new corporate headquarters buildings, like the new offices and warehouse of Tootal, Broadhurst Lee (a very large integrated merchant and manufacturer of cottons), and the Calico Printers' Association, both on the Oxford Road, further down which stood grand new university and teaching hospital buildings.

By another measure of modernity – multinational operation – British cotton firms also stood out. The sewing thread company Coats (headquartered in Glasgow) had some 39,000 foreign employees by 1913.[5] It established manufacturing in the USA, Russia, Brazil, Canada, France, Mexico, Portugal, Switzerland, Hungary, India, Bulgaria, Italy, Spain, Japan and Belgium.[6] It lost its plants in Russia after the revolution, and in Eastern Europe after the Second World War. The Calico Printers operated not just printing works, but spinning and weaving in Shanghai, and also in India, Java and later Australia.[7]

The pre-Great War cotton industry was an expanding and world-dominating industry, and most people would have expected it to continue to be so. But in the interwar years, apart from a short-lived boom (in which there was much investment in textiles), the markets for British cottons did not resume their growth – countries put up tariff barriers against British goods (not least, as we have seen, India), and a major competitor appeared – Japan. By the 1930s the British national industry was no longer the leading exporter of textiles, even though textiles still accounted for a quarter of its exports. The result was that the industry, which remained oriented to exports, never retained the output of 1913 and was in perpetual trouble. Investment dried up, and most companies continued to use the equipment they had in 1921 (most of it of course pre-1914) until the firms closed, whether in the 1930s, or in the 1950s. For all that it was efficient overall, it could not hold its own against low-wage producers.

This is not to say nothing new happened in the textile industry after 1913. For a start, the man-made fibres, as they were called, expanded enormously. Viscose, or rayon, made from wood, was made by the British company Courtaulds, whose subsidiary, American Viscose, became the largest producer in the USA. The Calico Printers came up with the new synthetic Terylene (which was developed by ICI), one of the fibres of the second half of the century.

The British textile industry was also global in that its raw materials came from far away. Most of the raw cotton came from the southern United States, much of the rest from Egypt. Some wool was home-produced, but most came from the southern hemisphere, mostly from Australia. The interwar years saw, just as we have noted in the case of sugar (chapter 4), a determined attempt at imperialization of supply. British engineers and capitalists and the British state outdid the pharaohs many times over when it came to controlling the Nile, the British empire's Dneiper or Colorado, largely for cotton production. The first dam, the Aswan, was completed in 1902 (at the cost of a dreadnought). It was extended upwards almost as soon as it was finished, and again in 1929–33. On the Blue Nile, Lord Cowdray built the gigantic Sennar Dam (3 kilometres long and 40 metres high) which was central to the Gezira irrigation scheme. This was a semi-private enterprise developed by the Sudan Plantations Syndicate, which irrigated and controlled an area the size of a couple of English counties for cotton growing. Sir Arthur Gaitskell, brother of Hugh, worked on it for most of his career, becoming its head. One hundred or so British male graduates, mostly of Oxford and Cambridge, specialists in agriculture, oversaw the work of tenant farmers in the vast irrigated Gezira Plain.[8] The White Nile was itself dammed by British engineers in the 1930s, with what was then the largest dam in the world, just south of Khartoum, at Jebel Aulia, to further control the waters of the Nile for irrigation lower down. An important engineer in all these projects was Sir Murdoch MacDonald, who served as a senior engineer to the Egyptian government to 1921, and as a Liberal and National Liberal MP between 1922 and 1950, when he also ran a consulting engineering firm.

TRANSATLANTIC AND EUROPEAN CONNECTIONS

The connections to Africa and Asia should not be overstated. British firms were making products and equipment for the rich world, and for communications in the rich world. In 1906 the newly merged Swan Hunter and Wigham Richardson of Newcastle launched the *Mauretania*, then the largest ship in the world, which was to hold the record for the fastest transatlantic crossing into the late 1920s. This was the key passenger route of the world, and British ships dominated it. The coal-powered *Mauretania* was equipped with the new steam turbines, also built by the new firm. They had been invented by the Honourable (for he was the son of a peer) Sir Charles Parsons, also of Newcastle. She was built for Cunard with a government loan and subsidy, under arrangements which kept Cunard British, unlike its great rival, the White Star Line. Swan Hunter & Wigham Richardson was employing up to 6,000 men on its formation in 1903.[9] The Quaker John Wigham Richardson, whose shipbuilding firm went public in 1899, was multilingual, well travelled and well connected to the local intellectual elite.[10] His sister Alice was married to John Theodore Merz, Newcastle industrialist and author of *A History of European Thought in the Nineteenth Century*.[11] Merz was a key figure in making Edwardian Newcastle the site of the largest integrated supplier of electricity in Europe, with engines made by Wigham Richardson, one of the clients for its electricity. He sent his daughters as well as his sons to Oxford and Cambridge. One son (Sir Philip, as he was later) went on to become a Tory MP and chairman of Swan Hunter & Wigham Richardson.

There was nothing backward about Newcastle or other centres of British shipbuilding. The *Lusitania*, the very slightly smaller and slower sister of the *Mauretania*, was built by John Brown of Clydebank in Scotland, part of a Sheffield-Clyde complex of firms, in steel, armaments and ships, that built the dreadnoughts. The chairman of that company was Charles McLaren, who studied at Edinburgh, Bonn and Heidelberg Universities and was called to the Bar, was in parliament as a Liberal, sitting till 1910 and then entering the Lords as Baron Aberconway of Bodnant, Denbigh. He was also chairman of the Metropolitan Railway Company, of the Tredegar Iron and Coal Company and of the Sheepbridge Iron and Coal Company. He published *The Basic Industries of Great Britain* in 1927.

The *Mauretania*'s world-size record did not last long – it was beaten by a trio of sister-ships built at Harland & Wolff in Belfast, for their associated White Star Line, which was owned by an American company controlled by the New York banker J. P. Morgan. The chairman of Harland & Wolff was Lord Pirrie, who had, like MacLaren, been a Liberal MP. The *Olympic*, *Titanic* and *Britannic*, though huge, were slower than the Cunarders and conventionally powered with triple-expansion engines and, like the Cunarders, were coal-fired, all destined for the New York route.

The connections across the Atlantic were very important in manufacturing industry. Clydebank was also the home of the largest sewing-machine factory in the world, which by 1911 had over 10,000 workers. At its peak in 1913 it made more than 1 million machines and employed 14,000, including thousands of women, making it one of the largest factories in the world, certainly in Britain. It was owned by the American company Singer. Singer supplied the whole world with this transformative piece of domestic and industrial equipment from Clydebank. Even its labour relations were global. A drive to intensify work and lower wages at Clydebank led to a strike and victimization and defeat for the workers. The strike, which started among some women workers, was called by the Industrial Workers of Great Britain, an offshoot of the US Industrial Workers of the World, known as the 'Wobblies', whose slogan was 'one big union'. The British Wobblies, and the associated British Socialist Labour Party (founded 1911), were a Glasgow phenomenon but were to have continuing influence in the radical industrial politics of the city. Many of their leaders would migrate to the new Communist Party of Great Britain on its foundation in 1920.

Manchester's connections with the United States were longstanding, as the American South had always been the main source of raw cotton for its cotton spinning industry. From the 1890s Manchester was connected directly to the sea by the new Manchester Ship Canal, linking the city to the River Mersey. The new canal generated a new industrial estate enclosed in a bend as it approached the new Manchester docks. The green fields of Trafford Park estate were to be the home of many enterprises. In 1910 Manchester United Football Club moved into a new stadium adjacent to it (Old Trafford). The first big arrival was British Westinghouse, subsidiary of the US electrical engineering firm. Other firms included the Brooke Bond tea factory, supplied by its own tea plantations in India, Ceylon and Kenya, and the US breakfast cereal firm Kelloggs, also processing imports. In the early 1920s the coal-fired Barton Power Station was built on the site, with much locally sourced equipment. Another new industry established in Trafford Park with US capital and expertise was the motor industry.

The United Kingdom was a vigorous early user of largely foreign motor cars, taxis, buses and lorries. It imported more cars than it exported before 1913, from the United States (for cheap cars) and from France (for luxury models) – they came in free of duty. By 1913 there was a substantial local industry, of which the biggest producer was the Ford Motor Company of Detroit, Michigan. Ford had arrived in Trafford Park in 1911, where it first assembled and then manufactured the Model T, the most popular car in the United Kingdom, as it was in the USA. US capital continued to play an important role in the British car industry. Vauxhall was a subsidiary of General Motors (GM) from 1925. From the late 1920s Ford built the largest car factory in Europe in Dagenham on what was a greenfield site on the River Thames, with workers housed in a new council estate, Becontree, built by the London County Council. The British car industry received protection from 1915, which no doubt promoted the entry of foreign companies who could avoid tariffs by building their own British factories. They included tyre makers such as Firestone. British firms emerged behind these tariff barriers, like Austin in Birmingham and Morris (Nuffield) in Oxford, along with many others. They needed the protection: even in imperial markets they lost out to US cars – New Zealand or Ceylon or the Gold Coast all preferred US rather than British cars and lorries.

Americanization affected the United Kingdom and the empire more generally, long before 1945. Many US businesses came to be headquartered on a new street built in London in the Edwardian years, with modern business very much in mind: Kingsway, a wide thoroughfare from the Strand to Holborn.[12] At the southern end stood Bush House (first part opened 1925), an American project, decorated with a statue commemorating Anglo-American friendship (it was from this building the BBC overseas services operated from 1941). Kodak, of Rochester, New York, which had its showroom at headquarters on Kingsway, was before 1914 the United Kingdom's and the world's largest photographic firm. British Thomson-Houston was there, a subsidiary of the US General Electric. GE would form and control Associated Electrical Industries, based on Kingsway, which from the 1920s owned both Metropolitan-Vickers and British-Thomson Houston. Metropolitan-Vickers was British Westinghouse of Trafford Park, which had been taken over by British interests

(Vickers and Metropolitan Carriage) but had been sold to GE, Westinghouse's competitor. Westinghouse controlled English Electric, also on Kingsway. The only major British electrical company was on the same street, in Magnet House. General Electric, led by Lord Hirst, had fought off the Americans, restricting voting shareholding to the British empire.

The emergence of corporate headquarters in London was an important phenomenon of the interwar years, reflecting the growth of firms with plants not only in the United Kingdom but around the world. The headquarters of Unilever, Shell, British Petroleum (Britannic House), Imperial Chemical Industries, at Millbank, were in central London, in monumental interwar buildings still standing today. These buildings, with the exception of ICI, were the headquarters of importing firms.

US capital was, like British capital, global, and went to where British capital had already gone. Like British firms, US firms began to export from other parts of the world to the United Kingdom. Thus Chicago meatpackers such as Armour and Swift came to be of importance in the River Plate meatpacking trade, supplying London and Liverpool in competition, and collusion, with Vestey and others. Elders & Fyffes, a banana importer, was taken over by United Fruit in 1913 and in the interwar years achieved a near monopoly in the banana trade in the British Caribbean and the United Kingdom. On the other hand, British capital, with Bolivian capital, dominated the world tin industry. In the United Kingdom smelters smelted Cornish and Bolivian ore for the British and European markets; British smelters in Penang and Singapore dominated the smelting of Malayan (and far Eastern) ore, which went overwhelmingly to the United States, which did not smelt until the Second World War. British companies in Malaya dominated world rubber production, for which the main world market was also the United States. Indeed, there were important British companies operating inside the US, including American Viscose and Shell.

The connections to Europe in terms of communications were much less glamorous. It was a matter of routine tramp-ship operations. Much was in what was called the 'home trade' – which covered ports from the Elbe to Brest – itself a huge quite open market in which

British trade was a central feature. The United Kingdom was integrated by sea into the European economy, especially before 1914. We have already noted the importance of British coal to the continental and Baltic economies. Baltic timber was vital for building, and for coal mining. The British steel industry had national reserves of iron ore, but even before 1914 more than half the iron produced came from richer foreign ores, mainly from Sweden, Spain and North Africa. Belfast, the centre of the world linen industry, relied on flax from the eastern Baltic.

There were also significant imports of manufactures from the rest of Europe. The United Kingdom imported finished steel from Europe, which it made into ships and the like. Furthermore, Germany was a vital supplier of many specialized manufactures from dyestuffs to pharmaceuticals to optical glass, magnetos and more.

There was also significant direct investment in the United Kingdom from the continent. Nobel Industries in Scotland was the local subsidiary of the Swedish multinational enterprises of Alfred Nobel. The German electrical giant Siemens Company was making telegraph cable and electric motors and much else in London and elsewhere. Furthermore, German dye and pharmaceutical firms were producing in the United Kingdom before the Great War. Brunner, Mond in Cheshire, was the licensee of the Belgian Solvay company for the making of alkali using the Solvay process. Friedrich Engels was hardly the only German businessman in Manchester and the northwest in the nineteenth century. Among the others were the great capitalist Ludwig Mond, Hans Renold of Renold Chain, Henry Simon of what became Simon Engineering, and Ivan Levinstein, who created Levinstein Dyes.

TOWARDS PROTECTION

The story told above is of an economy integrated with the European and world economies before 1914, and in the 1920s and beyond. Yet the Great War imposed extraordinary temporary changes, and in the longer term strongly encouraged protection. Before the Great War the broadly liberal trading system meant that many materials which were to prove essential in fighting a war came to the United Kingdom from continental Europe. The disruption of the war left the United Kingdom without necessary supplies. The result was a successful programme of import substitution. Perhaps the most spectacular case was dyestuffs, where state initiatives created a whole new state-backed firm, the British Dyestuffs Corporation. It was created to supply dyes which had come from Germany, but it was also intended to be a post-war competitor to the German firms. A similar story was repeated in optical glass, scientific instruments and nitrates. The war thus saw not only the expansion of the arms industry, but the establishment of many industries new to the United Kingdom. Many products of these industries were advertised with Union Jacks.

Opportunities arose to throw out 'alien' or semi-alien competitors. The new British Metals Corporation was created to destroy the Anglo-German Metalsgesellschaft, a dominant force in non-ferrous metals (copper, zinc, tin, etc.) trading and production. The campaign to create it was full of both anti-German and anti-Semitic themes.[13] This rhetoric drew on pre-war attacks on Jewish-German cosmopolitan business, especially finance, which was seen as undermining the British productive economy. It was not out of the blue that the association German/Jew/Liberal/traitor was made, for example in the scandalous Pemberton Billing trial of 1918. In this context it is worth noting that the two greatest British-owned companies in the chemical and electrical industries in the interwar years, Imperial Chemical Industries and the General Electric Company, were led by men of German-Jewish heritage, Alfred Mond (Lord Melchett) and Sir Hugo Hirst. Both were influential protectionists, and Hirst tried to restrict shareholding in GEC to residents of the British empire. Mond, who had been a Liberal and then a coalition MP, and minister, became a committed protectionist. Imperial Chemical Industries, GEC and many others were supported by the protectionist measures under the Safeguarding of Industries Act, and the support for industrial research. They were the sheltered trades, focused on the domestic market and protected; this would become more pronounced in the interwar years.

The formation of Imperial Chemical Industries (ICI) in the 1920s exemplifies a very significant transformation. It was formed by the merger of Sir Alfred's firm Brunner, Mond, created by his father and Sir John Brunner (who was also Liberal MP for the constituency of the main factory until 1910), with the other main British chemical firms. They were the United Alkali Company, Nobel Industries, and a wartime creation, the British Dyestuffs Corporation. Formed in 1926, ICI developed synthetic fertilizer and later synthetic fuel, as well as dyestuffs and general chemicals. With government support Brunner, Mond created a subsidiary, Synthetic Ammonia and Nitrates, at Billingham, on Teesside, to make nitrate for fertilizer and explosives. It was the largest spender on scientific research in the country and one of the three most important chemical companies in the world. The well-protected Imperial Chemical Industries (ICI) had the largest private research effort in the country, much of it copying, developing and improving on German developments in synthetic nitrates and oil-from-coal. Among its notable inventions of the 1930s was the later universal plastic polythene. It was, and saw itself as, a national and imperial enterprise, closely connected to the British state.

The large electrical concerns, such as Metro-Vickers, GEC and British Thomson Houston, also protected, were also notable for their large R&D efforts. Some were owned outright by US electrical giants GE and Westinghouse, who between them controlled the industry by the early 1930s, but less so by 1939.[14] Some firms were unambiguously foreign-owned and did research in the United Kingdom, some on a considerable scale, such as British United Shoe Machinery, Kodak and Mond Nickel (from 1929 US owned).[15]

Although the scale of research and development was certainly very much lower than in the USA, it was comparable to that in German industry and more important than the industrial research of any other nation. If British industry had lagged behind German in research in 1914, it probably did not in 1939, and certainly not in 1945 or 1950. Characterizations of British industrial research effort in this period as deficient, over-dependent on limited state funding and failing to follow the German and especially the US model of large corporate research laboratories just got the British story wrong.[16] In addition, the Department of Scientific and Industrial Research of

1915/16 was to fund university research and fund and develop research associations and new government laboratories. It supported research at arm's length, with collective research organizations partly funded by industries as a whole. The idea was that the research associations would do what was called fundamental research on the principles underlying an industry, to the benefit of all, but the exclusive benefit of none, a liberal non-interventionist politics of research.[17]

Indeed, the government's broadly liberal policy meant that it did not spend huge sums on research and development to create a national self-sufficient economy, as did Germany in the 1930s. The USA, as an essentially continental power, could supply itself with nearly everything it needed, with the exception of tropical products. The United Kingdom, the greatest trading nation in the world, could not hope, at least in the medium term, to be autarchic given the scale of its needs and its small size. It was in any case happy to rely on imported petrol, rubber, cotton, wool and food.

In the tariff reform controversies of the Edwardian years the threat to British manufacturing was seen as coming from both Germany and the United States. In the 1920s the economic ascendancy of the United States was most strongly felt, not just in the United Kingdom, but in the British empire as a whole. Many of the safeguarding of industry controls were directed against US industry, for example in tyres and cars. The Kinematograph Films Act of 1927 introduced quotas for non-empire films, directed against Hollywood. One consequence was that US companies set up production facilities in the United Kingdom, from film companies making 'quota quickies' to car and tyre companies like General Motors and Firestone. US finance also took control of many British enterprises, notably in the heavy electrical industry. But there were still important European dimensions – protection for chemicals was principally directed against Germany.

The Great Depression, starting in 1929, led to spectacular falls in world trade, world output and world prices. The Conservative Party, which lost the 1929 election, was attacked by radical protectionists. The Canadian Lord Beaverbrook, owner of the best-selling *Daily Express*, launched his Empire Crusade (with the little crusader logo which still adorns his old, now much-diminished newspaper) to achieve what he ingeniously called Empire Free Trade – in other words imperial protection. In 1930 he and his fellow right-wing press lord, Lord Rothermere (of the *Daily Mail*), formed the United Empire Party. It was supported by the greatest of industrialists, such as Sir Harry McGowan of Imperial Chemical Industries and Sir Hugo Hirst of the General Electric Company. Their aim was to push the Conservatives towards protection. The challenge was perhaps at its height at a by-election in London in March 1931, when the hard-right Sir Ernest Petter (owner of Petters, an engineering firm, and Westland Aircraft) stood, supported by the press magnates, against the official Conservative, not just on empire free trade, but on a more general die-hard imperialist platform. He lost, and Stanley Baldwin and therefore a more liberal Conservatism, survived.[18] It was during this campaign that Baldwin complained about the press exercising 'power without responsibility, the prerogative of the harlot through the ages'.

Tariffs on most manufactured imports came in 1931 and were made permanent in 1932. What the overall effect was is difficult to say, but in the case of steel at least the effect was positive. With protection, and the expansion in domestic demand, a new steel industry was created. The Ebbw Vale steel works closed down in the Depression, but a new steel works was built there from 1936 by Richard Thomas. This was the first wide strip mill in the United Kingdom, designed by US engineers to supply cheap steel sheet (the USSR and Germany also got US-designed strip mills at this time). It would become, according to some, the largest steelworks in Europe. A second wide strip mill was started later in Shotton (Summerson) and came into operation during the war. The third was built in the 1940s.

The home market was to become much more important for British industry. This was reflected in a switch of industrial activity from the exporting areas of the north to the national suppliers of the south. It was in this 'inner Britain', as it was called in the 1930s, that manufacturing prospered. It was centred on London and the Midlands, though some other places benefited too, in all cases reflected in increases in population. London was to expand and expand, reaching a peak in size and its contribution to manufacturing around 1939.[19] As an industrial centre 1930s London had few rivals. To the east was the largest car factory in Europe, Ford's Dagenham works; to the west EMI and Nestlé. To the north were aircraft companies like De Havilland and Handley Page, with others such as Vickers and Fairey towards the west. The Thames was as never before a great industrial river, with such manufacturers as the flour millers, Tate & Lyle, Siemens and many others, as well as new power stations, gas works and more.

In the northern export industries, which tariffs could not protect, there was contraction, including the coordinated scrapping of machinery and factories. In cotton and in shipbuilding firms got together to scrap particular factories and yards. Under the Cotton Spinning Industry Act 1936, the spinners raised a levy which was used to buy up and destroy machinery, in the hope of making the rest more profitable. In shipbuilding, the companies joined together to buy up and 'sterilize' shipyards, the most famous example being Palmers shipyard in Jarrow. One notable and largely forgotten development was called industrial self-government. The idea was that industries could collectively come up with policies for the whole industry, which could be backed by legislation. A key example was the cotton textile industry, where enabling government legislation, culminating in the Cotton Industry Act 1939 (which never went into operation) allowed the industry to come up with schemes to scrap capacity and much else. Industrial feudalism critics called this a collectivist approach.

WAR PRODUCTION

The United Kingdom had by 1939 the full range of industries required to produce for modern war, many developed behind protectionist barriers. In a remarkable change from 1914, it now had its own optical glass, dyes and a full chemical industry. It was in a much better position internally to provide the ways and means of modern war. In 1944 there would be 10.3 million people in the forces and the arms factories, 32 per cent of the working population. This compared with 7.3 million in 1918 (28 per cent). The main reason was there were 2 million more employed in arms factories in 1944 than in 1918, while the size of the armed forces themselves was only a little larger.[20] The key was to reduce British exports, which allowed reductions in imports of some raw materials, and the expansion of war production. This was 'to a large extent the consequence of a deliberate act of policy' designed to maximize arms output.[21] It was the policy essentially of the United States – for without Lend-Lease, and indeed without the rest of the world supplying raw materials in exchange for promises to pay in the future (the sterling balances), it could not have happened. The empire, the southern hemisphere food providers and above all the United States made this seemingly national effort possible. The impressive war production record cannot be understood nationally.

International support of the economy allowed the creation of an extraordinarily powerful warfare state. The armed forces were expanded with new stations, barracks, regiments and ships. The building of aerodromes, military communication systems and the like put pre-war rates of investment to shame. Newly tractorized and extended British agriculture provided standardized outputs including a mere four types of industrial cheese. Vast new arms factories were built, which turned out new weapons in prodigious quantities.

In the Second World War, as in the First, it was the expanded arms factories which dominated arms production. Vickers (which had merged with Armstrong Whitworth in the 1920s) was once again producing nearly every armament modern armed services needed, from the Spitfire and Wellington to the Valentine tank. There were government factories of very many types, some run by the government itself (such as the Royal Ordnance Factories), some by private firms (for example, the shadow factories for aircraft and aero-engines), and extensions to the works of arms contractors. Vast new industrial spaces were built with government money, around £1 billion worth, comparable in value to an entire major infrastructural sector like the railways. Trafford Park welcomed back the Ford Company, which operated a new state-owned aero-engine plant, making Rolls-Royce Merlin engines. Rolls-Royce itself operated a government-owned factory in a new industrial estate south of Glasgow. It was in these new state-financed factories and extensions that most of the young women drafted into war production worked. These were factories for a hygienic, electrical age of production.

The other side of this commitment to war production was deliberate restriction of domestic consumption and exports. This meant the shrinking of whole sectors, such as textiles, furniture, pottery. They were, following Lend-Lease, 'concentrated', releasing labour and factory space for other uses. These industries, which would be vital to the export drive after the war, had no investment in them. The great bulk of civilian industry was not mobilized for war, but creaked on. There emerged a bifurcated British industry – that which was central to the war effort, the arms industry, and the rest.

Even with the extraordinary commitment to produce arms, the British and imperial armed forces demanded and got even more than the United Kingdom could produce. British factories never made enough rifles for the British army, let alone the other British armies. They also came from Canada, the United States, Australia and India. Lend-Lease sent a great stream of goods to the United Kingdom and the British empire, from transport aircraft to the bulk of petroleum products. They were given free, but one can think of them as manufacturing imports, and they arrived on an unprecedented scale. Far from being national, the British war effort was in many dimensions the product of a radical internationalism, economically as well as politically and ideologically.

EXPORT OR DIE

However, with the end of the war the United Kingdom found itself economically alone. It now lost free supplies of goods through Lend-Lease and it had to start paying in the form of exports for the supplies it had got from the empire and from foreigners. It still needed imports on a huge scale but had given up the export trade, and thus began a unique period of state policy in which the promotion of exports of goods became central.[22] It was not simply a matter of getting back to the pre-war position. In the past the United Kingdom had had a substantial deficit in trade in goods, compensated for by a surplus in shipping (one-third roughly of the deficit) and investment income (two-thirds roughly). Now it faced a future with a diminished shipping fleet and lower net investment income. Exports would have to pay for more of the import bill. There were also greatly increased commitments to overseas expenditure on the military, in effect imports, to pay for. Furthermore, the character of exports needed to change. There was very little coal to export, but lots of capacity to build up manufacturing production. Britain's bread now, and only now, hung by Lancashire's thread.

The post-war drive for exports was a coordinated national effort, one which bit deep into the economy. Exorbitant domestic taxes, such as the new wartime purchase tax, were put on things like cars and kept very high, and steel was allocated preferentially to those firms who exported. The result was a full decade where the national fleet of private cars did not increase, and for the first and only time the United Kingdom became the largest car exporter in the world. An exhausted but essentially undamaged nation brought back into operation factories full of old machinery which would in other circumstances never have reopened. Film upon film was made to encourage workers, including women, to return to make a career in once-doomed industries, for example *Cotton Come Back* of 1946.[23] Employment in cotton went up, as it did in mining. In shipbuilding employment was at its historical peak at around 300,000 workers in 1950. This was twice as many as in the worst year of the Depression and considerably more than the 200,000 or so employed before the Great War. This build-up, it has been suggested, postponed the inevitable decline of these industries.[24] The export drive was in its own terms a success. Around 1950 the United Kingdom contributed 22 per cent of the world's manufacturing exports. This put it behind the US, but way ahead of everyone else. Yet that level of exports was not from the point of view of the British economy a natural one – it relied on forced exports. That is not to say the difficulties lay in finding customers overseas. On the contrary, a war-devastated Europe and Asia, and Latin American and African markets which had been deprived of imports by the war, were keen to buy. The difficulty lay in depriving British people of goods so that they could have necessary imports.

Restriction of imports was a central plank of policy. Food imports continued to be controlled by state purchasing, which went on into the 1950s, with demand kept down by rationing. Raw material imports were handed back to the private sector progressively, but these were destined in significant measure for export industries. In the case of manufactures there were new restrictions. While during the war the United Kingdom was awash with manufactured goods from abroad, from machine tools to weapons, these had mostly come free through Lend-Lease. After the war the government bore down hard on manufactured imports. They were minimal, though there was no avoiding the import of Hollywood films and long-range passenger aircraft from the United States. The United Kingdom depended on direct support from the USA. First came the 1945 loan to support imports from the USA. From 1947 there was Marshall Aid, which went to the United Kingdom alongside Western Europe. Both made it possible to buy food, tobacco, raw materials and industrial goods from the USA, the only place with supplies to spare.

Even with the encouragement of exports, and the restriction of imports, there were difficulties. Imports were too great for the quantity of exports. The result was a stupendous devaluation of the pound by 30 per cent against the dollar in September 1949, a move which led to devaluations by all other major currencies against the dollar. This was a much more significant devaluation to the comparable ones of 1919 and of 1931, which were both reversed, one brutally and slowly the second quickly and easily. It was also larger than the 1939 devaluation which pegged sterling at the $4.03 from which it was devalued in 1949. This time, in the new regime of fixed exchange rates, it stayed down at $2.80.

The national export effort led to a more national and technocratic conception of the economy. Part of that was a greater focus on the technicians and managers who organized production and created new products rather than the capitalists who owned manufacturing firms. Stafford Cripps at the wartime Ministry of Aircraft Production, and in post-war years as president of the Board of Trade and chancellor of the exchequer, was very keen on management, on science, on efficiency, as befits a scientist who had acted as a patent lawyer for ICI. So too was Harold Wilson, his successor at the Board of Trade, an economist, and the son of an industrial chemist. They were more national technocrats than socialists.[25]

The new national era, also an era of labour shortage rather than over-supply, encouraged a fresh concern with efficiency as well as the rights of workers. Comparative studies of what was called productivity emerged, showing a very large difference between British and US levels. This was long known; what was new was the systematic nature of this knowledge and the determination to act upon it at national level. What mattered now was national productivity, not merely the efficiency of this or that firm. This is not to say there were no important differences between industries. US miners each dug five times as much coal as did British miners. But in shipbuilding, British yards had the edge. Despite the small physical size of British yards and the need to produce quickly, on man hours on the finished product 'we still claim to maintain the lead' said the wartime film *Clyde Built*.[26] Indeed, they were right. In making aeroplanes, too, productivity was comparable. But overall there was a huge gap in national productivity, with the USA perhaps twice as productive per worker. The gap between British and US industry in labour productivity was the greatest it would ever be. Determined efforts were made to change this.

While the government thought in terms of the national interest, and bent the tools of government to force enterprises to export, there were limits to its power. In contrast to coal and the infrastructure industries and the one significant exception of the steel industry, manufacturing industries were not nationalized. The exporting industries, like the importing ones, were kept in the private sector. More than this, the mass of state-owned capacity created during the war was not used to create new state manufacturing enterprises. It was sold or leased to the private sector or kept in reserve, with few exceptions.

There were tensions between the national interest and particular private interests. Film provides a good example. Two companies dominated film distribution in the United Kingdom; both were important film-makers too. They preferred to buy cheap Hollywood films rather than make their own. Just as Rank bought wheat from overseas, the Rank Organization set up by J. Arthur Rank in 1937 bought films from Hollywood. The Labour government, for largely economic reasons, wanted to reduce the outflow of dollars to Hollywood but met unbreakable resistance not just from the United States but also from the British distributers/producers of films. Thus it was that British film had only a brief moment of national glory in the 1940s.[27]

The British economy was now understood in a national frame as a single economy which produced, imported and exported. It was taken to have national features such as particular levels of national labour productivity and research and development spending and investment. Such measures were not entirely new but they gained currency and salience in what was now a highly protected and controlled national economy for which there was a tendency to see the balance of payments as a national profit and loss account. Furthermore, this post-war industrial export-or-die moment helped establish the notion that Britain had always depended on manufactured exports. Manufacturing not only became the central discussion point in relation to foreign trade, but stood for the economy as a whole. That resulted in the underplaying of many other sectors of the economy and the significance of shipping and investment income to the national accounts, as well as the export of non-manufactures, essentially coal. Indeed, the whole pre-national economy became difficult to understand in this new national frame.

Yet for many on the left Labour's productionism did not go far enough. Aneurin Bevan made a point which would reverberate through the later writings of the Labour left: 'I therefore seriously suggest to the Government that they should set up a production department and put the chancellor of the exchequer in the position where he ought to be now under modern planning, that is, with the function of making an annual statement of accounts.'[28]

6

Knowledge and Power

Liberalism was still embodied in a large political party; it enjoyed the support of philosophy and religion; it was intelligible, it was intelligent, and it was English.

George Dangerfield, The Strange Death
of Liberal England *(1935)*

What socialists proclaim as a duty towards the fellow members of the existing states, they are not prepared to grant to the foreigner ... That socialism so long as it remains theoretical, is internationalist, while as soon as it is put into practice, whether in Russia or in Germany, it becomes violently nationalist, is one of the reasons why 'liberal socialism' as most people in the Western world imagine it is purely theoretical, while the practice of socialism is everywhere totalitarian.

F. A. Hayek, The Road to Serfdom *(1944)*[1]

The idea that the United Kingdom had no intellectuals was once a commonplace. It was a good thing for conservatives in that instead of egg-heads peddling dangerous advanced doctrines, in the United Kingdom practical common sense ruled. It was a bad thing for left intellectuals in that for them the world of ideas seemed populated by old and bad ideas. But the United Kingdom had a galaxy of thinkers that in other contexts would have been called intellectuals. It is just that many of them spread the idea that they themselves did not exist, and that if they did their influence was negligible. As a result of these ideas, which were to be influential, the history of British knowledge and its relation to power became impossible to write. There seemed to be little modern knowledge and no connection to power. Within this capacious framework there was plenty of room for self-interested stories about economists ignored, scientists sidelined and medical reformers brushed aside. An elaborate story of progressive ideas being at best rejected to be taken up too late was to become a central assumption of British histories. This has been inadvertently strengthened because much of the concern with British ideas and ideas of the British was focused on the novel, and on the relatively small university subject of English.[2]

Instead of thinking in terms of deficits and backwardness we need to note that, as in most similar places, experts fought, preached, pleaded, judged, healed, argued, invented and made. Forms of knowledge about the world shaped how the world was acted on. Knowledge shaped the understanding of what was possible, what was calculable, what was mere common sense. Knowledge and knowing was associated with power, not least economic clout, and shaped and constrained how politics was conducted, and histories written, and everything from war to love understood. Some striking differences are evident, however. Perhaps the least commented on and most important is that there was very little serious anti-modern thought in the United Kingdom. Even the hereditary aristocracy managed to produce advanced liberal thinkers such as Bertrand Russell. Russell was not only a peer, but the grandson of a prime minister, a member of an immensely rich family, a mathematician and later a notably scientistic philosopher. The second issue is the exceptional importance of elite universities in all sorts of knowledge production – thus even the chief ideologue of the British communists, Rajani Palme Dutt, and the country's greatest contributor to the occult, Aleister Crowley, were Oxbridge graduates. Also among the Oxbridge-educated were popular writers Dorothy L. Sayers and J. B. Priestley and many early women MPs in the Labour Party.[3]

It is too easily assumed that British universities were there to turn out national and imperial civil servants when this was not even true of Oxford or Cambridge. Apart from Oxford, British universities were very technical places. Cambridge was especially strong in mathematics and engineering. The new civic universities, many created around 1900, were there to train doctors (some one-third of the national student body), and the reason new buildings were built next to new hospitals and large medical schools – as was typically the case for civic universities. The sciences and engineering were also important. The arts were for a minority and at the beginning of the century focused on classics; the new humanities, such as history, were small beer, English, for example, emerged on a tiny scale in the interwar years. The social sciences, primarily economics, also attracted very few students. Going to university was necessary only for entry to teaching in grammar and public schools, to enter medicine and the most learned parts of other professions, and the tiny national and imperial administrative civil services. Only a small proportion of grammar- and public-school leavers went to university – for there were many professions, such as the army or the imperial police services, which recruited at eighteen for officers. Naval officers entered at thirteen in most cases.

Nor was religion especially important. To be sure, the connections between the Anglican Church and elite education remained deep and strong through most of the colleges of Oxford and Cambridge and the major public schools and many old grammar schools too. It had been a long time since a major intellectual was an ordained minister, but the heads of the Church were expected to be men of some secular learning. In any case it was hardly likely that the Church that had buried Charles Darwin in Westminster Abbey in 1882 would stand in the way of scientific ideas. The politics of the established churches were never reactionary. Archbishops of Canterbury were generally solidly Tory, though intellectually the pole of the Anglican political position was on the liberal right, as can be seen in the case of the ecumenical Christian intellectual discussion group 'The Moot', which met between 1938 and 1947 and included Anglicans such as the poet T. S. Eliot, the exiled continental sociologist Karl Mannheim and the scientist Michael Polanyi and other big names. But there were exceptions. William Temple, archbishop of Canterbury 1942–4, was a Christian socialist who had briefly been a member of the Labour Party.[4] There was a 'red vicar' in East Anglia, and a Stalinist 'red dean' of Canterbury, author of The Socialist Sixth of the World. Catholic intellectuals and writers cleaved to the right, as is evident in the cases of Hilaire Belloc and the converts G. K. Chesterton and Evelyn Waugh. All showed a disdain for the modern, the materialist machine order and British liberalism. Thus Hilaire Belloc tilted at H. G. Wells' phenomenally successful *Outline of History* of 1919, though with little effect. British ideas were much more Wellsian than the ideas of the professors of Greek and priests he despised.

POLITICAL ECONOMY

Writing in the 1960s, the historian E. P. Thompson argued that political economy, alongside natural science and Protestantism, was characteristically powerful in England.[5] Although his principal focus was on the nineteenth century, it can be argued that for the first half of the twentieth century especially, political economy was the language of British public life. The dominant tradition was liberal political economy, which emphasized the virtues, economic and moral, of laissez-faire and free trade and looked to state action with the suspicion that there was a corrupt and corrupting aspect to it. It remained important much longer than the Liberal Party, and longer too than the economy remained liberal. War was bad for liberalism, but liberalism as an ideology persisted, not least in the mode in which war itself was understood.

The multi-faceted nature of political economy is clear when we consider some key intellectuals of the first half of the twentieth century. John Hobson was not merely (as he is remembered today) a theorist of imperialism, but a political economic thinker concerned with underconsumption, free trade, international government, production and war. William Beveridge was an expert on the administration of unemployment, director of the London School of Economics, advocate of internationalism and rationalizer of the British social services. Norman Angell, the founder of 'International Polity', the study and commentary on international relations, was active from the Edwardian years into the 1940s and winner of the Nobel Peace Prize 1933. In book after book he celebrated international trade and interchange, and denounced all manner of nationalist militarists, especially abroad. Maynard Keynes, a journalist as much as an academic, wrote on everything from international relations to public finance. His friend and colleague at Cambridge, the economist Hubert Henderson, was editor of the Liberal *Nation*. Political economy was the language not just of orthodox policy, but of critics. It was the language of socialism and anti-imperialism, as much as of liberalism; it was also, though less so, the language of nationalism and imperialism.

Political economy was something much broader than economics. Economics was a remarkably small academic discipline, but political economy was everywhere. It lived in the daily press, in the weeklies and quarterlies, and in books, and in the administrative and investigative systems of government. It was characterized not by quantification (of which there was little) but rather by abstraction. It focused not on concrete nations or policies or firms, but on the essential economic principles of production, or unemployment, public finance or war. It was a language of analysis of everything from war to social policy. Its assumptions represented the common sense of public life.

British intellectuals – British liberal intellectuals – were typically internationalists. They argued, typically, that free trade would break down the influence of their two bugbears, nationalism and militarism. The internationalism of the liberals did not see any difference between a British buyer and a foreign buyer – the idea that nations were in economic competition with each other was seen as dangerous.[6] It was individuals and firms who competed, not nations. Individuals were both producers and consumers, and it was wrong to favour producers over consumers, or to suggest that exports were worthier than imports. They were often anti-imperialists too, as in the case of the original Little Englanders, who, far from being inward-looking nationalists, were anti-imperial liberal internationalists. Being anti-imperialist was, as we have seen, not the same thing as being against the British empire.

Liberal internationalists were not naive pacifists blind to the dangers of the cruel real world. They identified the enemies of progress and peace very clearly. Thus, Norman Angell argued that although there were no gains from war, as it would disrupt trade and make everyone poorer, there were nevertheless many who believed there were. This was the *Great Illusion* (his book of 1911), an illusion which existed and was dangerous. Angell, like many others, was deeply concerned by the rise of militarism and nationalism, not just before 1914 – he was active in denouncing the danger of Nazism.

Others saw dangers in particular groups taking control of the state, particularly certain capitalists. Thus, John Hobson argued that the new imperialism of the early twentieth century was the result of capitalist interests driving the state to open up poor markets for investment abroad. Thus, while free trade served all the people, and while protection and imperialism impoverished the majority, some could and did benefit from them, and that is why it happened.

Liberal internationalists argued that free trade gave the United Kingdom military strength. For John Hobson, as for many others, the United Kingdom's strength in the Great War rested in the end on naval and mercantile muscle, its dominance of finance and commerce, which all rested on free trade.[7] John Hobson thus denounced a 'New Protectionism' emerging during the war and railed once more against what free traders took to be the fallacies of the protectionists. After the Great War Angell argued, as of course did so many others, that the UK absolutely needed a free trade world, or it could not feed itself.[8]

The 1930s were thus an era of despair for liberal internationalists. For them tariffs and trade wars meant not just economic losses, but political nationalism, militarism and war.[9] This gave them a particularly acute sense of the historical danger of Nazism. They worried too about what protection and imperialism (and rearmament) might do to the United Kingdom. It is no accident that British liberal intellectuals were in the forefront of calling for a League of Nations, collective security and federations of various sorts. They looked to conciliation and arbitration, but also to the use of international armed forces, and the weapon of the economic boycott.[10] One of the clichés of the interwar years was the call for international government, for a world state, which would put down miscreant nationalists and militarists with force. While not uniquely British, it found much expression in British liberal internationalist circles.[11]

The greatest popularizer of the notion was H. G. Wells, who like many writers on scientific topics, dressed up standard liberal internationalist theses in scientistic and futuristic garb. His *Shape of Things to Come* of 1933, which was filmed in 1936 as *Things to Come*, is a perfect illustration of the argument. It shows a future where an international air police bring peace to a world descended into nationalism, war and backwardness. The international air police would in some future extirpate militarism and nationalism from the world. One of the advocates, of many, was the coal owner and endower of the study of international relations David Davies, who financed the New Commonwealth Society to promote the idea. The League of Nations Union organized a Peace Ballot in 1935, which was once cited by historians as evidence of pacifist sentiment, but is now more likely to be used to show how powerful was the view that international peace should be secured by sanctions and by the use of force, especially international force.

The liberal internationalists gained new strength in the Second World War. In 1941, before the US entered the war, the National Labour MP Commander Stephen King-Hall (from February 1942 an independent) wanted an Anglo-American naval fleet and air force, a 'Peace Force' as he called it. The fleet would be three times larger than any other, and twice as strong as three other fleets; the air force would be four times larger than any other, and twice as large as two others combined.[12] The idea was that unilateral aggression be crushed instantly by multilateral counter-aggression.[13] Others too dilated on the theme of an Anglo-American air force which would 'lead the way ultimately to a World Federation of the Air . . . a guarantor of a co-operative international system'.[14] David Davies got the Liberal Party conference in September 1942 to vote for an international police force, the internationalization of civil aviation and a federation of English-speaking peoples.[15] J. M. Spaight, one of the leading British air propagandists, a retired Air Ministry civil servant, wrote a book called *Bombing Vindicated* in 1944 whose flavour is captured by the title of chapter one: 'The Bomber Saves Civilisation'. For Spaight the bomber was 'a murderous weapon. Its only merit is that it can murder war'.[16] Liberal internationalism well described the position of Sir William Beveridge at the end of the war.[17]

Churchill himself should be seen in part as a supporter of these ideas, as he himself suggested. He prevented British diplomats from turning down a Soviet proposal for an international force at the 1944 Dumbarton Oaks conference, reminding them he had supported such an idea in the 1920s and noting that the 'proposal will gain very great acceptance in Great Britain and it certainly seems by weaving the forces of different countries together to give assurances of permanent peace'.[18] Churchill continued to believe in it, and it would form a crucial but neglected part of his famous 'iron curtain' speech in Fulton, Missouri in 1946, where he proposed the temporary assimilation of national air squadrons into a United Nations force. Otherwise he claimed, in his inimitable style, but in a clichéd sentiment, 'the Stone Age may return on the gleaming wings of science, and what might now shower immeasurable material blessings upon mankind, may even bring about its total destruction'.[19]

To a striking extent the internationalist arguments about aeroplanes were transferred to atomic bombs, and indeed made to seem novel by the unprecedented explosive power of a single device. The key phrase was now not 'international police' but 'international control'. These ideas were real enough and influential enough to make the bomb seem even more of a world-transforming thing than the aeroplane. In public and in private liberal internationalists toyed, and more than toyed, with the idea that the non-liberal USSR should be subject to pre-emptive atomic bombing before they got a bomb of their own.[20] Bertrand Russell argued that while they were a US monopoly they should be used to enforce peace through preventative attack on the USSR. This wasn't a shocking indiscretion but essentially a repetition of the Wellsian international police arguments, transferred, as so many other liberals had already done, to atomic weapons. Both the US and British governments claimed to be in favour of handing the bomb over to an international body, while determined to keep national control in the US case and to develop a national bomb in the British case. Churchill wanted an Anglo-American bomb, a pipe dream almost as silly as international control.

The Second World War was seen by liberals in internationalist terms, and indeed the war promoted such ideas. 1939 saw the establishment of the Federal Union, a classic liberal internationalist body, which helped shape thinking at the beginning of the war, the years of a deepening Anglo-French alliance, which prepared the grounds for the British proposal to France to create a complete union in June 1940, an offer which came too late.[21] The war was presented in liberal internationalist terms, not as a war between nations, but as a war for freedom and civilization against barbarism, a giant police action against militarism and nationalist racism. From January 1942 this was, we will recall, a war fought by the 'United Nations'. And indeed the United Nations set up in 1945 was obviously deeply influenced by liberal internationalism.

War itself was thought of by liberals in very particular political economic terms. That wars still happened was explained using one of the clichés of the age, the cultural lag argument. A tedious common-place, it sees modern war as a tragic clash of old and new, arising from lack of education and modern thinking among the masses and the politicians. The ignorant drifted into nationalism and militar-ism.[22] Modern war, when it happened, was seen as a matter of civilian, industrial effort, in which the most advanced machines mattered most. Such accounts were shared even by the most passionate and outspoken of anti-bombing campaigners.[23] The pacifist writer Vera Brittain was typical in seeing modern war as defined by chemicals, aeroplanes, tanks and the radio.[24] The RAF's wartime PR man Squadron Leader John Strachey (who in the 1930s was the United Kingdom's leading Marxist intellectual) discussed bombing in a thor-oughly economic analysis of war which was typical of official thought: 'the German army, and the German economic system which supports it, are inseparable; they stand or fall together; an attack on one is an attack on both . . . The object of war is to bankrupt your enemy.'[25]

ANGLO-MARXISM AND SOCIALISM

The UK did not have a Karl Kautsky, Rudolf Hilferding or Rosa Luxemburg, let alone its own Lenin or Plekhanov. But it had its radi-cal political economists. One cannot understand British socialism and its advocates without noting the centrality of political economic modes and focuses. Political economy was the language of John Strachey's *The Coming Struggle for Power* (1932) and *The Theory and Practice of Socialism* (1936), key works in the intellectual history of British communism.[26] H. N. Brailsford of the ILP wrote classic political economic works on war and militarism such as *The War of Steel and Gold: A Study of the Armed Peace* (1914) and *Property or Peace?* (1934) as well as works on any number of other topics. The Labour Party's intellectuals of the 1930s and 1940s, such as Hugh Dalton, G. D. H. Cole, Evan Durbin, Hugh Gaitskell and

Harold Wilson, were typically political economists; indeed, many were academic economists. The New Fabian Research Bureau of the 1930s was likewise a producer of political economic studies.

The key differences between the Marxists and the liberal-radicals and the Labour socialists essentially amounted to a different analysis of capitalism. For the Marxists all capitalists, industrial, financial or agricultural, were equally exploitative. Radicals and socialists criticized only very particular types of capitalist – landlords and rentiers and perhaps monopolists were the problem. The socialism of men like Hobson, Brailsford and the economic historian R. H. Tawney was based on a critique of the functionless rentier, rather than the productive capitalist. This was essentially the position of the Labour left. Marxists did also dwell on rentiers and monopolists, but for them all capitalists, and capitalism itself, were becoming economically redundant, if still extraordinarily powerful. Marxists were also very sceptical of liberal internationalism, as they differentiated between capitalist states and the one workers' state, however deformed, the USSR, and were less likely indeed to differentiate between good and bad capitalist states. Hence, for some Marxists, the early phase of the Second World War, like the Great War, was literally an imperialist war in which monopoly capitalist states fought each other.

British Marxism was for decades the province of a tiny group of activists, often autodidact artisans. In 1900 the President of the Trades Union Congress for that year was William Pickles of the National Amalgamated Society of House and Ship Painters, also an Independent Labour Party activist. His presidential address mixed Marxism with Darwinism, natural history and anthropology in a manner which German social democrats would have been familiar with.[27] There were but few graduate Marxists. Walton Newbold, of the University of Manchester, was the author of *How Europe Armed for War 1870–1914* (1916), originally meant as a joint work with Karl Liebknecht. He was elected as a Communist MP in 1922. He sat for Motherwell until the 1923 election, one of three communists in the House at that time. The Communist Party of Great Britain had as its chief theoretician from the 1920s the remarkable Rajani Palme Dutt, a brilliant product of Oxford: as the son of a Bengali doctor practising in Cambridge and a Swedish poet mother, he was not the typical

Oxonian of his time. He was a stout anti-imperialist who influenced communists throughout the British empire, but was also the most rigid of Stalinists.

The 1930s were the key decade for intellectual Marxism in the United Kingdom. There was a vibrant new 'Anglo-Marxist' culture.[28] It was experienced as an intellectual liberation not merely from liberal political economy but from orthodox literary criticism, history and more besides. It opened eyes to other parts of the world, not just the USSR. It also stimulated critical examination, in an empirical mode, of at least some aspects of the British state and industry. John Strachey rethought international relations; Maurice Dobb economic history, and John Desmond Bernal the place of science in society (with a distinctively political economic approach). Bernal was part of a remarkable group of scientist-activists – including Lancelot Hogben, Herman Levy, Patrick Blackett, J. B. S. Haldane and Joseph Needham – who criticized British society and the use it made of science.[29] Another notable figure was the non-graduate Christopher Caudwell, a writer on aviation, physics and culture.[30] The Left Book Club produced work like Ellen Wilkinson MP's *The Town that Was Murdered* (1939), an account of the history of Jarrow (Wilkinson was a historian), and (writing as 'Simon Haxey'), Arthur and Margaret Wynn's pioneering analysis of the links between business and members of parliament in *Tory M.P.* (1939). Yet perhaps the most interesting was a Trotskyist from Trinidad rather than the Communist Party intellectuals of Cambridge. C. L. R. James, while in London, wrote his astonishing history of the Haitian revolution, *Black Jacobins* (1938).

Perhaps the key claim put forward by the communists was that capitalism, especially British capitalism, was in decline. 'For British capitalism, under the domination of the big monopoly capitalists, is decaying. The masses of the people of Britain are being ruined by the big trusts and their millionaires. Unless we put an end to capitalism, the lot of the masses will become worse and worse,' declared the Communist Party in 1935.[31] Marxists looked not only to workers but also to the 'technical and professional workers, the scientists and the administrators', whose inventions were misused, to change the world. Their critique of British capitalism would prove very influential.

THE RISE AND FALL OF THE BRITISH NATION

From 1941 there was a new emphasis on criticizing British business for not being efficient enough (and shop-floor Trotskyists as fascists and wreckers).[32] British capitalism, communists argued, was oriented to owning assets abroad, which only paid their way if they resulted in imports into the United Kingdom.[33] British capitalists were fundamentally importers who had no interest in stimulating domestic production. It was hardly surprising, then, if war production was insufficient and inefficient, given that government controls were in the hands of monopolistic importers and restrictionist producers.[34] The national and nationalist focus of the critique was to inform socialist critiques in the rest of the war and beyond. For example, in 1944 Aneurin Bevan, a left-Labour MP, attacked the idea that exports needed to be increased after the war, and foreign investments built up again. He saw this plan as a Tory plot to deprive British workers of goods and to allow capitalists to benefit from higher rates of profit abroad. His alternative was to invest at home and stimulate home demand.[35] The communist critiques of British capitalism continued after the war. They complained that production fell way behind the USA, where output per hour worked was three times greater (they claimed).[36] The post-war United Kingdom was suffering from a 'crisis of under-production' because labour was being allowed to drift into parasitic distribution, entertainment and similar industries which characterized British capitalism.[37] By 1951 the Communist Party had adopted a deeply nationalist policy, called, appropriately enough, the *British Road to Socialism*.[38] The left critique of British capitalism took on a distinctly nationalist hue. It is a telling but not well-known point that Friedrich Hayek's *The Road to Serfdom* (1944) was a classical liberal attack not so much on socialism, as on planning, on scientism and on nationalism.

IMPERIALISM AND NATIONALISM

As well as providing the language of liberalism, socialism and communism, political economy was also there in imperialism and in tariff reform. However, partly through the influence of German historical economics, this political economy was not only more historical but rather more concrete and specific than liberal political economy. William Ashley, William Hewins (the first director of the LSE) and William Cunningham (also an Anglican clergyman) were supportive of tariffs.[39] The second director of the LSE, Halford Mackinder, a geographer with a background in science and history, famously adopted a land-centred view of history and geopolitics. He switched from being a liberal imperialist free trader to a protectionist imperialist; he was a powerful advocate of his cause and served as a Unionist MP 1910–22.[40]

Such imperialist thinking was clearly present in the interwar years. However, those worlds of opinion are only now being mapped properly and were for long disregarded.[41] There was a great deal of conservative writing, often in the form of essays in quarterly and monthly periodicals, which circulated in clubland, such as the *English Review*, *Nineteenth Century and After* and *National Review*.[42] Some of these reviews were run by figures from the hard right, sympathetic to fascism, such as the Catholic Douglas Jerrold of the *English Review* (1931–5), and Sir Arnold Wilson MP of the *Nineteenth Century and After*. Wilson was an extraordinary character – as a soldier he helped shape Iraq out of Mesopotamia and went on to become a senior figure in the Anglo-Iranian oil company. More prominent imperialist Tories in the realm of letters and ideas connected to politics included John Buchan, novelist, MP, governor-general of Canada and later peer. Another might be the historian G. M. Trevelyan, friend of Baldwin and master of Trinity College Cambridge. While we remember the Left Book Club, we too easily ignore the Right Book Club, run by the popular historian Arthur Bryant. Bryant co-authored *Britain Awake!*, a hard-right imperialist protectionist tract in 1939–40.[43]

When we think of British nationalism, it is hard to find it in the world of ideas – few declared themselves British nationalists, for reasons we have given. There is one notable exception, as we have seen – Oswald Mosley. Surprisingly, this aspect of his thought has not been highlighted – he is seen as a fascist and anti-Semite. He has been thought of as a proto-Keynesian. By contrast, his radical economic nationalism, which was distinctive and central to his politics, has been played down. Following his resignation from the Labour government in 1930, Mosley already called for planned and *reduced* trade. 'You cannot build a higher civilisation and a standard of life which can absorb the great force of modern production if you are subject to price fluctuations from the rest of the world which dislocate your industry at every turn, and to the sport of competition from virtually slave conditions in other countries. What prospects have we, except the home market, of absorbing modern production?'[44] His thoroughgoing nationalism was also evident in the plans he put forward with other Labour MPs in 1931, before establishing the New Party. He and his supporters called for the 'insulation' of home economy through rigid import controls (rather than just tariffs), the development of national planning, extending to the 'Imperial Commonwealth' later. They called for a radical extension of domestic agriculture, less emphasis on exports, and expansion of research, notably in coal carbonization. They were also highly critical of the revaluation of the national debt.[45] All these ideas were central to the British Union of Fascists. In his *Greater Britain* Mosley called not only for scientific protection, but also maximizing national food production, oil-from-coal, and scientific research, themes echoed in all fascist literature.[46] Mosley's BUF had an imperialist side, but, as we have seen in relation to India, Mosley had a national conception of empire as a place to be exploited for the nation. His policy was one of maximizing national self-sufficiency, within the context of a self-sufficient empire, isolated from the world economy.[47] Mosley claimed: 'It is necessary for us to choose between the interests of those who have invested their money abroad and those who have invested their money and lives in the land of Great Britain', a distinctly non-imperialist position.[48]

The BUF, arguing for the 'rebirth of a nation', increasingly attacked the City of London, and indeed the Conservative Party as the party of the City. The City, driven by foreign investment, from which followed high imports, undermined the economic nation.[49] This nationalist thesis (which was, as we have seen, important on the left) was turned into a farcical one by William Joyce, once a senior figure in the BUF. Writing from Nazi Germany, this anti-Semite echoed not just the standard nationalist complaints about the decline of British agriculture, the failure to make oil from coal and the importance of overseas investment but explained this as the result of cosmopolitan Jews controlling British industry, the press and finance. There is no more conclusive proof that anti-Semitism was the socialism of fools.[50]

Historians argued for the idea that a new British (and sometimes an English) nationalism of the left can be seen coming into being in 1940. They have ignored its older right-wing manifestations, and see it instead as the product of an anti-fascist people's war. Indeed, the rise of left nationalism in 1940 is seen as central to the politics of the war. Much rests on readings, often very particular ones, of two writers, J. B. Priestley and George Orwell.[51] In fact Priestley cannot be described only as a nationalist, for there was a clear imperialist, and a weaker internationalist, side to the wartime talks and writing cited in evidence for his nationalism.[52] He was, to be sure, a critic of capitalism (and a founder of Common Wealth), but a mild one, in line with many other public figures of the 1930s.[53] As the *New Statesman* noted of the right-wing imperialist Arthur Bryant's *English Saga* of 1940, it was saying much the same thing as J. B. Priestley, although their politics were very different.[54]

George Orwell's nationalism has also been misunderstood. *The Lion and the Unicorn,* a long essay published in 1941, argues for the *lack* of British patriotism among those on the left, and that *existing* types of patriotism were very obvious after the retreat from Dunkirk.[55] However, and this is the source of the misreading, Orwell sought to bring the left and nationalism together (while denying it was happening in general). Orwell was critical of the wartime United Kingdom and the Labour Party, rather than celebratory.[56] The *Lion and the Unicorn* attacked English capitalism, imperialism and the war effort, which he saw as weak because of the character of British capitalism and imperialism. Orwell was far from unique in this. As we have noted above, this *critical* left nationalism was a central feature of the communist position and parts of the labour left during and indeed after the Second World War.[57] The British ruling class was seen by many on the far left as a *Traitor Class,* to give the title of a 1940 book by well-known communist filmmaker and class traitor Ivor Montagu.[58] Thus it was that J. T. Murphy, an ex-communist, called in 1942 for a 'full-blooded patriotism' to 'transcend the vested interests of all classes and parties and subordinate all property and all service to the all-in war against Nazism'.[59] Murphy wanted a full-scale takeover of private property as well as a general militarization and bringing-together of the military and people.

TECHNOCRATS

British technocrats, a species supposed not to exist, advanced, and very influentially so, a thesis which suggested that the British scientist and engineer was in a systematically weak position, excluded from power. Thus, the British Science Guild was formed in 1903, led by the astronomer Norman Lockyer, who also served as editor of *Nature* (owned by the publisher Macmillan). The guild expressed the view that the British elite was far too indifferent to science and scientists. These complaints were reinforced during the Great War; H. G. Wells and leading scientists complained of the 'Neglect of Science' in a memorandum of February 1916. This was the dominant mode of intervention by the scientists: they claimed they did not have enough power, and the established elite did not have enough knowledge. It was a technocratic critique of the government, civil service, parliament and elite education, usually a highly selective and misleading one. The solution they gave was always much the same – more scientific education, especially for the elite.

The influence of this argument has led to an extraordinary downplaying of the importance of scientists and engineers and doctors in public life and of the impact of scientific ideas in the public realm. Yet, as one would expect, the elite of a rich and strong nation and empire included many figures trained in science, engineering and medicine and more receptive to and supportive of technocratic tendencies. Even among British prime ministers one finds evidence of education and interest in science. A. J. Balfour (brother-in-law to the Nobel Prize-winning physicist Lord Rayleigh) published work on the philosophy of science. Ramsay MacDonald was keen on biological metaphors, the product of a deep interest in natural history. Winston Churchill had as his close personal adviser over decades Frederick Lindemann, professor of physics at Oxford, the only academic scientist ever to rise to the cabinet, as well as being himself deeply enthusiastic about science and machines. As we have seen, both Baldwin and Chamberlain studied science at university level, if only briefly.

Once one looks, it is clear that there were more scientists, engineers and doctors in politics than would be enough to sustain the view that they were the exception to prove the rule. The doctor Christopher Addison served in Liberal and Labour cabinets. H. Fletcher Moulton, a mathematician, was a very successful patent lawyer and a senior judge, and sometime Liberal MP. He was the first chairman of the Medical Research Council and played a key role controlling explosives production in the Great War. A. V. Hill, a Nobel Prize winner, was a member of parliament in the Second World War. Among the very longest-serving MPs was Sir Murdoch MacDonald, builder of the Sennar Dam.

Even the higher administrative civil service, notorious in crude technocratic analyses for being made up of classicists, certainly had people of technical backgrounds. Two, rather extraordinarily, became cabinet ministers in the Second World War. The most important, Sir John Anderson, studied the chemistry of uranium and became one of the most noted civil servants of the interwar years, ending his career as a state servant as governor of Bengal. He rose to become chancellor of the exchequer in wartime, the main coordinator of the domestic economy and additionally a central figure in atomic politics. As well as administrative civil servants there were many professionals, whether doctors, engineers, naval constructors or research scientists, including men like Sir Henry Tizard and Charles Drysdale, a senior naval scientist who had been the president of the Malthusian League.

Men of science and industry were elevated to the peerage. In 1892 Sir William Thomson was the first; in 1902 he was one of the founding members of the new Order of Merit. Lord Kelvin, as he became, died in 1907 and was buried in the Anglican Pantheon, Westminster Abbey, alongside Newton and Darwin. Kelvin designed many instruments, electrical and navigational, made by his own company. He also served as scientific adviser and consultant and board member of many enterprises. In 1899 he became, for example, vice chairman of Kodak Ltd (which at that time controlled the main enterprise Eastman

Kodak); he was also on the board of British Aluminium. Also elevated to the Order of Merit in 1902 was the 3rd Baron Rayleigh, once professor of natural philosophy at Cambridge, and soon (1904) to win the United Kingdom's first Nobel Prize for Physics (the first was for Peace, the second for Chemistry). Rayleigh was a landed aristocrat and an advanced farmer in Essex, and he served as chairman of a committee on explosives, and as first chairman of one of the most long-standing advisory committees, the Advisory Committee on Aeronautics. The 3rd Baron Rayleigh's achievement may be compared to those of the 3rd Earl Russell, Bertrand Russell, who was raised to the Order of Merit in 1949 and garlanded with the Nobel Prize for literature in 1950. Later scientific peers included Lord Rutherford, the great Cambridge physicist, and Lord Cadman, the mining engineer who was chairman of British Petroleum.

Science was very much part of elite culture. The mathematicians and scientists (Lord) Maynard Keynes, Sir Alfred Egerton, Sir Alexander Carr-Saunders, Sir Julian Huxley, Henry Moseley, Sir Thomas Merton, and J. B. S. Haldane all went through Eton within the same decade.[60] Elite families produced both scientists and literary figures. The liberal journalist J. A. Spender was the father of the architect and photographer Humphrey Spender, the engineer and photogrammetrist Michael Spender and the poet Stephen Spender. The Oxford physiologist J. S. Haldane was the brother of the lawyer and politician R. B. Haldane and the father of the writer Naomi Mitchison and the scientist J. B. S. Haldane. The writer Leonard Huxley was the father of the biologist Julian Huxley, the writer Aldous Huxley and, by his second wife, the much younger biologist Andrew Huxley. The public health physician George Auden was the father of the geologist John Auden, who served with the Geological Survey of India, and the poet W. H. Auden. The writer Lytton Strachey's brother became chief engineer on East Indian Railways; their father was an irrigation engineer in India. J. Neville Keynes, a teacher of economics at Cambridge, was the father of J. Maynard Keynes, graduate in mathematics and economist, and Geoffrey Keynes, surgeon, bibliographer and biographer. The economist and politician Hugh Gaitskell was the younger brother of Arthur Gaitskell, one of well over 100 British agricultural officers supervising the growing of cotton for the Sudan Plantations Syndicate. Marriage also brought together science and arts – A. V. Hill, the physiologist, was married to J. M. Keynes' sister. J. B. S. Haldane was married to the writer Charlotte Haldane. There were also many novelists with backgrounds in science, engineering and medicine, H. G. Wells being the most illustrious, including Arthur Conan Doyle, the creator of Sherlock Holmes, W. Somerset Maugham, best known for the semi-autobiographical *Of Human Bondage* (1915), A. J. Cronin, best known for the best-selling *The Citadel* (1937), Eric Ambler, creator of the leftist detective story, and C. P. Snow, whose risible later 'two cultures' thesis we may thus dispose of.[61] Even foreign writers and intellectuals with technical backgrounds flourished in the United Kingdom, among them Elias Cannetti (chemistry), Arthur Koestler (engineering) and Ludwig Wittgenstein (engineering).

It is hardly surprising in this context that science appears everywhere in British public life. It is there in election manifestos, in policies for agriculture and coal. Chamberlain had argued for a 'scientific tariff'. It is there in thinking about the empire, and even modern electioneering.[62] In the 1930s there was a distinctive right version of support for science in public life. Sir Arnold Wilson was a long-standing chairman of the Parliamentary and Scientific Committee; he was also one of the most fervent admirers of the Nazis in the House of Commons. Scientists and engineers themselves spoke out but it would be a mistake to assume they did so, though they claimed to, with a distinctive voice. They generally spoke as liberals or nationalists, and sometimes as Marxists. Among the latter were a very few atypical academic scientists such as J. D. Bernal and J. B. S. Haldane. There were also scientists among the radical liberals who emerged in the 1930s and 1940s, most notably the chemist Michael Polanyi. Science came in all sorts of ideological shapes and sizes.

Yet in some areas there was a particularly direct relationship between scientific thought and policy. The body politic was very concerned with biological politics. The science of eugenics in the United Kingdom had a distinct tendency to assume the poor genetic quality of the urban working class. The need to reduce the poorest and weakest from reproducing, what was called negative eugenics, was a powerful idea in the Edwardian period, and still strong in the interwar years. There was little sense that healthy country people should be encouraged to breed, though there were strains of this thinking among Liberals and Tories before 1914.[63] The nation was in danger from the breeding of the mass, rather than finding its true self in the people. Eugenics was no pseudo-science. There was a eugenics laboratory in the University of London and a Eugenics Education Society (EES) made up of distinguished men of science. Eugenics was very popular (though not with Catholics and socialists) but had no actual impact on policy before 1914.[64]

Yet the association of human qualities with genetic features hardly went away. The experts all maintained there were huge numbers of feeble-minded people, more who carried feeble-mindedness, that these unfortunates bred faster, and that without control, therefore, the population would continue to degenerate. Politics stood in the experts' way. There was a campaign for the sterilization of the 'feeble-minded' in the early 1930s. A Labour MP, Major Archibald Church, also the long-standing general secretary of what was then known as the Association of Scientific Workers, attempted to introduce a bill to that effect in the Commons, but it was rejected, with opposition most vocal from the left and from Catholics. The issue did not go away, and indeed a committee of the Ministry of Health proposed voluntary sterilization in 1934.[65] Yet the same people had success in other areas. The most important British educational psychologist of the era, Sir Cyril Burt, advised government committees on education and drove forward his argument that intelligence was hereditary and stable and could be tested. This work strongly influenced the testing of children at eleven to allocate them to what became known and generalized after the 1944 Education Act as secondary modern schools for the majority, and grammar schools for the minority. Thus it was that interwar eugenics affected the lives of millions of children in much later years. It should be remembered, though, that the grammar schools did not educate the national elite, a task which fell to some public schools.

7

Tomorrow, Perhaps the Future

In pre-war London a Sacre, a Nijinsky, a Stravinsky, a Mat-isse, a Van Gogh, seemed to be the very sound and shadow of times wingèd chariot, which, with its terrible occupant, was still at the back of a doomed world, unheard, but hurry-ing near. The lofty shade, the hastening sound, are not to be heard in the poems of Rupert Brooke. And yet, in the opin-ion of his friends . . . he was the poet of young England . . .
George Dangerfield, The Strange
Death of Liberal England *(1935)*

It is clear that our future as an industrial nation depends largely upon a regular supply of coal at a moderate price. We consider that the careful, systematic and continued applica-tion of science to the practices of the coal mining industry is one of the most important essentials necessary to achieve this end . . . It is also essential that that industry as a whole should become imbued with the spirit of science, in order that it may utilize to the fullest extent the results of modern scientific developments.
Report of the Royal Commission on the Coal Industry
(1925)

We don't alas yet have a history of the British future. Yet we may surmise that the future became more important between 1900 and 1950 as its possibilities appeared to be clearer, and the possibilities of managing them greater. Manifestos, declarations to electors, shifted somewhat from being statements of political principles to being plans for the future. What the modern world was to be like became an important political issue; there was never ever one modernity. Even those who wanted to keep everything the same knew they needed new ways of doing it.

Making the future was not just an ideological project, but a material one. Creating the future required command of resources. The creator – individual, enterprise or nation – needed the ability to afford to forgo immediate needs for the uncertain business of investing in making a world which might not come to pass. Making the future was the business of the powerful. Yet the creative power of the elite, so very obvious when one thinks about it, has been obscured by strong traditions making them seem merely conservative or even reactionary. Especially since the 1950s, a persistent drone of commentary insisted on the dangerous conservatism of British elites, whether political, ideological, business or military. They were forced to take up the new, it was suggested, only in extreme circumstances, like war. Only then were experts given their due. Another set of arguments pointed to the supposed inability of industry and government to innovate at all – there simply was not enough resources or commitment to successfully create the new.

The creators are too often taken to be outsiders, radicals, leftists, hoping not to maintain existing structures but to release the world from the past. Furthermore, British radicals, leftists and outsiders have themselves been seen as unable to break the stranglehold of a conservative and backward elite even in the realm of ideas. One wonders how anything changed at all. The assumption of a heavy elite inertia has thoroughly distorted political histories also, which can read as if everything new in politics and society came from advanced liberals and the Labour Party, and that conservatives merely grimly acquiesced in the new future. One can't properly understand British history as a matter of progressives of the left and reactionaries of the right – all wanted change.

Yet things did change and radically so, in the United Kingdom as in other rich nations. The supposedly conservative and reactionary British elite was dominant in the creation of futures, which followed its priorities. The United Kingdom was one of the inventive centres in the world in the first half of the twentieth century, though not the only one, or the best. Yet the plans and schemes of the elite for free trade and for empire on the whole failed. Indeed, it is important to note that most plans fail, most schemes for the future are not realized. To study futures we need to focus on the unfilmed treatments, the unfinished novels, the unexploited patent, policies not adopted; in short we need to open up an archive of failure.[1]

The United Kingdom did not rely only on its own ideas or inventions and was in fact a very ready adopter of foreign ones. It was a great importer of novelties just as it was an importer of food. Equally, British inventions were made use of abroad, though these inventions were also typically exploited at home, often very quickly. In the Edwardian years the United Kingdom understood itself as a participant in a cosmopolitan world of invention, but war and economic policy drove invention, political and technical, in more imperial and national directions, culminating in extraordinary self-assessments of British inventiveness. In the 1940s, 1950s and 1960s, the United Kingdom prided itself on being the single inventor of such things as the jet engine, Penicillin and even key parts of the atomic bomb, not to mention parliamentary democracy and the welfare state. No other country, it seemed to suggest, had invented so very much of modernity; yet the modern world had as surely made the United Kingdom as much as it was made by it. Later generations, overcompensating for this bombast perhaps, underplayed its inventiveness in the first half of the twentieth century.

It later became common to point to other countries as pioneers of the modern, whether in writing, painting, film-making, philosophy, history, architecture, in the sciences, in the making of war, in nearly everything. What would characterize the United Kingdom of the era for the writers of the 1960s to the 1990s was a deep creative backwardness born of being stuck in earlier modes of thought and action. The basic idea was that the United Kingdom pioneered in an earlier wave – the industrial revolution – and, stuck in its industries and rhythms of thought, barely kept up with innovations of the late nineteenth and early twentieth centuries. The case for British backwardness was easily made and indeed reinforced by observing just how much modern creative talent came from abroad. Yet the case needs to be made carefully – everywhere in the world modern forms competed with older and different forms not in the canon of modernity. That canon, whether in industrial forms or paintings or literature, is in any case a creation of interested parties, and for nowhere a good reflection of what was actually being created and invented. We have barely begun to study not only how the future was imagined, but how the future was actually created.

Perhaps the appropriate overall picture might be of a general innovative performance roughly what one would expect from a comparatively very rich country, but with no evidence of superiority in much or anything. It was perhaps not even notable as a place where talent gravitated to – for Paris and Berlin benefited a good deal from foreigners – though from the 1930s the United Kingdom was by force of circumstance a particular place of refuge. Yet it was impressive in the extent to which it took up foreign innovations and made them its own, especially where this really mattered.

The standard indicators and impressions of British creativity yield a not very flattering picture, but a closer examination points at least to a more varied one.[2] To 1939 there were around twenty British winners of the Nobel Prize in the sciences and medicine, only just ahead of France, and a long way behind Germany. In the case of the Nobel Prize for Literature the only English, Scottish or Welsh winners into the early 1950s were John Galsworthy, Bertrand Russell and Winston Churchill, hardly modernists. On the other hand, a wider definition of British would include the Indian-born Rudyard Kipling, the Bengali Rabindranath Tagore, the Irishmen William Butler Yeats and George Bernard Shaw and the US-born T. S. Eliot. Among the writers working in the United Kingdom not so honoured were the Pole Joseph Conrad, the American Ezra Pound and the Englishwoman Virginia Woolf. The Irishmen James Joyce and Samuel Beckett made their names elsewhere. In the case of music Edward Elgar, Ralph Vaughan Williams and William Walton do not have the musicological status of, say, Stravinsky or Schoenberg, though Elgar was perhaps the first British composer to make any mark at all on the continent for centuries.

In the modern art galleries of the world, selective records of innovation as they are, the United Kingdom does not rank as a creative place in the first half of the twentieth century. Spain, through Picasso and Miró, is far better represented. In modernist painting, nothing British troubled the canon-making walls of US museums before the 1940s. More precisely, London hardly compares with Paris or Berlin, or even Moscow, as a centre of modern art creation. British post-impressionism, futurism, surrealism, constructivism, cubism are minor derivative forms. Yet Percy Wyndham Lewis and Paul Nash, say, were hardly of no consequence.[3] The fifty greatest art films of all time will not usually have a British entry. In documentary film, there is a little more of a claim, but nothing radical compared to Soviet cinema. There was indeed hardly a national cinema at all. Hollywood products dominated British screens even at the very height of British film production in the 1940s, a rare moment of distinction, which saw work like that of Michael Powell and Emeric Pressburger, David Lean and Carol Reed. In architecture it is clear enough no British schools had the impact of the Bauhaus. Indeed, exiles play a large role in the story of modernist architecture. Serge Chermayeff designed not only the De La Warr Pavilion in Bexhill, but also a warehouse and offices for Gilbey's Wine and Spirits, and a vast research laboratory for Imperial Chemical Industries in Manchester. Berthold Lubetkin did the penguin pool at London Zoo, Highpoint flats and the Finsbury Health Centre. Yet there were some notable British efforts from three engineers. Oscar Faber was engineer for the new Bank of England, one of the important new corporate headquarters of the interwar years, and engineer-architect for modernist flour mills for Spillers in Avonmouth, Cardiff and Newcastle docks. The latter was the largest flour mill in Europe and would process 250,000 tons of grain per annum.[4] His contemporary Sir Owen Williams, a specialist in concrete, built a new Boots factory in Nottingham, the *Daily Express* buildings in London and Manchester, the Empire Stadium, Wembley and the Empire Swimming Pool at Wembley. A third architect trained in engineering was the Canadian-born Wells Coates, designer of the Isokon flats. Furthermore, the Garden City was an influential British invention of 1898 – the first was built before 1914 in Letchworth, the second mainly between the wars at Welwyn. Hampstead Garden Suburb, smaller but on similar lines, was started in 1906. These were private efforts, with a long tail of influence in public efforts in the post-Second World War British New Towns project and many examples abroad. Perhaps, to reverse a misleading cliché, the United Kingdom was bad at inventing but good at developing?

ARMING THE STATE OF THE FUTURE

In the case of preparation for war and the development of new weapons the British armed forces were hardly laggards. Despite the mythology concerning the technical conservatism of British officers, they pursued, in peace and in war, a policy of developing new technical means of warfare which sought a transformation in the nature of war. Far from being forced to take up the new created by civilians in conditions of emergency, they were themselves the sponsors of new ways of war. Thus nearly all the weapons of the Great War were developed and in use in armed services before 1914 and continued to be developed through the war and beyond it, typically by the existing naval-industrial complex. Take the superdreadnoughts launched just before 1914 and during the war. These oil-fired giants aimed their guns with mechanical computers and were powered by steam turbines. They communicated by radio, much provided by the Marconi company, a London enterprise created by the greatest Italian inventor of the century, Guglielmo Marconi. Many were later modernized and were still in service to 1945. Military aeroplanes were being developed before 1914, by private firms including the armourers, and also by the government's Royal Aircraft Factory, a notable centre for design and research. Though they were not a British invention, the British army and navy were by 1914 peculiarly well endowed with aeroplanes. The submarine too was eagerly adopted and developed pre-war. Any notion that British forces were unprepared for technical war is seriously misplaced.

During the war itself technical development of weapons accelerated, notably in aviation. The aeroplanes being made at the end of the war were very much larger, faster and heavier than those of 1914. They included four-engined bombers which could reach Berlin from East Anglia. The tank was invented during the war, by a group of men including the first lord of the Admiralty, Winston Churchill, and was deployed by 1916, and in large numbers later in the war. By 1918, as we have seen, the British forces were, though now very large, still the most machine-intensive in the world.

In the interwar years the British armed services were pioneers of large-scale organized research and development efforts. They created large staffs of civilian researchers collaborating (and sometimes competing) with the technical arms of the forces. Directors of scientific research were appointed for the navy (1920) and the air force (1925), though not until 1938 for the army. Some of the defence laboratories were much bigger than academic laboratories, for example the Research Department at Woolwich, the Royal Aircraft Establishment at Farnborough and the chemical warfare establishment at Porton Down.[5] There was a powerful military scientific complex in the interwar years, developing new weapons for the future. It was creating new aeroplanes and aero-engines (including the jet engine); new techniques to bomb and aim bombs; new means for detecting submarines; indeed every sort of equipment for fighting new sorts of wars. Most of the famous innovations in military technique came from state servants: radar (not a uniquely British idea) was developed by government radio experts, the jet engine by civil servants and an RAF officer, Frank Whittle; and sonar (ASDIC) by naval scientists. These efforts were surrounded by a vast array of speculative literature on wars of the future, which was generally to be won by those with the best machines. In the Second World War, many academics and young scientists were also recruited into long-established projects in aeronautics, poison gas, explosives, ballistics and so on. Though academic scientists came to head the old Woolwich research department (which would later create the British atomic bomb) and the army radar effort, newer enterprises such as the Telecommunications Research Establishment (the key radar laboratory) and the Royal Aircraft Establishment remained in the hands of pre-war scientific civil servants.[6]

Just as in the supply of arms, and the higher direction of the war, wartime weapons development had a distinct internationalist element. Penicillin, a wonder drug which followed hot on the heels of another, the sulphonamides, was developed by both British and US industry.[7] British developments, such as the resonant cavity magnetron for radar, were shared. The British atomic bomb project, the greatest in the world in 1940–41, in which ICI took a leading role and which was directed by a senior Oxford-trained chemist from the company, became a joint project, based in the USA and to a lesser extent Canada.[8] When the atomic bombs were dropped the British government claimed more than its fair share of the credit. On 6 August 1945, the new prime minister, Clement Attlee, read a statement by Churchill outlining the history of the bomb project, summing up by saying: 'By God's mercy, British and American science outpaced all German efforts.' This greatly exaggerated the British contribution and also subtly ignored the contribution of continental European exiles to the project.

Winston Churchill was not particularly keen on the long-established organized methods of weapons development. He encouraged individual inventors and promoted any number of devices, from the Blacker Bombard, to Hobart's funnies, to his own earth-moving NELLIE, a machine which dug a trench through which infantry could advance. He was very keen on anti-aircraft rockets. He helped promote the idea of the artificial Mulberry harbours. These, along with Barnes Wallis's bouncing bomb and the PLUTO petrol pipeline, were celebrated for a very long time as testaments to British inventive genius. They were technical extravagances rather than necessities.[9]

There was to be indeed a great deal of mythologizing about British weapons development, which played up the contributions of academics and promoted the view that the armed forces were backward. The underlying reality of a British commitment to the development of new weapons of war was rarely if ever captured. But its flavour is clearly there in a long-running Belgian cartoon, published in the *Tintin* magazine, from the late 1940s. *Blake et Mortimer* featured Blake the RAF officer and Professor Mortimer, the inventor of a wonder-weapon, who are called to save the world from the Yellow Peril.

MAKING AN ELECTRIC FUTURE

In 1900 British cities had transport, heating, lighting, entertainment and more, all powered by coal and by gas. Many of the largest cities were no longer growing very fast; in 1950 they would still be roughly the size they were in 1900 and dominated by buildings of that earlier time. Many major cities and towns had approximately the same population in 1950 as in 1900.[10] Many looked much the same. There were few great public buildings built in the interwar years, apart from some notable new town halls and extensions, hospitals and corporate headquarters.[11] But Birmingham, Coventry, Oxford, Cambridge, Bournemouth, Southampton, Southend, Ipswich, Bristol, Exeter, Blackpool and Wolverhampton, were all rapidly growing places.[12] So too was, until 1939, the County of London.

Within the interstices of the cities old and new there was one transformational development that many, though not all, saw as central to the future. Electricity, already available in 1900 in some places, would be pushed forwards everywhere, through a mixture of public and private plans. It found itself in many differing contexts and offered the promise of many sorts of new futures, but above all perhaps a clean one. The electric future of the years after 1950 was essayed for decades before.

In 1900 British cities still relied on horsepower for nearly all forms of public transport other than steam power for railways: there were horse tramways and horse omnibuses as well as horse cabs and carts. Electricity had a dramatic effect in many places with the introduction of electric tramways and later electric trolley buses in nearly all major cities, alongside motor buses. London saw the development of a vast network of electric railways in addition to the trams. The Underground Electric Railways Company of London, financed mainly by US capital, was run by the British-born American urban transport specialist Albert Stanley. The company owned, built and extended most of the London 'Underground', as it called itself starting well before 1914. The system continued to grow in the interwar years, and the company hired the architect Charles Holden to design its headquarters at 55 Broadway as well as many new and rebuilt stations in the 1920s. 55 Broadway was one of very few tall buildings in London, a city that would with rare exceptions avoid the early-twentieth-century craze for building skyscrapers – a startlingly modern feature of some US cities such as New York and Chicago. Stanley's company, which he continued to run, became the core of the nationalized London Transport in 1933. Stanley served as a Conservative MP during the Great War and president of the Board of Trade under Lloyd George and was elevated to the peerage as a result, as Baron Ashfield. The building and extension of the electric underground to 1939 (after which very little was built until the 1960s) was not the only electrification of transport scheme. The Southern Railway, formed as the smallest of the merged railway companies in 1923, set out on a complete electrification of its system, which was nearly achieved by 1939, and what was not achieved had to wait till the late 1950s and early 1960s. The Southern Railway had the largest electric mainline railway in the world and was quite distinct from the steam-powered services of the other main lines.

Electricity transformed not only the urban mobility of people but entertainment. Electric light replaced limelight in the theatre but also created a new kind of theatre entirely – the cinema. Born before 1900, it grew astonishingly large in the 1930s, when cinemas appeared as rare examples of modernist architecture in coal-encrusted cities. By the 1930s there were talking pictures and talking newsreels for the great mass of the British population every week. Hollywood provided most of the movies despite restrictions on their import. Rapid adoption also applied to domestic entertainment machines, above all the radio. Radio broadcasting was invented as a commercial activity after the war, with one company granted a monopoly. It was rather uniquely turned into a state-owned monopoly, run by the British Broadcasting Corporation (created 1926), funded by a compulsory levy on the listening public rather than advertising. It had extraordinary success: by the late 1930s there was hardly a home without radio. In stark contrast to the cinema, the radio programming was national. However, competition came from two radio stations on the continent: one Radio Luxembourg, the other, the International Broadcasting

Company, run by a Tory MP, the engineer Captain Leonard Plugge, broadcasting from France and financed by advertising. In the 1930s the BBC diversified into television, producing the first regular television broadcasting in the world. At first it used two systems – an all-British semi-mechanical system due to John Logie Baird and an electronic system which would soon take over entirely. This Marconi-EMI electronic system was the product of international capitalism, the Radio Corporation of America and its associated companies, including Marconi-EMI, rather than an independent British effort.

The electricity which powered all these systems was generated by a mixture of public and private companies. Some, like the Newcastle-upon-Tyne Electrical Supply Company, were integrated regional systems; others served much smaller localities. In a significant intervention the government created a Central Electricity Board (1926) to supervise and control the building of a new national infrastructure, the so-called National Grid, along with housing and roads a key case of interwar public works. 'The placing of contracts in respect of the constructional work on the transmission system has been pressed on, and the total value of orders already placed amounts to £8.5 million, all of which have been placed with British firms,' said the 1929 Conservative manifesto. Distinctive pylons marched across the countryside, carrying high-voltage current generated by the most efficient stations to unite regions, with national interconnection achieved in 1938. Power stations became symbols of modernity, most notably the Battersea power station, an art deco masterpiece built for the London Power Company in the 1930s by Sir Giles Gilbert Scott. (A second station of identical design was added in the 1950s, giving the four-chimney structure which remains.) This temple of power generated electricity from coal into the 1980s.

Then there were the roads and the private motor cars. These built up rapidly in the interwar years. A notable feature was new straight concrete roads, arterial dual carriage roads out of cities, bypasses and new interurban routes such as the Liverpool-East Lancashire Road, between Liverpool and Manchester. London was a great focus of road building, with the Western and Eastern Avenues in London, the

Great Cambridge Road, the Watford Road, the North Circular Road and many more, with a peak in the 1920s.[13] These were, like the construction of the National Grid, 'public works' – in the case of roads in the 1920s designed to help reduce unemployment.

INNOVATION AS PANACEA AND ALTERNATIVE

Not all research was done to effect great changes.[14] Some was done to avoid it. Through the early twentieth century national research provided a more palatable alternative than nationalist or imperialist polices. Demands for agricultural protection, for imperial preference, for subsidies for coal were met with research stations. Lloyd George's Development and Road Improvement Act 1909 promoted rural road-building and research. The Development Commission co-funded a large number of research institutes and university units in agriculture, botany, animal studies of various sorts. It was a pioneer of a mode of central government support for civil research.[15] In the case of new varieties of wheat, potato and grass, the impact of the research stations until 1939 at least was minimal – farmers preferred older commercial varieties, though the Cambridge 'Yeoman' wheat had some success. Research was controlled by academics interested in the fundamental aspects, rather than direct applicability, and in any case was generally directed to areas where British production was stagnant. By contrast, in expanding areas such as dairy farming, a hugely important sector in the United Kingdom, research was much less strongly supported.[16]

In the case of coal the claims for research had a prominent place. The Samuel Commission, set up as part of the process of delaying strike action by miners in 1925, devoted pages of its report to science and research, claiming it was 'essential that the industry as a whole should become imbued with the spirit of science'.[17] More research was indeed the *first* of the three things the industry needed to do, along with promoting larger units of production and distribution and a 'fuller partnership' between employers and employed.[18]

One process that attracted a lot of attention was the low-temperature carbonization of coal. It involved heating of coal to a lower temperature than when making coke (and thus gas), but enough to produce a smokeless fuel (semi-coke), and to produce liquids from which petrol could be extracted. The Samuel Commission noted that it was not yet a viable process but recommended more research.[19] Some schemes did come into operation on a small scale, for example Coalite in Bolsover and Rexco in Mansfield. Coalite produced low-octane 'coalene' petrol from 1939 and also diesel and fuel oil. The Department of Scientific and Industrial Research fuel research budget was about £100,000 per annum, half of the budget of the National Physical Laboratory, and more than was spent on road research, or on food research.[20] The Fuel Research Station at Greenwich, next to the large gas works, where the Millennium Dome was later to stand, was an important centre for working out how to turn coal into oil, and its work helped ICI with its oil-from-coal project.[21] But these initiatives made, for all the talk around them, a minimal impact on the demand for coal or on oil supplies.

MAKING THE EMPIRE

Research was also used as an alternative to imperial protection. The Empire Marketing Board, formed in 1926 and lasting to 1933, when it was no longer needed, was engaged in propaganda and research in favour of British goods and imperial goods, and in particular the promotion of imperial sources of supply. It was created in 1926 by the modernizing colonial secretary and imperialist Leo Amery, the heir to Chamberlain as the champion of constructive imperialism. Its work was divided in three – scientific research, economic analysis and publicity. The publicity machine included John Grierson, who with his EMB-funded film *Drifters* (1929) created the British documentary.[22] The research effort had a major success. It funded work on food preservation that had started in 1917, at the Low Temperature Research Station. The key discovery was that gas could be used in refrigeration chambers, which greatly improved the quality of the fruit imported from Australia and other distant points and was to make it possible, in the 1930s, to import chilled beef from Australia, otherwise only available from the River Plate. Gas refrigeration augmented the significance of those distinctively British machines, the reefer ships, indeed a whole generation of such ships of the 1930s, known as Empire Food Ships, used this technique.[23] In the late 1930s small shipments of chilled beef started coming from Australasia once the new gas-chilling equipment was fitted in ships of the Blue Funnel, Blue Star and Port Lines and others, as part of an attempt to imperialize meat supply.[24] But this imperialization had limited effect. However, from 1939 until the mid-1950s all meat was not only rationed, but imported frozen not chilled, to increase the capacity of ships and to allow for longer journeys and storage.

Empire was, it was said, outdoor relief for the aristocracy, but in the twentieth century it was outdoor relief for technocrats and their wondrous new machines. Empire did not retard modernity, or distort it, but promoted it. The conservative imperialist project so often condemned by liberals and the left as backward and backward-looking was anything but. Constructive imperialism did much more than to build the new imperial capital of New Delhi in the 1920s, the work of Sir Herbert Lutyens and Sir Herbert Baker. This great new city for state servants had residential areas divided into those for gazetted officers (overwhelmingly white) and 'European clerks', separate from 'Indian clerks', as well as a space for the nobility from the princely states. A modern empire needed modern machines. Specifically imperial communications got a great boost from state-led innovation. In 1924 the Labour government inaugurated the Imperial Airship Scheme, which would start with the design and construction of one capitalist one, built by Vickers, the other, labelled the 'socialist' one by its opponents, by the state. With the crash of the socialist R101, the whole scheme (which envisioned five airships) was abandoned by the second Labour government in 1931. Indeed, this is about all a Labour policy for the technical future would ever amount to – building machines for non-socialist purposes, but with a greater state input than might otherwise have been the case. In the mid-1930s Imperial Airways with state support started the development of new large flying boats. This led to it having more than twenty four-engined Empire Flying Boats. By 1939 there were three weekly flights to Australia (taking ten days) and three to South Africa (taking six days). Another twenty or so civil flying boats (Hythes) were added during the war, and more after it. No other country or empire had anything like this number of any kind of long-distance aircraft. Pan American had a mere nine Boeing clippers – though they could fly the Atlantic – three Martin flying boats for the trans-Pacific route and a handful of various Sikorskis. The development of new imperial communications went further still. In the 1920s an Imperial Wireless Chain for transmitting messages had been built, which was merged with the private and public telegraphs of the empire to form Cable and Wireless, nationalized by the 1945 Labour government. An Empire Service on short-wave radio was launched in 1932 from the BBC Experimental Station.

The future development of the empire involved any number of great projects. Thus the British Empire Cotton Growing Corporation supported research that led to development of cotton growing in the Sudan. There was a great deal of research into the agricultural problems of the empire; there were surveys, such as the African Research Survey of the 1930s. The search for new uses for imperial sugar was an important part of projects for imperial research, much increased in 1940, and especially from 1945, when a Colonial Research Council was established. From 1945 more was provided for colonial research than for the domestic Medical Research Council or the Agricultural Research Council.[25] As the economy imperialized after 1945, so did colonial research.[26] Projects to allow the use of raw materials from the sterling area rather than the dollar area (including, for example, making the wonder-drug cortisone from African sisal rayon from South African eucalyptus trees, an alternative to linseed oil from Nigerian N'gart seeds and sulphur from British and imperial minerals) were strongly encouraged.[27] British scientists and engineers, doctors and agriculturalists, teachers and policemen went out to the empire as never before. Not to India, of course, but above all to Africa. This future did not last either.

INNOVATION AND THE NATION

If the years after 1945 were great years for nationalist-imperialist plans and projects, they also inaugurated a new age of techno-nationalism. Research, development, design would be bent to specifically national purposes, along with the economy as a whole. It had many elements. The first was what might be called invention-chauvinism. The 1945 Labour manifesto proclaimed that 'The genius of British scientists and technicians who have produced radio-location, jet propulsion, Penicillin and the Mulberry Harbours in wartime, must be given full rein in peacetime too.' By the late 1940s the innocent Briton could be forgiven for believing that Britons had been the sole inventors of jet engines, radar, television, atom bombs. For example, the official film *Jet* (1950), by the Central Office of Information, presented Frank Whittle as the sole inventor of the jet, the man who through the company he was associated with had the patent, controlled the new machine, licensed it.[28] The Festival of Britain of 1951 was a great national exhibition, in which British scientific contributions were extraordinarily prominent, and not only in the Dome of Discovery. 'British leadership in particular areas of science and technology' was emphasized, but not contributions to war. It was recognized that some claims to British leadership might be questionable, and these were avoided at least in some cases.[29]

Radical nationalists called for great efforts to create a national economy. They were very clear too that this required new technical means. Thus support for various novel oil-from-coal processes and national agriculture research was a standard theme of nationalist futures for the United Kingdom from the 1930s. As we have already noted, both were prominent as a pair in the plans of Mosley's British Union of Fascists. But they were hardly unique. Labour, in its Immediate Programme of 1937, called for a 'national plan under the guidance of the state' under which science could be properly used; one of the few examples given was 'Oil from Coal'.

The Second World War inaugurated much closer interconnection between research and national production. For example, new grasses from Aberystwyth were widely planted under ministry of agriculture and food patronage.[30] A new British Coal Utilization Research Association was created by government and the coal industry in 1938, and grew to become, within a few years, the second-largest research association behind the Cotton Industry Research Association (though both would be overtaken after the war by the British Iron and Steel Research Association, created in 1944). It had 300 staff by 1943. Among them was Rosalind Franklin, who was doing a PhD on the structure of coal and would after the war use X-rays to determine the structure of DNA. It was led by a remarkable man called John G. Bennett. He had got into coal research in Greece and sought to find a way of carbonizing lignite to make domestic charcoal. He experimented in England with the help of the Fuel Research Station and Birmingham gas works.[31] He was a former Royal Engineer officer with a strong mathematical bent but no degree, who had been a spy, and was the main British devotee of the mystic Gurdjieff. In 1950 the National Coal Board created the Coal Research Establishment in Gloucestershire, under Jacob Bronowski, a mathematician and mystic about science, who also worked on smokeless fuel. Herbert Morrison looked to the new National Coal Board to 'conduct research in a far more effective manner than the eight hundred colliery companies': coal would move from being a source of heat, to the 'raw product for innumerable valuable commercial products'.[32]

Very much more was spent on developing new aeroplanes for the now fully nationalized airlines than on coal research. Here indeed, it was felt, the British future lay – in making aeroplanes the whole world would want. After the war the Bristol Company got finance to build its gigantic eight-engined 130-ton Brabazon airliner (which required a new factory, with the largest span of any roof in Europe, and an exceptionally long new runway). It would be powered (in its initial version) with eight Bristol Centaurus piston engines, a later version with the Bristol Proteus jet (turboprop). The Brabazon is quite well known, but the even larger contemporary 157-ton Saunders Roe Princess flying boat, powered by the ten Bristol Proteus engines, is not. Neither of these leviathans, amongst the biggest civil aircraft in the world, went into service. Other programmes, much smaller, proved more significant, including that leading to the Comet and the Viscount. Yet overall the programme failed – BOAC bought long-range aeroplanes from the USA from the 1940s.

Greater sums still went to making new weapons for deployment many years into the future. The warlike research and development effort was only a little lower than the wartime one. The state was developing all three ABC weapons – atomic, biological and chemical – also then known as weapons of mass destruction.

That the United Kingdom would build an atomic bomb was hardly in doubt. Moves towards it started straight after the war, with the creating of research facilities, plutonium production piles and more. In January 1947 the need arose to take a decision, for essentially bureaucratic reasons, to build the bomb itself, and to continue to keep the whole programme secret. So the decision was made, the direction of travel ratified.

What the UK wanted and needed was an independent *national* atomic bomb.[33] The building of such a national bomb was thought unnecessary during the war because there was a combined project. The USA withdrew from wartime agreements, and British ministers wanted a British bomb to show the USA they were not to be pushed around. Ernest Bevin, it is said, wanted a British atomic bomb so as not to be humiliated by the USA in an era before NATO or a Soviet atomic bomb existed. It is telling indeed that the British insisted that all the nuclear facilities be built in the British Isles, not the Commonwealth, though Australia provided sites for testing. The bomb development had been placed outside the normal machinery of government, in a 'holy of holies of its own'.[34] It cost £150 million to get a bomb, a vast sum spent with the highest priority, overriding exports, or other aspects of the defence programme.[35] This national bomb project shocked Winston Churchill: he had wanted a continuation of Anglo-American cooperation.[36]

To British astonishment, the Soviet Union exploded a bomb in 1949, a feat not achieved by the British project until 1952. The new British atomic bomb was made obsolete only months later by the first US and Soviet hydrogen bombs, which were 100 times more devastating, leaving the United Kingdom a nation with atomic bombs in a world of superpowers with hydrogen bombs.

CHANGE FROM BELOW

Was there a distinctive left future, as the thesis that it was the left which made the future requires? The Labour Party was exceptionally moderate, and coy, about the future it wanted to create. Its visions for the future, such as they were, owed a great deal first to Liberal thought, and then to a national productivism which hardly originated within the party. Its socialism was little more than radical railing against unproductive rentiers. In 1929 it said, for example, that 'A Labour majority would nationalise the Mines and Minerals as the only condition for satisfactory working. It would develop the scientific utilisation of coal and its valuable by-products, now largely wasted.' Other measures were very limited indeed. It was more radical in 1935, with 'schemes of public ownership for the efficient conduct, in the national interest, of banking, coal and its products, transport, electricity, iron and steel, and cotton', and the abolition of the House of Lords, but still hardly revolutionary. There was no plan really for a new society, only movement on the edges – better social services and education, lower taxes for the workers and so on.

But revolutionary parties were not necessarily much better in setting out what the future would look like. The communists did so in the 1930s and produced a document which is revealing both as to what would change and what would not. The fundamental change was that the new United Kingdom would not have capitalists; otherwise, apart from making the workers better off, many things would essentially be better versions of the present. It would be a more scientific future, with scientists and technicians having more of a say. They promised what capitalism promised and they claimed could not deliver – electrified railways, oil from coal (as usual), full use of resources . . .[37] One of the central arguments of British communism of the 1930s was, and would be later, that the problem with British capitalism was that it did not invent enough, did not use the latest machines and was retarding technical progress. Capitalism, and especially British capitalism, was a brake on technical progress. To restart it, make use of its bounty and spread it efficiently, state planning, guided by experts, would be needed. Essentially, though, there was no alternative innovation policy from the left.

The usual answer to the question about what difference Labour made concerns welfare. Its great innovation of the 1940s is taken to be the welfare state, a topic taken up in chapter 9. Suffice it to say here that the distinctively Labour approach to the social services was in large part abandoned in the late 1930s and 1940s. The welfare state that emerged had mainly Conservative and Liberal origins. In the case of the National Health Service (itself perhaps the greatest British medical innovation) there is a better claim for Labour innovation, in that a national, state-owned and -run service was created, a new nationalized industry, and Labour doctors had indeed called for a state-owned and -run medical service. But Labour was uncertain what kind of health service it wanted in 1945, and the National Health Service as it emerged in 1948 was not prefigured in the manifestos of the Labour Party. Yet it has been argued that the rationalized national health system followed from a managerial and administrative impulse rather than primarily a political one. A logic of efficiency driving towards specialism and hierarchy was common throughout medicine, though strongest in the state sector.[38]

Whatever the origins of the way of creating the future which characterized the 1940s, there were critics. Not everyone was convinced that the national, planned, future would be more creative. Some Conservatives saw state involvement and planning in innovation only as dampening enterprise and creativity. Thus the Conservatives said:

> we stand for the fullest opportunity for go and push in all ranks throughout the whole nation. This quality is part of the genius of the British people, who mean to be free to use their own judgment and never intend to be State serfs, nor always to wait for official orders before they can act.

They had also stated that 'Medicine will be left free to develop along its own lines, and to achieve preventive as well as curative triumphs. Liberty is an essential condition of scientific progress.'[39] The case of Penicillin, discovered by Alexander Fleming in laboratories of the voluntary St Mary's Hospital in London, was a cited case of such private initiative. Nevertheless the idea that radical invention came from freedom, not from social demands, and from genius rather than from organized research, became prominent in the late 1940s and beyond.

Scientist after elite scientist, though not those of the left, made comments like: 'Great scientific discovery is possible only for the gifted few, and only in an atmosphere of complete intellectual freedom: subordination to political or any other dogma is utterly destructive' – as was putting good scientists onto committees or having them do housework.[40] These views were more common than we might guess from a literature which was deeply imbued with the assumptions of the national technocratic left. This anti-socialist view is very evident in the novels of Nevil Shute and L. T. C. Rolt, where there is a distinct critique of socialism as bureaucratic and uncreative, lamenting very specifically the situation in the United Kingdom in the late 1940s. Nevil Shute, an aeronautical engineer, had run one of the smaller aircraft makers, Airspeed, and was writing novels from the 1930s, becoming a global bestseller after the war. L. T. C. Rolt had worked as an agricultural engineer and was best known as a pioneer of railway and canal preservation.[41] He was the chairman of the Talyllyn Railway, which opened the world's first preserved railway to the public in 1951. Rolt went on to write celebratory accounts of British engineer-entrepreneurs of the nineteenth century, which fed into the post-war story of an entrepreneurial past and a bureaucratic present. The greatest British reflection was in George Orwell's *Nineteen Eighty-Four*, published in 1949. As in the case of many other dystopian accounts of the future it envisaged a world of new machines, but one which was technically static. Orwell's picture is one of totally controlled knowledge dedicated to repression in Airstrip One, a province of Oceania, ruled by the ideology of English Socialism (Ingsoc in Newspeak). Orwell was influenced by liberal scientific intellectuals who criticized the scientific left's ideas for the planning of the development of knowledge.[42]

However, all these critiques, in relation to the United Kingdom, rather miss the point. Knowledge and innovation were controlled, but by existing elites, by corporations, by governments. Penicillin was not the product of individual genius, but large teams of researchers and industrial firms, funded and coordinated by the state. The issue was who should be in charge, not whether someone should be in charge. For the Conservatives the issue was not resisting change, but rather resisting change to the agencies of change. They wanted to keep the power of initiative or control in the hands of the private sector. For

Labour a national plan 'in the service of the nation' was essential in order to redirect that private effort. 'The nation needs a tremendous overhaul, a great programme of modernisation and re-equipment of its homes, its factories and machinery, its schools, its social services,' said Labour in 1945. Labour would actually achieve its national objectives, it said, by 'drastic policies and keeping a firm constructive hand on our whole productive machinery', it would deal 'decisively with those interests which would use high-sounding talk about economic freedom to cloak their determination to put themselves and their wishes above those of the whole nation'.[43] This needed to be a public plan, a mobilizing plan, and one to give authority to the actions of the state over those of powerful private interests. Therein lay the great asymmetry between a party of the powerful, and a tribune of the downtrodden.

8

A Mirror of the Nation at Work[1]

Most are accepters, born and bred to harness,
And take things as they come,
But some refusing harness and more who are refused it
Would pray that another and a better Kingdom come . . .
            Louis MacNeice, 'Autumn Journal' (1938)

New Year's Day 1948 – I attended the take over ceremony at
the pit at Ashington in Northumberland. The Communist
chairman of the trade union branch made a rousing speech,
the Union Jack was hoisted and the band played the National
Anthem.
            Michael Stewart MP, in his memoirs[2]

This great nation has a message for the world which is dis-
tinct from that of America or that of the Soviet Union. Ever
since 1945 we have been engaged in this country in the most
remarkable piece of social reconstruction the world has ever
seen. By the end of 1950 we had . . . assumed the moral lead-
ership of the world . . . There is only one hope for mankind,
and that hope still remains in this little island.
            Aneurin Bevan's speech resigning as minister of
                        labour and national service, 1951[3]

The United Kingdom was the most proletarian country in the world.
This was hardly the image it projected overseas, or within the empire,
or to itself. Yet it had the largest and perhaps the most uniform urban
working class – rivalled in size only by the German and the American.

In no place other than the United Kingdom could it be said that up to 80 per cent of the people were known as the 'working classes'.[4] The British people were 'manual workers', they were 'hands', 'house-wives'. Most were 'respectable', 'decent' indeed. A minority were so far from being 'gentle' they were labelled 'rough'. The people were not, as in most of the world, peasants, but proletarians living in a complex interconnected society. Their lives were recorded by the hand of a bureaucrat – a shipping clerk, a census enumerator, a War Office pen-pusher, an official in a labour exchange – not by their own hands.

Labour, work, toil were, aside from sleep, what most did with most of their time. Necessity's sharp pinch was never far away. Most owned very little – three-quarters had less than £100 (a low annual wage) in wealth.[5] They owned very little more than their clothes and furniture and kitchen utensils. They were branded on the tongue, speaking in local accents, different from those of the gentlefolk above them. They were marked by their clothing: they wore cloth caps if male, and if female might have, at the beginning of the century, covered their heads with a shawl.[6] They paid rent to private land-lords, and they worked for private employers. If employed, they were paid weekly, and from 1911 were subject to a specific working-class poll-tax, National Insurance. The great majority paid no income tax, and if they did they paid no National Insurance. They started work earlier in the morning than the middle class. There were special 'workmen's tickets' on trains running before 8 a.m.; such fares accounted for some 5 per cent or more of passenger revenue in the 1930s, and one-third of the ordinary number of tickets sold (exclud-ing season tickets).[7] They had schools, and many other institutions, exclusively to themselves too. So-called 'elementary' schools run by local authorities from the 1902 Education Act onwards divided from the interwar years into infants (to seven), junior (to eleven) and senior elementary schools (to fourteen), with an increasing distinction between the first two (primary schools) and secondary schools – terminology which remained even as the system changed radically. Unlike middle-class schools they were mixed gender. The spectator sport of the working-class male was football – not rugby or cricket – a game successfully implanted by the British working class all over the world, with, oddly, the exception of the former British empire. In terms of intellectual life the stark truth was that the working class did not have very much it could call its own.[8]

Yet this working class developed an unusually strong trade union movement, both for the skilled and the unskilled, especially for men. These trade unions created a political party itself steeped in the world of work which emerged as a national party in the interwar years. In the 1920s, and especially from 1945, it gave the House of Commons a significant number of working-class members and formed a majority government. In 1950 the United Kingdom still had one of the very largest working-class movements in the capitalist world, and certainly the most organized. By telling the story of the Labour Party as part of the story of labour, we can see that its power rested on a quite different basis from that of the other important parties. It was always subservient or in opposition to greater political powers. The Labour Party was in office from time to time; the industrial, military, financial and professional arms of the Liberal and Conservative parties were in power all of the time. Labour's primary task was to get workers, specifically trade unionists, into local government, and into the House of Commons. It was not a party with a complete alternative set of policies and prescriptions, for example in foreign affairs and military strategy.

WORK

The history of work in the United Kingdom has too often been the history of industrial relations, and within that of trade unions, and within that, strikes. Unions and strikes are things for which there are numbers, and they were otherwise also very visible. But much more significant were what workers did when they worked, what unions did other than striking, and more important still were the aspects of work in which unions had virtually no say – that is, what work was done, how it was regulated and by what mechanism it was paid for. On this the historical and statistical record is much less good.

Work outside the home, by men and boys, and girls and women, was long and wearisome. Long hours and many years of work, interrupted only by short weekends and holidays, were the norm. British people generally started work at age twelve, or fourteen after 1918, and worked into their sixties, typically then living for a short period in retirement. The state old-age pension for paupers was payable from the age of seventy; under the new contributory scheme from 1925 it was sixty-five; reduced to sixty for women in 1940. But until the late 1940s the pension age was not retirement age. Work accounted for, say, fifty years out of, say, seventy years of life (compared with today when for many it might be forty-five years out of say eighty years). In industries such as textiles, where regulations for women set maximum working hours, the 56.5-hour week was the norm; in many other industries hours were longer. In the engineering and many other trades, the standard was ten hours for five days, and four hours on Saturday morning, the fifty-four-hour week. This Saturday half-day was so unusual elsewhere that the French had a special name for this working week, *la semaine anglaise*; the Spanish referred to *la semana inglesa* or *el sábado inglés*. This was an indicator that the United Kingdom, and its workers, were rich by world standards, by European standards indeed. Some employers had moved to forty-eight hours (including Saturday morning), but this was rare, despite offering advantages in terms of intensification of work.[9] In the years 1919–20 there was a wave of cuts to forty-eight hours, and after the Second World War to forty-four hours. The great nineteenth-century call for the eight-hour day was yet to be achieved.

The position of men and boys, women and girls, was systematically and uncontroversially different. The adult male breadwinner, women workers, who were typically young, and young male workers were regarded as different kinds of worker. Men and boys worked outside the home. Women, most especially married women, did not, though girls and young women often did. Women were not regarded as being in the position of supporting a family, and where they worked they were generally unmarried and living with their families. By convention and sometimes by statute women were excluded from some industries, and from shift work. Married women specifically were excluded from many jobs, for example, into the Second World War, teaching and the civil service, where the marriage bar was not lifted until 1946. By contrast, adult men were regarded as having families to support and were paid, when they could demand it, a 'family wage'. The result was that wages for women were systematically lower than wages for men even in comparable work. For example, women weavers, skilled workers, were paid the same wages as unskilled men, labourers, rather than the wages paid to male mule spinners, who, like coal getters and engine drivers, were paid at skilled rates.[10] This was an important reason men resisted letting women into the workforce and kept them out of some trade unions (for example, the engineers until the Second World War). Similarly wages for boys and apprentices were systematically lower than for older men.

About half the number of women worked for wages as did men. Women nearly always worked indoors, most obviously in the case of domestic service, but also in industry. The single largest quantum of work was done unpaid, by housewives at home. Although much less studied than female work outside the home, this was the most important single economic contribution of women, who were mostly married.[11] The ability to keep house efficiently and economically was central to existence, not least that of working men. Even single men lodged in households where a woman washed and cooked for them. The house-wife performed laborious, skilled tasks, which were central to respectability, which men only did on board ship, or in the armed forces.[12]

More visible has been the work of women in the homes of others: paid 'domestic service' was the second major feminine occupation until the Second World War, one dominated by young, unmarried women. In the interwar years about one-quarter of young women and girls were in domestic service: in 1931 1.4 million women worked as 'indoor servants'. The next most common occupations for women were as textile workers (an industry whose workforce was two-thirds female), makers of clothing, shop assistants, teachers and nurses.[13] Female shop assistants often slept above the shop. Then came work in factories and shops and offices, generally also for unmarried women only. Much of this industrial work, though certainly not all, was in industrial kitchens, or working on industrial looms, spindles or sewing machines, industrial variants of domestic machines. A rather special and important case was Montague Burton of Leeds. Burton's factory was built up through the 1920s into the 1930s as an industrial wonder – the largest clothing factory in the world. In 1934 its canteen could hold 8,000 workers in one sitting, also the largest in the world.[14] Burton's, like other combined makers and retailers (multiples) concentrated in Leeds, sold made-to-measure suits rather than off-the-peg. Shops were places to be measured up and to order suits, which appeared within days. The factory employed 10,000 workers, nearly all women, and the company employed another 6,000 in Lancashire. The 600 shops selling the suits the women made were staffed by men. The women at Burton's sewed with essentially the same machine they used at home.

There were separate spheres within industry. Particular factories or factory spaces were reserved for either men or women. Women might work with other women only in packing, in light assembly, in restricted parts of factory complexes. Mixed working was very rare except that in general women workers were supervised by men (though never the other way around). Men and women, boys and girls, did different types of work and were generally separated from each other into definitely separate spheres of work.

A common feature was that men worked in very public ways, often in the open air – building and agriculture are perhaps the obvious cases. But hundreds of thousands of transport workers, such as the driver and fireman of a train, worked in the open, as did most railway station staff. Dockers, porters and delivery men also worked outside. So did hundreds of thousands of postmen. Manufacturing, too, was sometimes an outdoor industry, most notably in the case of shipbuilding. The spaces of indoor male work were in any case far removed from a normal domestic indoor space – steel works, mines, engineering works were dirty, hot and dangerous places.

There was also a stark contrast between what was called manual and non-manual work, between the blue-collared overalled worker and the white-collared, shirted or bloused worker. Manual work was typically physically demanding. Many miners cut coal by hand; firemen and stokers shovelled coal, dockers manhandled cargo. Work was often dirty too – the miner coming home covered in coal dust merely a particularly visible example. Many workplaces were noisy – the clatter of sheds full of looms, the racket of a steam locomotive, the constant noise of an engineering works were always remarked on by visitors. By contrast non-manual work was clean, indoor and quiet work, which did not leave calloused hands or damaged lungs.

It is hardly surprising, then, that official statistics distinguished between men and women, boys and girls, between manual and non-manual work, between staff and operatives. There were other divisions also clearly recognized in the statistics, between the skilled, the semi-skilled and the unskilled, between artisans, tradesmen and labourers. Furthermore, men were not simply tradesmen or indeed labourers, they were specialized and would describe themselves with pride as engineers, boilermakers, sheet metal workers, engineers, shipwrights, spinners, weavers, blacksmiths, stevedores, firemen, drivers, miners. The British craftsman was skilled through apprenticeship in highly specialized work. The most skilled and independent were sometimes referred to as the 'aristocracy of labour'. Skilled workers furthermore were at the core of the shop stewards' movement of the First World War, radical trade unionism more generally, and the labour left and especially the Communist Party. For example, Harry Pollitt, the longest-serving general secretary of the British Communist Party (1929–39; 1941–56), was a boilermaker.[15] Trade unions were referred to as either craft or general unions, the former organizing the skilled artisans, the latter the labourers.

In lectures, films and commentaries on industry into the 1940s, the importance of craftsmanship, and the significance of British craftsmanship, stand out. Here, craftsmanship referred to industrial skills, to the knowledge which went into the making of ships or cars or textiles. Now such claims are too easily read as inappropriate self-satisfaction, but that would be a mistake. The British industrial craftsman had been schooled over more than one generation. There was no reason to suppose that the British working class was less skilled than any European one, and good reasons to think it was more skilled than the US one. At the beginning of the twentieth century and well beyond, the British worker could spin cotton and build ships like no other workers in the world. These skills were admired the world over.

These skills were acquired on the job. The early years of work were typically a more important form of education than school years. In many fields, for example cotton textiles, there were no formal apprenticeships – workers started young, not even as teenagers, and just learned the job. In the male mule-spinning sector boys would enter as 'little piecers', working under the machines. The 'tradesman' or 'artisan' served an apprenticeship in a workplace to become a fitter or turner or shipwright. The 'time-served' worker was a skilled worker, more knowledgeable and capable than the mere labourer. They entered between fourteen and sixteen and served for five to seven years. Such apprentices were paid, but their wages would double or more on completion.[16] Apprenticeship was not confined to manual workers. It was the main form of training of higher technical staffs. Thus someone leaving grammar school at sixteen might well go into an apprenticeship, which might also involve courses at a local technical college, leading to special qualifications like the National Certificates and Diplomas, at both ordinary and higher level, which allowed access to the professional engineering institution – the higher certificates and diplomas corresponded to a university pass degree. These schemes started in the 1920s. Others might go into apprenticeships at age eighteen, and others after graduating from university in, for example, engineering science.

For many industries there was not a great deal of difference between the world of 1950 and that of 1900. Indeed, many grew, declined and were reborn in employment terms. There was the same number of miners – just under 800,000 – in 1900 as in 1950 (though the peak in the interim was over 1 million, and there were fewer in the Depression). In textiles the peak in 1913 was around 1.3 million workers, and there were 1 million in 1950, and again many fewer in the early 1930s. For some, such as shipbuilding, the peak in the early 1950s was higher than employment had ever been. This is not to say there were not important changes in these industries, but on average the textile workers, miners and shipbuilders of 1950 were very likely to be in mills, mines and yards in existence in 1914 and equipped with similar or indeed the same equipment. Similar observations might be made about working on the railways, or railway engineering.[17] Trains were still operated by a driver and a fireman, who shifted 1 ton of coal for every 50 miles; guards, station masters, signalmen, controllers, maintenance gangs, clerks and shunters all did jobs which had not changed much; neither had the maintenance or manufacture of engines.[18] Dock work, too, was not much changed. There were, however, great changes in employment in other sectors. There was a clear decline in domestic service, which was still the single largest female paid occupation to the Second World War. Some industries were growing – some 300,000 made motor vehicles by 1950, where there had been none in 1900.

THE ORGANIZATION OF WORK

In the early part of our period, to an extraordinary extent, workers organized their own work. In the textile mills spinners organized themselves. In the coal mines a gang system operated, with men working together under a gang leader who contracted employment with the mine. On the docks, too, established gangs of workers worked together and were paid collectively. Of course, in some industries managerial control was greater and impinged on the individual worker. This was to be the future. It was partly a question of machines. In a book of 1923, *The Wheelwright's Shop* by George Sturt, a former teacher, who took over the family woodworking business in the countryside, lamented the introduction of the gas engine and the mechanical saw it powered, the 'thin end of the wedge of scientific engineering', making the axe and adze, the saw and the saw-pit disappear. In the new world, 'untrained youths wait upon machines', 'Work is less and less pleasant to do – unless, perhaps, for the engineer or the electrician'. 'That civilisation may flourish a less-civilised working class must work,' he claimed.[19]

It used to be argued that British employers broadly speaking rejected modern management methods and modern forms of work, instead sticking to old methods, or developing a welfarist approach to management (especially in such firms as Rowntree). This fitted in well with the general declinist picture of backward British industry leavened by a few perhaps over-enlightened employers. Yet there was clearly, for a variety of reasons, a general move to design work for workers, and to devise systems to keep workers working hard and in standard patterns. In some industries, of course, the machinery itself imposed work patterns, in others workers were organized more directly (and of course most factories had many different types of machine). In the making of things by hand, pay was determined by a complex formula based on what was produced (piece-rates and systems like the premium bonus system); in others pay was by time spent working. In fact, British industry was a notable user of new work measurement techniques, certainly in the interwar period. It is difficult to find a major firm which did not use them, from ICI to Rowntree, from Powell Duffryn to Anglo-Iranian, from Kodak to Lucas. Indeed, the major consultancy which introduced work measurement, the Bedaux company, founded by the Franco-American Charles Bedaux, did more business in the United Kingdom than anywhere else, and its method of creating a standard unit of work, which it called the B, was copied by other consultancies and many firms who introduced it under different names, like Rowntree's 'Mark', ICI's 'Standard Minute', and Urwick, Orr & Partners' (a noted consultancy) 'Point'. Bedaux's own company, and offshoots created by former 'efficiency engineers' of his, were long to dominate British management consultancy. The chairman of British Bedaux was James Grimston, the 3rd Earl Verulam, of Enfield cables, a director of BTH and of Imperial Airways and a graduate electrical engineer.[20] Bedaux, a well-known socialite, womanizer, big game hunter and adventurer, became extremely rich. He hosted the wedding of the recently abdicated Edward VIII to Wallis Simpson at his French chateau. Following the couple's honeymoon, Bedaux accompanied them on a tour of Nazi Germany, where they met Adolf Hitler. This, and the fact that he stayed in France during the war and worked for Vichy, ensured a lurid reputation which impelled others to downplay his earlier influence and the spread of his methods.[21] But spread they did, pushed by large companies and consultancies, by wartime ministries and by the post-war Labour government. Out of all this emerged some of the largest management consultancies in Europe, and in the 1940s and beyond all sorts of academic studies and methods for the study of machines and work organization, in which nationalized industries played important roles.[22]

TRADE UNIONS

British workers were by international standards strongly unionized and were united into essentially one labour movement. Only a minority of workers were union members, and membership was weighted towards male, skilled workers. The history of trade unionism reveals a key divide, much changed over time, between the craft unions and the labourer or general unions, and the divisions too between skills, with many unions representing workers in each workplace. Full employment and rising prices stimulated membership, unemployment and falling prices made it less attractive. Membership doubled between 1900 and 1914 (starting at 2 million) and doubled again over the Great War, peaking in 1920. It then fell rapidly and then steadily got back to just over 1913 levels in 1931. Thereafter there was a rapid rise, with membership reaching the 1920 peak in the Second World War and expanding slowly after it.

The engineers' union was an early national union. The engineers (the Amalgamated Society of Engineers, the Amalgamated Engineering Union from 1920), were the ' "Brigade of Guards" of British Trade Unionism'. Not only were their commanders in the front rank of trade unionism, for example Tom Mann, but they provided the first trade union cabinet member – indeed two Great War cabinet members. They also heroically held out (though they lost) in the great engineering lockout of 1922.[23] But many unions were, like the cotton unions, in practice regionally specific. The Miners' Federation was just that: a federation of unions based in particular coalfields, such as the South Wales or Durham Miners' Federation. There was undoubtedly a trend towards national organization of trade unions, engaged in national collective bargaining with employers' organizations. Furthermore, unions were coming together. The Miners' Federation of Great Britain, which loosely organized the regional miners' federations, was greatly strengthened by the adherence of the Durham Miners in 1908. In 1910 a Federation of Transport Workers, made up of two general dockers' unions (one southern, one northern) and the sailors' union (its leader was a Liberal MP), was formed. A National Union of Railwaymen emerged in 1913 by merger (though the drivers' union, ASLEF, remained aloof). By 1914 these three groupings created a 'triple alliance' which was threatening a general strike.

Union organization was mirrored by employer organization, at the top level by the Trades Union Congress and the National Confederation of Employers' Organizations (founded 1919), at lower levels by the likes of the Engineering and Shipbuilding Employers' Federation and the Federation of Engineering and Shipbuilding Trades, which were already national before 1914. Indeed, one important aim of trade unionism was to get the same wages and conditions across the nation through national agreements, which involved getting government to recognize and deal with trade unions at national level. Trade unions wanted to be national social partners, not regional or firm-specific ones.

The main aim of trade unions was to negotiate with employers over wages, hours and conditions. Unions might negotiate with an individual employer or with an employers' federation, and thus negotiate conditions over a whole industry. These were all private initiatives and agreements, and the state stayed out of them. This was 'free collective bargaining'. The whole basis of the legal structure of trade union activity was a negative one – the granting of 'immunities' from contract law so that strikes were not illegal. These had been established in the late nineteenth century. But the doctrine was overturned in 1901, when the Taff Vale Railway (which carried coal to Cardiff docks) sued a railway workers union for the costs imposed by a strike. They succeeded, causing outrage among trade unionists and the strengthening of what became the Labour Party. The Trade Disputes Act of 1906 restored what had been understood to be the status quo. The railwaymen were the subject of another court defeat in the Osborne judgement, which made political contributions by unions illegal. This was countered by the 1911 Trade Union Act.

If the state had to intervene against judges, the state was also to be used in ways to support workers in particular industries, where such industries were regulated in aspects of labour conditions, for example the textile industries and the mines. There were gendered elements here – the work of women was much more tightly regulated than that of men. Indeed, legislation forbade the employment of women as miners. For these reasons trade unions sought representation in parliament, which was, as we have seen, dominated by men of property and employers. The Liberal Party supported the election of a small number of workers and trade unionists. An example was the United Kingdom's first winner of the Nobel Peace Prize, Sir Randal Cremer, a Liberal London MP, a carpenter by profession and a noted anti-suffragist. In the 1906 election twenty-five trade unionists were elected as Liberal members (they were known as the 'Lib-Labs'); most were miners in a grouping supported by the Miners' Federation – they were all miners' union officials. In 1900 some (by no means all) the trade unions formed a Labour Representation Committee, though it included the Fabian Society, the Independent Labour Party and, briefly, the Social Democratic Federation. Its aim was to put workers in parliament under their own party label. Railway workers and then cotton workers were among the first to affiliate to the LRC and send their officials to parliament through it. The Taff Vale Railway case was a major recruiter. LRC MPs were also elected with the cooperation of the Liberal Party (who stood down candidates in many single-member constituencies and collaborated in multi-member ones). After the 1906 election there were twenty-nine LRC MPs, the great majority union officials. Only a handful were ILP-sponsored or members of the ILP.[24] The Edwardian world of labour politics is well illustrated by the case of David Shackleton.[25] He was a cotton trade union official and was elected unopposed for Clitheroe at a by-election in 1902, and he and his union later affiliated to the LRC. As an MP and chairman of the Trades Union Congress he worked with both LRC and Lib-Lab MPs, and in this he was typical of trade unionists.

The Labour Party, as the LRC was renamed in 1906, was very greatly strengthened in 1910. In 1909 the Miners' Federation announced that its MPs, the bulk of Liberal-affiliated trade union MPs, would stand for Labour in the next election, as the Federation was now affiliated to the Labour Party. Labour increased its numbers in Parliament to forty in the first 1910 election, though this was fewer than the 1906 total of Lib-Lab and LRC combined. Labour MPs supported the minority Liberal government from 1910 but were only the fourth party, well behind the Irish Nationalists. The growth of the Labour Party indicated a rejection by trade unions of an association with the Liberal Party, a party of employers. Nevertheless, working-class voters in Great Britain still generally voted Liberal or Conservative, and one point in favour of a Labour Party for the Liberals was that it attracted working-class voters who would otherwise have voted Conservative. Labour wanted to bring a politically divided working class together in one party. It is worth noting that only just over half of trade unionists were in Labour Party-affiliated unions in 1914.

That the only barely socialist Labour Party was the fourth party in the British imperial parliament stands in sharp contrast to the position of socialists in the imperial parliaments of Germany and Austria-Hungary. In Germany and Austria, the imperial parliaments, elected on a broader male franchise than the British House of Commons, had social democratic (that is socialist) parties as the single largest party, though this did not give them any executive power. The contrast with Germany especially has exercised historians, who point to religion and the allegedly smaller size of British workplaces to explain this. It remains a mystery.

In the years just before and just after the Great War the working class was on the march, in the factories, the railways, mines and docks, rather than in parliament. These were times of strikes. Not till the 1970s and early 1980s would anything like it be seen again. Then, as in the 1970s, they were the product of grass-roots action, often against the wishes of the official trade union leadership (and of the Labour Party too). The great strikes of the years before the Great War were generally in the interconnected transport and coal industries rather than in factories. Nothing like these strikes had been seen before, not least because they often were led by socialists and syndicalists. In 1910 police from Bristol and London were deployed against the miners of Tonypandy, and, most controversially of all, troops were also deployed – Hussars and Lancashire Fusiliers. No shots were fired. 1911 saw the first national railway strike, lasting two days. Two railwaymen were shot dead by troops in Llanelli in South Wales. Transport strikes closed down Liverpool, where two workers were killed by soldiers' bullets. 1912 saw the first ever national miners' strike: over a million miners were on strike for thirty-seven days. Its aim was a national minimum wage, obtained through an act of parliament of that year.

During the Great War there were no longer such strikes, but there were unofficial strikes, especially in engineering factories, led by socialist shop stewards. The rise of a new revolutionary left, small though it was, came on the back of rapidly growing trade union strength and labour strife, especially in munitions work. A politicized working class was demanding better pay, shorter hours and a new politics, just as they were in the German and in the Russian empires. The years after the war saw, in the United Kingdom, as in many parts of the world from Buenos Aires to Barcelona, a great wave of strikes. The United Kingdom was no more immune to this global phenomenon than to the Spanish flu. In 1919 the riot act was read and armed troops were deployed in Glasgow and Birkenhead. 1919 saw advances for many workers, not least in shortening hours and increasing pay. The following years saw a series of defensive strikes and lockouts, notably by the miners in 1921, and the engineers in 1922. The workers and unions were seeking to defend wages and conditions as employers tried to push back against very significant wartime gains. In the 1920s wages were not much higher than before the war in real terms, but the difference between the wages of labourers and skilled men had narrowed. There were as a result fewer working people in poverty, a notable change from the Edwardian years.[26]

The management of industrial relations by the state became a vital matter in which Lloyd George was closely involved before, during and after the war. He was central to creating a system which has been called 'corporate bias', whereby the state dealt at a national level with single organizations of both labour and capital (newly formed during the war), which both understood their role as being partly agents of the state. There were, despite appearances, key elements of a new hidden constitution whose task was to marginalize ultras on both sides. At issue was not the parliamentary power of Labour, but the industrial power of labour. Labour were brought into wartime coalitions also, because wartime governments needed the support not of Labour

MPs, but of organized labour. The elite did not need to accommodate socialism, or even technocratic Fabianism, but workers. The fundamental politics of industrial society was not the politics of Westminster, but the extra-parliamentary politics of capital–labour relations.[27]

THE LABOUR PARTY

The experiences of the Liberal and Labour Parties during the war were in some respects similar. In both cases the parties supported the war, but in both there was dissent, with some significant figures leaving positions of leadership. Later there were splits in Labour as in the Liberals, though it is usually thought that the war split only the Liberal Party.[28]

Labour trade unionist MPs went into the wartime coalition governments. Five served in wartime cabinets: Arthur Henderson (the Labour leader) was an iron founder; John Hodge was a steel smelter; J. R. Clynes was a cotton and gas worker; George Barnes was an engineer; and George Henry Roberts was a printer. Henderson was a minister without portfolio from 1916; Hodge, a protectionist, was Britain's first minister of labour.[29] He was followed by Roberts. Barnes was minister of (war) pensions, and Clynes minister of food control. Of these five, three – Barnes, Roberts and Hodge – continued in office until 1920. That is, they remained in the Lloyd George coalition, which the Labour Party had left in 1918 to fight the election of that year as an independent party. Some of the defectors stood for election in 1918 as part of a new National Democratic and Labour Party, others as coalition Labour, mostly unopposed by the coalition. The NDLP grew out of the British Workers' League, formed in part by Lord Milner, and was pro-war, imperialist and protectionist.[30] The cabinet members were joined in the coalition by others who held junior office, or who had merely been MPs, most never to be heard of again (among them G. J. Wardle and James Parker). A very few later returned to Labour, including Stephen Walsh, a miner. The two wartime cabinet ministers who didn't leave Labour, Henderson and Clynes, were members of the ILP as well as trade unionists. The ILP was generally very hesitant about the war and opposed Labour participation in government. Henderson and Clynes would serve with Ramsay MacDonald in the 1924 and 1929 Labour cabinets. Both refused to go into the National cabinet with him in 1931.

One effect of the Great War was to create a new and fully independent Labour Party. It was based on a much larger trade union base and was much richer. In a move provoked by the likelihood of proportional representation being introduced in 1918, it for the first time contested the election with some pretension to do so nationally rather than locally (with candidates in over half of seats). It had a new constitution; it now had individual members in constituency parties as well as affiliated unions and other organizations. Its 1918 manifesto was a warning against 'reaction': Labour wanted an end to control of labour and conscription. It was very much a workers' party, claiming, for example, that 'the workers supplied the vast majority of our soldiers and sailors'. It stood for the 'Conscription of Wealth': 'In paying the War Debt, Labour will place the burden on the broadest backs by a special tax on capital. Those who have made fortunes out of the war must pay for the war.' And it stood for free trade.[31]

It did not do very well. By having a large number of candidates, its share of the national vote went up, but it remained the fourth party with only fifty-seven MPs. Ramsay MacDonald, Philip Snowden and Arthur Henderson, men who had had doubts about the war, all lost their seats, the last to the NDLP. The parliamentary Labour Party was not that much bigger than the twenty non-Labour Party Labour MPs. The NDLP put up only twenty-eight candidates, but ten were elected. Three were MPs elected for Henry Hyndman's National Socialist Party, including Will Thorne, general secretary of the gas workers, who represented West Ham South/Plaistow from 1906 to 1945 and Jack Jones, who defeated the official Labour candidate in nearby Silvertown in 1918. The openly anti-war left that emerged on the continent only had a weak echo in the United Kingdom, but the anti-war British Socialist Party and other small parties formed a Communist Party of Great Britain in 1920. Among its founders was the trade union leader Tom Mann, elected in 1919 as general secretary of the

Amalgamated Engineering Union. It would have two MPs elected in 1922, none in 1923 and one in 1924.

The Labour Party's growth as a party was a phenomenon of the 1920s. It was in many ways a surprising success, for the party was led by men rejected by the electorate in 1918, and its rise as an electoral force coincided with a weakening of trade unions. It rather caught up with the German SPD and indeed learned from the German party.[32] The Conservatives and Liberals took to calling the Labour Party 'the socialists', a tradition which lasted for many decades. They were more likely to be accused of being socialists than claim to be socialists. But most who saw themselves as socialist thought that at best the Labour Party might, one day, become socialist. There was a relatively clear socialist element in the Labour Party, the Independent Labour Party, which had played a key part in the party and had preceded it. It had a substantial bloc of members of parliament, from both the right and left of Labour (from Ramsay MacDonald to James Maxton). It left the Labour Party in 1932 but, far from thriving, lost most of its MPs and members very quickly. It had four MPs from 1935. The Communist Party repeatedly failed to get affiliation to Labour.

The parliamentary Labour Party had seven leaders to 1935, all essentially from the working class and all born between 1856 and 1869, making the youngest, J. R. Clynes, thirty-one in 1900. Although it remained very strongly a trade union party, it now included a stronger group of socialists in the form of a much larger ILP representation and also recruited Liberal MPs and intellectuals in the 1920s – for example, Josiah Wedgwood MP and Norman Angell, who joined in 1920 and was elected in 1929. William Wedgwood Benn had been a Liberal MP (and was secretary of state for India under Labour in 1929–31). It also recruited Tories. Among those who came from the Tory benches was Sir Oswald Mosley MP. Among the peers it recruited Lord Haldane, a former Liberal MP and minister, and Lord Parmoor, the lawyer Charles Cripps, who had been a Unionist MP. It recruited public school boys with Tory backgrounds, including Clement Attlee (elected 1922) and Hugh Dalton (elected 1924). Clement Attlee, leader from 1935, was born in 1883, and represented a radical generational as well as social change. Not surprisingly, Labour did not recruit from business or finance – with exceptions, George Strauss and (Major) Richard Stokes, who sat for Ipswich, where his family company was based, and John Wheatley, who ran a printing business. Wheatley and Stokes were Catholics, and Strauss Jewish.

If all the Labour cabinet members during the Great War had been workers, this was very far from the case in the Labour cabinets formed in the 1920s and beyond. The miner Stephen Walsh was one of about eight workers in a cabinet of twenty in 1924. The 1929 cabinet included only five workers. Among them was Margaret Bondfield, the first woman to sit in a British cabinet. She was a senior trade union official – secretary of the Women's section of what became in 1924 the National Union of General and Municipal Workers. She represented women workers on the General Council of the TUC, which she rose to chair. She continued the tradition of trade union ministers of labour, holding the post 1929–31.[33] (The National government of 1931 had only one working-class member other than Ramsay MacDonald, J. H. Thomas of the railwaymen, who had been in the 1924 cabinet.) There were seven workers in the cabinet in 1945, and only five in the 1950 cabinet. Among them were two miners, Jim Griffiths and Aneurin Bevan, who between them covered the social services. They had been trained up by the South Wales miners for leadership in the 1920s, through a Central Labour College, which closed in 1929. The working-class autodidact was a figure of significance in politics and in trade unions, but very rarely in high ranks.[34]

Labour's key positions in the 1920s were classic liberal ones – free trade and a deep hostility to protection, action to open up the trade of the world, support for the new League of Nations and financial orthodoxy. But they also had some distinctive policies. To deal with the greatest issue of public finance, war debt, they called for a capital levy; they wanted to increase the differential between the taxation of earned and unearned income. They looked to public works, and a reduction in the working lifetime, to increase employment. They called for the nationalization of land and mineral rights, and coal mines, and sometimes of railways. They wanted to abolish indirect taxes of all kinds. It is too tempting a thesis to see Labour as an offshoot from liberalism which replaced the original article, carrying forward the liberal programme of reform. It was structurally and politically a very different beast, even if its intellectuals inherited much from liberalism.

In office Labour achieved little. The minority Labour government elected in 1929 was at a loss, as so many others were, in facing the great global financial and economic crisis. They responded as they were told to – by cutting expenditure on the social services mainly to maintain confidence and the value of sterling. In its discussions with the Labour cabinet in the crisis of 1931, the TUC proposed a new levy to pay unemployment benefit, suspension of the sinking fund and a tax on interest-bearing securities (noting the appreciation of the value of war debt in particular). They did not propose anything on tariffs, mindful of divisions within the TUC.[35] These solutions were not acceptable. The government stuck to the proposed cuts, which proved too much for most of the cabinet. It was the cutting of benefits, not the creation of new ones, which was the issue – there already was a welfare state in existence. The result was a National government, which won a landslide victory in 1931.

In the years 1931–2 the parliamentary Labour Party split three ways. Six MPs went off with Oswald Mosley to the protectionist New Party, fourteen others went with MacDonald, in the form of National Labour into the National government.[36] The Labour Party itself remained intact as a trade union party, but in 1932 the ILP and its MPs disaffiliated. The left remaining in Labour would be small and centred on two rich men who could finance publications, Sir Stafford Cripps and George Strauss. The most significant specifically Labour intellectual was Professor Harold Laski of the LSE, also a figure of the left. The party was now dominated by trade unions again, a key figure being Ernest Bevin of the Transport and General Workers Union, the largest union, but with strong figures like the humbly born Herbert Morrison, who ran London, and the public school boys Attlee and Dalton. The party built its strength, as did the trade unions, but slowly and in a hostile atmosphere. It was down to fifty-two seats in a 31 per cent vote in 1931; but then rose to 154 seats on a 38 per cent vote (as good as it had ever got before 1945) in 1935. It was at this low parliamentary strength that it sat in parliament through the Second World War.

LABOUR AND THE SECOND
WORLD WAR

The demands of the Second World War quickly ensured full employment, which raised wages in many cases and strengthened trade unions. Although strikes were made illegal, trade union membership nearly doubled, and employers were forced to recognize unions in firms and industries previously resistant. In 1938–9 only 1 million manual workers paid income tax, and they paid barely £3 per annum each; by 1944 the number had increased to 7 million, paying on average just under £30 each.[37] The Second World War saw a newly assertive British working class, and film producers, and the state, sometimes, let through what was unthinkable before the war. No British worker would, before the war, have been shown on film saying that workers should be sticking together in the cause of 'smashing fascism', as happened in a film of 1943 about how ships were built. Ordinary people were now portrayed as people who could 'Build ships, win wars, and defy dictators'.[38] Generally speaking, though propaganda was inclusive, it was very rarely of the left.

As in the Great War, Labour joined the government, although again this was not dictated by parliamentary arithmetic. It did so in greater proportional strength than in 1915 as it was now the second party in the country and in parliament. It refused to join a coalition under Neville Chamberlain, and thus it was that Labour made Churchill prime minister in May 1940. Labour people took key positions, perhaps the most important being the Ministry of Labour and National Service, under the leader of the greatest union, the Transport and General Workers' Union, Ernest Bevin. But its ministers were involved in many aspects of the war effort, from running the contracting civilian trades and industries (Hugh Dalton as president of the Board of Trade), to the Home Office (Herbert Morrison), to one of the service ministries (A. V. Alexander was first lord of the Admiralty). Clement Attlee was deputy prime minister (from 1942). However, the common idea that Labour ran the home front while the Conservatives and Churchill controlled the fighting is a fantasy: the key domestic positions, not least in industrial and financial control, were in the hands of Conservatives. Wartime chancellors, ministers of production, health, supply, food, war transport, education, fuel and power, and agriculture were overwhelmingly Conservatives. Stafford Cripps was minister of aircraft production from 1942, but was not in the Labour Party through the whole war. That said, Labour and the trade unions now had a place in the system of administration they had never had before. But that administrative role, as the left of the party complained, came at the expense of the exercise of public political power and the acceptance of many policies and practices it would otherwise have rejected. As a party it could no longer attack the Tories; similarly the Tories could not attack 'the socialists', or indeed the trade unions. Silence was not consensus. Indeed, talk of consensus from 1940 is misplaced for another reason: even when practical politics suggested similar positions it mattered intensely who was in charge, it mattered whose agenda was in the background.

The left tended not to celebrate the wartime United Kingdom but to criticize it. The Communist Party was a critic between 1939 and 1941; thereafter the party sided very strongly with the Churchill government. They did, however, strongly criticize the war production effort, blaming the nature of British capitalism for poor performance, and also called for a second front. The left opposition in the factories came from parts of the ILP, Trotskyite groups and one or two Labour MPs, notably Aneurin Bevan.[39] George Orwell from his vantage point on the left called Attlee a 'tame cat', and a 'recently dead fish'.[40] A new party of the left, Common Wealth, called for a more robust war effort, for a proper people's war. The war did not stop opposition to the Tories and the elite: it intensified it in some respects, even if Labour was largely out of that game. However, by comparison with the Great War, domestic politics were very gentle, not least because the enemy had very little support at all, was clearly non-democratic and also because all the left was very solidly in support of the war, especially from 1941.

For some historians it is not particularly surprising that in 1945 Labour should win the election; perhaps it might even have won in 1940 had there been one then. Indeed, for many historians 1940 is a key break in political history.[41] But in a number of ways the 1945

Labour victory was a surprise. The few contested by-elections were generally won by incumbent parties, and not all the few independents who won were of the left – furthermore there was anti-party feeling directed not just at the Conservatives, but Labour too.[42] It is rather telling that the takers of the political temperature did not see a clear shift to Labour (though pioneering polls did). In 1945 Gallup polls suggested that a majority wanted the continuation of a coalition, but more weighted towards the left. With no coalition possible, the concern to throw out Tories pushed people to vote against the government.[43] Another explanation is that Labour attracted voters because it successfully combined patriotism and socialism more decisively than during the Great War.[44]

Labour got 47.8 per cent of the vote (one-third of the electorate). The really significant point was Labour's increasing proportion of the working-class vote, much of which had been Tory. This was a much more important factor than the increase in middle-class votes (the numbers in that class were smaller, and the shift smaller too).[45] Indeed, in many ways what needs to be highlighted is the scale of the defeat of the Conservative Party and of the National government it was the central element of. National government parties got 40 per cent of the vote in 1945, down from 53 per cent in 1935. The Conservatives alone got a mere 36 per cent, down from 48 per cent in 1935.

Labour's victory was a stunning political moment both because it was unexpected and because it potentially marked a very radical change in British and in world politics. The capitalist country with the largest organized working class in the world (now well unionized) had put a workers' party into office with a majority for the first time.

THE 1945 LABOUR GOVERNMENT

The standard view of the post-war Labour government focuses on its creation of a welfare state. In this view the welfare state is usually seen as an Edwardian innovation brought to fruition by Labour after 1945. Telling the story in this way seems to explain the failure of the Labour Party to be socialist and is an important concern for British socialists.[46] The other side of the story was the 'labourism', of the party. Its deep trade union consciousness itself made it a party limited in its aims. Critics then and since have rightly made much of its failure to fundamentally change the economy, state and society. The Communist Party insisted that 'the capitalist control of the State is as yet substantially untouched'. The 'British economy is still overwhelmingly capitalist. The leaders of the armed services and the people have not been changed.'[47] Its foreign policy hardly differed from what the Conservatives would have done.[48] The cabinet was dominated by public school boys, not just those in the leadership from the 1930s, but a new generation, among them Stafford Cripps and Hugh Gaitskell. It merely reformed an existing (and varied by local authority) education system rather than create a new one. It left elite education alone. Such conservatism, allied to the creation of the welfare state, has also been celebrated. Clement Attlee, an overrated prime minister, is applauded for his deference to tradition, and to the elite he belonged to, qualities one would not feel the need to praise in a Conservative, an implicit criticism of more original and significant Labour leaders.

Yet such criticisms miss the actual focus of Labour and its programme, which was not centred on welfare, in either 1945 or 1950. Instead, in both the manifestos and the policy pursued the main concern was with a national programme of economic development, in which exports were central. Social services and social security were secondary to production. As we have seen, Labour launched a quite extraordinary driving up of exports of manufactures. It is difficult to find the origins of these policies in specifically Labour programmes. They had had no distinctive plan for the economy beyond rather abstract calls for 'planning' and nationalization of coal and coal-using sectors. Their plans for the future of industrial policy as developed in the Labour-controlled Board of Trade under Hugh Dalton were extensions of Tory policies of the 1930s.[49] They pursued the policies of the 1930s and 1940s, though not, it must be emphasized, those of the 1920s, which were decisively rejected. There was no deflation, no windfall for the holders of debt and no free trade. Unions were more likely to be recognized and now had a place in some at least of the deliberations of government.

Once we ditch the assumption that we need to think of Labour either as liberal or socialist, we can begin to note the extraordinary importance of nationalism in its programme.[50] Labour presented itself in 1945 as the true national party. Its manifesto barely included the word 'socialism' (which appeared once), or 'socialist' (which appeared twice). It was, by contrast, full of references to 'Britain' (fourteen times) and 'British' (twelve times) and 'nation' and 'national' (nearly fifty times), more than 'public' (twenty-three)! 'Great Britain' appeared only once, and there was not a single reference to Scotland, Ireland, Wales or England. This was a national programme for a nation called Britain, with no reference to 'empire' and two passing mentions of the 'British Commonwealth' and one reference to 'Colonial Dependencies'. The party stood, in its own estimation, for the majority of the nation – its only overt enemies a small minority of not-well-specified non-workers, the profiteers of the Great War and the interwar period. It wasn't Tory-imperialist patriotism, or Edwardian liberalism, that was at the heart of the programme, but a distinctive nationalism built on a nationalist critique of free enterprise British capital. 'The nation wants food, work and homes,' said the 1945 manifesto. That in itself was not significant. What was significant was the claim that this policy needed to 'put the nation above any sectional interest, above any free enterprise'.[51] That meant not just nationalized, publicly owned infrastructural industries, but also publicly administered national social services. In other ways too Labour nationalism ran deep: as Aneurin Bevan exclaimed in 1948 (and similarly at other times):

> The eyes of the world are turning to Great Britain. We now have the moral leadership of the world, and before many years are over we shall have people coming here as to a modern Mecca, learning from us in the twentieth century as they learned from us in the seventeenth century.[52]

The 1950 manifesto was still deeply nationalist:

> the task now is to carry the nation through to complete recovery. And that will mean continued, mighty efforts from us all. The choice for the electors is between the Labour Party – the party of positive action, of constructive progress, the true party of the nation – and the Conservative Party – the party of outdated ideas, of unemployment, of privilege.

The document makes two references to socialism and one to social democracy, but these were far outnumbered by references to Britain, the nation and so on. The only difference to 1945 in this respect was that the Commonwealth appeared more often.[53]

Labour's nationalism helps explain many things. It helps explain the choice of the term 'nationalized industries'. Labour did not originate the term *National* Insurance, but *National* Assistance and the *National* Health Service were new. So were the *National* Coal Board, the *British* Transport Commission and *British* Railways. It also helps us understand Labour's contribution to the welfare state. For, as we shall see, what Labour did was not to create a welfare state, but rather to extend an existing comprehensive working-class welfare state to a universal welfare state for the whole nation. It also helps explain the

Figure 8.1: Trade Union membership and the Labour Party vote, 1880–1960

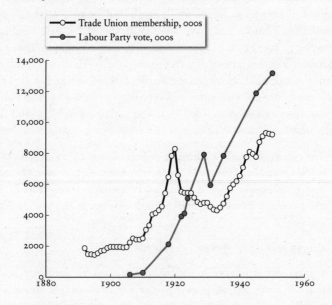

Source: A. H. Halsey (ed.), *Trends in British Society since 1900* (London, 1972), Tables 4.12 and 8.

party's admiration for the British state and elements of the elite. Tom Nairn suggested Labour

> 'stands not for class and nation – this is the ideological halo – but for class-in-nation; or more exactly, for nation-over-class. Labour is (to employ one of its own historic programme-words in a different sense) the nationalization of class. What it represents is not the class, in a sociological sense – the raw or material social reality of class – but the class as seduced by the nation.'[54]

It wanted a classless nation, one in which the working class would dissolve into its proper place in the nation. But the nation was a higher thing than class, or socialism. By 1951 workers voted as never before for Labour, who got nearly 50 per cent of the vote, the highest ever. But the nation's electoral system lost them their parliamentary majority. They left office without complaint.

9

From Class to Nation

On the birth, the proper feeding and the healthy upbringing
of a substantially increased number of children, depends the
life of Britain and her enduring glory.
                Mr Churchill's Declaration to the Electors, 1945

The first reason why a health scheme of this sort is necessary
at all is because it has been the firm conclusion of all parties
that money ought not to be permitted to stand in the way of
obtaining an efficient health service.
                Aneurin Bevan, House of Commons, 1946[1]

In 1945 and 1946, we were attacked on our housing policy
by every spiv in the country – for what is Toryism, except
organized spivery? They wanted to let the spivs loose.
                Aneurin Bevan, Manchester 4 July 1948

The story of the 'welfare state' as it came to be known in the 1950s, became one of the central stories in the history of the twentieth-century United Kingdom. It needs to be kept in proportion. In the first half of the century warfare was overall a far more important function of the state than welfare, and innovation in welfare was less important than in warfare than came to be believed. Another way we need to recalibrate the story is to get rid of the assumption that welfare was novel, and that only the state ever provided it. The story of welfare is not so much about whether welfare should be provided, but rather on what basis, and at what level, and of course who paid and how. We also need to refresh our sense of the timing of the welfare states's arrival, especially comparatively. The British welfare system of the interwar years was by international standards very comprehensive, the celebrated post-war welfare state much less so. Furthermore, although welfare expenditures were larger in the late 1940s than in the late 1930s, the largest increase in expenditure over the period came from the expansion of the warfare state.

We need also to beware the common and politically charged thesis that the welfare state was invented by the Edwardian Liberal Party and made complete by the Labour Party after 1945. This thesis, the standard history of the British welfare state, was first outlined by Richard Titmuss in the 1950s. His story is one of 'the great surge in legislation ... during the decade before the First World War' and then of how 'the second great revolution of this century in social care, beginning after Dunkirk and quickening into effect after 1945, continued the process'.[2] In this account the poor quality of recruits to the Boer War led to school medical inspections, school meals in elementary schools and efforts to reduce infant mortality. The Second World War had a more general effect, for it depended on 'virtually the effort of all citizens', united by calls for 'social justice'. In the Second World War, 'The social measures that were developed during the war centred on the primary needs of the whole population irrespective of class, creed or military category.' The trend was towards 'universalizing public provision'; the reforms of the 1940s were the result in part of wartime strategy which needed to 'fuse and unify the conditions of life of civilians and non-civilians alike' with a particular emphasis on support for dependants. By contrast, the Boer War and First World War are seen by Titmuss as imposing costs down to the 1950s, including war pensions and widows' benefits.[3] This account continues to structure textbook accounts to this day, though the positive effects of the First World War have become more prominent, and the Second has been treated more critically.[4] It is, however, very misleading about the actual development of the welfare state, which, as we shall see, owes a very great deal to innovations of the 1920s. Reluctantly, under great pressure, and with an eye to constraining expenditure, the state moved in as a key agent in organizing for the support of people afflicted by sickness and unemployment and in old age. By 1950 the United Kingdom had a uniquely universalistic system of health service provision, of pensions and of unemployment and sickness benefits which did away with much of the private and mutual provision. It was, however, not generous, or in many respects novel.

WELFARE MYTHS

The story of state welfare is encrusted with myths. One of the most persistent is the assumption that before the 1940s there was little welfare of any kind, public or private. There was plenty of both types. Welfare was not just a matter for central government, and it flowed through both public and private channels. Indeed, insurance companies had agents who penetrated down to perhaps a majority of households, rather like the rent-collector. Working-class mutual organizations – not least trade unions – had an important role as what were called 'friendly societies', providing insurance benefits for their members – from unemployment to sickness benefits and even pensions. For example the Durham Miners' Relief Society, for a 6d (2.5p) weekly contribution from miners (the only source of funds) provided a retirement pension (at sixty) or disability pension of 8s weekly. Nearly 90 per cent of miners in the northeast and Cumberland were covered by this and similar schemes by 1913.[5] But most people were outside such organizations, usually because they could not afford to be in them, and in any case before 1914 only a small percentage of employees were in unions. The state, especially at local level, provided services for the indigent. There was a 'mixed economy' of welfare.[6] The most needy did get support from the community in 1900, as they were to do in 1950. However, the basis of that support, its nature, and its justification, and its extent, would change.

Just as we should not equate poverty and misery with the lack of a welfare system, nor should we attribute its diminution to the advance of a welfare state. The so-called welfare state had little to do with the reduction of poverty – as it advanced it made poverty more bearable than it would otherwise have been. Dearth was eased primarily by the increased earnings of the poorest, helped by trade unions. As dearth decreased so did disease, dirt and despair. In that process state-provided education, housing and public amenities and health services made their contribution, but they were not the only factor.

Between 1900 and 1950 life chances were transformed. The greatest change was not in that people lived longer but that death rates for children went right down. At the beginning of the century the first years of life were exceptionally dangerous, 14 per cent of infants died within a year of birth, and down to around the age of ten death came easily. Children up to four years old were as likely to die in 1900 as people from their mid-sixties to mid-seventies, and at more than ten times the rate of twenty-year-olds. For children under one year, death rates were down to 10 per cent by 1914, and 5 per cent by 1938. By 1938 young children were as likely to die as fifty-year-olds. For those who reached old age there was little change in later life chances. For over-sixty-fives, death rates fell only slightly. Already in 1900 the most common age of death for adult males was in the late sixties; by 1950 it was in the seventies.[7]

That astonishing progress in the life chances of children, such that they ceased to be as likely to die as the elderly, was common to many rich countries. It was not due to medicine – the standard treatable or vaccinated-against infectious diseases accounted for small proportions of deaths; immediate causes of death were very varied. The most dramatic medical intervention was thanks to the rapid introduction of the sulphonamides in the 1930s, which led to a radical fall in deaths of women in childbirth from puerperal fever. One of the most important changes in the overall health of the nation came from the drastic reduction in drinking during and after the Great War, brought about by tighter licensing of pubs, and higher duties on beer and spirits. Drinking was very largely a matter of men drinking beer in pubs. The consumption of both beer and spirits halved between 1900 and the interwar years. Improvement in the life expectancy of young children came from better nutrition, housing and the environment of the very poor in particular, including sanitation. Indeed, British children grew, on average, physically taller through these years.

Another powerful myth is that the world wars improved civilian health by virtue of improved nutrition, and public health (and for some, more economic equality) led to health improvement. In fact both world wars saw a temporary worsening of health. Infant mortality saw a slight worsening in 1915.[8] In 1940–41 similarly there was a setback. But in both cases there was a resumption of progress at the pre-war rate.[9] The temporary worsening of this, and other measures of health, was not due to bombing or differential recruitment into the military – it applied to all ages, and all places. Nor was it due to road traffic accidents. The phenomenon is itself only very partially known, and has tended to be explained away. Wartime improvements in health, attributed to specific wartime effects, became a cliché in celebratory commentary about the Second World War in particular.

Lastly, state welfare was no more a drain on wealth than private welfare. Nor, in the period we are concerned with in this chapter, did it redistribute income – it was confined to workers and very largely paid for by them, through special taxes. Tax allowances (for children, for saving, for pensions), for example, though financially equivalent to benefits, are given very different political (and thus historical) treatment. Secondly the welfare state was not the only state welfare system. There were more generous state welfare provisions for servants of the state, whether veterans, or other employees of the state, than for mere citizens.

BEFORE THE GREAT WAR

In the Edwardian years the welfare measures of the central state were limited compared to the continued efforts of the local state. Under the ancient, but amended, poor laws, there was local provision made for the destitute through means-tested poor relief. It was carried out by Poor Law Guardians, financed by local property taxes (the 'rates') increasingly subsidized by central (sometimes known as 'imperial') taxes. It included outdoor relief and indeed hospital care too. Poor law institutions and methods, taxation rather than insurance funding, and the means test, under different names and often shifted to central government control, remained important, though a politically necessary account stressed its supersession in stages by a new welfare state. To put it another way, the means test never went away.

The first major national partial departure from the *local* poor law model through centralization was the 1908 Old Age Pension Act. It provided a non-contributory pension to the very old (over seventy), and very poor (determined by means test), at a level which was not meant to be sufficient to live on, but a supplement to other income, a miserly maximum of 5s (£0.25) a week, one-eighth of a worker's wage. It was paid through post offices. A clear majority of the recipients were women. It was meant to reach those who would not apply for degrading poor relief, and indeed to take some aged poor off poor relief (as it did). The number of old people on poor relief went down very markedly and quickly, once various restrictions applying to those who had claimed poor relief were lifted.[10] As we have seen the increased funds come from the tax hikes of Lloyd George's so-called 'People's Budget' of 1909, although, as we have also seen, at least as much went to *additional* battleships.

The second important welfare reform of the last Liberal government was the National Insurance Act of 1911. This provided compulsory state-backed, but essentially worker- and employer-financed, sickness insurance for workers earning less than £160 per annum, the level below which no income tax was paid; this covered four-fifths of the employed population. Its aims were limited to the financial support of the worker, the breadwinner, when sick, and to provide non-hospital medical care, again for that breadwinner only. It was a compulsory insurance system, which David Lloyd George claimed gave the worker a package of 'ninepence for fourpence', only 2d came from the state, the rest from workers and employers. The support it gave was distinctly ungenerous: sickness benefit was a flat-rate 10 shillings (50p) a week. A skilled male worker might be on £100 a year, or £2 per week, so sickness benefit was only one-quarter of his wage. These figures were for men in Great Britain; men in Ireland paid and received less, as did women everywhere. National Insurance contributions were a poll-tax on workers, independent of income. National Insurance was administered through 'approved societies', including friendly societies which had previously supplied health insurance to a minority of workers, and also by private life assurance companies engaged in 'industrial assurance', that is, insurance for the working classes, such as the Prudential Assurance Company, which insured over 4 million workers under the scheme by 1946.[11]

This was far from a comprehensive health insurance scheme. It paid sickness benefit to the usually, but not always, male breadwinner when incapacitated. In terms of access to doctors it applied to workers only, not their families; it did not cover hospital services for all. It was not, nor was it ever intended to be, an insurance-based health service for all. This is not to say there was no medicine for the poor. On the contrary, there was government support for hospitals, through poor law infirmaries, and municipal hospitals too. There was also voluntary provision, with many savings schemes available to workers and their families. Medicine was always largely of the people, and largely free, at least for the working class. There was also a notable set of developments under local authorities outside the poor law regime. One important form which concerns about 'national efficiency' took was worry about the health of infants and children, and indeed the Edwardian period saw many developments of local government effort in this direction, and the extension of specific welfare measures for infants and children was a feature of the Second World War.[12]

The 1911 act also provided compulsory unemployment insurance (which required an additional flat-rate contribution) for a small fraction of workers, some 2 million in total. The rationale was that support was needed in industries where work was seasonal (building and civil engineering), or where the business cycle was strong (hence the inclusion of shipbuilding and vehicle building).[13] The flat-rate unemployment benefit came to only 7s (35p) a week. It was assumed only men worked in these industries; there was no separate rate for women.

State funding for the new National Insurance was minimal, as intended. This, as well as the low flat-rate contributions (though, as we have noted, with different rates for women, etc.) leading to low flat-rate benefits would be central to the future British social insurance model. The system was attractive precisely because it had a built-in limit to contributions and benefits – increasing both would harm the lowest paid most. Although often compared with the German system from which it in part originated, it was in fact crucially different in that continental systems had graduated contributions and benefits. They were also available to many fewer workers.

National Insurance was a way of preventing the redistribution of tax income. It was largely self-financed by workers and employers. This is not to say that tax funding would have in itself been progressive. Only the middle class and above paid income tax. However, workers were taxed through excise duties. Beer duty raised £13 million before the war (enough for the old-age pension) and £70 million in the interwar years (enough for the entire Royal Navy). In the pre-war years 10 per cent of the cost of a pint of beer went on duty, and some 5 per cent of the income of a working man might go on beer duties in the 1920s.[14] In the 1920s an 'ordinary fairly careful working man' who smoke and drank might in effect end up paying 10 per cent of his income in tax.[15]

BENEFITS FOR WARRIORS

The Great War was not so much a mobilization of society as the bringing of millions into the direct and indirect service of the state, notably in the new volunteer and conscript armies. Employment by the state implied support for widows and dependants and also for the families with an absent breadwinner on a low wage. Military officers, like senior civil servants, had long had retirement pensions and other benefits; their widows too were supported, with payments through the Post Office. Other ranks' wives 'on the strength' (that is, part of the army) got a widow's pension from the Boer War, at 5s (25p) a week. But off-the-strength wives depended on organized philanthropy.[16] At the beginning of the Great War, widows' pensions for all wives of other ranks were introduced. With conscription came a Ministry of Pensions to pay this and other aid to the forces and families. It remained in place after the war to pay pensions to widows and dependants, and also to veterans. The vast system of support for injured veterans and widows was the main spender on welfare in 1920s United Kingdom (see table 9.1). War pensions were not based on contributions, were rank dependent and were more generous than civil benefits. After the war the old-age pension and the new contributory widow's pension (1925) was at a flat rate of 10s (50p), less than half the war widow's pension of a widow of a private. This comparison should not be read as a criticism – they were intended to be very different sorts of payments. Indeed, war pensions were not as generous as many wished, and in contrast to Germany, there was very significant charitable and voluntary support for disabled servicemen, which was one reason for the political quiescence of British veterans.[17]

The new armies required the general recognition of the existence of wives and dependants. They and dependants were to be paid separation allowances (once available only to on-the-strength wives). These were payments, part of the wages of the soldiers, but paid to wives. At first there was a very heavy charitable and voluntary element.[18] The allowance was also a benefit, in as much as it depended on the number of children, and of course was not paid to unmarried soldiers. Officers' dependants would not have separation allowances until the end of the war.

There was another, specifically military benefit. Immediately after the war, for a little over a year, a generous scheme of unemployment benefit specifically for ex-servicemen and munitions workers operated. The Treasury funded an 'out of work donation' which lasted to March 1921 (for servicemen: for civilians in the arms industry it lasted only to November 1919). It paid out £60 million, the number of claimants peaking at just over 1 million. It was highly discriminatory and outside the insurance and poor law systems. It was more generous financially and included provision for dependants (as had the separation allowances granted to service personnel).

INSURANCE FOR THE WORKING CLASS

The welfare state for veterans and dependants run by the Ministry of Pensions, and the 'out of work' donation, raised the issue that it was not just military and arms personnel who had served; others too had worked for their country. In response to this and the great labour agitation of the immediate post-war years, the Liberal-Conservative coalition created a comprehensive welfare system for the working class based on the National Insurance model. In 1916 the National Insurance unemployment insurance was extended to munitions workers, taking the total insured to over 3 million. The great change in unemployment benefit provision came with the 1920 National Insurance Act, which created compulsory unemployment insurance for the great majority of workers (12 million) earning below £250 per annum (major exclusions were domestic and agricultural workers, and permanent railway workers, civil servants and local government employees). It was not generous: benefits were restricted to fifteen weeks and to 15s (75p) for men and 12s (60p) for women. As under the 1911 act, unemployment benefit was paid at a flat rate (though different for men, women, boys and girls) irrespective of circumstances. However, 1921 saw a vitally important emergency change, which became permanent in 1922: the introduction of dependants' allowances, because the sum was simply not enough to fund a family.[19] Another important extension to the insurance system was the 1925 act which created compulsory contributory widows', orphans' and old-age pensions (again for workers earning less than £250 per annum), provisions extended in 1929. This gave contributory pensions for sixty-five- to seventy-year-olds and maintenance for widows (with no government contribution) at 10s (50p) for the single pensioner or widow, that is, well under unemployment benefit. At seventy the pensioners moved on to the provisions of the 1908 act, where the pension was also, as of 1919, 10s per week. The contributions were paid by all who contributed to national health insurance with the same stamp (on a form now labelled National Health and Pension Insurance).[20] All were managed, using approved societies, by the Ministry of Health (established in 1919). This ministry, also responsible for local government, was thus responsible for the bulk of the complex system of social services: pensions, health insurance, hospitals, the poor law and housing. The new Ministry of Labour ran unemployment insurance.

Table 9.1: Central and local government expenditure on social services, 1920–38

	Gross public expenditure, central government, on selected social services £million (for contributory schemes, only the amount paid by central government is given).					Local government total expenditure on selected social services £million	
	Old-age pension (non-contributory, over 70s)	Ministry of Pensions (Armed Services and dependants only)	Contributory pensions (ages 65–70)	Ministry of Labour unemployment	Ministry of Health/National Health Insurance	Poor relief (local)	Housing
1920	19.3	99.4	–	3.3	10.7	19.2	1.4
1925	25.8	69.0	–	14.4	21.1	31.5	18.1
1933	39.7	46.9	11.0	77.9	22.2	32.7	41.8
1938	45.4	40.2	16.0	23.7	25.7	34.3	42.3

Source: B. R. Mitchell with P. Deane, *Abstract of British Historical Statistics* (Cambridge, 1962), Table Public Finance 4a, p. 400; Table Public Finance 10, p. 418. In this period the combined employees' and employers' contributions added up to £70–100 million, with employers paying slightly more than half. These contributions, not included above, accounted for most health insurance expenditure, and most of the contributory pension too (Charles Mowat, *Britain between the Wars, 1918–1940* (Chicago, 1955), pp. 496–7). In calendar year 1938, the insurance fund paid out £51 million in unemployment benefit, and got in £42 million from employees and employers. Ministry of Labour. *Report for the Year 1938, 1938–39* [Cmd. 6016], Appendix XXI.

Table 9.2: The structure of interwar social services: expenditure and contributions

Public social services expenditure and receipts, 1936, England and Wales £000					
Expenditure	Receipts				
	Total expenditure	Contributions, etc.	Parliamentary vote	Local rates and block grants	Total receipts
Unemployment benefit	38,319	38,407	19,078		57,485
Unemployment allowances	34,708	-	34,708		34,708
National health insurance	35,553	32,221	6,742		38,963
Widows', orphans' and old-age pensions*	40,487	27,924			27,924
Old-age pension	40,009		40,009		40,009
War pensions	35,535		35,535		35,535
Education	100,454	7,999	46,670	45,785	100,454
Public health hospitals	14,261	934	63	13,264	14,261
Housing	37,304	19,788	13,911	3,605	37,304
Poor relief	44,283	3,453	3,987	36,843	44,283
Total (including small sums not included above)	431,550	133,471	201,574	107,230	442,275

* The balance came from Exchequer contributions but was not technically a vote so not included.

Source: Public Social Services (Total Expenditure under Certain Acts of Parliament), etc. 1938–39 [Cmd. 5906].

The Liberal–Conservative and Conservative welfare state for nearly the whole working class was remarkable for its scope and for its nature. Crucially the programme was based on a flat-rate contribution and benefit insurance principle, as a very deliberate way to constrain expenditure to what the poorer working class could pay.[21] Rights accrued to the employed payer of the contribution, and through them to dependants, who were now (in contrast to pre-war sickness insurance and the old-age pension) supported. Benefits for dependants had gender implications – most workers were men; most women were married and did not work outside the home. This raises the question of whether this dimension was a product of the wartime separation allowance or the post-war decision to use the insurance principle.[22] It is clear that the insurance system based on workers was quite different from Labour's ideas of benefits to those who needed them funded by taxation.

These insurance measures were for the long term but could not cope with the mounting unemployment from 1920–21, as many of the unemployed had either not paid in enough yet to qualify or their unemployment outlasted the fifteen-week limit. A new act of 1921 introduced limited additional 'uncovenanted benefit' or 'extended benefit' (later called 'transitional benefit') at the discretion of the state, a provision which changed from discretion to right back and forth over the 1920s. From 1921 onwards, the supplementary schemes paid more (just) in each year than the standard benefit.[23] These benefits were administered by poor law authorities and successors, until taken in hand by a new national Unemployment Assistance Board. Local committees were often quite generous, and the nationalization of 1934 generally lowered rates, which is why it met with protests. From 1931 and to some extent earlier, these benefits were means-tested, and on the basis of the household means test, which caused deep resentment. In 1936 most of the unemployed were supported roughly equally by the insurance scheme and the new Unemployment Assistance Board, and a further 20 per cent came under the Public Assistance Committees.[24] It should be noted that the insurance system was not (as the scheme intended) self-financing. It was kept going by loans from the state, loans paid back in the late 1930s; by the Second World War the insurance fund was in surplus.

Liberal-Conservative and Conservative governments created, and adapted, a remarkably comprehensive welfare system. For all the excoriation of scroungers, and the indignities and unfairness of the household means test, no Briton, even an able-bodied one, would be left to starve, nor crucially were most left to be cared for under poor relief. The expenditures were huge and marked a transformation of the state. The pre-1914 central state spent half its expenditure on the armed forces; the major expenditures of the interwar state were welfare (both for war pensions and the civil welfare functions) and debt interest (welfare for the rich). By contrast with the pre-war years the interwar state was a welfare state.

Conservative central government also transformed local social services. A notable development was the abolition of the poor law authorities under the Conservative 1929 Local Government Act (the responsibility of the minister of health, Neville Chamberlain), and their replacement by public assistance committees. Poor law hospitals, municipal hospitals and voluntary hospitals all expanded, as did provision for child welfare (under the Maternity and Child Welfare Act 1918).[25] In Manchester fairly comprehensive municipal hospital and other welfare facilities were available from the 1930s. Even in the case of the voluntaries – which had contribution schemes – 'the provision was for the community'.[26]

There was also expansion in municipal housing provision following the Housing Act passed by the Labour minister of health John Wheatley, in 1924, building on the Housing Act of 1919. This was the origin of very significant 'council house' building in the 1920s, often in the form of 'estates' on greenfield sites, some the size of towns, such as the Knowle estate in Bristol, Wythenshawe in Manchester, or Becontree outside London. Becontree had 25,000 houses by 1935 and was described as the largest public housing project in the world. Most of the estate was built in a time when coal fires and gas lighting were still the future. It was to provide housing for the new Ford works at nearby Dagenham, and other modern enterprises.

Workers, the richer among them, could move into well-appointed, council-owned, three-bedroom, semi-detached housing, and along with the middle class into similar private homes financed by cheap mortgages (a direct consequence of the new economic policies of the

1930s).[27] In terms of numbers, in the 1930s, there was a private build-ing boom: some 1 million houses in a few years (350,000 per annum). Never had so many houses been built, and the total would only be exceeded in the very late 1960s. By 1938 owner-occupation had increased from 10 per cent before the war to around 30 per cent; council-house occupation from very little to around 10 per cent. At the bottom of the housing market were appalling private rented slums.

MAKING INSURANCE WORK

The idea that the post-war Labour government created the welfare state out of little, and that it did so in the wake of the great popular mobilization of the war, dies hard. This interpretation became cen-tral especially from the 1960s. Thus A. J. P. Taylor ended his *English History* with the claim that in the war 'the British people came of age. This was a people's war ... Imperial greatness was on the way out; the welfare state was on the way in'.[28] In the nation 'which faced defeat between 1940 and 1942,' wrote Angus Calder, in *The People's War* (the book title that essentially coined the term in the standard sense used in British historiography), were the 'seeds of a new democ-racy'; the rulers had to ensure the cooperation of all society by making 'concessions in the direction of a higher standard of living for the poor, greater social equality and improved welfare services'.[29] A whole historiography developed, claiming a wartime consensus around the need to create a welfare state, brought into being after 1945.[30] This has been challenged in three distinct ways: firstly, whether there was a consensus;[31] secondly, to what extent the welfare measures were as generous or novel as they appeared;[32] and thirdly, by taking a fresh look at the war from a perspective much broader than that of the historiography of the social services, noting the new inequalities the war produced, and the diminution of the social ser-vices for civilians during the war.[33] Yet the key point was long in the literature, though seemingly forgotten. This was that in the 1930s there already was an elaborate system of welfare for the working class (that is, around 80 per cent of the population): all was ready for Sir William Beveridge to rationalize, and 'by the legislation of

1945–1948 the gaps were filled, the walls finished, and a roof put over all'.[34] That was for the future – the United Kingdom went through the war with weakened pre-war welfare services; what was promised for the future was their extension, not a radical change. The United Kingdom went to war in September 1939 with a welfare state already in place.

The tendency in the older arguments was to stress the often unachieved desire and need for universal, unifying, welfare measures in the British case, stimulated by the necessary unity brought about through war. But this is to misunderstand both war and welfare. Modern war, and especially British war, did not put everyone in the same boat. New discriminations arose. War divided society into those needed for the war effort and those who were not. As in the Great War there were very different provisions for the armed services and arms workers in the war, with important new discriminations arising. Firstly, although conscripts' wages were low, benefits for dependants were higher than for dependants of the unemployed. The war widow's pension remained considerably higher than the state widow's pension or indeed unemployment benefit or public assistance. These were all £1.30 per week in 1948; while a single war widow got £1 15s (£1.75) to £2 if the widow of someone who had served in the ranks; an officer's widow was given a yearly sum of £150 to £350, say £3 to £7 per week (all figures for a single childless person).[35] During the war the disparity was even greater, as the civil widow's pension was only 10s (50p) (see below). Service personnel got better food than the average civilian. Their food allocation, known as the Home Service Ration, was very generous and included significantly larger quantities of foods than covered by the civilian ration, including at least twice the quantity of meat.[36] Many arms factory workers could get additional quantities of otherwise rationed foods in canteens.

Health provision during the war became increasingly discriminatory. The Emergency Medical Service, sometimes wrongly seen as the wartime predecessor to the NHS, was not designed to improve health care in general but to deal with military and air-raid casualties. It led to the emptying of hospitals. Some new hospitals were built for the EMS, such as the Churchill, near Oxford, but after lying empty it was handed over to the US army. Civil doctors went into the forces, leaving fewer doctors to deal with civilians. It was service personnel who got the Penicillin or the vastly increased supplies of sulphonamides.[37] In some cases, however, civilians directly engaged in dangerous warlike operations were hardly in a different position from before the war – the merchant navy stands out here.[38] The war was bad for social services; so bad indeed that this in itself promoted post-war reform. It was the dire treatment of the old, for example, that pricked people's consciences.[39] As Titmuss put it: 'Somebody had to pay the price of war by going without, waiting longer, getting less or being pushed about to make room for others', noting that 'among those who suffered most were the poorest, the most helpless and the "useless" members of the community.'[40] Far from being universal provision of hospital treatment, there was a hierarchy at work, with the aged and chronic sick at the bottom, followed by the ordinary sick and expectant mothers in need of beds, air-raid casualties, evacuees and, at the top, 'Service patients, the most favoured group of all, who got the lion's share of hospital care throughout the war'.[41] The war 'deprived the civilian population of a large part of its pre-war medical resources', not only in hospitals, but in dental surgeries, schools, maternity and child welfare clinics and public health. GP services were badly affected, a decrease of over one-third, and of those left many were old.[42] In 1943, in the United Kingdom, there were five times more doctors per soldier than per civilian.[43] Only minimal claims may be made for wartime extensions of social services: the increase in the number of school meals, their provision beyond the really needy, the national milk scheme for nursing mothers and children and improvements to the old-age pension. Some groups, children, nursing mothers, the infirm had special supplements and concessions. It might be noted that the focus was on areas of welfare pioneered before the Great War, a maternalist and pronatalist emphasis which was important through the Second World War, especially for Conservatives. Indeed, many of the programmes highlighted were extensions of growing 1930s provision.[44]

There were in fact two other areas of wartime reform of some note in the social services. There was a relaxation in the means test from the interwar household system to one focused on individuals or couples, which meant it ceased to be so contentious.[45] A significant reform was made during the war with the Old Age and Widow's Pension Act 1940. It was clearly not the war, but the pre-war conditions and campaigns, not least by pensioners, which led to it – it was indeed passed by the National government, before the formation of the coalition in May 1940. This act reduced the contributory pension age for women to sixty, but made supplementing it with means-tested benefits a matter for the central state (the Assistance Board, as the Unemployment Assistance Board had become), not local authorities. A key point was that the act did not raise the dire level of the pension (indeed the war was used as an argument against doing so, though proponents noted that money was not short for fighting the war), but applications for relief were very much larger than expected – 1.5 million pensioners applied, rather than the anticipated 0.4 million.[46] For the poorest of these pensioners the overall benefit they got was nearly twice the standard pension, bringing it up to almost £1.[47] It is notable that there was no increase in the basic pension (10s, or 50p) from 1919 to 1946.[48]

During the Second World War there were, in many countries, plans for fresh universalistic and social services.[49] In December 1942, the economist, expert in social insurance and former director of the London School of Economics Sir William Beveridge published his famous report advocating a new system of 'social security', as he called it, based centrally on compulsory 'social insurance'. In a broadcast to accompany the publication of his December 1942 report on *Social Insurance and Allied Services*, Sir William Beveridge started by invoking the Atlantic Charter, which he said 'speaks of securing for all improved labour standards, economic advancement and social security', going on to say that his scheme gave effect to those last two words, 'social security'.[50] He was reflecting the liberal internationalism of the time rather than the nationalist framing which later historians have given the proposals.

He called for 'social insurance against interruption and destruction of earning power and for special expenditure arising at birth, marriage or death'.[51] 'The State should offer security for service and contribution. The State ... should not stifle incentive, opportunity, responsibility; in establishing a national minimum, it should leave room and encouragement for voluntary action by each individual to provide more than that minimum for himself and his family.'[52] He was very aware of the gendered nature of his focus on earners. Rhetorically it called for compulsory social insurance (for all, not just the working class) at the core, with national assistance and voluntary contributions filling holes. Beveridge endorsed the flat-rate contribution, and flat-rate benefits, with no means testing or time limit.[53] Benefits were to be set at 'subsistence' level (but see below). There were, however, some important novelties which were required by this plan: the universal family (that is children's) allowance and the new comprehensive health system, which owed little to Beveridge. In short, what was novel was not all due to Beveridge; and what was due to Beveridge was by no means all novel.

The problem for Beveridge was that the near-comprehensive insurance system of the 1920s had not in fact worked very well. Unemployment insurance could not cope with high levels of unemployment, one important reason for Beveridge to stress the low unemployment condition. High unemployment implied a different system. The coalition committed itself to maintain a high level of employment in the 1944 Employment Policy White Paper. The problem was wished away and did not arise in practice for many years. The second major problem was that Beveridge's scheme could not provide subsistence-level pensions. So great is this problem that it in effect makes the whole Beveridge scheme take on a new look. Pensions, some two-thirds of the projected expenditure (and about one half if children's allowances are included) were – in Beveridge's plan – to stay very considerably lower than other subsistence benefits (Beveridge proposed 14s (70p) as compared with the existing 10s (50p), a tiny increase in real terms). 'Universality legitimated the insurance principle, and the insurance principle legitimated inadequate pensions.'[54] Insurance-based universal subsistence pensions could not be funded by flat-rate insurance. In Beveridge's scheme poor pensioners were forced to remain on supplementary means-tested benefits (as under the 1940 act) to get them up to subsistence, only after twenty years would the subsistence universal retirement pension be payable.[55] Furthermore, the new pension was paid not as of right to old women as under the still-operating 1908 act, but on the basis of the working partner's contributions.[56] In short, except in universalization, this was no advance on the position of 1940, in this, the crucial benefit. This position was not forced on Beveridge – he, and Keynes, wished it so.[57] What Beveridge proposed was in fact politically unacceptable, and the government was forced to concede, in 1943, and in public, under pressure from Ernest Bevin, that the full pension would be paid from the beginning of the new scheme.[58] The 1944 White Paper (which rejected subsistence, stressing the importance of contributions), set the pension at 20s (£1), markedly higher than Beveridge, though still at a very low level. Under Labour, a full rate adjusted up to 26s (£1.30) was adopted immediately (that is before the beginning of the new scheme in 1948). The 1940s universal subsistence pension was thus due to Labour, and not to Beveridge.

Beveridge's proposed system was also dependent on two new tax-funded and comprehensive schemes: children's allowances for all families, whether on benefit or not, and comprehensive health and rehabilitation services, also for all. Family allowances were voted for under the Conservative caretaker government, which ruled briefly between the end of the coalition and the general election in 1945, as a result of a long campaign by the Independent MP Eleanor Rathbone (who sat for Combined English Universities).[59] They were both a pro-natalist, pro-family measure, to give non-taxpayers the support for children that taxpayers got, and in the context of Beveridge a necessary prop to the insurance system, for without family allowances to all, there would be many with families who would be better off unemployed than employed, given that the unemployment benefit was flat-rate. The health services of the 1930s, varied as they were, were not regarded at the time as being in a state of crisis, rather the contrary. They were well regarded generally speaking. Furthermore, the call for something like an NHS as it emerged was a minority taste.[60] But there was a move towards thinking about a more planned and coordinated system, and crucially one which was free, but the form it would take was up for discussion.

NATIONALIZING THE SOCIAL SERVICES

The National Insurance Act of 1946 was the key Beveridgean measure. It was passed into law by the minister of national insurance, Jim

Griffiths, a former Welsh miner. It extended to everyone (with special contributions for those not working or self-employed) and not just workers below a certain threshold (which had been raised to £420 in 1940), a compulsory insurance system based on a flat-rate contribution for many benefits previously restricted and only available under separate schemes from the 1920s – it provided unemployment, widow's, orphan's, sickness and retirement pensions, all at around 26s (£1.30) for a single person. Unemployment benefit and sickness was still time restricted (though more generously than before the war): Beveridge had suggested no limit, but the 1944 White Paper proposed them, and Labour stuck to a limit. The flat-rate insurance and contribution principle made the system regressive. Indeed, it had been consistently opposed by the Labour Party for just this reason, but by 1937 the Labour Party accepted insurance pensions and was to endorse their continuation and the extension of the insurance principle. However, the new universal near-subsistence pension for all which Labour insisted on was a major change, as it did not require a build-up of contributions, as Beveridge had suggested. There was another major change. The role of private and mutual bodies in the provision of insurance was eliminated. The new Ministry of National Insurance (established in the former German Embassy in 1944) ran the whole system and would also take over all the benefits from the other ministries after the war, as well as the (military) Ministry of Pensions in 1953.

There were three important tax-based benefits. The Family Allowances Act came into force in 1946. Allowances for second and subsequent children were set at 5s (25p) (paid to 4.5 million children), rather than the 8s (40p) suggested by Beveridge. That it was below subsistence is clear from the fact that from 1951 the unemployed were not expected to depend on family allowance alone for second and subsequent children – a supplement to the allowance was added. Already another key principle was eroded, with low universal benefits meaning that recourse had to be made to supplements to benefits, or to national assistance. The second tax-based benefit was national assistance, under the National Assistance Act of 1948 which gave central and local support, on a means-tested basis, for those not provided for, or insufficiently provided for, by the insurance system (which included more than a quarter of pensioner households in the mid-1950s). It took over the Assistance Board. The third was health-care under the National Health Service, providing the only universal benefit giving services at a level the middle class would consider adequate.

The National Health Service Act provided a health service out of taxation (though many believed it was funded by the insurance stamp) on a universal basis. The NHS radically generalized the existing but limited principle of free service at the time of need, now for all. Importantly, the NHS did away with national health insurance, with private health insurance for the family, with municipally funded hospital services, with contributory schemes for voluntary hospitals and, for the middle classes, much private medicine. The NHS was a distinctly Labour creation in that it was a national and nationalized service, but it was not the only sort of health service which Labour could have created. Some had argued for in effect a radical extension of municipal health services. Indeed, one of the great novel strands in British medicine – social medicine or public health – suffered a defeat and went into decline, marginalized by remaining in local authority control. The National Health Service was the creation of the Ministry of Health, under another Welsh miner, Aneurin Bevan. He made a deal and entrenched the medical elite, the voluntary hospital consultants, not only in their hospitals and associated medical schools, but in the medical system more generally.

It was a huge reorganization, but it did not involve any extension of actual medical services. No significant civil hospital was built in the late 1940s, and what expansion in capacity there was during and after the war might not have been enough to raise bed provision per capita.[61] Essentially the NHS continued the health services of the 1930s, varied as they were, because they were not regarded at the time as being in a state of crisis, rather the contrary.[62] The break was not perhaps as radical as popular history suggests. Instead, 'the NHS built on one of the great virtues of the previous hospital arrangements. It inherited the goodwill enjoyed by pre-war hospitals as community institutions . . . Hospitals seemed to be provided by and for the majority of the population.'[63]

The Ministry of Health under Aneurin Bevan was still the interwar ministry and was thus still responsible for local government and housing. The war saw a collapse in investment in housing, with slow recuperation in the late 1940s, typically not reaching the levels of the 1930s until the 1950s. However, in the 1940s, the proportion of public housing being built was significantly greater than in the 1930s. Bevan was notable for insisting on high specifications for these post-war council houses and, in another sign of the significance of universalism, changed the law so that councils could build houses for anyone, not just the working classes.

The great legislative activity of the late 1940s, important as it was in establishing new universal systems on both old and new principles, should not be confused with a massive extension of welfare spending. 'Labour in the 1940s constructed an austerity welfare state', in which new consumption of resources was minimal.[64] The biggest new expenditure was on the pension. The total of public expenditure, whether from rates (local taxes) or taxes, on the social services (that is excluding employer and employee contributions) was 2.1 per cent of national income in 1900–1901, 2.9 per cent in 1910–11 and essentially unchanged a decade later. But through the interwar years the increases were notable: to 5.2 per cent by 1925–6 and 8.2 per cent a decade later; the proportion actually fell to 6.8 per cent in 1947–8, only to increase with the creation of the NHS in 1948–9 to 10.7 per cent.[65]

The rise in welfare spending was much greater following the Great War than the Second World War, and after around 1950 the rise in public spending was remarkably low, certainly lower than in the interwar years.[66] Sidney Pollard cautioned long ago that: 'In spite of a widespread belief to the contrary, the United Kingdom did not spend significantly more on the social services after 1948 than she did before 1939 apart from the retirement pension.'[67] In the mid-1930s total public and private health spending amounted to £150 million (about 3 per cent of GNP, of which public expenditure was around 1.2 per cent).[68] That would have been worth around £300 million in the late 1940s, which suggests, since in the early years the NHS was spending around £400 million, a hardly revolutionary increase of about 25 per cent over a decade. A revised analysis of post-war poverty suggests, contrary to contemporary claims, that post-1936 welfare measures (excluding food subsidies) reduced the number of working-class households below the poverty line by only 3.7 per cent.[69]

The really big expansion in state expenditure between the 1930s and the late 1940s and the early 1950s was not in welfare but in warfare. In the years before the Great War, expenditures on social services (by all public authorities) were lower but similar to expenditures on the armed forces. In the interwar years, by strong contrast, they were notably greater than warfare expenditures. In the years after the Second World War, although welfare expenditure was higher than warfare expenditure, the gap had narrowed. The post-Second World War state had a higher warfare-to-welfare ratio than in the interwar state.[70] In 1950–51 the Labour government put warfare spending well above welfare spending in its priorities. It rearmed on a huge scale, while imposing NHS charges at a trivial but politically significant level. As the Communist Party put it, 'the boasted Welfare State is to be turned into a warfare State' (sic).[71] Aneurin Bevan, now minister of labour, Harold Wilson at the Board of Trade and John Freeman resigned from the government, at least as much over the unrealistically large rearmament programme as over the NHS charges. They were proved right on this. Indeed, the great expansion in British welfare expenditures started in the 1950s, as the huge burden of warlike expenditure decreased, and not in the 1940s, as an old political narrative appeared to dictate.[72] Furthermore, comparative statistical sources, though not the older histories, consistently show that the post-war United Kingdom was a low spender on social services, by comparison with other European nations.[73]

To think of the post-war welfare system as Beveridgean is itself misleading. Beveridge's focus on insurance remained more typical of the continent's system than the British one. A significant element of the British system was in effect a nationalized universal poor law.[74] In the United Kingdom, much expenditure went on either universal provision from taxation (the National Health Service and family allowances) or taxpayer-paid public assistance to the poor not covered or insufficiently covered by the insurance system. In the longer term, the flat-rate contribution, the core of the Beveridge system, was seen as regressive, and the fixed benefits too were seen as too low, and both were abolished.

PART 2

1950–2000

This second half of the book is concerned with the building of the new nation which emerged in the 1940s, and its later dissolution. It deals with but rejects the argument that the period is best thought of in terms of left-overs from liberalism and imperialism, with the novel development of a weak social democracy followed by the rise of neo-liberalism. The focus on the development of the nation in Chapters 10–15 cover the years from 1950 into the 1970s and allows for new ways of framing the key issues in recent British history. The chapters tell of economic development of unprecedented speed, of the creation of an economy more focused on industry than ever before, of a developmental state, a warfare state and a welfare state. Chapter 15 discusses ideas, particularly nationalism and declinism and the writing of new national histories, which characterized this era.

The following two chapters look at different aspects of the crises of the 1970s and early 1980s as important ends and beginnings. They deal with domestic and external affairs. The last three chapters take the story on from the mid-1980s, showing how the economic, political and social nation created in previous decades was consciously downgraded by deliberate moves to European economic integration and globalization. I end with the economic and political triumph of post-national politics, and its apotheosis in British participation in the Iraq War.

The chronological division helps make sense of the story, but for this period in particular creates a problem. Governments were concerned with the very long term (and not as in the cliché only with the length of a parliamentary term). Thus, we cannot understand the limited success of the post-Thatcher economy if we don't appreciate how much it owed to state investments made up to the 1970s.

Parliaments, governments and prime ministers, 1950–2000

Parliament	Government	Prime Minister
1950	Labour	Clement Attlee
1951	Conservative	Winston Churchill
1955		Anthony Eden
		1957 Harold Macmillan
1959		
		1963 Sir Alec Douglas-Home
1964	Labour	Harold Wilson
1966		
1970	Conservative	Edward Heath
1974 February	Labour minority	Harold Wilson
1974 October	Labour Labour minority from 1976	1976 James Callaghan

1979	Conservative	Margaret Thatcher
1983		
1987		
		1990 John Major
1992		
1997	New Labour	Tony Blair

NB: detailed election results are available online. Note that into the 1970s results for the Conservatives usually include those for National Liberals and Ulster Unionists.

10

A Nation in the World

We are proud of the British Commonwealth and Empire. We believe it has a part to play in the future of the world. By its action in 1939 it saved the forces of freedom and democracy from extinction. We reaffirm the principle of Imperial Preference, believing that it will help both us and Empire peoples to solve our economic difficulties.

Margaret Thatcher, 1950, General Election Address[1]

The Communist Party fights for the national independence and the true national interests of the British people and of all the peoples of the British Empire. The subjection of Britain to American imperialism is a betrayal of the British people in the interests of big business and of those who are planning a new world war. In the economic sphere, Britain has been turned into a satellite of America, and an American monopolist placed in supreme command of Britain's industry and American economic controllers and supervisors established in London and reporting to Washington.

Communist Party of Great Britain,
British Road to Socialism 1951

Ignoring an overwhelming vote by the United Nations Assembly, they put Britain into a hopeless military venture which split the Commonwealth and all but destroyed the Anglo-American alliance. The Suez gamble was not only a crime, it was also an act of folly, hopelessly misconceived,

bungled in execution and covered with a tissue of lies told by
the leading Ministers concerned.

Britain Belongs to You: The Labour Party's
Policy for Consideration by the British People, *1959*
Labour Party manifesto[2]

So we today, at the heart of a vanished empire, amid the frag-
ments of demolished glory, seem to find, like one of her own
oak trees, standing and growing, the sap still rising from her
ancient roots to meet the spring, England herself. Perhaps,
after all, we know most of England 'who only England know'.

Enoch Powell, speech to the Royal Society of St George
in London on St George's Day, 23 April 1961

The prime objective of any British Government must be to
safeguard the security and prosperity of the United Kingdom
and its peoples. Since 1961 successive British Governments
have taken the view that these fundamental interests would
be best served by British accession to the European Com-
munities. It has accordingly been their declared policy that
the United Kingdom should become a full member of the
European Communities provided that satisfactory arrange-
ments could be negotiated for our entry.

The United Kingdom and the European
Communities *(1971)*[3]

The Conservatives were returned in 1951, remaining in office for
thirteen years, under Churchill, then Anthony Eden, Harold Macmillan and lastly Sir Alec Douglas-Home, formerly the 14th Earl of
Home. These were, in the conventional view, the years of attempts to
hold on to both imperial and great power status, evident in the invasion of Egypt in 1956, which was followed by rapid decolonization.
Imperial illusions were such that the British government missed the
European unity bus in the late 1950s. They were, however, the years
of affluence, of rising living standards, of the birth of the consumer

society. These were the years of social democracy, of the welfare state. Yet the relative performance of the British economy came into question, the British decline became a live issue. Through immigration from the 'New Commonwealth' the United Kingdom was becoming a multiracial, multicultural society. Thus we can sum up much of British history in this period.

But if we take the story of the British nation seriously, other aspects stand out more clearly, and we can rethink the question of national power, empire, Europe and immigration. The place of the nation in the world was central in ways in which a focus on residual imperialism and liberalism does not capture.

On taking up the premiership again in 1951, Churchill took charge of a second-rank power. Stalin and Truman commanded vastly greater forces. Only ten years before, Churchill's forces were second to none. This spectacular decline in relative British power meant the United Kingdom now lived in a world of a dominant US capitalism and Soviet communism more powerful than ever before. The national interest, and domestic politics, were in new ways, inseparable from questions of international relations. Central was the Cold War, the great stand-off between communism and capitalism which was at danger point in the early 1950s and remained the towering issue in both international and national politics into the 1980s.

Just how complex the connections were is clear from the tiny Communist Party's new programme published in 1951. It was called, significantly, *The British Road to Socialism*. It was a British nationalist tract written under order from Stalin, who told British communists, once committed to fighting British imperialism and capitalism, to turn into British super-patriots and aim their fire on the greater enemy, the raw capitalism and imperialism of the United States of America.[4] On other sides of British politics, there were those who looked to forge new relations with the rest of the world in pursuit of different domestic and international agendas. There were those who looked to strengthen what was left of the empire, others to a close alliance with the United States, and others to linking up with Europe, and with France in particular. None of these programmes were exclusive – some involved all three orientations.

One remaining way forward was potentially, at least for some, the empire. Among the young members elected to parliament in 1950 was a Tory who set out to draft a book to rally the Tory troops and to recharge the 'imperial dynamic'. 'Unless the people of this country can be made to feel the British Colonial Empire and our Commonwealth association is worth preserving,' he wrote, 'nothing can stop the present disintegration.' He complained of the 'exploitation and expropriation' overseas of 'British work and enterprise' by, for example, the Persians (who had nationalized BP) – he could see no reason why they 'should be allowed to make good their corruption and effeteness at the expense of our enterprise and work'. He had in mind to discuss 'Britain's uniqueness; the oceans and the air above them'. He intended to extol 'the two-fold community of nation and Church, which lies at the heart of Toryism'. He would be lamenting the impact of the welfare state and social security on the 'quality of character' of the nation.[5] The intending author, Enoch Powell, was no aged diehard, no blockhead aristocrat, no dim knight of the shires, but rather until 1939 the youngest professor in the British empire, a brilliant classicist and a scholarship boy from Birmingham, who to cap it all served with distinction as an intelligence and staff officer, rising to the rank of brigadier.

The scholar-soldier, the would-be philosopher-king, made his first important speech, on the Royal Titles Bill, in March 1953. At issue was what the British monarch ruled over. George VI, a man, like his wife, of 'High Tory opinions', died young in 1952. He had been the last real emperor – the only two who continued to use the title were the emperors of Ethiopia and Japan. Princess Elizabeth, who came to the throne while on a trip to Kenya to help settle the nerves of the white settlers there, would not, of course, be empress of India, but nor would she be an empress in a more informal sense. What she would be queen of was in fact a problematic issue. As Powell noted, she was proclaimed queen in 1952 'by an unknown style and title and one which at that time had no statutory basis'. She was made 'Queen of this Realm and of all her other Realms and Territories, Head of the Commonwealth, Defender of the Faith', a neat way to avoid specifying what her realms actually were. For the coronation, her style, as stipulated by the Royal Titles Act, was to be, in the United Kingdom only, queen of 'the United Kingdom of Great Britain and Northern Ireland and of Her other Realms and Territories . . .' Elsewhere she had different titles, granted by different legislation. Enoch Powell denounced this change, which marked a transition from a single empire to no empire at all, not even to a *British* Commonwealth.[6] He was right. The *British* Commonwealth had ceased to exist with the declaration of London of April 1949 which recognized the British monarch, as the symbol of the free association of independent member nations, as 'Head of the Commonwealth'.[7] When she spoke to the Commonwealth, she spoke to her many peoples, not a singular people.[8]

The colonial territories she was monarch of by virtue of being queen of the United Kingdom shrank very rapidly indeed. Yet she acquired some new queenships as some mere provinces of empire became independent monarchies. In the 1960s, she became, for example, Queen of St Vincent and the Grenadines, and of St Lucia. However, the great majority of former colonies chose not to have her as head of state; indeed many African colonies were discouraged from doing this, though she was temporarily queen of some.[9] Elizabeth was, as Powell feared, queen of many nations. Even monarchy was nationalized.

NATIONALITY

After the Second World War, all the way through to the 1980s, emigration from the United Kingdom was larger than immigration into it. The 1950s and 1960s saw a renewed emigrant traffic, mostly to the antipodes, in large new ships. The last and greatest were the SS *Oriana* (1959) and the SS *Canberra* (1960), but there had been many more launched in the 1940s and 1950s – even in 1966 the Peninsular and Oriental Line (now incorporating the Orient Line) had nine passenger ships on the Australia run, with two sailings per month. Between 1945 and 1972 more than 1 million people emigrated from the United Kingdom to Australia with subsidies from the British and Australian governments.[10] They were encouraged to go by officials who wanted to populate the country in the name of Commonwealth defence, despite labour shortages at home, and a more national conception of citizenship. By the 1960s and 1970s, the 'Ten Pound Poms' had ceased to be part of the British story, turning into Australians.[11]

By contrast, movement into the United Kingdom from the empire was not encouraged. In the 1950s a comparatively small number of incontrovertibly British citizens, Christian and English-speaking people from the very oldest British colonies, arrived in the United Kingdom. They were, under the 1948 Nationality Act, citizens of the United Kingdom and Colonies. They came from the Caribbean, to where their antecedents had been transported by the British before the colonisation of Africa or Asia. They had every right to expect to be regarded as British and to be treated accordingly. Yet they were not. Everywhere there were visible and invisible barriers put up. Black boxers were not permitted into the 1950s, when the ban was breached by British-born mixed-race boxers.[12] Some shops and pubs operated 'colour bars', which were only made illegal for such establishments in 1965. Employers also operated a 'colour bar'. Such discrimination in employment was also perfectly legal until 1968 (though it remained lawful in Northern Ireland). For example, the Cowley car works only opened all positions to non-white workers in 1967. By the end of the 1960s 20 per cent of the assembly workers were black.[13] Another example was the publicly owned Bristol Omnibus Company, which employed only white drivers and conductors until forced to change by a boycott by black Bristolians. Racial discrimination in housing was perfectly legal and common until 1968 (again excepting Northern Ireland). Notoriously, private landlords used to indicate 'No blacks, no Irish' when advertising for tenants or lodgers. Less well known is the common formulation 'Europeans only'.[14] The category 'British' could not be a racial category since the immigrants, so called, were British. But to be British was not the same as being a Briton. Race mattered profoundly.

The idea that British racism was a product of empire, that it was a domestic consequence of imperialism, should not be uncritically accepted – it was associated as much with nationalist anti-imperialism as with imperialism. Perverse and unlikely as it might now seem, British imperialism often cast itself in distinctly non-racial terms. In the 1940s and 1950s, imperialism implied to some at least the free-moving imperial subject. However, the United Kingdom reacted just as the rightly named white dominions had earlier in their histories when they faced non-white immigration from within the empire. They devised means of barring entry to non-whites.

The late 1950s and early 1960s saw a three-pronged transformation of the situation. Ending the empire was a fundamental part of it. As nationalist movements mobilized in the colonies, so a British nationalism shook off even a pretence of noblesse oblige. Firstly, most of the colonial empire was granted independence, including the most populous Caribbean colonies, Jamaica and Trinidad. It was from these colonies that the immigration of the 1940s and 1950s overwhelmingly came. Their people thus ceased to be citizens of the United Kingdom and Colonies, and mostly became citizens of the Independent Commonwealth. Roughly simultaneously, immigration from this expanded Commonwealth was curtailed. The 1962 Commonwealth Immigrants Act imposed controls (through labour vouchers) on all Commonwealth citizens but also on some Colonies citizens (a diminishing group), those who had passports not issued by UK governments. This second aspect of control was strengthened by the 1968 Commonwealth Immigrants Act. The third was the 1961 application, rejected, to join the European Common Market, which included the free movement of overwhelmingly white workers. It will be recalled that in the 1940s and indeed beyond there were more immigrants from Europe than from the empire. Though never articulated as such, there was a choice between a white nation, a white Europe and a black empire, and the former two were chosen.

Preparation for accession to the European Economic Community in the early 1970s was accompanied by the 1971 Immigration Act, which restricted free immigration to 'patrials', those with very close connections to the United Kingdom. This was a move towards a standard European form of nationality, tied to specific European territories. This move was strengthened by a new Nationality Act (of 1981 – the first since 1948), a bipartisan measure, which essentially limited right of abode to a new category of British citizen. Commonwealth citizens were now fully alien in terms of citizenship, with others in intermediate categories. Women as well as men could pass on British citizenship, though only the children of permanent residents or citizens could gain British citizenship by being born in the UK. One important effect of the act was to deny full citizenship to Falkland Islanders, which became an embarrassing problem following the war of 1982; full status was restored in 1983. In 1966, when the Commonwealth Relations Office and the Colonial Office were merged into the Foreign and Commonwealth Office, the old and powerful general distinction between relations with 'British countries' and those with foreigners was thus much reduced, though certainly not eliminated. Vestiges of a different system remained. To this day citizens of Commonwealth countries (including India and other former colonies), and citizens of the Irish republic may vote in British parliamentary elections if resident. A Commonwealth citizen may find it very hard to settle, but once here can vote, whereas a freely entering EU citizen can only vote in local and some other elections.

In the 1950s and 1960s there was a party consensus to keep racial language out of politics, moves which silenced overt racism in public and marginalized racist parties such as Oswald Mosley's anti-immigrant but pro-European integration Union Movement (founded in 1948). Tellingly the immigration control was rhetorically and in terms of legislation coupled with measures to improve what were called 'race relations'. Neither Conservative imperialism nor Labour internationalism were consistent with racism. Nationalists were not so restricted.

Enoch Powell, who considered the possibilities of a revitalized empire in 1950, had by the early 1960s consciously rejected imperialism, seeing it as a mere passing phase of a much longer and deeper English history.[15] He became a pungent critic of imperial delusions. He was also in favour of British entry to the Common Market. It was this nationalist Powell, now a front-bench politician, who made a notorious racist speech in 1968. He claimed there were 'areas that are already undergoing the total transformation to which there is no parallel in a thousand years of English history'. He went on: 'We must be mad, literally mad, as a nation to be permitting the annual inflow of some 50,000 dependants . . . It is like watching a nation busily engaged in heaping up its own funeral pyre.' The existing British population, he said, 'found themselves made strangers in their own country'. He

wanted support for re-emigration and warned that race relations legislation (then going through parliament) and an increasing immigrant
population would lead to the sorts of race riots that were happening
in the USA. It was the end of his career in the Conservative Party,
where he was defence spokesman, and a critic of the nuclear strategy
of the British state. But it propelled him to national fame, and he was
to become one of the leading *anti*-Common Market activists of the
1970s, and a notably anti-American one too.

For all the dramatic changes of the early 1960s, immigration from
the former empire was not in fact cut off. It grew, with increased flows
from the Caribbean, and later strong ones from parts of the Indian
sub-continent, especially those with a long connection to the United
Kingdom, such as Sylhet, home of many lascars, and from zones of
war and dislocation. Significant waves of ethnic Indians came from
East Africa in the late 1960s and early 1970s. Smaller communities
were formed of Chinese from Hong Kong, and Cypriots.

A new racially inflected category, the 'New Commonwealth', was
invented in the 1960s. It had no legal or official standing. Its only
basis in history was that white dominions had got independence and
thus become members of the Commonwealth before India and
the colonies. It artfully conflated the very different imperial stories
of the West Indies, India and Africa and implied that the last to leave
the empire had the least right to live in the United Kingdom. It should
be noted that much of the 'New Commonwealth' had been formally
closer to the United Kingdom than the Commonwealth and indeed
had been part of empire for centuries. Indeed, for those seeking to
develop an overt politics of whiteness, the very term 'Commonwealth', not just the 'New Commonwealth', came to imply former
black colonies, and they openly attacked the close royal association
with it. Right-wing nationalists of the 1980s argued that the existence of the 'Commonwealth' was a fig leaf for loss of world status,
claiming that in the 1950s liberal Tories would even pay the price of
immigration to maintain it.[16] The argument is nonsense, not only
because, as we have seen, the immigrants of the 1950s came from the
Colonies and not the Commonwealth, but because immigration controls were imposed early and strongly on the Commonwealth.

THE RISE AND FALL OF THE BRITISH NATION

While hostility to immigration should not be conflated with imperialism, a racialist outlook on empire did persist. The Conservative right looked with favour on the white supremacist regimes in Rhodesia and South Africa. They formed the Conservative Monday Club in 1961 in the wake of Harold Macmillan's 'Wind of Change' speech in South Africa, which reaffirmed the United Kingdom's non-racialist programme of independence for colonies, and of the ejection of South Africa, soon declared a republic, from the Commonwealth. Many members, such as Julian Amery and Geoffrey Rippon, wanted entry into the Common Market. There was no necessary opposition between supporting racist regimes and being pro-Common Market, just as racism was increasingly likely to be nationalist rather than imperialist. For the Conservative right the causes of white supremacist South Africa and Rhodesia, also seen as bastions of anti-communism in Africa, were significant political markers well into the 1970s.

ECONOMIC NATION

The decisive shift to a national United Kingdom nationality mirrored a profound economic transformation. The economy became more national through many different processes. First was the sequestration, destruction, forced sell-offs and nationalizations of British capital abroad. This led to an estimated loss of 40 per cent or more of business assets abroad between 1938 and 1956.[17] Second was the taking of major industries into public ownership, which resulted in the state and its agencies controlling perhaps half of all investment at home in the 1950s and 1960s. Third was the control of movements of goods and capital across the nation's borders. In the 1950s and early 1960s the proportion of GDP traded was falling. Imports, though not exports, were even below the average for the 1930s, a period of low import prices, into the 1960s.[18] In this the United Kingdom was out of kilter with Europe, for European economies were internationalizing, though from a lower base. The result was a convergence, with the United Kingdom becoming European, and the Europeans becoming a little more British in their extent of trade. Indeed, an economic freedom index, including measures of protection, shows the

UK ranked in the middle of the OECD countries in these years – whereas before the 1930s (and from the 1980s) it was at or very near the top of the list.[19]

That nationalizing of British trade rarely merits even a mention in economic histories. This is partly because of the focus on the balance of payments (the difference between imports and exports) rather than the changing dimensions of both. It is also because rising British economic nationalism does not fit the standard story of post-war economic liberalization, which correctly emphasizes the search for new ways to re-establish global economic relations rent asunder by the Great Depression and the Second World War. If historians have noted the existence of a national political economy at all in the British case, they have deemed it weak.[20]

Figure 10.1: Goods trade as a percentage of GDP, 1900–2000, Lend-Lease supplies excluded

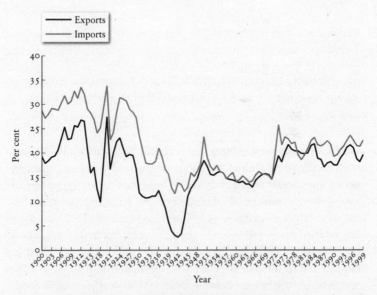

Source: Catherine Schenk, *The Decline of Sterling: Managing the Retreat of an International Currency 1945–1992* (Cambridge, 2010), figure 1.2, p. 16.

Figure 10.2: Trade as a proportion of GDP, main Western European economies, 1950–90

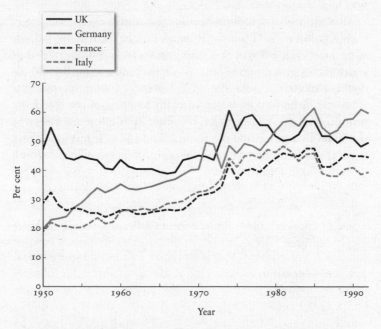

Source: Bradford DeLong, 'Post-WWII Western European Exceptionalism: The Economic Dimension' (UCLA and NBER, 1997), available at http://www.j-bradford-delong.net.

In fact the nationalization of the economy was profoundly important. The post-war United Kingdom was a land of tariffs, quotas, import surcharges – of 'Buy British'. Direct controls of quantities of imports were complicated, chaotic, rapidly changing, but nevertheless were 'a cornerstone of post-war reconstruction'.[21] They alone reduced the import bill by around 10 per cent, but a very important 10 per cent, allowing industries to develop and grow and invest in research and development. They were particularly directed at strategic industries in manufacturing. National self-sufficiency, in food, oil refining, sulphuric acid production (then seen as a major index of industrial strength) and manufacturing generally were strongly

encouraged. So powerful was this economic nationalism that governments were quite prepared to establish or increase import controls
even against the Commonwealth, as in the case of textiles from the
1950s, and imports in general in the 1960s, including a large sur-
charge between 1964 and 1966, which included tariffs against the
other members of the so-called European Free Trade Area (EFTA), in
which the United Kingdom was by far the largest economy! As we
shall see in chapter 12, new industries were developed to replace
imports from both the Commonwealth and EFTA. Opposition to the
maintenance of tariffs was weak – the only party advocating this was
the now tiny Liberal Party, and even it called for reductions rather
than, as it did into the 1920s, call for general free trade.

AN IMPERIAL ECONOMY?

As the national economy became more national, the United Kingdom's still very large external trade was, in shorthand, more imperial
than it had been at the height of imperialism, whether in the Edwardian or the interwar years. In the 1950s, 50 per cent of British trade
was with the empire and the Commonwealth. This did not reflect
some natural state of affairs – it was rather an aberration caused by
depression, autarkic policy and the World War.

There was even less prospect than before the war of empire free
trade, and indeed imperial preferences were lower than in the 1930s.[22]
Most of that trade was, as imperial trade had always been, with the
fully independent former white dominions, which were themselves
now more connected to other trading partners. Yet parts of the colonial empire did play newly important roles. The dollar exports of
Malaya (rubber and tin) and Gold Coast/Ghana (cocoa) were vital to
the overall strength of sterling. Some colonies also became important
in dollar-saving initiatives (that is avoiding importing from the US
and areas which operated in dollars). Thus it was that the welfare
orange juice provided to British children as a free source of vitamin C
increasingly came from new plantations and factories, not in Spain or
Florida, but Jamaica and British Honduras, under a contract with the
Ministry of Food. The Windward Islands started producing imperial

bananas on a large scale from the mid-1950s. The sterling area, which was not quite the same as the empire, was a distinctive trading bloc in the 1940s and 1950s.

Private investment in the sterling area represented a deliberately uncontrolled flow of capital out of the United Kingdom, one which later was seen as undermining a strategy of national renewal.[23] Yet in practice it was low (never more than 1.6 per cent of GDP) and was significantly directed to mining and oil, needed for the home economy.[24]

The idea of an imperial economy was still a feature of Tory politics, but there was a distinct shift away from it. The 1951 Tory manifesto promised that 'To foster commerce within the Empire we shall maintain Imperial Preference.' Yet the empire was clearly not the top priority. As the manifesto put it: 'In our home market the Empire producer will have a place second only to the home producer.'[25] In the case of investment the language of empire was also important in the early 1950s: 'Conservative policy will stimulate the flow of private and public capital from London for sound Empire development,' they said. They celebrated the 'Great wealth-creating projects . . . under way in all the Commonwealth countries and in the Colonial territories too'.[26] However, the largest development projects in British colonies were now funded by the World Bank, including the Kariba Dam in Southern Rhodesia, built by Italian contractors. In 1959 the Tories are still hailing investment in the Commonwealth, but the 'empire' disappeared, and 'overseas' investment, at over 1 per cent of national income, was what was now seen as important.[27] There was indeed a very marked change in emphasis away from any idea of an imperial economy, to doing more trade wherever it was growing fastest, and that place was Europe. Within a decade the great cause of Conservatism of nearly the entire first half of the century was dropped.

EUROPE AND HOPES FOR FREE TRADE

In the 1990s the idea that the United Kingdom had once stood aside from 'Europe', preferring instead empire/Commonwealth, or sometimes the world and the USA, was a commonplace.[28] Thus it was suggested that an imperial history, and perhaps a deluded commitment to a special relationship with the USA, prevented the British elite from recognizing the nation's destiny as part of Europe. There is a parallel argument that an irrational commitment to recreating the international role of sterling after the war had serious negative effects on the British economy. Recent work rejects both these arguments.[29] We should see these arguments not as reflecting historical realities, but rather as a version of the very odd historical claims of some of those opposed to entry into the Common Market, in the 1960s and later. *They* contrasted British liberty, enterprise, its maritime, global and imperial orientation with continental order, bureaucracy, agriculture and nation. For good measure some threw in British Protestantism and European Catholicism. There were opponents who made different sorts of arguments, not least national-protectionist arguments.

But there are two very important objections to taking this kind of thinking too seriously. Firstly, it did not explain the majority elite view, not least of the Conservative Party, which was that the United Kingdom should align itself with Europe. It does not explain why the United Kingdom applied for membership as early as 1961 and again in 1967, before being admitted in 1973. If it missed the boat in 1956–7, within a very few years it was trying to scramble aboard. Secondly, to the extent that material differences existed in reality between the United Kingdom and Europe, they were being reduced, radically and consciously so. Things had changed. Those who invoked a contrast between the United Kingdom and Europe were at best describing 1914 or 1929, but not 1961, 1967 or 1973. The folly of uncritically overemphasizing a continuous British exceptionalism is evident.

The case of sport provides a telling instance of the realities. After the Second World War as before it, but on a larger scale, British football clubs played in Europe and against European clubs, from both sides of the Iron Curtain, indeed. Football, a British invention of course, was not much played in the empire, where middle-class cricket and rugby thrived, but was taken up in both Europe and South America. Rather than standing aloof from Europe, British teams were, with a few exceptions, keen participants in European competition.[30] Thus it was that in 1958 the Manchester United team found themselves in Munich, where they suffered a terrible air-crash on take-off.

They had stopped in the city to refuel, on the way home from beating Red Star Belgrade in a European Cup match.

In the 1950s and 1960s the United Kingdom was no longer, as we have seen, the free-trading, liberal, globally oriented economy it had been. It was more national, and its policy was to increase national food production, and increase self-sufficiency in other areas too. Indeed, the attraction and the danger of going into the Common Market was precisely that it offered a more liberal economic future to the United Kingdom. An important concern of British farmers was that Common Market producers would flood the British market. Although, as the government put it in 1967, negotiations with Europe had to address the 'special problems of New Zealand and of the Commonwealth sugar producing countries',[31] the United Kingdom was now growing its own sugar and raising more sheep than ever (on which see chapter 11). What requires explanation, then, is not why the United Kingdom remained aloof and trapped in an imperial, liberal, global mind-set and rejected the Common Market. What needs explanation is the opposite – why a nation which found itself with a strong imperial and especially national orientation after the war should choose to give both up, to open up its markets to European competition.

It is not so surprising if we recall that in the past the United Kingdom had in fact traded more with Europe than with empire. Recent history had disturbed a long-standing and very important set of economic relationships. On the other hand, British military engagement with Europe after 1945 was profound. After the Second World War the great concentration of British forces was and remained in Germany, and not the empire. Membership of NATO (created in 1949) was as much about engagement with Europe as with the USA; so was membership of the OEEC, the body that oversaw Marshall Aid, the US aid which flowed in Europe from the late 1940s. To cap it all, there was the cornerstone of British military planning, the long-standing Anglo-French alliance, which took them to war together in 1914, in 1939 and in 1956.

Furthermore, there was a powerful argument in the 1940s, led by Winston Churchill and Leo Amery (though rejected by the Labour government), that the United Kingdom needed the empire *and* economic integration into Europe to remain strong – the close union of the British and French empires was essential to maintaining a place in the world distinct from both the USA and the USSR.[32] Churchill was committed to a United Europe with the United Kingdom in it, as his great campaign of the late 1940s testified. It was an argument with strong liberal-internationalist aspects and was fully compatible not only with the UN, but also the relationship with the USA, and the Commonwealth.[33] Churchill's campaign was funded by British big business: ICI, Rothschild, General Electric, Vickers, Lever, Boots, Austin, Ford, Rolls-Royce, Monsanto, the Lancashire Steel Corporation and United Steel all contributed.[34] This Churchillian perspective was influential in part of the Tory Party, not least in the case of Harold Macmillan. Its mere existence should have been enough to disprove the thesis that imperial feeling held back European integration.

The move towards Europe needs to be understood as a move towards free trade, not away from it. The United Kingdom pursued a rational national strategy based on post-war economic realities (and not on misplaced nostalgia for empire) in the 1940s and 1950s.[35] The national strategy of the 1940s and the 1950s was to break out of the redoubt of unprecedented economic nationalism and imperialism to a world again much more open to British trade, and one with freely exchanging currencies. In other words to get back to the world before 1929, to get back into Europe, into the USA. It was about going back to a future, one of free trade. Opening up Europe was a priority. As the Conservative Party manifesto of 1959 put it: 'our aim remains an industrial free market embracing all Western Europe'. The problem was that the six partners who had signed the Treaty of Rome in 1957 wanted a very much smaller free trade area, not restricted to industry, with a common external tariff. The British project failed, and EFTA, in which it was joined by Austria, Denmark, Norway, Portugal, Sweden and Switzerland, was no substitute. EFTA allowed the United Kingdom to maintain Commonwealth and other preferences and trade in food (which was what mattered) but it could not join the six.[36]

The formation of the Common Market of the six (established by the Treaty of Rome of 1957) was a threat to British interests in

Europe, because in many cases it meant *higher* tariffs against the United Kingdom, because the common external tariff was often higher than the tariffs of particular trading partners.[37] By 1961 there were no serious alternatives to joining the Common Market, and that is why the government applied for membership. Being within a free trade zone (with an external tariff) in Europe had major attractions. It meant opening the home market to *manufacturing* competition for the first time in decades; and it also maintained and extended the business British companies were doing in Europe already.[38] Continental Europe had a very large, increasingly wealthy population, where business prospects were much better than in the Commonwealth, which was growing much less quickly. Western Europe, for decades beset by low growth and ravaged by war, was now rapidly transforming. In time even its poorest parts would begin to approximate the levels of income of the areas of white settlement in the new world.

The elite, and the press, wanted to go in, and were prepared to throw overboard Commonwealth preferences, and a common set of Commonwealth citizenships. The elite, here defined as those still active who were listed in *Who's Who* (around 10,000 people, overwhelmingly men, who lived in the southeast, read *The Times*, had graduated from Oxbridge *if* they went to university, and so on), were strongly of the belief that British prestige had declined. Strong majorities, the survey suggested, were in favour of the EEC, NATO, the Special Relationship, the United Nations *and* the Commonwealth. There was no either/or for the majority, who wanted all these relationships. Tellingly those most against the EEC were exceptionally strong in their pro-Commonwealth views and less enthusiastic about *all* other international entanglements.[39] The Confederation of British Industry, created in 1965 by a merger of the Federation of British Industries and the British Employers' Confederation, came out strongly in favour of Common Market entry, because of the larger market and also because it preferred the legal and fiscal regimes the Common Market offered.[40]

It was not British objections, or even European ones, which scuppered this project. In 1963 and again in 1967 it was specifically the French President de Gaulle who said 'non'. *He* feared that the United

Kingdom represented something alien to the European project, an island with a maritime orientation, industrial rather than agricultural, which bought its food from abroad. But he too missed the key point that the United Kingdom was becoming, by these measures, much more European, by choice.

There was British opposition to entering the Common Market, but it lost against a determined elite which was in favour. Imperialist arguments were important to anti-marketeers. The Canadian Lord Beaverbrook's best-selling conservative *Daily Express* opposed entry vehemently, still arguing for empire free trade, kith-and-kin imperialism and anti-Americanism.[41] Much of his argument was in fact economically nationalist, defending subsidized British agriculture against subsidized European agriculture. The Labour Party, though not the Labour-supporting *Daily Mirror*, was against entry to the Common Market. Hugh Gaitskell, in a famous speech in 1962, denounced the 'end of a thousand years of history' as an independent state and that the Commonwealth could not exist if 'the mother country' became a 'province of Europe'.[42] This was a more nationalist than imperialist objection.

The Labour left was generally anti-Common Market on the grounds that the EEC was a capitalist club, closely linked to NATO. The Communist Party was also opposed. It noted that wages were higher in the United Kingdom, worker contributions to social services were lower and there was a danger of harmonization of social services on the contributory (that is Beveridgean) model on joining. There was no Common Market commitment to full employment; the Common Market meant discrimination against the Commonwealth in trade, and higher food prices.[43] There were those on the Labour left who disguised their own nationalism by claiming that the Common Market represented continental protection and that the United Kingdom should look outwards, to remain truly internationalist, committed to the Commonwealth and the United Nations.[44]

Harold Wilson rather niftily endorsed this line of thinking. In opposition Wilson deftly suggested there were opportunities to supply Russia and the countries behind the Iron Curtain with British chemical plant and to do research to feed the millions in Asia and Africa. It was 'very nice', he claimed, to do research on colour television and put effort into producing bigger and better washing machines to sell in Düsseldorf, but instead 'we should be mass producing simply ploughs and tractors' and researching 'one or two horsepower steam engines, because that is what the world needs' – the now redundant British steam locomotive works could help here.[45] The anti-affluence, anti-consumerist theme in anti-Common Market argument was also sounded by J. B. Priestley, who was opposed on the grounds that the Common Market was all about an alien business efficiency. He was an 'off-shore island man' who didn't like the continental way of doing things, did not want to lose cheap food, did not trust this Tory policy. 'We might be happier out in the wind, risking the loss of colour television, holidays in Spain, more and more cars, prepared to make audacious experiments, so many odd but exciting islanders,' he thought.[46]

Once in office in 1964, Harold Wilson's position would change. The Labour government got a positive vote in parliament, with dissenters, and a narrow victory at the party conference for a second application to join. Once more the process was vetoed by President de Gaulle. Surprisingly, Wilson lost the 1970 election, allowing in a new kind of Conservative leader, the humbly born Edward Heath. His achievement was to finally take Britain into the European Economic Community: a very few years later, after de Gaulle had retired, the Conservatives applied and were accepted, with only a few dissenters on their side. But with votes from the Labour right, the Conservative Party won the vote in parliament to join and led the United Kingdom into the EEC in 1973, together with Ireland and Denmark. Entering was a great personal achievement for Heath, a long-standing enthusiast for Europe who had been involved in negotiations in the early 1960s. That he had been elected as leader in 1965 was itself testimony to the pro-European orientation of the Conservative Party.

The bulk of the Labour MPs had voted against joining. Labour, as a party in opposition from 1970, remained opposed. Labour promised to renegotiate the terms of entry and, having returned to office in 1974, achieved minor changes which it put to a referendum in 1975. It is a measure of the significance to the elite of staying in the EEC that this constitutional innovation was not objected to, for its purpose was to take the decision out of the hands of the divided Labour

Party. Generally speaking, the Labour left was against membership, the right in favour. The yes campaign was better funded and better organized and confidently confirmed what the political, administrative elite had long decided on. Every government since 1959 had been in favour of membership, including the Labour government itself, and the Conservative Party consistently so in government and in opposition. The Conservative Party, now under Margaret Thatcher, remained strongly in favour.

The anti-marketeers of both left and right had an extraordinary love-in with British institutions.[47] The anti-American, anti-EEC, state interventionist nationalists of the labour left, led by Tony Benn, were patriots and nationalists, defending the rights of the British parliament. They wanted to pursue a nationalist economic policy of modernizing the British economy through state action, if necessary behind import controls. The anti-American, anti-EEC free-market nationalists of the right – of which there were few, were led by Enoch Powell, now an Ulster Unionist. Powell had been in favour of entry until 1969. He echoed an image of the nation as a free-trading Edwardian idyll. Enoch Powell would claim in a speech in 1976 that because the United Kingdom had been at the crossroads of the oceans it was the richest country in the Old World. Self-sufficiency in and high prices of food did not suit a compact and highly industrialized nation. Yet it was not just a matter of the price of butter, there was the question of sovereignty. It was intolerable that the United Kingdom become the province of a European state; it could not be what it ought to be, a nation-state.[48] He had advised the British people to vote Labour in 1974.

The vote, two-thirds in favour of continued membership, represented a crushing defeat for the Labour left in particular. British economic nationalism of a general and serious kind was now decisively rejected.[49] The impact took time to be felt. Entry to the EEC came in January 1973 and was confirmed in 1975, but the process of joining was a staggered one. The integration of the United Kingdom into the Common External Tariff, the abolition of tariffs with the rest of the EEC and the transfer into the Common Agricultural Policy were all achieved, in stages, by the end of 1977. It was only then that the United Kingdom was open to free trade within the Common

Market, and was behind the Common European Tariff. Only then was Commonwealth preference over. So too was the economic nation.

AMERICA

One of the main claims of the anti-marketeers was indeed that the United Kingdom would surrender its national sovereignty by entry into the Common Market. Yet there was an existing, and more significant, loss of sovereignty to the USA. It was, however, much easier to create an anti-EEC movement than an anti-American one. This was less true of the left than of the right, but true of both. While pro-Americanism was a common enough feature of British life, the relative lack of overt anti-American feeling is notable. One reason is that Churchill and his successors were committed to the US alliance and told a story which celebrated it and made it seem natural and fair. They could hardly advertise their own subservient position, much less their failure to achieve serious interdependence. The imperialist right had bigger fish to fry, and its anti-Americanism only came out sporadically. Both preferred to be under the wing of the US to being under that of a British left. In later life Enoch Powell was the great exception. He was anti-EEC, anti-American, anti-nuclear and anti-imperialist.[50] It made him a marginal figure.

The US–UK relationship was not, after the 1920s, primarily a trade relationship. The United Kingdom tried to minimize US imports, as part of its wider aim to reduce 'dollar imports'. It launched efforts to develop national and imperial substitutes, which could be bought in sterling. Exports to the US were hard to achieve – there was little British production the US needed, in contrast to the rubber and tin from Malaya. In any case the USA was protectionist and applied tariffs and quotas on trade. In some cases which particularly agitated the British government they did indeed damage British economic interests. Woollen goods was one such.

The key economic relationship arose from US investment in the UK, a very long-standing phenomenon, but one which grew strongly from the 1950s. The USA was easily the largest foreign investor in the United Kingdom. US firms were long significant in such fields as cars

(Ford and GM), photography (Kodak), oil (Esso) and calculating machines (IBM). These and other companies significantly extended their interests after the war. Among the new ones were Chrysler in cars (which arrived in the 1960s) and new oil companies who built major refineries in the 1950s and 1960s. There was through this investment a measure of Americanization, or rather re-Americanization, of the economy.

It was in military and overseas matters that the US relationship was closest and most important. Both states, independently, shared an aversion to the Soviet Union. Both abhorred the economic nationalism of others, though not their own. Again and again the US and the UK acted together, or rather the UK followed the US lead. In the Korean War (1950–53), a Commonwealth division (58 per cent British) was part of a nominally United Nations force, under the leadership of the United States. This was the last United Nations war until the end of the Cold War, and was made possible only because the USSR was temporarily boycotting the UN Security Council. A second case was the US-led destruction of the Iranian nationalist government which had nationalized the Anglo-Iranian oilfields and refinery in 1951. First the British and US and other oil companies enforced a total embargo on Iranian oil. In 1953 the Americans took the lead, with help from the British secret service, in the toppling of the legitimate Iranian government, installing a pro-US government under the shah, who had been forced into exile. Anglo-Iranian, renamed BP, got back only a minority share in its old oilfields and refinery.

The nationalization of another asset, the Suez Canal, in which, as in the case of BP, the British government was a shareholder, led to war against Egypt. With the French and Israelis the British government, newly in the hands of Anthony Eden, decided to teach the Egyptian nationalist leader Gamal Nasser a lesson. They thought they had the tacit approval of the United States. The chancellor of the exchequer, Harold Macmillan, believing himself to be a wily Greek slave to the Roman emperor, Dwight Eisenhower, his old wartime colleague in North Africa, went to Washington asking the new Roman empire to turn a blind eye. The Greek slave did not understand the emperor's demurral, taking it to be endorsement of his cunning plan – for obviously it was in the US's interest to have Nasser overthrown. There was in fact no such approval, and the US used its power over money and oil to bring the whole adventure to an end in short order. The USA had more important business than punishing Egypt – the Soviet Union had at the same time crushed the Hungarian revolution.

The 1956 war against Egypt was neither a United Nations war nor a war within the empire, nor yet a war which involved the Commonwealth. It was a national-European war, a joint enterprise with the French and Israelis, which was opposed by the United Nations and the Commonwealth, as well as the USA. It was, for these reasons, and for others, an aberration. It was essentially the work of an insecure and unwell prime minister. Goaded by die-hard Tories organized as the 'Suez group', he took actions which many inside the government machine thought insane.[51] The Suez group was formed not in 1956, but in 1954, to campaign against the British withdrawal from the military bases in the Canal Zone in that year.

The British government wanted to go *back* into Egypt. It was not a matter of *keeping* an imperial possession or vassal. However, the British government couldn't decide what the aim of the invasion was actually to be. Was it to retake the Canal Zone it had left two years earlier? Or was it to topple Gamal Nasser, the Egyptian leader, a heavier task still, which would not be achieved by just taking Port Said and the Canal Zone? British planners went back and forth, ending with a limited mission. They certainly were unable to mobilize domestic Egyptian opposition, as the CIA had done in toppling the Iranian and Guatemalan governments in the immediate past.

The Anglo-French invasion was done under the pretext of intervening in a pre-planned Israeli attack. The Israelis invaded on 29 October 1956; the British and French started bombing on 31 October. They destroyed much of the Egyptian air force, made up of British and Soviet aeroplanes. They bombed from bases in Malta and Cyprus, and from five British aircraft carriers. The British in stages sent in one infantry division, one parachute brigade and one commando brigade. The first forces landed in Port Said on 5 November. The very next day they stopped fighting. They did so following a United Nations General Assembly resolution calling for a ceasefire. The USA made clear that it would not support sterling or make up oil shipments now blocked by Arab nations. The United Kingdom did not even have the support of the Commonwealth, whether India or Canada. There seems little doubt that British and French forces could have completed their mission and captured the Canal Zone. But the whole scheme became pointless, as they would have had to deal with a hostile world, as well as hostile Egyptians. The United Kingdom and France were lucky that their folly was so rapidly stopped in its tracks.

Furthermore, there was opposition at home. 'Law not War' was the slogan of the moment. The Labour Party, including its leader Hugh Gaitskell, were solidly against it, partly because so were the Americans. There was a large demonstration in Trafalgar Square, where Aneurin Bevan claimed Eden had 'besmirched the name of Britain'.[52] The trouble was not merely that the stated intentions of action were false, but no sensible policy was to be found. It was not merely wrong, it was stupid, was the claim. Yet it must be remembered that the war had a great deal of support, and that it took courage to stand against it – after all, Nasser was in British propaganda a new Hitler or Mussolini, and the British and French had invaded, they claimed, to bring peace, to separate the warring Egyptians and Israelis. They had pretended to act to ensure the peace of the world.

There was a temporary rupture with the USA, but the result was ever more dependence in military matters rather than estrangement. The issue was not so much the alliance – that was firm – but the room for independent action. Neither Harold Macmillan nor any other British prime minister would ever again make the mistake of presuming to act alone. Never again would the United Kingdom initiate an attack on a sovereign state independently of the USA. Under Macmillan the British state gave up not only any idea of any such operation in future, but much more importantly the central elements of its independent military power – atomic weapons and delivery systems, as we shall discuss in chapter 13. It now sought 'interdependence', not independence. Indeed, one of many reasons the British government turned to seek application to the EEC in the early 1960s was that 'interdependence' with the USA on weapons had proved chimerical – the turn to Europe (though encouraged by the USA) was a response to the discovered reality that there was no special relation-ship of near equality with the USA.[53]

The turn to Europe was real, and the wariness towards the USA in some respects also. The United Kingdom refused to send troops to Vietnam (when, for example, Australia did). Edward Heath was also much less keen on the 'special relationship' with the USA than his predecessors or successors.[54] Following the Arab oil embargo during the Arab-Israeli war of 1973 he joined with the EEC in calling for a solution to the Israeli occupations along the lines of Resolution 242, a declaration which made the United Kingdom able to continue to import from Arab oilfields. The US was not pleased and withdrew intelligence collaboration. Heath also refused permission for the US to use spy planes from Cyprus and, implicitly, to use UK air bases in support of Israel. He was soon to shift position and sided with US proposals in the light of EEC disarray, but crucially against the wishes of the French.[55] In the end the USA called the shots.

EMPIRE/COLD WAR

It is often implied that British failure in Egypt marked, or even accel-erated, or caused, the end of empire. There is something in this, but the argument needs to be made carefully. As we have noted, it was not an imperial war, but a post-imperial, national war. What Suez marked was not the end of empire, but the end of the possibility of being a national player on the world stage. It resulted in a national humiliation, which demanded a reassessment of the United King-dom's place in the world. However, it did not lead to the drawing-back from real imperial wars, not least where there were British military bases. The United Kingdom could no longer decide to fight foreign-ers, but it did not stop British forces fighting British subjects, or the subjects of allies. Thus active fighting continued for years afterwards in Malaya, independent from 1957 (Singapore was still a British base), in Cyprus (now the replacement Middle East base), in Borneo, in Kenya, in Aden (where there was also a very large air base).

When did the empire end? The empire that mattered in military and population terms, the Indian empire, went in 1947. The white dominions, which mattered economically, were politically independent already, and increasingly economically and militarily so. Egypt and Persia were lost to British power by 1954. The empire left in the 1950s and 1960s was the demographically, economically and militarily least important part, the colonial empire. It had been freshly exploited from the 1940s and was also important to British prestige, but it had not been, by a long way, the central focus of British power.

The great British overseas concerns were with the Cold War, not with the colonies, and when the colonies became a liability in these and other bigger questions, they went. There was no question of generating conflicts in which there was a risk that the colonies might go communist; nor could the United Kingdom be seen to be defending white supremacy. All this was made very clear by Harold Macmillan, who took over as prime minister from Anthony Eden in January 1957, in a six-week tour of Africa in early 1960. At its end, in South Africa, he made a famous speech which articulated the central arguments. Macmillan's main theme was the rise of nationalism, first in Europe, then in Asia and now in Africa. He complimented his white hosts by declaring theirs the first African nationalism. Nationalism, in his view, was the product of science, of education, of the West. 'The wind of change is blowing through this continent, and whether we like it or not, this growth of national consciousness is a political fact,' he told them. Not only that, but:

> We must all accept it as a fact, and our national policies must take account of it. We've got to come to terms with it. I sincerely believe that if we cannot do so we may imperil the precarious balance between the East and West on which the peace of the world depends.

That was indeed the crucial issue in what he insisted in many ways was an interconnected and interdependent small world. Speaking globally, he noted that: 'As I see it the great issue in this second half of the twentieth century is whether the uncommitted peoples of Asia and Africa will swing to the East or to the West.'[56]

He told his white South African audience that the United Kingdom would continue to grant independence to African nations and would do so on a non-racial basis. This was not a new policy, but its affirmation was important and led to a strong reaction from white supremacists in the empire, and in the Conservative Party, as we have seen. This was far from the end of the matter. British colonists in Southern Rhodesia fought on, declaring independence in 1965, under Prime Minister Ian Smith. Indeed, it is significant that while in the 1950s British troops operated at huge distances, in the 1960s there was no question of using British forces to put down a white settler rebellion in Rhodesia. Rhodesia and South Africa remained causes for the British right and left and became active theatres of the Cold War. The latter fought, directly and by proxy, the new governments of the former Portuguese colonies to the very end of the global Cold War.

The policy of granting independence on a non-racial basis was already in action. Malaya (later to grow into Malaysia) was independent from 1957, as was Ghana (formerly the Gold Coast). From the autumn of 1960 a great wave of declarations of independence would follow with Cyprus, Nigeria, Kuwait, Sierra Leone, Tanzania, Jamaica, Trinidad and Tobago, Uganda, Kenya, Malawi, Malta and Zambia independent by the end of 1964. Remaining colonies would soon follow. One former colony returned to the British crown very briefly in 1979–80 so that it could be made independent on the non-racial basis that had proved impossible in the 1960s. In the process Rhodesia became Zimbabwe. It was Mrs Thatcher's government, not Harold Macmillan's, which presided over the end of the white supremacist empire. It agreed to the inevitable in promising to hand over all of Hong Kong, not just the leased territory, to China, which took place in 1997.

II

Building the Future

Cement and Bricks – Bricks and Cement – these fill the day,
morning, noon and evening – till far into the night!
              Harold Macmillan, Minister of Housing and
                              Local Government, 1953[1]

. . . the strength, the solvency, the influence of Britain, which
some still think depends upon nostalgic illusions or upon
nuclear posturings – these things are going to depend in the
remainder of this century to a unique extent on the speed
with which we come to terms with the world of change.
              Harold Wilson, Speech at the Scarborough
                              Conference, 1963[2]

Traffic control is, for most people,
Their most intimate, and direct,
Experience of government –
              Heathcote Williams, 'Autogeddon' (1991)

In many ways, then, the United Kingdom emerged as a nation, separate from the empire and Commonwealth, more economically
nationalist, more oriented towards Europe in matters material and
military. As it did it was also being transformed internally, with
changes as fast and dramatic in the internal material constitution as
in its foreign relations. If the relations outside can be seen as shrinking in scope and scale, internally the story is one of dramatic growth
and transformation. A British developmental state focused on changing the nation, on building a new national future.

Yet there is really only one prime minister who is remembered for being an enthusiast for modernization. Harold Wilson is indeed famous for his promise to create a New Britain, pulsating with the energies of the white heat of the new scientific revolution. The record of his 1964–70 government in this respect is generally thought to be terrible. Among the few achievements credited to the government are its presiding over a social and cultural revolution, doing away with capital punishment, decriminalizing abortion and homosexual relations and making divorce more humane. However, what is striking is the commitment of every government into the 1960s, and to some extent the 1970s too, to transform the very infrastructure, industry and nature of the nation. Wilson is not the exception which proves the rule, but rather made an exceptional speech on the topic, which is remembered for a line he did not in fact utter – 'the white heat of the technological revolution'.

The ground had been prepared by war and by the post-war Labour government. As Herbert Morrison, a senior Labour politician, had put it in 1947: 'If production is now universally recognised as national duty No. 1, that is because the Government, without as much help from others as I should have liked, have placed it firmly in that position on the national agenda by a sustained campaign.'[3] In his leaden way Morrison was right. For example, 'A MODERN, INCREASINGLY PRODUCTIVE NATION' was the message of a government propaganda film of 1950, an economics lecture designed to explain 'the vast productive machine by which we live'. It stressed the need for investment in new productive capacity, giving as examples electrified coal mines, new steel works, jet-powered locomotives and tractor-powered agriculture.[4]

Yet, if the idea came from the 1940s, it took decades to transform the old economy, the old industries and social services, in a process which culminated in the 1970s and early 1980s. From 1950 to the early 1980s, the United Kingdom was indeed remade. In very many respects over these thirty years the changes were much greater than in the previous thirty. They were especially dramatic because of the stagnation in the civil infrastructure from at least the late 1930s, and in many cases longer. In the early 1950s there was little new rolling stock; there were barely more private cars and buses than in the late

1930s; the most modern public buildings from pubs to council buildings dated from the 1930s. In 1950 there were still about the same number of private telephones as there were business telephones. The number of TV owners was at 1930s levels, the newest cinemas were the great palaces of the 1930s. The schools, hospitals and employment exchanges of the 1950s were those of the 1930s. To cap it all, the British diet was the 1930s diet set in aspic by a decade and a half of food control and rationing.

The greatest change of all was to be in the size of the national cake. Its size came to be measured almost as a matter of routine by the increasingly familiar estimates of national income or gross domestic product. This number was increasing year by year and at a sustained rate which would never have been seen had it been measured as systematically earlier. From the late 1940s into the early 1970s growth averaged 2–3% per cent of GDP per annum. Even by later standards, growth was not only fast, but also smooth. The high point of 'growthmanship' was 1964, when both the Conservative manifesto and Labour's National Plan of 1964 called for 4 per cent per annum growth, which was never achieved on a sustained basis. There were spurts lasting a year in the 1960s when growth reached 6 per cent; the record was and is 1973, with 7.4 per cent annual GDP growth. Still, the size of the national cake measured by real GDP more than doubled between 1950 and 1975 (a greater growth than between 1975 and 2000). Furthermore, the population was growing as the result of baby booms in the late 1940s and early 1960s – due to couples marrying younger than ever.

Not for nothing were the terms 'affluent society' and 'consumer society' applied to these years of transformative growth. An economy producing more than twice as much in 1975 as 1950 resulted in all too real changes in the lives of nearly every British person. The working class, the vast majority of the population in both 1950 and 1975, went from austerity to relative plenty. They now enjoyed at least some of the perquisites of the middle class of the 1930s, the motor car and the telephone, the camera and any number of electrical goods. In the 1960s more than half of households got washing machines and cars. British acquisition of new domestic machinery was reaching the levels achieved in the USA in the 1920s. In the course of the 1970s more than half got colour television, central heating and a telephone.[5] As a result, there was a transformation in the technique of domestic production of heat, cleanliness and food, in domestic leisure and indeed in transport.

But to see the changes just in terms of the growth of incomes is not enough. The character of the national infrastructure had changed in particular ways to make all this possible. Projects were planned, programmed, imagined in advance and put into effect by agencies granted great powers of investment, coordination and decision. In the 1950s and 1960s, government and nationalized industries, which accounted for around a half of all investment, made political choices, some overt, some covert, some not even thought of as political choices, whose upshot was the conscious if contested transformation of the nation. Some of these changes, such as the creation of a welfare state, are well known, if not always well understood. Others, such as achievement of self-sufficiency in food, the quintupling of electricity production, the rise of the private motor car to dominate transport, are less readily invoked in histories. These were epochal changes. In 1950 the United Kingdom was still the same coal-fired, food-importing area it was in 1900. By the mid-1970s it had been changed into an electrified, motorized nation which could easily feed itself.

FOOD

In the early 1950s West Germany and the United Kingdom were very different in one still crucial respect. Twenty per cent of the German population was on the land, about four times more than in the British case.[6] Germany supplied 80 per cent of its own food, the United Kingdom only about half, with some foods, such as butter, cheese, meat and sugar, still coming mostly from abroad. Through to 1954, as since 1940, these foods were rationed, as before as a means of import control. Still Britons ate more than Germans. By the 1970s the two countries had grown alike, as a result of radical changes in the United Kingdom especially. It ceased to be a major food importer and turned to growing its own. While in 1953 net imports of food, drink and tobacco amounted to 6.1 per cent of GDP, by 1980 they were a mere 1 per cent, which, together with reductions in net imports of raw materials, amounted to a saving of over 9 per cent of GDP.[7] In the mid-1980s the balance of trade in food was down to a negative £11 billion (in 2013 prices), half the level of 1936.[8] From the 1980s onwards the United Kingdom was as self-sufficient in food as any of the main European economies.

After the war there were determined efforts to increase domestic food supplies in the long term. The 1947 Agriculture Act introduced permanent subsidies for UK agriculture. Farmers were paid the difference between import prices and their costs of production – known as 'deficiency payments'. Land was put under the plough in peacetime as never before. Fertilizer, now made from oil and gas, rather than, as before, using coal, was poured on to British fields.[9] A new 'power agriculture' of tractors and combine harvesters, also dependent on oil, reduced labour requirements. In plant breeding, government-funded organizations came to dominate the supply of new varieties.[10] On the farm, the old, complex process of making silage (fermented wet fodder, used as winter food instead of hay) was radically expanded so that by the 1980s it was a commonplace way of generating food for the vastly expanded cattle herd.[11] Both old and new techniques consistently applied transformed both levels of production and the productivity of land and workers.

There were also linked transformations in food manufacture. Using low-protein (or soft) British wheat to make bread required a new method. The Chorleywood Bread Process, a fast method of bread making, which could use this wheat, came into being in 1961. It was the product of the British Baking Industries Research Association, established in 1946 in the leafy outskirts of London, one of a new batch of such bodies created after 1945. The cheap, cotton-wool-like British loaf was the product of national research for national purposes.[12]

In the 1950s and 1960s self-sufficiency in food increased steadily but slowly. For food which could be grown in the United Kingdom, the proportion of food supplied domestically was 61 per cent in 1956. This rose steadily to a peak of 95 per cent in 1984, falling to 80 per cent by the end of the century. The figures for all food, including, for example, tropical products, were, for the same dates, 47, 78 and 67 per cent.[13]

Figure 11.1: UK food, feed and drink imports and exports at 2011 prices £000 (GDP deflator)

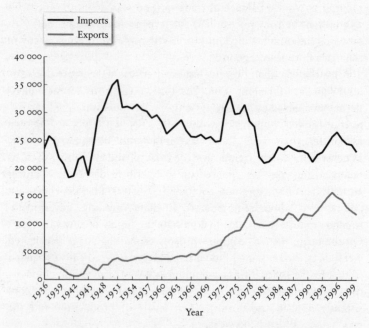

Note: The peaks in the early 1950s and 1970s are the result of relatively high world food prices at those times rather than increased volume of imports.

Source: http://webarchive.nationalarchives.gov.uk/20130103014432/ http://www.defra.gov.uk/statistics/foodfarm/food/overseastrade/.

Self-sufficiency was to get a major boost from 1975, with the United Kingdom now part of the EEC. Being in the Common Market turned out not to mean more European food, but very much more *British* food. A White Paper was published called *Food from Our Own Resources* – which, based on the argument that both world and European Community prices for food were rising, called for large increases of domestic supply. That rise in prices, usually ignored in treatments of the period which focus only on the oil price and domestic problems, was important and caused by global weather conditions.[14] The

White Paper called for increases in national output, especially in milk (and consequentially beef), sugar beet, cereals and sheep.[15] And indeed production did go up. There were increases in sugar beet output, once the great symbol of autarchic economics but now just a crop; the amount of land under wheat, already much higher even than the very sharp wartime peak, continued up. The number of cattle peaked at 15 million in the mid-1970s, at twice the interwar number. Beef production tonnage in the 1970s was double pre-war and wartime levels.[16] British farmers took to making a living by the copulation of continental cattle. French Charolais and Limousin, huge animals, were producers of lean beef and replaced small British breeds such as the Aberdeen Angus and Hereford. Sheep numbers increased sharply from the mid-1970s into the 1980s and 1990s – from under 30 million to nearly 45 million. There was nothing ancestral about the hill farming of sheep; it was the product of policy.

The only trends that were clearly and consistently downward were the human population of farms and the number of orchards. In 1950 there were slightly more agricultural workers than miners. In 1970 there was a wider gap though numbers in both had fallen dramatically: 400,000 on the land and 300,000 under it. The great difference was that coal output fell, while agricultural output increased. Labour productivity growth in agriculture was much higher than in mining, indeed than in the economy as a whole, higher even than in manufacturing industry.

The British diet was to change quite radically as Britons got richer and ate British food. As rationing disappeared, the British diet changed back to what it had been before the war, with more meat and sugar and less grain and potato, and stayed stable.[17] Thereafter the old staples of bread and potatoes drifted downwards. Milk consumption, through an organized system of distribution to every door, grew and remained very high. Every home that wanted it – and most did – had milk delivered every day, at the same price as in the shops, in an extraordinary semi-socialized system of distribution on a national scale. Much was done by special electric lorries known as milk floats. Beef and veal, now increasingly domestically produced, were augmented and to some extent displaced by the arrival of the (national) frozen chicken in the 1950s, closely allied to the rise of supermarkets, which turned poultry from a luxury into a staple. From the 1970s there was a distinct move away from a diet heavy in red meat, potatoes, bread, sugar and tea. For example, household beef and veal consumption was from the 1980s below, soon well below, Second World War levels; for mutton and lamb that had happened in the 1960s.

The new food regime had its critics, liberal and socialist. In 1973 Liverpool MP Eric Heffer, protesting about entry into the Common Market, claimed that 'most northern working-class families at Sunday evening tea have tinned salmon with salad followed by tinned peaches and tinned cream'. This 'traditional working-class Sunday-evening tea' was to be made more expensive by the external tariffs of the Common Market, which taxed food coming in from outside its borders.[18] They were the global preserved foods the United Kingdom would now leave behind. A national agriculture now supplied the nation which once prided itself on being fed by the agriculture of the world. It would soon import fresh peaches from southern Europe and be awash in fresh cream. The salmon, too, would be fresh, and home produced. Astonishingly, the United Kingdom became an exporter of food and indeed became a *net* exporter of wheat, and a significant exporter of beef. In sheep meat United Kingdom was a small net exporter in some years.[19] All this was unthinkable in 1950.

THE END OF THE REEFER

The expansion of domestic agriculture transformed not only the British countryside, but the foreign relations of the nation and its shipping. It in itself meant that one of the most important trades with the Commonwealth – that in meat and wheat – was coming to an end. For example, within two decades the enormous and unique British meat trade from the River Plate and to a great extent from Australasia stopped. With the end of rationing in 1954, frozen imported meat gave way to premium chilled meat once more. The trade never returned to its pre-war scale, in part because as population increased in the River Plate so did local meat consumption, leaving less for export (as had happened in the USA half a century earlier). Still the

Figure 11.2: Household consumption (grams per week) of selected foods (from the National Food Survey)

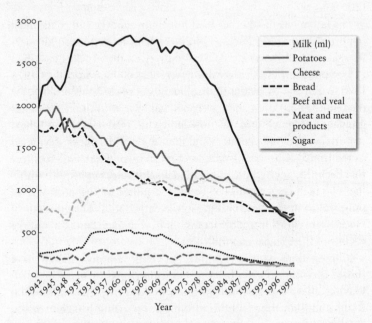

Note: Food eaten outside the home is excluded.
Source: National Food Survey, archived at webarchive.nationalarchives.gov.uk.

national reefer fleet was renovated in the 1940s and again in the late 1950s. The Blue Star Line had five ships sailing to the River Plate, all built in the 1940s, among them the *Uruguay Star*. The Royal Mail Line operated four *Highland* meat ships (built in the 1920s) to 1959–60 and four 1940s ships into the 1960s.[20] It built a new generation launched in 1959–60 – the *Amazon*, *Arlanza* and *Aragon* – which carried passengers in its cabins and meat in its holds. They were among the last passenger ships to be built at Harland & Wolff; the *Arlanza* was launched just before the *Canberra*. The last Royal Mail sailings to the River Plate, using these ships, were in 1969.[21] They were transferred to a then related company Shaw, Saville and Albion, sailing to New Zealand. They lasted only a very few years, before all were converted into early car-carriers operated by a Norwegian company. The Blue Star service ended in the late 1960s, and the ships were scrapped in 1972. The Australasian trade lasted only a very little longer.

The fall in meat and other food imports meant the end of the most important of the older docks. There were many fewer 50–100-kg quarter sides of chilled beef for dockers to carry on their backs ('backing') to load on to lorries.[22] There were fewer sacks of sugar from the Caribbean, Brazil and Mauritius to manhandle out of the holds of ships, for the refineries at Love Lane, Liverpool and Silvertown, London. Sugar growing and processing was now largely an inland industry. Wheat imports, to the grain elevators and flour mills of the docks, decreased as the United Kingdom came to process its own wheat. And tobacco, too, declined, not because of a national substitute, but because smoking, like high consumption of bread and potatoes, was no longer as universal as in the past, peaking in the early 1960s. The great Royal Docks were closed in 1980, victims not of containerization, but of the decline of these staple imports.

Many nations who have wanted to create themselves anew have shifted their capital cities from cosmopolitan ports to inland, inward-looking cities, or at least sought to do so. Moscow, Ankara, Brasilia, Abuja and Islamabad took over from great ports for just this reason. Yet while no one thought seriously of replacing London – there was nowhere sufficiently inland in the United Kingdom in any case – London itself turned inwards, to managing the nation, not the world, and was fed by the nation, not the world. Liverpool, too, was deeply affected by this change. Both were cities in decline, particularly in the areas around the docks. The politics changed too, in that London and Liverpool dock workers, and the workers in its dockside industries, were central to the working class, the unions and the politics of these cities. The docks were places where into the 1960s labour was casual and organized in gangs and where the main union, the Transport and General Workers' Union, was regarded by the rank and file as a tool of management. After the mid-1970s there were none of the strikes which had been such a feature of Britain back to the Edwardian years and beyond. The great British dock strike was over. More than that, the nation turned its back on the sea – ships, ports, shipyards were no longer a staple feature of the visual life of the nation. It was now no longer an island – an image which, like that of the British ship, was pushed back into the eighteenth and nineteenth centuries.[23]

The United Kingdom did not stop importing, far from it, but what it imported changed. Imports were to come in containers and tankers. Liverpool built the new Seaforth container dock in the 1970s; London developed Tilbury as a container port, while Southampton used tidal facilities for the container trade. Felixstowe emerged out of nowhere as a container giant, pointing towards Europe, not the Atlantic. These docks were mere transport nodes, not great industrial centres. They imported manufactured goods. The really large new bulk trades also moved to new places, becoming invisible in the process. Oil, the most important, was imported through jetties close to refineries rather than to traditional ports.

NATIONAL ENERGY

The case of energy provides another astonishing example of rapid state-led change. Energy supply was a national effort by interconnected nationalized industries – coal, gas, electricity and nuclear research and development. These national enterprises, many very capital intensive, effected great transformations, such that by the 1970s whole systems had been renewed. In the context of rapidly growing total supply, oil, natural gas, nuclear and some hydro were all added to the coal supply, creating a world of plenty in energy. From 1950 there was no stopping domestic electrification and every index of consumer durable consumption, as it was called. It is perhaps better to think of these things as machines for domestic production and domestic entertainment. Washing machines, and then dishwashers, fridges and freezers, spread slowly, changing the routines of domestic labour. Central heating, too, diffused slowly, following on from gas and electric heating, eliminating what in 1950 was still standard, the open coal fire. Radios, record-players and especially television, which all sold very much faster than machines for the production of heat and cleanliness and food, domesticated and privatized entertainment – as they expanded, so the cinema and theatre declined. The coronation of 1953 gave a great boost to television. Services were extended, with great masts being put up on peaks around the country. Television took over from radio in the 1950s as the main source of news, and even some popular programmes shifted over from radio.[24]

In the 1950s the United Kingdom was still a coal-based economy, and one in which coal was short. Output increased to a post-war peak in 1955, while the number of miners peaked in 1948 (though both output and employment were still well under 1913 levels). Domestic coal consumption reached its historic peak in the 1950s, when it still powered most of the railways, most of industry, produced all the gas and heated homes. In less than twenty years coal went from being a universal fuel to one used by the 1970s essentially for two purposes – to generate electricity and to make steel. Its functions as the main sources of domestic heat, gas and power for transport was replaced by natural gas, and various derivatives of oil.

Table 11.1: UK final energy consumption, 1948–98, million tonnes of oil equivalent

	1948	1958	1968	1978	1988	1998
Coal/coke/ other solid	101.5	83.3	50.7	22.8	16.3	5.3
Petroleum	13.2	30.5	61.2	68.2	62.0	66.1
Natural gas			0.2	37.8	46.3	55.9
Town gas/ coke oven gas	12.5	13.4	12.2	1.0	0.8	0.4
Electricity	4.2	7.4	14.7	19.3	22.8	27.1
Renewable and waste					0.4	0.9
Total	131.5	134.7	138.9	149.1	148.6	155.61

Source: DECC 60th Anniversary: Digest of United Kingdom Energy Statistics (London, 2009).

In electricity supply coal remained king despite the best efforts of planners. An extraordinarily powerful futurism, more radical than in any other country, gripped the state. In gushing terms – nuclear was 'the energy of the future' – the 1950s Conservative government launched the most ambitious nuclear programme in the world. In 1955 it announced a programme of nuclear power and declared that 'Our future as an industrial country depends both on the ability of our scientists to discover the secrets of nature and on our speed in applying the new techniques that science places within our grasp.'[25] According to the 1955 plan, by 1965 the United Kingdom would be producing 25 per cent of its electricity from nuclear; something like 25 per cent of the investment in new stations would be in nuclear. It envisaged that after 1965 no more coal stations would be built.[26] This plan was made before the Calder Hall reactor, whose main function was to make plutonium for bombs, had generated any power. That success, which came in 1956, and the oil embargo following the failed invasion of Egypt, prompted the more radical 1957 plan. This envisaged nineteen rather than twelve nuclear reactors.[27] What is remarkable is not the technical originality of Calder Hall – it was obviously neither the first atomic pile nor the first to generate electricity. What made the British project different was the deep commitment to the large-scale exploitation of nuclear fission.

Although in the 1960s the United Kingdom had generated more nuclear power than any other nation, nothing like the first or second plans came about. The reason was simple. British coal remained cheaper than British nuclear, despite the claims of the nuclear barons, and imported oil was cheaper still. Nevertheless, all through the 1950s and the 1960s the government claimed that nuclear was and would be cheaper than coal.[28] Nuclear stations continued to be built, as well as linked pumped storage schemes which used off-peak nuclear electricity to pump water into reservoirs, which was discharged at peak times to generate hydro-electricity. Four of these were built, by far the largest being the last one, in North Wales, completed in 1984, the largest civil engineering project to that date, which could produce power at a rate greater than any nuclear station.

British governments, until 1979, chose British reactors even when it was clear that US reactors were cheaper. The first generation of reactors was wholly British, and although foreign sales were hoped for, there were to be only two. The British advanced gas-cooled reactor (AGR) won a rigged contest against the American PWR (pressurized water reactor) in 1965, when the CEGB chose it for Dungeness B.

Though ordered in that year, the station did not produce power until 1983. The other AGRs were completed between 1971 and 1989. Not one was exported. In 1974 the government planned a large order of steam-generating heavy water reactors (derived by British teams from the Canada deuterium uranium (CANDU) reactor) against the wishes of the CEGB and the major contractor, GEC, and it eventually came to nothing. Instead, two final AGRs (the last throw of Build British) were ordered by Labour in 1979, and a single American-designed PWR by the incoming Conservative government, which planned (but did not bring about) a massive PWR programme. The AGR in particular was claimed to have been one of the worst investment decisions in the history of mankind, alongside Concorde.[29] With all these reactors working – the Magnox reactors ordered in the 1950s, the AGRs ordered in the 1960s and the one US-designed PWR ordered in the 1980s – nuclear output peaked in the mid-1990s, at the proportion it had been planned to reach in 1965.

Coal-powered electricity won out. From the 1960s coal was used to fire new power stations ten times the size of those of the 1950s, and bigger than any nuclear station. For example, the 2.5GW Longannet, in full operation in 1973, drawing from local mines, consumed 4.5 million tons per annum. From 1968 Didcot A, rated at 2GW, consumed nearly 4 million tons of coal per annum. There were many others of this vintage and scale: Cottam, Eggborough, Ferrybridge C, Fiddler's Ferry, Kingsnorth, Ratcliffe-on-Soar, West Burton A and Drax. Drax was the last coal power station to be completed in the United Kingdom and the largest power station in Europe. These stations were equipped with 500 MW sets (in the 1960s) and 660 MW turbo-generating sets (in the 1970s), which compared with the 30 and 60 MW sets of the immediate post-war years.[30] These coal stations were connected to distant areas of consumption by the new supergrid of 400 KV, built from 1965. Much less well known than the nuclear stations, they were more important in terms of electricity produced and continued to produce electricity into the twenty-first century.

From the late 1950s to the mid-1970s there was a spectacular fall in coal output. It nearly halved as coal-gas, coal-powered locomotives, coal-heated homes and coal-fired factories were eliminated. This is not to say the industry decayed; rather, it was transformed by new machinery. The National Coal Board developed a coal-cutting machine, the Anderton Shearer Loader, which equipped the mines and sold all over the world.[31] New pits were dug, including the 'Big-K', the Kellingley colliery in North Yorkshire, the largest in Europe. A new coalfield was discovered in Selby, Yorkshire, and from the 1970s coal started being produced in a new superpit (in fact a complex of interconnected pits) which was in full production from the 1980s, with peak output of over 10 million tons in the early 1990s.

Coal came to matter more in the 1970s than it had since the 1940s. The miners were in a strong position – domestic coal was now an attractive alternative to expensive imported oil following the recent quadrupling of the oil price in 1973. There was hope for an increased demand for coal in the future, and investment poured in. The 1975 plan for coal envisaged increasing output, to replace oil, for a steel industry expected to expand, and for new uses. There was thought of re-coaling the British economy – but new houses could not burn coal, they had not been built with flues. Once again scientists were paid to research the processing of coal to make smokeless fuel, chemicals and oil. Coal production never got up to expected levels, though 1980 saw the peak use of coal in power stations, now its main use by far. However, output ceased to fall as it had in the late 1950s and 1960s; its long and pronounced decline was decisively interrupted. Through the 1980s coal production fell slowly – from 125 million tonnes in 1980 to 100 million tonnes in 1990. The dramatic fall in production came under John Major and continued under New Labour.

OIL

The story of energy growth in the 1950s and 1960s is mainly the story of oil. The reasons for this were simple. It was a new and versatile universal fuel and a source of chemicals, from plastics to fertilizers. Only oil could cheaply power the expanding number of motor vehicles. It began to be used as heating oil, and to make gas on a small scale. It was also used as a primary or reserve fuel in some power stations. Oil overtook coal as a source of energy in 1970 – and then kept roughly constant shares for a decade.[32]

However, there was relatively little British nationalism in oil, in contrast to nuclear and coal. This perhaps reflected British strength in oil, for the United Kingdom was very unusual in having not just one, but two global oil majors, Shell and BP, two of the 'seven sisters' which dominated world oil. One was state-owned though autonomous, but both had intimate connections with the British state. The lack of nationalism was reflected in the fact that US oil companies continued to be important within the United Kingdom. US companies were among those who built the new refineries of the 1940s and 1950s. Four refineries belonging to US firms started operating in Milford Haven between 1960 and 1973. And of course the crude oil itself came from overseas, now largely from the Middle East, at first through the Suez Canal, but increasingly in tankers too big to pass through that waterway. The new oil terminals which fed refineries were now among the greatest importing ports by bulk, to be compared with great coal-exporting ports of the past. The United Kingdom had become a net importer of energy, just like most European nations. For all the centrality of considerations of national security of supply of energy, the most important source by the early 1970s was vulnerable.

The hike in oil prices orchestrated by Middle East producers in 1973 had a profound effect on the British economy, just as on the European and world economies. Oil had been cheap but was now expensive enough to register in the balance of payments. The United Kingdom developed a balance of payments deficit, which reached 4 per cent of GDP, the same as the proportion of GDP accounted for by oil imports at their peak in value.[33] The upshot was an end to the growth of the oil economy. The growth of refining ended in 1973; oil was no longer routinely used in power stations.

But the United Kingdom was quite exceptionally fortunate. North Sea oil started coming ashore in 1975, and within a decade the United Kingdom was a net exporter of oil, the peak corresponding to even higher world oil prices following the Iranian revolution in 1979. To produce oil at a time when oil was so expensive was supremely lucky. It gave hope for plans for a new national reconstruction in the 1970s. Even from the late 1960s refineries were built on the east coast to take advantage of the oil which would soon be flowing in: three on Teesside (two by Philips and ICI and one by Shell) and two on Humberside.

The very early 1970s saw finds of new fields – Ekofisk (Philips), to be connected to Teesside, Forties (BP), to be connected to Cruden Bay, and then to the great BP refinery at Grangemouth, and Brent (Shell), which was to be connected to Sullom Voe, Shetland, were the largest. The Piper Field (Occidental and Thompson) was to be connected by pipeline to Flotta, Orkney.

Less well known is the case of gas. Gas was found in the North Sea, off Norfolk in 1965. From then there was a boom in investment, and a remarkable changeover of the whole nation, in the space of a few years, from coal and oil gas, to North Sea gas, an immense task. The supply of town gas peaked in 1969. From then it fell at an incredible pace as vast quantities of North Sea methane flowed in. The huge gasometers which dominated many urban skylines were now as redundant as the gasworks which fed them. By 1973 gas supply was double that of 1969 and would continue to increase very rapidly. All this was the work of the nationalized British Gas. By 2000 gas supply was three times greater than 1973; one-third was used to generate electricity.[34] By 2000 gas was the single largest source of energy for the United Kingdom.

By the mid-1980s, thanks to oil and gas production, total domestic energy production was back to 1913 levels. The North Sea was producing around 150 million tons of oil and gas annually, at a time when just over 100 million tons of coal were still mined. The peak surplus in the crude oil trade came in 1984, with 48 million tonnes of surplus.[35] This was comparable in tonnage to exports of coal in the interwar years. The value of oil and gas peaked in 1984–5 at 7 per cent of GDP; in that year 7 per cent of government revenues came from oil and gas taxes. A second peak in output, not value, came in 1999 and was considerably higher than the first in 1986, as the proportion of gas was going up.[36] North Sea oil and gas production was alone now about the same as the coal output of 1913.[37]

Despite the return of the United Kingdom to being a major energy producer, oil and gas production hardly figured in the self-image of the nation. The whole sector was much less visible than coal had been or still was, especially perhaps in retrospect. The oil industry was very different from coal – it was private and employed only around 60,000 people in the early 1980s.[38] The miners were all-British and unionized; the oil workers typically neither. Oil was only temporarily visible. 1988 saw an explosion and fire on a US-owned rig in the North Sea, the Piper Alpha. This rig, one of the earliest, took oil and gas from the pioneering Piper field, the equivalent of a gigantic coal mine. 167 men died, in what was the biggest industrial disaster since the Gresford mine disaster of 1934, where 266 men died in a coal mine in North Wales.

The oil production of the world outside the USA was, in the 1970s, largely in the hands of the producing states. However, the British government exercised relatively little control. While gas was in the hands of a nationalized industry, oil was not. The nationalized BP was not the agent for developing the North Sea on behalf of the state: it was too independent, more so from 1977, when the Labour government actually sold 17 per cent of it. When Labour returned in 1974 it quickly established a new petroleum revenue tax and a British National Oil Corporation (BNOC), which took a share in the production in fields, negotiated with the oil companies and gave the government expertise in oil. It was led by a formidable businessman, Lord Kearton, an Oxford chemist who had worked for ICI and the bomb programme and later ran Courtaulds – the sort of technocratic businessman supposed not to exist in the United Kingdom. Yet, in a move unthinkable in other energies, there was no great fuss as to whether British or foreign oil companies used British equipment. The investment involved was huge: in 1976 40 per cent of what was being invested in manufacturing.[39] However, only a paltry 35 per cent of the orders went to the United Kingdom as of 1974 – the rigs and supply vessels were foreign, the platforms British, but built by foreign firms; the vast steel pipelines from Japan were not even laid by British ships.[40] Even France built more oil rigs than did the United Kingdom.[41] Norway, tiny and barely industrial, did much better in supplying material and created a significant offshore industry. This private oil, dependent on overseas equipment, was to be a portent for future energy policy.

INFRASTRUCTURE

The transformations in food and energy supply were just two examples of infrastructural renewals led by the state. Between the 1950s

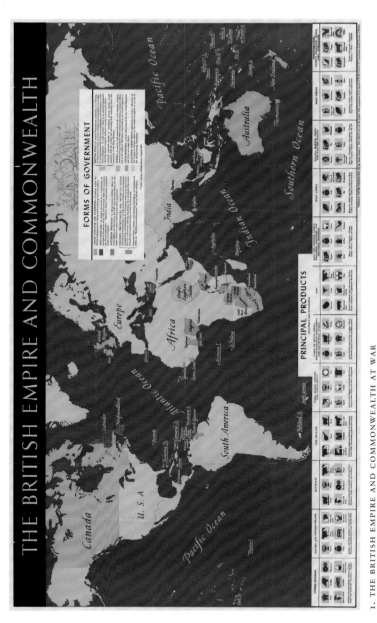

1. THE BRITISH EMPIRE AND COMMONWEALTH AT WAR

A Second World War Canadian propaganda poster showing the very different administrative regimes it incorporated. Egypt and Iraq are not shown, as they gained formal independence in 1922 and 1932.

2. PATRIOTISMS AND POLITICS
(*left*) The Edith Cavell monument in
London. At the top is written, 'King and
Country'; below, added during the 1924
Labour Government, is the phrase,
'Patriotism is not enough. I must have
no hatred or bitterness for anyone'.
(*above*) A Great War recruitment poster,
one of many emphasizing that allegiance
was due to the Empire as a whole.

3. THE PEOPLES' WAR, AND
PEOPLES' WAR IN PROPAGANDA
(*above*) British children in a bomb
shelter. (*right*) An Indian soldier
arriving in Singapore 1941 or 1942.
The original caption read 'He gives
the "V" sign from a port-hole of a
ship as he arrives at Singapore –
and his "V" is backed by a million
Indian troops and the rest of the
empire as well.'

FORCIBLE FEEDING.

4. POLITICS AND POLITICIANS

(*top*) A cartoon by Stanger Pritchard, 1913, from *Truth*, December 1913, setting out the issues of the time and showing, among others, David Lloyd George, Herbert Asquith, Emmeline Pankhurst, Edward Carson, Keir Hardie, and Winston Churchill. (*below*) Prime Minister Stanley Baldwin (*centre*) with Foreign Secretary Austen Chamberlain (half-brother of Neville) and Chancellor of the Exchequer Winston Churchill in 1925.

5. A NATION AMONG SUPERPOWERS (*above*) Clement Attlee,
newly elected as Prime Minister, with Harry Truman, US
President since April 1945, and Joseph Stalin, recently elevated
to Generalissimo of the Soviet Union, in Berlin, August 1945.
(*below*) Sir Winston Churchill, with Anthony Eden, visiting
President Dwight Eisenhower, shown with Secretary of State
John Foster Dulles and Vice-President Richard Nixon.

6 and 7. THE POWER OF COAL
(*top left*) The Temple of Peace and Health, Cardiff, endowed by Lord
David Davies, coal-owner and philanthropist, advocate of an international air police. (*below left*) The new Battersea Power Station,
designed by Sir Giles Gilbert Scott, photographed in 1935. Scott
would go on to design the new House of Commons, completed in
1950. (*above*) Coal-powered chemistry on display in the ICI pavilion
at the Empire Exhibition, Glasgow, 1938, designed by Sir Basil Spence.

8. GLOBAL CAPITALISM

(*top*) Coal out and wheat in at the Roath Dock, Cardiff, in the 1930s. The architect of the new 24,000-ton grain silo to the left was Oscar Faber, to be engineer of the new House of Commons, completed in 1950. (*above*) The new Retiro station (completed *c.* 1915) of the Central Argentine Railway in Buenos Aires. This British-owned railway was nationalized in 1948. The station, and the railway it served, is still in use.

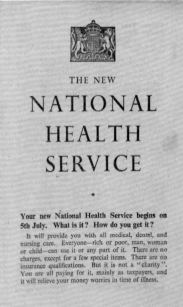

THE NEW
NATIONAL
HEALTH
SERVICE

*

Your new National Health Service begins on 5th July. What is it? How do you get it?

It will provide you with all medical, dental, and nursing care. Everyone—rich or poor, man, woman or child—can use it or any part of it. There are no charges, except for a few special items. There are no insurance qualifications. But it is not a "charity". You are all paying for it, mainly as taxpayers, and it will relieve your money worries in time of illness.

9. THE WELFARE STATE

(*top*) A Ministry of Health leaflet from *c.* 1960, advertising orange juice made in new plants and plantations in the colonies of British Honduras and Jamaica. (*above left*) A Ministry of Health pamphlet explaining the new National Health Service (1948). (*above right*) A ministry poster by H. M. Bateman, 1950.

10 and 11. NATIONAL MODERN
(*top left*) This gigantic hangar, completed in 1949 by the
Bristol Aeroplane Company at its Filton factory, was used
to build the eight-engined Brabazon airliner and, later, the
Concorde. (*below left*) Railway property, in this case a
lorry, becomes British. (*above*) Making the peanut-based
fibre Ardil at ICI Dumfries in 1956.

12 and 13. THE OLD AND THE NEW
(*top left*) The Royal Mail *Amazon*, one of the last great meat and
passenger liners, shown in 1965. (*bottom left*) Union Jack hat with
flags of state industries and enterprises, *c.* 1970. (*top*) Cleaners at
work on the first British Concorde, at the British Aircraft Corporation (BAC) works at Filton, Bristol, in 1967. (*above*), women
in Matlock, Derbyshire, machining clothes in 1968, in a factory
dating from 1784.

What does possession mean to you?

7% of our population own 84% of our wealth

The Economist, 15 January, 1966

14 and 15. ONE NATION?
(*above*) *Possession*, by Victor Burgin (1976). (*top right*) Opposition
leader Harold Wilson with the Labour Party's slogan and symbol for the
February 1974 General Election. (*below right*) Prime Minister Margaret
Thatcher with cows. In the 1970s the British cattle herd peaked at
double the size of the interwar period, part of the successful effort to
make the United Kingdom nearly self-sufficient in food, a pre-condition
for the UK becoming a net importer of manufactures in the 1980s.

16. THE END OF THE NATION?

(*top*) Diana, Princess of Wales, speaking to machinists at Ford's
Halewood Plant on its twenty-fifth anniversary in 1988. Twenty years
earlier, these machinists followed their sisters at Ford's Dagenham
plant out on strike for equal pay for women. In the following decade,
the 'People's Princess' seriously damaged the legitimacy of the House
of Windsor. (*above*) Tony Benn, Arthur Scargill and Dennis Skinner at
the miners' rally in London on 21 October 1992, walking down
Kensington High Street, where the locals, 'moved by the sheer
numbers and quiet dignity of the marchers, broke out into clapping
and cheers'. In the 1990s, British coal gave way to imported coal.

and the 1970s and 1980s, roads, pipes, electricity lines and bridges were built on a vaster scale and faster than the railways of the Victorian age.

The first (and very short) motorway was opened in 1958; the last major projects were completed in 1986 (M25) and 1990 (M40), though each of these had started decades before.[42] They were generously proportioned and almost theatrically laid out, with well-designed sign-posting which still has an air of modernity about it and would be used as a uniform national road sign system. The 1960s and 1970s were also a great age for building road bridges, many for motorways, such as the Severn, Avonmouth, Forth Road, Frairton, Cromarty and Humber bridges and the Bromford viaduct. 'Juggernauts', heavy lorries, now became the main means of transport. Motorization did not at first imply private ownership. Labour had nationalized road haulage (as British Road Services) in the 1940s, but under the Conservatives private road haulage expanded, with BRS, later called the National Freight Corporation, taking only a minor role. Here, there was a huge relative expansion of the private sector, as in the case of the intimately related shift to oil.

As far as people were concerned, in 1950 the bulk of movements took place in publicly owned public transport. Publicly owned buses, trams and coaches were the largest single mode of transport, with public rail and private cars about equal. By the mid-1950s private cars had overtaken buses and coaches and grew inexorably, such that by 1970 or so car usage had quintupled as bus and rail usage fell. The motorization of the country was made revolutionary by its new scale rather than its novelty. It was achieved with British-made cars, buses, and trucks.

The state also took the lead in promoting the building of new housing, on a historically unprecedented scale. By the 1950s, hundreds of thousands of new houses were being built, many by local councils. Total and council building peaked in the late 1960s. The result was more private ownership by occupiers, but also an unprecedented number of council houses which were rented (reaching a peak of over 30 per cent of households in the 1970s). The private landlord, increasingly associated with the rack-renting of slums, was nearly eliminated. Creation of new suburbias, public and private, was the rule.[43] New forms of building were encouraged, not just tower blocks, which remained few, but many different kinds of alternative configurations. The council house was still mainly the interwar semi-detached type. Yet critics of modernism and the welfare state would conflate the tower block and the welfare state. The tower block was rather the product of special subsidies and was promoted by large construction firms using industrialized building systems in the 1960s into the early 1970s. Some were huge – the Red Road flats in Glasgow were the tallest residential buildings in Europe. They were cheap and nasty, poorly insulated and – a telling detail – with tiny lifts.[44] They were exceptional but marked a move away from the council house as a superior alternative to a private landlord and were a cynical abuse of the taxpayer and the humble.

There were also New Towns, planned conurbations on greenfield sites, on a scale not seen earlier in the twentieth century. They were often centred on new or enlarged industrial facilities. Thus Irvine and Runcorn New Towns were close by ICI plants. Tellingly, they were connected to motorways. Many were looking to the future and were built for cars, with some notable for separating car traffic from pedestrians. North Bucks New City, which was to emerge as Milton Keynes, was exceptional in that it was meant to have had a high-speed automated monorail system for internal transport. It too was built for the car.[45]

The railways were in near-permanent decline in the face of the motorways and the private car. Yet they too were transformed by state investment. Although a programme of national dieselization was announced in 1955, new coal-powered steam locomotives were being built into 1960. From the early 1960s British Rail would be scrapping both old and recently built steam locomotives. British Rail, under Dr Beeching, a former ICI scientist, cut many branch lines in the 1960s, essentially eliminating steam services. This was the period of a rapid switch to diesel and electric traction, but it was not until the very late 1960s that steam traction was eliminated. British Rail itself developed, from the 1960s, the APT tilting train and the interim diesel Intercity 125. The high-speed 125s were in service from the mid-1970s into the twenty-first century. The APT, though abandoned, led to the 225 electric trains on the East Coast main line, introduced in the 1980s.

This story of state late modernization coming to fruition in the 1970s and early 1980s can be told for other sectors too. The Post Office spent decades designing systems for the mechanical sorting of letters. These came into operation in the 1970s, continuing a radical reduction in Post Office staff.[46] Electrical engineering companies were building System X, a pioneering digital exchange system for the nationalized telephone system. Only in the 1970s did telephones spread to most of the population.

One of the ways in which daily life as well as the infrastructure of state and industry was changed was by the reform of currency and weights and measures. The United Kingdom had been distinctive in both. Its currency, the pound sterling, was divided into twenty shillings – with 'silver' coins for five shillings (the crown), two-and-a-half shillings (the half-crown), two shillings (the florin), and the sixpence – each of which was divided into twelve pennies – there were 'coppers' for the threepenny, penny, halfpenny and farthing (quarter of a penny); the guinea (twenty-one shillings) was the unit of account for elite professional services and luxury goods. Weights and measures in imperial units (so named because they were established by act of the imperial parliament, as the United Kingdom parliament was often referred to in the early nineteenth century, in 1825) were many and various, and in many different bases. There were twelve inches to a foot, and three feet to a yard. There were also chains and furlongs, fathoms and miles. There were sixteen ounces to the pound, and fourteen pounds to the stone, and eight stones to the hundredweight (cwt) and twenty hundredweight to the (long) ton. It was little wonder, then, that many nations, including members of the Commonwealth, had switched to much simpler systems of money and of weights and measures in which units were divisible by ten. 'Metrication' of weights and measures and the 'decimalization' of currency were national projects predating entry into the Common Market. Metrication was led by industry starting in the 1960s and was clearly in place by the 1970s for most purposes. There were exceptions made for some consumer goods – miles for roads and vehicle speeds, pints for beer and milk. 'Decimalization' of currency was announced in 1966 and implemented in 1971. Thus came to an end a great marker of difference not only with Europe, but with the rest of the world.

THE WELFARE STATE

Thinking of the social services as a set of publicly owned and run service industries helps one see that there is a common history here with the conventionally labelled nationalized industries. Here, too, the state took over a rather decrepit set of institutions and modernized them and expanded them, but only really from the 1960s. The welfare state of the 1940s and 1950s was very oriented to production, to work. Some indeed argued that there ought to be a shift in the focus of welfare from production to consumption, and that consumption, unlike modern production, had the family at its heart.[47] That shift, together with many others in welfare, took decades to come about.

The health services in the 1950s were in many respects leftovers from the 1930s – they relied on old surgeries, hospitals and equipment. The Guillebaud committee was appointed by the Treasury in 1953 to seek to *constrain* growth in health spending. What the committee found and reported on in 1955 was in fact that health spending was falling as a proportion of GDP in the early 1950s, and that building remained at a small fraction of the interwar rate. Hospitals were getting ever older. Hospital building started only in the late 1950s, with a major boost in the 1960s under the Tories. It was only in the early 1960s that expenditures started to move steadily up. There were, and long continued to be, chunks of medical opinion opposed to the whole idea of the NHS.[48]

The 1950s system had over 500,000 beds, nearly half of which were for mental illness, learning disabilities and geriatric cases – there were indeed many more people in mental asylums than in prison. Asylums incarcerated the unruly and the unhappy and made many mentally ill. The NHS embarked on a process of closing hospitals for the mentally ill and for learning disability (with bed numbers reduced to one-quarter and to one-sixth respectively by 2000), as well as cutting back the number of geriatric beds. These processes gathered pace in the 1970s.

It was only with the great reorganization of 1974, with the emphasis on redistributing health resources, planning for fair delivery and consensus management, that a truly national approach was taken to the health of the nation, remembering that there were a number of National Health Services. There was an important move to eliminate what the left saw as a major anomaly – the existence of private beds within the best public hospitals, where patients were attended to by NHS consultants in time they were allowed to reserve for private practice. Labour reduced the number of private beds but did not eliminate them, but in the process promoted the private hospital industry.

The 1940s welfare system was eroded in significant ways by the Tory government of the 1950s and early 1960s. The real value of family allowances which were available to second and subsequent children fell. This benefit, starting at 25p, was paid to all, irrespective of income. (It was taxed, though tax-paying families additionally benefited from tax allowances for children.) This was meant to be a subsistence-level benefit, and thus unemployment and other benefits did not need to have additional sums for second and subsequent children. The drift down meant that the unemployment benefit system had to include a supplement for second and subsequent children, effectively destroying the point of the system, a central pillar of the Beveridgean plan for unemployment benefit. The Labour Party document *Labour in the Sixties* was clear that 'the British Welfare State was not only the pride of the nation but a pattern for our neighbours' in 1951, but that in 1960 'we are a backward country', 'our family allowances, measured against their original purpose, are a farce ... the only social service which is being steadily developed under the Tories is, in fact, National Assistance, conceded after a means test'.[49]

In pensions, Conservative governments of the 1950s reduced the exchequer contribution and kept the upper earnings limit on National Insurance low, making the system still more regressive than it had been.[50] The Conservatives promoted private occupational pensions subsidized through the tax system. In the mid-1950s the Treasury paid more through this hidden 'fiscal welfare state' than in its contribution to National Insurance pensions.[51] The subsidies for the middle class were significantly added to by the effective introduction of a subsidy to mortgage interest payments for homeowners in 1963.

From the mid-1970s Mortgage Interest Tax Relief cost more than the subsidy for council housing. Furthermore, there were generous pensions for public sector employees, for example those of the National Health Service, which pointed sharply to the difference between being employed by the welfare state and being subject to it.[52]

The Beveridgean welfare state was not set in stone. Indeed, one of the least understood and most important points in the history of the welfare state is that key aspects of the Beveridge scheme were rejected not only in practice but in principle. The Labour Party moved to reject the key Beveridgean notion of the fixed contribution and benefit for pensions. It instead proposed (for the 1959 election) a new national superannuation scheme with graduated contributions, a significant tax contribution and earnings-related pensions at half-pay for most, and more for the lower paid. Instead of a miserly pension funded by a regressive poll-tax, the state pension would provide at the same level as civil service and military pensions.[53] Under the Tory 1959 act there was a measure of increased contributions (determined by pay) and an increased pension too, but it was nothing like a system to provide a decent pension for the majority.

The means-tested national assistance that Beveridge hoped would wither away with the expansion of his new comprehensive system not only did not, but indeed expanded, filling the gaps in the Beveridge system. The means-tested benefits of the national assistance supplemented the benefits of, among others, many pensioners. In 1964 a central feature of the Labour campaign was the claim that the Tories wanted to create a 'Means Test State'. There was something in this criticism. For what distinguished the British welfare system from others was not social insurance but national assistance; the dreaded means test was not abolished but became central. In benefits, the creation of the supplementary benefit in the 1960s, to replace national assistance, made available more generous benefits, sought to get benefits to those who had not claimed national assistance and more generally led to more integration with the insurance system. The combination of low insurance benefits and the rise of need of people who were non-insurable in the usual way led to an expansion in means-tested benefits, especially in the 1970s. As in the interwar period, it was discovered that the insurance system on its own could not cope; Beveridge and post-war governments patched it up to try and get it to work, but yet again it did not. There was no escaping the need for tax-funded benefits to which everyone was entitled irrespective of their employment status.

Furthermore, the very core of the Beveridgean system, the flat rate of contribution and of benefit, came to be seen as a bad rather than a good thing. As well as seeking to do away with it for pensions in the 1950s, Labour was generally critical. 'The flat-rate national insurance contribution imposed a regressive poll-tax on the lower-paid,' said the 1970 Labour manifesto. Labour introduced a measure of graduated contribution for National Insurance in 1966, leading to a time-limited, earnings-related element for short-term unemployment and sickness benefits. However, the really big change came in the 1970s. National Insurance charges became a percentage of income as the result of a Conservative measure which came into effect under Labour in 1975. There was still a regressive element in that there was still an upper earnings limit.[54] This was indeed the last vestige of the days when workers paid National Insurance and the middle classes income tax. The other side of that coin was the creation of the State Earnings Related Pension and the continuation of an earnings-related element to unemployment benefit. Another great change of the 1970s was the introduction of child benefit. This was payable to the mother for all children, replaced both the family allowance (also paid to the mother) and the tax allowances, but was well under the level of support for children in the benefits system. But it had the distinction of remaining one of the very few benefits paid to very large numbers of people, the other being the state pension. In the 1970s the social security system was also computerized with, of course, British computers. A new computerized central National Insurance register replaced the paper ones dating to the origins of National Insurance.[55] This led to further networked computerization from the 1980s, but that was the last large state-organized computing project.

Far from representing the end of the welfare state, the 1970s saw its consolidation and radicalization. This was not a uniquely British phenomenon, far from it. The first post-war SPD German Chancellor, Willy Brandt (1969–74), for example, transformed welfare provision in West Germany. What did this amount to in terms of benefit levels in relation to earnings? Comparatively the British welfare system was less generous than that of other rich countries. The years from 1945 to 1965 or even 1970 were not the golden years of the welfare state, to judge by generosity.[56] The ratio of benefits to average earnings in fact peaked in the 1970s, at 25 per cent for the basic state pension, and 20 per cent for unemployment benefit, falling markedly thereafter.[57] These 'replacement ratios' were typically much lower than those found in continental welfare systems.

Education provides another example of the delayed impact of the welfare state, and of important changes which took place in the 1960s and 1970s. It took till the 1970s to raise the school leaving age to sixteen, as had been promised in 1944. It had been fifteen from 1947. The second change was the abandonment in most places of the distinction between the grammar school and the secondary modern. The great majority of local authority school places were in secondary modern schools, the old senior elementary schools. Few (if any) new grammar schools were built after 1944, and in new communities 'comprehensive' schools were created – single types of secondary schools. There was to be a decisive shift to a comprehensive system. Already from the 1950s Labour was pushing the development of local authority education without the eleven-plus, a unified high-quality system – 'grammar schools for all'. By contrast, the Conservatives repeatedly said they favoured grammar schools, meaning selection at eleven as well as different kinds of schools. At the national level there was a clear, contentious policy difference. However, at local level, while Labour was more in favour of comprehensive schools than the Conservatives, the latter nevertheless promoted them. 'Many of the most imaginative new schemes abolishing the eleven-plus have been introduced by Conservative councils,' noted the 1970 Conservative manifesto, calling only for the retention of local choice. Parental pressure, acting locally, on education authorities was the key here.[58] By the mid-1970s the system, in as much as it was a system, in that local authorities controlled education, was nearly fully comprehensive. The old direct-grant grammar schools were also lost – most became 'independent' schools, the euphemism for private schools.[59]

THE DEVELOPMENTAL STATE

The stories told above about remaking the nation discredit a common claim made from the late 1980s onwards, that the United Kingdom did not have what was called a 'developmental state'.[60] This argument was used to explain poor economic performance – that the British state, stuck in its liberalism, in its deference to parliamentary forms, could not, and did not, develop the means to intervene in the economy in ways the modern world demanded. This was, even if the term was not always used, a central argument of declinists.[61] Other countries had such modernizing states, focused on national development, the argument went. The story in this book also contradicts the erroneous cliché often invoked in explanation for the lack of long-term development, that the change in government every few years precluded long-term planning. There was no difficulty in planning for the long term, it was the norm. Decisions on many important matters took decades to become effective.

The remaking of the United Kingdom by the planners and technocrats was to have its critics. Some complained that they did more damage to some of the cities of the nation than the bombing by the Luftwaffe in the Second World War. Others claimed that the tower blocks destroyed communities, or that modern industry destroyed natural resources. It was thus for some a salvation that plans were halted in the 1970s as the economy stalled. Most of the planned inner-city motorways (for example, the London Motorway Box, as it was called) were abandoned in the early 1970s, never to be built.[62] Areas of old houses were not torn down but remodelled. The gigantic Maplin Sands airport for London, to be built on the Thames Estuary, was stopped. This represented a rather sudden and radical transformation in the nature of the nation-building process. These criticisms and critiques did not come only from a new left, or environmentalists – a new feature of the 1970s – but from various species of the right as well. It came from within and without bureaucracies and the state.

Just as important were the claims being increasingly made that nationalized industries were prone to make terrible decisions. Some such charges are surely correct – the decision to build the many advanced gas-cooled reactors and persevere with them was an example of the crassest techno-nationalism trumping respect for efficiency. On the other hand, the switch to natural gas was a success achieved at a stunning speed. But whether efficient or inefficient, right or wrong, deluded or rational, the nationalized industries and state investment more generally were key to making a new country. For without the investments of the post-war developmental state, the Thatcher revolution would hardly have been feasible.

As we shall see, the dismantling of this developmental state in the 1980s would render it historically invisible, and in doing so it made a proper understanding of both the role of the state and of Thatcherism impossible. In the case of welfare measures Conservative politicians of the 1970s came to complain of what they called 'social engineering', the use of state measures to change the structure of society. This was deemed illegitimate. It was telling, perhaps, that the other engineering projects of the state were not so denounced. In particular there was no criticism of the great transformations to which the state contributed so much, such as creating a society of motorists and home-owners.

12

National Capitalism

Far from leading in the race for higher productivity, Britain in these last years has been outpaced by almost every other industrial nation.

> Britain Belongs to You: The Labour Party's
> Policy for Consideration by the British People, *1959*
> *Labour Party manifesto*

A New Britain – mobilising the resources of technology under a national plan; harnessing our national wealth in brains, our genius for scientific invention and medical discovery; reversing the decline of the thirteen wasted years; affording a new opportunity to equal, and if possible surpass, the roaring progress of other western powers while Tory Britain has moved sideways, backwards but seldom forward.

> The New Britain, *1964 Labour Party manifesto*

We are the people who, among other things, invented the computer, refrigerator, electric motor, stethoscope, rayon, steam turbine, stainless steel, the tank, television, penicillin, radar, jet engine, hovercraft, float glass and carbon fibres. Oh, and the best half of Concorde.

> *Margaret Thatcher, first speech to Conservative*
> *Party Conference as leader, 1975*[1]

It is too easily assumed that the United Kingdom was at its most industrial in the distant past, when it was the workshop of the world in, say, the 1850s. The economic statistics tell a different story. It was in the 1950s and 1960s that the United Kingdom was most focused on industry, and on manufacturing industry in particular. If it was the workshop of the world in the nineteenth century, the nation itself was most like a workshop in the 1950s and 1960s. The share of manufacturing workers in total employment peaked in the 1950s, the absolute number of workers in manufacturing in the 1960s. This was British manufacturing's moment; the moment too of the industrial working class. This was the time of the fastest ever British economic growth, putting the industrial revolutions, both first and second, to shame.

The nationalization of the post-war economy and the great emphasis on production in this national context appears to support the argument that economic nationalism and production went together, a suggestion which has been central to critiques of the British economy. Yet to the extent it supports the abstract proposition, it undermines the analysis of the British case it is used to support. For even when the British economy was liberal, it was the most production-intensive in the world. If nationalization of the economy promoted productivism, that started from a uniquely high base. More important still, the very fact the economy nationalized and became even more production-oriented undermines the argument usually applied to the British case. That was that because British capitalism was so global, there was no British national economy and no strong national industrial capitalism. In reality, then, post-war economic nationalism merely reinforced an existing orientation to industrial production, making it a doubly strong bit of evidence against the thesis that global capitalism undermined national industry.

The British national economy stood out as the most manufacturing-intensive economy in the world in the 1950s, barring only Germany. In terms of proportion of output represented by manufacturing it was 37 per cent in 1950 and 36 per cent in 1960, declining slowly to 29 per cent in 1975. If calculated in constant prices, to take account of the relative fall in manufactures' prices compared to prices in general, then the proportion (in 1963 prices) remained essentially constant at 30 per cent between 1950 and 1975.[2] By one measure from 1948 into the early 1970s manufacturing expanded more than services in output (see table 12.2). It was the policy of governments to push manufacturing. For example, the selective employment tax of the 1960s was designed to discourage employment in industries other than manufacturing.

Manufacturing, which, rather tellingly, began to stand for the economy as a whole, was a national enterprise to be encouraged by national and nationalist policy – protection, support for investment, discriminatory taxes and nationalistic procurement. Although manufacturing industry was, unlike the utilities and mining, not nationalized, it makes sense to think of it as a national capitalism in contrast to the global capitalism of the first half of the century. In the 1970s, in an era of crisis for manufacturing, many of the great names of British manufacturing were in fact nationalized in a last-ditch attempt to save them.

Manufacturing was regarded as particularly important not only because its products were exportable, but because it was seen as the place where the gains in labour productivity were to be made. In the 1950s, British manufactured exports accounted for 10 per cent of GDP, and the United Kingdom had more than one-quarter of the world's manufacturing exports; only just behind the US, and well ahead of everyone else. However, the fall in the United Kingdom's share in world exports of manufactures was a notable feature of the period. It was down to 14 per cent in 1965 as other countries either returned to or entered the world market for manufactures.[3] Furthermore, the share of exports in GDP fell, as we have seen, into the late 1960s. As we have also seen, exports of manufactures and imports of all kinds of goods roughly balanced through to the 1970s. Within these totals were significant changes, as the United Kingdom became a significant importer of manufactured goods. From the early 1980s the United Kingdom imported more manufactures than it exported. In the manufacturing-focused picture of the economy this was a calamity, and a central bit of evidence for the notion of a serious British economic decline. Not only had the United Kingdom lost its seemingly rightful share of the world market, it had lost much of its home market too.

A different analysis is needed. The main determinant of manufacturing export shares was what happened not in the United Kingdom, but in other countries. It was perfectly possible to be succeeding in promoting manufacturing, and indeed manufacturing exports, and to lose market share at an expanding world level. Secondly, the move to becoming a net importer of manufactures was the mirror-image of the fact that the United Kingdom no longer needed to import food or energy on a large scale. The basic relations of the economy to the rest of the world had changed, in ways in which the manufacturing-oriented fables did not grasp. Furthermore, while the net trade in manufactures became negative, exports of manufactures continued to increase. Essentially the economy was becoming more open, another way in which the characteristic notions of the 1950s and 1960s no longer applied. The very structures of specifically national capitalism were by then coming apart.

The economic benchmark in the 1950s and 1960s in terms of income per head was the USA. It was roughly twice as productive per capita. In terms of rates of growth the standard was not set by the USA but by France, Germany, Italy and Japan. They grew faster than the UK, but from a lower base of income per head. The fundamental process was that of convergence – with the poorer of these economies growing faster than the richer ones. Slow growth was for a country like the United Kingdom a sign not of backwardness, but of wealth.

BRITISH BUSINESS

In the 1950s and 1960s the United Kingdom had capitalist businesses, some of the very largest and most successful in the world. The important British firms were national, headquartered in London, produced largely within the United Kingdom and were closely connected to government. They were also close to finance, through interlocking directorships as well as financial relations. The term 'finance capital' did not necessarily mean banks, but rather the union of business and finance.[4] 'The City' did not mean finance as opposed to industry, but the centre of all British business, including the industrial groups. Only very much later would an overwhelmingly financial City take over.

The 1950s saw the return of the high place of the businessman in public esteem. In the 1950s the boss, the industrialist or banker, was becoming something of a hero. He, for this was an almost exclusively masculine domain, was more of a manager than a capitalist, an employee with an expense account rather than a capitalist or simply a rich man. More generally, 'With business so prosperous and prestigeful, the upper classes have naturally moved into its command positions.'[5] The public schools were training future businessmen. Indeed, in the 1950s politicians and some professionals with political or government experience were going on to run businesses. As one critic put it:

> As a Professor of Moral Philosophy, Sir Oliver Franks [who had served as a very senior civil servant and diplomat] may have been a man of some influence; as the Chairman of Lloyd's Bank, he is a man of power. As the leading barrister of the day, Sir Hartley Shawcross [a former Attorney General] may have been on the fringe of the power elite; as a member of the board of Shell and Ford's, he is right in it.[6]

Powerful and respected politicians such as Walter Monckton (Midland Bank) and Oliver Lyttelton (Lord Chandos, who went to Associated Electrical Industries) also went into business, or bigger business than they had come from.

It was notable that the industrialists elevated to the peerage in these years were managers rather than owners and, also in contrast to earlier years, generally had not first been in the House of Commons. They included Ernest Hives of Rolls-Royce, Clive Baillieu of Dunlop Rubber, Peter Bennett of Lucas (who had been an MP), men from Shell and BP, three from ICI, as well as from Pilkington, British Leyland, Courtaulds, Rootes, English Electric, BICC, the Rank Organisation, Sainsbury, Marks and Spencer and Great Universal Stores.[7] From the 1970s onwards fewer industrialists went to the Lords, as the new peerage was dominated by professional politicians, with the proportion of senior serving officers, as well as businessmen, diminishing. Lord Weinstock of GEC, Lord Tombs of Rolls-Royce and a few others, and one nationalized industry head, Lord Marshall, were the exceptions.

At local level, and through representation in the House of Commons, there was a profound diminution of business influence from the 1940s onwards. The bourgeois cities became cities without a bourgeoisie, only a service middle class; they had factories but few head offices; they were no longer centres of opinion or elites connected to national power. Local banks, stock exchanges and commodity exchanges disappeared.[8] Capitalist concentration, and nationalization, had denuded the industrial cities of their active, local haute bourgeoisie. Whereas in 1914 it made perfect sense to think of a Manchester bourgeoisie, and still to an extent in the interwar years, by the 1960s things were different. The *Manchester Guardian* became the London *Guardian*, and Manchester, like other cities, lost most or all of its Conservative MPs and councillors. Liverpool lost its last important shipping firm in the 1960s.[9] The case of Newcastle was studied by a community history project in the 1970s, which showed how local coal families such as the Peases and shipbuilders such as the Wigham-Richardsons no longer commanded local enterprises, though they might retain country houses in their region.[10] Of course, there were exceptions. Ronald Colville, 2nd Baron Clydesmuir, joined the family steel works in Scotland in 1945, becoming a director in 1958. He was also a senior Scottish banker, rising to become governor of the Bank of Scotland and a director of Barclays. He held important honorary royal and military posts in Scotland. Sebastian de Ferranti, managing director and later chairman of Ferranti, took cultural posts in Manchester in, for example, the Halle Society. His brother was a director of Ferranti and Tory MP for a northwest seat 1958–64. Such links, though once common, were now exceptional.

But the Ferrantis and Colvilles were deeply dependent on other sorts of relations with the state. Ferranti depended on state purchases of everything from computers to guided missiles. Colville, Scotland's main steel maker, was subject to the direct and indirect influence of the state. Steel was nationalized in 1951 and mostly quickly privatized. It was nationalized again in 1967. Whether public or private, the state was involved in a transformation through which, by 1970, steel output was twice as great as in 1940. The expansion and renewal came in phases. The late 1940s and early 1950s saw a new Dorman Long plant at Lackenby. The Steel Company of Wales built the Abbey Works at Port Talbot 1947–53, which became the largest steel works in Europe, with a new strip mill. In the late 1950s it fell to Harold

Macmillan as prime minister to give one plant to Wales and the other to Scotland – critics argued that a single plant in Wales would have been better. The Scottish plant was for Colvilles at Ravenscraig, to which a strip mill was added from 1959. The Welsh plant was built at Llanwern by Richard Thomas and Baldwin Ltd. Generally there is no evidence for technical backwardness. The Llanwern hot strip mill pioneered the first successful use of a computer for complete mill control. The United Steel Companies developed 'management cybernetics'.[11] British steel companies were as fast as those elsewhere in introducing new steel-making processes too.[12]

Industry saw itself as national, sometimes even still imperial. Imperial Chemical Industries, the greatest chemical company, was never nationalized, but in 1955 a company book for employees and shareholders sought to explain 'in what manner it discharges its responsibilities to Great Britain and the British Commonwealth of Nations'.[13] It was, the book stated, a company 'essential to the life of the nation'.[14] The new plant at Wilton, it intoned, 'was being developed into one of the world's greatest and most modern centres of chemical manufacture'.[15] Wilton ran on petroleum, imported raw material, but it produced mostly polythene, polypropylene and Terylene, boasting two plants which were the largest in the world, connected by pipeline under the Tees to Billingham. Polythene and Terylene were British discoveries from the 1930s, one made by ICI, the other taken up by ICI from the Calico Printers' Association. By 1970 Wilton had 14,900 workers.[16] Petroleum chemicals, including refining, Wilton included, were 'perhaps the most successful British example of import substitution in an infant industry protected by quantitative import restriction'.[17]

ICI was also national in that its single largest customer was British agriculture – it was a huge maker of fertilizer especially. The works at Billingham were the hub of its ammonia and nitrate factories. Billingham also made sulphuric acid and expanded production in the early 1950s from local anhydride (in a notable import-substituting initiative). This huge chemical complex, once the great hope for coal-powered British national modernity, changed over to oil from the late 1950s and early 1960s and to British natural gas from the late 1960s.

NATIONAL SUBSTITUTES

Manufacturing was there to supply national needs, and to export in order to obtain imports. Less well known was the development of manufacturing capacity to replace imports. Yet it is an important case for it shows very clearly that nation trumped empire and Commonwealth in manufactures as well as in food. Even if it had been the case in the past that overseas production for the United Kingdom was promoted by British capitalism at the expense of the national productive base, this was certainly not true of the post-war years.

'Will peanuts oust Sheep?' asked a worried Australian newspaper in 1951.[18] The reason for their alarm was a process to turn peanuts into artificial wool. The fibre (Ardil) had been invented by ICI in the 1930s, working with a physicist at the University of Leeds (Yorkshire was the centre of the wool industry) who was studying the structure of wool.[19] Small-scale production started in 1946. The new ICI plant at Dumfries costing £2 million was built in 1949–50, at a time when industrial building was restricted to what were taken to be vital projects. Unilever built a new £1 million plant on the Mersey to extract the oil from peanuts, from which it made margarine, the residue going on to Dumfries.[20] Ardil, hailed as 'one of the greatest textile discoveries of the century', was actively promoted by the government: the president of the Board of Trade, Harold Wilson, even wore an Ardil suit.[21] While the infamous groundnuts scheme (from whose peanuts Ardil would have been made) had failed by 1950, Ardil was in production till 1957. It was doomed by its low strength when wet. The failure caught the attention of the US humorist Art Buchwald, who noted rather cruelly of the project that 'Dumfries squirrels started hoarding peanuts in hopes the price would go up, the imperial monkey institute was working on a synthetic peanut just in case they couldn't get the real thing any more, and a rival company was hoping to come out with a cloth made of popcorn'.[22] The story was a real-life parallel in some ways to the brilliant Ealing comedy *The Man in the White Suit* (1951), in which the young scientist played by Alec Guinness invents a revolutionary new textile.

A second example was national synthetic rubber to compete with imperial natural rubber. A synthetic rubber plant was built in the early 1950s and came into operation in 1958, even though Malaya, in the empire, was one of the largest rubber growers in the world. The Dunlop Rubber Company, although it had its own Malayan plantations, wanted synthetic rubber, and this helped override the interests of great plantation owners such as Guthrie and Harrisons & Crossfield, who also operated from the United Kingdom.[23]

Aluminium provides one of the last examples of such strategies. In 1967–8 it was decided by the government that it would support the building of two, which ended up as three, aluminium smelters, two powered by nuclear power stations, the other by a new coal station. The argument for them was that they would reduce imports mainly from Canada, in the Commonwealth, and from Norway (in EFTA). Hardly debated in parliament, the plan was controversial and contested from abroad, especially from Norway, a close ally.[24] The plants were all subsidized through special electricity and coal contracts, and through loans and investment grants.[25] The Rio Tinto Zinc plant in Anglesey was 15 miles from the Magnox reactor at Wylfa – both started operating in 1971 and closed in 2009. British Aluminium's plant at Invergordon, the largest industrial project ever seen in the Highlands, took its power from the new AGR at Hunterston B and ran between 1971 and 1981.[26] The third was fed by a new coal-powered station next to it – at Lynemouth in Northumberland. It opened in 1974 and closed in 2012. For economic liberals this represents a serious misuse of resources.

In the case of textiles the situation was different in that Commonwealth imports were threatening an existing British industry. Remaining Commonwealth preference gave producers in Hong Kong, India and Pakistan access to the British market no one else could have. Imports flooded into the United Kingdom, though in the late 1950s the government imposed (high) supposedly voluntary quotas on Commonwealth imports, an early version of the later much more general Multi-Fibre Agreement, to keep the textiles of poor countries out. The home industry continued to contract, however, and in 1959 the Conservative government passed a new Cotton Industry Act, which financed the closing-down of much of the industry, subsidizing most of the destruction of machinery and redundancy, and also providing investment grants. Courtaulds and ICI stepped in to reshape textiles as a large-scale, integrated capital-intensive industry with synthetic fibres, of which they were the major makers. The mantra of large firms, research and modernity, was put into action but failed, both in the face of cheap imports and later in an inability to compete with high-quality European production. By contrast, the German, French and Italian textile industries, better protected individually and then collectively through the EEC, expanded. By the late 1950s Germany and France were making more cotton textiles than the United Kingdom, with Italy following in the early 1960s.[27] What looked like continental backwardness – protected small and medium firms – turned out better than British large-scale modernity.

There was an unexpected aspect to the new textile industry. Being more capital intensive, it required shift-working, indeed continuous operation, which had not been true of most of the older textile industry. Furthermore, the work was no longer so skilled. Night shifts were special in that they required men, as women were banned from such work. For this reason, and because local men and women did not want to work in what was a low-wage industry, the factories started recruiting Asian, mostly Pakistani, *men* in what had been a predominantly female industry. This happened from the 1960s through the 1970s, creating entirely new communities. Not only did Pakistani workers make textiles for the United Kingdom in Pakistan, but in the old textile centres of Oldham, Blackburn, Rochdale, Bradford and many more.[28]

CARS AND SHIPS

Textiles were clearly a dying industry, but there were many industries which were extraordinarily successful. The British motor car industry was very large and fast-growing, and rapidly changing. In 1950 it was not only the largest car producer in Europe but the largest exporter of cars in the world. It accounted for 17 per cent of British exports in the early 1960s, and one-quarter of world exports of cars. Into the early 1970s the industry remained a very significant exporter – around 40 per cent of its output went overseas. The British Motor Corporation, a merger of the giant Austin and Morris firms, was the largest car maker in Europe in the late 1960s and the United Kingdom's largest single exporter.[29] It exported over a third of its production. It went multinational and bought factories in Italy and Belgium. Imports were minimal, though edging higher, already over one in ten new British cars by 1970. It was, however, the British car industry which brought cars, easily the most expensive family purchase other than a house, to the British masses by the 1970s.

The car industry had modern equipment. Many of the wartime aero-engines and aircraft factories in the West Midlands were turned over to cars. Vast new plants were added with government support in the early 1960s, taking the industry away from its centre around London and the West Midlands. The US-owned firms were in the lead. Ford built a new factory in Halewood (it made Anglias, later Escorts) while General Motors went to Ellesmere Port (making Vivas). Both factories soon grew to over 10,000 employees each. Rootes (soon to be taken over by Chrysler) went to Linwood in Scotland.[30] The industry succeeded in expanding production into the early 1970s, not least through these new plants.

British car production peaked in 1972 and went into a rapid absolute decline. The change came with the opening of markets to foreign cars. Not only did the general British tariff fall but it was abolished within the Common Market, such that by the late 1970s, European cars came in for nothing. Japanese cars paid 11 per cent. In the 1970s British Leyland, which succeeded BMC, saw its production halved. It was nationalized and closed many factories. By 1981 it was a small producer, concentrated in Longbridge and Cowley, and was smaller even than LADA of the USSR, not to mention FIAT, Renault, Citroën and Peugeot, or Volkswagen. The British nation now produced more cars than Spain or Canada, though not by much.[31] It was telling that the two long-established American firms in the United Kingdom, Ford and General Motors (Vauxhall), both did relatively well, and did so by integrating their production across Europe. The Ford Escort (1967–) was built in Halewood and in Germany and had been designed as a European car; the Vauxhall Viva was a variant of the Opel Kadett. Opel was the German arm of General Motors, Vauxhall the British.

The case of shipbuilding is another one of early success followed by a failure even in the domestic market. In 1950, as well as building for its own register, it was supplying one-third of foreign registrations, and nearly half in 1951.[32] The shipyards in the 1950s employed more people than ever before. But shipbuilding could not expand production very much – it kept producing at roughly the same level into the 1970s. However, had it kept its world share of ballooning output, by 1970 it would have had to be ten times larger, which would have been physically impossible, showing the absurdity of taking falling global shares of production as an index of failure. Other nations did expand production and as early as 1954 British shipyards were overtaken on world markets by Germany, and by the following year by Japan.[33]

Into the 1960s British yards were producing a full range of ships. In 1961 the Harland & Wolff shipyard in Belfast, which had built the *Titanic*, completed its last large passenger liner, the *Canberra* for P&O (having recently completed the last passenger reefers for the Royal Mail Line). Some years later the John Brown yard on the Clyde built the last great British passenger ship, the *Queen Elizabeth* 2 for Cunard, successor to the *Queens* of the 1930s, which had come from the same yard. Vickers at Barrow-in-Furness, which had built five beautiful passenger 'Strath' liners for P&O in the 1930s, completed its last liner, the *Oriana*, in 1960 for the Orient Line. The very last passenger liner built in the United Kingdom was built by Swan Hunter & Wigham Richardson, builders of the *Mauretania*: the *Vistafjord*, completed in 1973. These ships, like many other liners of the 1950s and 1960s, were to be switched to cruising. But when new cruise ships came to be built from the 1980s British shipyards got none of this work, which went to yards in Italy, Germany, France, and Japan. British yards lost all sorts of business in the 1970s. An exception was the Liberty Ship replacement SD14, designed like the Liberty Ship itself by a shipbuilder on the Wear, in this case Austin & Pickersgill, a progressive firm.[34] From the 1960s, and overwhelmingly so in the 1970s, British shipping lines generally had their ships built abroad. With a few exceptions the yards failed to diversify into the booming market for equipment for the North Sea oil and gas industry. The result was dereliction on the shores of the Tyne, Wear, Clyde and Mersey, with a few yards kept going only by warship business. Like the British car industry, British shipbuilding was nationalized in the 1970s while in a state of terminal decline.

LABOUR AND THE NEW
INDUSTRIAL STATE

For the British working class the years from 1950 to at least the late 1960s were years of success. In contrast to the interwar years, there was no permanent cadre of the unemployed and no underused industrial capacity. These were the years of the long boom where there was sustained demand for labour as well increasing productivity. Indeed, the productivity of the workforce was increasing as never before. The relations of output, productivity and employment varied by sector. As we have seen in agriculture, increased output went with falling employment, while in mining decreasing output and decreasing employment went together. Manufacturing was an intermediate case, with increases in output and employment. British workers were going into manufacturing jobs as never before, and each worker was producing more and more. This obvious point needs stating because so much attention has focused on the productivity deficit with the USA that the fact of growth in productivity, which needs explanation, is ignored.

The reasons for the increasing productivity of labour are difficult to pin down, but the conventional story has the ring of truth. In some sectors the scale of the machinery made processes more efficient in terms of capital and also required fewer operators. An example would be in very much larger chemical plants. Secondly, new techniques replaced labour, for example in the making of motor car engines, where transfer machines moved work automatically between machine tools. Another very important reason was changes in the organization of work, partly in relation to scale of operation. There may have been an element of the deskilling of a large section of manual work, though by no means all. Even more than in the interwar years, the years of the long boom were those of the management expert, the white-collar organizers and measurers of blue-collar work. The idea that British business was slow in taking up new machines and methods is not borne out by studies.[35] Increasing the productivity of labour was the routine concern of managements, and of the state.

High levels of employment, and a culture committed to production, gave trade unions a strong place in the private economy. The largest unions were overwhelmingly in the private sector and some of the nationalized industries. Still the largest was the Transport and General Workers Union, with over 1 million members in 1960. It was, as its name suggested, a general union, with many members in manufacturing industry. Second was the Amalgamated Engineering Union (the AEU, 'the engineers'), third the National Union of General and Municipal Workers, then the National Union of Mineworkers and the National Union of Railwaymen (at over 300,000 members).[36] There were then electricians and shop workers, and some public-sector-only unions. Then came a mass of very small unions, among which by 1960 came the once-mighty textile unions.

The largest unions were national unions, operating in every part of the country. Furthermore, they entered into national agreements with groupings of employers, employers' federations, to set wages and conditions at national levels, or at least setting national minima. In the economy nationally organized 'free collective bargaining' became the norm, not because it had not existed before, but because the unions were now in a much stronger position than between the wars. Wages were set by national processes and, at least in part, at national levels. This can be seen, for example, in the large national wage strikes in shipbuilding and engineering in 1957.

Trade unions were involved in the management of society and economy in other ways too. One important legacy of the war and the post-war Labour government was what was called 'tripartism'. In many areas of industrial policy boards of various kinds were created, made up of representatives of employers, trade unions and independents, chosen by government, and sometimes government officials. Examples would be the Development Councils for particular industries, one of which was the Cotton Board, or the National Economic Development Council (NEDC) established in the early 1960s, and its sector working parties. Trade unions were also represented on all sorts of other tribunals, boards, and committees, balancing the employer interest. In another country they would have been called 'social partners'. Trade union officials were thus a part of the system of administration of the nation, part of the extended machinery of government.

These tripartite bodies were in the end creatures of the state, there to perform work for the state. One important role was to bring the trade unions and employers' organizations into the orbit of administration as a way of exerting control of both, in particular to marginalize those who wanted to act outside the system. Thus the state attempted to limit the range of legitimate action. While they looked to be independent and representative, these bodies were in part representing not their members but government, or at least the highest interests of government. Through this 'corporate bias' the state managed society, privately, outside the frames of party politics and parliament.[37]

That said, trade unions were very visible. The general secretary of the Trades Union Congress and the leaders of transport workers, engineers, miners and others were well-known public figures, often far better known at the time and since than the heads of the largest corporations or even nationalized industries. Among the well-known leaders were Frank Cousins and Jack Jones of the transport workers; Joe Gormley of the miners; Clive Jenkins of the white-collar workers; Tom Jackson of the postmen; Hugh Scanlon of the engineers and many more.

In the 1960s a new politics of productivity developed in which attempts were made to get industry and trade unions to agree to procedures to improve productivity in such a way that both would benefit. Workers would be encouraged to leave declining industries by a new system of 'redundancy' payments as well. In addition, there was a great enquiry into labour relations in the late 1960s which recommended action against emerging unofficial industrial action. The idea was essentially to reach high-level agreements between capital and labour, and find means of enforcing them further down.

Through the post-war years there was a constant drone of criticism of the British worker, as peculiarly unproductive, far too prone, at best, to take too many tea breaks and to indulge in 'wild cat' strikes, and 'Spanish practices'. Even in the later 1950s Harold Macmillan privately referred to paying the price of 'industrial appeasement' in the early 1950s Churchill government, when Walter Monckton was minister of labour.[38] The criticisms of the British grew louder in the 1960s and reached a peak in the 1970s. The reason was that after decades of industrial peace strikes were back to the levels of the early 1920s. In the late 1960s the rising concern in government with shop stewards and unofficial strikes led to a proposal to repress such actions, in the form of the White Paper *In Place of Strife*. It was opposed by union members, and then union leaderships. It was replaced by a TUC undertaking that unions would exercise more control over their members.

The response of the Conservative government elected in 1970 was a major innovation in industrial relations legislation, the Industrial Relations Act of 1971. This brought the law into industrial relations, in contrast to the practice since the late nineteenth century of keeping potentially applicable law out through what were called immunities. In positively regulating industrial relations through the law, it consciously echoed continental European practice, at the very moment that the UK was to enter the Common Market. Other important acts regulating employment practices were the Race Relations Act, 1968 (which did not apply in Northern Ireland) and the Sexual Discrimination Act, 1975. The unions were mostly hostile to Common Market entry, and in particular, their members did not like the Industrial Relations Act, and there were mass demonstrations and boycotting of the law such that it became a dead letter. Five dockers imprisoned under the act were released by an obscure legal mechanism in the face of mass disobedience. The act remained in place into the 1974 Labour government, and it was in this period that the Industrial Relations Court ordered the sequestration of the funds of the Amalgamated Union of Engineering Workers (AUEW, formed 1971), which had participated in an illegal strike in a small firm and had refused to pay a fine. The AUEW called an immediate national strike, which led to the total collapse of the act. The Labour Party in office 1974–9 restored the status quo.

British workers were not more strike prone than others. Everywhere strikes were increasing in the face of the rising cost of living, as workers sought to keep their standard of living. In any case strikes were a minor cause of loss of labour – it was, in a bad strike year, comparable to that from industrial accidents and an order of magnitude less than sickness or unemployment.[39] Furthermore, strikes were concentrated in particular industries, most notably in the car industry.[40] For example, 1971 saw a strike in Ford, the largest-ever strike against a single employer.

British workers were productive. The negative image arose certainly in the 1950s, as it had in the 1940s, and to some extent earlier, through a comparison with the US worker, but a comparison with European workers told a different overall story. The productivity of the British worker was about the same as the German, who had the lead in Europe.[41] Yet in the 1970s especially the idea that the British worker and trade unionism were responsible for a large difference in productivity with continental Europe became established, though the evidence was often poor. There were differences, but these were too easily ascribed to worker problems, and not enough to differences in equipment, management and so on.[42] The idea that British workers or trade unionists were 'Luddites' was itself misleading. The Luddites were the rioters and machine-breakers of 1811 who were hostile to the capitalism that was putting them out of work, not to machinery itself. Indeed, there were no greater enthusiasts for new machines than trade unionists and large parts of the left.

Improving the quality of British industry for the Labour Party in particular meant taking state action to support and restructure key industries. In the early 1960s the centre and left of British politics in particular came to the conclusion that, contrary to the image of the 1950s, British business was backward, in its management, its investment in new products and processes, and even in the generation of innovation. In the period of declinism (see chapter 15) British capitalism was seen as seriously deficient compared to US and German capitalism, and even French. For Labour, in office from 1964, the answer was a new drive extending the breadth and depth of state intervention in industry. Particularly notable was the creation of the Ministry of Technology (1964) with a brief to take measures to stimulate the industry making machine tools and computers in particular. Its first minister was Frank Cousins, the leader of the Transport and General Workers' Union. An Industrial Reorganization Corporation facilitated and encouraged mergers to create large national champion firms such as GEC, a merger of all the large electrical engineering firms, and smaller ones such as a national ball-bearing firm and a national computing champion (ICL). There were also state-backed mergers in shipbuilding leading to Upper Clyde Shipbuilders (UCS), and motor cars, leading to the British Motor Corporation (BMC). An Industrial Expansion Act (1968) gave the state increased powers of support and intervention. By the end of the 1960s the Ministry of Technology was a comprehensive industrial ministry with great powers of intervention across civil and military industry, and it also had control of the energy industries.

While in opposition in the late 1960s the Conservatives increasingly rejected the notion of industrial policy, or investment grants, or 'picking winners', or supporting what they called 'lame ducks'. They came into office in 1970 and quickly put their strategy into action, disbanding the Industrial Reorganization Corporation and the Ministry of Technology.

However, the policy unravelled, and the party was to launch industrial policy initiatives which were more radical than had gone before. In 1971 the government saved Rolls-Royce, which would otherwise have gone under because of losses on its RB211 engine programme. It did so by nationalizing the company, a drastic step for a Conservative government. Following this intervention it refused to save Upper Clyde Shipbuilders, in which the government had a substantial shareholding, when it went into liquidation. The workers organized a famous work-in, and the government relented in early 1972, with the saving of most of the yards under new structures: Yarrow, Fairfields (Govan) and John Brown (Marathon). The one profitable one (Yarrow) left the group. A new Industry Act of 1972 gave the government huge interventionist powers. In 1972 the government announced a £3 billion modernization of the nationalized steel industry. It was extraordinarily ambitious, with six major bulk steel plants to be built. There was expansion in capacity at Port Talbot (to 6 million tons), to add to ongoing development at Llanwern. There was another round of growth at Ravenscraig and a new 7-million-ton plant next to Lackenby, giving a combined total of more than 12 million tons output on Teesside. All this investment envisaged a workforce continuing to fall.[43] What was remarkable in retrospect was the optimism of the plan – they were aiming for 35 million tonnes per annum by the late 1970s. Output would never reach anything like that – in fact steel production peaked in the early 1970s. This 'technocratic, production-led vision' did not survive the crisis of the 1970s.

TECHNO-NATIONALISM

One of the strongly recurring features of British industrial policy through to the 1970s was a powerful belief in the peculiar British genius for invention and brain work. In 1950, a socialist journalist, a former soldier, Alan Wood, commented that he 'believed that Britain to-day is in the same position as Athens after the Peloponnesian War, still leading the thought of the world after losing its military supremacy'.[44] The nationalist reverie *Family Portrait*, made for the Festival of Britain, hailed British inventiveness, the marriage of the poetry of science and the prose of engineering, exemplified by the jet engine, and also Penicillin, with a prominent role for radar and radio. Sir Dennis Robertson, professor of political economy at Cambridge, in lectures in the USA in 1953 referred to British 'scientific and inventive genius which has flowered forth in Penicillin and the Comet and the atomic pile'.[45] The *Sunday Express* boasted in 1961 how 'the jet engine, the development of television, the first nuclear power station' all 'came from our tiny country . . . Household names like radar and penicillin – they were products of British genius'.[46] All this went beyond idle, repetitious propagandizing. In his memoirs Harold Wilson made an extraordinary claim for British inventiveness. He believed that, after a period in decline, British inventiveness rose to new heights in the Second World War. The key British inventions of the period, which he took to be radar, jet engines, antibiotics and advances in nuclear research, were in his estimation powering an industrial revolution in the whole developed world. Had Churchill been able to get a proper royalty deal on these crucial advances, he claimed, then the whole wartime and post-war balance of payments issue would have been very different.[47] There, in extreme form, is the techno-nationalist analysis of post-war history. Crucial elements of this view were in fact shared by others. The view that the United

Kingdom had sold its wartime technological patrimony cheap was held by Harold Macmillan. The president of the United States, General Eisenhower, apparently recognized the claim, one reason, it is suggested, why he was willing to share nuclear secrets with the United Kingdom in the late 1950s.[48]

It should not be thought that the thesis was correct – none of the inventions Wilson cited could be claimed as uniquely British, nor were they in fact anywhere near as significant in transforming the world as he claimed. The jet engine, television and radar were invented in many places. All the great developments in nuclear science of the late 1930s and the war came from outside the United Kingdom. There were plenty of other over-egged techno-nationalist puddings after the war. The US pilot Chuck Yeager was rather surprised that the British film *The Sound Barrier* (1953) overlooked that he had flown faster than the speed of sound long before any Briton had. The much-celebrated world speed record held with the Fairey Delta FD2 experimental jet aeroplane in the mid-1950s lasted for around eighteen months, and was beaten by an aeroplane already in service with the USAF. The importance of the Calder Hall nuclear reactor was overblown. Still, the claim for British inventiveness was politically potent.

Ideas of a uniquely brilliant British inventiveness helped bolster extraordinary levels of support for inventions. British governments were at great pains to develop within the nation, for the nation, products of what they took to be a particular British genius. In its first television party political broadcast (1953) the Labour Party called for more production to meet the balance of payments problem. This meant not just an increase in domestic food production and increasing exports of low-import industries, but also making the inventions that were the fruit of British brainpower. The party gave a list which included the very familiar examples of aircraft, jet engines, television equipment and radar.[49] Other great British inventions came along and were enthusiastically supported over long periods. The fuel cell, invented by F. T. Bacon (Eton and Trinity College Cambridge), who had worked for Parsons in the 1930s and was in Cambridge University after the war, was for decades a device of immense promise lauded and funded by politicians; it found only minor use in the US space programme in the 1960s.[50] Sir Christopher Cockerell's hover-craft was hyped and financed into the 1960s. These crosses between ships and aeroplanes were powered by jet engines. Six were built between the 1960s and early 1970s, and they plied the cross-Channel trade until 2000.

Indeed, one reason for subsequent failure in many industries was an over-commitment to the idea of British technical genius, and that the future would be determined by the latest inventions. The Ministry of Supply, and then Aviation and Mintech, with the aircraft makers, supported any number of innovative British aircraft. Far from the home sales being a springboard for export success, they were often the only sales, to an unwilling customer. The nationalized British airlines had to be forced to take on, or were indeed given, every large British aircraft produced. They ranged from the Comet IV, the Britannia and the VC10 to the Concorde. Despite using them, they depended on US aircraft for most of their long-distance operations. Yet a mythology developed that the government had failed to support British aircraft enough.

Barnes Wallis, one of the most celebrated wartime inventors, went around complaining of the failure of the government to support his swing-wing aircraft, the Swallow. For a decade he toured the public schools with a lecture on 'The Strength of England', advocating the building of short-take-off airliners and nuclear-powered merchant submarines – between them these distinctly British and un-American machines would put the United Kingdom back at the centre of the world.[51] The creativity of its engineers and their new technologies of trade and communication, he argued, could arrest national decline and reinvigorate the British Commonwealth. His 'second Elizabethan Age' (a 1950s cliché) was backward looking, imperialist, anti-American. Yet there was a powerful nationalist element too. Wallis disliked emigration (which imperialists liked) as well as immigration (which imperialists could not always be seen to dislike). Like the other celebrated aeronautical inventor of the Second World War, Sir Frank Whittle, he also spoke out against non-white immigration.[52] Both ended up addressing the Monday Club.

The United Kingdom had a politics of invention and development which can be characterized as 'bipartisan technological chauvinism'.[53] It was bipartisan, to the extent of stretching from the far left to the far right, though some elements in the middle were critical. The supersonic Concorde passenger aircraft is a case in point. The key committee which led to its development was established in the Ministry of Supply in October 1956. The treaty to build it with France was signed in 1962 by Julian Amery, formerly a key figure in the Suez group, and still a hard-right, anti-American and pro-European figure associated with the Monday Club. Both the British and French Communist Parties were strongly supportive of Concorde – support for technology and anti-American nationalism were central features of their ideology too. How could they not be, given that the USSR very much believed in the notion of the 'scientific-technical revolution' and supported anti-American nationalism? The Anglo-French Concorde went into production and service in the 1970s; the USA and the USSR had, wisely, cancelled their own programmes.

Concorde, and the Europa rocket, which used a British first stage based on the cancelled Blue Streak missile, were important gestures towards European technical integration around the first British application to join. Concorde had an informal precedent in the very successful French Caravelle airliner, which, like Concorde, was essentially a French airframe powered by British engines. In 1967, a key part of the United Kingdom's second move to join the EEC was to suggest the creation of a European Technological Community. Never fully spelt out, the idea was in part aimed at giving technical expertise to Europe, sharing in order to reap economies of scale. It was not just a matter of British superiority (which even some British officials thought should not be exaggerated), but that Europe could learn from the United Kingdom's experience, which meant taking care not to develop machines with no market, which alas in practice included British-French and British-European projects. The United Kingdom wanted to pursue a much more industrially focused approach and for Europe to do so also.[54]

There was increased concern about the value of such a national-technical policy. Would it not be better to leave things to the market, to import aeroplanes and reactors and anything needed from the best suppliers rather than keep buying perhaps second-best and expensive

British equipment? One answer was to focus research and development on real needs – the policy of the 1960s and 1970s – the other was to give up the game as a hopeless one.[55] For example, Lord Rothschild argued that ministries should determine 'the needs of the nation' and get the research done by a contractor, to ensure less undirected, unproductive research was done.[56] The difficulty was that for years the idea that British machines, whether the hovercraft or new kinds of nuclear reactor, would lead to successful exports was a central propagandistic notion. To be against these developments was to be against exports! But the exports never came – no large hovercraft, no AGR, no Concorde was ever sold abroad. By the late 1960s, in private, within government, this was already known to be likely, but this truth was too scandalous, too unpatriotic to utter. But there would be no more Concordes, and no more AGRs.

It should not be thought that the support of innovation came only from government pursuing deluded techno-nationalist policies. In the industrial and military sectors research and development boomed. Enterprises like ICI continued to dominate industrial research, with multiple laboratories, which now had hundreds of research staff. ICI in the early/mid-1950s spent £5 million per annum on 'research', using 4,500 people, around 1,500 graduates or equivalent. It spent around £100,000 on supporting research in universities and £3 million on development (building and operating pilot plants) and technical service, of which £1 million and 900 workers (300 graduates) were on technical service.[57] In fact, the 1960s and 1970s were a moment of creativity in British state and industry in smaller-scale activities away from the glare of state policy and often connected internationally. For example, in the 1960s in the STC (the British subsidiary of ITT) laboratories in Essex Charles K. Kao, born in China, trained in Hong Kong and the United Kingdom, devised the fibre-optic cable, for which he much later won a Nobel Prize. Also in the 1960s Donald Davies of the National Physical Laboratory developed packet-switching, a key element of the internet. Sir Geoffrey Houndsfield of EMI developed the CT-scanner, introduced in the 1970s, and Sir Peter Mansfield of Nottingham University invented MRI imaging, also introduced in the 1970s. Neither had been to Oxford or Cambridge, very unusually for Nobel Prize winners, as they too became. The artificial hip can be seen as an NHS contribution to the world. It was developed in the 1960s by a surgeon, Sir John Charnley, working in a Manchester hospital, not a laboratory.[58] Academic research entered into a golden age, financed by the state. Between 1950 and 1984 there were only two years without a British Nobel Prize, a much higher tally than before 1950. The scientists of the United Kingdom stepped into the place once occupied by German professors. They did so in a world where a new scientific nation dominated – the United States.

Outside the sciences, too, the years from the 1950s were much richer than earlier periods in many fields. British artists such as Francis Bacon, Lucien Freud, Henry Moore, Richard Hamilton and David Hockney found a place on the walls of global art galleries denied to their predecessors. The Beatles (on the national scene from 1962–3) and the Rolling Stones (on the national scene from 1963–4) conquered not only the rest of the world, but the USA too. The Beatles were awarded the MBE in 1965, which caused a scandal; some believed a myth that they were awarded it because they were great dollar earners.[59] They certainly earned more for the country than Concorde or the hovercraft or fuel cells. Jimi Hendrix achieved success and died in London; Bob Marley made his name in Kingston, Jamaica and London. British groups of the late 1960s and 1970s (the Kinks, the Who, the Yardbirds, Cream, Yes, Genesis, Queen, Pink Floyd, Deep Purple, Black Sabbath, Led Zeppelin) made global impressions where British record players or transistor radios were not known. Elton John and David Bowie were outer Londoners who conquered the Anglo-American charts as individuals. The Rock and Roll Hall of Fame is almost entirely an Anglo-American affair. Punk may have had roots in New York but it grew in the United Kingdom like nowhere else, where it had a distinctive local political and sartorial impact. On the other hand, British film became noticeably worse than that of the 1940s. It descended to Norman Wisdom vehicles (inexplicably, they were popular not only in the United Kingdom but in Albania), the *Doctor* series of seven films (four with Dirk Bogarde), the so-bad-they're-good *Carry On* films. The 1970s saw the last of the Hammer horror flicks and dismal TV knock-offs (*Dad's Army*, *Up Pompei . . .*). What could be achieved is shown by the work of US directors working in the United Kingdom. The blacklisted

Joseph Losey made the cool and dark *The Servant* (1963) and *Accident* (1967) (both with Dirk Bogarde, and both adapted for the screen by Harold Pinter), and Stanley Kubrick made the immortal *Dr Strangelove* (1963). The Bond films were manufactured by British crews in British studios but were American/Canadian productions for a global market.

One way out of the seeming conundrum of historically unprecedented creative activity combined with disappointing economic performance is to explain away what is seen as a paradox of high innovation and low growth. But there is no paradox to explain. We should expect rich countries to grow relatively slowly and to innovate. We should not expect, in a world of shared innovations, for national innovation to lead to national growth. A counterfactual question can help us get at a core issue. After the war the United Kingdom, as we have seen, hitched its waggon to the United States, creating a relationship of deep dependence. It was, some thought, the fifty-first state of the Union. Imagine that was the case and that perhaps for strategic reasons this state was banned from doing any inventive activity or directed industrial policy. Would that state be richer or poorer than the United Kingdom? The first inclination is to assume that anywhere that doesn't invent will be poor; on the other hand we know that all industrial areas of the USA were richer than the real United Kingdom. Why wouldn't a fifty-first British state be richer too, by using everything the other states had to offer? Buried in these points are key issues which were contested through the post-war years – what was the relationship between economic, strategic, inventive, and political boundaries? What *should* they be?

In the late 1960s and 1970s it was noted that British-based businesses were expanding abroad. Similarly overseas businesses, especially from the US, were increasingly important in the United Kingdom. Manufacturing industry was being concentrated in fewer very large firms, and these were now typically multinational. The scale of British business overseas was contrasted with the seeming weakness of business in the United Kingdom. It was noted that Britain was second only to the US in the league table of who owned the largest businesses in the world. It was the 'very strength of the cosmopolitan activities of British capital, which has helped to undermine further its strictly domestic economy' was one conclusion from the left, a new version of a much older critique. British capital looked abroad for the best investment opportunities, weakening also the capacity of the British state to control it. British capital, it seemed, no longer needed the British state. Thus one analyst concluded, 'leading sections of the British bourgeoisie have been effectively 'de-nationalized', not through their own weakness but through the weakness of the British state and their own home base'.[60]

British capitalism put class before nation, while the left put nation before class.[61] This, to the left, helped explain why an ailing British industrial capitalism, like turkeys voting for Christmas, wanted to enter the EEC. A rational, national capitalism would have preferred to stay behind the protectionist barriers of the nation rather than be exposed to unfettered trade, which would destroy so much of it. There was no question that business was in favour of entry to the Common Market/EU in 1961, in 1967 and on the moment of entry in the early 1970s. Another argument was that British capital was furiously pro-EEC because it was financial capital, the brains of capital, which was in the saddle, and that it had won the decisive victory back in the Edwardian years.[62] In other words that finance's interests overrode those of productive industry. But there was little evidence that manufacturing took a different view to finance.

The other side of the same story is the increasing hostility of business to national industrial policies. The capitalist class took very different views of actions taken with respect to industry by Conservative and Labour governments. While the Industrial Expansion Act of 1968 was opposed, and later repealed, by the Tories, the more radical Conservative Industry Act 1972 was not. The Labour 1975 Industry Act was the subject of the most strenuous attack when it was barely more significant than the 1972 act, which indeed was the one through which key interventions were made. Great enterprises attacked Labour governments for their policies while being mostly dependent on government funding. Labour's problem was not simply that capital was not national, but that even national capital was hostile to it. This had always been the key problem for Labour's national project, and it never went away. As we shall see, Labour as a party attracted hardly anyone from business, indeed it was treated with suspicion by business. As far as state action was concerned, who controlled the state mattered as much as what it did.

THE DECLINE OF MANUFACTURING?

British manufacturing industry essentially stopped growing in the early 1970s. It lost market share abroad and at home. The dominant way of understanding this has been to postulate a deep-seated failure, one with causes intrinsic to the 1940s, 1950s and 1960s, but often to a much earlier period, usually the period 1870–1914. A better story than one of early and continuing failure is one which points to the quite exceptional and extraordinary strength of British production in the 1950s and 1960s, with total dominance in the home market and an exceptional short-term dominance in exports, not just to the Commonwealth. Such a position could not have continued to exist as other countries entered export markets more strongly as they developed their industries faster, and certainly not once protections to the home market were progressively removed. The United Kingdom was peculiarly oriented towards manufacturing in the period 1950–73 and peculiarly successful in it, but this large manufacturing sector could not compete against new, rapidly growing and similar manufacturing industries elsewhere. The issue was not so much the failure of British industry, as the success of foreign industry.[63] It might also be that the state was no longer in a position to support manufacturing, as it continued to do in agriculture and in basic infrastructure.

That there was no failure of manufacturing to explain, only relative success before the 1970s, helps us make sense of the fact that most of the explanations for the failure of manufacturing simply did not work even on their own terms, though many have had great authority. The British were not, for example, weighted towards old industries, for some 'old' industries were precisely the ones other European countries did increasingly well in. Equally, British industry was exceptionally strong in new industries such as cars, electronics and aviation in the

Table 12.1: Manufacturing shares of output, labour and capital in the whole economy (per cent)

	Share of output at current prices	Share of output at constant prices	Share of labour	Share of capital
1924 industrial classification				
1924	30.9	30.9	32.9	20.3
1937	31.3	34.8	32.9	19.0
1958 industrial classification				
1937	29.5	29.5	30.4	19.5
1951	35.7	34.6	35.1	23.8
1964	33.6	37.0	36.1	25.5
1973	30.1	38.2	34.7	22.8
1995 industrial classification				
1973	31.9	31.9	26.1	14.5
1979	29.0	28.7	23.7	12.9
1990	22.8	25.7	16.3	10.0
2000	17.3	21.3	13.0	8.7
2007	12.4	18.7	9.5	6.7

Sources: 1924–37 and 1937–73: Matthews et al. (1982: pp. 222–3); 1973–2007: EUKLEMS database (O'Mahony and Timmer, 2009), in Professor Stephen Broadberry and Dr Tim Leunig, *The Impact of Government Policies on UK Manufacturing since 1945*, London School of Economics, October 2013, Government Office for Science, 2013.

1950s and 1960s, and these industries too suffered in the 1970s. The popular thesis was that trade unions and workers were to blame, but the strike record was not radically different from elsewhere, and strikes were highly concentrated. The high labour productivity levels – except in particular industries – did not suggest a general problem of work either.[64] There was no convincing evidence either of a reluctance to take up new production techniques.[65] The idea that

Table 12.2: Output of manufacturing and services,
1948–2000 (1948 = 100)

	Manufacturing CKYY	Services GDQS	
1948	100	100	
1949	107.1979	100	
1950	115.1671	101.581	
1955	135.2185	113.0435	
1960	156.5553	126.4822	
1965	182.5193	144.664	
1970	209.5116	162.0553	
1975	212.5964	182.6087	
1980	202.5707	199.6047	
1985	206.6838	224.5059	
1990	244.473	263.6364	
1995	250.3856	294.0711	
2000	266.838	360.8696	

Source: *The ONS Productivity Handbook: A Statistical
Overview and Guide*, edited by Dawn Camus, Office for
National Statistics (2007), figure 7.5, associated data.

there was a failure to be sufficiently committed to the future, and to
support technical innovation, has proved especially attractive to
declinists. Yet the evidence is simply not there. Huge expenditures,
peaking at 3 per cent of GDP in the early 1960s, went into 'research
and development'. At that time, this was a very much greater commitment to creating the new than that of any nation except the USA or
the USSR. This high expenditure was only partly due to government.
Industrially funded research and development expenditures boomed
from the end of the war.[66] Into the mid-1960s these private, civil
expenditures were absolutely and relatively greater than those of German or Japanese industry. Furthermore, British industry distributed
its effort across different fields in much the same way as the Germans

and the Japanese – into chemicals, mechanical and electrical engineering. By the late 1960s Japanese and German firms were catching up and taking over; indeed the growth of British private industrial research came to an end in 1968 – spending actually fell into the early 1970s. It was not a historical aversion to innovation which led to low spending from the 1970s onwards, but rather disappointment that previous high levels of research and development had not produced more benefit. It was the extraordinary, indeed reckless, futurism of the 1950s and 1960s not its lack, that made later decision-makers reluctant to invest further in making the future.

13

Warfare State

Britain's position and influence in the world depend first and foremost upon the health of her internal economy and the success of her export trade. Without these, military power is of no avail and in any case cannot in the long run be supported. It is therefore as much in the interests of defence as of prosperity that the country's financial and commercial position should be consolidated.

Outline of Future Policy, *1957 Defence White Paper*

'the independent British deterrent' . . . will not be independent, it will not be British, and it will not deter. Its possession will impress neither friend nor potential foe.

The New Britain, *1964 Labour Party manifesto*

After the Second World War Britons built not only a new Jerusalem but a new Sparta. Though no longer one of the greatest powers, in the 1950s the United Kingdom was militarized to an unprecedented peacetime degree. In the early 1950s, a period of generalized rearmament, defence expenditure amounted to around 10 per cent of GDP, much more than in 1913 or 1938. There was a conscript army, which did not exist in 1913 or 1938. This was to change with the ending of conscription in 1960 and a reorientation of British power around nuclear weapons, especially US ones. Even so the warfare state consumed more than the education budget or the health budget into the 1960s and 1970s. Even in the 1970s defence spending was, at around 5 per cent of GDP, higher than it had ever been in times of peace

339

before 1938 (in 2017 it is 2 per cent). It took till the 1970s for the relationship between welfare and warfare spending to return to the levels of the interwar period. Indeed, it was the slow relative decline of the warfare state from the mid-1950s which in part allowed the welfare state to grow.

The warfare state was a vast national machine. It consisted not only of the armed forces themselves, each with a ministry to itself until 1964, but civilian ministries whose main business was the supply of equipment. The main ones were the Ministry of Supply until 1959 and the Ministry of Aviation from 1959 to 1967, when the Ministry of Technology took over. The Ministry of Defence, established in its modern form in 1964, took over what was now called defence procurement only in 1970. These bodies controlled the bulk of state expenditure on research and development, military and civil. They were at the core of part at least of the post-war developmental state. The warfare state also extended into industry, into government-owned factories and to private armourers. Understanding it is essential to appreciating the nature of the British state, especially so as it was routinely left out of analysis of what was thought of as a 'welfare state' by social scientists and historians until at least the 1990s. If before then the level of defence expenditure was appreciated, the full significance of the warfare state was not.

THE IMPACT OF THE WARFARE STATE

The warfare state was active and present in people's lives, at least as much as the developmental state or the welfare state. The warfare state required men more than women, which resulted in the relative strengthening of masculine industries and occupations. The profound militarization of the 1950s went along with a new masculinization of the public sphere, the other side of the much-noted promotion of feminine domesticity. The 1950s saw a campaign for the repression of homosexuality which led to increased prosecutions, which in turn led to the Wolfenden Committee being set up, and eventual limited decriminalization in 1967. It also coincided with another phenomenon, which welfare-oriented accounts have trouble explaining. The 1950s saw elements of a religious revival and, at the very least, continuity with the stable religiosity of the first half of the century. That there was a connection between religion and the Cold War is evident in the success of the US evangelist Billy Graham, whose 'crusades' in the United Kingdom in 1954 and 1955 attracted over 2 million people each.[1] It was also the age of the war film, films about the Second World War which were much more focused on military operations, and on men, than the war films of the war itself. This was the era of *The Cruel Sea* (1953), *The Colditz Story* (1953), *The Dam Busters* (1955), *The Bridge on the River Kwai* (1957) and *Dunkirk* (1958), to name just a few that remain famous.

The warfare state, rather than the welfare state, was strongly associated with the monarchy. The Coronation Naval Review at Spithead in June 1953 featured over 300 ships at anchor, headed by the battleship HMS *Vanguard* and representatives of the USA, USSR and France. More than 300 aircraft of the Fleet Air Arm and other Commonwealth forces took part in a fly-past.[2] The Royal Air Force had if anything a grander spectacle. An air base in Hampshire had 300 aircraft on display on the ground, while over 600 flew past overhead, including the prototypes of the three V-Bombers, and new fighters such as the Hawker Hunter.[3] These extraordinary spectacles of force were never to be repeated on such a scale, but the connections of royalty to the military would continue to be very obvious, as indeed was the association with modernity. Prince Philip was indeed a prince consort for a jet age.

The warfare state helped maintain the highly masculinized university that had emerged in the late 1930s. Even within science faculties the proportion of female students was lower than before the war because state and industry wanted men, and graduates in the most masculine of sciences – physics, engineering and mathematics. By the late 1960s a majority of male students were studying science or technology (excluding medicine), up from 30 per cent in the late 1920s.[4] The huge new demand of the state and industry for male scientists, engineers and to a lesser extent doctors led to a radical expansion of higher education, especially in London and the major civic universities, which were now funded largely by central government. By the 1960s, universal funding for student maintenance as well as fees meant that all universities were, for the first time, overwhelmingly dedicated to full-time residential education geared towards the three-year honours degree (or four in Scotland). Universities were now not merely either for the education of national or local technicians and elites, but producers of national manpower for the state and national industry.

The warfare state conscripted young men, not young women. For young men, military service, from age eighteen, was a nearly universal experience, taking them from workplaces and homes (and a minority from school and university) to a hyper-masculine environment. It was also one in which class divisions were more rigid and authoritarian than those of the factories from which they had come. Since 1946 women had a permanent place in peacetime armed services, though the proportion of women would be lower than during the war, and were all volunteers. Women were not unusual in being non-combatants in the armed forces; the point was they could not gain access to combatant roles which were open only to men.

The warfare state also affected the culture of the state. It was a secret state, with far more restriction on information than had applied to the military in the interwar years. Information given to parliament became less detailed. Some things were so secret that not even most of the cabinet knew what was going on and were carried on without serious internal or external scrutiny, much less challenge. The technocrats got away with a lot. Yet the relations between secrecy and openness were rather complicated. Nuclear weapons were known about: they were very public as well as very secret. On the other hand, British chemical and biological weapons were both secret and hidden.

Spin, rather than secrecy, has been the most responsible for the failure to get to grips with the outlines of the warfare state. There was always enough information in the public sphere to estimate its total size, its impact on the economy and its key products. Yet it was and remained largely invisible to critics from the left, and to British intellectuals. For them it was impossible, it seems, to think of the British state as a warfare state, even though it might have occasionally succumbed to foreign pressure to become so. The two world wars have not, remarkably enough, been generally thought of as involving an expanded warfare state.

MILITARY-INDUSTRIAL COMPLEX

Into the late 1950s a future war was thought probable, and it was anticipated that it was likely to be a war of production much like the Second World War. After the Second World War a great deal of military factory capacity was kept in being in case it was needed. 'War potential', an important concept, was understood to include the ability to produce all sorts of specialized equipment that was needed in warfare. This served as the justification for building up industries such as the watch and clock industry, adaptable to fuze-making, and many others with military applications.

During the early 1950s, a great deal of this capacity was brought back into operation. This is sometimes called 'Korean War rearmament', but that is misleading. Little new equipment was needed for the small British force fighting in Korea. The rearmament programme was a very general one, directed towards countering the Soviet Union in Europe. For this expansion in output new capacity was also built, with new factories for tanks and aero-engines, as well as the nuclear installations which were being completed.

The British warfare state believed in new machines and created an extraordinary military-scientific complex to generate them. Six aircraft carriers were commissioned in the 1950s, which saw the development and production of three types of long-range nuclear jet bombers, the so-called V-Bombers, the Valiant, Victor and Vulcan. A second generation of jet fighters was developed and deployed, the most successful of which was the Hawker Hunter. Anti-aircraft rockets and an intermediate-range ballistic missile, the Blue Streak, were designed. Warlike research and development expenditures dominated government funding of research. Many new installations were built – from atomic research centres at Aldermaston to rocket-testing facilities.[5] At Porton Down, work on chemical warfare was supplemented with a programme of development of biological weapons.[6]

Astonishingly, in the mid-1950s, more than half of all research and development expenditure, public and private, in the United Kingdom was for the warfare state, and it employed 40 per cent or so of qualified research and development staff.[7]

The military-scientific complex was dominated by scientific civil servants – obscure figures unknown to most historians of British science. They lived in Whitehall and the military laboratories and had no presence in the newspapers. They were powerful figures who usually got their way – men such as Sir Frederick Brundrett of the Ministry of Defence, advocate of the rocket and the H-bomb, and his protégé Sir William Cook, who organized H-bomb research and went on to get the Chevaline project going in the late 1960s.[8]

The influence of scientific and futuristic thinking was very clear in the 1957 Defence White Paper. It spoke of 'sensational scientific advances', of hydrogen bombs and rockets 'steered by electronic brains'. As Harold Macmillan put it, the White Paper made clear '*all* our defence – and the economies in defence expenditure – are founded on nuclear warfare'.[9] What mattered was the ability to fight nuclear war – only nuclear facilities would be defended. British forces would be smaller but of high quality. At the very centre was the British H-bomb, which would be going into production, and would be carried by the V-Bombers and then by a new ballistic missile. Conscription would go, as had already been announced. It went in stages from 1957, with the last draft (of previously deferred men) entering in 1960. The United Kingdom was the first power to put the nuclear deterrent at the heart of its strategy, to abolish conscription and to run down the bloated military-industrial complex. It was returning to liberal militarism, to professional capital-intensive forces in order to reduce expenditure to more manageable levels. It was a matter of back to the future.

The 'central aim of military policy must be to prevent war rather than to prepare for it' was a central doctrine of the 1957 White Paper. This meant an end to the whole doctrine of war potential by which the state kept a close eye on the capacity to produce in a future war. Reserve capacity would very largely go. Many wartime Royal Ordnance factories were only now disposed of. The private arms industry, especially the aircraft industry, would be rationalized into a few large firms, BAC, Hawker Siddeley, and in engines Bristol-Siddeley and Rolls-Royce. There would be no new supersonic fighter aircraft or bombers; their functions would be taken over by missiles. There would be some new types of aircraft, but only complex ones with new capabilities.

The new programmes proved to be extraordinarily expensive and overambitious. The driving factor was essentially the dream of competing with the USA, rather than the USSR. Of course, the Soviet threat was invoked but was not the yardstick. Within a few years most of the advanced aircraft programmes were cancelled and replaced by straightforward orders for existing US aircraft, which were to enter British service in the 1960s – the C130 Hercules transport and F4 Phantom supersonic fighters. By the 1960s it was also looking to projects developed with European partners for its important aircraft. The large missile programme was cancelled in 1960. There were further cancellations in the late 1960s, notably of two proposed very large aircraft carriers in 1966. This, too, was of enormous symbolic importance. It meant the navy would in the not-too-distant future no longer have equivalent or even smaller versions of the ships which would remain at the heart of the US navy. The biggest ships in the future navy looked like being nuclear submarines.[10]

In 1961 President Eisenhower lamented the power of the military-industrial complex, a state dominated by a 'scientific-technological elite' and the encroachment of the state on the world of scholarship. There was barely any equivalent criticism in the United Kingdom, which appeared to many not even to have a state-centred scientific technological elite or indeed a military-industrial complex. Nevertheless certain sorts of criticism were central to the polities of the left.

Aneurin Bevan, Harold Wilson and the junior minister John Freeman resigned from the Labour government in 1951 over the issue of excessive funding of rearmament, which led to the introduction of health service charges for spectacles and the raiding of the National Insurance fund. The objection was not to rearmament as such, but to a programme so large that it could not be achieved, as was to prove to be the case. More than that, it was argued, it would wreck the national economy and the project of reconstruction that Great Britain had embarked upon. As Bevan put it: 'we must not follow behind the anarchy of American competitive capitalism which is unable to restrain itself at all, as is seen in the stockpiling that is now going on, and which denies to the economy of Great Britain even the means of carrying on our civil production.' The charges that the Labour chancellor, Hugh Gaitskell, was imposing for NHS spectacles and dentures were themselves trivial, so trivial up against the costs of rearmament, that it was clearly a political gesture, with ominous implications for the future of democratic socialism.[11]

Bevan went on to be the acknowledged leader of the Labour left of the 1950s, and the issues on which they fought against the official position of the Labour Party, as well as that of the government, were mostly matters of war. Bevan and his Bevanites rebelled over German rearmament, a policy supported by the Tory government, and Labour in opposition. Bevan resigned from the shadow cabinet over this. In 1955 he led sixty-two MPs to vote against the hydrogen bomb, defying the Labour leadership, which also supported the government on this. Bevan had the whip removed and was nearly expelled from the party. He soon returned to the shadow cabinet. At the 1957 Labour Party conference Bevan supported the British hydrogen bomb. That might itself indicate the crushing power of the consensus. However, as shadow foreign secretary (from 1956), he, with Gaitskell, was outspoken in his opposition to the whole Suez operation. Still, the Bevanite rebellion was a flash in the pan, with little by way of a political programme behind it, but the key to understanding it was the politics of the warfare state.

But where the Bevanite revolt finished a new extra-parliamentary campaign took off. The Campaign for Nuclear Disarmament was formed in 1958 in the wake of the British H-bomb test in 1957. It organized a march from London to the Atomic Weapons Research Establishment at Aldermaston in 1958. In 1960 its influence peaked when the Labour conference passed a unilateral nuclear disarmament motion, ignored by the party leadership and reversed the following year. This was one of two significant conflicts between Hugh Gaitskell's leadership and the party membership (the other was on nationalisation). CND's campaign was narrowly focused on nuclear weapons, not on defence strategy. Its rhetoric betrayed a moralistic imperialism – if the United Kingdom renounced nuclear weapons it would assume a powerful position of moral leadership in the world.

In pursuing grandiose projects which ended up being cancelled the British war machine was wasting scarce technical and administrative resources better used in developing the nation.[12] This was the essence of the Labour Party's criticism in the early 1960s. Indeed, its distinctive defence policy along these lines was a significant part of its election campaign in 1964.[13] Harold Wilson, who had a reputation amongst his colleagues, and historians, for being shifty, was more straightforwardly honest about science and the military than most technocrats of the era.[14] Wilson knew very well something scientific intellectuals, who were often disingenuous to the point of mendacity on this, did not wish to be frank about: that the British state was by far the biggest investor in research and development other than the states of the US and the USSR. He wanted to redirect this effort: as he put it, Labour would be 'mobilizing Britain's scientific wealth for the task of creating, not the means of human destruction, but the munitions of peace'. They needed to be used to 'increase Britain's productive power'. Wilson wanted to find good productive work for the scientists and engineers who would, in the wake of proposed cuts in defence research, be made redundant. The plan was that the state would adopt for the civilian economy the sorts of state support the military sector had. Research and its products needed purposive planning. The results needed to be applied through R&D contracts (as in defence). The military-industrial-complex was, for Wilson, a model for how the state could and should operate in other areas.

Indeed, Wilson was to build an industrial ministry out of the main procurement ministry, the Ministry of Aviation, which became the heart, after 1967, of a gigantic Ministry of Technology. Its policy was to shift money and expertise away from military development to civilian projects, especially those with commercial potential.

Wilson was also critical of the United Kingdom's role as a major seller of arms. Increasingly, arms were sold not to democratic partners, but primarily to dictatorships. In 1964 the Conservative government negotiated to sell the designs of the new Leander class frigates to Franco's Spain. As Harold Wilson objected: 'Must a country whose economy, according to the Prime Minister, has seldom, if ever, been stronger,' he asked, 'sell drawings and details of frigates to a Fascist country for a few million pounds?' 'So low have we sunk as a result of Ministers' nuclear posturings,' he suggested, 'that all we can do now is to try to get money by an arms deal with Spain.'[15] Labour's opposition killed that deal. In another indication of the weakness of consensus, Harold Wilson put a stop to new orders from South Africa for arms; there would be no follow-on orders from those agreed by the Conservative government in the Simonstown naval agreement which transferred the British base to apartheid South Africa, but allowed continued British use (which ended in 1975). Furthermore, he faced down strong pressure from within his cabinet to agree to new arms deals in the late 1960s, in what was a serious controversy within government.[16]

But in office Labour was to come round to arms sales to some dictatorships. In the 1960s, in a huge deal engineered with the United States, the United Kingdom sold Lightning fighters (which no one else would buy) to Saudi Arabia, a deal which set in train a succession of sales of the following generations of new European fighters – the Tornado and the Typhoon – in corrupt deals systematically covered up by British governments.[17] These were to be by far the most important arms deals of the future. The United Kingdom's link to the Gulf states was a matter of arms as much as oil.

HEY, BIG SPENDER

How is the high level of military preparedness of the post-war United Kingdom to be explained? One common explanation is imperial throwback. This argument needs to be used carefully because the main orientation of British forces, as before, was not maintaining empire, but confronting European powers. These were operations, in the empire, largely by conscripts, which should get more attention than they normally do in British histories. They were, however, small by

French, Portuguese or US standards. There was no equivalent to the French wars in Indochina and Algeria of the 1950s and early 1960s, or the Portuguese wars in Africa which ended in 1974, or the involvement of the USA in Vietnam to 1975. In terms of costs British military operations – from Korea to Aden – were trivial compared to total warlike expenditures.

Better might be the argument that an antique ruling class was committed to high expenditure because that was the way things had always been. But they had not: post-war expenditure was at historically unprecedented levels; peacetime conscription was unprecedented too. A third, and connected, explanation, is the subservience of the British elite to the US – it was the Americans who forced, or helped, the British elite, to spend. Militarism was, heaven forbid, not a characteristic of the British, but an alien import. This was analogous to the argument that the United Kingdom was a land without capitalists, in contrast not just to the United States, but also to the Common Market. However, this does not explain the desire of the British elite to develop its own very expensive and, in the context of the alliance with the US, unnecessary systems.

There was a powerful domestic urge to be a modern world power, with a full military-industrial complex. The elite put a great deal of energy and effort put into the devising of new weapons to compete with the USA, not the USSR. In many ways, for the United Kingdom the story of armaments was the story, not of the logic of the Cold War, but of the domestic politics of Anglo-American relations. And in that context being clear about the small relative role of the United Kingdom was politically difficult, and thus delusions of grandeur were important in constraining political choices, though they didn't drive the process.

There was also a desire to fight communism, to take a full part in the Cold War. This was never an enterprise the United Kingdom engaged with alone – at every level it saw itself as a minor partner to the USA. This 'first and more exacting task' of British defence (the other was the defence of, and preservation of order in, colonies), was a collective effort to defend capitalism.[18] Many British leaders, and fewer Americans, have lauded a not-very-well-specified 'special relationship' with the United States, explaining it in terms of ideological similarity and common objectives. Of course, many responded that the ideology was not that similar, nor the objectives the same. The USA had special relationships with many countries. The UK was hardly the only country outside the USA to drink Coca-Cola or to have an elite deeply committed to Washington or to be dependent on US arms. But there was a special relationship – that existed essentially in secret – over matters of the highest importance to the sovereignty of the state in intelligence and weapons of mass destruction. Uniquely, from the late 1950s, the United Kingdom relied on actual US nuclear weapons and US nuclear designs, as well as, increasingly, US delivery systems as well. There was sharing and exchange of intelligence between intimately connected state intelligence services. There were particular intelligence and military relations between the forces of the USA, the United Kingdom, Canada, Australia and New Zealand, but the United Kingdom was part of, not the centre, of this network.

ATOM BOMBS

The most important nuclear story affecting the United Kingdom is not the history either of British nuclear weapons, or nuclear weapons on British armaments, but rather the stationing of US nuclear forces in the United Kingdom. The first atomic bombs, hydrogen bombs, intermediate-range ballistic missiles (IRBMs) and submarine-launched nuclear missiles, and cruise missiles on British soil were US-owned and operated. There were airfields for B29, B47 and B52 nuclear bombers operated by the USAF, and later for many other nuclear-armed aircraft, under development from 1948. Between 1959 and 1963 the United Kingdom hosted sixty US Thor IRBMs (with 1.4 MT warheads). Between 1961 and 1992 it was a base for US Polaris-missile-carrying submarines (Holy Loch), as a result of an agreement made in 1960, when the USA offered the Skybolt missile, then in development, to the RAF. British equivalents to US nuclear systems (where they existed) followed years later: the V-Bombers entered service in the late 1950s, years after the B29s, the Thor missiles came before the ill-fated Blue Streak was even meant to be operational; British Polaris-missile-carrying submarines arrived at their base in Faslane years after the US equivalents arrived at Holy Loch, only a few miles away along the Clyde. Use from British bases of US nuclear weapons by US forces was subject only to an ambiguous 'joint decision'.[19]

British forces also used US nuclear weapons, indeed more US than British bombs: 'by the end of 1959, the RAF had a national stockpile of only seventy-one fission bombs, but was planning to deliver one hundred and sixty-eight US fission bombs on its own aircraft'.[20] Into the 1960s British forces had more US nuclear weapons than British ones – over 300, compared to around 250 or so British-made ones. The power of British bombs was at its highest in 1967 at 150 megatons. Only in the 1970s with the multiple warheads on Polaris were UK-made bombs more common (the 1970s were the peak years for British nuclear weapons in numbers). It was not until 1992 that the US weapons were gone from British forces. Thus for much of the Cold War the most important nuclear weapons in the UK were operated from US bases, and the second most important were US weapons to be used by British forces. To this we must add, as an addendum, British-designed and -built weapons, and the British versions of US warheads made from 1958.

When he returned to office in 1951, Winston Churchill argued that Labour should not have built an independent British bomb, but should have held the Americans to wartime collaborative agreements.[21] This was not a unique view. Harold Macmillan, visiting 'keen and buoyant' Aldermaston, where the British bombs were designed, as prime minister in 1957, noted that 'the tragedy is that . . . the American and British effort has to be duplicated, instead of shared'.[22] Within the arc of British nuclear history the national British bomb was an aberration. But a British national bomb did, briefly, exist.

The United Kingdom was the third member of the Security Council of the United Nations to have an atomic bomb; the permanent members of the Council became all-nuclear only in 1964. In 1952 a British A-bomb, a near-copy of the US plutonium bomb, designed by scientists who had been involved in the Manhattan Project, detonated on an island just off Australia. Later tests were done on the

Australian mainland. The first national atomic weapons were deployed in 1955 (Blue Danube), for only then were the bombers ready (a result of the fact that the bomb had had overriding priority but not the bombers).[23] The Blue Danubes were replaced by the smaller Red Beards from 1960. The United Kingdom also made a gigantic fission Green Grass weapon, the first and last all-British 'megaton range' (actually only 400 kiloton, but still the equivalent of twenty-five of the bomb used on Hiroshima) weapon to be deployed, and it was in service only between 1958 and 1963.[24] By 1963 the era of the fully national independent deterrent was over. It had lasted a mere eight years.

It was meant to last much longer. In the early 1950s there was a cross-party consensus that the United Kingdom should also develop a national hydrogen bomb to follow on from the A-bomb programme. Some, like the imperialist Julian Amery, saw the H-bomb making the United Kingdom a great power again, given its one-hundred-fold increase in power over the atomic bomb. Development went ahead, and various devices were tested in 1957 and 1958. The closest the nation came to having its own H-bomb was one tested in September 1958, named FLAGPOLE.[25] However, no British H-bomb was ever deployed. These test devices were destined to become entry tickets to the US nuclear design laboratories rather than weapons. From 1958, when a comprehensive nuclear agreement was made with the USA, the United Kingdom was to manufacture amended US designs for its own use.[26] The Red Snow, based on the American W28, went into the Yellow Sun Mk2 bomb and the Blue Steel stand-off missile (which was in limited service from 1961) and would have gone on Blue Streak. The WE177B deployed in V-Bombers from 1966 and the Polaris warhead deployed from 1968 were both based on US designs. These two last bombs and variants were in service into the 1990s.

If the H-bombs were not British, at least the delivery systems were, though only at first. The design of the V-Bombers started in the 1940s; they were in service from the mid-1950s, the Valiant being the first. They were to be superseded by a missile, the Blue Streak, which was not quite as all-British, as it had some US technical input, but this was cancelled in 1960. It was killed off because the Royal Air Force wanted British bombers using the American Skybolt air-launched missile. Duncan Sandys managed to keep a civil version of Blue Streak going, and this became the first stage of the planned Europa space launcher.[27]

'Interdependence' with the United States was a key idea for Harold Macmillan, who like Churchill had an American mother.[28] Indeed, he gave a speech about it in a university in his mother's home town.[29] In October 1957 the British and the Americans made what the British, with perhaps sardonic humour, called a 'declaration of interdependence'. This involved secret joint working groups to address areas of common concern, in an echo of the Second World War, where Macmillan and Eisenhower had themselves worked together. Progress was rapid. July 1958 saw the new atomic agreement. In 1960 came the decision to buy Skybolt. The British side took interdependence to mean that in return the US or NATO would use British equipment. But the Americans would not play – for example they sold their Sergeant missile to NATO rather than allowing the British to sell their Blue Water; they also sold ground-to-air missiles to Israel, after supposedly leaving the field to the British Bloodhound. Macmillan was incensed and wrote to Kennedy of his 'disgust and despair' about this 'trickery'.[30] This was nothing, however, compared to the unilateral cancellation by the US of the Skybolt, on the basis of which the United Kingdom had given up Blue Streak.

The hugely embarrassing cancellation of Skybolt in 1962 could easily have been the end of Anglo-American nuclear relations, and either the end of the British deterrent or the creation of a new independent one. Instead, at difficult negotiations at a summit in the Bahamas (then a British colony), Harold Macmillan got agreement that the United Kingdom could buy the Polaris missile and that it could be used independently of NATO/the USA in extreme circumstances. It was an interdependent deterrent first, and an independent one second.[31] As Macmillan put in his diary, betraying a certain nervousness, it was a 'proper contribution to *interdependent* defence, while retaining the ultimate rights of a sovereign state'.[32]

Although this is often forgotten, there was a distinct difference in nuclear policy in the 1964 election. The Labour Party went into it with an anti-Polaris position: in its manifesto it got the essential point, which was often made by the party leader, Harold Wilson: there was no 'independent British deterrent' being proposed, Polaris being neither independent, British nor a deterrent.[33] The Liberal position was that it was against Polaris, indeed following its position through the 1950s, echoing its historical position on weapons of mass destruction: it wanted an international, allied bomb, not a national one.[34] Despite Labour winning the election, in a complicated fudge indicated in part before the election the United Kingdom did in fact deploy this non-British, non-independent, non-deterrent on the first of four submarines, HMS *Resolution*, which went on patrol in 1968 and remained in service till 1994. The Labour cabinet was given the convenient fiction that the submarine programme was too advanced to cancel.[35] It was, however, put under NATO control, with a British veto. Wilson never believed it was independent. Thus matters continued, with Conservatives making clear that the independence was limited to particular circumstances: 'We believe that Britain must *in the last resort* retain independent control of its nuclear weapons to deter an aggressor; as at present, those assigned to NATO *can be withdrawn if supreme national interests are at stake*' [emphasis added].[36]

Not all opposition to nuclear policy came from the left. There were those on the right who wanted a properly independent, fully British deterrent. Enoch Powell, as Conservative shadow secretary of state for defence in the 1960s, argued from a nationalist perspective that the United Kingdom, without India, could only be a European and North Atlantic Power and that far too much was being spent on futile overseas military expenditure; he argued for pulling back from east of Suez.[37] He himself came out against nuclear weapons, noting that all they deter is nuclear war, not war itself.[38] He went as far as to state, as shadow defence secretary in the 1960s, that 'The last self-protective layer of imperial delusion was the nuclear deterrent, independent or otherwise.'[39] There is a case then for a strong element of party political consensus on the warfare state, but one which needs to recognise significant dissent.

HOLDING ON TO EMPIRE AND BASES

The protection, from internal and external threats, of the British colonies and protectorates was the second, less expensive and complex defence issue. It was less controversial in political terms too. It was, however, long-running and involved the use of the conscript British army overseas in counter-insurgency operations, often to defend territories with British bases. The least-known British operation was before 1954 in Egypt, which, while independent, housed the most important British base overseas other than Germany, holding at its height in the early 1950s some 70,000 troops, mostly from the United Kingdom. There was anti-British feeling in Egypt: British forces had killed fifty policemen in the Canal Zone in 1952, which had led to riots in Cairo that destroyed much British property. These events led to the formation of a new nationalist government in Egypt in 1952, which forced the British out of the Canal Zone in 1954. But in the interim more than 400 members of the British armed forces had been killed, many more than died in the Suez operation of 1956.

The typical operations were in internal counter-insurgency against British subjects, notably in Malaya, Kenya, Cyprus, Aden and Northern Ireland (the last of which peaked at over 20,000 troops). The so-called 'Malayan emergency' ran from 1948 to 1960. The campaign was fought against the fighters of the Malayan Communist Party, which was made up almost entirely from the poor Chinese minority of Malaya. A guerrilla force of perhaps 10,000 fighters held out for many years against British troops (with Commonwealth support), who used bombing and defoliants to clear vegetation and destroy crops and interned 500,000 people in 'New Villages'. In Kenya, another part of the colonial empire, the British put down the Mau-Mau rebellion (1952–60) – as in Malaya, Lincoln bombers were used, and 1 million Kikuyu were locked into 'protected villages'. Many more Mau Mau were killed (the number is uncertain) than guerrillas in Malaya, and the extraordinary total of 1,000 were executed.[40] These were not the only major operations. In Cyprus (1955–60), another crown colony, the Greek Cypriots who wanted union with Greece were repressed. Cyprus was the main post-Egypt Middle Eastern base, central to the United Kingdom's anti-Soviet nuclear capability. The United Kingdom conceded independence in 1960 but retained the bases. Then there was Aden (1963–67), part colony, part protectorate, where another war ended with the granting of independence to what became South Yemen. Aden was the home of a vast air base, RAF Khormaksar, a key staging post for the RAF for both Africa and Asia. This was to be the last counter-insurgency operation outside the UK until the return to Iraq in 2003. We should not pass over these operations too quickly, for they were by previous standards quite extraordinary. There were many more British killed in imperial repressions between 1950 and 1970 than in the interwar years. Indeed, the scale of operations was much greater, and campaigns were generally longer.

Other bases were transferred while remaining in British use, or transferred to US forces. The Royal Navy withdrew from the naval dockyards at Malta (in 1959, though the Royal Navy used Malta as a base until 1979) and Singapore (1971) and transferred Simonstown to South Africa in the 1950s (though it was used by the Royal Navy until 1975). The remaining protectorates in the Gulf got independence in 1971 as Qatar, Bahrain and the United Arab Emirates, and the UK withdrew its forces. The USA used or took over a number of other British bases, including Ascension Island (in the 1950s), Bahrain (1971) and Singapore (1971). From the late 1960s the British hived off from newly independent Mauritius a new British colony called Diego Garcia, which became a US base which would grow to monstrous proportions later. The British were paid indirectly for its use and forcibly displaced the local population. Nor was withdrawal total. The United Kingdom retained a small interest in the defence of Singapore through a five-power treaty with Malaysia, Singapore, Australia and New Zealand. A joint British, Australian and New Zealand force was based in Singapore to 1974.

Such Commonwealth collaborations could not conceal the fact that the dominions were no longer part of a British war machine. Their primary connection was now with the USA. Canada was to buy all its jet aircraft from the USA. Australia bought its first generation of jet fighters and bombers from the United Kingdom but turned in the 1950s to first US and then French designs. Of the former dominions, only apartheid South Africa was still buying British military aircraft in the 1960s.

Table 13.1: Nine major conflicts by operational deaths, UK armed services, 1945–

Place	Deaths	Dates
Malaya	1443	1948–60
Northern Ireland	1441	1969–98
Korea	1129	1950–53
Palestine	754	1945–8
Canal Zone	405	1951–4
Cyprus	358	1955–9
Falklands	237	1982
Iraq	179	2003–

Source: Ministry of Defence, 'UK Armed Forces Operational Deaths Post World War II' (4 November 2014).[41]

THE SHIFT TO EUROPE

The Labour government had decided in the late 1960s to pull out armed forces from bases and protectorates and colonies in the Middle East and the Far East. These 'East of Suez' dispositions, in the fanciful imperialist language they were described in, really meant very little. The United Kingdom could exert very little power over those distances. The United Kingdom, as even Conservatives knew and said, was only ever going to be a serious power in its immediate vicinity, in Europe.[42] It even lost control of the eastern Atlantic – the NATO Supreme Allied Commander Atlantic was to be a US admiral, with headquarters in the United States. Churchill had protested, to no avail.[43]

Withdrawing slowly and sometimes reluctantly from these bases was a key part of a process of maintaining what had always been the primary orientation of British force: Europe. By far the most important bases, including airfields, were in Germany. Here roughly four armoured divisions were permanently stationed, plus many RAF squadrons. The British Army of the Rhine, or 1st Corps, at times amounted to well over 50,000 men. Maintenance of such a large force in Germany cost precious foreign currency, but it was kept in place. It was a Potemkin army: large enough for show, but nowhere near large enough on its own to defeat the forces that would be ranged against it.[44] It is important to note that Labour and Conservatives were hardly at one on the Labour decision to pull out of bases East of Suez in the late 1960s.[45] Labour were in part right to claim in 1970 that 'Labour's fundamental and historic changes in Britain's defence and foreign policy have given Britain a more credible and realistic position in world affairs than we ever enjoyed under the last Tory administration.'[46] This shift went along with defence intellectuals criticizing the idea of a distinct 'British way in warfare', which was now interpreted as the imperial delusion that the British could exert force on the continent without a continental-style commitment to an army.

British defence expenditures remained high, over 5 per cent of GDP into the 1970s. The retrenchment was difficult and slow. In the 1970s and 1980s especially, the left of the Labour Party said it was inappropriately high but also damaging to the national economy, as it took resources, not least scientific and technological ones, from civil industry. And that was probably right. There had, however, been major changes. In the 1970s the British military effort was essentially the Polaris force, the British Army of the Rhine, anti-submarine warfare in the Atlantic and the defence of the United Kingdom. It was focused on Europe. It was no longer in its equipment an overwhelmingly national force. While the ships and submarines were British, and most of the army equipment, in the air things were different. Around 1980 the newest RAF aircraft were the European Tornado, the Anglo-French Jaguar, the US Phantom and the British Harrier. There were still many older British aircraft, including the Buccaneer, the last all-British bomber, introduced in 1962, and the Lightning, the last all-British fighter, which had first gone into service in 1959, as well as remnants of the V bombers of the 1950s. And, of course, the Polaris missiles came from the USA. In the 1970s the United States air force stationed in the United Kingdom was more modern and larger than the British fighter and bomber forces stationed in the UK.[47]

The limits of British military power became painfully obvious in the 1970s. Tiny Iceland was able to force the United Kingdom to capitulate to its extension of its territorial waters to 200 miles from the coast in the face of a threat to withdraw from NATO. This mattered – the United Kingdom distant water fishing fleet depended on access to these seas, and the Royal Navy had sent in a naval force to defend the fishermen, mostly from Hull and Grimsby, as they trawled for cod. In a determined action the Icelandic coastguard cut trawls and rammed British frigates, damaging fifteen of the twenty-two which were deployed in total. It was the third cod war, the other being in the early 1970s and late 1950s, and all ended with a British defeat. The consequence of the 1976 defeat was the end of distant trawling. It was a potent symbol of the collapse of British power, which was not overturned by a victory in the South Atlantic in 1982.

14
Two Classes, Two Parties,
One Nation

By raising living standards and by social reform we are
succeeding in creating One Nation at home.

The Next Five Years, 1959 *Conservative manifesto*

In social security, we still have austerity National Insurance
benefits that impose poverty standards on the retired, the
sick and the unemployed.

The New Britain, 1964 *Labour Party manifesto*

In 1950 the House of Commons moved from the House of Lords, where it had sat since the bombing of 1941, into a new steel and concrete House. Designed by Sir Giles Gilbert Scott (of the red telephone box and Battersea power station) and engineered by Oscar Faber (of modernist flour mills of the 1930s), it was disguised to look like the old one. Much remained the same in the political system too. Labour had retained the House of Lords, only limiting its powers. It had abolished university seats and other forms of plural voting but retained the first-past-the-post system. After 1950 the pace of change was glacial. In 1958 life peerages were introduced, for men and women, who were now allowed into the Lords for the first time. From the 1964 Labour government onwards, except in some odd cases, no new hereditary peerages were created. The Lords continued otherwise unreformed until 1999. As far as the House of Commons was concerned the changes were minimal. The voting age was reduced from twenty-one to eighteen in 1969; because the Northern Ireland parliament was abolished in 1972–3 the number of seats for

Northern Ireland was increased from twelve to seventeen, under an act passed by the Labour government in 1979, which came into effect only for the 1983 election. There was nothing as significant as happened on the continent, where politics were substantially restructured sooner or later after the Second World War, with the abolition of monarchies, new constitutions and the creation of new governing parties. But the very foundations of British politics had also changed. Politics was no longer, with important exceptions, about empire, free trade, the constitution or religion or territory. Instead it was the politics of the policy of the nation, and the politics of class. Parties of national scope now dominated politics.

However, the real politics of industrial society was now more than ever conducted elsewhere than parliament. This was reflected in the fact that neither big businessmen, nor big local manufacturers, nor indeed big trade unionists now sat in parliament. In this world of the hidden politics of industrial society there was accommodation, or mutual recognition of interests, rather than consensus. There was no great capacity to forge significant agreed positions. The actual attitudes of business were more economically liberal than an assumption that they shared in some Keynesian, interventionist consensus suggested.[1] Organized labour also was less enamoured of the status quo than 'consensus' might imply. Hence in part the usefulness of the notion of 'corporate bias', by which the state, as the crucial active party, used high-level national organizations representing capital and labour essentially to neutralize dissent.[2]

Nevertheless, open party politics mattered also. It was conducted by two very different dominant political parties, who indeed saw themselves as very different. They disagreed on much and had different priorities and interests. There were also important disagreements within parties over crucial issues. There was an unsteady agreement to disagree and to acquiesce, on both sides, which limited freedom of action. It was more like an armistice than a 'post-war settlement', more an agreement to differ than a 'consensus'. Stability, legitimacy did not require consensus.

Capital and the majority who owned no capital faced each other on more equal terms than before the war. There was some redistribution of wealth and income, and wealth and status could not be displayed as

THE RISE AND FALL OF THE BRITISH NATION

nonchalantly as before the war. The wealthiest 1 per cent owned
around 40 per cent of the wealth (as measured from tax returns and
death duties) compared with 56 per cent in 1936–8. For income from
property, 1 per cent got 60 per cent and 10 per cent got 99 per cent.[3]
As before, the great majority had negligible net assets. Public debt, a
debt for the poor and an asset for the banks, individuals, and foreigners, despite being much greater than that of the Great War, paid low
interest and was inflated away.[4] Furthermore wages rose with respect
to salaries, and top pay failed to rise with inflation as low pay did.
The share of wages in national income went up. Differentials narrowed. Through indirect means – supporting trade unions, the tax
and benefit systems, a certain amount of redistribution was effected.

THE TWO-PARTY SYSTEM

Although the basic structures of the early twentieth-century political
system remained, their outward appearance, and the effects they generated, was very different. The first-past-the-post electoral system
now entrenched two class-based parties covering nearly the whole
United Kingdom. The Conservative and Labour Parties were now
roughly equally matched. Labour, in opposition, had 47 per cent of
the seats in 1951 and 44 per cent in 1955. Other parties were driven
out of the House of Commons. In 1964 only the Conservative Parties,
Labour and a handful of Liberals had seats. In 1966, apart from
Gerry Fitt, sitting for Republican Labour in Northern Ireland, and
twelve Liberals, all MPs belonged to the Labour Party or the Conservative Parties. As recently as 1945 there had been twenty-seven
members of small parties, including two Communists, two ILP, two
Irish Nationalists and more. After 1966 the smaller parties would
return, not least Scottish, Irish and Welsh Nationalists. By the 1970s
there would be eight parties in parliament, though most were tiny.

Also in contrast to the situation before 1945, the electorate now
had the decisive say in changing governments. Now, with one exception, only elections changed governments. The great majority of
administrations were single-party ones with absolute majorities.
There were no more coalitions. There were periods of minority

Labour government. The minority Labour government formed in February 1974 went to the polls in October 1974 but only got a majority of three. This disappeared in 1976, and for the remainder of its life the government depended on some of the small parties voting for it. It also negotiated an agreement in 1977–8 called the Lib-Lab Pact, under which the Liberals voted with the Labour government but would pre-agree legislation, and in a 1978 vote of confidence were supported by the Ulster Unionists. The government lost a vote of confidence and fell in March 1979; the first to do so since the Labour minority government of 1924.

The final important difference with the pre-1945 political system was that the two governing parties were different sorts of beasts, in a way which was not true of the Liberal and Conservative Parties when they dominated politics between them. Labour was the party of workers and welfare professions; the Tories the party of wealth and warfare. Nearly all the manual workers and teachers sat for Labour; most of the barristers, businessmen and military officers for the Tories. Politics was fundamentally asymmetric. Society was not pillarized into political/religious segments of equivalent status and power. As in the years before 1950, in the years 1950 to 2000, the Conservative Party dominated – it was in office for thirty-five of these years.

THE CONSERVATIVE PARTY

The Conservatives staged an extraordinary recovery in the 1950s. They won the election of 1951 with fewer votes than Labour but in 1955 and 1959 the Conservative block got nearly 50 per cent of the votes. The core Conservative alliance was doing better than in 1935, or the 1920s; only in 1931 had it got a higher proportion of the vote.[5] In the 1950s it was a mass organization, with an estimated, perhaps exaggerated, membership peaking at nearly 3 million, nearly three times peak Labour individual membership.[6] This comparative success requires some stressing and explanation. What it meant was that a very significant proportion of the working class must have voted Tory, more than before the war. Indeed, although the working class now, and only now, *tended* to vote Labour, its lead over the

Conservatives with these voters was not huge. In 1951 the Labour lead among the working class was at around 10 per cent, though it had been over 20 per cent in 1945. Even in the 1950s Labour did not have, as indeed it had never had, a complete dominance even among trade unionists. In 1957 Harold Macmillan noted his party needed 'at least 3 million Trade Union votes'.[7] Still, Labour could easily be identified by the Tories with the male manual producer. For there was also an important and changing gender dimension to voting behaviour. In 1951 and 1955 the Conservatives had a more than 10 per cent lead over Labour among women, and most women were, of course, working class. The Conservatives had set out to be the party of consumers, and of housewives, and reaped the benefits.[8] Yet if it was the party for women, it was not the party of women. During the whole period from 1951 to 1974 there were only two Tory women in cabinet, both in what was considered a woman's job: minister for education. They were Florence Horsbrugh, 1951–4 (in Cabinet only from 1953), and Margaret Thatcher, 1970–74.

The Conservative Parties consisted of essentially four non-competing parties into the 1960s, operating in every part of the United Kingdom. They were the Conservative and Unionist Party, the [Scottish] Unionist Party, the Ulster Unionist Party (dating effectively from 1905) and the National Liberals. The (Scottish) Unionist Party merged into the English and Welsh party in 1965. The Ulster Unionists stopped taking the Tory whip in 1974 and would leave the Unionist family of parties in 1985. The National Liberals were more important than the independent Liberals between 1950 and 1964, though they petered out in the 1960s. Indeed, in 1951 and 1955 the Liberals returned only six MPs, with 2.5 percent of the vote.

The Conservatives and Unionists were posh parties. The English and Welsh Conservative and Unionist Party was led by the aristocratic Winston Churchill to 1955; by Anthony Eden, from a minor aristocratic family, to 1957; and by Harold Macmillan, married into the grandest of aristocratic families, until 1963. Macmillan was succeeded by a fully titled aristocrat, the 14th Earl of Home, or Sir Alec Douglas-Home, as he became on renouncing his peerage. The ministers in Conservative governments of the 1950s and early 1960s were overwhelmingly public school and Oxbridge educated. Around one-sixth were aristocrats, and fully one-third Etonians.[9] The Labour Party, excepting a small part of its leadership, was very different. Those with secondary and university education had, as in the case of the Tories, tended to have been to public schools and Oxbridge. Where Labour differed was that part of its front bench (and most of its MPs), had no secondary or university education. Neither parliamentary party, in other words, had a strong cadre of the emergent grammar school/civic university middle class. In Parliament, Labour was the party of the elementary school, the Tories of the public school.

The Tory Party was also the party of the officer class. In the 1950s, after years of conscription, high warlike expenditure and continuous military operations, the martial virtues were very evident in public life. To have had a good war was an advantage. Many young men who reached high army rank prospered in the party, among them Brigadier Enoch Powell (elected 1950), Colonel Frederick Erroll (elected 1945), and Lieutenant-Colonel Edward Heath (elected 1950). Sidney, Viscount De L'Isle, was a dashing officer who won the VC in Italy. Major Peter Carrington MC, 6th Baron Carrington, was remarkable for holding many ministerial positions from the 1950s to the 1980s, including foreign secretary, entirely from the House of Lords. Major William Whitelaw MC (elected 1955) was to be home secretary and deputy prime minister (and was one of two childless men elevated to hereditary viscountcies by Margaret Thatcher). By contrast, the younger Labour leadership tended to come from men who were dons and wartime civil servants rather than soldiers, for example Hugh Gaitskell, Harold Wilson and Douglas Jay, though many had served as relatively junior officers such as Captain Tony Crosland, Major Denis Healey, Major John Freeman, Captain Roy Jenkins, Squadron Leader Merlyn Rees, Flying Officer Peter Shore, Pilot Officer Anthony Wedgwood Benn and Lieutenant James Callaghan RN.[10] None served with elite regiments. By contrast in 1953 the Tory cabinet had four former Grenadier Guards officers in it.[11]

The Tory Party was also without question the party of business. The very great majority of their MPs, when they were not ministers, had serious external interests (unlike most Labour MPs). Only twelve Tory MPs in 1966 had no identifiable remunerative job outside parliament; and some of these were simply retired from such work and others had private income.[12] In 1966–7, 243 Tory MPs held 290 positions of chairman, deputy chairman, or managing director of enterprises; and 601 had directorships. The comparable figures for Labour were 32 and 70. While 123 of the 363 Labour MPs had been manual workers, and 99 teachers, the number of Tory former workers or teachers was negligible.[13]

The businessmen were not just backbenchers. Churchill brought back his own key businessmen from wartime, Woolton, Leathers, Lyttelton and Bennett, into government. Oliver Lyttelton, as colonial secretary, was in charge of Malaya from 1951. He had been chairman of the largest group of tin-mining companies in that territory. Percy Mills of W & T Avery came into his own under Macmillan, as did Frederick Erroll (a Cambridge engineer who served as president of the Board of Trade and minister of power). He was later to be chairman of the papermaker Bowaters and of Consolidated Goldfields. Harold Watkinson, another businessman and engineer, served as minister of defence. Aubrey Jones, an economist who worked in steel, was minister of supply. But perhaps most obviously and importantly, Harold Macmillan was himself a businessman, chairman of the family business, the publishers Macmillan & Co.

From 1965 the party was led by Edward Heath. Very unusually for a Conservative, he spent some time after the war as a civil servant, and as a journalist for the *Church Times*. From his election in 1950 he was a professional politician. Men from business played important roles in his shadow cabinet in the late 1960s and in government 1970–74. For example, Sir Keith Joseph (of the builders Bovis) spoke on industry and trade in opposition. When Heath came into office in 1970 he brought industrial people into key positions. Robert Carr, an MP since 1950, went to the Department of Employment to introduce the new Industrial Relations Act, a major innovation. Carr was a Cambridge-trained metallurgist and had been head of research and development in his family's business, John Dale Ltd, makers of non-ferrous tubes and aluminium products. John Davies of BP had been director-general of the Confederation of British Industry and came in as secretary of state for trade and industry. Peter Walker was in finance. Heath brought in Lord Rothschild, of Shell, as head of a new think tank: Rothschild was a man of power – aristocrat, scientist, and former member of the security service.[14] There were younger men from business, such as the publisher Michael Heseltine and the engineer Nicholas Ridley of a Tyneside civil engineering firm, Brims and Co.

The contrast with the Labour Party was clear here too. For while it did have its Oxbridge graduates, and men who served as officers in the Second World War, its connections to business were minimal. Labour-affiliated and Labour-funding business people were typically Jewish. The Conservative Party, by contrast, attracted both Jewish and non-Jewish businessmen. Harold Wilson in particular was associated with Lord Kagan (ennobled 1976), who made Gannex raincoats in Huddersfield. Captain Robert Maxwell of Pergamon Press, who later owned the only Labour-supporting paper, the *Daily Mirror*, was briefly a Labour MP. The main financial experts in the party were Harold Lever, Edmund Dell, Joel Barnett and Robert Sheldon, all businessmen, Jewish and from Manchester.[15] They all chaired the Public Accounts Committee; indeed, they were the only Labour MPs to do so between 1970 and 1997. They also all served in the Treasury, while Dell was in addition secretary of state for trade. He had worked for ICI between 1949 and 1963. Other Jewish businessmen/experts on management were Ian Mikardo (who applied his management skills to canvassing, inventing the Reading Pad, named after his constituency), and Austen Albu, an Imperial-College-trained engineer who served as minister of state in the short-lived Department of Economic Affairs in the 1960s.[16]

THE LABOUR PARTY

The Labour Party was a conservative organization. It was dominated by the right of the party in the House of Commons. Clement Attlee was leader until after the election of 1955; he was succeeded by another public schoolboy and Oxford graduate, Hugh Gaitskell, who was leader until his death in 1963. This leadership was supported by right-wing trade union leaders, who dominated organized labour. Its socialism was muted and concentrated in the ranks of its individual members in the local constituency parties. One way to look at this is that the fundamental aim of the Labour Party has always been extremely modest. It was to get trade unionist and/or workers into parliament, to nationalize the coal mines and related industries, and to obtain a comprehensive welfare state providing a national minimum of what was first called 'maintenance'. That may indeed have been the limit of its ambitions, leaving it with little more do after 1951.

Yet Labour was a complex coalition of ideas, and the history of these ideas, and of its policies, is not well understood from within the arguments of the factions, which still dominate the histories.[17] For example, Hugh Gaitskell came out emphatically and decisively against the Suez adventure (not least because the US was not on board) and was against the Common Market (and in favour of the Commonwealth). Gaitskell thus went against the patriotic-imperialist end of Labour in 1956 and the right-wing pro-Common Market revisionists (and in particular his ideological spear-carriers such as Roy Jenkins). By later standards these stands, and his welfarism, would put Gaitskell at the far left of the party. The Labour right preferred to remember his failed attempt to get rid of the party's entirely notional commitment to total nationalization by dropping Clause IV of the party's constitution, and his success in reversing a temporary position of the party (though not the parliamentary party) in favour of nuclear disarmament.

From 1955 to 1983 Labour was led by four men all born between 1906 and 1916. Gaitskell, Wilson and Michael Foot studied at Oxford; Gaitskell and Foot had been to public school. The fourth, James Callaghan, was a white-collar trade unionist. They were representative of Labour's front bench, though not its MPs. First, these were products of grammar and public schools and overwhelmingly of the (mostly 1930s) University of Oxford: such as Denis Healey, Roy Jenkins, Michael Stewart, Barbara Castle, Harold Wilson, Patrick Gordon Walker, Richard Crossman, Anthony Crosland, Anthony Wedgwood Benn and Michael Foot. Some had taught at Oxford; most, but not all, were on the right of the party. Then there was the trade union officer class: men who rose without university through the ranks of trade union officialdom. These were men such as James Callaghan (tax officers), Ray Gunter (TSSA), George Brown (T&G), Bob Mellish (T&G), Reg Prentice (T&G), Richard Marsh (NUPE),

Fred Lee (AUEW), Roy Mason (NUM) and Eric Varley (NUM). Some had served in the war and were typically commissioned, for example James Callaghan, Ray Gunter, Bob Mellish and Reg Prentice. Some had higher education, sponsored by their union or the TUC, such as Roy Mason (LSE), Eric Varley (Ruskin), Richard Marsh (Ruskin) and Reg Prentice (LSE). They were also, with the exception of Fred Lee, on the right of the party. Reg Prentice defected to the Tories in 1977, Richard Marsh who had left politics to run the railways, indicated support for Thatcher in 1978. Mellish resigned in 1982 and joined the government's London Dockland Development Corporation. Varley left politics and became chairman of Coalite, which owned the Falkland Islands. George Brown was hostile to Labour in the 1970s and joined the Social Democratic Party, formed in 1981.

Among the leadership of the party the left was weak. Aneurin Bevan, once a miner and mining union official, was the leader of the left from the 1940s into the 1950s. Thereafter the leadership of the left included a number of figures – Richard Crossman, Barbara Castle and Michael Foot and from the 1970s, Tony Benn, who as Anthony Wedgwood Benn had inherited Cripps' Bristol seat. Cripps and Benn had much in common. Both were sons of peers appointed for political service, one Liberal, one Unionist. Both were younger sons, but Benn inherited the title because his elder brother had died in the war. Both were independently wealthy, Christians and vegetarians. Both had a particular connection to science and technology, the first as a chemist and patent lawyer, the second as an enthusiast for all sorts of new machines; Benn was Labour's modernizing whiz-kid of the 1960s. Stafford Cripps had been Minister of Aircraft Production during the Second World War; Benn ran its much enlarged successor, the Ministry of Technology. The difference was that Cripps moved rapidly to the right after 1939. Benn moved to the left after 1970.

In the general election of 1951 the Labour Party got its highest-ever proportion of the national vote. It lost votes in opposition in 1955 under Attlee, and in 1959 under Gaitskell. There was, even in the 1950s, a thesis that as society became wealthier, and supposedly less class conscious, so the self-identifying working-class Labour vote would fall.[18] It was an argument designed to shift the position of the Labour Party to the right, reflecting the belief that it was the

Conservatives who were more in tune with the times and the likely future. However, the British working class did not vote Labour by nature, as the argument assumed. Had they done so Labour would have been the majority party since its creation. Labour did far better among the affluent workers of the 1950s than the relatively impoverished workers of the interwar years. Looking forwards, the thesis does not work so well either. Labour was to continue to increase its vote as the working class got richer and smaller: in 1966 Labour got as good a result as in 1945, with 48 per cent of the vote (in 1964 it had been 44 per cent).

On one possible measure, trade union membership, class consciousness increased over time. In the 1950s and early 1960s trade unions hardly grew at all and were dominated by the right. Most of the unions were affiliated to the Labour Party and supported the Labour leadership against the more left-wing constituency membership. The trade unions were there, as before, to represent a largely male industrial workforce, in the private sector and the nationalized industries. From the late 1960s trade unionism grew rapidly, especially among white-collar workers in industry (the Association of Scientific, Technical and Managerial Staffs (ASTMS) grew notably) and in the public sector, bringing many more women into the trade union movement. Instead of members leaving unions as they became middle-class, the middle classes were joining unions! It is not clear then what was going on – were workers joining unions for individualistic rather than collectivist reasons? Was union membership a measure of the collapse of collectivism? What was clear was that, as union membership increased, the Labour vote fell. The Tories returned in 1970 with 46 per cent of the popular vote. In 1974 Labour were the largest party in a hung parliament with 37 per cent in February, with the Tories out-voting them (38 per cent). They won an overall majority in October with 39 per cent. In 1979, the Conservatives won with 44 per cent, with Labour down to 37 percent. Peak trade union membership was in 1979, and the Labour vote was nowhere near its highest.

The central revisionist argument of the 1950s was not about the working class but about capitalism. Revisionists argued that capitalist business had been transformed into an economically creative force, controlled by its managers, not its owners. Capitalism, even British capitalism, was then seen as successful. Anthony Crosland's *Future of Socialism*, in 1956 *the* revisionist text, should really have been called the future of welfare capitalism. Labour, it was argued, no longer needed to transform capitalism, but to tax it and spend in order to achieve greater equality. Fiscal measures could and should replace concerns with ownership. Labour had in fact already given up on nationalization. In 1950 there was quite a list of industries still to be nationalized – sugar, cement, 'appropriate sections' of chemicals, 'all suitable minerals', water, meat-importing and wholesaling, cold storage and insurance. By *Challenge to Britain*, a policy programme of 1953, the contenders had shrunk to a few machine-tool firms, some mining machinery firms and any inefficient aircraft establishment. By the 1957 party document *Industry and Society* nationalization seemed to have gone entirely.[19]

The logic of the revisionist position became clear in the 1959 Labour manifesto. The Labour programme was now for the first time focused on welfare. The central plank of the welfare programme was a radical reform and upgrading of the National Insurance pension, rejecting the Beveridgean flat-rate scheme. The 1959 manifesto was to be the most welfarist Labour manifesto ever. Practically its only industrial policy was to renationalize steel and long-distance road haulage.[20]

Hugh Gaitskell died young in 1963 and was replaced by a leader apparently from the centre left, Harold Wilson, the first non-public-school leader since 1935. He won the general election in 1964 with roughly the same vote Gaitskell got in 1959, but a Liberal revival now ate into the Tory vote.[21] He won on a very different manifesto than the 1959 one. It was overwhelmingly national-productivist, which was much more representative of Labour manifestos of the past, and of the future too.

In contrast to the earlier revisionist stories, Wilson stressed that *British* capitalism was deficient – run by gentlemen, financiers, speculators and amateurs. This analysis was attractive to the left, mixing as it did a traditional Liberal-Labour attack on rentiers, with its commitment to technicians and managers. He was very much in tune with national declinism of the time (see chapter 15). Wilson was a more complex and interesting figure than caricatures of him as merely slippery suggest. As we have seen Wilson was hostile to 'British' nuclear weapons and the sale of arms to fascists; he wanted to rein back the British military-industrial complex and was against Common Market entry, at least at first. Later the success would be put down to Wilson's modernizing, white-heat rhetoric, admired for its vacuous futurism rather than for its serious content. By the standards of the 1980s he was a politician of the extreme left – but the left of the 1960s and 1970s did not see him as such.

CONSENSUS?

The social polarization between the two parties pointed to their very different relations to power in economy, society and state. The Conservatives were the party of multiple overlapping elites; the Labour Party that of the organized working class, and some renegades from the elite. The Conservatives were the party connected to the great warfare functions of the state, the Labour Party at best to welfare. The Conservatives also had most of the newspapers, which reached all classes, on their side. *The Times, Telegraph, Mail, Express* and *Sketch* were Tory daily papers. The bias towards the Conservatives increased over time. In 1960 the Liberal (but which supported the Labour right) *News Chronicle* was sold to Lord Rothermere and was absorbed into the *Daily Mail*, and in 1964 the *Daily Herald* (the Labour paper) was renamed the *Sun* and in 1969 sold to Rupert Murdoch, leaving the *Mirror* as the only major Labour-supporting newspaper. Most of the very high-selling Sunday newspapers were Conservative, such as the *News of the World* (selling 7 million), the *Sunday Express, Sunday Mail, Graphic, Empire News* and others; the Labour-supporting Sundays were *Reynolds News*, the *Sunday Pictorial* and *Women's Sunday Mirror.*[22]

We should, for this reason alone, resist the tendency to discuss politics in the 1940s, 1950s and 1960s in terms of consensus, or the post-war settlement. The concepts came to frame the history of an entire era because from the 1970s historians and others wanted to defend what they took to be the good progressive post-war arrangements, while a minority were critical of it as stultifyingly retrogressive.[23] For both, the notion of a consensus served their purposes. Consensus embodied a naive claim that what mattered was party politics.

The concept of 'consensus' was only partially about whether there was agreement – it is at least as much about what there was supposed to be agreement about. For consensus was defined in relation to very particular issues, most notably those labelled Keynesianism and the welfare state. Yet the increasing welfare of the British people was not due to Keynesianism or to the welfare state. Economic growth, low unemployment and a whole raft of measures and policies were much more important than demand management or the social services. It was also not the case that the welfare state was the central concern of the elite, or the government or, indeed, political parties.

The very notion thus embodied a particular analysis and choice of what was or ought to be considered central to the life of post-war Britain. By centring consensus on Keynesianism and welfare, the argument was that the origins of the consensus or settlement were found on the liberal-left, and that the right therefore had accommodated to their position. It is no mere thesis about post-war agreement, it is a thesis that made particular claims about the character of the whole of politics over the century. Perhaps the richest version is that there was a national consensus, in which the Conservatives were allowed to dominate in questions of national greatness, and Labour was given the welfare state.[24] But most accounts ignore the warfare and foreign aspects and assume the centrality of welfare to the state.

What were Keynesianism and the welfare state? 'Keynesianism' is taken to mean very different things. Sometimes a very wide definition of Keynesianism was used as a label for all economic policy, including nationalization and sometimes even the welfare state. It has been suggested that Keynesianism even created the concept of a national economy, but this is unconvincing. The idea not only existed before Keynes, but the Keynesian notion of demand management itself depended on the existence of a national economic space. National economies were defined by economic controls at borders, not economic doctrines. Where this argument is helpful is in making clear the significance of the national economy as an analytical and conceptual category which was real and powerful, even if not Keynesian.

Sometimes Keynesianism is defined narrowly, as demand management, in order to argue that because policy was Keynesian in this sense it ignored 'the supply side' or did not lead to a 'developmental state'. But while this was true of many commentaries and histories it was not true of the history itself. Keynesianism as an idea does not capture more than a fraction of what was distinctive about the control of the economy of the long boom. Keynesianism per se had nothing to say about economic nationalism, the development of agriculture, or nationalization, or regional policies, or industrial policy, or indeed the control of prices and incomes (a feature of the entire 1960–79 period, with a 1948–50 incarnation also). To think about the economy as Keynesian or non-Keynesian is to miss the most important policy levers and transformations in the economy.

As an economic doctrine Keynesianism was the idea that managing the total level of demand in the economy was the way in which government managed to generate the historically unprecedented rates of economic growth (well over 2 per cent per annum on average) which were sustained from the war years into the 1970s, with historically low rates of unemployment. Yet even in this quite narrow sense the concept is unhelpful. Demand management was used, but mainly, as in the Second World War, to restrain inflation rather than to promote growth. It was more stop than go, even with Labour in the late 1940s. The notions that Keynesians were inflationists and those opposed to inflation were anti-Keynesian are both false.[25] It was not the case that an inherently sluggish economy was brought to life by stimulating demand. Indeed, this point was made by anti-Keynesians, some of whom regarded Keynesianism as the management of the economy and society by too-clever-by-half men with no families, indifferent to the future, who undermined the moral basis of capitalism, a capitalism which was in fact already generating growth and employment despite them.

The repeated invocation of 'Keynesianism' does, however, need to be taken seriously. What Keynesianism, and later monetarism, did was to provide a language around government budgets – a particularly visible parliamentary occasion – which dominated reporting, with the language of expansionary or deflationary budgets, reflation and deflation, stop and go, and later the Public Sector Borrowing Requirement and the Medium Term Financial Strategy of the monetarist period. This filtered into histories telling the story of the post-war economy as stop-go, balance of payments crises, sterling taking the strain, inflationary and disinflationary budgets and so on. This was not unimportant, but was only part of the story. Demand management and a sense of how the macro-economy was to be conceived (which did owe something to Keynes) was only one small dimension of economic policy.

The second key concept was that of the newly-created 'welfare state'. This is of course associated with another liberal political economist, William Beveridge, though he did not use the term. In the standard consensus account a novel, newly large-scale model of welfare provision rested on a new conceptualization of citizenship, born in the Second World War. These assumptions are, as we have seen, very questionable. The welfare state was largely not new, and what was new was not centrally due to Beveridge. In any case, multiple principles were in play. Furthermore, it was not the welfare state which lifted the British people out of poverty, just as it was not Keynesian economics which kept them fully employed from 1940 into the early 1970s.

The term 'welfare state', appeared in English for the first time in the 1920s but was not common, or used in its modern sense, until the 1950s. It first appeared in the work of the then Bishop of Manchester, William Temple, in 1928, meaning something like a democratic state which stood in contrast to a 'power state'. In was also used in this sense by Sir Alfred Zimmern, Montague Burton professor of international relations at the University of Oxford between 1930 and 1944.[26] It was utterly disconnected from the 'social services' as can be seen from the fact that Temple and others did not use the term when writing about the social services.[27] The modern sense – that of extended social services provided by the state – emerged only in the late 1940s, and became established in the 1950s. By 1960 the sociologist of welfare Richard Titmuss wrote of the myth of the welfare state: the idea that the state had indeed got rid of poverty and misery. The welfare state was, for Titmuss and his colleagues, something yet to be achieved. As we have seen, they and the Labour Party came to the view that in order to do this the key Beveridgean ideas needed to be rejected.

Focusing on the idea of the post-war state as a welfare state gets the state very wrong. What was most novel in British public spending in the 1950s was not, as we have seen, welfare spending, but high levels of warfare spending. Comparatively speaking, the United Kingdom was a low spender on welfare and a high spender on warfare, in the 1950s and indeed later too.[28] If there was a welfare state in post-war Europe it was not most obviously the United Kingdom.

It is in fact very doubtful whether Keynesianism or welfarism were at the centre of politics, let alone state practices. The economy was discussed in terms of exports and imports, investment, planning, production, at least as much as in terms of budget deficits or surpluses. Welfare policy was not the main focus of politics or policy, even rhetorically, even for the Labour Party, as we have seen. The first time Labour had used the term 'welfare state' in a manifesto was in 1955. But this is what it said:

> In order to strengthen our Welfare State still further and at the same time to play our part in assisting the under-developed areas of the world, our own production must rise every year. Only a government prepared to plan the nation's resources can do this. Labour will ensure that the claims of investment and modernisation come first.[29]

The Conservative manifesto of that year paired the welfare state with military expenditure:

> In an armed Welfare State the demands on taxable resources cannot be light. This makes it all the more necessary that government, central and local, should be run economically. There are today over 50,000 fewer civil servants and four fewer Ministries than when we took over. Conservatives will persist in the drive for simpler and less expensive administration.[30]

There was hardly a political consensus about the welfare state either. Policies, and practices, clearly differed between the parties, and both, especially Labour, distanced themselves from the Beveridge programme.

Big differences in approach were evident in economic policy. Stories of 'Butskellism' (originally a jokey conflation of the name of R. A. Butler, the Conservative chancellor of the exchequer in the early 1950s, and his shadow, and predecessor, Hugh Gaitskell), grossly exaggerate the degree of agreement between the parties – Labour was much more committed to planning, to economic nationalism, than the more market-oriented, more economically internationalist Conservatives.[31] The Tories denationalized steel in the 1950s, and it was renationalized by Labour in the 1960s. The Conservative government introduced 'commercial' television in 1955, known as 'independent television' to its promoters. It was funded by advertising, on the American model, and was decried as vulgar from the outset and for decades to come. The Conservatives allowed large-scale private road transport, a vital change. Labour opposed entry into the Common Market in the early 1960s, under Gaitskell and Wilson, when the government was firmly committed to it. There were also important disagreements on industrial policy in the late 1960s and 1970s. Edward Heath, later held up as the very embodiment of the consensus, was understood in 1970–71 to have decisively broken with the consensus on industrial relations and the role of the state in industry, repealing key bits of interventionist legislation and abolishing whole ministries.[32]

Where the concept of consensus might be salvaged is in foreign and defence policy. This is an area to which the idea has not generally been applied. Here the key point is that policy was not so much a matter of consensus between parties as the product, not of party politics, but of the state itself. There are indeed striking continuities across administrations which are in part a story of lack of political input. Such consensus as existed in politics here might indeed stem from the fact of relative lack of expertise and engagement with these issues by Labour (that asymmetry again). Furthermore, the Cold War forced the domestic left onto the defensive, it was in important respects a war *on* the domestic left, whether communist or not. And the left did suffer – in 'Natopolitan' culture, as one new left activist called it, it did not have the intellectual impact it had had in the 1930s or the 1940s.[33] But while there is a case for a consensus on defence policy, it is not an overwhelming one. There was, as we have seen, a contested politics of the warfare state. It was mostly a matter of parts of the Labour left criticizing a consensus which generally included the Labour leadership (as in the cases of 1950s British rearmament, German rearmament and the H-bomb). But there was also dispute over nuclear policy in the early 1960s *between* the front benches, which is too easily forgotten.

A second area of consensus, with some dissent, was protectionism, the obligation to buy British and the promotion of British technology. Here, too, parliamentary politics was not relevant – a deeper state and administrative culture was in control. These were central features of what has been called Do It Yourself Economics.[34] It was essentially economic nationalism, with a very strong dose of techno-nationalism thrown in. We might also call it Listianism, after the nineteenth-century theorist of economic nationalism, or indeed scientific nationalism, as Listianism has been called by analogy with Marx's scientific socialism. It is difficult indeed to find a textbook of DIYE, by definition, and hard also to find economists who were openly economically nationalist. Thomas Balogh of Oxford, an economic adviser to Harold Wilson in the 1964 government, was perhaps a partial exception in that he was openly in favour of Commonwealth preferences and hostile to the EEC on economic grounds.[35]

Economic nationalism was an elusive idea which, if it did not exist as formal doctrine, was nonetheless a fundamental aspect of economic discourse, and clearly of practice. Everyday economic discussion in the 1940s to the 1970s was remarkably focused on the nation, on the balance of payments as a national profit and loss account, on exhortations to export or die, on production, efficiency, productivity, science and that new key word, technology, all in a national context.

Thus, while the proponents of the view that there was a consensus tend to focus their attention on ideas from the liberal-left, on which there was in fact little consensus, we find a very different picture. The issues on which there was a greater measure of consensus – the warfare state and protection – were historically policies not of the liberal-left, but rather the right and of the state. Post-war Labour came to accept protection, conscription and a measure of imperialism, the long-established policies of the Tories. It is rather telling that Harold Wilson so liked the popular historian Arthur Bryant, a national-imperialist protectionist of the 1930s, knighted by the Conservatives in 1954, that he raised him to the Companionship of Honour in the 1960s.

15

Social Democracy, Nationalism and Declinism

There is no more dangerous illusion than the comfortable doctrine that the world owes us a living. One of the dangers of the old-boy network approach to life is . . . that it is international, that whatever we do, whenever we run into trouble, we can always rely on a special relationship with someone or other to bail us out. From now on Britain will have just as much influence in the world as we can earn, as we can deserve. We have no accumulated reserves on which to live.

Harold Wilson, speech at Scarborough, 1963

The old idols of gentlemanly sloth and corpse-like 'stability' had to give way to the over-riding demands of one new, hard god: production. British capitalism, which had dominated the world without severing itself from a semi-feudal past, had now to come nakedly of age.

Tom Nairn, 1964[1]

Our island is one of the very few provinces of Europe which has not in this century suffered from civil or international war upon its own soil; and which has escaped the consequences – gas chambers, 'quisling' regimes, partisan movements, terror and counter-terror – which have coloured the outlook of whole nations, East and West. It is very easy for us to fall into insular, parochial attitudes . . .

E. P. Thompson, 1957[2]

Our jobs, our living standards, and the role of Britain in the World all depend on our ability to earn our living as a nation. That is why Britain has to pay her way in trade and transactions with the outside world. In the last financial year, 1969/70, our national surplus was £550 million – the largest we have ever had.

Now Britain's Strong – Let's Make It Great to
Live In, *Labour Party manifesto*, 1970[3]

It is telling that efforts to anatomize British power still evoke the cliché the 'Establishment'. The term appeared, though perhaps not for the first time, in the *Spectator* in 1955 and became famous because of the furious reaction the article it appeared in elicited. What was meant, and not meant, by it provides a rich illustration of the limits of the concept. Anyone, wrote Henry Fairlie, the author of the piece:

> who has at any point been close to the exercise of power will know what I mean when I say that the 'Establishment' can be seen at work in the activities of, not only the Prime Minister, the Archbishop of Canterbury and the Earl Marshal, but of such lesser mortals as the chairman of the Arts Council, the Director-General of the BBC, and even the editor of *The Times Literary Supplement*, not to mention divinities like Lady Violet Bonham Carter.

But this was about civic, public power; power over what was said, not what was done. The focus was on religion (an indicator that it was still important), royalty, the arts and letters. The cases he gave were the rallying around the Soviet spies Guy Burgess and Donald MacLean, and a story of how Clement Attlee stopped a very mildly critical article by an MP about Princess Margaret.[4] No doubt ideological power lay in such interconnected places, but in this account of the 'Establishment' there is no City, no military, no business, no United States, no science, no technology. It was hardly an analysis of who ran the United Kingdom, a question rarely addressed well, nor even who did the influential thinking. We are left with neither an account of the elite nor elite thought.

Histories of the ideas which animated political action in the United

THE NEW CABINET

"A COUNTRY NEGLECTS ITS EGGHEADS AT ITS PERIL ... IT IS TIME WE GOT TOGETHER"
— LORD HAILSHAM

Illustration 15.1: 'The New Cabinet', by Vicky. In the centre is Lord Hailsham. L to R, John Boyd-Orr, nutritionist, A. J. P. Taylor, historian, John Osborne, playwright, T. S. Eliot, poet, Edith Sitwell, poet, Malcolm Muggeridge, journalist, Bertrand Russell, philosopher, Victor Gollancz, publisher, Basil Liddell Hart, military intellectual, Kingsley Martin, journalist, and Vicky, cartoonist. (British Cartoon Archive VY1066, published 1958)

Kingdom after 1945 seem to imply that social democracy and/or liberalism dominated. Social democracy essentially means the policies of the Labour Party, understood as the creation of a welfare state, and an accommodation with capitalism. Historians of the left tend to favour liberalism, and make the point that British social democracy was but weakly developed. They might speak indeed of the myth of social democracy.[5] This argument is essentially a liberal continuity thesis supported by references to the post-war ideas of two liberals, Keynes and Beveridge, the importance of Edwardian liberal innovations in welfare and of the supposed failure to transform the nature of the state and state intervention in the post-Second World War years. Both stories, as has already been suggested, are not only misleading in different ways, but also insufficient. This is not to say there were no liberal ideas in play – there certainly were – for example in the powerful arguments which seemed to explain why liberal conservatives and right social democrats sought the bracing competition and rational transnationalism of the Common Market. But these were far from the only ideas in play – we cannot usefully characterize British ideas as liberal and/or social democratic only.

What is notable, or rather should be, is the post-war importance of critiques, often implicit, but deep and strong, of liberalism. These were certainly not only social democratic. In the years after 1950 especially the argument would repeatedly be made that the United Kingdom had not been Prussian enough, not continental enough, in terms of both the economy and military practice. These criticisms came from left and right and were evidence of British nationalism, whose model of a successful nation was decidedly continental.

SOCIAL DEMOCRACY

If liberalism and social democracy, like Keynesianism and the welfare state, won't do as place holders for the key ideas and assumptions which shaped state and society, what, then, were they? Political economy is indeed central, but what kind of political economy? Was there, for example, a distinctive social democratic political economy?[6] Or sociology? It is difficult indeed to find an economics which was distinctly social democratic, committed to the Labour Party, with a distinctive analysis of capitalism. There were powerful economists who advised prime ministers such as Sir Donald MacDougall, Sir Alec Cairncross, and Lords Roberthall, Balogh and Kaldor, but few if any had a distinctly social democratic outlook.[7] Only the last two were brought in as political appointees, to Harold Wilson. Harold Wilson was himself an economist, but we have no study of what was distinctive about his economic thought beyond his commitment to planning, and his rejection of a policy of devaluation of sterling in 1964 (though he was forced to devalue in 1967). Wilson did, however, show a marked understanding of the need of government control over firms so that they would follow the national interest rather than their own interest.

Labour's analysis of capitalism and that of Labour-sympathizing intellectuals was weak. Anthony Crosland's *Future of Socialism* (1956) in essence argued that the class of capitalists that had ruled the world no longer existed. Individual capitalists had lost the power to control large enterprises, which were now in the hands of managers, not shareholders, and they were not concerned just with the pursuit of profit. As far as control of industry was concerned, the state had all the power it needed, and, furthermore, it was suggested, the new managerial controllers were not as averse as the old capitalists to working with the state. The problem was that this was supposition – the actual nature of the policies and programmes of enterprises was not discussed.[8] Critics of Crosland did not get very far either. For the new left that emerged after 1956 analyses of the capitalists in particular was an urgent task in the light of Crosland's revisionism. 'Analysis of the power structure of British society . . . is thus the greatest present research need.'[9] The aim was to show individual capitalist control, control over many firms by interlocking directorships and the links between finance and industry.

One looks in vain (until the 1970s) for an elaborated set of arguments from the left for alternative ways of running the economy to that practised by the Conservatives in the 1950s, except for making general arguments about planning and putting the interests of the nation first. What is harder still to find is anyone setting out a general case, and methods, for a new national calculus which would work

out what was best for the nation in terms of both equity and efficiency. There were no distinctive criteria for nationalized industries,
though they were nationalized on the basis that they should indeed be
run on principles reflecting their national importance. The government produced criteria which merely aped the profit criteria for
private firms, which often made nationalized industries unprofitable
when they did what they were supposed to do – behave differently
from a private enterprise.[10] This is not to say that nationalized industries and other state enterprises did not in fact operate to distinctly
national and other criteria – they did, most notably in buying British
and ignoring the costs of doing so – the point here is that these crucial
issues were not the subject of sustained analysis on the left. To put it
another way, the Labour Party generally relied on state experts rather
than on its own, not just in matters of war, or research, but even in
its own area of special concern, the nationalized industries. It did not
have, as the much more politically marginal communist parties of
France and Italy did, a cadre of intellectuals of renown developing
party-specific positions. Indeed, the levels of political education
within the Labour Party were notoriously low.

The exception that proves the rule is the economics and sociology
of the welfare state. Here, there was a left tradition of investigation
and policy prescription operating on assumptions as to what was best
for the nation. For example, in criticizing the notion of the NHS as a
cost to the individual through taxation, and private medicine as a
saving to the taxpayer, one found the response that both private and
public medicine cost the nation money, the issue was which system
was more equitable and more efficient. The NHS could convincingly
come out best on both grounds. Thus the National Health Service, it
was argued, was a cheap as well as equitable way of providing the
nation with the health care it might provide itself by less equitable
and more expensive private means. Similarly, a national state pension
scheme of a generous kind might well be the most efficient from a
national point of view. The issue is whether one system of giving
money to particular people was more efficient and equitable than
another. Similarly, one finds objections to the idea that benefits were
a cost and tax allowances a saving. After all, they are both transfers
from a public pot to private individuals. The argument for child

benefits was made on this basis. This was the sort of argument indeed put forward by the applied economists of the welfare state, who served on Royal Commissions and advised the Labour Party on the NHS and on pensions.[11] It is crucial to recall that, far from arguing from a Beveridgean consensus, they generally rejected Beveridge's central policy, the flat-rate contribution and benefit.

This is not to say these were the only views on these matters, or that the only policies were those of the left. An assumption of uniformity of view, of experts in favour of the actually existing welfare state, is belied by a group of doctors and others who continued to oppose the NHS, including health economists, through the 1950s into the 1960s and 1970s.[12] Much of the application of efficiency thinking to the NHS was the sort of work study and operational research already in use in government and industry to reduce costs.[13]

The extent to which professionals concerned with the state represented or pushed policy in a progressive direction remains open. The assumption that the state-connected professionals were of the left is based on the prior assumption that the state was overwhelmingly a welfare state.[14] There were small numbers of lawyers, architects and sociologists concerned with welfare, from health, to labour law, to race relations, but whether the welfare state professionals were generally progressive has not been established. Taking a broader look at the experts connected to the state, not least the warfare state, suggests that this is far from a safe generalization.

The thesis of the left that British social democracy was weak is thus surely right. Where I think the argument goes wrong is in assuming that therefore liberalism triumphed or at least continued to have the dominant influence. There were alternatives to liberalism in the past, and in the present. In the past the dominant one was imperialism; after 1950 it was nationalism, which liberals had always regarded as a powerful anti-liberal view.

BRITISH NATIONALISM

Because British nationalism did not label itself as such, it has barely been noticed by historians, who might see in it only a residual imperialism and racism. It is recognized in the forms of *anti*-British nationalism such that nationalism in British history usually means Scottish and Welsh and Irish nationalism. British nationalism barely seems to exist at all, nor indeed does English nationalism. This tends to be associated with a very few figures – often no more than Enoch Powell and Margaret Thatcher.[15] They were, however, not economic nationalists.

Yet British nationalism of the left did exist. It was a post-imperial nationalism, similar to the post-imperial nationalism of other parts of the British empire. It was not derivative from these other post-imperial nationalisms, as has been suggested.[16] It was a critical rather than celebratory nationalism. Indeed, on the left especially, but not exclusively, the failure to be national enough was seen as the central problem with the United Kingdom in the past, and into the present. As we have seen, during the war many communists and others on the left promoted a nationalist critique of British liberalism and imperialism. As I suggested in Part I, Labour could be seen as a nationalist party after 1945, indeed as *the* nationalist party. It put nation before class, it invoked national victories from the past, and not class victories (or defeats).[17] It is not accidental that Labour prime ministers invoked the national interest again and again, nor was it a mere cliché.

As in the past and elsewhere, nationalism was important in the writing of history. The 1950s to the 1970s saw the writing of very national, though certainly not necessarily celebratory, accounts of recent British or English history. Histories typically ignored or downplayed the empire and abroad, telling a story of the coming-together of the British people. Just as Australian nationalists, long after the event, created national stories around ANZAC and Singapore, so post-war British nationalists chose 1940 as the moment in which the island nation discovered itself. Histories began to tell a national story in which 'Britain stood alone' in 1940, that is, the island nation stood alone. The war was given a national framing and was seen as having been fought by a mobilization of the left and the people. The war was a good war, in its aims, and in that it was good for the people who fought it. What was to be regretted was that its progressive logic did not endure longer, that its promise was betrayed. The complex politics of history and memory projected a hoped-for national future onto the past (and especially 1940). Then it took that invented past for the actual past, so the future looks nostalgic.

A. J. P. Taylor's *English History 1914–1945*, has as a key theme of the story of the Second World War that of a nation coming of age by looking to itself, by fighting a 'people's war' in which the left was prominent. Success came from mobilizing the British people. Angus Calder in his *People's War* also told a story of a nation, not an empire, which found its strength by turning inwards and binding together to create a successful national effort, led by the left. Calder and many other historians of the left take 1940 not 1945 as the key moment in which the new nation is born, making it clear that, although the nation is to be interpreted in terms of class, what was important was nation trumping class. For Calder the years from 1945 represented a betrayal of the potential of 1940. That has proven a powerful historical argument, whatever its grasp on reality.[18]

The war came to be seen as the one moment in which the nation or perhaps just the elite could be raised from its lethargy, in a way post-war Labour governments, for example, could not. Where, say, the white heat of the 1960s failed, the wartime spirit had succeeded. A. J. P. Taylor insisted that it was the war which brought the British economy into the twentieth century. The communist historian Eric Hobsbawm saw it as the moment of national renewal and of technical advance. After 1940, the United Kingdom was turned 'in the interests of survival, into the most state-planned and state-managed economy ever introduced outside a frankly socialist country' in part because of 'implicit political pressure of the working classes'.[19] He also celebrated national agricultural production. That image of the war as the national and industrial moment of exception recurs in many more instances.[20] He and others developed the genuinely national critique in which internationalist British capitalism failed, except in the moment it was national, taken to be the Second World War.

It is notable that the right did not write histories of the nation at war. Winston Churchill wrote a semi-official history of the war in its entirety, not just the role of the United Kingdom, or even that of the

British empire. If anything, its focus was on the Anglo-American alliance. Historians of the right have followed him in telling stories of the Second World War as a whole rather than specifically writing about the British experience. Histories of the fighting British empire did not appear until the twenty-first century.[21] It is indeed worth noting the absence of imperialist (rather than imperial) histories of the twentieth-century United Kingdom, and the few that are supportive of the British empire write from a liberal point of view portraying the empire as diffuser of trade and enlightenment, rather than as a trading bloc or the basis of military power.[22] The reason is perhaps obvious – there were bigger fish to fry in the Cold War – and the US alliance was central. Imperialism was a fringe activity confined to private spaces. One of the spaces it can be found hinted at is in the suggestions by some historians that it would have been better to do a deal with Hitler in 1940, and thus have preserved a powerful empire. Churchill discovered the reality of British weakness and made it worse by fighting the war. By 1945 the empire was finished, the UK depended on the USA, a Labour government was in power, and the USSR dominated half of Europe: 1945 was 'the end of glory'.[23]

The left's critical nationalism had a core weakness. It had no analysis of the local British elite, relying as it did on the idea of a non-national British elite. The nationalism of the left in particular helps explain the failure to actively criticize the actual policies and practices of the British elite, except where they are seen as the stooges of foreigners: Americans, the 'Gnomes of Zurich' (that is, Swiss bankers) or later the bureaucrats of Brussels. In nationalist left fantasies the United Kingdom was militaristic because it sold out to the USA, capitalist because it was in hock to American business, or the high authorities of the Common Market. It also helps explain the lack of an alternative theory of society, the constant invocation of the nation, the admiration for British forms and the explanation of weakness in national terms. It was also weak in that it could not beat the Conservatives when it came to claiming the imagery of the nation. Thus nationalism remained, as Tom Nairn suggested, focused on the symbolism of monarchy, armed forces, parliament – on mystificatory forms rather than on possibilities of popular mobilization.[24]

DECLINISM

There was, however, one very important nationalist critique of the British elite. The failure of the national elite was central to proliferating arguments about a supposed British 'decline'. Declinism may be defined as the explanation of relative decline, by what are taken to be national failings. The most notable exponent of this sort of analysis was Correlli Barnett, writing from the 1960s. He argued that the British nation was not nationalist enough, too militarily weak, too geared to abroad. Empire was a drain on national power. The United Kingdom should have been more like Germany – more national, more militarist, more scientific, less imperial, naval and liberal. Correlli Barnett created a negative, inverted story in which, in the Second World War, the United Kingdom did not mobilize nationally but became dependent on the USA.[25] Weakened and distracted by empire, it was saved in 1940 by the United States and became its pensioner during the war. Such theses later found strong echoes on the left. In 1991 Angus Calder was to argue that the whole myth of the Blitz was designed to cover up that momentous transfer of power to the US in 1940.[26]

For the nationalist left the empire and British internationalist capitalism were also a central cause of decline. Empire (allegedly) gave the United Kingdom protected markets for low-quality manufacturers, provided prestigious careers which drew the elite away from industry and led to wasteful warlike expenditure of the wrong sort. Empire cushioned the United Kingdom from the realities of the cruel real world for too long and gave an old ruling class prestige and power they would otherwise have lost. Investments overseas, a distinctive feature of British capitalism, required a payback, which came in the form of imports, undermining the national economy.[27] These were central arguments of post-war nationalist histories, as they were of nationalist political economy earlier. Declinism, a central feature of intellectual discourse from the 1950s into the 1990s, was a very important expression of anti-imperialist, anti-liberal nationalism.[28]

Declinism arose from a sense that the nation was weakening relative to other nations, expressed, for example, in the number of national comparative statistics which emerged in the 1950s. The central observation was that the British nation was not growing as fast as others. The new league tables of rates of growth of GDP had the United Kingdom as a straggler especially, but not only, in Europe. As a result of low relative (but high absolute) rates of growth the British economy was shrinking relative to the world economy as a whole, and others were thus grabbing larger shares of world production and indeed trade. Low relative rates of growth got confused with low efficiency. Poor countries were regarded as paragons of modernity because they grew faster.

An internationalist framing would note that the United Kingdom was bound to weaken relative to other powers, as they became more successful. That was to be expected and welcomed in any internationalist calculus of well-being, in which everyone was getting richer, and the poor faster than the richer. It would also have led to the conclusion that even if the UK had the most efficient workers, the most ruthless entrepreneurs, the most inventive engineers, it would still have declined relatively. It could only have been avoided if, say, places like Germany and Japan had been turned into poor agricultural countries and the Soviet Union bombed out of existence.

Declinism has to be seen as the unwitting last refuge of great power delusions. Fix those national failings, the implication went, and the United Kingdom would once again be a top dog. Indeed, the very centrality of declinism, while it insisted on decline, was evidence of unwillingness to come to terms with its reality, taking solace in the idea that it might be reversed. Declinism was, paradoxically, a reason why the UK has not been able to adjust to inevitable, and welcome, relative decline. It is useful to think of it partly as a response to an elite that was shamed by Suez, as part also of the anti-deferential mood of the 1960s; and also something which affected policy by undermining the confidence of the elite, not least with respect to the Common Market.[29] It was a common declinist theme that empire had been and continued to be too important in the political imagination, that too much attention was granted to the maintenance of sterling, and defence expenditure.[30] Yet it was also a form of jingoism, a delusion about inherent superiority, dressed up as critique.

Declinism was at the core of the early 1960s attack on the elite, understood as a political class, an economic class, a social elite. These criticisms took a particularly rich form among left intellectuals, though it needs to be recognized that it came in many ideological varieties. Thus Eric Hobsbawm in his widely read *Industry and Empire* (1968) claimed that British industry, formed in the 'archaic phase of industrialization', had not needed much in the way of science, and as a result the new sciences and technologies of the late nineteenth century, these 'winds of change . . . grew sluggish' as they crossed the Channel.[31] British scientific and technical education was in this and so many other accounts, negligible. Hobsbawm saw economic decline as a palpable fact in the interwar years. There was a move to larger firms, but merely a defensive anti-competitive one which did not improve the basic condition of the economy.[32] Only the state promoted new techniques, for example, the jet and radar.

Declinism was also central to the analysis of the British condition by the new left. In the early 1960s Tom Nairn could write: 'As is well-known, every major index of economic development shows the inferiority of British capitalism to its main competitors.'[33] The key idea was that the British elite was aristocratic, old-fashioned and inefficient; the industrial middle class had succumbed to the aristocracy; elite culture became fixated on the countryside and aristocratic rather than bourgeois virtues.[34] This led to immobility, archaism, rigidity, crystallization, petrification, indeed 'stale constipation and sedimentary ancestor-worship'.[35] Perry Anderson dismissed the British intellectuals and technocrats as useless. He discounted the importance of British intellectual Marxism of the 1930s, which was, in his view, dominated by 'poets and natural scientists – the two vocations most unsuited to effect any lasting transformation of British culture'. He went on: 'where there was a bid to "apply" their formal beliefs, the outcome was frequently bad art and false science: at its worst the rhymes of Spender and the fantasies of Bernal'.[36] For all this dismissal of British intellectual traditions, Anderson was a very British analyst of his time, reproducing in his own distinctive language the key theses of the declinists: 'Today Britain stands revealed as a sclerosed, archaic society, trapped and burdened by its past successes.' He claimed the causes were old: 'under-investment at home, lagging technological innovation since the end of the last century'; the Treasury, after the City of London (the financial centre), was 'the second great albatross round the neck of British economic growth'. The British state needed to be interventionist, technocratic, but all it offered was 'universal dilettantism and anachronistic economic liberalism', while the British educational system was only belatedly scientific. And so on and so forth.[37] The key underlying point was that the elite was stuck in its Edwardian globalist liberal imperialism.

On the left the critique of British capitalism's internationalism echoed left nationalist critiques in post-colonial contexts, where the lack of a national bourgeoisie, rather than a cosmopolitan one connected more to global capital than the nation, was the central element of 'dependista' political economy. The United Kingdom came to be written about as if it were Argentina. This sort of argument was to have especial prominence in the work of Scottish left-nationalists.[38] The Scottish elite was by implication more industrial, more scientific, more democratic than the English, or at least had been.

Just as Anderson and Nairn's arguments are not known for their declinism, not least because it was a commonplace, E. P. Thompson's famous response, similarly, is not known for its anti-declinism, its invocation of the importance of science and political economy, or its hints at the significance of the warfare state.[39] Thompson noted the 'uncomfortable affinity of tone' between the pronouncements of Perry Anderson and Tom Nairn on the one hand and 'the journalistic diagnosticians of the British malaise whom they profess to despise . . . Mr David Frost, Mr Shanks, and Comrade Anderson are saying different things but there is the same edge to the voice.' Thompson worried that they all overlooked 'certain strengths and humane traditions' in Britain, but more importantly, in attacking what they saw as left-overs from Old Corruption, they were blind to the reality that a 'new, and entirely different, predatory complex occupies the state'. He asked whether it was not to this new Thing of vast power and influence, 'rather than to the hunting of an aristocratic Snark, that an analysis of the political formations of our time should be addressed?'[40]

Interestingly he did not give the Thing a more specifically modern name – nor indeed did he complain of a British military-industrial complex or a British warfare state; he had a wide and rather vague concept in mind. But there was an inkling here of something the rest of the left implicitly denied existed, except as yet another archaic remnant.

By framing decline in the way it did, declinism took to explaining what never happened with explanations which didn't work. It sought to explain a supposed catastrophic failure, by invoking the power of finance, or the aristocracy or imperial thought, or literature, or the classics. All these explanations were blown up to monstrous proportions. The supposed lack of entrepreneurs, large corporations, research laboratories and technocrats that these explanations supposedly accounted for became deeply entrenched as authoritatively established historical reality. Thus, what should have been the most obvious features of twentieth-century British history were consigned to near non-existence. For example, Margaret Gowing, an official historian of the war economy and the British nuclear programme, could state in the 1970s that 'My own research in atomic energy shows that at the end of the Second World War, which had strengthened British industry, the industrial base of scientific technology in Britain was extremely thin.'[41] She was hardly alone in this kind of distorted account, though she was one of the few that had studied the history of British science and technology. Yet at most what any index of strength showed was that British capitalism was behind US capital and perhaps German capitalism, but that it was by most indicators one of the top three capitalisms in the world, with, one might add, a base of industrial scientific technology not much thinner than that of Germany or of the USA either.

Declinists managed the extraordinary feat of not seeing what one might have thought was in plain sight. But of course declinism was never merely descriptive, it was primarily prescriptive. To judge from its explanations of British failure and what it appeared to take to be the reasons for the success of the nations it compared the United Kingdom unfavourably with (Wilhelmine Germany was a favourite), its prescription was a strong technocratic state and economic nationalism. It is telling in this context that the early critics of declinism were typically economic liberals such as Lord Hailsham and Enoch Powell, and free-market-supporting US economic historians examining the British case.[42]

Historians, mostly still believing in decline, disputed particular explanations for it into the early 1990s. Thereafter, while declinism was discredited and assumed to have dissipated, its deep assumptions still lingered on, deeply embedded in the historical literature.

THE TECHNOCRATIC CRITIQUE

In the British post-war case the discourse on experts was a very strange one (quite different from that in the USA). National declinism peddled the fanciful doctrine of the anti-technocratic British elite. It insisted on the lack of significance of the expert in the United Kingdom, consequential low investment in innovation and all the rest. This was a very peculiar attempt to write out of history the actual experts who were in fact so central to British history. The denunciation was essentially that the elite was old-fashioned, trained in the wrong subjects, had the wrong attitudes – these criticisms applied particularly to the business, political and civil service elite, and it usually came from those with the background they themselves were criticizing – public school boys who studied arts subjects at Oxbridge. There was little original in the critique. Remarkably it came from experts themselves, and their dismal failure to tell empirically coherent stories about themselves has seriously misled historians as to their significance.

One of the prime culprits was C. P. Snow, the scientist-novelist, in his *Two Cultures* lecture of 1959. Sir Charles Snow was a living refutation of his own thesis, as he was a major cultural figure of the 1950s and 1960s, who was a company director, was elevated to the peerage and had a position in government. He inherited the mantle of H. G. Wells as diagnostician, prophet, critic, politico and all-round sage.

His idea was simple, indeed simplistic. It was that British elite culture was peculiar in that it was particularly divided between the cultures of 'science' and of 'literature', and that these divisions were increasing. The scientists (academic physicists he meant) had the future in their bones, while the literary men, novelists and poets were 'natural Luddites', indeed proto-fascists. The former were to the left, and of more humble origin, than the literary types whose culture dominated the state. Questions of class, power and knowledge were mixed up with ignorant gusto. Snow's thesis was taken as reportage from a man who was famed for understanding the elite, but it is laughably wrong.

The literary scholar F. R. Leavis attacked Snow's childish fictions, from the perspective not of literature, but of the engaged and enraged intellectual. That such an intellectual nullity as Snow, wrong on literature, and on science, could be taken seriously in the modern metropolitan world of culture (he was the lead book reviewer for *The Sunday Times*) was for Leavis a sign of the corruption of that world. The significance of Snow was not what he said, but that he was granted enormous significance by the knowers and shakers of the modern United Kingdom, showing them up for what they were. Leavis' potent attack has been disparaged for a lack of politesse, and as the predictable riposte from literature. But they were arguing about very different things. Snow was making a crass, historically ignorant plea for 'science', while Leavis was outraged that such tat could be taken seriously. Snow's thesis would have been much more plausible had Leavis won the ideological battle, had we remembered Snow as the unfortunate victim of Leavis's demolition, a minor Ludwig Feuerbach or Eugen Dühring (of whom we know only because they were the butt of theoretical abuse by Marx and Engels) of the British literary or perhaps scientific scene. But the point is that Leavis lost and knew he was losing. As a result we cannot escape repeated invocations of Snow's thesis as if it described reality, or at least a serious basis for discussion, not just in the past but in the present.

Two Cultures, or rather the tradition it exemplified and sustained, is centrally about making the case for science, for action, for modernity. It does so by systematically downplaying the significance of what it supports. It sucks science, technology, modernity out of British history, leaving it over-populated with caricatures of literary intellectuals, anti-scientific mandarins and the like. While celebrating science it removes it from history except as the odd exception which proves the rule. It is what I have called an anti-history, forced to take out of history that which is central to it for the history to make sense. Alas Snow's argument, though certainly not originally his, is found implicitly and explicitly in much writing about the United Kingdom, manifest in studies of the civil service which deal only with the administrative class and not the scientists and engineers, which treat universities as if they consist only of arts faculties, books as if they were all novels and science as if it were all academic physics. It is impossible to understand British knowing, the history of the universities and the history of education if one believes Snow to have been right, or simply shares his assumptions. Equally, it is impossible to understand the world of British ideas if one does not appreciate why such empirically dubious accounts could hold such sway in the world of ideas, and even affairs of state.

The Fulton Report of the 1960s provides an example. The philosopher John Fulton, vice-chancellor of the University of Sussex, chaired an inquiry into the civil service. It was set up in 1966, in the technocratic moment, and reported in 1968. It took up the classic long-standing technocratic critique of the civil service and made it official. Its structures were made, it claimed, in the nineteenth century, making it unfit for the twentieth; the key administrative class were 'amateurs' or 'generalists'; they were too concerned with policy and incapable as 'managers'; the divisions between classes, that is the separate hierarchies of administrators, scientists, engineers, lawyers, economists, prevented the professionals influencing policy, the domain of the administrators.

It was all very convincing within the intellectual frameworks of the time, and the civil service was interpreted as resisting the proposed reforms – not least the unified grading structure at the top, and the opening of all top jobs, in principle, to all professionals. The problem was that the report, and subsequent analysis, remained fixated on the administrative class and refused to recognize the enormous power and authority of the professionals. For it was they who were critical in pushing the *grands projets* of the post-war state, from nuclear weapons, to nuclear reactors, to Concorde, and all the other cases we have looked at. Many of these projects, especially in the 1960s, were run by joint teams of professionals and administrators, with the professionals very much in charge. It can be put this way – the standard account of the civil service focused on the assistant, under-deputy and permanent secretaries – the administrators – and ignored the power and influence of the directors, directors-general and controllers – the professionals. There was a position called director-general Concorde, for example, filled by an engineer.[43] There were controllers of guided weapons and the like. Indeed, in many ministries unified hierarchies long pre-dated Fulton, and this was especially true of the Ministry of Technology.[44] Fulton suggested reforms which as far as the warfare state were concerned were redundant.

John Fulton was an example of an important new phenomenon, the academic taking on state roles and political roles. To be sure, some academics had been prominent as intellectuals before the war – men such as G. D. H. Cole, a reader in economics in Oxford from 1925 and the first Chichele professor of social and political theory (1944), and Professor Harold Laski of the London School of Economics. In Oxford Gilbert Murray, a liberal classicist, was a major public intellectual prominent in the League of Nations Union, as was, from Cambridge, the liberal conservative historian G. M. Trevelyan, author of the bestselling *English Social History* (1944). There were also a few academics who took on important advisory roles for government: for example, Sir William Beveridge, the LSE director in the 1930s, Sir Henry Tizard, the rector of Imperial College (1929–42), and John Maynard Keynes of Cambridge, though he was only a part-time don, best thought of as a London figure, a man who made himself independently very wealthy in order to enjoy metropolitan life to the full. During the Second World War many young and ambitious dons from across the system (though typically Oxbridge graduates) went into state service. The worlds of thought and action were peculiarly conjoined, which helped shape a future of close interconnection of state and university in the aid of a national project of reconstruction. Many of these men were to become great academic and state panjandrums. Oliver Franks, professor of moral philosophy at Glasgow, joined the ministry of supply as a principal, rising to become permanent secretary just after the war. Among his government work was an inquiry into the Falklands War of 1982. P. M. S. Blackett and Solly Zuckerman were academic scientists in and out of government. Senior academics chaired Royal Commissions:

for example, the economist Lord Robbins looked into higher education and recommended its expansion in 1963. Academics, most of them scientists, chaired Royal Commissions on the press (1949), the civil service (1952–3), environmental pollution (1971–2011) and the National Health Service (1975–9). Thus it was that the chairman of the Royal Commission on broadcasting (1977), a historian of the British intellectual elite, could call the post-Second World War years 'Our Age'.[45]

Where we find British technocrats in the public sphere is not in arguments celebrating them, extolling their achievements or even analysing their importance in business and the state. We find them complaining that they are not taken seriously, that they have no power, expressing Snow-like arguments. In his first speech as leader of the Labour Party in 1963 Harold Wilson claimed that 'Those charged with the control of our affairs must be ready to think and to speak in the language or our scientific age.' However, the standard declinist point was central. He said, indeed, that 'for commanding heights of British industry today to be controlled by men whose only claim is their aristocratic connections or the power of inherited wealth or speculative finance' was as irrelevant to the twentieth century as the purchase of commissions in the nineteenth. In 'science and industry we are content to remain a nation of Gentlemen in a world of Players'. That is one reason the speech is important – it is a powerful instance of Wilson's *technocratic critique* of the British business elite.

Yet it can be read another way. Wilson was one of the most technical of prime ministers, an economic historian and statistician, who had been a civil service professional, not an administrator. His father was an industrial chemist. His most famous speech has one of the most famous misquoted phrases in British political history – the white heat of the technological revolution. That speech was a celebration of the machine, of science. Wilson claimed that:

> In all our plans for the future, we are re-defining and we are re-stating our Socialism in terms of the scientific revolution . . . the Britain to be forged in the white heat of this revolution will be no place for restrictive practices or for outdated methods on either side of industry.

"A NATION NEGLECTS ITS EGGHEADS AT ITS PERIL . . ."
—MR. QUINTIN HOGG (LORD HAILSHAM AS HE THEN WAS), NOVEMBER 30, 1957

Illustration 15.2: 'A Nation Neglects Its Eggheads at Its Peril', by Vicky. From L to R Lord (C. P.) Snow, Dr Thomas Balogh, Professor Patrick Blackett, Professor Sir Solly Zuckermann, and Harold Wilson. (British Cartoon Archive 06099, Associated Newspapers Ltd, published 1964)

He went on about the scientific revolution, machine tools, computers, fertilizer, steam engines and plant breeding. He talked about automation and computers and he claimed that 'the essence of modern automation is that it replaces the hitherto unique human functions of memory and of judgement'; computers now commanded 'facilities of memory and of judgement far beyond the capacity of any human being or groups of human beings who have ever lived'. The 'programme-controlled machine tool line' could 'without the intervention of any human agency' produce a 'new set of machine tools in its own image'; machine tools had acquired 'the faculty of unassisted reproduction'. He called for the production of more scientists (mentioning large-scale Russian production), he called for 10 per cent of young people to go into higher education, and for a university of the air. It could be taken as a measure of the commitment of the audience, as well as the speaker, to such a technocratic vision of the country.

One consequence of the relative fame of the speech has been the belief that British technocracy was only of the left, and that the failure of technocracy was also the failure of the left. Indeed, the war and the Wilsonian 1960s are seen as the two left technocratic moments in British history. There is a big problem with the thesis, and that is that, as we have seen, state, industry and military were all committed to technical means, too much so perhaps. British technocracy was far from being exclusively of the left. Wilson was hardly the only occupant of No 10 Downing Street to be enthralled by science and machines.

There were technocrats of the right, and in many ways the 1950s and 1960s was their moment rather than Wilson's. Sir Roy Fedden, the aero-engine designer who had been with Bristol until 1942, was one. He decried the lack of leadership in government and industry which led to the loss of British air power in the 1950s. Complaining about the 'Welfare State', he noted that 'A "something-for-nothing" philosophy will never build a virile new Britain, capable of expanding and advancing in the age of supersonics and atomics which is now dawning.'[46] After the war the country had been 'fired by well-meaning new building and reconstruction generally in order to lay the foundations of the Welfare State, all of which was outlined in over-optimistic promises of a better world to live in'.[47] The problem was that 'our present culture is basically antipathetic to engineering and science'.[48]

Barnes Wallis and Frank Whittle too were clearly aligned with the right; they were voluble, especially Wallis, in condemning lack of support for their machines. Although this right was less vocal than the left, it is hard to avoid the conclusion that the bulk of state-backed aviation and its industry was in tone and demeanour of the right.

There was a technocratic moment in British ideology in the early 1960s which had its obverse in the decline of religion as a public force. Technocrats railed against aristocrats, bankers and civil servants but hardly needed to bother with priests. British official religion had hardly been averse to capitalism or science, though this was not of course its primary terrain. Even so, there was a sudden secularization of the higher public sphere. Religious observance, essentially steady into the 1950s, saw some increase in that decade, but a dramatic and sustained fall from the early 1960s, whether in attendance, membership or the use of churches for rites of passage. Furthermore, the influence of religion weakened in the higher reaches of public life and the educational system. The Lords spiritual were hardly as important as the Lords scientific and industrial, or indeed political.[49] Of course, religion did not disappear. In Ireland, especially Northern Ireland, it did matter, as the expression and cause of a profound discrimination between the dominant Protestant churches of many types and the Catholic and nationalist minority. That was a division which, far from going away, intensified. Nor did religion go away on the mainland: it was a feature of certain revivals and political movements, for example the anti-pornography campaigns of Mary Whitehouse. Furthermore, immigrants from outside Europe brought religion – Caribbean immigrants revived Christianity in the inner cities, while Hinduism and Islam put down roots across the whole country.

However, from the late 1960s and 1970s disenchantments with modernity of many different kinds became stronger. There was a greater degree of contestation of ideas, or the power of elites, and authority more generally, than at any time since the 1930s, and this was expressed in stronger terms. Technocrats, in fact, celebrated in the 1950s and 1960s, would meet some serious questioning only in the 1970s, from both the left and the right. Middle-class morality and its bastions in the churches would not be ignored but flouted. Nationalism would be challenged by new internationalisms, of both left and right.

16

Possibilities

It was on a motion of the Labour Party that the House of Commons threw out the Chamberlain Government in 1940. It was thanks to the Labour Party that Churchill had the chance to serve the country in the war years. Two-thirds of the Conservative Party at that time voted for the same reactionary policies as they will vote for tonight. It is sometimes in the most difficult and painful moments of our history that the country has turned to the Labour Party for salvation, and it has never turned in vain. We saved the country in 1940, and we did it again in 1945. We set out to rescue the country – or what was left of it – in 1974. Here again in 1979 we shall do the same.

Michael Foot, closing the confidence debate,
28 March 1979[1]

What we face today is not a crisis of capitalism, but of Socialism.

Margaret Thatcher's first speech as Conservative leader, 1975[2]

It was not so long ago that the shop stewards at Elswick invited management to their annual dinner and united with them in a toast to the monarch.

The Workers' Report on Vickers (1979)[3]

Inglan is a bitch
dere's no escapin it
Inglan is a bitch
is whey wi a goh dhu 'bout it?

'Inglan Is a Bitch' (1980), lyrics by Linton Kwesi Johnson

The British Police are the best in the world
I don't believe one of these stories I've heard
'Bout them raiding our pubs for no reason at all
Lining the customers up by the wall
Picking out people and knocking them down
Resisting arrest as they're kicked on the ground
Searching their houses and calling them queer
I don't believe that sort of thing happens here

Sing if you're glad to be gay
Sing if you're happy that way
    'Glad to Be Gay' (1978), lyrics by Tom Robinson

I don't much go for a 'siege economy' and import controls,
which I regard as a lot of nationalist claptrap.
    Paul Foot, Three Letters to a Bennite *(1982)*

The 1970s are usually treated as a moment of crisis, of an old system crashing into reality. They represent the end, the collapse, of the post-war settlement, the consensus and economic growth. In fact, far from expiring, British social democracy and the welfare state were to be at their peak. It was also the moment in which the modernizing state investments were bearing fruit and were indeed still underway. Oil promised the possibility of national regeneration (though the Dutch disease – an overvalued currency as a result of having gas – was a live worry). It was a moment, too, when the state did actively and powerfully intervene in industry. It was a moment of transformation that did not end up as expected.

It was also a moment of revolt, and of possibility, one too often pushed back into the 1960s.[4] In part it was also a moment of the restarting of old battles harking back to another moment of contention. Unfinished business, old grievances, were plain to see. Four issues re-emerged, having last been significant in the early 1920s. The first was the legitimacy of Northern Ireland, with the result of new armed struggle between nationalists and unionists (see the following chapter). Second, British workers were organizing, and taking strike action, at a level not seen since the early 1920s, in the face of the worry caused by rising prices. Unemployment returned, at the level of the 1920s, though not yet that of the 1930s. Third, there was a great debate about protection and free trade around the EEC referendum of 1975 and subsequent debate about the EEC, an echo of 1906 and 1931. Fourth, these were the years of challenge to intellectual, cultural and political authority – there was a resurgent feminism, now stronger than ever before – of intellectual revolt and of a more general crisis of legitimacy in the state and nation. New movements and new parties were born as perhaps had not been seen since the Edwardian years.

In hardly any of this was the United Kingdom unique. The 1970s saw changes everywhere in the world economy. The long global boom, in the capitalist and socialist countries, came to an end. Growth was lower and more intermittent. Everywhere low growth, even falls in output, were associated not with falling prices, but with high inflation. Economists called this new global phenomenon 'stag-flation'. The quadrupling of the oil price by the cartel of oil-producing countries in 1973 and their flexing of political and economic muscle was a new phenomenon in world history, and it led to huge transfers of wealth to them. There was industrial unrest all over the world and in many places revolution too. New ideas were everywhere.

EXPECTATIONS DASHED

In the late 1960s and early 1970s there was talk of an emerging post-industrial society. It was to be a society with high and increasing industrial output, greater levels of research and development and, because of higher productivity, much more leisure. It was post-indus-trial not because there would be less industry, but because industry would not need so many people. Indeed, British planners, like their counterparts elsewhere, were looking forward to higher levels of pro-duction of all sorts. Thus it was, as we have seen, that new power stations and motorways were being built in the late 1960s and 1970s, and expansion plans for steel and cars assumed much greater demand in the future. In this it was similar to the 1940s and 1950s, when investing for a richer future was the order of the day. Some, however,

called for a new kind of post-industrial society – a radically less industrialized society which would be in better relationship with nature.[5]

Neither was to be the sort of post-industrial society that would be
talked about in the 1980s and neither predicted what happened. Far
from continuing to grow apace, British industrial production would
stagnate, and employment in industry would fall drastically as
imports surged. Demand for energy tailed off. The most obvious feature of the development of the British economy since the 1970s is
perhaps the rise of the service economy. The economy essentially grew
from the 1970s by adding new activities over and above a roughly stable level of agricultural, industrial and manufacturing production (see
figure 19.4). Showing these changes as shares, the usual way, misses the
key dynamic of expansions and cumulation. It is the case that the share
of manufacturing workers in the workforce declined very fast, as other
sectors crudely labelled as 'services' grew very much faster, but this was
all primarily due to the growth of other sectors, not the decline of
industry, except in employment terms. The direct connection between
growth of the economy and growth in energy supplied would
end – growth and energy input were uncoupled as growth took place
with small energy input increases. By the 1980s 'post-industrial' did
not mean high-tech leisure and abundance of resources, but rather a
move to harder, longer, less-well-paid work. Furthermore, rather than
being planned and organized, the future turned out to be one of violent
swings in economic activity, with major recessions in 1974–5 and a
very great one indeed in 1979–83 (which was comparable to 1929–33
in depth and extent). Unemployment at levels not seen from the 1930s
returned, after 1979 especially. The future was not as the technocrats
had so confidently and authoritatively claimed.

By the 1970s British was no longer best. No one wanted the products British technocrats had argued would be essential to a successful
economy. British R&D spending fell. The products of British genius
went unsold. Whether it was cars, TV sets, nuclear reactors, or capitalism or socialism, foreigners did it better. It was clear that by the
measure of GDP per head, or GDP per hour worked, the nation was
no longer the richest or most efficient in Europe. Germany had overtaken it in the 1960s, and France in the 1970s. As the result of a
re-estimation of the black economy, Italy overtook it in the 1980s – *il*

sorpasso. Declinism got such a grip on the elite imagination that grotesquely exaggerated accounts of relative economic failure proliferated. For example, the valedictory despatch by the ambassador in Paris, Sir Nicholas Henderson, leaked and published in the *Economist* in June 1979, claimed French and German GDP per capita were 41 and 46 per cent higher than that of the UK in 1977.[6] That could be justified statistically, but it was not a sound comparison.

1940S REDUX?

There are parallels to be drawn between the first moment of British social democracy in the late 1940s and that of the 1970s. The first is that both periods saw exceptional problems with the balance of payments. By the 1970s the British economy, like that of every country in Europe, depended for a majority of its energy on what had been cheap imported oil. The decision of the main oil-exporting countries, now organized in a cartel, to increase prices in 1973 meant the balance of payments went into deep and long-term deficit, reaching over 4 per cent of GDP in 1974. Both balance of payments crises forced the British government to take out loans, from the USA in 1945 and from the International Monetary Fund, dominated by the USA, in 1976. In both cases the loans served purposes that were not advertised – in 1945 to maintain expenditure abroad and in 1976 to legitimate the policy of holding back reform and welfare. Furthermore, both sets of loans met a temporary problem. Indeed, just as the economy was in better shape in 1950 than 1945, so it would be by 1979, by quite a margin.[7]

As in the 1940s the crisis of 1976 was met by further promoting of national production (for example, in coal and in food). There were subsidies to hold down food prices, in both cases, as a counter-inflationary strategy and as a means of assisting the poorest. In the 1940s and early 1950s many foods were subsidized; in the 1970s the Tories started with milk and butter subsidies, and Labour added cheese, butter, bread and flour. There was much discussion about the imposition of import controls, as existed in the 1940s, but these were now ruled out by British membership of the EEC. There were also export drives, now not so much for dollars but the so-called petrodollars of the Middle East: the

United Kingdom offered Concorde, nuclear reactors and arms to the new oil potentates of the Orient – they only bought arms.

There was another similarity. There was a strong sense of a shift in power in society towards the workers, and in both periods there were important moves to extend the welfare state, to democratize society, schooling, even industry. Far from representing the end of the welfare state, the 1970s saw, as we have seen, its radicalization, with the end of the regressive National Insurance stamp, the new State Earnings Related Pension, universal child benefit, the comprehensivization of education. This was the highest point social democracy reached in the United Kingdom: bringing social partners into a discussion as to how and for what purpose elements of the national cake should be distributed – between wages and profits, between wages and benefits. It was in this period that inequality in income and wealth was at its lowest in the twentieth century.

INDUSTRIAL RELATIONS

The idea of the backward British worker whose organizations had to be broken, whose culture of solidarity had to be despised, became powerful in the 1970s. It was implied in many such arguments that unions lived embedded in a society of equals where other than trade unionism there were no sectional interests. Of course, the rationale of trade unions was precisely that workers were weak in the face of the private interests of particular employers and the sectional interests of all employers. Yet the very limited power of workers and unions could be presented as much greater than it actually was because this could only express itself in visible ways – in trade union organization, in trade union elections, in strikes.

There is no doubt about the relative strength of organized labour in the 1970s compared to earlier periods. Through the 1970s the number of trade unionists rose, peaking in 1979. The proportion of unionized workers was higher than ever before, reaching to more than half the workforce. Trade unionism expanded into new areas – into white-collar work and the public sector. The relations between the Labour Party and the trade unions changed also. Some large trade unions elected leaders who were on the left of the Labour Party, which created, for the first time, a trade union left block in the labour movement. The two key figures were Jack Jones of the TGWU and Hugh Scanlon of the engineers. Compared to the 1940s, the trade unions were less inclined to accept the entreaties of government, even a Labour government. The 1970s were a high point in workerism.[8] Yet this trade unionism did not necessarily imply greater collectivism or real trade union organizational strength.

Although historical memory implies otherwise, there was more strike activity under the Conservative governments of 1970–74 and 1979 onwards than during the Labour governments of 1974–9. There were for the first time, in 1970, national strikes of municipal workers, and in 1971 of postal workers. The case of the miners is instructive. They were relatively low-paid workers before a strike in 1972, their first national action since 1926. They were briefly well paid, but then lost out quickly, so that in 1973–4 they were asking for more than the average increase. They worked to rule and struck again. The Heath government made standing up to the miners an election issue, asking whether the miners or the government ruled. It was a silly question, and the response of the electorate was: you don't. The point was not that the miners wanted to bring down the government, it was that all workers were potentially in conflict with the government in that directly or indirectly it was involved in all pay disputes. This was because it sought to keep wage growth down as a central part of its strategy to deal with inflation – wage increases increased inflation, which cut the value of wages, which made for pressure for higher wages.

The period 1971–82 was one of notably high price inflation. The peak was in 1975, when the average rate reached nearly 25 per cent per annum, stoked by the huge oil-price rises of 1973. Why prices rose – and they did nearly everywhere in the world – was difficult to work out because of the interlinking of causes and effects. For example, did wage rates follow prices, or vice-versa? But efforts to bring down the rate of price increase was a central concern of the state. One important reason was that it had a differential effect on people. Because real interests were negative, savings lost their value (see figure 18.2). On the other hand, organized labour could ensure it got pay rises matching or perhaps outstripping price increases.

Governments went to great lengths to attempt to control inflation by controlling pay rises through what was called 'incomes policy' and also through attempts to control price increases. The Labour government was able to drive down inflation to around 8 per cent in 1979, but the Conservatives allowed it back up to nearly 20 per cent before forcing it down.

The Labour government and the unions established what was called the 'social contract', under which the unions agreed to limit pay claims in return for action in favour of all workers and the poor – in the form of benefits, control of prices of necessities through food subsidies and rent freezes. Unions got repeal of industrial relations legislation and important new legislation on health and safety, equal pay and more. This was the context in which an inquiry was set up into 'industrial democracy' which recommended worker representation on boards of companies, where management and workers would be equally represented, with a smaller number of independents acceptable to both (the famous formula was $2x + y$, where x was the number of employer and workers' representatives and y the number of independents). This is not to say that unions were always gaining, far from it. For example, a film-processing factory (photographic films were sent by post to such factories, and the prints returned by post) in northwest London called Grunwick refused to recognize a trade union, leading to a strike by its workforce of around 400 mostly Asian women. The dispute, involving picketing and large police action, went on for two years from 1976, and pitted the trade unions and the left against an emergent anti-union right. The workers lost.

In the Tory mythology which was to dominate from the 1980s, the Thatcher government was elected as a result of the 'winter of discontent' of 1978–9, in which unions showed they had too much power over government. The reality was different. There was a strike wave in early 1979, but that was because the unions *did not* have power over the government. The strikes happened because the Labour government was not prepared to give in to the unions, not because the unions wanted to strike. What had happened was that under the fourth phase of inflation control, the government limited pay settlements to 5 per cent. Yet Ford workers, with official union support, went on strike and broke the barrier, as did others. The public sector workers tried to do the same, and it was they who were faced down by government, which thus brought on strikes.[9]

The new Conservative government elected in May 1979 also provoked large-scale strikes. Indeed, most of the strike activity of the year 1979 took place in the Conservative-ruled half of the year. Thus, while the 29.5 million working days lost in 1979, the highest since 1926, are usually unthinkingly allocated to the Labour years, and indeed specifically to the 'winter of discontent' strikes of January and February, the real picture is that fully 20.7 million of these working days were lost between July and December 1979. This was itself only just under the total for the previous whole year record since 1926, 1972 under Heath. September 1979, with 11.7 million working days lost is the most strike-intensive month since monthly records began in 1931 and remains a record. Much of the loss came from the engineering strike for shorter hours, which the unions won, which involved rolling short strikes by 1.5 million workers, leading to the loss of 16 million working days. This now unknown strike was larger than the miners' strikes of the 1970s and may well have been larger than the general strike of 1926 (excepting the massive lockout of miners).[10] By contrast, the winter of discontent months, January and February 1979, had 3.0 and 2.4 million working days lost respectively. This was lower than the time of the miners' strikes of 1972 and 1974, and comparable to the early months of 1980, with 2.8, 3.2 and 3.3 million days lost.[11] The first major strike of 1980 was that of the steel workers, who had hardly gone on strike at all in the whole century. They were on strike for three months, over pay and a closure programme. They won some pay, but by the end of the year closures of plants had left an industry of half the size it had been in 1967. The support they got from other unions was weak, and the survivors reciprocated this later. One large strike which did not happen was a potential miners' strike over pit closures in 1981. Thatcher's government backed down and started to prepare for a likely strike of miners in the future. When it came, it was the greatest strike since 1926 and dwarfed anything else in the 1970s or 1980s. It was a spring, summer, autumn and winter of discontent, lasting from March 1984 to March 1985.

INDUSTRIAL RESTRUCTURING

As we have seen there was major industrial restructuring in the 1950s and 1960s, with workers leaving the mines, the railways and the land, often shifting into manufacturing. The 1970s, too, were an era of restructuring, but with differences. As we have seen, coal stopped contracting, and agriculture expanded especially strongly. Yet the most important difference was that the lower overall rate of economic growth gave less room for change, and as a result unemployment increased. Manufacturing in particular ceased to be a source of new jobs and indeed was the main sector of the economy from which jobs were lost. One of the most spectacular cases was the motor car industry, which had been growing rapidly until 1972. Thereafter output and employment collapsed, not because car purchasing fell, but because exports fell and imports increased. Another was steel, where both output and employment also both fell. For example, the once gigantic Ebbw Vale steel works was closed down and demolished in stages from 1972. The local MP, Michael Foot, was secretary of state for employment 1974–9.

In the face of job cuts in many manufacturing industries a new kind of industrial action arose. Workers' cooperatives were formed to keep businesses going, as in the earlier case of the Upper Clyde Shipbuilders. Workers and unions made plans for alternative products to keep old arms factories in production. As never before, trade unions were researching, thinking about and discussing the import of new machines, new ways of working. The most famous case was that of Lucas Aerospace, where engineers hoped to no longer design weapons, but socially useful products. 'Defence conversion', a concern of the left since the early 1960s, entered a new phase where workers themselves would redirect work to make the munitions of peace. These possibilities for the future came to nothing, but they were part and parcel of a whole new way of thinking about the social shaping of invention for better purposes. The 1970s was a period when all sorts of alternative technologies popped up, from electricity from waves and wind to new forms of human-powered transport. At the same time a new scientific left – much less elite and much more critical of science – emerged notably around the British Society for Social Responsibility in Science. Their key concerns were the abuse of science in war, of biology (for example in IQ testing), industrial hazards, environmental degradation and state use of new repressive technologies.[12]

The main thrust of Labour policy was not nationalization, but rather intervention and support of private enterprises as part of an attempt at a comprehensive industrial strategy based on a hoped-for partnership in industry. Labour developed proposals for a state holding company which would take control of twenty-five top manufacturing enterprises, proposals which turned into the National Enterprise Board, the BNOC and the nationalization of shipbuilding and aircraft.[13] The National Enterprise Board took over government companies such as Rolls-Royce and added to them as more and more went into crisis. Among the acquisitions were British Leyland, Ferranti and the machine-tool maker Alfred Herbert. The upshot was that in the 1970s, for the first time, there were large portions of manufacturing industry in public ownership, including by accident and design some of the greatest names in British manufacturing. Previously the main exception was steel, in public ownership briefly in the early 1950s, and again from 1967.

In the 1970s there was concern that the UK was being left behind in many areas of computing, other than software, but there was also much enthusiasm and investment.[14] Sinclair Research and ACORN computers were among the pioneers of the table-top computer, the latter getting a lot of support through the BBC, which gave it the contract for a BBC Micro. The National Enterprise Board supported and took over Clive Sinclair's Sinclair Radionics and launched the semiconductor company INMOS, established in 1978.[15] In the early 1980s their computers were everywhere: the Sinclair ZX series, much cheaper than the first Apples and Commodores from the USA, and the BBC ACORN computers. Sir Clive Sinclair, as he became in 1982, was a symbol of British entrepreneurial activity in this area.[16] The 1970s were hardly lacking in entrepreneurship or innovation. In illegal drugs also British entrepreneurs did well. Operation Julie in 1977 busted the biggest LSD-producing operation in the world.[17]

LABOUR

On the left there was disappointment that the Labour governments had done so little to change the United Kingdom. The new left saw Labour as a mere electoral machine, a party which was part of a system which managed a stultifying consensus in the 'national interest', really the interests of the new capitalism, not the poor.[18] That sense of disillusionment with Labour was expressed in the new student movement that emerged in the late 1960s, in the growing militancy of trade unions, and in revolutionary parties of the left in the 1970s.

In opposition from 1970, the Labour Party moved to the left. It was returned to office as a minority government in February 1974, and as a government with a tiny majority in October 1974. It stood on a much more left-wing manifesto than ever before, one centred on serious intervention in the economy. It was committed to nationalizing land for development, and introducing a wealth tax. The left, which pushed for the EEC referendum in 1975, and the leader of the left, Tony Benn, made a serious attempt to get public involvement and proper taxation of North Sea oil, and to develop the industries which might supply the very capital-intensive off-shore oil industry. Benn found that attempts to subsidize these industries met determined opposition from the EEC, which added to his sense and that of others that the EEC stood in the way of state-led national regeneration.[19] There was now a split in Labour between the pro- and anti-marketeers, which would intensify and become one of the central dividers between the right and the left of the party. The defeat of the anti-market side in the EEC referendum of 1975 was a major defeat for the left.

The 1974–9 government, in the view of the left, was an even greater failure than the 1964–70 government, pursuing policies they believed no Labour government should have. That the decisions of the party conference, and plans in manifestos, were manifestly not implemented led to the campaign to make the party structures, rather than MPs, dominant. After 1979 moves were made to allow local parties to deselect MPs and the election by the party of the party leader. The aim was to hold the party to democratically decided-on policies. For the Liberals and Conservatives the power of the parliamentary party was no problem, for party machines were there to get parliamentarians elected. Labour had been different but now it was split between a parliamentary and a broader party orientation division aligned with clear left–right division.

After 1979 the left of the party won. In 1980 even the parliamentary party elected a leader from the soft left, Michael Foot, an anti-nuclear, anti-EEC campaigner. Foot, though old, had only reached the Cabinet in the 1970s. One important consequence was that the party lost the support of a significant section of its parliamentary leadership. A group of senior politicians with elite intellectual backgrounds broke away in 1981 to form the Social Democratic Party. For Roy Jenkins, Shirley Williams, David Owen and Bill Rodgers, the so-called Gang of Four, the Labour Party now challenged the established social and economic order in unacceptable ways. There was indeed a notable shift in sentiment among those who thought of themselves as meritocrats from association with Labour in the early 1960s to Conservativism and Social Democracy in the 1970s and 1980s.[20] They were right to note that Labour had changed. But that is not to say it was not in line with contemporary European socialism, which itself moved to the left in the 1970s and achieved electoral success. Most important of all was the election of François Mitterrand to the presidency of France in 1981 with a mandate for nationalization and expansion. The Greek socialist party, PASOK, formed a government in Greece in 1981, and the Spanish socialists, PSOE, in 1982. Indeed, the left was advancing across the world in the 1970s.

The 1983 manifesto, caricatured as the 'longest suicide note in history', committed Labour to deal with the mass unemployment of the moment, and it offered a non-nuclear defence policy, which meant getting rid of US nuclear bases but staying in NATO, though reducing defence expenditure to the European average and not ordering Trident. It struck many nationalist notes, including a promise to abandon the 'Tory PWR' (the US-designed nuclear reactor) and rethink the 'British AGR'. 'We intend,' said the manifesto, 'to create new companies and new science-based industries – using new public enterprise to lead the way'; they would renationalize what the Tories had so far privatized, but for the future, 'We will establish a significant public stake in electronics, pharmaceuticals, health equipment and building materials; and also in other important sectors, as required in the national interest'. This was no more than was in the manifestos Harold Wilson and James Callaghan had presented. A key difference was that the manifesto now argued explicitly against EEC membership. The next Labour government, 'committed to radical, socialist policies for reviving the British economy' was bound to find membership 'a most serious obstacle' to, among other things, industrial policy and increasing trade, 'and our need to restore exchange controls and to regulate direct overseas investment'. Moreover, by preventing 'us from buying food from the best sources of world supply', it 'would run counter to our plans to control prices and inflation'.[21] The Alternative Economic Strategy, as it was called, once rejected by the Labour government, was now Labour's programme.

This Alternative Economic Strategy, while presented as novel, was the last gasp of the logic of post-1945 Labourism. Its key advocate, Tony Benn, was indeed not primarily a socialist but a 'radical patriot' and economic nationalist.[22] As we have seen, Labour had been all about a modernizing, techno-nationalist, productionist, autarchic programme. What the Labour left was now wanting to bring into being were the means to make it workable. Yet there was little if any awareness that Labour had made serious attempts at such a policy in the recent past. Labour's left was nostalgic for a past they had forgotten and looked forward to bringing into existence.[23] This is not to say the past was ignored. Economists of the left probed the history of economic planning in the 1940s for the first time; new historical accounts of British capitalism as financial and global flourished and were at the core of a powerful left historical declinism. In this frame the Thatcher revolution was seen as the latest version of the untrammelled power of internationalist finance making itself felt. Thatcherism was seen as a radical version of the policies which had led to decline in the first place.

The 1970s and 1980s were the only time one can speak of a thought-through attempt by the Labour party to plan in advance of taking office what the policies it ought to pursue might be. There was fresh investigative and critical energy in coming up with alternative policies for it, on every aspect from defence to the economy and social policy.[24] The policies sought to effect a transformation in society in the face of opposition to make the United Kingdom both more efficient and more equitable. Yet one thing they did not do was reflect critically enough on what had been attempted and achieved since the 1950s.

THE COMMUNIST PARTY
AND NEW LEFT

One important feature of the left that came to the fore in the 1970s and 1980s was its particular concern with what happened abroad. In the late 1960s, the Vietnam Solidarity Campaign was a mobilizer. In the 1970s the left was active in support for the victims of the repression in Chile after 1973, and for the Sandinista revolution in Nicaragua. The Anti-Apartheid Campaign had long been important and continued to be. Close to home, the issues were trickier. It is telling that there was no 1968 moment against the British state. While in Northern Ireland there was an armed insurrection, the Angry Brigade were a very pale imitation of the German Red Army Faction or the Italian Red Brigades, who were in conflict with their states on a significant scale. The Troops Out (of Northern Ireland) movement was relatively weak.

Generally speaking, the far left was weaker in the United Kingdom than on the continent. There was nothing like the communist parties of France or Italy in terms of electoral strength or intellectual influence. Yet the Communist Party remained a strong presence in the trade unions, where its knowledgeable, disciplined and cautious approach appealed particularly to skilled workers. The autodidact communist trade unionist (especially in the high engineering industries, including armaments) was a recognizable figure with Labour Party equivalents.[25] The Communist Party was never merely workerist and had a continuous intellectual tradition, which developed many interesting currents of analysis of the United Kingdom in the 1970s and 1980s, when *Marxism Today*, of all publications, became the prime site for discussions of, among other things, 'Thatcherism'.

The 1970s was the moment of various Trotskyist parties, that is, revolutionary left parties hostile to the USSR. All survived longer than the Communist Party but were finished by the 1990s. The three main groupings were led by three figures from outside the United Kingdom but within the empire who had been active from the 1940s.[26] Ted Grant's Militant Tendency pursued a policy of entryism into the Labour Party and peaked in the 1980s, when there were two Militant MPs elected in 1983, and a further one in 1987.[27] They had about fifty councillors, and 250 full-time employees (more than the Labour Party itself).[28] Tony Cliff was the leader of the International Socialists, later the Socialist Workers' Party, notable in the 1970s for their work with the Anti-Nazi League, a powerful cultural counter to the National Front, and in the trade unions. Gerry Healy's Workers' Revolutionary Party was the only one to have celebrity endorsement and a daily newspaper, the *Newsline*. They put forward sixty parliamentary candidates in 1979; the only other Trotskyite party to put forward candidates under its name was the tiny Revolutionary Communist Party.

Although they attracted intellectuals and publicists of talent, such as the economist Andrew Glyn (Militant) and the journalist Paul Foot (Socialist Workers' Party), their ideas for the future were in many ways limited and traditional. They were very keen on new technology. The Workers' Revolutionary Party was proud of its advanced printing presses in the 1970s. Militant were keen on the microchip: as they claimed, 'A free democratic society under the control and management of the working class could carry through the new microchip transformation of industry, which would clear the way for the complete transition to socialism.' The problem was that 'The microchip and the capitalist system are in complete contradiction,' with socialism 'bringing the working class to a six-hour, four-day week on the basis of micro-technology and science' and onto 'a two-hour day, two-day week, and even a one-day week in the future, as mankind, beginning with a socialist Britain and Europe, moves in the direction of socialism'.[29]

The London Labour left was to be of particular importance. The Labour left took control of the Greater London Council (GLC) in 1981, under Ken Livingstone, the most intelligent and interesting politician of the left, a man from the lower middle class without university education. The 'loony left' as it was called in the right-wing press, and in much of the Labour Party, was the inheritor of much of the counter-cultural work of the 1970s. The GLC supported new

rainbow coalitions, social forms, municipal entertainments, commitments to an inclusive public sphere and industrial possibilities.
Sheffield became the 'Socialist republic of South Yorkshire' in the late
1970s and early 1980s.[30] These centres of left power were seen as a
threat. Margaret Thatcher abolished the GLC and radically restricted
the powers of local authorities, not only through rate-capping, but
also by forcing them to sell housing, and also to do such things as get
rid of their direct works organizations – through which councils
employed builders and other workers for public projects. In effect
council political and economic functions as well as assets were
privatized.

A WORLD OF POSSIBILITIES

The 1970s were a time of significant cultural and social change.
Structural change in the economy, the shift to white-collar work of
various kinds, was the main cause of what was called social mobility.
As measured, it did not result from an increased openness of the
small elite occupations, nor from any downward mobility of the
existing elite. It was was a statistical concept, which would have been
better called 'the expansion of higher occupational categories',
another way of saying that the nature of work had changed. There
was movement indoors, into offices and out of factories, into clean
and quiet jobs, from manual to mental work.

Perhaps the greatest change of all not well captured by occupational
categories was the growing number of women who worked outside the
home. Of course, many had long worked – the novelty was that now
many married women were working outside the home, especially married women with children. In 1931 80 per cent of single women 25–34
were in work; for married women of the same age it was 13 per cent,
and 24 per cent by 1951. By 1966 the figure was 34 per cent, but significantly higher for older married women (around 50 per cent).[31] Smaller
families, families started younger and a partially refashioned world of
domestic work and production came about with readily acquired new
machines of domestic production, which were around in the interwar
years, but had been restricted to the wealthy and the electrified.

Women who worked outside the home typically still did so working with other women, in jobs reserved for women, for which women were paid less than men. However, a gap emerged between the public and private sectors, between white-blouse and blue-blouse work. In the early 1950s female teachers, civil servants and local government officers got equal pay with men (measures a Royal Commission had proposed during the Second World War). In these cases the jobs men and women did were the same. But for industrial jobs the position was different, and unequal pay remained standard. By the late 1960s there was pressure to equalize pay and jobs. In 1968 female sewing machinists in Ford, the only female production workers in what was a male-dominated firm, wanted to be regraded from the second-lowest skill level to a higher one. They went on strike, and in order to end the strike the women were granted equal pay for the same job (the actual regrading would happen many years later, after a six-week strike in 1984). That is to say in this case, as in many others, the women had been doubly discriminated against – the skill of their jobs was under-rated, and on top of that they were paid less than men on the skill grade they were put on. The results of the strike, and the need to comply with EEC regulations, was the Equal Pay Act, 1970 (in force 1975), which stipulated the same wage for the same job. That was a major advance in that a real and long-standing discrimination was removed, but the crucial issue of comparability between different jobs into which men and women were still segregated was not addressed.[32]

These were just signs of a revolution in the position of women which would take decades to work through. One important way in which things changed subtly but importantly was in the breakdown, by earlier standards, of gender segregation at work. This was very evident in the world of graduates. The proportion of female students was increasing from the 1960s but accelerated in the 1970s, reversing the masculinization of the 1930s to the 1950s. With the outlawing of gender discrimination, the exclusively male colleges in Oxford and Cambridge were eventually opened to women (from the mid 1970s). Women started entering into medicine and pharmacy in large numbers. But in routine office work, too, men and women increasingly worked together.

The nature of domestic relations changed too – the average age of marriage for both men and women increased, from the historic lows of the 1950s and 1960s; the extent of marriage decreased too – cohabitation began to appear as a legitimate option, before, and even instead of, marriage. This would have been unthinkable except for a tiny minority in earlier decades. Spreading use of the contraceptive pill, and other contraceptive devices, separated the trinity of sex, marriage and children into different issues. There was free NHS contraception from 1974, and indeed a marked increase in contraceptive use by the married and not-married in the early 1970s. More and more children were born 'outside wedlock', a condition no longer categorized as 'bastardy' or 'illegitimacy'. Divorce rates increased strongly too, made easier and more humane by the Divorce Reform Act of 1969, which made marriage breakdown (which might be evidenced by separation), rather than matrimonial offences, the grounds for divorce. Sex outside marriage was no longer 'pre-marital sex', which assumed it would be generally followed by marriage, but a normal phenomenon. The net effect was that practices which the respectable and the churches abhorred and stigmatized became much more common and lost their exclusionary potency. All this was underway in the 1970s – the full changes would take time to become very large; just as educational opportunities in the 1970s only manifested themselves in greater numbers of senior medical women, politicians and so on at the end of the twentieth century.

PERMISSIVENESS AND LIBERATION

Harold Wilson promised to create a New Britain, pulsating with the energies of the white heat of the new scientific revolution. Although it is often thought that Wilson's government signally failed to do this, it is more commonly accepted that he presided over an era of permissiveness, a social and cultural revolution, doing away with capital punishment and decriminalizing abortion and homosexual relations. This account relies too much on an assumption that the law had come down hard, and that the weight of repression was lifted by liberalizing legislation in the 1960s. In fact, laws were much less harshly imposed than assumed, and change in the law had less effect than might have been thought. Although the death penalty was mandatory for all murder, and so-called capital murder after 1957, about half of all male murderers and nearly all female murderers were reprieved by the home secretary. Hanging was a political act. In any case the number of murder convictions was very low, around thirty per annum in 1950s England, when homicides ran at about 300 per annum. Killers were overwhelmingly either not caught or declared insane or convicted of manslaughter. Thus, although in theory murder was punished with death, capital punishment was rare – the average was about one hanging in England and Wales per month before the Homicide Act of 1957, and fewer thereafter. Hangings were concentrated in a few large prisons; the tiny number of executioners were very part-time. Albert Pierrepoint (the son and nephew of executioners) was primarily a grocer and then a publican. Hanging was effectively abolished outside Northern Ireland in 1965, following a private member's bill, although the last execution in Northern Ireland was in 1961, it was not abolished there until 1973. The death penalty was not abolished for all crimes until 1998, and the remaining set of gallows was taken out of commission. For years figures on the right wanted to reintroduce it under the mistaken belief both that it had been applied mercilessly and that it had been an effective deterrent.

A similar belief perhaps explained the opposition to the legalization of abortion (Abortion Act, 1967) and the partial legalisation of homosexual acts between men (the Sexual Offences Act, 1967), neither of which applied in Northern Ireland. In fact abortion and homosexuality were practised before the acts and rarely led to conviction. This is not to say liberalizing measures were not important in, for example, bringing abortion into the public medical sphere and taking the law on homosexuality out of most bedrooms. What happened in the wider public sphere was a separate issue, raising different concerns. New obscenity legislation, for example, was concerned mainly with what could be public rather than what was private. Indeed, it is notable how much opposition there was not so much to particular private practices, but to the fact that they might take place in, or be reflected in, the legitimate public sphere. This was denounced as permissiveness, as were many other violations of previous rules governing the public sphere, like men wearing their hair long. What was in play was the boundary between public and private: it was not just what went on that mattered, but whether activities could be discussed in the public sphere.

Permissive legislation as to what might happen in private was probably a minor element in what were significant modern changes. Important campaigns started in the 1970s to change not so much the law as social practices, including the actions of police forces. This was the era of *Spare Rib* and *Gay News*. Here the greatest influence was probably immediately previous developments in the USA. The Women's Liberation Movement (hence 'women's lib') was formed in 1970. There were campaigns against violence against women (the first refuge for women who were victims of domestic violence was set up in London by Erin Pizzey in 1971), for wages for housework, for better support for single mothers and more. The Gay Liberation Front was set up in 1971, bringing the term 'gay' into general use and transforming the public and private lives of gay people.[33] The use of the term 'liberation' was a conscious echo of the names of many other liberation movements in the 1960s, not least the National Liberation Front of Vietnam. And a liberation it was, bringing into the public arena injustice and violence previously private and hidden, through direct action and through political activism and publications.

It would be decades before feminism and gay liberation would be features of mainstream politics. Within the world of parliamentary politics the most radical female politician was probably the independent Irish republican Bernadette Devlin, elected at the age of twenty-one in 1969 and soon to be an unmarried mother. There were no openly gay members of parliament. Indeed, the gay leader of the Liberal Party, Jeremy Thorpe, was charged with attempting to have a blackmailing former lover killed rather than risk exposure. His party, and the establishment, rallied around him, denying he was gay, and he was found not guilty of attempted murder in 1979. His political career and reputation were destroyed, but the façade remained in place. By contrast, the Labour MP Maureen Colquhoun, elected in 1974, was outed by the press as a lesbian, making her the first openly gay or lesbian MP in the house. She was almost deselected by her local party as a result and lost her seat in the 1979 election. Lesbianism had never been illegal but was repressed nonetheless. In Northern Ireland the Reverend Ian Paisley led a campaign to 'Save Ulster from Sodomy' in a last-ditch attempt to stop decriminalization of homosexuality in the province, which did not happen until 1982. In 1983, in a by-election in South London caused by the Labour MP Bob Mellish resigning to run the London Docklands Development Corporation (the body which took over the closed London Docks), the Labour candidate and gay activist, Peter Tatchell, was subject to an openly homophobic campaign, not least by the Liberal Party, whose candidate, Simon Hughes, would win the seat. Behind the scenes the story was very different – the bisexual Mellish had repeatedly propositioned Tatchell; Simon Hughes was also a closet bisexual.

A third focus of activism, also with US roots, was focused on the plight of the Afro-Caribbean community, especially the extent to which it endured sustained police harassment. An early locus of contention was routine police intervention in the Mangrove Restaurant in Notting Hill. A protest led to mass arrests and the trial of the 'Mangrove Nine' in 1971, most acquitted of most charges. Their leader was Darcus Howe, who went on to edit *Race Today*. Police racism led to the systematic and excessive use of the 'sus' (suspicion) laws to arrest young black men when there was no evidence of criminal activity. The late 1970s saw the beginning of a much larger-scale annual Notting Hill carnival – sometimes marked by confrontations between black youth and the police. A second focus of political activity was in opposing the growing racist party the National Front. The National Front, founded in 1967 and very visible in the 1970s, was overtly racist – its aim was the 'repatriation' of specifically non-white immigrants. At the 'Battle of Lewisham' in 1977 activists stopped the NF marching, though they were faced with police using riot shields for the first time outside Northern Ireland. The racist politics was confronted on the streets by the Anti-Nazi League, set up in a deliberate echo of the 1930s by the Socialist Workers' Party. The party was involved in Rock against Racism, a march and concert at Victoria Park in the East End of London in 1978. The politics of rock music was not straightforward, yet broadly punk and reggae, novelties of the era, aligned with the left, and the latter obviously with anti-racism. Black political and cultural activism began to find a place on a wider political and cultural stage, as was the case for the poet Linton Kwesi Johnson, and for Bob Marley and the Wailers and other Rastamen. British reggae emerged too. Tellingly the term 'black' was used in an inclusive way to indicate non-white rather than only Afro-Caribbean. This was a political definition of blackness – one which united in the face of racism. It was itself transitory – it was rare from the mid-1980s when politically and culturally and indeed economically there emerged marked differences between the children of different groups of what had once been immigrant communities.

An explosion in what were being euphemistically called 'the inner cities' came in the early 1980s. Riots in 1980 in St Pauls in Bristol, and then in 1981 in Brixton in London and Toxteth in Liverpool, were on a scale not seen for decades. They were far from race riots, in that the white youths acted alongside black, but race discrimination, especially by the police, was a key factor. The official line was rather different. Emphasis was placed on problems in what were called 'race relations', a term imported from post-war southern Africa, where it was used by white capitalists and experts. The issue was how to deal, in this scheme, with a series of issues generated by friction between communities. The answer was to recognize communities, and their 'community leaders', as if this was a problem of governing a colony with many potentially warring tribes. What this also meant was a toleration of cultural particularity, as in the case of Sikhs, who were permitted to ignore the obligation to wear crash helmets on motorbikes so that they could sport their turbans.[34]

The 1970s saw a ferment of ideas and organizations perhaps unknown in earlier history.[35] There was fresh anti-nuclear activism, and the green and ecological movements were established. The hunting of foxes was disrupted by the hunt-saboteur movement. New histories unearthed unknown stories, such as Peter Fryer's *Staying Power: The History of Black People in Britain* (London, 1984) about the long-standing presence and racial persecution of black people. In literature, and in the academy, too, it was a moment of experimentation, by older and new writers – the future Nobel Laureates Doris

Lessing, V. S. Naipaul and Harold Pinter among them, and the likes
of Angela Carter, J. G. Ballard, Ian McEwen and Martin Amis. While
there was little that matched the continental cinema, on either side of
the Iron Curtain, state-controlled TV was another matter – its golden
age started in the late 1960s and continued into the early 1980s, with
everything from historical documentaries to dramas. A new critical
awareness entered into the understanding of the UK, lasting into the
1980s, not least dramas like *Boys from the Blackstuff* (BBC, 1982,
but written in the 1970s). The theatre, too, was transformed by small
radical touring companies, and in the state-supported theatre at least,
a move to more intelligent, more political plays. The age of Noel and
Ratty seemed truly over.

These new ideas brought forth counter-movements. The 1970s saw
other organizations of the right formed, including the National Association for Freedom, founded in 1975. It was a determinedly anti-trade
union organization set up by Norris McWhirter after his brother
Ross (they both created and ran the *Guinness Book of Records*) had
been murdered by the IRA following his call for restrictions on the
Irish in Great Britain. Among its founders was Viscount De L'Isle, a
former Conservative cabinet minister. It was very active in the Grunwick dispute. Although past its peak by 1979, the National Front fielded
303 candidates in that general election. There was also a significant
activist Christian right, exemplified by Mary Whitehouse and her
National Listeners and Viewers Association. She was hostile to the
point of obsession with swearing on television, and to pornography and
sexually explicit material. She was especially hostile to homosexuality.
She brought a case for blasphemous libel in 1977, the first since 1922,
against *Gay News*, for publishing a poem by James Kirkup. *Gay News*
was fined, and the editor sentenced to prison, a judgement reversed at
appeal. In 1980 Mary Whitehouse's group contrived a private prosecution of Howard Brenton's National Theatre play *The Romans in Britain*
under the Sexual Offences Act. The case fell apart in court. The play
became notorious through this prosecution for its portrayal of homosexual rape, but its point was lost: it was a critique of imperialist
violence, not just by the Romans in ancient Britain, but, quite explicitly,
by the British state in Northern Ireland.[36]

17

Defending the Nation

*Britain, as it enters the 1980s, offers itself as a caricature of
an exterminist formation. The imperatives of 'defence' poison the nation's economy; the imperatives of ideology deflect
even profitable weapons-manufacture into the hands of
United States contractors. The subordinate inertial thrust of
the national weapons-system-complex augments the imposts
of NATO . . .*

E. P. Thompson, 1980[1]

*And so today, we can rejoice at our success in the Falklands
and take pride in the achievement of the men and women of
our Task Force. But we do so, not as at some last flickering
of a flame which must soon be dead. No – we rejoice that
Britain has re-kindled that spirit which has fired her for generations past and which today has begun to burn as brightly
as before. Britain found herself again in the South Atlantic
and will not look back from the victory she has won.*

Margaret Thatcher, Speech in Cheltenham, 1982[2]

While the 1970s saw the high point of the welfare state and Labour's
social democracy at a time of economic convulsion, the 1970s and
early 1980s also saw a strengthening of the power and influence of
the warfare and security states. Questions of war were on the agenda
as they had not been since the late 1950s and they, as much as the
politics of production, were the issues of contention in what was an
age of controversy. Yet governments, whether Labour or Conservative, followed similar policies.

THE TRAGEDY OF NORTHERN
IRELAND

The greatest crisis in the United Kingdom in the 1970s is the one least written about in histories of the Kingdom, the bloody crisis in Northern Ireland which erupted in 1969.

Northern Ireland had its own government and parliament. The parliament was dominated by unionists; nationalists did not even contest elections outside a very few areas. It was effectively a one-party state, with a sizeable disenfranchised Catholic minority. That minority protested in 1969, and London sent in troops to keep order in place of the clearly partisan local police. The result was an escalation of violence, indeed a war between the new Provisional IRA, founded in 1969, and the British state. The Catholic population (represented from 1970 by a new Social Democratic and Labour Party), wanted to eliminate discrimination against it, and wanted union with Ireland; the unionist population wanted to remain in the United Kingdom and keep its privileges. The central British state defended, if not the status quo, then the integrity of the United Kingdom. From 1969 until the late 1990s Northern Ireland was a very major commitment of British forces, second only to Germany. Some 10–20,000 soldiers were there at any one time.

In the early 1970s conflict deepened, with, for example, British troops firing on unarmed demonstrators (Bloody Sunday, 1972), and the PIRA (in the acronym used by the army) attacking British troops and others with guns and bombs. Internment without trial, introduced in 1971, radicalized republicans and strengthened the Provisionals. Special courts without juries operated. The last ever sentence of death in the United Kingdom was handed down in Northern Ireland in 1972. Liam Holden had his sentence commuted to life. He served seventeen years, and his conviction was quashed years later when a court accepted that a false confession had been beaten from him by British troops.[3]

The war, for such it was, led to more deaths in the British army than in all the services in the Falklands War, and about a third of the deaths in Korea and Malaya. In proportion to population, the number of

United Kingdom civilians killed was greater than in the Blitz. No other rich country in the capitalist world saw similar levels of domestic political violence after 1945; no part of a rich country was so intensively policed or so subject to special laws.

The war revealed there was no British genius for light and effective counter-insurgency – it was a nasty, long business. British forces constrained and contained the PIRA but never defeated it. The war quickly reached a stalemate, with the army and the Royal Ulster Constabulary sometimes working with paramilitary unionist organizations which were involved in their own sectarian war.

Lives were lost not just in Northern Ireland, but on the 'mainland', most notably the bombing of two pubs in Birmingham in 1974, with the loss of twenty-one lives. In 1982 twenty-one soldiers were killed outside Hyde Park Barracks, and in 1984 the Conservative Party conference hotel in Brighton was attacked, killing five and narrowly missing the prime minister. Two Conservative politicians were assassinated, as was Lord Mountbatten of Burma.

In an echo of the suffragette campaign of the Edwardian years, the IRA made a major impact with a hunger strike in 1981, to back a demand for the recognition by the British that the PIRA and Irish National Liberation Army (INLA) prisoners were not mere criminals but in effect political prisoners or prisoners of war. Ten hunger strikers starved themselves to death, led by Bobby Sands, who was elected to the Westminster parliament in a by-election. The deaths reverberated around the world. In Northern Ireland sixty died in violence around this time.

The Northern Ireland parliament, which had sat from 1921, was dissolved in 1972, with direct rule from London introduced, and abolished in 1973. These were extreme measures, revealing of the lack of legitimacy of the Northern Irish government and institutions, and of the seriousness of the war on the ground. In 1973 a Northern Ireland assembly, elected by PR, was established, with a power-sharing government and a Council of Ireland. It was brought down by unionist opposition, and especially by a general strike by Protestant workers in 1974, which the British government was not willing to break. Direct Rule was reimposed, which lasted until a new Northern Ireland assembly and government was established on similar lines to that of 1973, after the Belfast/Good Friday Agreement of 1998. In the interim an assembly was elected (1982–6), but no powers were devolved to it.

The war had profound effects. It led to a strengthening of the security services, including the development of all sorts of security measures from CCTV recognition of car number plates to the mundane searches of bags at the entrance to public buildings. It transformed the security arrangements for the political class, now banished behind security controls. The complete blocking of Downing Street in 1989 with heavy gates was a telling late indicator. Not surprisingly the powers of the police, the development of new security measures and the enforcement of state secrecy caused increasing unease in critics on the left and elsewhere in the early 1970s.[4]

FALKLANDS

In the early 1980s the United Kingdom found itself, extraordinarily enough, fighting a right-wing dictatorship in Argentina. Sensing British weakness and taking advantage of a long-stoked nationalist view that the Falkland Islands were Argentine territories, the Argentine military regime landed forces in (now) uninhabited South Georgia and then the Falkland Islands in April 1982. What followed was the only war since December 1941 that the United Kingdom waged because its imperial territory was attacked. But it was different in that the people of the islands were considered British; the islanders were 'kith and kin' in a way the inhabitants of other colonies such as Hong Kong were not. British nationalism was aroused rather than imperial feeling; analogies were made with 1940, not with a forgotten 1941. The war burst onto a British public who had barely heard of the Falklands, and had lost its memory of Argentina as having once been a critical source of food. If Argentina was now known at all, it was for football.

In better days for both, the two countries had been tied to each other by powerful bonds of liberal sea-borne commerce. Now Argentina only bought British arms; the United Kingdom had no need of Argentine beef or wheat. They were two countries in economic turmoil, which had both suffered relative decline and were both experimenting with free market policies. For both, the Falklands were materially inconsequential. The islanders had lost their British nationality in 1981, and the ice patrol ship HMS *Endurance* was to be withdrawn.[5] Argentina had no economic interest in the islands. The Argentine writer Jorge Luis (Georgie to his intimates) Borges, who had British blood in his veins, famously remarked that the war was like two bald men fighting over a comb.[6] However, the islands were ideologically of extreme significance to Argentine and, from April 1982, to British, nationalism.

The House of Commons was recalled to sit on a Saturday immediately following the invasion. The call for action came from Michael Foot, leader of the Labour Party.[7] He had been MP for the naval dockyard town of Devonport between 1945 and 1955 and came from a liberal family from the area and was very much a navalist. He was old enough to have agitated against Chamberlain and the 'Men of Munich' in 1940 and to have called for a second front in 1942. And now again he faced, in his view, a prime minister who had betrayed British interests to fascists. Indeed, throughout the debate that day there were many conscious allusions to May 1940. One of the first speakers was Julian Amery, son of Leo 'in the name of God go' Amery who called on Chamberlain to resign in the Norway debate. Many contributors alleged that Thatcher's government had fallen asleep on its watch, unlike the Labour government, who had warned off the Argentinians in the 1970s. On that Saturday the war that was to come to look like Thatcher's war was parliament's war: all parties except the Welsh nationalists were in favour.

The taking of the Falklands, in the austral winter, from a large conscript army so far from any base was a triumph for British arms, though luck as ever played its part.[8] The British armada successfully landed one royal marine commando brigade and one infantry brigade of elite army troops, who 'yomped' their way across heathlands to take Port Stanley on 14 June 1982, having landed on 21 May. It was a small war – 255 British servicemen died, and 649 Argentines. 11,000 Argentines were taken prisoner. It was a war of equipment from another era. The commandos sailed to war on the last great emigrant liner, the *Canberra*, and most of the infantry on the last

Illustration 17.1: On board HMS *Incredible* the nuclear-powered armoured punt, by Steve Bell, 1982, the greatest political cartoonist since Low. (© Steve Bell)

Illustration 17.2: Harry Hardnose, red-nosed, red-top journalist, by Steve Bell, 1982. Bell captures the historical memory of the joint development of the UK and Argentina and the sordid genius of the tabloid press. (© Steve Bell)

transatlantic liner, the *QE2* (the remainder were aboard the *Norland*, a more modern Bremerhaven-built ferry). The British flagship, HMS *Hermes*, was a small aircraft carrier from the 1950s, converted to helicopters and Harriers. The *Belgrano* was a 1930s US cruiser which was sunk by British torpedoes of interwar design; the Vulcan bomber of the 1950s was used by the British, and the slightly older and also British Canberra bomber by the Argentines. The British aircraft carriers (with short-range Harriers aboard) were nothing like those of earlier generations, or the many floating airfields the USA could deploy.

The Falklands War was the last independent military action of the British state, the last gesture of British nationalism, at a moment when the British economy was still profoundly national too. John Bull rolled up his sleeves for a last quixotic adventure. British victory meant an expensive new airfield on the islands and the saving of the pair of *Invincible*-class small carriers, one of which was going to be sold. But there was no refocus on a large navy capable of distant operations; it shrank further.

Ideologically it was a very important war. Victory gave prestige and influence to the prime minister and diminished that not only of her opponents, but of many colleagues. In the midst of rising unemployment at home it turned people's minds to contemplating British greatness. While the effects on opinion were electric, the Conservative share of the vote in the 1983 election actually fell compared to 1979.

The war prompted a discussion among left intellectuals about British national identity which would go on for decades. It was as if they had noticed British nationalism for the first time. The war was seen as confirming, indeed revealing, the grip of a new nationalism created in 1940.[9] It was argued that Mrs Thatcher had been able to understand and exploit this form of nationalism, which was interpreted as descended from imperialism. The empire was, again, the problem for the left.[10] In response some wanted to recreate the left nationalism of the Second World War. That the war was accidental, the British response contingent and opposed (in secret) by many Conservatives, was ignored, as was the push to war from large sections of the left.

THE COLD WAR AND SECOND
COLD WAR

The 1970s were a period of increasing confrontations between the United States and its communist rivals across the world. In 1975 South Vietnam and Cambodia fell to forces supported by the Soviet Union and China respectively. In Africa liberation movements supported from the Soviet bloc and China were victorious in the Portuguese empire and making progress in Rhodesia and South Africa. In Europe, Portugal and Spain lost their fascist dictatorships. In Central America guerrillas were fighting the USA's own 'sons of bitches' in Nicaragua, Guatemala and El Salvador. A brutal counter-revolution was underway in the southern cone, where the military had taken over with US support in Uruguay, Chile and Argentina.

International relations were reflected in domestic political contestations. In the 1970s the Labour government did not stop the completion of orders of warships and engine repairs for what was now the Pinochet regime in Chile.[11] It also allowed delivery to the Argentine junta of two British Type 42 warships – the same type as HMS *Sheffield*, which was sunk by Argentine aircraft in the Falklands War. So little concern was there that at official level consideration was given to offering Argentina the small aircraft carrier HMS *Invincible* as well as Harriers and even aged Vulcan bombers.[12] The Thatcher government actively sought to sell Chile new materiel and succeeded.

By the late 1970s the Labour government was pushing to increase defence expenditures in what became known as the second Cold War. The new Conservative government pushed up defence expenditures from 4.5 per cent of GDP to a peak of 5.2 per cent in 1985; at the same time expenditure on education fell, so that by 1985 it was below defence expenditure again. The levels of both warlike and educational spending were back to the levels of the late 1960s as a proportion of GDP, and up one-third in real terms. New US nuclear weapons appeared. The installation of cruise missiles with nuclear warheads, while agreed to by Labour, was announced by the

Conservatives in December 1979 and would lead to the astonishing revival of the Campaign for Nuclear Disarmament, in concert with other anti-nuclear movements across Europe.

During the late 1960s and 1970s an extraordinary secret project was underway to upgrade the capacities of the Polaris missile. It was feared that Polaris could not be effective in future against anti-missile systems, so the government set out to create a new re-entry vehicle which could allow bombs to fall on a defended Soviet target – the so-called 'Moscow Criterion'. Full development started in 1975, under the Labour government, but the programme was a deep secret, kept even from the cabinet. Its existence was not revealed until 1980. The Chevaline system became the payload of the Polaris missiles between 1982 and 1996, when Polaris was withdrawn.[13]

Contrary to the Labour manifesto of 1974, the Labour government conducted studies for a replacement of the Polaris submarine-launched nuclear missile systems, with officials, the prime minister and the minister of defence coming out in favour of another US system, the Trident C4.[14] The government rejected not only non-replacement, but also cheaper systems, including cruise missiles. It took a preliminary decision to acquire Trident from the USA and got approval from the Americans for this. But the final decision was left to the incoming Conservative government. Tridents (in the event the D5 rather than the C4) were to be carried by four new British-built submarines. These came into service in 1994–6, well after the end of the Cold War. The missiles came from a common pool of rockets, and the warheads were of unclear nationality.

Why the continuing commitment to the dependent, or at best inter-dependent nuclear bomb by both the Labour government and the incoming Conservative one? It was not because, as an independent nation, the United Kingdom needed a bomb, whether to defend itself or punch above its weight. The idea that it was a truly independent British deterrent was for the public only. Internally the government repeatedly rejected actual independence in favour of dependence. Thus in 1979 the Conservative government was advised that the C4 missile could not be kept going for more than six to twelve months without US support – that was the extent of full British independence.[15] Officials and politicians worried that the USA would feel it unnecessary to let the UK borrow US weapons. Indeed, an official rationale for a bomb only partly controlled by the British needed to be invented. It was that the alliance deterrent was made more credible by the prospect of a potentially suicidal action by a British prime minister: a 'second centre' of decision-making made deterrence more credible and locked the USA into nuclear escalation. What was made to appear a symbol of British national sovereignty depended for its value on a willingness to destroy the country for the sake of a wider alliance.

That increasing the effectiveness of deterrence was the motive behind acquiring Trident is, however, dubious. It is far more likely that giving up even the pretence of a national bomb was too difficult. The bomb seemed to emanate power and influence (expressed in the false belief that being a member of the Security Council implied having a bomb, but only the US had the bomb when it was set up). In any case it was inconceivable that France should have a bomb, while the United Kingdom did not (that only France had an independent bomb was not mentioned in this context). But the bomb was no mere irrationality. It gave power to the prime minister, and of course to its controllers and builders. The bomb was beyond the purview of the cabinet, who were rarely if ever given a chance to discuss it seriously. Even senior ministers with reservations were marginalized. It was a presidential weapon.

It was also a very important political weapon to be used against anyone who opposed it. As we have seen, there was no real difference between the policies of the Labour government and the Conservative opposition on nuclear matters. However, after 1979 much of the Labour Party became openly hostile to nuclear weapons. From 1980 it had an anti-nuclear leader, a veteran of the first efflorescence of the Campaign for Nuclear Disarmament in the 1960s, Michael Foot. It adopted an anti-nuclear policy for the 1983 election, one hostile to US nuclear bases, as well as Trident. 'One-sided disarmament' was how proposals to get rid of nuclear weapons were labelled by the Tory government, or 'unilateral nuclear disarmament' – as if there was no debate to be had about the value of nuclear weapons, as if it were inconceivable that getting rid of nuclear weapons might be a way of making British forces stronger. A nuclear defence policy was also promised by the right-wing breakaway from Labour, the Social Democratic Party, and indeed the Liberal Party with which it fought the 1983 election. Rather importantly, they both wanted to cancel the Trident programme, but this idea was denounced as extremism when proposed by Labour.

FOREIGN RELATIONS

The victory of the Conservative Party in the 1983 election meant a continuation not only of nuclear policy, but also of membership of the EEC, from which Labour had intended to withdraw. Mrs Thatcher strongly supported British membership of the EEC. However, she demanded a rebate on the British contribution and got it. She was seen as a reluctant European, though she was very keen on the development of ever freer trade within the EEC, which is what the Single European Act of 1986 strongly pushed forward. However, it was clear that the primary British relationship was with the United States. In that sense Mrs Thatcher's premiership was distinct from that of Edward Heath, and indeed that of Harold Wilson.

Mrs Thatcher was an enthusiastic Cold Warrior. She attempted to force a British boycott of the Moscow Olympics following the Soviet intervention in Afghanistan, supporting President Carter's action. Globally famous as the 'Iron Lady', she was personally close to Ronald Reagan (in office from January 1981) and supportive of his strong anti-left actions across the world. That implied support for many brutal regimes of the right. But the USA could still treat the UK with contempt, as over the invasion of the Commonwealth nation of Grenada in 1983. The humiliation was not that, as claimed, it came out of the blue, but that London was aware from its diplomats in the Caribbean that US action was likely; indeed they reported troop build-up. Furthermore, the United Kingdom was asked by Caribbean nations to take part in an invasion of Grenada and refused. London told Washington of its opposition to military action: Margaret Thatcher expressed the gravest concern to Reagan, by telephone, before the invasion went ahead anyway.[16]

Mrs Thatcher was quick to recognize that the new Soviet leadership under Mikhail Gorbachev (from 1985) wanted change and helped thereby to bring a sudden and peaceful end to the Cold War in 1989. Yet this had potentially dangerous consequences for her. One of her concerns was that the United Kingdom would have to get rid of its nuclear weapons as a result of a US–Soviet deal. Mrs Thatcher was roused to fury by Ronald Reagan: 'He nearly gave away the store,' she told Boxing Day guests at Chequers, by which she meant he had nearly given away the nuclear weapons the United Kingdom oversaw.[17] This outburst exposed the weakness of the claim that the United Kingdom had nuclear weapons in order to trade them away by multilateral nuclear disarmament.

Questions of foreign relations led to Mrs Thatcher's deposition. She nearly fell as a result of the so-called Westland Affair of 1986. Defence secretary Michael Heseltine wanted to pursue a European alignment for the British helicopter company Westland (whose business was making US-designed Sikorski helicopters for British forces). Margaret Thatcher preferred a direct link with the US firm Sikorski, which went ahead, but proved temporary. Westland was eventually to link up with an Italian firm and to make European helicopters. The dispute had led to the resignation of Heseltine, and the industry secretary, Leon Brittan, who had backed Mrs Thatcher. Heseltine would lead the challenge which brought her down four years later. That challenge, and her defeat, resulted from her increasingly anti-EEC stance. Her chancellor and foreign secretary had been in favour of the European Exchange Rate Mechanism for stabilizing currencies and proposals for a 'hard ECU' (the ECU was a Common Market currency), which Margaret Thatcher noisily and publicly rejected. This led to the resignation of Sir Geoffrey Howe, her foreign secretary, in 1990, the move against her by Michael Heseltine and her rejection by her parliamentary party in 1990. What motivated the animus towards the EEC of Margaret Thatcher is hard to fathom; anti-Germanism in the face of a unified Germany is one explanation.[18] But what is more significant was the deep pro-EEC consensus which toppled her. This was one Mrs Thatcher could not break, any more than could Michael Foot.

THE INTEGRITY OF THE
BRITISH STATE

Margaret Thatcher also restored the emphasis on the unitary character of the British state by rejecting devolution. For the first time since
the Edwardian years there were calls, from the 1970s especially, for a
measure of Home Rule, in this case for Scotland, and for Wales. This
arose from the demands of and as a response to the growth of nationalist parties. In Wales Plaid Cymru (formed 1925) grew rapidly in the
1960s (winning a by-election in 1966), and from the 1970s was contesting all Welsh seats, winning three in 1974. Much more dramatic
was the Scottish case. During the 1970s the Scottish National Party
(SNP), founded in 1934, grew very considerably, eating into both the
Tory and the Labour vote in Scotland. Its rise was promoted by the
prospect of new riches for Scotland. It was Scotland, Shetland and
Orkney where most of the oil would land, making it, rather than
England, a major oil producer. The SNP won a by-election in 1970
and advanced strongly, taking eleven seats in October 1974. There
was for the first time since 1918 a significant group of nationalist
MPs in Westminster.

As in the case of the Liberal government after 1910, the Labour government was to depend on nationalist votes as its slim majority was
lost in by-elections by 1976. Labour proposed a measure of devolution,
opposed by the Tories and many Labour MPs. Queen Elizabeth made
it very clear she believed in the Union. During her silver jubilee celebra-
tions (1977), when the issue of devolution to Scotland and Wales was
being debated, she noted that she recognized a revival of 'awareness of
historic national identities in these Islands' and said: 'I number Kings and
Queens of England and of Scotland, and Princes of Wales among my
ancestors and so I can readily understand these aspirations.' 'But,' she
made scandalously clear in the rider, 'I cannot forget that I was crowned
Queen of the United Kingdom of Great Britain and Northern Ireland.'[19]
That is, for all the informal references to her as 'Queen of England', not
least by Enoch Powell, she has never been any such thing.[20]

A Labour backbencher, George Cunningham, a Scot sitting for
Islington South, put in an amendment which required 40 per cent of

the electorate (not merely those who had voted) to say yes. The amendment was passed. Scotland voted yes, but not enough to pass this very stiff additional test. Wales voted no. As a result the SNP lodged a confidence vote against the government, which was taken over by the Conservative opposition. Others who felt betrayed voted with them, with the result that the vote was lost by one. Into the lobby with the Conservatives, who were implacably opposed to devolution, went the SNP, turkeys voting for an early Christmas, it was said. With them went most of the Ulster Unionists, and the Liberals. Two Ulster Unionists voted with the government, as did Plaid Cymru and Scottish Labour. However two Irish nationalists abstained. Because Labour decided not to bring in a dying MP, they lost by one vote. Thus fell the Labour government, in an echo of the territorial politics of another era.

With the return of the Conservative and Unionist party to power in the resulting election, devolution was dead. The economic and social policies of the new government, as well as its hostility to devolution, meant the near elimination of the Conservative and Unionist Party from Scotland, once one of its centres of strength.

REFLECTIONS ON DEFEAT

By the early 1980s the power of the central state against political opposition had been powerfully demonstrated. It held firm in Northern Ireland, it went to war to get back the Falkland Islands and it had dealt with opponents to nuclear weapons and bolstered the alliance with the United States. Membership of the EEC was confirmed. The nationalists had been thrown back, along with the left.

In the process the legitimacy of the British state suffered grievous blows. The British state and constitution, its courts, police and parliament, were, deservedly or not, legitimate until the 1970s. There was pride in British democracy, fair play, decency and honesty. The United Kingdom had the mother of parliaments and the best police force in the world, famous for being unarmed, if one discounted Ireland, as most British people of course did. But from the 1970s especially this legitimacy was eroded, slowly, and for that reason more damagingly. The victory of conventional authority woke people up to the nature of its power. As a result it was now the subject of investigation and critique as never before. There was sustained criticism of the police who used the 'sus laws' to stop and harass young black men. It became clear how official secrecy, upheld by powerful and intimidating laws, was used to suppress the politically difficult. Two journalists and a former soldier were tried by the Labour government for spying in 1978; they had in fact collated open source material and, while found guilty, were released.[21]

Real state secrets began to be revealed. It became clearer that British governments had a lot to hide. It was shown in the 1970s that the decision to build an atomic bomb in the 1940s was taken by a carefully selected group of ministers and then kept secret. It was only in the 1970s that the greatest wartime secret of all – the mass breaking of German codes – was made public. 1980 saw the revelation of the Chevaline programme, and its huge costs, which had been kept secret, even from most of the Labour cabinet. It was revealed that the state-owned BP and Shell, deliberately and with the covert support of the state, maintained oil supplies to white supremacist Rhodesia. This rendered absurd the Royal Navy's decade-long 'Beira Patrol', with which it had prevented oil getting to Rhodesia via the Portuguese colonial port of Beira between 1965 and 1975. To cap it all, Margaret Thatcher told parliament that the state had covered up wartime espionage for the Soviet Union by elite figures.

Yet many scandals of the era were successfully covered up until very much later. Six men convicted of planting IRA bombs in Birmingham in 1974 were innocent. Rejecting their appeal, Lord Denning, a famous judge, argued that their case relied on the police having perjured themselves, using violence against them, inventing confessions. This 'appalling vista' was so preposterous it could not be true. And most people agreed. They were not released till 1991. The Guildford Four and the Maguire Seven, convicted for the Guildford bombings of 1974, were entirely innocent but not released till 1989 and 1991. There would be many other cases of serious misbehaviour and cover-ups by the authorities, endorsed and upheld by inquests and other inquiries, where years later the lies, and the credulity of the inquirers, were painfully and at cost exposed.

The 1970s saw the rise of critical analysis of the secret British state and institutions from the left.[22] There were exposés of the existence of GCHQ, police surveillance and new technologies of political control and a fresh concern for civil liberties. The issue of war, nuclear war especially, animated large parts of the left, at least as much as unemployment. The Campaign for Nuclear Disarmament produced much more thoughtful and engaged research than the first CND. There was a powerful new feminist critique of militarism which resulted in a permanent encamped protest by women outside the Greenham Common United States air Force base. The warfare state, and its relations to the USA, was becoming a little more visible. One of the enlighteners was the historian E. P. Thompson, who threw himself into this campaign as he had earlier against the new secret state. Thompson was among the war veterans who called for alternative forms of defence. Another was Peter Johnson, wartime bomber commander, who argued for a non-aligned United Kingdom, one which should reorient its policies around defence of the United Kingdom, rather than defence of West Germany; that would lead to lower costs and more defence.[23] Duncan Campbell's book *The Unsinkable Aircraft Carrier: American Military Power in Britain* (London, 1984) was revelatory about the realities of military power in the United Kingdom, as was a hit BBC series *Edge of Darkness* (BBC 1985).

18

Rulers' Revolt

*This election is about the future of Britain – a great country
which seems to have lost its way. It is a country rich in natural resources, in coal, oil, gas and fertile farmlands.*

Conservative Party manifesto, 1979

*Remember the conventional wisdom of the day. The British
people were 'ungovernable'. We were in the grip of an incurable 'British disease'. Britain was heading for 'irreversible
decline'. Well, the people were not ungovernable, the disease
was not incurable, the decline has been reversed.*

The Next Moves Forward, Conservative manifesto, 1987

Politics changed in the 1970s, but in ways that are not well described
by the concept of an end to consensus. Much more was changing than the politics between parties. Intra-party politics were
especially important. For some the main division lay between the
right and left of the Labour Party; for others between the New Right
of the Conservative Party and the rest of parliamentary politics.[1]

The two key political drivers of new ideas in the 1970s, Tony Benn
and Margaret Thatcher, represented positions which were critical of the
positions of their own parties. For both, 1975, their fiftieth year, was
particularly important. Tony Benn, without question the leader of the
left, led the anti-EEC campaign of that year, losing decisively, and as
a result was demoted from the Industry to the Energy portfolio in the
Labour government. Margaret Thatcher stood against and defeated
Edward Heath as leader of the Conservative Party and took the party
sharply to the right. She campaigned for a yes vote in the referendum.

Both came into their moment of greatest power in the late 1970s and early 1980s: Margaret Thatcher as prime minister, Tony Benn as leader of a Labour left which was able to change the policies of the Labour Party very substantially. If there had ever been a post-war consensus they would both certainly have broken it.

Margaret Thatcher became prime minister in 1979. Under her determined leadership, the trade unions were brought to heel, and the British decline, her supporters claimed, finally began to be reversed. Industries nationalized in the 1940s and earlier and later were now privatized and liberalized. So were industries born from within the state machine. There was an economic transition from manufacturing to services in which, it was claimed, British firms did very well, creating a uniquely competitive European economy which became a model for many. Margaret Thatcher, in office for eleven consecutive years, was forced out in 1990, to be replaced by John Major, who won the 1992 election with the consequence that the Conservatives would be in power for a remarkable eighteen years. The country was transformed, economically and ideologically, to a degree not seen since the 1940s.

For both Margaret Thatcher and Tony Benn, their push for new policies was in part about recapturing a past. Margaret Thatcher's policies were in some respects about a *return* to the 1950s, a period she identified with. This was a period with high defence spending, a clear bipartisan commitment to national nuclear weapons, to close relations with the USA, to the capitalist economy and to limited welfare expenditure. All this was threatened in the 1970s by the rise of the unions and the left in the Labour Party. Thus, the 1979 Tory manifesto did not attack a post-war consensus, but what had happened in the recent past, pointing to the fact that Labour governments had dominated by being in office for eleven out of the previous fifteen years. Certainly in some respects the 1974 Labour programme broke with the previous one, but the really big break came after 1979. By 1983 the left had pushed the Labour Party into a position which involved withdrawal from the EEC, rejection of nuclear weapons and elimination of US nuclear bases, and a strong dose of nationalist economic planning. By this standard the Conservative Party certainly stood for the post-war consensus in substance though not in style.[2]

And yet, one could also see the Labour programme of 1983 as a plea for a return to the past. Though it was never expressed in this way Labour advocated the national, protected economy, with an interventionist state, outside the EEC, which had been the post-war norm. In many respects the left was looking to finally bring about the promise of those years, which they saw as unrealized because of the political power of British capitalism and the political and ideological weakness of previous Labour governments. The difficulty was that business, the Conservative Party and the Labour right had long moved from this past, to decisively support the EEC and to reject economic nationalism.

Perhaps the best way to think about this is to cast out any thought of a general consensus being broken and rather to see both major parties revising their positions radically, both looking to recreate semi-mythical pasts and to create a new future. Furthermore, the policies of the parties interacted with each other – the Tories reacted to the extension of social democracy in the 1970s, just as Labour reacted to the market liberalism of the Conservatives after 1979. In both cases they reacted in ways which drove their positions, always different, further apart.

The key difference in the politics of the 1980s from what went before was the preparedness of government to fight dissenters very hard and to exert the rights of elected authority very strongly. That is not the same as breaking a consensus – it is rather a willingness to press on with one's own policies in the face of odium. Thus it was not a matter of moving from agreement to disagreement, but rather a change, a very important one, in how to deal with disagreement. From the war both parties accommodated disagreement – Mrs Thatcher did so much less. She was admired and loathed for being what she said she was – a conviction politician. She broke through an unsteady equilibrium of forces. Push came to shove, and the forces on her side could shove an awful lot harder.

There was indeed a crucial transformation in the power and self-confidence of the British elite. Sometime in the 1970s a chunk of the British upper class said enough is enough. For parts of the middle class, too, a future with stronger unions and a more comprehensive welfare state, was not attractive. In the 1970s there emerged the idea that the United Kingdom was becoming ungovernable; that the state had been captured by unproductive groups; that there was an inexorable tendency to use the state to exploit producers in favour of a parasitic public. The answer to everything, it had seemed, was the government must do something, which it couldn't. Government not only dominated economic activity, it actively prevented private sector operation, by making it illegal in certain fields and uncompetitive in others. Democracy was thus destroying the sinews of production and of national power. The answer was, of course, 'rolling back the state', rhetorically speaking, but it also involved making the state more autonomous, more powerful. There were models. In Chile from 1973 and in Argentina from 1976, military governments opened markets, privatized state industries and crushed organized labour. There were also think tanks and pressure groups in the United Kingdom arguing for a robust economic liberalism and talk of anti-socialist private armies of the right among a fringe of business and military people.

LA PASIONARIA OF PRIVILEGE

In 1975, in a dramatic shift, the leadership of the Conservative Party changed in style, substance and its deep nature. It was the result of a coup, the first against a Conservative Party leader. It was to be called, very misleadingly, 'the Peasants' Revolt'. But Margaret Thatcher was voted in by 'toffs, country gents and Treasury specialists', 'men of old money, old regiments and old school ties'.[3] Edward Heath, leader since 1965, when he was the first leader of the Conservative Party to be elected by members of parliament, was thrown out of office. Conservative MPs replaced Heath by someone not much younger, of similar social origin, who had studied also in Oxford. But Heath was a man who had visited republican Spain during the civil war; where he had met Jack Jones, then fighting in the International Brigades, later to be leader of the TGWU. By contrast, Margaret Thatcher had no positive feeling for the anti-fascist compact of the 1930s or the war and its aftermath. Just before becoming leader she was called the 'La Pasionaria of privilege' by the Labour chancellor, Denis Healey. She was a nationalist with a very different sense of the nation and one who clearly communicated that nationalism in an overt way.

Heath was able at least in part to play the role of party grandee, but Thatcher was 'that awful woman' even to some who were extremely loyal and helpful to her. In a telling anecdote, the Labour MP Dennis Skinner, a stalwart of the parliamentary left, recalls being taunted for being a grammar school boy (which, unusually for a former miner, he is) by a crowd of braying Conservative public school MPs seated around her in the tea room of the House of Commons in the late 1980s. He embarrassed them all by telling them that 'Maggie', who sat silently among them, also went to a grammar school.[4] Margaret Thatcher was in part a creature of the old party who spoke directly to the membership of the Conservative Party and to a wider public in ways Edward Heath plainly did not.

Margaret Thatcher's ascent and success were not inevitable. She won the election in 1979 with a lower vote percentage than Edward Heath gained in 1970. The Conservative vote share decreased from 44 per cent in 1979 to approximately 42 per cent in 1983, 1987 and 1992. She was a minority taste and remained so. The electoral victories depended, particularly in 1983, on a strong performance by the new SDP–Liberal Alliance, which split the opposition and nearly replaced Labour as the second party. Furthermore, the Falklands War could have finished differently, she could have lost against the miners, she could have been thrown out as a result of Westland and she could have been left isolated by the abolition of nuclear weapons by the USA and the USSR. Yet she dominated politics like no other politician since Churchill, drove through changes against strong opposition and indeed destroyed British socialism. She was admired around the world and had an extraordinary personal following within her own party. She represented and led a reinvigorated ruling class. As she herself put it, 'We have ceased to be a nation in retreat. We have instead a new-found confidence – born in the economic battles at home and tested and found true 8,000 miles away. That confidence comes from the re-discovery of ourselves, and grows with the recovery of our self-respect.'[5] She had power, and great self-belief, if little popularity.

Yet Margaret Thatcher was the first British prime minister to be

dumped by her party while in office. Challenged by Michael Heseltine, whom she beat but not strongly enough, she resigned at the
end of 1990. Not since the defenestration of Neville Chamberlain in
May 1940 had something similar happened. But Chamberlain at least
remained leader of his party and a senior minister. Edward Heath
was got rid of in opposition. In earlier times Asquith and then Lloyd
George were kicked out of office, but largely by coalition partners,
not their own parties. What is plain is this. When she threatened a
key policy of the Conservative elite, and the business elite – engagement
in the EEC – she was forced out. While Margaret Thatcher was
clearly useful for a project of transformation, she was far from indis-
pensable. There was indeed a party and class project for which she
was, temporarily, a brilliant political figurehead. For she was thrown
out not by the actions of 'the wets', but by the resignations of two
deeply Thatcherite senior ministers, Nigel Lawson and Geoffrey
Howe. Finally, despite the strong sense that Margaret Thatcher
achieved what she set out to do, it is not clear that this was the case.
For it could be argued that what she appeared to want was a strong,
self-confidently British and socially conservative nation, with a powerful regenerated manufacturing industry led by British entrepreneurs,
which would reverse the decline as it had been defined by declinists.[6]
By these measures she undoubtedly failed.

IDEAS

Mrs Thatcher's Conservative Party was strongly influenced by many
different sorts of ideas often in contradiction with each other. Some
were socially and politically conservative and authoritarian, others
were libertarian. It was not just about conserving the old, but also
about creating something new. It was thus not easily comprehended
by those who saw Conservatives as mere reactionaries, and the promoters of change only on the left. One strand was a growing body of
economic reflection which was profoundly critical of economic
nationalism, of the notion that the state could or should guide economic development. The new right, as they were called by the left,
believed in free trade and in letting the private sector decide on

investments, on what machinery to buy, what research to do, where to locate and so on. The nation, as had been the case for the Liberals of old, should not be a factor.[7] This was the big issue on which there was a clear divide, and it is not summed up by the difference between something called Keynesianism and something called monetarism. It was a matter of political-economic principles, not particular kinds of macro-economics. It was not the control of demand or the money supply which was really at issue, but the place of free trade, and of the capitalist, in a global market. It was more profound than hostility to nationalized industries – it was a matter of who or what was in charge. And it was also about any number of different kinds of government measures for the support of industry, from education to taxation, on which neither 'Keynesianism' nor 'monetarism' had anything distinctive to say. It was crucially about the distribution of power in society, an expression of the feeling that an active state had supported the unproductive rather too much.

It was a movement centred on business-financed private think tanks, rather than British universities. Indeed, it ran in opposition to the academy and what it took to be conventional elite thought (and of course socialist ideas). Its central academic influences came from abroad. Friedrich Hayek, who had been at the LSE between 1931 and 1950, went to Chicago. Milton Friedman was a US academic.[8] In terms of economic theory there was a very significant difference between the Austrians, like Hayek, who were hostile to macro-economic ideas and scientism, and the neo-classicals like Friedman, who were macro-economists schooled in proudly scientistic economics. The British think tanks which took up these ideas sought influence not in the universities but in the press, in politics and policy, with success, though they also set up their own small private university. Their success came in the 1970s, but their ideas were not as marginal in the 1950s and 1960s as they were later made to seem.[9]

Among the politicians and thinkers associated with these ideas and institutions there were those who attacked both British economic nationalism and techno-nationalism. For example, Enoch Powell imagined, in 1968, getting rid of all industrial and agricultural subsidies. Nicholas Ridley wrote a 1973 pamphlet attacking the civil service for its *support* of high-tech industries. Duncan Burn was a fulminating critic of the extraordinarily wasteful British nuclear programme. David Henderson claimed the Concorde and the AGR programmes, while still underway, were some of the worst imaginable investment decisions. Naive techno-nationalism resulted in giving too much power to engineers and not enough to market forces and was in their view to be rigorously avoided. These critics focused on civil programmes, though the bigger problem was in the military sector.[10]

Mrs Thatcher was the first British prime minister to have completed a science degree. Yet this did not make her a technocrat.[11] Indeed, British academic science had an important tradition of liberal-individualist thinking in it. Its ablest ideologue was the Hungarian émigré Michael Polanyi, professor of physical chemistry and then of social philosophy at Manchester, and who closely associated with classically liberal philosophers and economists such as Hayek and John Jewkes. They were profoundly hostile not only to Marxism but also to centrist scientism, and their writings of the late 1940s onwards were well supported by the CIA.[12] Jewkes was to become a notable critic of claims for bureaucratized invention.[13] Rather strikingly, there were British scientists who prospered even outside the university. Peter Mitchell, a biochemist with personal wealth, left the academy completely to research in his country house in the 1960s; he won the Nobel Prize for chemistry in 1978. Another country-house scientist of the 1960s and 1970s was the inventor James Lovelock, later famous for his Gaia Hypothesis.[14] Nevertheless, in the academy at least few scientists had any sympathy for the politics of the first fully-trained scientist in No. 10.[15]

The relationship between the Thatcher revolutionaries and the universities was fraught. Universities had been marginal to the development of the new liberal economics, or indeed thinking from the right more generally, and were (laughably) regarded as strongholds of the left. Mrs Thatcher was refused an honorary degree by her own university, in a calculated and controversial insult. The Royal Society elected her, as it did most prime ministers, but with more reason, given she was a chemist, but even this was a commented-on election. She also had a tense relationship with the established churches and promoted an evangelical to the see of Canterbury. However, she did not favour the sort of cynical born-again Christianity that the US right promoted at this time, though this was prominent in Northern Ireland in the case of the Reverend Dr Ian Paisley, who had an honorary doctorate from a US fundamentalist university.

In arguing for a free market economy, from which political freedom would flow, the economic liberals were very poor indeed in describing the actually existing economy and its history. They blamed its faults on 'socialists of all parties' and foreign ideas. An early and blatant example was John Jewkes' *Ordeal by Planning*, of 1948 and 1968, which lambasted the post-war Labour government for planning while ignoring the wartime planning in which he had been a major player. Indeed, there was no convincing economic-historical account of the British economy to support the economic revolution which was being proposed. Perhaps this was not surprising in that the most elementary examination of the historical record would show that phases of slow growth corresponded to full exposure to the market, and that the greatest growth had taken place in the years after the Second World War in a protected economy with significant state intervention and control. Tory histories of the twentieth century did little more than lambast past Tory governments for appeasing Labour and letting in too many black people.[16] They might at most hint that it might have been a good idea to stay out of the Second World War, hiding behind imagined imperial ramparts.[17] There was essentially no useable, positive Tory history of the twentieth century, a reason perhaps for the popularity of the nineteenth century, with its 'Victorian values'.

Yet histories which purported to explain poor British economic performance were important to arguments for an economic revolution. Revitalized declinist histories were central to the ideological baggage of Thatcherism. Martin Wiener's reiteration of a 1960s thesis on the elite educational system sucking the entrepreneurial spirit out of the British bourgeoisie was a huge success in 1981.[18] Even more spectacular was that of Correlli Barnett's *Audit of War*, another version of the same thesis, which also blamed the post-Second World

War British decline on high welfare spending and a do-gooding British elite schooled in Christian moralism and determined to create a New Jerusalem rather than a thrusting industrial nation. The academics generally liked these works – the higher reading public, of left and right, were generally ecstatic, especially about Barnett.[19] They did not detect, perhaps because they shared, his nationalistic-militaristic-technocratic world view. Thatcherism was never ideologically consistent. It took time for the claims of these histories to be shredded, and they remained influential even so.

The Thatcher government was very self-consciously going to do something about the British decline. When Margaret Thatcher talked about reversing decline and releasing enterprise she, like others thinking about the issue, was thinking primarily of manufacturing industry.[20] Yet ministers in the first Thatcher government were 'notable for the lack of contact with the industrial values that they extolled'.[21] While this is true of manufacturing industry, there were many businessmen in the government, including David Young from the world of property, Nicholas Ridley, a civil engineering contractor, from a business and aristocratic family, Sir Keith Joseph, a hereditary baronet whose father had created the building firm Bovis, Patrick Jenkin, a director of Distillers, and Michael Heseltine from publishing. There were also important advisers from business in No. 10 Downing Street.[22] Yet it was also the most donnish set of ministers since the 1960s, though of a distinctive sort, including many Fellows of All Souls in its leadership – for example, in the later years, Keith Joseph, John Redwood, Robert Jackson, Lord Hailsham and William Waldegrave, and at least three PhD historians, Rhodes Boyson, John Redwood and John Patten.

POLICIES

The Thatcher government came in at a very inauspicious moment – a new Great Depression, comparable to that of the 1930s, had hit the world. Yet this crisis of capitalism, global as it once again was, far from discrediting capitalism, as had happened in the 1930s, actually strengthened it ideologically, especially in the United Kingdom and the USA, where Ronald Reagan became president in 1981 on a very economically liberal agenda. One important reason for this shift was that there were no cases of apparently radically better economic performance by non-capitalist countries. Indeed, what was very obvious in the 1970s and 1980s was the poor recent performance of the Soviet bloc and its satellites. In any case, the crisis was interpreted by most not as a crisis of capitalism, but as a crisis generated by interventionist states (however implausible this was). Yet it was clear that something was wrong – rapid growth had stopped in the mid-1970s, inflation surged nearly everywhere, together with unemployment. On top of this, the established order was threatened by stronger trade unions and the rise of the left. However, economic doctrine, and economic policy, were a changeable mess between 1979 and the late 1980s.[23]

What was particularly astonishing was the response to the crisis, one which conventional economists thought was making it worse. Instead of Keynesian reflation there was Keynesian deflation. This was partly a question of economic doctrine and partly of objective. The long-proclaimed central aim of the Thatcher government was bringing down inflation. Inflation in their view undermined freedom, a key word. They saw inflation as debasing savings, weakening the middle class against the workers. Furthermore, though this was not stated, it favoured the debtor, rather than the creditor. They also had a theory of inflation – that it was due not to high demand, or trade unions pushing up wages, but rather to the supply of money in the economy. Reducing inflation meant, in their terms, control of the money supply, which meant high interest rates and cuts in public spending and higher taxes. This they did. In fact their measures at first pushed inflation upwards such that it went up from 8 per cent to 18 per cent. However, as the economy crashed, so did the rate of rise of prices. Real interest rates were raised for a prolonged period to levels last seen in the 1920s and were in stark contrast to most of the 1970s, when real interest rates had been negative, as they had been from the Second World War into the early 1950s. These high rates were a gift to owners of property – real owners that is, not mortgagees.

High interest rates, and a high pound, exacerbated the problems of tradeable manufacturing industries in particular. Manufacturing output fell much faster than that of the economy as a whole – there was a fall in two years of nearly 15 per cent, taking manufacturing output back to that of the late 1960s. ICI lost 30 per cent of its workers between 1979 and 1983 and by 1984 was employing equal numbers in the UK and overseas.[24] The United Kingdom became a net importer of manufactures. Mass unemployment followed but was often seen within government-supporting circles as a necessary shake-out of labour from 'over-manned' industries.

The attitude to the national economy was critical too. Economic nationalism was out. There was in time an all-out rejection of Labour's refreshed economic nationalism. One telling early indicator was the abolition of exchange controls in 1979. These had once affected even holiday spending money, but was now really a matter of overseas investment. British investors were now free to invest abroad as they wished, and they did. From its beginning, then, the Conservative government was encouraging the bringing-down of economic barriers around the nation – which would lead step by step to the fall of the nation as an economic unit as it was understood into the 1970s.

Another crucial element was a change in attitude to trade unions. They were no longer to be seen as social partners but as an economic danger. Trade union legislation was passed, but of a very different sort from Heath's ill-fated Industrial Relations Act. Successive legislation ate away at the various immunities that allowed trade unions to act. In effect there was a return to the practices of past Tory governments. Trade unions were derecognized in very significant ways, and this was all the more important because unemployment was increasing very radically in the early 1980s. Among many changes, unions were made liable for damages for strikes unless they took place in very particular conditions and were voted for in postal ballots. An extreme case, but a potent symbol, was the 1984 banning of trade unions at GCHQ, the central electronic espionage facility which had only recently had its existence acknowledged. This led to the sacking of fourteen workers who refused to renounce union membership. The implication that trade unions might be traitorous was as offensive as it was deliberate. This was the only anti-trade union measure repealed by the 1997 New Labour government.

The power of organized workers was broken by high unemployment and the collapse of unionized industries. The changes were
palpable – the heads of the TUC diminished in stature, the names of
union leaders were increasingly unknown, the industrial correspondents disappeared from television and newspapers. From the late 1980s
the working class disappeared from the public sphere. The poor, the
unsuccessful, were stigmatized in the media in ways which would
have been unthinkable earlier.[25] The tripartite apparatus that involved
trade unions in public life was abolished or ignored. The NEDC was
sidelined, though not abandoned till 1992. The discourse around the
economy was now one of flotations and enterprise and the state of the
stock market, rather than the balance of payments and production.

LEGACY ASSETS

A crucial factor in the Thatcher revolution was submerged in accounts
stressing crisis and decline in the 1970s. The Thatcher government
claimed it had inherited a fundamental economic crisis caused by
government intervention in the economy. Yet the developmental state
had created the very economic conditions which made Thatcher's
approach possible. The transformations under Thatcher were only
feasible because of previous state investment, because of the success
of the state, not by its failure.

Her government had inherited, for the first time since the late nineteenth century, a nation self-sufficient in food, indeed an exporter
of wheat and meat. It had also taken over a nation which was about
to become, for the first time since 1939, a net exporter of energy. The
implications were extraordinary: the United Kingdom no longer
needed to be a net exporter of manufactures to balance its earlier
needs for energy and food. This epochal transformation has barely
registered in political discourse or the history books.[26]

When the Conservative Party came to power in 1979, there was a
mass of modern public capital that had not been there in 1950, or
1960, or even 1970. There were modern electricity supply, railway,
telephone, gas, postal and other systems newly in place. As we have
also seen, there was an inheritance of a motorway system, new steel

works and more, including new coal mines. Council houses, in their millions, now existed.

These valuable assets could be sold. Two million council houses were sold to tenants. North Sea Oil was the first significant state-owned industry to be privatized, though this is not very well known.[27] First went part of Britoil, formerly BNOC, in 1982 for over £600 million. In 1983 a £500 million tranche of BP was sold, the biggest privatization of the year. In 1984 nearly £400 million was raised from Enterprise Oil, spun out of British Gas. In 1987 another large chunk of Britoil went, and in 1987 £5.5 billion of BP.[28] The first huge sale was that of British Telecom, which had been part of the Post Office, which came at the end of 1984. Just over 50 per cent was sold, for £4 billion. This was followed by the massive £7 billion privatization of British Gas in 1986. The other utilities would not be privatized until the 1990s.[29]

It should not be thought that the Thatcher government modernized nationalized industries by selling them off – they were modernized further under state ownership prior to privatization. There was continued, indeed increased, activism by the state in these industries. However, it was not like that of old, which consisted in investment in new equipment. Now the focus was on reducing the workforce and on closing facilities. The most radical case was the coal mines, not privatized till a tiny rump was left in the 1990s. But British Airways (1987), British Steel (1988), British Telecom (1984), British Gas (1986) and others were all privatized as lean, profitable enterprises, which had all first shed labour under public ownership. Among the others were the warship yards (1985), British Leyland (1988) and Rolls-Royce (1987). Even in the case of nuclear energy, there was a transformation in performance of the old reactors, but under public ownership. The best that can be said for the positive impact of privatization on performance is that it resulted from the need to be ready for privatization. But of course, the argument for privatization was precisely that the state was incapable of modernizing, or even shrinking, industries. Thatcherism was not so much the release of entrepreneurial power, but rather the creation of a brutally activist state, directly and powerfully transforming society, ideas, as well as the economy. For all the complaints about social democratic state intervention, there had never been state intervention this strong until

Thatcher. Indeed, there was a strong bureaucratization and an extension of central controls, of planning and of the state. The rulers' revolt did not push aside the state, it strengthened it and made use of it.

Furthermore, it could be argued that the devastations to the productive economy caused by government policy were only sustainable because the government inherited a newly comprehensive and, by historical British standards, generous welfare state. There was an extensive safety net onto which many millions could, and did, fall. The official number of unemployed rose to over 3 million and stayed at that level for years. Many who would otherwise have worked went onto disability benefits. The number of people on invalidity and sickness benefit doubled between 1980 and 1993, to 2 million people.[30]

THE GREAT MINERS' STRIKE 1984–5

Under the plan for coal of the 1970s the British coal mining industry would be modernized and its output expanded slightly. The rapid decline of the late 1950s and 1960s was over. The future was to be based on new, much more productive mines, notably the complex being developed at Selby in Yorkshire. The new Conservative government, elected in 1979, wanted to cut subsidies to coal, and thus its use, but U-turned in 1981, giving the miners what they wanted.[31] By 1981 the Conservative government wanted to close what were called 'uneconomic' pits. The miners rebelled, threatening strikes, and a general programme of closures was called off. But mines continued to close, and more were expected to close, especially in Wales and Scotland. In 1984 the miners correctly believed there was a plan to close over seventy pits (a claim denied by the Coal Board and government). They went on strike following the announced closure of Cortonwood colliery in Yorkshire. Despite the long strike, there was no significant loss of electricity production, because of coal stocks, coal imports and the switching of many power stations to oil.[32] This was a very different outcome from the work-to-rule and strikes of the 1970s, which had brought the three-day week and power cuts.

Why did the strike happen at all? Plenty of mines had closed in the 1960s, more than the Conservative government of the 1980s planned to close. As a result, the number of miners in 1984 was a fraction of what it had been in 1954 or 1964. The difference between the 1960s and the 1980s was that this was a closure in the face of mass and rising unemployment. There were no jobs for miners to go to, or their children to go to, as there had been earlier. To leave the pit for the car factory was one thing, for the dole another. 'Coal not Dole' was the slogan of the striking miners.

The strike was a wrenching event. It was a defence of communities, rural rather isolated communities, conservative, and law-abiding, white, patriotic communities. Most miners were not fighting for their own jobs, but for jobs for other miners. They demanded British power stations burn British coal. They became, nevertheless, the 'enemy within', associated in the eyes of the conservative media with violence, picketing and intimidation. That the miners did not have a national ballot was used against them, despite the fact that they voted with their feet. A near-national strike was achieved, by talking, by picketing, by area ballots, and it was without doubt legitimate in the eyes of the strikers: its extraordinary length is eloquent testimony to that. The miners were in fact difficult to organize nationally; there was no national action between 1926 and 1972. The national strikes of the early 1970s were exceptional and were over pay, which affected everyone. Indeed, the National Union of Mineworkers was, despite the name, really a continuation of its predecessor, the Miners' Federation, that is a federation of various local mining unions. In 1977 the union had agreed an area incentive scheme (destroying national solidarity), despite a national ballot against it. This weakness at national level was a reflection of a strength at local level, most obvious in the close links between living and working in mining.

The state, and the Conservative Party, set out to destroy the union. The gloves were off, the assumptions of corporatism finished. Union members were encouraged and financed to bring actions against the union, leading to the quite unprecedented sequestration of its funds. The union was infiltrated, and an extraordinary campaign was launched to unseat the leaderships, one in which the *Daily Mirror* and the secret services were involved. The police were set onto the miners, with on average 4,000 officers (4 per cent of the male police force) policing the strike each day, with many more on some

occasions.[33] The miners were crushed by distinctly continental practices – a shielded and visored police force tore up British liberties
during the strike.[34] Yet this ghastly vista found no strong opposition
on the right, though there was some coded distaste in the 1984 Christmas broadcast from Buckingham Palace.[35] Yet the strike held, and
there was a real possibility of victory. The miners were not doomed,
they were defeated. Had the dockers struck, as they nearly did, and
the National Association of Colliery Overmen, Deputies and Shotfir-
ers (NACODS), as they nearly did, the outcome could very easily
have been different. It would undoubtedly have been messy – for it
would have been a victory against the might of the state, and against
the unsympathetic Labour Party parliamentary leadership, not least
its leader, Neil Kinnock.

The great miners' strike of 1984–5, like the lockout of 1926, was not
an offensive, but a last redoubt, the tail end of a period of some trade
union influence. It was understood by all that a defeat for the miners
was the defeat of the organized working class as a whole, for the left
too. The miners agreed to return to work unconditionally in March
1985, as the drift back became an issue of survival for the union. Their
defeat was complete, but the fight to save mines was not over. The
director Stephen Daldry saw miners marching to save the pits again in
1992 down fashionable Kensington Church Street 'full of antique
shops and coffee shops – and there were people cheering out of their
windows and bringing out tea. Suddenly the miners are the underdogs
and it's OK.'[36] But the sympathy not only came too late, it meant nothing: the mines closed faster than before, and production now fell
quickly.

The 'Britain that found herself' in the South Atlantic did not find
itself to be a nation that included the pit villages of Yorkshire, Scotland or Wales. The defeat of the miners was much more important
than a defeat of organized labour. It marked, more fundamentally,
the end of British economic nationalism, just as the Falklands War
was the last national military operation. Although coal production
remained roughly level till 1990, the defeat of the miners opened up
the possibility of not using British coal at all, but importing it on a
large scale. This is what would happen in the 1990s (see chapter 19).

Figure 18.1: Defence, NHS, education, social security and public investment as percentages of GDP, 1948–2000

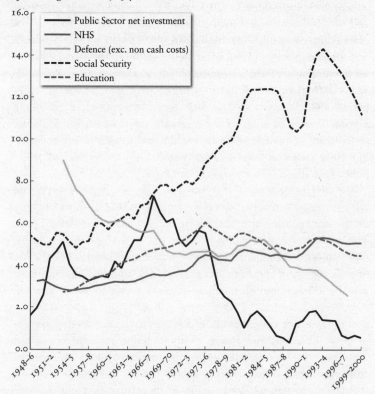

Source: IFS, UK *Historic Government Spending by Area, Guardian* datablog, 18/10/10.

ROLLING BACK WELFARE?

There are those who still believe that the Thatcher governments (1979–90) rolled back the state and cut taxes. In fact Thatcherism at first involved an increase in the proportion of national income passing through the state and an increase in the tax burden. Only income taxes went down, with great publicity – the more-hidden taxes increased. Value Added Tax, a form of purchase tax, was increased and was by comparison with income taxes, regressive, though not quite as regressive as the additional taxes which were levied on alcohol and tobacco. National Insurance, itself regressive, was increased from 5.5 per cent in 1975 (the beginning of National Insurance as a percentage of income up to a limit) to 9 per cent for most of the Thatcher period and increased slightly later too. Furthermore, while many aspects of state funding were cut, notably investment, the Thatcher government in its early years increased spending in absolute and even in relative terms on welfare taken overall. Only in the late 1980s did public spending fall as a proportion of GDP.

The welfare state was transformed, not abolished. After increasing with earnings in the 1950s, 1960s, and 1970s, the incomes of those on the state pension and benefits were quite deliberately left behind. The welfare system provided benefits that were stuck in real terms, representing a decreasing proportion of average earnings.[37] The ratio of unemployment benefit to average earnings, and the basic state pension to average earnings, fell to levels very much lower than in comparable countries. This was not a rejection of a long-standing generous welfare state, but rather a return to the low levels of generosity of the 1940s and 1950s.[38] This fundamental change was not very visible and resulted from the delinking of pensions and benefits from earnings, so that they rose only in line with prices.

Apart from pensions, two areas of increasing expenditure were especially prominent. The first was disability allowances, the result in part of wanting to take people off the unemployed total. The second was housing benefits – a subsidy for landlords – arising from the increasing lack of cheap housing. Total house building was stagnant through the late 1970s, 1980s and 1990s, at half the peak of the mid-1960s. Under Thatcher education and NHS spending as a proportion of GDP fell.

Although local government had been shorn of many powers by the nationalization of the 1940s (in health, electricity, gas), it still retained important functions and a good deal of autonomy. Under the Thatcher governments extraordinary controls were placed on the ability of local authorities to raise taxes (rate-capping), and government grants became a central means of control of local government. Most importantly, they were forced to sell off most of their housing stock, much recently built, and prevented in effect from building much new stock. The government abolished the greatest local authority in the country, the Greater London Council, descendant of the London County Council. Councils were forced to buy services they would once have provided for themselves, part of a much larger trend whereby the state paid for but did not directly supply services of many different kinds. What really changed was not the funding, but the nature of the services and how they were provided, reversing the great nationalizations of the social services of the 1940s.

As well as controlling the level of spending centrally, the government moved to replace the one British property tax, the rates, with, of all things, a poll-tax. Named the 'community charge', it was introduced first in Scotland and then England and Wales, as a fixed charge for local authority services. It was designed just like the old flat-rate National Insurance contribution to act as an automatic restrictor of the level of benefits. The idea, a theoretical one but which aimed to force the poor themselves to reduce expenditure, was that the poor, the hardest hit by the new tax, would vote for lower taxes and thus lower council services. Property was spared, and the poor penalized. It was poor politics, but it gave a good insight into the priorities of the government. It lasted only a few years, having been a factor in the ejecting of Mrs Thatcher from the premiership in 1990.

The Thatcher governments clamped down on educational spending (the province of local authorities) and also introduced centralizing reforms. In a distinctly continental move teaching content was directed through a National Curriculum, in the context of British history a remarkable turnaround. It was introduced in stages, starting in 1989. At the same time a rather more hidden revolution was to take place – although the school-leaving age remained at sixteen, many more students began to stay on, especially from the late 1980s. The expansion in secondary education increased demand for higher education, which had been reined back in the early 1980s.

Thus began, in the late 1980s especially, an unexpected expansion in publicly funded higher education. In a British university city of 1950, there might be fifty professors; fifty years later there might be 1,000. In 1950 the university might have been a small feature of a bustling industrial city centre; in the post-industrial city the university might be one of the major employers, and the middle-class students a motor of the town's economy. Universities, once close to production and associated with a certain austerity, were now congregations of up-market consumers.

The expansion took place in a new ideological context, and a new more controlling funding regime. In the early 1990s the binary divide between local authority polytechnics and the independently chartered universities was dissolved. This removed the former polytechnics from the local authorities, but subjected the older universities to oversight which had been more familiar in the polytechnics. Universities would in a short time become (again) conformist institutions, their vice chancellors not representatives of learning, but managers of vast enterprises and property portfolios. The massified university, irony of ironies, was put in place by the inheritors of those who believed more is worse.

PROPERTY'S PROGRESS

Although the economy continued to grow in the 1980s and 1990s, it did not do so as in the 1950s and 1960s by the expansion of manufacturing and by the growth of large manufacturing firms. Manufacturing output was at best stagnant, and manufacturing employment was falling very rapidly. Firms shrank in size, yet returns on investment increased. The stock market boomed. The rich simply got richer by being rich. A key minimal indicator was that real interest rates (interest rates discounting inflation) were exceptionally high – at levels last seen in the 1920s. This was a very marked contrast to the negative real rates of the 1970s, the

Figure 18.2: Inflation and interest rates, 1900–2000

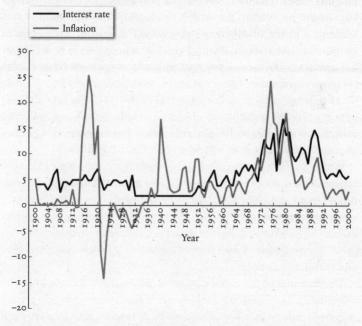

Source: http://www.economicshelp.org/blog/1485/interest-rates/historical-real-interest-rate/.

low rates of the 1950s and 1960s, and the negative rates of the 1940s. This in itself yielded a powerful trickle-up of income and wealth and power. Property, capital and wealth were once again central.[39]

The 1980s saw a massive reversal of the long trend culminating in the 1970s towards increasing equality in income and wealth. Inequality was driven by higher unemployment, by lower rates of benefit, by the pushing-down of wages and by increases in the returns to capital in many forms. The greatest and easiest rewards came from ownership of property, not work, much less building a business. The massive rise in house prices, temporarily halted in 1987, and the early 1990s, meant that many in the middle class accumulated capital in larger annual increments than their salaries. They made money simply by sitting in the right sort of homes. House price inflation was the one kind of inflation that seemed to be liked; just as the mortgage was the exception to the remaining social prejudice against debt. The tax relief on mortgage interest grew to a gigantic subsidy for the middle classes and, for those owning homes outright, boosted their value. Here was the new politics of property in action, a profoundly unproductive politics.

With vast elite salaries and rising investment incomes came new tastes and new outlooks, or rather the renewal of old haute-bourgeoise taste. Opera and elegant restaurants expanded. A new anti-egalitarian snobbism was permissible, a certain reactionary chic possible. Private schools thrived. Money and merit tightened their grip on each other. Houses divided into flats became houses once more; servants and nannies returned.

This renewal of the elite bears some exploration because one self-presentation and indeed analysis of Thatcherism and its effects suggested otherwise. Was Thatcherism a revolt against rulers or a rulers' revolt? Much was made of the claim that both Thatcher herself, seen as incorrigibly middle-class and unrefined, and Thatcherism challenged the ruling class, that business now trumped aristocracy, and merit the old school tie. There is something in this in as much as the state-oriented high bourgeoisie, in the limited sense of 'the establishment' – the top echelons of the BBC, the universities and the civil service, the gentlemen of *The Times*, the heads of great professions – saw their status and power fall. Furthermore, it was suggested that there was a downgrading of the leaders of manufacturing and an elevation of financiers. Yet this should not be overdone. The House of Lords did not fight for the old order – it was overwhelmingly, until 1999, a Conservative-voting body that followed the party line. The BBC, never radical, was hardly even neutral in, say, the miners' strike and was put firmly under the control of government sympathizers in 1986 and 1987. The Confederation of British Industry remained close to and very supportive of the main thrust of policy.[40]

There is some evidence of hostility from the monarchy and more importantly to the monarchy from the guardians of the new order. In 1986 journalists briefed by Palace officials wrote that the queen was concerned about the policies of the government, not merely about its resistance to the Commonwealth view on sanctions against South Africa, but also about damage that was being done to social cohesion at home, not least in the coalfields.[41] Certainly there was a fresh critique of monarchy in the air. From the left Tom Nairn launched a scintillating attack on the notion that the monarchy was irrelevant. It was in his view at the absolute core of a diseased and decaying nationalism and elite. The new right came to agree, and the Murdoch press in particular destroyed much of the mystique of monarchy. There was much tut-tutting about an intrusive press gawping at the private affairs of Prince Charles and Diana, Princess of Wales, until the rare moment of honesty which revealed the 'War of the Waleses' involved both sides putting essentially true stories into their favoured newspapers. By the mid-1990s royalty was indeed in a very different place in the public eye. A BBC *Panorama* interview in 1995, in which the Princess of Wales dished the dirt, would have been unthinkable in 1985. Diana's death in August 1997 unleashed an emotional response from the public unheard of in recent history, which put the monarchy in more danger than it had ever been in since the nineteenth century. Yet it was a revolt of celebrity against crown, not of a republican spirit.

Generally the elite presented a united front: old and new both prospered together as both were changed.

19

A Nation Lost

*... when American and Japanese companies invest in
Europe, we are their first choice. Britain no longer has an
overmanned, inefficient, backward manufacturing sector,
but modern, dynamic industries.*

Margaret Thatcher's last House of Commons
contribution as prime minister, 1990[1]

*Free trade is the greatest force for prosperity and
peaceful cooperation ... I would like to see the European
Community – embracing ... the former Communist countries to its East – agree to develop an Atlantic free trade area
with the United States.*

Margaret Thatcher, speech at The Hague, 1992[2]

While UK Ltd had certainly existed, UK plc very quickly did not. As
a phrase, 'UK plc' suggested a tough-minded approach to the nation,
a nation competing economically with other nations. Its duty was to
export, its beating heart was manufacturing industry. However, the
idea of a national economy, the economic nation, became ever less
important from the late 1980s. A new kind of economy emerged in
which there was no longer any concern for national champions, for
the ownership even of firms operating within the UK, or the balance
of payments. From the 1990s talk of any problem in productivity had
become much more muted, though some, such as the future Labour
chancellor Gordon Brown, saw low productivity as a continuing British problem.

In one sense there was a return to the cosmopolitanism and free

Figure 19.1: Percentage of UK stock market owned by foreign capital, by value, 1963–2000

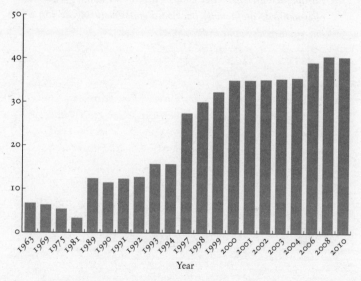

Source: ONS, *Ownership of UK Quoted Shares: 2010* (ONS, 2012), figure 3.

Figure 19.2: Real GDP, logged, 1948–99 (£ billion)

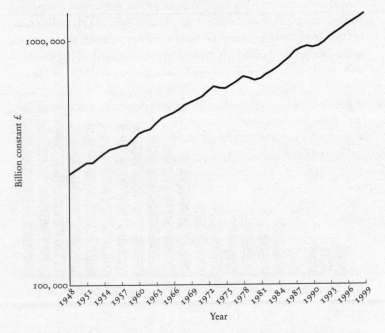

Source: ONS, *Long-term profile of Gross Domestic Product (GDP) in the*
UK, release August 2013.

trade of the Edwardian years. But there was a profound difference. At the beginning of the century a small measure of democracy, strong national sovereignty and integration into the world market could be combined, in the British case at least. In 1914 British capital owned the infrastructure, the banks, the ships, the communications of half the world; it was flush with the incomes of these investments. But in 2000 London was not a centre for the export of capital, but a tax haven attracting it. The United Kingdom was, to an extent not known before, owned by foreigners – the big City institutions, the service companies, the infrastructure operators, the car makers, even the chocolate makers were now owned abroad. Global capitalism was unleashed into the United Kingdom, but British capitalism itself suffered. What had been unleashed was not British entrepreneurial genius, but that of foreigners. What Mrs Thatcher and above all her successors did was to change the country and the economy, but not its relative economic standing in the world. Now the question arose for the United Kingdom as for any other nation – was it possible to combine democracy, national sovereignty and integration into the new world economy?[3]

Of all this, politics could take only passing cognisance, by invoking clichéd terms such as 'globalization' and 'neo-liberalism'. The terms 'entrepreneurship' and 'innovation' were bandied around, implying a transformation in the supply side of the British economy. The economy was now 'post-industrial', a creative or 'knowledge' economy. Thus a powerful contrast was implied between the post-war settlement, social democracy, consensus, Keynesianism, welfarism and the new neo-liberalism. But what had changed the most was what this analysis did not deign to discuss – the instruments of industrial policy, trade, trade union legislation, taxation and much else. Nor did 'neo-liberalism' as a notion speak to the realities of a transformed economy. It sometimes meant little more than the free market, at others (rather oddly) a rationalizing, technocratic state.[4] What had changed above all were assumptions about the nature of a national economy, the nationality of capital and indeed even of machines. There were still important nationally-organized elements, an increased welfare budget notably, but overall the economy was thought of and acted on in a radically less national way.

A NEW BRITISH CAPITALISM?

The late 1980s, and especially the 1990s, saw a change in elite self-understanding. For many, Thatcher had saved the country, reversed the decline, made Britain great again. This revivalism was as unfounded as the declinism of earlier years. There might have been a minor temporary small change in relative performance with respect to the richer parts of Europe, but the relative decline with respect to the rest of the world continued. The rate of growth of the economy was not greatly changed by the liberalization and globalization since the 1980s. To be sure, from the depths of the early 1980s, the rate of growth was slightly higher than the post-war average, but never enough to make up for the effect of the depression. Growth from the late 1980s was at a lower rate than that in the long boom of the 1950s and 1960s (See figure 19.2). To put it another way, the average rate of growth of the economy was higher and steadier in the years 1948–79 than between 1979 and 2000. Looking at the United Kingdom comparatively shows that in 2000 it still lagged behind the European leaders in labour productivity. Compared to France and Germany, GDP per hour worked was in these countries 20 per cent higher in 2000 than in the UK.[5] If the problem the United Kingdom had was poor growth, and low labour productivity, the changes of the 1980s and 1990s did little to change this.

If the problem to be solved was a weakness in the balance of payments, as many had suggested in the 1970s and before, the record since 1979 was catastrophic. Before the 1970s the British economy was in fact generally in surplus on the current account, while in the last decades of the twentieth century it was generally in deep deficit. In particular, to take the net figures, the United Kingdom went, from the early 1980s, into a permanent and very large trade deficit in manufactures. None of this was a matter of concern; in itself it was a marker of a change in economic thinking and practice. In nationalist political economy the balance of payments was talked of as if it were a national profit and loss account. In the new internationalist political economy, it was merely a record of the net flow of one kind of money, necessarily balanced by inward flows in the capital account.

Finally, if the problem was unemployment – 'Labour isn't working' was the nice, ambiguous slogan the Conservatives used on a 1978 poster – the record was disastrous. Not only did it climb to nearly 4 million, it did not return to 1970s levels until the twenty-first century. Unemployment was one cause of a heroin and crack cocaine use explosion from the 1980s onwards – heroin and cocaine had been in much more limited use in the 1960s and 1970s, concentrated among students. Unemployment, and the new hard-drug epidemic among the young unemployed, among other factors, drove a relentless increase in crime, which peaked in the early 1990s.[6] Drugs and criminality were very much more significant in the late 1980s and 1990s than during the supposedly lax and permissive 1960s and 1970s. The prison population surged by more than 20 per cent from the early 1990s to 2000 – 'prison works' was the policy. By the end of the century there were roughly half as many prisoners as there were hospital beds.

One unexpected development was a remarkable expansion in financial services which radically changed the nature of the elite, and of the capital city. It was the product of the liberalization of many activities especially in and around the London Stock Exchange. Stock Exchange membership had been limited to UK firms, which were restricted to particular activities, and charged cartelized prices. In 1983 the decision was taken to introduce a wholly new regime all at once in 1986 – hence the name, 'Big Bang'. In this case deregulation, unlike in most other cases, really did lead to new business on a huge scale, to huge increases in employment as well. There was a much larger change in the City, which grew as a centre for the trading of offshore dollars and other financial transactions on a global scale. The City sold itself as an exporter of 'financial services'.[7] But it was not British-owned businesses which prospered most, but giant foreign banks which moved in, taking over small enterprises, and transforming the culture of the City from a leisurely, gentlemanly one to something distinctively meritocratic and money-driven and American. It operated within the EEC, as well as within a wider global economy. The power of the City was not a left-over, but something new and not particularly British.

The Big Bang, and other developments, transformed London. The City rebuilt the city. It had been a city in decline: its population had been falling since the war, reaching a trough in 1981. Its expansion as a financial centre was a key factor in driving up population, and indeed diversifying it. The financial sector spread from the City eastwards, into those parts of London which had been the home to the docks. The London that had traded things became the London that traded money. Trading in money yielded huge salaries for a few. At the very top end of the City, young men (typically) could earn not simply a lot more than their fathers, but could imagine earning in a year what their fathers earned in a lifetime as, say, a bank manager.

One important change not noticed was the displacement of national elites, old and new, by a new cosmopolitan elite. In the first *Sunday Times* Rich List, that of 1989, its publication in itself a notable indicator of a change in the treatment of wealth in the public sphere, the richest were British. In the top ten, the British rich with interests primarily in the United Kingdom were the queen, the duke of Westminster, the Sainsbury family, Sir John Moores, the Vestey family and Sir James Goldsmith. Two others, including Garfield Weston of Associated British Foods, were rich through British interests. A decade later most of these were still in the top twenty. But of that top twenty fewer than half were British with mainly British interests, of which only one was a manufacturer, Sir Anthony Bamford of JCB. The United Kingdom was now the residence of rich people from around the world, with interests largely outside the United Kingdom, for example, the steel magnate Lakshmi Mittal, who did not own British steel mills. It was far removed from the kind of capital the Thatcherites dreamed of – a dynamic *British* capitalism, perhaps even manufacturing capital.

We can get a sense of the profound changes in the direction of capital by returning to the London Stock Exchange. This market in shares boomed through the 1980s, and especially the late 1990s. The FTSE 100 index, created in 1984, and accounting for the bulk of the stock market by value, surged to a peak in December 1999. It did this because investors had come to believe in what was called the New Economy. Extraordinary price to earnings ratios resulted as investors piled into enterprises which ultimately found the laws of economic gravity all too real. The bubble burst, and the FTSE 100 did not reach these unsupported heights again for more than a decade.

Over that time the composition of the index changed. In 1984 the largest firms by capitalization on the London Stock Exchange included a number of manufacturing companies, most of whose workers were in the United Kingdom. Some, such as Imperial Chemical Industries, once without doubt British, now had half their employees abroad, some, such as BAT, a much higher proportion. But most of the others were more British than multinational in their workforces, notably GEC, an enterprise employing more than 130,000 in the UK, by far the largest manufacturer in the UK.

In 2000 the composition of the index was very different. Firstly, most of the large firms in the FTSE 100 were much less representative of economic activity within the United Kingdom. Most of the top manufacturing firms in the FTSE 100 had more employees abroad than in the United Kingdom. This was almost certainly true of the large pharmaceutical companies with headquarters in the UK like Astra-Zeneca and GlaxoSmithKline. Large overseas employment was also typical of the oil companies, some of the main banks (HSBC and Barclays), service companies such as Compass, and Serco, and even supermarkets such as Tesco. Even a company such as Rolls-Royce had perhaps a third of its employees overseas; the arms firms BAE, inheritor of the airframe and military electronics industries, had more than half its employees overseas. The national companies were firms like Sainsbury, Lloyds Bank, Marks and Spencer.[8]

A second critical point is that the London Stock Exchange was a place where the global elite invested, not just the British elite. By the end of the twentieth century nearly 40 per cent was owned by overseas owners (see figure 19.1). Remarkably, for all the rhetorical ambition under Thatcher to create a share-owning democracy, the proportion of shares held by individuals was lower in 1989 than in 1975 and would fall even lower, down from 38 per cent in 1975 to 16 per cent in 2000.[9] The controllers of British capitalism were no longer necessarily in the City of London, and if they were, they were no longer necessarily British.

A third – and this was perhaps the most critical and least understood point – was that very many of the large employers in the United Kingdom were no longer in the FTSE 100. They were often listed on foreign stock exchanges, or not listed at all. The FTSE cannot include the US and European and other investment banks in London, the foreign owners of energy infrastructure, the owners of the motor car industry and much else besides, which as we shall see came to hold a new and vitally important place in the British economy.

One should not assume that British capitalism became more successful at the global level, whatever its fate at home. Of the top fifty global companies by revenue in the recent past, only one and a half were British: the Anglo-Dutch Royal Dutch Shell and BP, both very old oil companies. In a listing by market capitalization these would also be in the top fifty with at other recent times perhaps Vodafone or HSBC. In short, the United Kingdom no longer stood out as the headquarters of more large global enterprises by size than, say, France or Germany. Internationally it is where one would expect a country of its size and wealth to be. Nationally, however, it was not. In no other major capitalist economy was there no approximation to a national major car firm, chemical firm, electrical engineering or electronic firm operating on its territory. Nor did it have any large 'technology' companies like Facebook or Google. Whatever it did, the programme of Thatcher, Major and Blair did not revive a decaying British national capitalism, but rather brought the benefits of international capitalism to the United Kingdom.

The opening up and expansion of the EEC was of fundamental importance. The United Kingdom joined the six, with Ireland and Denmark, in 1973. But the European Union, as the new body was called following the Treaty on European Union (the Maastricht Treaty of 1992), was very much larger than the EEC the United Kingdom joined. Greece (1981), Spain, Portugal (1986), Sweden, Finland and Austria (1992) had joined, as well as the former GDR (1990). The 1986 Single European Act, strongly supported by the Conservative government, aimed to remove all sorts of non-tariff barriers within the expanding Community, changes which came into full effect in 1992. These were transformative developments leading to a radical liberalization of European trade, in the context of more liberalized global trade. From 1992, trade within the European Union was as free as it was previously within national economies. Technical norms, specifications and all the hidden apparatus of trade and regulation were the province of the EU, an instance of a politically rather invisible change with major administrative and economic consequences. The white dominions, once so central to British trade, were now minor trading partners, but Canada, Australia and New Zealand now had a combined population comparable to that of the United Kingdom. Indeed, in terms of global heft we would do well to think of the United Kingdom at the end of the twentieth century as a large Canada rather than, say, a small United States of America.

THE NEW ECONOMY

This opening of markets was of significance in ways that grew less visible as it became the norm. For example, it would have been unthinkable in the 1950s and 1960s to have our telephones or cars or computers made abroad or by foreign companies. Now it was unthinkable to deprive the British consumer of such devices. There was a great internationalization of British life, well expressed in the case of elite football. In the 1980s it was rare but not unknown to have foreign-born players, for example the Argentine Ossie Ardiles. In the early 1990s, around 70 per cent of top English league players were English. However, by 2000 the proportion was down to fewer than half.[10] Boxing Day 1999 saw Chelsea start a premier league match with an entirely foreign XI on the pitch. Among the greats of the 1990s were the Frenchmen Eric Cantona and Thierry Henry. Furthermore, the United Kingdom, once an exporter of football managers, started importing them towards the end of the 1990s, especially to the biggest teams – notably Arsène Wenger at Arsenal and Ruud Gullit and Gianluca Vialli, both player-managers at Chelsea.

Trade was no longer a matter of importing food and raw materials and exporting manufactures. It was a swirl across political (rather than economic) boundaries of everything from food to manufactures. Indeed, such was the movement of components that to speak of the nationality of a motor car made little sense. A vast service industry grew up importing, storing, distributing and retailing manufactures from abroad. The jobs they provided in, say, a warehouse, or driving a lorry, were less skilled than the average of the older manufacturing

Figure 19.3: United Kingdom estimated gross value added by sector at constant prices, 1948–2000 (£m)

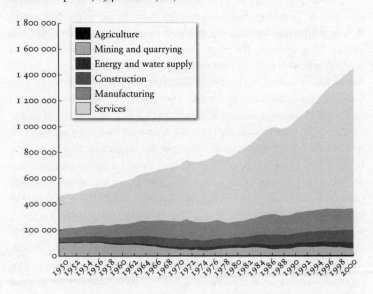

Source: Estimated from ONS, UK GDP(O) low level aggregates (Q2 1916 edition). Industry classification SIC2003.

jobs and were highly routinized. The new and expanding retailers were now the largest employers of labour, not the old manufacturing firms. The retailers, and their warehouses, were, with the partial exception of food stores, emporia of foreign manufactures.

In this new world, importing ports were now central once more, but this time were an invisible feature of the British economy. New importing ports for manufactures were built, such as Thames Port and Sheerness, sometimes on the sites of older industrial enterprises like oil refineries, which imported raw materials. A whole new method of importing came into being with the creation of the Channel Tunnel. This long-discussed venture came of age in the late 1980s. It was 'high time we became involved in an industrial enterprise of this scale' was the sentiment expressed about the Channel Tunnel by Mrs Thatcher in 1984, as long as it was privately funded. She herself was keen on a road tunnel, but it was not to be.[11] Instead it was a railway tunnel, which took passenger trains, freight trains and, by special train, freight lorries too. Opened in 1994 it in effect became a major new port, handling nearly 20 million tonnes by 2000. From the point of view of the private investors the Tunnel was a costly failure. The private sector could also produce white elephants but at least this one was useable. Airports, too, became enormous places moving millions of people and increasingly goods too. By the end of the twentieth century more people were employed, about three times as many indeed, within the perimeter of Heathrow airport as had been employed within the port of London at its peak.

Another rapidly expanding sector also dealing with things was the many-faceted food supply system. By 2000 the streets of British cities had been transformed by the appearance of astonishing numbers of places to drink and eat. The selling of food – standardized branded food, though some prepared within the shops – took off, replacing all manner of older businesses. Labour intensive, profitable and expensive compared to home preparation, but cheaper than formal restaurants and cafés, coffee and sandwich shops were now everywhere. Catering businesses (canteens, restaurants, coffee shops, etc.) were now employing more than food and drink retailers, each more than 1 million.[12] The United Kingdom had become a land of servers, waiters and cooks, not of shopkeepers but of shop-workers.

Then there were the service industries as they are more usually thought of – the retail banks, the estate agencies, the call centres. By 2000, armies of proletarianized office workers and call-centre operatives were making a mockery of the earlier notion that white-collar work was superior in status to a manual manufacturing job.

Finally, there were the public sector and publicly financed service jobs. They were far more important than a politically driven picture of the recent past would suggest. The welfare state continued to grow, and the United Kingdom was far more of a welfare state in 2000 than in 1990 or 1980.[13] In both absolute and relative terms such spending was high at the end of the twentieth century (and higher still in 2018). British state expenditure has never been as welfare oriented as in 2000 (or 2018).[14] Increasing welfare expenditures by the state were a significant aspect of the rise of the 'service economy'. Benefits represented 10 per cent of GDP and health 5 per cent in 2000. State education, too, was an expanding industry (see figure 18.1). The welfare state peaked at a time it was supposed no longer to exist.

The result of the rise of necessarily local service provision and an expanding national welfare system was that there remained an important national element in the economy. It was, however, very different from the earlier situation when the national impinged very much more generally across the economy.

The economy continued to grow from the 1970s, if not at such a sustained pace as before. Between 1975 and 2000 total income nearly doubled. Society was affluent as never before, more devoted to consumption than ever. Superior goods, often more expensive ones, drove out inferior ones. Holidays overseas replaced a week in Blackpool or Skegness. The pet budgerigar, a little parrot from Australia, was on its way out. 3.3 million were kept as pets in 1965, and only 1 million in 2000 and falling. By contrast, the more expensive dogs increased from 4.7 million to 6.1 million and cats were overtaking, growing from 4.1 million to 8 million, between the same dates.[15] On average, life became very much fuller of things. The quality of food and services generally increased.

While seen from the perspective of the economic nationalist much of the discussion above would have a critical tenor, from the internationalist perspective it is a story of progress, of equalization across now disappearing economic boundaries. It was surely a good thing that efficient foreign enterprises drove out poor British ones. Didn't the quality of football improve? What did the nationality of capital matter to workers, a left internationalist would say. British people now had access on a routine basis to the goods of Europe and to a lesser extent the world, and more goods than ever before. That made the British economy, and society, much like that of the rest of Europe, in particular, in a way it had never been before. There were other benefits. The British people were free of the huge burdens of arms spending and of the techno-nationalist delusions that led to wasting resources, which could otherwise have provided prosaic pleasures for millions. Openness to the world, to other people as well as other things, brought many benefits, and much happiness. The new internationalized economy was overall more productive than the old national one. There were indeed good reasons to believe that things could only get better.

We need, partly to complete our story, partly to illustrate further how profound the changes had been, to return to the economic activities which were at the core of British life into the 1970s: energy, agriculture and manufacturing. In each there was an extraordinary transformation as well as *relative* decline in their place in the economy.

ENERGY AND AGRICULTURE

Returning newly nationalized manufacturing companies to the private sector or selling shareholdings in oil companies was one thing. Selling utilities, most built up by the state and state agencies from even before the 1940s, was another thing altogether. Here matters of principle were more obviously important, and measures had to be taken to prevent abuse of monopoly power. Privatization in this sector also involved another element – that of direct sale to small investors, as an attempt to create what was called a 'share-owning democracy'. It concerned essentially two privatizations only. The first was that of British Telecom, formerly part of the Post Office, which came at the end of 1984. Just over 50 per cent was sold, for £4 billion.

This was followed by the massive £7 billion privatization of British Gas in 1986. The other utilities would not be privatized until the 1990s.[16]

That the opening up of markets and the ending of protections for British industries were central can be clearly seen in the case of energy supply. From a national perspective one might assume that the decline in British coal mining was due to a process of modernization by which coal was replaced by more modern fuels. But coal was not a fuel of the past. At a global level its use was increasing. In the United Kingdom usage was dropping slowly. In the new energy regime coal was far from redundant, but British coal and British miners were.

Coal remained essential to electricity supply. Apart from nuclear reactors ordered in the 1970s the only new capacity came from cheap and quickly built combined-cycle gas turbine power stations, powered by North Sea gas. All the rest of the electricity supply system in place in 2000 consisted of 'legacy assets'; the focus was on 'sweating inherited assets', rather than creating new ones.[17] At the core were the coal-powered stations of the 1960s and 1970s. From the early 1990s the consumption of coal in these power stations fell from a position close to the peak to, by 2000, the level of around 1960.

The second great change was that coal for these stations now came from abroad, though this was barely noticed. By 2001 more coal was imported (35½ million tonnes) than was produced (32 million tonnes); the level of home production was equivalent to that of the very early nineteenth century. Coal imports were at levels similar to the coal exports of the 1930s. So large were they that they increased the overall bulk of British imports to unprecedented levels.[18] By 2000 Grimsby/Immingham overtook London as the busiest port by bulk, not least because of this. It had once been one of the great coal-exporting ports. Even in the 1970s British Steel and the National Coal Board had built a new *export* dock for coal and steel there alongside a major oil import centre for new refineries built nearby, and for iron ore. The same story was repeated elsewhere. Hunterston, built as an iron-ore-importing facility to supply the blast furnaces at Ravenscraig, became a coal-importing port, connected by rail to both Scottish and English power stations.

Mrs Thatcher, her government and the nationalized CEGB wanted to import coal from the 1980s, but it did not happen quickly. It was

only in 1993, when coal contracts had to be renewed by a newly privatized electricity industry, that the prospect for British coal became
catastrophic. In the face of political pressure (the defeated miners of
1993, and miners who had worked through the strike, had more sympathy than the striking miners of 1984–5 had), a partial reprieve was
engineered by the government.[19] But it was only temporary, and
domestic coal production continued downwards. A barely existing
coal mining industry was privatized in 1994, or rather the operation
of remaining mines – the huge liabilities remained in the public sector. There were now only 7,000 miners, down from 50,000 or so in
1990, and a mere one-hundredth of the employment of around 1950.

Liberalization and internationalization of energy could have
destroyed British national nuclear supply as well. However, government was more concerned to protect the nuclear reactors than the
coal mines. In the late 1980s privatization plans for the CEGB
included one company with the nuclear 'fleet' and another without.
Since no one wanted the nuclear part, plans were changed, and the
nuclear stations remained in state ownership. The efficiency of the
AGRs improved radically, because the managers were now interested
in doing this, as opposed to arguing for PWRs.[20] British Energy,
which had only AGRs and the one PWR, and promised to build no
more, was privatized in 1996; the price achieved revealed that the
AGRs were valued at zero.[21] The market, not rational public or
expert inquiry, stopped the nuclear juggernaut.[22] The state was left
with the retiring Magnox stations of the 1960s and their clean-up
costs. Indeed, nuclear waste management was a case of a costly last
gasp of techno-nationalist enthusiasm for nuclear. In 1978 parliament (with cross-party support) approved the construction of the
THORP nuclear reprocessing plant at Windscale (following a large
public inquiry) – the plant was not completed until 1994 and closed
in the next century, having amassed huge losses.

The national technocrats who had once had so much power were
destroyed by liberalization and privatization. A singular case was
state nuclear physicist Walter Marshall. He was, unusually for a British nuclear baron, an advocate of the PWR and was appointed to run
the CEGB by Margaret Thatcher, who also wanted many of these
US-designed reactors. He was instrumental in getting the CEGB

ready for the miners' strike. He kept the lights on and was rewarded with elevation to the House of Lords. But the government decided to break up the CEGB in order to privatize it in parts, as we have seen, and he resigned. Sir Denis Rooke, a chemical engineer of distinction, ran British Gas. Unlike Marshall, he succeeded in keeping British Gas as one, on technical grounds. But it too was later broken up. Many of the bits would end up in the hands of European companies. The electricity generator Powergen was taken over by the German E.On in 2002, National Power by RWE, again German, in the same year and Scottish Power by the Spanish Iberdrola in 2006. British Energy, which had the AGRs and the PWR, collapsed in 2004 and was effectively renationalized; it was then sold on to the French nationalized company EDF, Electricité de France.

In the case of food the dynamics of internationalization were rather different. Agriculture was under an EEC regime, the common agricultural policy, not a national one. British agriculture, as part of Common Market agriculture, was protected by a high common external tariff and supported by subsidies. As a result it did very much better than coal mining. By 2000 there were still around 200,000 farm workers, but there were hardly any coal miners left. By 2000 self-sufficiency in food diminished from its peak in the 1980s, though it was still much higher than in the 1950s. What was radically different from the 1950s was the source of imports. They now generally came from the EU. Indeed, there was a continentalization of British food tastes. With imported Mediterranean foods, from citrus to tomatoes to avocados, aubergines and courgettes, the British diet became varied and interesting. Tea consumption fell, while coffee increased, beer gave way to wine, potatoes to pasta. Where bottled mineral water had once been rare, in a country with good drinking water, pointless French and Italian mineral waters were now everywhere. Yet the United Kingdom remained a significant exporter of food, mainly to the EU. It sold grains and meat and more. The case of beef is exemplary of what would have been unthinkable in 1950. In the mid-1990s the United Kingdom was almost wholly self-sufficient in beef, with one-third of production exported. However, because of the intensive production methods which led to the BSE

Figure 19.4: UK manufacturing output, 1948–2014

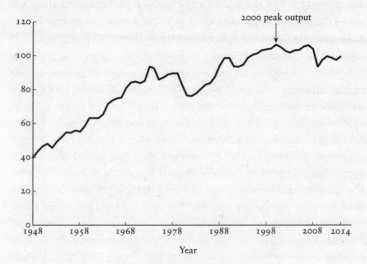

Source: ONS data via BBC, http://www.bbc.co.uk/news/
business-35414075, accessed 29 January 2018.

infections, the EEC responded with a ban of exports (partial in 1990, full in 1996), causing total exports to fall to nearly nil. There was an extraordinary massification and mass production of food, largely hidden away, a story exemplified by the rise of chicken meat to dominate meat consumption.

MANUFACTURING

In 1980 Dr Sir Monty Finniston, a metallurgist, and a former head of British Steel, reported on the engineering profession, calling his report *Engineering Our Future*. It argued for the centrality of manufacturing in national terms. One of its recommendations was that 'The national objective should be to produce as many engineers as possible.'[23] Such naive techno-nationalism would by the 1990s seem risible. Manufacturing was no longer regarded as central, and there was little or no concern with the nationality of manufacturing firms.

Manufacturing did not decline; but it too was transformed. Manufacturing output was in 2000 higher than ever before, though the rate of growth from the 1970s had been low. Between 1948 and the early 1970s, output doubled. Between then and 2000, it increased only by about 10 per cent (see figure 19.4). Manufacturing became less visible not because it produced less, but because it employed many fewer people, and because it was a smaller part of the economy. There was nothing uniquely British about this development. Nearly all rich countries saw increases in manufacturing output, falls in manufacturing employment and falls in manufacturing as a proportion of GDP. However, in the 1950s and 1960s the United Kingdom was clearly a nation with an especially heavy bias towards manufacturing (comparable only to Germany). By the 1990s it was a nation with a comparatively weak manufacturing sector. It was not like Germany and Japan; it was now clearly much more like the USA or France. History is not destiny.

Most of the leading sectors of manufacturing had been rescued by nationalization in the 1970s. As in the case of utilities, many were then made very much smaller under public ownership in anticipation of privatization. British Aerospace, nationalized in 1977, was privatized in 1981 but relied on an expanding arms budget. The state-owned British Shipbuilders closed half its yards by 1982. In 1985 the profitable warship yards were sold as a group; in the meantime the remaining civil yards were sold or closed individually. British Steel also saw huge cutbacks under public ownership. Following the 1980 national steel strike, the industry was rapidly shrunk, though with huge subsidies continuing to, for example, keep Ravenscraig going. Privatization of a much smaller but profitable British Steel came in 1988; Ravenscraig, a huge plant started in the 1950s, closed in 1992. Between 1980 and 2000, British steel production was roughly constant at just over half the peak levels of 1970 or so, but employment in 2000 was one-third of what it had been in 1980.

The great cutbacks in the workforce and in plants in the nationalized British Leyland had started under Labour. The investment of the 1970s paid off in the launch of the Metro in 1980, made on a new robotic assembly line completed at Longbridge in 1979. It was launched with an extraordinary nationalist TV advertising campaign – it was 'A British car to beat the world', the means to fight back against the recent invasion of the United Kingdom by the Italians, Germans, Japanese and the French. The advertisement showed them repulsed by Metros landing on a beach from Second World War landing craft, with 'Rule Britannia' playing in the background.[24] The company was sold to BAe in 1988. The Metro was its last British-designed car. Far from the invasion being repulsed, more and more imported cars came in; on top of that, foreign car companies were invited to produce in the UK such that there were soon no all-British car producers at all. While the United Kingdom became more and more motorized, that ceased to be driven by domestic car manufacturing.

Rolls-Royce and its large civil engine, the RB211, had been saved by nationalization in 1971. The engine proved to be very developable and led to many subtypes and the Trent engine, which were all to be successes. These were financed by government, who also underwrote the losses. In the mid-1980s the company became profitable. It was privatized in 1987 and continued to receive 'launch aid' to finance engine development. Rolls-Royce's engines gave it nearly one-half of the world's civil engine market, an astonishing development, unthinkable without the hundreds of millions of pounds in state support it received.

There was a powerful techno-nationalist streak in Mrs Thatcher's thinking and certainly that of her government. This worried one thoughtful economist.[25] There were in fact expensive and ambitious programmes for fifth-generation computing (the Alvey programme) and much muscular discussion about the need for new technology, a new culture and new ambitious national capitalism. 'Information Technology' became the new buzzword, the focus of British state-supported R&D indeed.[26] However, Margaret Thatcher's time in office disproved the persistent and silly belief that more scientists in high office means more money for research and greater enthusiasm for its results. Across government, and industry, with the exception at first of the military, research budgets were cut back. Far from releasing the innovative energies of the private sector, what happened was that companies no longer felt obliged to do research for national reasons, and national champions and their R&D programmes went by the board. She may have been a nationalist, and a scientist, but she presided over the end of significant British techno-nationalism.

As well as falling manufacturing employment the other obvious change has been that the United Kingdom became a net importer of manufactures. This was a shocking development for the former workshop of the world, but more especially for those brought up on the notion that a net positive manufacturing balance was needed to then import food and raw materials. But although the net balance went strongly negative, British manufacturing exports increased, though imports increased very much more. There was a related change these figures did not in themselves capture. The United Kingdom's manufacturing exports now included many parts made abroad, and its imports might well include parts made in the United Kingdom. Neither the balance of trade nor the import or export quantities meant what they once did. The United Kingdom manufacturing economy barely existed as a unit – firms and factories in the United Kingdom now operated in a much larger non-national economic arena.

Motor vehicles make this very clear. For most of the twentieth century the United Kingdom was the most significant car-using and car-producing place in Europe. By 2000 production in Germany and France (both richer countries) and poorer Spain was far higher than in the United Kingdom. In the early 1970s a mostly British vehicle industry was still a net exporter. In 2000 the United Kingdom imported 1.8 million vehicles through Grimsby/Immingham, Bristol, Southampton, London and Medway and exported 1.2 million (much more than in the 1960s), with London and Southampton docks dominating.[27] In 2000 imports of motor vehicles accounted for 65 per cent of home demand and 45 per cent of home demand plus exports. Production in the United Kingdom was undertaken in a largely European market where raw materials, components and finished vehicles moved freely, and in which the British economy was a net importer of components, just as it was of finished cars.

The industry within the United Kingdom was nearly all foreign-owned. The main British-owned enterprise (formerly British Leyland, renamed Rover) had been part privatized in 1984, when it was already producing Japanese-designed cars. In 1994 it was sold on to the German company BMW, which in 1999 sold it all off, except Cowley. The remainder, the historic Longbridge plant, was essentially closed, though sold on to a Chinese car company. Nissan started manufacturing in a new factory in Sunderland in 1986; within a decade it had produced a million cars and a million engines. In Swindon, Honda started producing engines in 1989 and cars in 1992. Toyota started manufacturing in 1992, with an engine plant in Deeside and a car plant in Derbyshire (100,000 each in 2012). Volkswagen bought Rolls-Royce (and Bentley) Motorcars in 1998. Ford and General Motors were long US-owned and themselves long integrated into the European operations of these companies.

The car sector was much more successful than others. In many important sectors production went abroad to a much greater extent. For example, the last major new all-British trains on British tracks appeared in the 1970s and 1980s. The Pendolinos on the west coast main line of the 1990s were merely assembled in the United Kingdom; the Eurostars for the new cross-Channel services were derived from TGVs and made abroad. 1998 saw the beginning of delivery of 250 class 66 locomotives built in Canada for General Motors of the USA, replacing British-designed and -built freight locomotives. The only things made in the United Kingdom were smaller regional trains and tube rolling stock. These are not special cases: the combined-cycle generating stations came from abroad. Indeed, the former nationalized industries, no longer forced to buy British, generally no longer did.

What is striking is not simply the small number of surviving national companies with strong places in world industrial markets and the loss of most, but that very few new large enterprises were created. Two large enterprises in engineering continued to supply the United Kingdom and to have significant export markets – J. C. Bamford in earth-moving equipment and above all Rolls-Royce, as discussed earlier.

ENTREPRENEURS?

One of the new words introduced into everyday language was entre-preneurship. It suggested a risk-taking capitalist creating new firms, replacing the staid bureaucratic businesses of the past with fresh energetic start-ups. The term 'entrepreneur', and the allied term 'innovator', came to be used quite indiscriminately to describe the owners of standard small and unadventurous firms and mere employ-ees of large corporations, including banks. The cult of the entrepreneur, which continued to 2000 and well beyond, was not one to look too closely at economic realities.

The list of great entrepreneurs whose animal spirits were unleashed in the new dispensation of the late 1980s and 1990s is rather thin. Sir Richard Branson is a brand, and his firms, many no longer owned by him, operate aeroplanes and trains, in the latter case highly subsi-dized. He was nothing like as pioneering as an airline boss as Sir Freddie Laker of the 1960s and 1970s. Sir James Dyson invented a new vacuum cleaner and a public lavatory hand-drying system, no longer built in the United Kingdom, but continues to invest in devel-opment. This is not the sort of transformational success that, say, Lord Nuffield had with motor cars in the interwar years. Lord Sugar, founder of Amstrad (which once rose to the FTSE 100), made and sold computers in the 1970s and boomed in the 1980s (taking over

Sinclair Research), but he was no Bill Gates. He was not even a Lord Weinstock, the chairman of GEC, a 1960s creation.[28]

Yet there were, as one might expect, successes, though the real ones were less visible than the promoted ones. Vodafone, formed out of Racal, launched mobile phones in the United Kingdom in the 1980s and was by 2000 the largest mobile telephone operation in the world. Psion, founded by David Potter, supplied software for Sinclair computers in the 1970s and early 1980s and then went on to make Psion organizers, whose software became the basis for the first smartphones, including those by Nokia. It too reached the FTSE 100. But the only company that was a high-tech start-up in the FTSE 100 as of 2013 was ARM holdings, designers of special chips – they employed under 2,000, licensed their technology but did not build. The company, based in Cambridge, was established in 1990 and grew out of ACORN computers, one of the pioneering computer firms of the 1970s. A telling success in the media was the expansion of the *Financial Times* and *The Economist*, which boomed in circulation, with by 2000 more copies sold overseas than in the UK and *The Economist* especially becoming a global rather than a British magazine.

The most celebrated case of British innovation and successful business practice since the 1980s has been without doubt the pharmaceutical industry. It boomed through the 1980s and 1990s and was responsible for increasing proportions of research and development spending. But its success was largely on the basis of drugs that pre-dated the Thatcher revolution. In the 1970s and earlier, Beecham developed new antibiotics, especially very successful semi-synthetic Penicillins, leading to Augmentin, developed in the 1970s. Sir James Black (another industrial Nobel Prize winner), working for ICI, developed the first beta blockers, Ternomil/Atenolol (1976), and for Smith, Kline & French (an American company) from their British laboratories, the first anti-ulcer H_2 blockers (Tagamet, launched 1975), both huge sellers. Tagamet was followed by an even more successful British development, Zantac, launched in 1981 by Glaxo, successful as a me-too drug, essentially a patentable small variation of an existing drug; it transformed Glaxo.

Small start-ups based on 'biotechnology' were supposed to revolutionize this industry. However, since the launch of Celltech (strongly supported by the National Enterprise Board) in 1980, there has been 'a dearth of outstanding successes, whether in terms of consistently profitable firms or high selling innovative drugs' among new pharmaceutical firms.[29] British research only produced three molecular-biological biologics, all brought to market by US companies. This disappointing performance cannot be pinned on the usual suspects – anti-business universities, an indifferent stock market and government – for such characterizations are not accurate for the period since 1979 (and in my view never were). Nor did the rest of Europe, with its allegedly backward capitalism and universities, do markedly worse, or better, than the United Kingdom. The core of the two significant biotech-proper firms, Celltech and Cambridge Antibodies Technology, both out of the famous Laboratory of Molecular Biology at the University of Cambridge, still operate as research centres in the UK, but for multinational 'Big Pharma'.

Despite an increase in R&D spending by multinational Big Pharma in the UK (as elsewhere), overall innovative activity in British industry in fact fell. The proportion of GDP devoted to R&D overall drifted downwards, to 1.8 per cent in 1999 – levels not seen since the 1950s, and distinctly lower than the USA, Japan, Germany and France. Even in 1981 it had been at 2.4 per cent, the same as the US or Japan, and only slightly behind Germany. Research done in business fell from 1.5 per cent of GDP, to 1.2 per cent over the same period, again leaving the United Kingdom adrift. Some of this fall was due to the relatively smaller size of manufacturing within the economy, but in manufacturing itself the proportion of R&D in output fell, and also fell relative to that of other manufacturing nations.[30] It was also telling that the British subsidiaries of foreign multinationals performed higher proportions of research, and increasing proportions of the industrial research expenditure came from abroad.[31] Far from unleashing British innovation, the new dispensation reduced it and made what there was more foreign controlled.

The sinews of state innovative power also shrank. With the ending of large-scale civil development programmes, expenditure by government on R&D fell from 0.9 to 0.5 per cent of GDP by the end of the 1990s. The state's key civil R&D organizations were reduced and privatized: the Plant Breeding Institute and the National Seed Development Organisation were sold to Unilever, and then in 1998 to the US firm Monsanto. The National Research Development Corporation, set up in 1948 to exploit public sector research, was privatized in 1992. The atomic weapons research establishment was 'contractorized' in 1993, and the National Physical Laboratory in 1995. In 2001 all the military laboratories, most with Edwardian origins, were, with the exception of the nuclear, and the biological and chemical warfare centre at Porton Down, put into the modishly named QinetiQ plc and were intended for the private sector. A US private equity group took a large stake in 2002, and the company was floated in 2006.

The cuts in industry and government research were severe but partly compensated for from the 1990s, especially by increases in state-funded university research. Quite unrealistic expectations were placed on this spending, which was directed in theory at generating commercially worthwhile invention. This was essentially about the appearance of doing something – research policy once again as substitute for an industrial policy as it had been in an earlier period of free trade. Research funding was a form of masterful inactivity, masquerading as action, strategy and commitment. Government got itself into an absurd position of wanting to direct research funding towards the priorities of UK plc when it did not believe in UK plc, and indeed UK plc no longer existed. Policy destroyed an entrepreneurial state, which did about all one could expect, and replaced it with an entrepreneurial culture that was more rhetoric than reality.

The reality was that there was no radically disruptive entrepreneurial culture; there was a culture of passive conformity, managerialism and imitation. Order and control were more obvious than freedom and imagination. To call the new order neo-liberalism is to flatter it, for there was little original or new, or liberal, about it. It was a culture which was increasingly global in its sameness and its lack of political contestation. But it was also a richer world. If it did not have what it claimed to have, it did not mean that in its own terms it did not work, and work well. The great thing was that it did not need entrepreneurs, or great creative energy, or novelties, or to generate great crises. To live in uninteresting times was, to many, a blessing.

THE NEW CONSENSUS

The 1990s were a time of consensus. The political figures in charge of the new era of the non-national economy were John Major and Tony Blair. John Major was a longer-serving prime minister (1990–97) than is often recalled. It was under Major that many of the paradoxical changes of the previous years would settle down into a new political and economic order. He had been elected to parliament only in 1979. From a modest background and with no university education, he had worked in old-fashioned banking and in local politics. He rose without much trace in the government, becoming chancellor and foreign secretary, and won the 1990 leadership election as the choice of the right. He beat the Labour Party in 1992, unexpectedly but decisively, and in effect set the agenda for New Labour. It was he, not Mrs Thatcher, who finally destroyed old Labour. He brought back Michael Heseltine, the pro-European, to undo the Community Charge and later to be supremo for industry, taking up the old title of 'president of the Board of Trade'.

Major clearly was not cut from the same cloth as the 1980s right. He was perhaps the 'first Conservative premier to believe in race and sex equality'.[32] Furthermore he reduced the warfare state and brought the war in Ireland to an end, both particularly impressive achievements for a Conservative. He negotiated the Maastricht Treaty, which led to the creation of the new European Union. While he achieved opt-outs for the United Kingdom from a commitment to participate in the future European currency, the euro, and the 'social chapter', which guaranteed social rights, he was clearly committed to the view that the United Kingdom had to be part of the new liberal Europe. This was no small matter, as he was hounded by the emergent 'Eurosceptic' 'bastards' and much of the right-wing press, previously very loyal to the Conservative government. He suffered one significant defeat over Europe – with his chancellor he poured billions into defending the rate of sterling, which was fixed within a narrow band on entry to the European Exchange Rate Mechanism (ERM) in 1990. They were forced to allow sterling to come out of the ERM and to devalue by around 15 per cent, a change which was taken by

Eurosceptics to account for the steady growth which followed the recession of the early 1990s.

Euroscepticism marked the emergence of a new politics of private wealth. Rich right-wing businessmen, setting themselves up as the heirs of Thatcher, but deeply hostile to Major and European political integration of any kind, created political parties. In 1997 a new Referendum Party, funded by Sir James Goldsmith, ran an astonishing 547 candidates. It wanted a referendum on further integration into the European Union, from a clearly Eurosceptic position, hostile to what it took to be a plan for a federal European super-state, in which Britain would be a mere province. EFTA was presented as a good, free-trading alternative.[33] Goldsmith's own position was unusual and confusing – he was hostile to political integration but a strong believer in European free trade, though one who believed that the European economies should be strongly protected against the rest of the world, in effect by a European economic union.

The Referendum Party was not the only one to emerge from one day to the next, though it put forward by far the largest set of candidates after the main parties. In the 1997 election next in the ranking of candidates was the Natural Law Party (transcendental meditationists).[34] They were followed by another new party, the UK Independence Party, then led by a non-racist liberal historian of the Austro-Hungarian Empire. The Green Party trailed in the number of candidates.

Major devoted immense energies to bringing peace to Northern Ireland, an unfashionable and neglected issue. In 1993 the Provisional IRA let it be known, following overtures from the British government, that it wanted to end the conflict, which had reached stalemate on both sides and was imposing enormous costs. Working closely and intensively, and taking political risks, John Major set to work. A PIRA ceasefire came into effect in 1994. It was broken in 1996 but then restored. This work prepared the ground for the Belfast/Good Friday Agreement of 1998. Overall, the agreements were more of a defeat for the unionists – for all that they insisted on Britishness, and their loyalty to the United Kingdom and the crown, they were increasingly regarded not as models of patriotism but as an embarrassment. The nationalists, while they did not gain union with Ireland, achieved recognition of the reality of connection with Ireland, a government in which they were recognized and had authority, and a change in the ethos of the state and its machinery. A cross-community government was formed in Belfast between Sinn Féin, the political wing of the Provisional IRA, and the more radical of the two unionist parties, the DUP.

In 1989 the Berlin Wall, and the whole Iron Curtain, came down, and the communist regimes in Eastern Europe collapsed. The USSR itself began to disintegrate and, following an attempted 1991 coup to retain it, came to an end; the Soviet Communist Party was dissolved. This was a world-historic victory for capitalism, and John Major's government cashed in a peace dividend. It was under John Major that the cost of the armed forces were substantially cut in real terms, from 4 to 2.6 per cent of GDP. Total personnel in the armed services was cut by one-third between 1990 and 2000, to around 200,000 men and women, lower than at any point in the twentieth century. Service personnel abroad were cut from around 100,000 to 50,000 or so, largely by halving the size of the forces in Germany from around 70,000 to 30,000. Both education and NHS expenditure increased in real terms (though only a little as a percentage of GDP). The warfare state was now marginal; the welfare state a very much larger and continuing spending commitment.

There was much talk of a new world order, one with just one superpower. Thus the Iraqi invasion of Kuwait in 1990 was reversed by a US-led coalition, which sent huge bodies of troops into the Gulf. On the coat-tails of the US forces, John Major took British forces into combat, and in the very places the United Kingdom had retired from in the 1970s, when they had withdrawn from 'East of Suez'. A total of 45,000 British service men and women were deployed in naval and air forces and the 1st Armoured Division. That war, short and decisive as it was, would have unhappy consequences, hardly imaginable at the time.

20

New Times, New Labour

*If we are to rebuild and recover in this country, this Labour
Party must be the party of production. That is where our
future lies. It is not a new role for us, but it does require a
fresh and vigorous reassertion. Over the years our enemies
and critics – yes, and a few of our friends as well – have given
us the reputation of being a party that is solely concerned
with redistribution, of being a party much more concerned
about the allocation of wealth than the creation of wealth. It
was not true; it is not true; it never has been; and all our history shows that – from the great industrial development and
nationalization acts of the Attlee government, which gave
this country a post-war industrial basis, through to the Wilson government's investment schemes and initiatives that
brought new life to where I come from, to South Wales, to
Scotland, to the Northeast, to Merseyside, to the new towns
of the Southeast, right through to the actions of the last
Labour government, which ensured that at least we retained
a British computer industry, a British motor industry, a
machine tool industry, a shipbuilding industry. We . . . need
give no apology for being the party of production.*

> Neil Kinnock, speech to the 1985 Labour
> Party Conference

*The great British–American alliance led the way – morally as
well as militarily – in both world wars.*

> Margaret Thatcher, speech to the English-Speaking
> Union in New York, 1999

You are Neville Chamberlain, I am Winston Churchill and Saddam is Hitler.

Tony Blair to an official 2002/3[1]

I think it's my job to maximise global welfare, not national welfare.

Sir Gus O'Donnell, permanent secretary to the Treasury, 2002–5, cabinet secretary, 2005–11.[2]

The Communist Party, in the vanguard of all the progressive forces of mankind, brought tidings of new times even in the 1980s. Now the news was not good for the left. In its *Manifesto for New Times* (1989) the party told its workers that socialists did 'not yet confidently speak the language of the future', that capitalism was entering a new phase – of robots, computers, satellite television – and that what was needed was an alternative to Thatcherism's 'regressive modernisation'.[3] The party journal, *Marxism Today*, opened its pages to politicians to its right, including Tony Blair, before he became Labour leader.[4] The central idea of *New Times* was a classic vulgar-Marxist technological determinism, which, it must be noted, is, while vulgar, generally rather richer than the usual non-Marxist variety. The postwar 'settlement' was being remade, it was claimed: Fordism, standardized mass production, was giving way to post-Fordism ('the economic and industrial core of the new times'), a more flexible system of production. The end of Fordism meant the end of large, unionized workforces in nationally organized welfare states. There were, they suggested, two ways of managing post-Fordism – the Thatcher way and an alternative which involved creating new solidarities, a new politics of *consumption*, an 'alternative socialism adequate to the post-Fordist age'.[5] The appeal was real – it was time to get rid of the grim, old-fashioned politics of production and embrace consumption, where the politics was essentially environmental, at this time focused on pollution, rainforests and whaling.[6] It was also attractive in that it pointed to new forms of intellectual enquiry for the left – towards culture and consumption, identities and ideology, and away from political economy, production, international relations and indeed politics.

Theorists of technical change now celebrated information technology as a paradigm shift – the high unemployment unleashed on the world, and especially on the United Kingdom, was the product, not of policy, but of a technical development. Capitalism, they claimed, developed in long waves of growth followed by years of painful restructuring, which repeated every fifty years. The depression of the 1980s, like that of the 1930s, would usher in a new world.[7] The new information or knowledge societies would be much more environmentally aware, and indeed it was in the late 1980s that politics took up what would later be called greenwashing. It was a feature of the 1987 SDP–Liberal Alliance manifesto, which had a section called 'Green Growth' – which called for cutting air pollution, and pollution of water by nuclear waste, protection of the green belt and more insulation. It was anti-nuclear and called for modernization and the expansion of coal.[8] The Labour Party Policy Review of 1989 also mentioned the environment as a new concern.[9]

As is so often the case, these technological determinist arguments failed to identify the key technologies, and indeed the social phenomena they sought to explain. For all the confidence of analysis, it was derived not from serious analysis of machinery and society but from boosterist commentary of the moment. Realities, as ever, were rather different. For example, for all the talk of post-Fordism, the Ford Motor Company itself had a giant new engine plant come into operation in 1980, in Bridgend, which was to become the largest engine plant the United Kingdom had ever seen, making a very small range of globally standardized engines. Of course, technical change in manufacturing reduced labour needs, often very radically, as in the Ford case, but the new small, flexible manufacturing hardly replaced mass production. The new foreign car plants mass-produced; new forms of mass white-collar work emerged. In any case, mass production had never covered all of manufacturing, and manufacturing was rather less than the whole capitalist economy. And car use went up and up. The more post-industrial the commentators claimed the world was becoming, the more metals, plastics and nearly every kind of product was produced in factories the world over.

These arguments in any case missed the really important transformations of the economy we have described. What had changed was not so much the means of production, as political economy, and it did so, as we have seen, in surprising ways. Capitalism, not technology, was the issue. The transformation in the nature of the labour force would indeed have dramatic impacts. The new jobs were to be found in highly routinized services of many different sorts. In the 1950s, 1960s and 1970s it still made sense to differentiate between manual and non-manual work, between white-collar and blue-collar, wage- and salary-earners, between working-class and middle-class. Though this distinction has continued to be used by pollsters and advertisers (C2 is skilled manual, D is semi-skilled and unskilled manual), the statistical authorities recognized before the end of the millennium that working with one's hands was no longer a sensible definitional criterion. This is not to say that manual jobs disappeared, rather the contrary. They multiplied in the 'service' sector, which was about caring, cleaning, shelving, serving in restaurants. These were often low-paying jobs, with wages so low in some cases that workers were also on benefits.[10] In some parts of the country especially immigrants were important in these jobs. In a notable, though hardly noticed development, immigration exceeded emigration from the 1980s. It was to continue to increase (with very great increases in the twenty-first century), but the invisible need for people to perform routine tasks created a new foreign-born workforce of a scale never seen in the history of the United Kingdom.

Trade unionism, like the welfare state, did not disappear but changed, again in surprising ways. In 1950, as in 1900, the trade unionist was typically a male manual worker – a miner, an engineer, a cotton worker (though this was an industry with many women, and women trade unionists), a docker – overwhelmingly working for a private employer. By the 1970s trade unionism was more oriented towards the public sector and had expanded to non-manual, white-collar workers including many more women. By 2000 trade union density, the proportion of workers in unions, was back to the relatively low levels of the 1940s, but now a majority of trade unionists were female, and over 60 per cent were in the public sector. Trade unionism was indeed now a middle-class phenomenon. While the miners' and steelworkers' and transport unions had shrunk, there were now large unions of teachers, university lecturers and nurses. The National Health Service had, in 2000, three times the number of employees it had in 1948, and these were more likely to be unionized as well. The number of teachers grew, indeed by the early 1990s the number of university teachers exceeded the number of miners. The most unionized parts of the private sector were those that had been public industries into the 1980s – transport, mining, electricity, gas and telecommunications.[11]

The weakening and the transformation of trade unions had an impact on the Labour Party. As the party of the trade unions, it lost influence and power in society and the economy. It was also weakened because for the first time since the Edwardian years a large (and growing) section of organized workers were not affiliated to the party. They included teachers, university lecturers, many of the nurses and other health workers and the largest civil service union.

The Labour Party itself went through an extraordinary transformation. The historical Labour Party had come of age in the 1970s and 1980s; only then did it achieve a certain intellectual coherence, and a programme reflecting its historical ambitions. But this moment did not last long. It lost the 1983 election very badly, admittedly in rather exceptional circumstances, garnering only 28 per cent of the vote. Its vote went up to 31 per cent in 1987 then to 34 per cent in 1992, significant but hardly earth-shattering increases, which left the vote share well below the 37 per cent achieved by James Callaghan in 1979, when he was defeated. The marginal increases in electors were achieved as the party went into a defensive shedding of its actual policies. The Labour Party which last won an election in 1974 never returned to office. James Callaghan was the last Labour prime minister, and the last prime minister to have served in the armed forces. Labour left office claiming to be the saviour of the nation but was not called to save it again. As the party of the nation, it found life in a post-national economy and society difficult to adjust to or respond to.

After the electoral defeat of 1983 the leadership of the Labour Party passed from Michael Foot to a so-called dream ticket combining the soft left and the right. The new leader and deputy leader were figures of much less substance than those they replaced. Neil Kinnock was neither an intellectual nor a worker, and for all the claims made for him as orator and parliamentarian, he was merely more prolix than Michael Foot. Roy Hattersley, the deputy leader with strong support in the parliamentary Labour Party, was a *littérateur* (like Michael Foot) rather than a robust specialist in international relations, as was his predecessor, Denis Healey.[12] Kinnock and Hattersley were both formed by residues from the Labour Party of the 1950s: Hattersley by Croslandite reformism, Kinnock by Bevanism.[13] The potential leaders of the left formed by the politics of the 1960s and 1970s, Tony Benn and Ken Livingstone, could not stand because neither were at that moment members of parliament.

With Kinnock and Hattersley came not new policies, but diminished and diluted versions of the radical 1983 ones. The overall aim was to overthrow and reverse what Kinnock called 'Thatcherism', which was interpreted not merely as morally wrong, but economically calamitous too. The central claim around the 1987 election was that 'Labour would rebuild' on the basis of its productionist agenda: it would repatriate capital (let loose by the lifting of exchange controls), focus on industry and production and create a Ministry of Science and Technology. While Labour would 'reject EEC interference with our policy for national recovery and renewal', it would (unlike its position in 1983) stay in. Labour was still committed to abandoning the Trident system and would invest in conventional defence, emphasizing new kinds of weapons.[14] Following the defeat in 1987, Labour abandoned any remaining opposition to the EEC and to the Trident submarine and missiles. The claim from the left was that Labour did not stand for fresh ideas: it did not generate them, or fight for them, but rather fought them off if they came from further left. This seemed truer than ever.[15] As Ralph Miliband scornfully put it, the Labour leadership has never ever wanted its members or supporters to be *more* active, to conduct campaigns with more vigour, or with greater resources.[16]

Labour advanced slowly by eating away not at the Tory vote but at the SDP–Liberal Alliance vote – which had nearly reached Labour's in 1983. It looked as if the three-party politics of the 1920s was back, and indeed it was. However, the Alliance peaked at just below Labour's trough in 1993. The politics of the SDP–Liberal Alliance, for all the insistence on their novelty, represented continuity. Although they criticized the other parties as class parties, fighting a class war, and presented themselves as committed to practicalities, there was a large element of the programme of the Labour right in it. They were appalled at unemployment levels and wanted to reflate the economy to create 1 million jobs; they were concerned, too, about the weakness of British manufacturing. While not rejecting nuclear weapons, they wanted to reduce their number and crucially were in favour of cancelling Trident. They were strong supporters of NATO and the EEC and wanted to reduce trade barriers. They did not see a case for the PWR and wanted the expansion of coal production.

For the 1987 election the SDP–Liberal Alliance was still close in spirit to old Labour productivism. It spoke of the need to leap through a second industrial revolution ('micro-electronics, biotechnology and new materials'), which required more R&D spending above all, noting correctly that this was in fact falling. They claimed, as many did still, that 'Manufacturing industry is the driving force at the core of our economy. Its decline must be reversed.'[17]

By 1992 the SDP had merged with the Liberals to form the Liberal Democratic Party. In their programme manufacturing was no longer the driving force at the core of the economy; there was much less emphasis on industrial revolutions and much, much more on free trade and competition. 'We are committed,' they said, 'to a free market, to free trade and to the creation of a competitive and enterprising economy.' The role of government was merely enabling, for example, 'playing a positive part in the construction of the new European economy and, above all, bringing greater stability to national economic management'.[18]

Labour was to abandon much more than the policies the left of the 1970s had got it to adopt. First, it rid itself of its national-productionist agenda, which, with the exception of the late 1950s, had been its guiding policy since 1945.[19] It did this slowly, without advertising or perhaps realizing the import of the change. The policy review of the late 1980s called for a new industrial ministry with status equal to the Treasury, which would pursue a 'Medium Term Industrial Strategy'. It still complained of low R&D investment and wanted the United Kingdom to be at the 'leading edge of technology', and to have a minister for science and technology in the new Industry Ministry. It wanted a Defence Diversification Agency to stimulate civil research.[20] It was as if the white heat policies of the 1960s had never happened;

the talk was 1960s talk but with no recognition that Wilson had once walked the walk. But by 1992 only a few dying embers of this white heat rhetoric were left in the manifesto, which claimed that 'Britain's industrial future depends on transforming our inventive genius into manufacturing strength'.[21] But the industrial policy was gone, and a firm commitment to the European Exchange Rate Mechanism was an indicator of a new enthusiasm for the EEC.[22] The diagnosis was still declinist, but the proposed cure was unrelated to the disease. Labour was out of office, and desperate for it, through all the 1980s and most of the 1990s – feeling that its policies were discredited and increasingly discreditable. Yet this was as much the product of polit-ical defeat as its cause, and one must wonder what policies a more confident and successful party might have come up with.

One possibility would have been a rethinking of welfare. Labour kept its welfare commitments into the 1990s. It aimed to restore the link between pensions and earnings, rather than merely keeping them constant in price terms; and it committed itself to a new State Earn-ings Related Pension. It was now once again what it had briefly been in the late 1950s: the party of progressive welfare rather than the party of production. That last vestige of what Labour had stood for would go under New Labour.

NEW LABOUR

Neil Kinnock resigned as Labour leader after two election defeats. He was succeeded, briefly, by John Smith, who reiterated some Labour themes. For example he noted that 'One of Britain's most important resources is our immense coal reserves. It was ready access to coal that put Britain at the front of the industrial revolution and it is the plentiful remaining reserves that give us an edge over most of our European competitors.' Yet, he complained, 'Britain's present government is proposing to abandon half of all the pits that remain. That is vandalism . . . it will destroy whole communities built around their role of providing the nation with coal . . . it will destroy a national asset which could meet Britain's long-term energy needs.'[23] He rejected any idea that the Thatcher-Major years were ones of success. 'These have been fourteen years of waste, years of neglect, years of decline. Fourteen years of casino economics – a speculators' paradise – have plunged British industry into two record-breaking recessions.' He noted, accurately, that economic growth was 'lower than in the 1960s and the 1970s; investment in manufacturing – the vital wealth creator of our economy – lower than in 1979'. There were huge deficits in public finance and trade, and still 3 million out of work. He called these and others the 'facts that mock the Tory hype and propaganda . . . that explode their so-called economic miracle: the so-called Thatcher revolution'.[24]

John Smith died suddenly, and with him this renewed Labour critique. He was succeeded by another barrister, Tony Blair. Blair, working closely with Gordon Brown, created a new party leadership, committing the party to policies which both the old right and the old left would have thought unthinkable. It was indeed *New* Labour rather than Labour which went into the 1997 general election. Labour won it with 43 per cent of the vote, an astonishing jump from 1992. The proportion would fall with each subsequent election, along with turnout, but New Labour was to be in office until 2010, when it got only 29 per cent. The Conservative Party, which had done so much to reshape the United Kingdom, not least New Labour, languished at around 30 per cent of the electorate, essentially where Labour had been in the 1980s and early 1990s. But much less changed than met the eye.

New Labour was born out of Labour but not of Labour. It was not, however, a new party. The party as a structure continued to exist, and there was no great transformation in membership. Old loyalties still mattered a great deal. The key difference was that the party leadership acquired quite extraordinary power over members of parliament and the party as a whole. It silenced its opponents and promised to succeed where Labour no longer did, a claim of enormous attraction to a party membership which believed that the Tories were vermin. Anything that could turn out the Tories was not to be sniffed at by Labour members and activists. The paradox was that this very hatred of the Tories made it possible for them to tolerate a party which adopted Tory policies.

For what was remarkable was not only that New Labour was not

Labour but that it was barely New either. It owed a good deal to the policies long espoused by the Conservative Party.[25] Indeed, it aspired to, and to some extent succeeded in, becoming a party much like the Conservative Party or the Liberal Democratic Party in both structure and policies. It was a party in which the parliamentary leadership dominated, was comfortable with plutocrats and had slight and wary connections to the working class. Millionaires, including Lord Sainsbury, funded New Labour. The plutocratic Murdoch press, which had vilified Neil Kinnock, and indeed John Major, supported New Labour, as no capitalist newspaper with the exception of the *Mirror* had. It was telling, too, that as they lost ministerial office the Labour high command took to going off to join boards of regulated companies, lobbying firms and aspiring private health providers.[26] It was the party of the management consultants, the PR agencies, the outsourced public services and the aspiring public sector high-fliers. Whereas the left had been strongly declinist in the 1980s, and indeed saw Mrs Thatcher's policies as strengthening the forces that led to decline – finance, free markets, trade liberalization – by the late 1990s these ideas were weakening even on the left. For New Labour there was no longer a problem of underperforming British capitalism.

There was, it seemed, a New Economy, a new weightless, past-less economy, which appeared to defy what seemed like old-fashioned laws of economic gravity, not least in the stock market boom which ran into 1999. People made fun of Gordon Brown for talking of 'neo-endogenous growth theory', but it was rather revealing that he was making a very general economic argument which suggested that what really mattered in growth was R&D and 'human capital', and not such things as investment or trade policy. For Brown, 'It is a knowledge-based economy, in which the key to success and profitability is to get the best out of our people and all their potentials.'[27]

The 1997 manifesto was quite clear that, as far the economy was concerned, we 'accept the global economy as a reality and reject the isolationism and "go-it-alone" policies of the extremes of right or left'.[28] It was 'a new and revitalised Labour Party that has been resolute in transforming itself into a party of the future,' claimed the 1997 manifesto. Labour promised a fresh re-engagement with the global forces of modernization, a rejection of class politics, a

Illustration 20.1: Tony Blair as New Labour Prime Minister, by Steve Bell, 1999. Blair as the modernizing e.pope at a time when e.government and e.commerce were popular. The cart-horse representing the TUC is in homage to Low, who created the image. (© Steve Bell)

commitment to efficiency. It presented itself as the modern, aspirational party, engaged with the deepest historical processes:

> We aim to put behind us the bitter political struggles of left and right
> that have torn our country apart for too many decades. Many of these
> conflicts have no relevance whatsoever to the modern world – public
> versus private, bosses versus workers, middle class versus working
> class. It is time for this country to move on and move forward.

'New Labour is the political arm of none other than the British people as a whole.'[29] The rhetoric of novelty, newness, modernity, the global, was central to New Labour.[30] It was an argument for the obliteration of the past. In welfare policy too there was no return to the past. New Labour never promised to restore the link between the basic state pension and other benefits and earnings, another crucial change from the Kinnock–Smith years.

New Labour was close to the Liberal Democrats, and particularly to Roy Jenkins. He certainly pushed the idea of a progressive alliance in the United Kingdom, harking back to the New Liberals of 1906. There were continuities between Jenkinsite enthusiasm for Europe, social liberalism and New Labour. Yet the analogy should not be overdone. The Jenkinsite Labour right of the 1950s and 1960s believed in taxing and spending to redistribute income, to make society more equal. Roy Jenkins as Labour chancellor in the 1960s had fought and won battles to cut defence spending and get out of east of Suez, because, as he insisted, the United Kingdom needed to rid itself of the notion it was a world power. These policies were not ones which would appeal to New Labour.

In other words, what was striking about New Labour was not that it was a response to Thatcherism but its child.[31] As Eric Hobsbawm put it in 1998,

> the difficult truth seems to be that the Blair project, in its overall
> analysis and key assumptions, is still essentially framed by and mov-
> ing on terrain defined by Thatcherism. Mrs Thatcher had a project.
> Blair's historic project is adjusting Us to It. That touches half – the
> modernising part – of the task, as *Marxism Today* argued it. But the

other, more difficult, half – that of the Left reinventing a genuinely modern response to the crisis of our times – has been largely abandoned. . . . Mr Blair seems to have learned some of the words. But, sadly, he has forgotten the music.[32]

Anyone looking for consensus in British political history will find it in 'Blatcherism' or 'Blajorism' rather than 'Butskellism'. The period from the mid-1990s was the period of the greatest identity of view between the major parties since 1950, or indeed since 1900. The lack of contestation over the key issues and practices of government was by twentieth-century historical standards extraordinary. It was an achievement of Mrs Thatcher and John Major that they converted one party to radical economic liberalism and had a hand in the creation of another committed to the same policy. There was agreement on free trade, for example. This was pointed out by one of the few remaining protectionists, Alan Clark, who was 'still not ashamed to argue the archaic but traditional Tory case that we should protect our manufacturing industry . . . The choice will be between the welfare of our constituents as producers and their welfare as consumers.' But he complained that both sides of the House now subscribed to the 'consumerist ethic, and that the service industries and the ephemeral earnings of show business, with all its shallowness and triviality, will support a major economy of 55 million people'.[33]

This achievement went deeper than merely destroying a certain kind of opposition dangerous to capitalism, it involved weakening the very idea of opposition. Labour was always in part a party of protest; New Labour was nothing but a party of power. For all the weakness of the Labour project, it always needed to mobilize on the basis of a distinct truth about society; it needed to expose, to criticize the nature of power in society. It had a crucial critical function, prided itself on being empirical, public, honest in contrast to the necessity of obfuscation imposed on parties of the status quo. Much as it rejected too-radical critiques of society, it was nevertheless in a world of critique. New Labour was very different. It took to dissembling about the nature of power with polished cynicism. Its task was not to generate any critique of economy or society; its publications were characterized by obfuscatory management speak. This gave rise to 'Bullshit Britain', as it was called, with reason.[34]

It operated in a world where parliament was marginal to real politics. The level of debate fell – by the end of the century members aimed to get reported not in the national press (which no longer covered parliament, except in sketches), but their own local press. They thus raised issues more appropriate for a local council and failed to discuss the key issues in which only parliament was competent with much seriousness or knowledge. Members of parliament, especially Labour members, given the nature of their constituencies, were overwhelmed with local casework which should have been the province of social workers or local councillors. Politics was the province of lobbyists – much better paid than MPs – special advisers and ministers. Those, like the majority of Labour MPs, with no external income, had lower incomes and status than the lobby correspondents or indeed the lobbyists who entertained them. Party conferences were places not of political debate between activists but lobbying sites protected from the world by heavy security barriers. MPs, like public opinion, were there to be manipulated.

At first New Labour promoted itself as an alternative to the Tories, armed with fresh concepts such as 'stakeholders' and 'the Third Way', a concern with the need to develop autonomous regional poles of economic development. It was, to be sure, much more consistently pro-European, more socially liberal, more open to constitutional change, to freedom of access to state information, to the minimum wage, than were the Conservatives as a party, though the contrast with the policies of John Major was far less clear.

There was talk of something called 'Cool Britannia', which effortlessly generated new industries in the bright new knowledge economy. In the 1990s 'Cool Britannia' stood for a celebration of a new swinging London and a revitalized pop and art culture – it was lost on New Labour that it was a term of 1960s irony. Neither the art nor the music was original: it was at best a replay of the 1960s, but without any radical or critical edge. The Rolling Stones were still playing, the Beatles still selling. It was perhaps telling that the plays chosen for revival in the 1990s were those of the 1950s – indeed those of J. B. Priestley, Noël Coward and Terence Rattigan, with only the occasional Arnold Wesker. The 'creative industries', as they came to be called, had little actually original about them. By contrast, by the end of the 1990s the declinist emphasis on the poverty of British science gave way among elite scientists to an emphasis on the strength of British academic science in comparative terms. This new argument for support, congruent with the emergent anti-declinist accounts, had evidence in its favour, long overlooked by declinists.[35] Academic scientific research was expanding strongly, with funding supported by the argument that in the new economy national R&D would indeed produce economic growth. The reality was that funding academic research gave the illusion of action; it was little more than a safe and cheap substitute for a real industrial policy. It had been discovered earlier in the century that funding research, or even just talking about it, was a wonderful alternative to, for example, agricultural protection, or protecting the wages of miners. It was as if this notion had found its way back into the methods of liberal governance.

The ascendancy of New Labour meant the total marginalization of what remained of the Labour left. The Labour left, like the independent left parties which had grown up in the 1970s and 1980s, shrank radically or disappeared. A telling indicator of the fate of the left within Labour was what happened to Ken Livingstone. Livingstone was elected to parliament in 1987 but made no progress. He was even actively prevented by New Labour from being the candidate for the new mayoralty of London it created. Forced to stand as an independent, he beat the New Labour as well as the Conservative candidate in the first mayoral election of 2000. The first mayor of London, one of the greatest centres of global capitalism, was the only socialist politician of significance left in the United Kingdom.

The London left also had other small but significant victories. It was critical in getting non-white politicians into the House of Commons for the first time since the interwar years. In 1987 Diane Abbott, Paul Boateng and Bernie Grant were all elected for London seats, and Keith Vaz for a seat in Leicester. Most had started in politics in London local government. Bernie Grant had been leader of Haringey council between 1986 and 1988, one of a handful of black council leaders. All were condemned in the press and much of the Labour Party as loony leftists. The Labour Party had indeed been hostile to the creation of black sections within the party. The London left of the 1970s and 1980s had also been critical in making a public space for gays and lesbians, and the GLC played a key role in this. In the 1980s there was only one out gay MP, Chris Smith, who sat for Labour in Islington South in London. In 1997 he became the first out gay cabinet minister. New Labour repealed the notorious, though essentially unused section 28 of the Conservative Local Government Act, which sought to counter the example of the GLC in promoting gay rights, one of the very few bits of Tory law to go. After 1997 there were many more openly gay, lesbian and bisexual MPs, in all parties. The equalization of the age of consent came in 1999, though it must be noted that it had been reduced to eighteen under John Major and nearly equalized at sixteen under him.

By far the greatest change in the composition of the House of Commons in 1997, though much less associated with the left than the advance of black MPs, was in the extraordinary and sudden increase in the number of women. In 1997 the number of women sitting doubled, from sixty to 120, overwhelmingly now with the Labour Party. This was a huge change – for most of the years since 1945 the number of women was far fewer than working-class MPs before 1918, and they tended to focus on women's issues: that would change from 1997.[36]

NEW LABOUR IN OFFICE

The Millennium Dome, planned to mark the arrival of the year 2000 by the Conservatives but taken up by New Labour, was perfectly emblematic of the new politics. It seemed to look to the future but plagiarized the past. It was not much more than a set of Skylons from the Festival of Britain of 1951. Peter Mandelson claimed it would display an amazing new computer game called Surfball. Why a computer game needed a gigantic dome to house it was not asked. Nor was Surfball looked into. It never existed.[37] In that and much more it was rather like the notion of a distinct New Labour ideology, which, if it did exist, dissipated like the thinnest of mists.

When New Labour came in there were some gestures towards an alternative programme. A national minimum wage was established, and trade union representation at GCHQ restored. But there was no significant change in the Conservative trade union legislation. One of the first New Labour economic measures was the granting of control over monetary policy to the Bank of England, a point it was still proud of long after the financial crash of 2008.

It stressed that it was not going to increase public spending in the beginning and it didn't. It claimed it had to make 'hard choices'. In fact, it made, from the point of view of its political programme, the easy choices, just to follow the previous government. A particularly telling case is the National Health Service – something which New Labour, like Labour, particularly associated with itself. Did New Labour have a different approach to the NHS than the Conservatives? Did it have a fresh plan? The answer must be no. The New Labour government spent no more on the NHS than the Tories had planned for the first two years – it had committed itself in advance to do this for all public sector spending. It did, however, seem to promise a pushing-back against the internal market which the previous government had created whereby GPs became purchasers of health services for their patients. Yet the reform was cosmetic, and the internal market became an increasingly important feature of the system. Another example was domiciliary care. Under John Major there began a process of shifting from local authority homes to privatized care homes. Under New Labour the programme continued with no discernible break such that by 2000 more than half of the sector had become private.[38]

There was, as we have seen, no promise to renew the links between benefits and earnings. This was profoundly important, as it first drove down the basic pension as a proportion of average earnings to 16 per cent, where it stayed essentially to the end of New Labour in 2010. It had stood at 26 per cent at its peak during the 1970s Labour government.[39] New Labour was content, it seemed, with extending special measures for a rediscovered underclass of the 'socially excluded' and for poor children and pensioners. It radically extended means-testing as the means of raising benefits for the poorest.

Under New Labour public spending fell to its lowest level as a proportion of GDP since the late 1950s. After 1999 public spending did increase under New Labour, notably in health and education and in benefits for the poorest. But it remained below the highest levels achieved under both

Mrs Thatcher and John Major, though after 1999, above the troughs in spending (as a propotion of GDP) of their times.We should not think, however, that this tax and spend made New Labour like Old Labour. As we have seen, tax and spend had been the policy of the revisionists of the 1950s, not of Labour in general. Old Labour was committed to higher universal benefits, New Labour to means-testing and targetting.

New Labour took up ideas which the Conservatives had found difficult to pursue on any scale. The Private Finance Initiative (PFI), by which the private sector built facilities for the public sector to lease, only really got going under New Labour, with its hospital building programme, which stood at the centre of the PFI, renamed Public Private Partnerships (PPP), programme. The theory was that the private sector would build more cheaply, despite the higher cost of capital it faced. A more real accounting advantage was that the spending could be kept off state accounts. The truth was that costs were higher overall, and the state got lumbered with high-cost contracts it could not get out of. The contractors were also able to get leasing contracts at exorbitant prices. Accounting tricks and poor supervision allowed rich investors to loot a public sector left with huge long-term liabilities. It was as if New Labour created a new rentier class, living not on interest on the national debt, but on very much richer skimmings of the national tax take. Yet New Labour remained deeply committed to the PPP, not just for hospitals but for all manner of state investments. It was pronounced a good idea by New Labour think tanks funded by private companies and consultancies with interests in this lucrative business.[40]

Public money was paid in increasing quantities to private corporations to deliver public services, corporations whose only business this was, though often in more than one country. Central state services and local government services expanded, but through contractors, who paid high salaries to top management and miserable wages to the rest. New Labour greatly extended the transformation of the public sector not only by bringing in 'outsourcers' but also by bureaucratizing the state and para-state sectors, which were now clogged with performance indicators, targets and form filling.

There was not merely an accommodation to the existing ideological regime, but active conversion to it. The former socialist Gordon

Brown was felt by some to be to the left of the prime minister he soon came to resent and plot against. Yet as an exceptionally powerful chancellor of the exchequer he was a strong supporter of the PFI. He came to read, quote and approve of US conservative thinkers.[41] This was a powerful indication that New Labour was itself more than a mere tactical accommodation to the reality of the 1990s – it embraced the Conservative agenda at a deep level.

It was perhaps only in the constitutional sphere that New Labour obviously did things the Conservatives would not have. A new Northern Ireland government and assembly was formed, with important elements of co-jurisdiction with Ireland under the Belfast/Good Friday Agreement of 1998. Here, acknowledgement of the long and patient work of John Major is needed. However, in the cases of creation of the Scottish parliament, the Welsh assembly and the London assembly the story is rather different. Tellingly, all these bodies were given different electoral systems to the first-past-the-post used for the House of Commons, and that for the European parliament changed.[42] These were New Labour initiatives, as was the reform of the House of Lords to eliminate most hereditary peers. However, the crucial House of Commons remained determinedly unreformed. New Labour had promised a referendum on a new electoral system to be proposed in the future. A commission under Roy Jenkins was set up which rejected an enhanced Alternative Vote system. New Labour kicked the proposal into the long grass – the old system was working only too well for them.

TO WAR

Another area in which New Labour was a dogged follower of the Conservatives was in matters concerning the warfare state. In its 1987 manifesto Labour promised to get rid of the Trident programme and to use the money to increase conventional defence spending. In 1989 the Berlin wall came down; in 1991 the Soviet Union was dissolved. In 1992, and 1997, Labour and New Labour nonetheless backed Trident. The first deployment was in December 1994. The last of the four submarines went into service in 2001. New Labour went to extreme lengths to keep up defence expenditure (which had been falling under the Tories). By the late 1990s the United Kingdom spent about the same proportion of GDP on defence as France, but more than the European average. It is not clear that it had the general technological edge over Europe it once clearly held, not least since most weapons systems were shared (for example, the main RAF aircraft was the European Tornado fighter and bomber). Nor, importantly, did it have the capacity to wage a serious war independently. In 1998 New Labour staged a defence review quite unlike previous ones – the aim was to define new roles, not to eliminate unaffordable ones. Indeed, the review led to the start of the design of two aircraft carriers, bigger than those cancelled in the 1960s (the first started its sea trials in 2017). The aim was to provide a complete but small air, sea and land force, to assist US operations. Without that, the whole justification for forces beyond those needed for home defence, for military budgets above German levels, collapsed.[43]

New Labour would create a story of British exceptionalism to justify a newly global orientation of British armed force. It reinvented the United Kingdom as a global contender, retrieving long-established clichés, of bridges, or overlapping memberships of international organizations, which required a global military role. They implied that the 10 million British citizens living abroad needed defending, presumably from the Americans, French, Australians and Spaniards among whom they lived. They invoked the fact that the UK exported a lot proportionally and that it invested a lot abroad; it did not note that the UK attracted a lot of investment, which by the same argument meant others should defend the United Kingdom. They even claimed dependence on foreign oil, when the UK was still a major oil producer. 'We have particularly important national interests and close friendships in the Gulf,' they claimed, not stating that these concerned arms sales, not oil. The key export market became Saudi Arabia – the United Kingdom had supplied Lightning fighters from the 1960s, and from the 1980s European Tornados. There were a series of state-to-state deals involving corrupt payments, all shrouded in deep secrecy. As a result of these deals in the early 1990s 75 per cent of all British arms exports went to Saudi Arabia. Discounting this rather special contract, the United Kingdom's share of the world's arms trade slumped dramatically.[44] It was claimed that 'The British are, by instinct, an internationalist people ... We do not want to stand idly by and watch humanitarian disasters or the aggression of dictators go unchecked.' This was projecting into the future what had once been true many decades earlier. Lurking was the notion that the United Kingdom could maintain a seat at the 'top table' by virtue of its military prowess – the familiar idea that the United Kingdom 'punches above its weight' in matters military.

But the upshot was that the United Kingdom was returning permanently, consciously, if not to bases East of Suez, then to a commitment to intervene East of Suez. Not that this was a New Labour innovation. In 1991 British forces (including an armoured division) had taken part in the war to get Iraq out of Kuwait. Nineteen British died, nine by mistake by US aircraft. But into global action New Labour did go. In 1998 British aircraft bombarded Iraq from Kuwait. In 1999 British forces were in action, again with others, in Kosovo. In 2000 they went in, on their own, to Sierra Leone, a former British colony in Africa. Something called the 'military covenant' was invented in the year 2000, as if it had been an eternal bond of obligation between nation and soldier. In 2003, the 1st Armoured Division was back in Iraq alongside a very much larger US force. In total forty British service personnel, from all services, were killed in Iraq in the course of 2003. The toll would mount to 179 British; the Iraqi toll at the very least 1,000 times more.

IRAQ

The decision to join in with the USA in its extraordinary war against Iraq was in effect made long before 2003. It was implicit in the decision that the United Kingdom military policy was to supply additional forces for US operations. The armed forces were eager to participate. But to uphold it in the circumstances that arose was difficult too. Tony Blair found himself having to make a case for war, for many months, in opposition to the views of important allies such as France, Germany and much of the rest of the world, as well as many people in the United Kingdom. From this all the distortions, exaggerations and mendacities followed. In order to justify this basic decision to ally with the USA, not itself unreasonable, an extraordinary set of misconceptions had to be created.

The USA had decided to invade Iraq to topple Saddam Hussein in the light of the false belief or pretext that he was connected to Al-Qaida, who had destroyed the Twin Towers in New York in September 2001. Tony Blair nailed his colours to this policy early and decisively, working himself up into a world-historical frenzy in the process. In the crucial Iraq debate of 18 March Blair claimed that 'many people' thought that the danger from the Nazis was 'fanciful' or 'worse, put forward in bad faith by warmongers'. Such a view was not at all widely held in the 1930s, not least because the political and military threat from the Nazis was obvious, at least to the left. Blair was as wrong about history as about Iraqi 'weapons of mass destruction' (WMD).

The case for war against Iraq was doubly misleading. It centred on WMD proliferation and mass-casualty terrorism: 'This fusion of longstanding concerns about proliferation with the post-9/11 concerns about mass-casualty terrorism was at the heart of the Government's case for taking action at this time against Iraq.'[45] The problem was that Iraq neither had WMD nor supported terrorism. Sir John Chilcot's post-mortem was brutally clear on this crucial point: 'While it was reasonable for the Government to be concerned about the fusion of proliferation and terrorism, there was no basis in the Joint Intelligence Committe (JIC) Assessments to suggest that Iraq itself represented such a threat.'[46] It is also telling that the British did not believe their own propaganda. While British troops went into action, 'The risk of CW [Chemical Warfare] attacks was assessed as low, but the UK's NBC [Nuclear, Biological, Chemical] protective capability while there for troops, would be "initially fragile".'[47] No clearer confirmation is needed that the invasion was about regime change and not chemical weapons. Yet the claim that such regime change was justified because Saddam was an especially vile dictator in that he killed his own people with chemical weapons was itself a serious distortion. He had used gas attacks against Iran, and its Kurdish allies, at a time when the British and US governments supported him and covered up the attacks.

Tony Blair's Iraq adventure was often compared to Anthony Eden's Suez. They were both much criticized for not telling the truth, but this was not their greatest crime. This was that they acted against the best interests of their nation, as well as against international norms. But there was one important difference. Eden was taking the lead in a British-French-Israeli rather than a US position. The serious charge against New Labour is not that they were deluded, but that they blindly followed the deluded policy of a particular foreign leader. The blame cannot be Blair's only. The war was decided on by the New Labour cabinet and by a majority of Labour MPs; the majority of newspapers and the BBC were in tow. The Tory opposition was strongly in favour. The military and the intelligence services were keen; the army became desperate when the original plan to use a British division invading from Turkey was shelved. There was in 2003 no anti-war party in the United Kingdom, with the temporary exception of the Liberal Democrats. Yet many saw through all this, most notably a former foreign secretary, Robin Cook, who denounced the policy in parliament in the debate on 18 March 2003. People from all political positions did not believe it either and marched through London in what was and still is the largest political demonstration in British history.

The domestic consequences of the war were minimal. Tony Blair won a general election in 2005 and sent troops to Afghanistan, where they would die and be wounded in much greater numbers than Iraq. The reputation the army had created for itself in counter-insurgency did not survive Basra and Helmand. The wars in Afghanistan and Iraq continued for longer than the First and Second World Wars combined. They brought not victory, but civil war, chaos and suffering of all sorts.

These extraordinary failures destroyed the last vestiges of a belief that the British state and its agencies told the truth if not the whole truth; the sense that the British state was primarily concerned with British, or European, interests. They also showed that the British state machine had lost the capacity for rational and critical examination of policy.[48]

OLD TIMES

Just as the adventures in Iraq and Afghanistan could be read as a return to previous times, so could other features of the twenty-first-century United Kingdom. Although British capital no longer dominated, even at home, London was restored to its Edwardian cosmopolitan pomp. Free trade, a laboriously created reality, made national economic borders non-existent in many key respects, again in ways which echoed the beginning of the twentieth century. Furthermore, the number of working-class members of parliament was reduced to 1910 levels.

Yet it was at this moment of the ending of the nation that the Labour chancellor, Gordon Brown, attempted to make 'Britishness' real. In a doubtless unconscious echo of the Edwardian campaign for Empire Day, he proposed a British National Day, a United Kingdom equivalent of 4 July and Bastille Day, to supplement St George's Day, St Andrew's Day, St David's Day and St Patrick's Day. Of course, politicians, even those with PhDs in History like Gordon Brown, are not required to be historically accurate or describe the present adequately. What is of interest is the vision, which in this case was one of both astonishing banality and great political import. He defined Britishness in ways that insulted the intelligence, and European partners. 'British patriotism is, in my view, founded ... on enduring ideals which shape our view of ourselves and our communities – values which in turn influence the way our institutions evolve,' he intoned. These 'enduring British ideals' were 'in addition to our qualities of creativity, inventiveness, enterprise and our internationalism', nothing less than 'a commitment to liberty for all, responsibility by all and fairness to all'. He repeatedly invoked the trinity 'liberty, responsibility and fairness', as if this tawdry trio could match up to 'liberty, fraternity, equality'. Indeed, the speech barely mentioned Europe and implied a distinction from Europe. The central references are contained in the following extract:

> I believe that, more sure of our values, we can become a Britain that is an increasingly successful leader of the global economy; a global Britain for whom membership of Europe is central; and then go on to help a reformed, more flexible, more outward-looking Europe play a bigger part in global society, not least improving relationships between Europe and the USA.[49]

Again, the implication was of British difference and superiority ('helping' Europe!); it was 'global Britain' with a special link to the USA. This was a moment of post-truth politics, as it would later be called. Blair *and* Brown in complex ways opened the way to UKIP and to non-fringe Euroscepticism, not least by encouraging fantasies of transformative revival and distinctiveness.

New Labour's futurism, and Brown's ideas about Britishness, wiped out the Labour past, not least its national past. But New Labour paid its dues to history, and in revealing ways. General Augusto Pinochet was arrested in London in October 1998 on a Spanish warrant for human rights violations in the 1970s and 1980s. He was arrested and held under house arrest into 2000, when the Labour government contrived to have him freed on health grounds, to avoid a ground-breaking legal judgement that he was liable to arrest and extradition. In doing so, New Labour undermined a new global human rights regime in favour of the most notorious butcher of socialists since the Second World War. Pinochet was called, without irony, 'Britain's only political prisoner' by the right-wing press. Margaret Thatcher was voluble in his support, as well she might be, given his free market views and his help in the war against Argentina. Her last speech to the Conservative Party conference, in 1999, was on his arrest.[50] It is even more telling that while in office New Labour agreed to an all-but-state funeral for Lady Thatcher, a ceremonial funeral with military honours. Big Ben was muffled, and Prime Minister's Questions cancelled. Most prime ministers were buried privately: Winston Churchill was the only one since William Gladstone to have had a state funeral. The country saw her passing, when it came in 2013, rather differently. Her body was carried on a gun-carriage from the National Gladstone Memorial at the Aldwych, at whose unveiling in 1905 crowds had thronged years after his demise, along Fleet Street into the City of London and St Paul's Cathedral, where her funeral service was held.[51] There were no cranes left to be dipped in respect by dockers in the unprecedented honour the London proletariat gave Churchill in 1965. In the old and distressed pit villages of England, of Scotland and of Wales, forgotten former miners celebrated bitterly. Tony Blair, meanwhile, was making money working for some of the vilest torturers and dictators on earth.[52] Only satirists, not historians, could do justice to this turn of events.

Notes

INTRODUCTION

1. See William Mulligan and Brendan Simms, *The Primacy of Foreign Policy in British History, 1660–2000: How Strategic Concerns Shaped Modern Britain* (London, 2010).
2. See Linda Colley, *Britons: Forging the Nation 1707–1837* (New Haven, Connecticut, 1992) for the question of British identity around 1800.
3. The term, by analogy with methodological individualism, I have taken from Andreas Wimmer and Nina Glick Schiller, 'Methodological Nationalism, the Social Sciences, and the Study of Migration: An Essay in Historical Epistemology', *The International Migration Review* 37.3 (2003), pp. 576–610.
4. Tom Nairn observed the 'obsessive English tendency to scrutinize society exclusively in terms of "class", rather than in terms of "nation" – sociologically, as it were, rather than politically, from the point of view of civil society rather than of the State and the totality'. Tom Nairn, 'The Left Against Europe?', *New Left Review* 1.75, September–October 1972, p. 45, n. 49.

CHAPTER 1: THE COUNTRY WITH NO NAME

1. Sir Dennis Robertson, *Britain in the World Economy* (London, 1954), p. 82.
2. Available at https://www.nationalchurchillmuseum.org, accessed 12 January 2018.
3. Ibid.
4. Stefan Zweig, *The World of Yesterday*, trans. Anthea Bell (London, 2009), p. 205.

5. Peter Mandler, *The English National Character: The History of an Idea from Edmund Burke to Tony Blair* (London, 2006); Frank Trentmann, *Free Trade Nation: Commerce, Consumption, and Civil Society in Modern Britain* (Oxford, 2008).

6. Listen for example to the H. G. Wells broadcast 'Whither Britain?', 9 January 1934, available at   http://www.bbc.co.uk/archive/hg_wells/12404.shtml, accessed 12 January 2018.

7. Trentmann, *Free Trade Nation*, pp. 95–100.

8. *The Manifesto of Lloyd George and Bonar Law*, 1918 Conservative Party manifesto, available at http://www.conservativemanifesto.com/1918/1918-conservative-manifesto.shtml, accessed 12 January 2018.

9. *Labour's Call to the People*, 1918 Labour Party manifesto, available at http://labourmanifesto.com/1918/1918-labour-manifesto.shtml, accessed 12 January 2018.

10. *Report of the Proceeding of the 62nd Annual Trades Union Congress*, Nottingham September 1930, pp. 257–87; the report of the Economic Committee on pp. 208–17, available at http://www.unionhistory.info/reports/index.php.

11. Sir Oswald Mosley, *House of Commons Debates*, 28 May 1930, col. 1354.

12. Ibid., cols. 1355–6; Robert Skidelsky, *Oswald Mosley* (London, 1975), pp. 214–20.

13. Skidelsky, *Oswald Mosley*, pp. 226–7, 229, 232, 237.

14. Ibid., p. 309.

15. *Labour's Call to Action: The Nation's Opportunity*, 1931 Labour Party manifesto, available at http://labourmanifesto.com/1931/1931-labour-manifesto.shtml, accessed 12 January 2018.

16. John Davis, *A History of Britain, 1885–1939* (London, 1999) is a rare example of a book which sees the 1930s as the triumph of the key Unionist programmes.

17. Tim Rooth, *British Protectionism and the International Economy: Overseas Commercial Policy in the 1930s* (Cambridge, 1993).

18. Charles Loch Mowat, *Britain Between the Wars 1918–1940* (Chicago, Illinois, 1955), pp. 399–419.

19. Lecture on 'National Self-Sufficiency' given at Dublin, April 1933, Robert Skidelsky, *Keynes* (London, 1992), pp. 476–80.

20. Keynes, broadcast on the 'pros and cons of tariffs', BBC, November 1932, John Maynard Keynes, *Keynes on the Wireless* (London, 2010), p. 91.

21. National Institute of Economic and Social Research, *Trade Regulations and Commercial Policy of the United Kingdom* (Cambridge, 1943).

22. Skidelsky, *Oswald Mosley*, p. 325.

23. Andrew Muldoon, *Empire, Politics and the Creation of the 1935 India Act: Last Act of the Raj* (London, 2009).

24. B. Chatterjee, 'Business and Politics in the 1930s: Lancashire and the Making of the Indo-British Trade Agreement', *Modern Asian Studies* 15.3 (1981), pp. 527–73; Muldoon, *Empire, Politics*; Martin Pugh, 'Lancashire, Cotton, and Indian Reform: Conservative Controversies in the 1930s', *Twentieth Century British History* 15 (2004), pp. 143–51. See also for the politics of jute, Jim Tomlinson, 'The Deglobalisation of Dundee, c. 1900–2000', *Journal of Scottish Historical Studies* 29 (2009), pp. 123–40, and 'De-globalization and Its Significance: From the Particular to the General', *Contemporary British History* 26 (2012), pp. 213–30.

25. *This Is the Road: The Conservative and Unionist Party's Policy*, Conservative Party, 1950, available at http://www.politicsresources.net/area/uk/man/con50.htm, accessed 12 January 2018.

26. Richard Toye, 'The Attlee Government, the Imperial Preference System and the Creation of the GATT', *English Historical Review* 118 (2003), pp. 912–39, though there were also free-trading tendencies in Labour still.

27. Harry Pollitt, *Looking Ahead* (London, 1946), p. 40.

28. John Darwin, *The Empire Project: The Rise and Fall of the British World-System, 1830–1970* (Cambridge, 2011).

29. Colin Kidd, *Union and Unionisms: Political Thought in Scotland, 1500–2000* (Cambridge, 2008), chapter 7.

30. I am grateful to my then student Graham Harding for his analysis of inscriptions found on the Imperial War Museum's Memorial Register; see: http://www.iwm.org.uk/memorials/search.

31. *Statistics Relating to the War Effort of the United Kingdom, 1943–1944*, Cmd. 6564.

32. 'A Speech by the Queen on her 21st Birthday, 1947', broadcast from Cape Town, 21 April 1947, available at https://www.royal.uk/21st-birthday-speech-21-april-1947, accessed 12 January 2018.

33. Board of Trade, *Statistical Abstract for the United Kingdom for Each of the Fifteen Years 1924 to 1938 Eighty-third Number*, Cmd. 6232, p. 363, figures for the 1920s and 1930s.

34. See the pioneering work of Peter Fryer, *Staying Power: The History of Black People in Britain* (London, 1984, 2010), pp. 298–316, 356–71.

35. Central Office of Information/Crown Film Unit, *Spotlight on the Colonies*, 1950. This film is held by the BFI (ID: 18147), available at http://www.colonialfilm.org.uk/node/757, accessed 5 February 2018.

36. Robert Winder, *Bloody Foreigners: The Story of Immigration to Britain* (London, 2005), pp. 322–7, 331.

37. Ibid., pp. 330–32.

38. For evidence see the cover of the 1966 World Cup final programme and the like. 'Empire Stadium' was still in use in the early 1970s, though 'Wembley Stadium' had appeared.

39. Jawaharlal Nehru, *An Autobiography* (1936) (New Delhi, 2004), p. 437.

40. Philip Williamson, *Stanley Baldwin* (Cambridge, 1999), chapter 9, 'Soul and Providence'.

41. Peter Gowan, 'The Origins of the Administrative Elite', *New Left Review*, 1.162 (March–April 1987), pp. 4–34.

42. Kevin Manton, 'Labour and the 1949 Parliament Act', *Contemporary British History*, 26 (2012), pp. 149–72.

43. Millicent Garrett Fawcett, *Women's Suffrage: A Short History of a Great Movement* (London, 1912), pp. 74–5.

44. Brian Harrison, 'Women in a Men's House: The Women MPs, 1919–1945', *Historical Journal* 29 (1986), pp. 623–54.

45. Peter Sloman, 'Partners in Progress? British Liberals and the Labour Party since 1918', *Political Studies Review*, 12 (2014), pp. 41–50.

46. Geraint Thomas, 'Political Modernity and "Government" in the Construction of Inter-war Democracy: Local and National Encounters', in Laura Beers and Geraint Thomas, *Brave New World: Imperial and Democratic Nation-Building in Britain Between the Wars* (London, 2012).

47. Movietone News, 'Mr Attlee Addresses You', June 1945, available at http://www.movietone.com/assets/BMN0418/wmv/BMN_45867_3.wmv, accessed 5 February 2018.

48. Colin Mellors, *The British MP: A Socio-economic Study of the House of Commons* (Farnborough, 1978), table 4.2, p. 41.

49. Richard Rose, 'Class and Party Divisions: Britain as a Test Case', *Sociology* 2.2 (1968), pp. 129–62, table 1, p. 131, and my own calculation from this. Definitions differ between sources. A. H. Halsey (ed.), *Trends in British Society since 1900* (London, 1972), table 8.6, p. 244, implies 117 'rank and file worker' Labour MPs on average in 1922–1935, 161 for 1945 and 135 for 1950. From the raw data in Mellors, *British MP*, Labour MPs in 1945 included 107 'workers' plus an additional 50 'trade union officials' (table 5.2, p. 63). To calculate this another way, no fewer than 210 (out of 400 of the 1945 parliament) were educated to elementary level, with 166 to elementary only and only 44 going on to secondary school from elementary school

(Mellors, *British MP*, table 4.2, p. 41). This all confirms that around 40 per cent of the 1945 Labour MPs were working class, much more than the sometimes reported 27 per cent which appears to be based on Mellors' 'workers' excluding the trade union officials.

50. See the discussion in chapter 15.

CHAPTER 2: MIGHTIER YET!

1. Sir Arthur Quiller-Couch (ed.), *The Oxford Book of English Verse* (Oxford, 1963), pp. 1123–4.

2. For a rebuttal see David French, *Raising Churchill's Army: The British Army and the War against Germany, 1919–1945* (Oxford, 2000), and his work more generally.

3. Commonwealth War Graves Commission, *Annual Report 2014/15*, available at http://media.cwgc.org/media/464598/cwgc-annual-report-2015-16.pdf, accessed 12 January 2018.

4. The jingoistic atmosphere is revealed in street names from the era: Mafeking, Ladysmith, Kimberley Roads and Avenues. I stayed briefly in Kimberley Avenue, Nunhead.

5. R. C. K. Ensor, *England 1870–1914* (London, 1936), pp. 412–13, put the budget in its dreadnought context; most recent histories put it firmly in the welfare context. The new pension would cost around £8 million per annum. Naval expenditures in 1900–1908 were always close to £30 million; those of 1909–1913 were well over £40 million.

6. The 1909–10 slightly extended financial year was a bumper one for dreadnought building, but the pace of building remained high. In the following three years five, four and then seven battleships or battle-cruisers were started each year.

7. The firm's Scotstoun works (one of three) was next to Yarrow on the Clyde. This was producing arms again from the 1930s into the 1960s. The original building appears still to stand, though it was added to very considerably between the 1920s and the late 1940s. For details and images see: http://canmore.org.uk/site/312087.

8. Matthew Seligmann, 'The Anglo-German Naval Race, 1898–1914', in Thomas Mahnken, Joseph Maiolo and David Stevenson (eds.), *Arms Races in International Politics: From the Nineteenth to the Twenty-first Century* (Oxford, 2016), pp. 21–40.

9. For the latest work see the special issue of *Journal of Strategic Studies* 38.7 (2015), edited by Matthew Seligmann and David Morgan-Owen.

10. For details of the national factories see David Kenyon, *First World War National Factories: An Archaeological, Architectural and Historical Review, Research Report Series*, Historic England Research Report 076-2015 (London, 2015). See also www.pastscape.org.uk, the website of Historic England.

11. Philip Hoare, *Wilde's Last Stand: Decadence, Conspiracy and the First World War* (London, 1997). See David Edgerton, *England and the Aeroplane: Militarism, Modernity and Machines* (London, 1991, 2013), pp. 24–6, for the connection to Supermarine, and Barbara Stoney, *Twentieth Century Maverick* (East Grinstead, 2004).

12. Adam Tooze, *The Deluge: The Great War, America and the Remaking of the Global Order, 1916–1931* (London, 2014), chapter 20.

13. Frederick Cooper, *Colonialism in Question: Theory, Knowledge, History* (Oakland, California, 2005), pp. 142–8; Jon Wilson, *India Conquered: Britain's Raj and the Chaos of Empire* (London, 2016).

14. See Martin Thomas, *Violence and Colonial Order: Police, Workers and Protest in the European Colonial Empires, 1918–1940* (Cambridge, 2012), chapter 9.

15. Ben Taylor, 'Science and the British Police Service: Surveillance, Intelligence and the Rise of the Professional Police Officer, 1930–2000' (PhD thesis, King's College London, 2015).

16. Tooze, *Deluge*.

17. Joe Maiolo, *Cry Havoc: The Arms Race and the Second World War, 1931–1941* (London, 2010).

18. This is very clear in the *Daily Mail*/British Movietone News film on the election: story no. 6263A, British Movietone News Archive, available at http://www.movietone.com/assets/BMN0267/wmv/BMN_6263A_3.wmv, combined with Pathé Gazette, *General Election Battle 1935*, British Pathé, film ID: 859.05, available at https://www.britishpathe.com/video/general-election-battle-1/query/85905, accessed 12 January 2018.

19. The Southampton dry-dock is now closed, but the Singapore dry-dock is still in action, repairing cruise liners.

20. Harry Pollitt's speeches to the 15th CPGB Congress, September 1938, available at https://www.marxists.org/archive/pollitt/1938/09/congress-report.htm, accessed 12 January 2018.

21. Evelyn Waugh, *Officers and Gentlemen* (1955) (London, 2001), p. 240.

22. R. A. C. Parker, 'The Pound Sterling, the American Treasury and British Preparations for War, 1938–1939', *The English Historical Review*, 98 (1983), pp. 261–79.

23. David Edgerton, *Warfare State: Britain 1920–1970* (Cambridge, 2006), pp. 56–7.

24. Christopher Bayly and Tim Harper, *Forgotten Armies: Britain's Asian Empire and the War with Japan* (London, 2005).

25. Jawaharlal Nehru, *The Discovery of India* (1946) (New Delhi, 2004), pp. 478–9.

26. *Statistics Relating to the War Effort of the United Kingdom*, p. 9.

27. 'No Part of the Reich Is Safe (The Lancaster Bomber)', British Movietone News (August 1942), available at https://www.youtube.com/watch?v=cLTP1U4Lz9k, accessed 30 January 2018.

28. Stafford Cripps, 'Mineral Resources and the Atlantic Charter', address to the BAAS conference on 25 July 1942, *The Advancement of Science* 2 (October 1942), p. 243.

29. *United Nations Day* (1943), British Pathé, film ID 108523, available at https://www.britishpathe.com/video/united-nations-day-parade/query/108523, accessed 12 January 2018.

30. S. D. Waters, *The Royal New Zealand Navy* (Wellington, 1956), chapter 24. *With the British Pacific Fleet*, available at http://nzetc.victoria.ac.nz/tm/scholarly/tei-WH2Navy-c24.html, accessed 12 January 2018.

31. Alan Allport, *Demobbed: Coming Home After the Second World War* (New Haven, Connecticut, 2009).

32. *Statistical Material Presented during the Washington Negotiations 1945*, Cmd. 6707, para. 2.

33. The idea has become very widespread. For a recent example, the left Labour politician Chris Mullin, in the *Observer*, 12 April 2015: 'Attlee and his colleagues Ernest Bevin and Herbert Morrison were more or less in charge of the home front throughout the last years of the war'. For the alternative view see David Edgerton, *Britain's War Machine: Weapons, Resources and Experts in the Second World War* (London, 2011), especially chapters 4, 5, 9. When the idea arose and got established is not clear. A. J. P. Taylor, *English History* (London, 1965), does not, for example, subscribe to it.

34. Edgerton, *Britain's War Machine*, pp. 129–31.

35. Taylor, *English History*, p. 29n.

36. A central key observation made by Alan Milward, *The Economic Effects of the Two World Wars on Britain*, 2nd edn (London, 1984).

37. Jim Tomlinson, 'Marshall Aid and the "Shortage Economy" in Britain in the 1940s', *Contemporary European History* 9 (2000), pp. 137–55.

38. Pollitt, *Looking Ahead*, pp. 10, 26.

39. Wilson, *India Conquered*, pp. 463–7.

40. Ronald Hyam, *Britain's Declining Empire: The Road to Decolonisation, 1918–1968* (Cambridge, 2007), pp. 160–62.

CHAPTER 3: GLOBALIZATION TO NATIONALIZATION

1. First published in *A School History of England* (London, 1911).

2. James Belich *Replenishing the Earth: The Settler Revolution and the Rise of Angloworld* (Oxford, 2009), pp. 442–52, correctly points out that it was in the twentieth century, not the industrial revolution period, that the ghost acres were really significant.

3. Board of Trade (in conjunction with the Ministry of Labour and the registrars-general), *Statistical Abstract for the United Kingdom for Each of the Fifteen Years 1924 to 1938*, p. xvii.

4. Ibid., pp. 392, 410.

5. A. H. Halsey (ed.), *Trends in British Society since 1900* (London, 1972), table 3.6.

6. *Report of the Royal Commission on the Coal Industry (1925) with Minutes of Evidence and Appendices*, vol. 1, report (1926), Cmd. 2600, pp. 44–5.

7. John Beckett and Michael Turner, 'Land Reform and the English Land Market, 1880–1925', in Matthew Cragoe and Paul Readman (eds.), *The Land Question in Britain, 1750–1950* (London, 2010), pp. 219–36.

8. Around 1900 US labour productivity in coal was around three times that of the British. *Report of the Royal Commission on the Coal Industry (1925)*, p. 127.

9. Ibid., p. 3.

10. Ibid., pp. 15–19.

11. Board of Trade, *Statistical Abstract for the United Kingdom for Each of the Fifteen Years 1924 to 1938*, p. 332.

12. *Report of the Royal Commission on the Coal Industry (1925)*, p. 23.

13. Ibid., pp. 46–7.

14. 'Presidential Address of Sir Richard A. S. Redmayne, President 1935', *Proceedings of the Institution of Civil Engineers* 239 (1935), pp. 1–35.

15. H. Stanley Jevons, *The British Coal Trade* (London, 1915), table on p. 752.

16. John Clapham, *An Economic History of Modern Britain*, vol. 3: *Machines and National Rivalries (1887–1914) with an Epilogue (1914–1929)* (Cambridge, 1938), pp. 387–9.

17. Christopher Lee, *Eight Bells and Top Masts: Diaries from a Tramp Steamer* (London, 2001).

18. *Report of the Royal Commission on the Coal Industry (1925)*, p. 6.

19. Charles Loch Mowat, *Britain between the Wars, 1918–1940* (Chicago, Illinois, 1955), p. 297.

41. On the politics of free trade and sugar see Anthony Howe, *Free Trade and Liberal England, 1846–1946* (Oxford, 1997), pp. 204–13.

42. For the passage of one such ship, the *Highland Princess* of the Royal Mail Line, in and out of the Royal Docks in London see Basil Wright (dir.), *Waters of Time* (1951), a film made for the Festival of Britain.

43. *Convention between the Government of the United Kingdom and the Government of the Argentine Republic Relating to Trade and Commerce … 1933–34*, Cmd. 4492, Treaty Series no. 2 (1934), and *Agreement between His Majesty's Government in the United Kingdom and the Argentine Government Relating to Trade and Commerce … 1936–37*, Cmd. 5324.

44. William Keith Hancock and Margaret Gowing, *British War Economy* (London, 1949), pp. 467–79.

45. H. M. D. Parker, *Manpower: A Study of Wartime Policy and Administration* (London, 1957), pp. 252–5.

46. Klaus Schmider, 'The Mediterranean in 1940–1941: Crossroads of Lost Opportunities?', *War & Society* 15 (1997), p. 31.

47. 'Sir John Russell's Presidential Address BAAS 1949', p. 179.

48. William Ashworth, *History of the British Coal Industry*, vol. 5 (Oxford, 1986), p. 25.

49. Ibid., p. 29. The now £80 million of Coal Commission stock was bought also – that is this stock was turned into government stock. See also Supple, *British Coal Industry*, pp. 649–65.

50. Ashworth, *History of the British Coal Industry*, p. 31.

51. I am thus perhaps strengthening Timothy Mitchell's thesis that coal production engendered social democracy. Though I have reservations about the thesis in relation to both coal and oil, it is suggestive; Timothy Mitchell, *Carbon Democracy: Political Power in the Age of Oil* (London, 2013).

52. Pollitt, *Looking Ahead*, p. 68.

53. Department for Business, Energy and Industrial Strategy, 'Historical Coal Data: Coal Production, 1853 to …' (January 2013, updated), available at https://www.gov.uk/government/statistical–data–sets, accessed 5 September 2017.

54. Arthur Horner, *The Communist Party and the Coal Crisis* (25 November 1945) (London, Communist Party of Great Britain), available at https://www.marxists.org/archive/horner/1945/11/coal.htm, accessed 12 January 2018.

55. Ashworth, *History of the British Coal Industry*, p. 152–3.

56. Ibid., p. 164.

57. Martin Chick, *Industrial Policy in Britain, 1945–1951: Economic Planning, Nationalisation and the Labour Governments* (Cambridge, 1998), pp. 45, 55–8.

58. Ibid., p. 45.

59. R. C. O. Matthews, Charles Feinstein, and John Odling-Smee, *British Economic Growth, 1856–1973* (Oxford, 1982), table 8.

60. See for example, Gavin Williams, 'Marketing without and with Marketing Boards: The Origins of State Marketing Boards in Nigeria', *Review of African Political Economy*, 12 (1985), pp. 4–15.

61. *A Plan for the Mechanised Production of Groundnuts in East and Central Africa*, cmd. 7030, quoted in Alan Wood, *The Groundnut Affair* (London, 1950), p. 252.

62. Wood, *The Groundnut Affair*.

63. *Let Us Win Through Together: A Declaration of Labour Policy for the Consideration of the Nation*, 1950 Labour Party manifesto, available at http://www.politicsresources.net/area/uk/man/lab50.htm, accessed 12 January 2018.

64. Ibid. On the background with respect to wholesaling see Kevin Manton, 'Playing Both Sides against the Middle: The Labour Party and the Wholesaling Industry 1919–1951', *Twentieth Century British History* 18.3 (2007), pp. 306–33.

CHAPTER 4: KINGDOM OF CAPITAL

1. James Connolly, 'Our Rulers as a Study', *The Worker*, 16 January 1915, republished in James Connolly, *Lost Writings*, ed. Aindrias Ó Cathasaigh (London, 1997), available at https://www.marxists.org/archive/connolly/1915/01/rulers.htm, accessed 12 January 2018.

2. Friedrich Hayek, *The Road to Serfdom* (1944) (London, 2001), p. 145.

3. Michael Powell and Emeric Pressburger (prod. and dir.), *I Know Where I'm Going* (1945).

4. Perhaps the most powerful is that in Alexander Mackendrick (dir.), *The Man in the White Suit* (1951), where there is a particularly sinister senior capitalist who comes up from London. The critique is largely balanced by the fact that labour and capital have the same interests in this case.

5. John Beckett and Michael Turner, 'Land Reform and the English Land Market, 1880–1925', in Matthew Cragoe and Paul Readman (eds.), *The Land Question in Britain, 1750–1950* (London, 2010), pp. 219–36.

6. Ibid., p. 222, see table, which is uncorrected for increased post-war prices.

7. F. M. L. Thompson, 'Presidential Address: English Landed Society in the Twentieth Century: I, Property: Collapse and Survival', *Transactions of the Royal Historical Society* 40 (1990), pp. 1–24.

8. In the interwar years the city had relatively few Jewish firms, being notably less cosmopolitan than before 1914. There was indeed anti-Semitism: it was rumoured that Montagu Norman was partly Jewish, but his anti-Semitism was clear. David Kynaston, *City of London: The History* (London, 1995), pp. 359–60.

9. The income from property, rentier income, is everywhere into the twentieth century. Jack Worthing's ward Cecily, Wilde tells us, has about £130,000 'in the Funds' (that is government debt). The central characters in *Howard's End* (1910) are cosmopolitan rentier intellectuals (Margaret is on £600 per annum); they are contrasted to the business family, national and imperial, in rubber, and currants, and much else, clearly.

10. Youssef Cassis and Margaret Rocques, *City Bankers 1890–1914* (Cambridge, 1994), p. 131. *House of Lords Hansard*, Lords Questions, 13 March 2003.

11. Charles Mowat, *Britain between the Wars 1918–1940* (London, 1955), p. 494.

12. Sidney and Beatrice Webb, *A Constitution for the Socialist Commonwealth of Great Britain* (London, 1920), p. xii.

13. She was the daughter of Richard Potter, once an MP and chairman of the Great Western Railway. A sister married Charles Cripps, father of Stafford Cripps.

14. For one example – note the lack of attention to the coal firms and the owners (and research); the discussion of industrial structure is abstract and statistical in Supple, *British Coal Industry.*

15. In each case the *Oxford Dictionary of National Biography* is tellingly inadequate on their business lives. For minor coal owners Michael Dintenfass notes that obituaries stress public life, but concludes from this the business was despised: see his 'The Voice of Industry and the Ethos of Decline' in Jean–Pierre Dormois and Michael Dintenfass (eds), *The British Industrial Decline* (London, 1999).

16. Ashworth, *History of British Coal Industry*, pp. 6–7. There is nothing like this listing of firms in the volume corresponding to the private industry.

17. F. M. L. Thompson, 'Presidential Address: English Landed Society in the Twentieth Century: II, New Poor and New Rich', *Transactions of*

the Royal Historical Society 1 (1991), pp. 1–20; F. M. L. Thompson, 'Presidential Address: English Landed Society in the Twentieth Century: III, Self-Help and Outdoor Relief', *Transactions of the Royal Historical Society* 2 (1992), pp. 1–23.

18. See the pithy account of his wealth and partial ascent in Richard Davenport-Hines, *Titanic Lives: Migrants and Millionaires, Conmen and Crew* (London, 2012), pp. 37–44.

19. For many more examples see F. M. L. Thompson, *Gentrification and the Enterprise Culture: Britain 1780–1980* (Oxford, 2001).

20. Stafford House (now Lancaster House) was the home of the Duke of Sutherland; Devonshire House, near Piccadilly, was demolished in 1924; Lansdowne House was bought by Gordon Selfridge; Dorchester House was rented out and demolished in 1929; Norfolk House, St James's Square, was demolished in 1938. Bridgewater House (Lord Ellesmere) became the headquarters of the British Oxygen Company in 1938 and was then restored as a house by John Latsis, a Greek billionaire, in 1981.

21. M. Worboys, 'Manson, Ross and Colonial Medical Policy: Tropical Medicine in London and Liverpool, 1899–1914', in R. MacLeod and M. Lewis (eds.), *Disease, Medicine and Empire: Perspectives on Western Medicine and the Experience of European Expansion* (London, 1988).

22. G. R. Searle, *The Liberal Party, Triumph and Disintegration* (London, 1992), pp. 102–7.

23. He fought North Paddington in 1918 as an independent Labour candidate and lost; his son George was to become an important wealthy figure on the Labour left, entering parliament in 1929 and again 1935, remaining into the 1970s.

24. Bernard Wasserstein, *The Secret Lives of Trebitsch Lincoln* (London, 1988). This brilliant book on an extraordinary conman echoes another – Hugh Trevor-Roper, *Hermit of Peking: The Hidden Life of Sir Edmund Backhouse* (Harmondsworth, 1978). Another foreignborn, though British-educated MP elected in 1910 was Frank Goldsmith, Tory MP for Stowmarket, who served until 1918. He was the father of Sir James Goldsmith.

25. Philip Williams, *Hugh Gaitskell: A Political Biography* (Oxford, 1982), p. 78.

26. J. A. Thomas, *The House of Commons* (London, 1958), cited in A. H. Halsey (ed.), *Trends in British Society since 1900* (London, 1972), table 8.5, p. 243. The tables in Halsey on p. 244 for the later period, by

imposing a distinction between business and professions, underestimate severely the connections of Conservatives to business in that many professionals were also in business in many ways.

27. This is my estimate from examining the new peerages of the interwar years. These are available online, and though they may be incomplete are unlikely to be biased towards business peers.

28. Sir William Wills, who had been a Liberal MP, was ennobled in 1906. Sir Frederick Wills, also raised to the barony, was a Liberal MP for Bristol North; his son was to be a Conservative MP. Other ennobled businessmen included: the textile magnate Lord Ashton; Lord Illingworth of one of the worsted spinners of Bradford, Liberal MP and minister in coalition; Lord Borwick of Borwick, makers of baking and custard powders; Lord Waring of furniture makers Waring & Gillow; Lord Vestey of the giant global meat combine; Lord Dewar, from the distillers Dewars (his brother became Lord Forteviot); Lord Austin of the motor company; the brewer Lord Daresbury, Gilbert Greenall of Greenalls; Lord Brotherton from chemicals; Lord Trent, Jesse Boot of Boots; Lord McGowan and Lord Melchett of ICI; Lord Hyndley of Powell Duffryn coal; Lord Greenway and Lord Cadman of the Anglo-Persian Oil company; Lord Lawrence of the LMS Railway and of the Antofagasta and Bolivia Railway; Lord Hives of Rolls-Royce; Lord Perry of the Ford Motor Company; Lord Hirst of Witton, Hugo Hirst of GEC; Lord Beaverbrook, Max Aitken (once a Unionist MP); Baron Merthyr, the coal owner Sir William Lewis; Lord Buckland, one of three ennobled Berry brothers; Lord Essendon, Frederick Lewis of Furness, Withy; Lord Inverforth, the brother of Viscount Weir, of a shipping line; Lord Kylsant, Owen Philipps, one of three ennobled brothers: his brother Laurence Philipps became Lord Milford, the other Viscount St Davids (a fourth brother was one of the three of the four who served as MPs – Sir Ivor Philipps was chairman of Schweppes, Ilford, etc.); Lord Inverclyde, John Burns of Cunard; Lord Invernairn, Sir William Beardmore, the armourer; Lord Kenilworth, Sir John Siddeley of Hawker Siddeley; Lord Woolavington, James Buchanan of the whisky firm; Lord Glentanar, George Coats of Coats sewing thread; Lord Hollenden, Samuel Morley, a Nottingham hosiery magnate; Lord Luke, George Lawson Johnston, founder of Bovril; Lord Cable, who ran one of the greatest merchant houses in British India; and Lord Rotherwick, Sir Herbert Cayzer MP, chairman of the Clan Line, Tory for Portsmouth South.

29. Later Lord Clydesmuir.

30. Philip Williamson, *Stanley Baldwin* (Cambridge, 1999), pp. 88–103.
31. Ibid., p. 259.
32. Peter Bennett of Lucas followed him in his seat (he was later ennobled).
33. Philip Murphy, *Monarchy and the Ends of Empire: The House of Windsor, the British Government and the Postwar Commonwealth* (Oxford, 2013), p. 29. Eire as part of an act to reduce the role of the monarch from Irish affairs; South Africa as a way of suggesting the divisibility of the crown.
34. Jose Harris, *Private Lives, Public Spirit: A Social History of Britain, 1870–1914* (Oxford, 1993), pp. 99–100.
35. Mowat, *Britain between the Wars*, p. 206.
36. Figures from ibid., pp. 205, 492.
37. Sidney Pollard, *The Development of the British Economy: 1914–1990* (London, 1962), p. 397.
38. Figures from Mowat, *Britain between the Wars*, p. 205.
39. Ibid., p. 494.
40. Kathleen Langley, 'An Analysis of the Asset Structure of Estates', *Oxford Bulletin of Economics and Statistics* 13.10 (1951), pp. 339–56.
41. B. R. Mitchell, *Abstract of British Historical Statistics* (Cambridge, 1962), pp. 377–8 (Feinstein data).
42. Ross McKibbin, 'Class and Conventional Wisdom: The Conservative Party and the "Public" in Inter-war Britain', in Ross McKibbin, *The Ideologies of Class: Social Relations in Britain, 1880–1950* (Oxford, 1990), pp. 259–93. Peter Clarke, *Hope and Glory: Britain, 1900–2000* (London, 1996, 2004), pp. 128–34, discusses sterling and prices in detail, but not the revaluation of the debt. Ross McKibbin, 'Political Sociology in the Guise of Economics: J. M. Keynes and the Rentier', *The English Historical Review*, 128.530 (1 February 2013), pp. 78–106, addresses the issue in theory but does not note just how big and important the effect was in reality.
43. Tooze, *Deluge*, pp. 353–73.
44. One of the few general histories which appreciates this is W. N. Medlicott, *Contemporary England 1914–1964* (London, 1967), pp. 147–9.
45. Arthur Bowley, *Some Economic Consequences of the Great War* (London, 1930), p. 110.
46. Joseph R. Cammarosano, *John Maynard Keynes: Free Trader or Protectionist?* (Plymouth, 2013), chapter 2.
47. J. M. Keynes, 'Alternative Aims in Monetary Policy (1923)', in J. M. Keynes, *Essays in Persuasion* (London, 1931).

48. *A National Policy: An Account of the Emergency Programme Advanced by Sir Oswald Mosley MP* [and sixteen other Labour members of Parliament] (London, 1931). It was drafted by Allan Young, John Strachey MP, W. L. Brown MP and Aneurin Bevan MP.

49. Martin Daunton, *Just Taxes: The Politics of Taxation in Britain, 1914–1979* (Cambridge, 2002), pp. 66–74.

50. As in Peter Cain and Anthony Hopkins, *British Imperialism: 1688–2000* (London, 2002) and in the works of many others who insist on continuity but ignore the actual history of domestic capital.

51. Sidney Pollard, *Britain's Prime and Britain's Decline: The British Economy, 1870–1914* (London, 1990), pp. 60–61.

52. Ibid., p. 109.

53. Ibid., p. 110.

54. By comparison the LMS Railway operated around 7,000 route miles of railway line, servicing 2,944 goods depots and 2,588 passenger stations, using 291,490 freight vehicles, 20,276 passenger vehicles and 9,914 locomotives. The company directly employed 263,000 staff and through its annual coal consumption of over 6.5 million tons could claim to indirectly employ a further 26,500 coal miners.

55. Iain Stewart, *Don Heriberto: Knight of the Argentine* (Ely, 2008).

56. Howard Cox, *The Global Cigarette: Origins and Evolution of British American Tobacco, 1880–1945* (New York, 2000), p. 291.

57. Ibid., p. 326.

58. *Statistical Material Presented during the Washington Negotiations 1945*, tables, 4, 6, pp. 9, 10.

59. Ibid., table 12, p. 14.

60. Cain and Hopkins, *British Imperialism*, p. 475.

61. Tom Nicholas, 'Wealth Making in Nineteenth- and Early Twentieth-Century Britain: Industry v. Commerce and Finance', *Business History* 41 (1999), pp. 16–36 shows that contrary to what is implied in the gentlemanly capitalist literature, it is wrong to imply that all the great fortunes came from finance and London. Raymond Dumett (ed.), *Gentlemanly Capitalism and British Imperialism: The New Debate on Empire* (London, 2014).

62. See Cain and Hopkins, *British Imperialism*, chapter 17, for this thesis for the interwar years. 'On the whole,' they claim, 'industrialists still lacked entry into the circles of influence to which the City had long been admitted' (p. 425).

CHAPTER 5: BRITISH CAPITALISM?

1. Herbert Morrison, *The Peaceful Revolution: Speeches by Herbert Morrison* (London, 1949), p. 85.

2. A. J. Brown, *Applied Economics* (London, 1948), table 20, p. 198.

3. Geoffrey Jones, *The Evolution of International Business* (London, 1996), pp. 30–31, 42–3.

4. David J. Jeremy, 'The Hundred Largest Employers in the United Kingdom, in Manufacturing and Non–Manufacturing Industries, in 1907, 1935 and 1955', *Business History* 33 (1991), pp. 93–111.

5. Kirsten W. Kininmonth, 'The Growth, Development and Management of J. & P. Coats Ltd, c.1890–1960: An Analysis of Strategy and Structure', *Business History* 48.4 (2006), pp. 551–79.

6. Ibid.

7. Calico Printers' Association, *Fifty Years of Calico Printing: A Jubilee History of the C.P.A.* (Manchester, 1949).

8. Maurits W. Ertsen, *Improvising planned development on the Gezira Plain, Sudan, 1900–1980* (London, 2015).

9. *Memoirs of John Wigham Richardson 1937–1908* (privately printed, Glasgow, 1911), p. 343.

10. Ibid., p. 255.

11. Ibid., p. 231.

12. I am grateful to John Ingram for discussion of the history of Kingsway.

13. Simon Ball, 'The German Octopus: The British Metal Corporation and the Next War, 1914–1939', *Enterprise & Society* 5 (2004), pp. 451–89.

14. Sally M. Horrocks, 'The Internationalization of Science in a Commercial Context: Research and Development by Overseas Multinationals in Britain before the Mid-1970s', *The British Journal for the History of Science* 40 (2007), pp. 227–50.

15. Ibid.

16. See in particular the arguments of David Mowery, 'Industrial Research', in B. Elbaum and W. Lazonick (eds.), *The Decline of the British Economy* (Oxford, 1986). For rebuttals, Edgerton, 'Science and Technology in British Business History'; D. E. H. Edgerton and S. M. Horrocks, 'British Industrial Research and Development before 1945', *Economic History Review* 47 (1994), pp. 213–38.

17. Sabine Clarke, 'Pure Science with a Practical Aim: The Meanings of Fundamental Research in Britain, circa 1916–1950', *Isis* 101 (2010), pp. 285–311.

18. Gillian Peele, 'St. George's and the Empire Crusade', in Chris Cook and John Ramsden (eds.), *By-elections in British Politics* (London, 1973).

19. Jerry White, *London in the Twentieth Century: A City and Its People* (London, 2001).

20. *Statistics Relating to the War Effort of the United Kingdom*, table 7.

21. *Statistical Material Presented during the Washington Negotiations 1945*, para. 6, p. 3.

22. Jim Tomlinson, *Democratic Socialism and Economic Policy: the Attlee Years, 1945–1951* (Cambridge, 1997), pp. 58–64.

23. Donald Alexander (dir.), *Cotton Come Back* (1946), 26 mins., ID 1210444, available at http://www.screenonline.org.uk/film/id/1210444/index.html, accessed 12 January 2018.

24. Barry Supple, 'Fear of Failing: Economic History and the Decline of Britain', *The Economic History Review* 47 (1994), pp. 441–58.

25. A rare early analyst to point this out was Paul Foot, *The Politics of Harold Wilson* (Harmondsworth, 1968).

26. Ministry of Information, *Clyde Built* (1943), film no.: UKY 502, accessed at http://film.iwmcollections.org.uk, but currently unavailable.

27. See Foot, *The Politics of Harold Wilson*, pp. 74–9.

28. Bevan resignation speech, 23 April 1951, *House of Commons Debates*, vol. 487, cols. 34–43.

CHAPTER 6: KNOWLEDGE AND POWER

1. F. A. Hayek, *The Road to Serfdom* (London, 2001), p. 146.

2. In part this is due to English academics pioneering in wider cultural studies, but the imprint remains important. See Raymond Williams, *Culture and Society, 1780–1950* (London, 1958); Raymond Williams, *The Long Revolution* (London, 1961). See also the work on Cambridge English in the interwar period, and the magazine *Scrutiny* in particular, Francis Mulhern, *The Moment of 'Scrutiny'* (London, 1979); and Christopher Hilliard, *English as a Vocation: The Scrutiny Movement* (Oxford, 2012).

3. Of the first three Labour female MPs, two (Susan Lawrence and Dorothy Jewson), were Cambridge-educated; the other was Margaret Bondfield, a trade unionist. Dr Marion Phillips, educated at Melbourne University and the LSE, was chief woman officer of the Labour Party and was elected to parliament in 1929. Ellen Wilkinson (Manchester), Jennie Lee (Edinburgh), Barbara Betts (later Castle) (Oxford) and Shirley Summerskill (London) were all graduates. So too were other

prominent women in politics, such as Eleanor Rathbone (Oxford), Lady Rhondda (Oxford) and Sylvia Pankhurst (Manchester). Amy Johnson, the most famous British aviatrix, was a Sheffield graduate.

4. Arthur Burns, 'Beyond the "Red Vicar": Community and Christian Socialism in Thaxted, Essex, 1910–84', *History Workshop Journal* 75 (2013), pp. 101–24.

5. Edward P. Thompson, 'The Peculiarities of the English', *Socialist Register* 2.2 (1965), also in slightly different form in E. P. Thompson, *The Poverty of Theory and Other Essays* (London, 1978).

6. J. A. Hobson, *The New Protectionism* (London, 1916), p. 3.

7. Ibid., p. 103.

8. Norman Angell, *If Britain is to Live* (London, 1923), available at https://archive.org/details/ifbritainistolivo00angeuoft, accessed 12 January 2018.

9. Listen, for example, to the H. G. Wells broadcast on 9 January 1934, 'Whither Britain?', bbc.co.uk/archive/hg_wells.

10. J. A. Hobson, *Towards International Government* (London: Allen & Unwin, 1915).

11. F. A. Voigt, *Unto Caesar* (London, 1938), pp. 211–12; Waqar Zaidi, ' "Aviation Will Either Destroy or Save Our Civilization": Proposals for the International Control of Aviation, 1920–1945', *Journal of Contemporary History* 46 (2011), pp. 150–78.

12. Stephen King-Hall, *Total Victory* (London, 1941), p. 217.

13. Ibid., p. 219.

14. M. J. B. Davy, *Air Power and Civilization* (London, 1941), pp. 161, 196.

15. S. W. H. Zaidi, 'Technology and the Reconstruction of International Relations: Liberal Internationalist Proposals for the Internationalisation of Aviation and the International Control of Atomic Energy in Britain, USA and France, 1920–1950' (unpublished PhD thesis, Imperial College London, 2008), p. 83.

16. J. M. Spaight, *Bombing Vindicated* (London, 1944), p. 152.

17. See also Sir William Beveridge, *The Price of Peace* (London, 1945), p. 54.

18. 'Prime Minister's Personal Minute, Foreign Secretary General Ismay for C.O.S. Committee (29 August 1944)', CAB 120/837, National Archives, in Zaidi, 'Technology and the Reconstruction of International Relations', p. 6.

19. Winston Churchill, 'The Soviet Danger: "The Iron Curtain" ', in David Cannadine (ed.), *The Speeches of Winston Churchill* (London, 1989),

pp. 295–308, quoted in Zaidi, 'Technology and the Reconstruction of International Relations', pp. 6–7.

20. Kevin Ruane, *Churchill and the Bomb in War and Cold War* (London, 2016), pp. 162–71; Alan Schwerin (ed.), *Bertrand Russell on Nuclear War, Peace, and Language: Critical and Historical Essays* (Westport, Connecticut 2002); Waqar Zaidi, ' "A Blessing in Disguise": Reconstructing International Relations through Atomic Energy, 1945–1948', *Past and Present Supplement* 6 (2011), pp. 309–31.

21. Andrea Bosco, *June 1940: Great Britain and the First Attempt to Build a European Union* (Cambridge, 2016).

22. Ibid., pp. 225–6.

23. Vera Brittain, *England's Hour* (1941) (London, 2005), pp. 128, 225.

24. Ibid., pp. 225–6.

25. Squadron Leader John Strachey, 'The Story of a Target', Home Service Broadcast. *The Listener* (1 June 1944).

26. Stuart Macintyre, *A Proletarian Science: Marxism in Britain, 1917–1933* (London, 1982). Jonathan Rée, *Proletarian Philosophers: Problems in Socialist Culture in Britain, 1900–1940* (London, 1984); Edwin A. Roberts, *The Anglo-Marxists: A Study in Ideology and Culture* (Lanham, Maryland, 1997).

27. Presidential address, TUC, Huddersfield, September 1900, *Report of the 33rd Annual Trades Union Congress*, pp. 44–54, available at http://www.unionhistory.info/reports/index.php, accessed 12 January 2018.

28. Roberts, *The Anglo-Marxists*.

29. Gary Werskey, *The Visible College: A Collective Biography of British Scientific Socialists in the Thirties* (London, 1978); William Mc-Gucken, *Scientists, Society, and State: The Relations of Science Movement in Great Britain, 1931–1947* (Columbus, Ohio, 1984); Timothy Shenk, *Maurice Dobb, Political Economist* (London, 2013).

30. Thinking of history, one is tempted to add George Dangerfield's brilliant *The Strange Death of Liberal England* (1935), except that Dangerfield had emigrated to the USA in 1930.

31. Communist Party of Great Britain, *For Soviet Britain: the Programme of the Communist Party Adopted at the XIII Congress February 2nd, 1935*, available at https://www.marxists.org/history/international/comintern/sections/britain/congresses/XIII/soviet_britain.htm, accessed 12 January 2018.

32. James Hinton, 'Coventry Communism: A Study of Factory Politics in the Second World War', *History Workshop* 10 (autumn 1980), pp. 90–118. See also the outstanding Richard Croucher, *The Engineers at*

War 1939–1945 (London, 1982) on both the Communist Party and on the centrality of production in the politics of 1942.

33. Argonaut, *Give Us the Tools: A Study of the Hindrances to Full War Production and How to End Them* (London, 1942), pp. 25–7. See the very positive review in the communist *Labour Monthly* 24 (1942), p. 160.

34. Ibid., chapter 5. See also the wonderfully clear Margot Heinemann, *Wages Front* (London, 1947).

35. Celticus (Aneurin Bevan MP), *Why not Trust the Tories?* (London, 1944), pp. 60–64.

36. Pollitt, *Looking Ahead*, p. 9.

37. Ibid., pp. 59, 63.

38. Yet perhaps Orwell, exceptionally, did pick up something of this in labelling (in *Nineteen Eighty-four*) the ideology of Oceania as 'Ingsoc' (English Socialism), which had a powerful dose of technocracy within it. See Ralph Desmarais, 'Science, Scientific Intellectuals, and British Culture in the Early Atomic Age: A Case Study of George Orwell, Jacob Bronowski, P. M. S. Blackett and J. G. Crowther' (PhD thesis, Imperial College London, 2010).

39. Bernard Semmel, 'Sir William Ashley as "Socialist of the Chair"', *Economica* (1957), pp. 343–53; Avner Offer, 'Using the Past in Britain: Retrospect and Prospect', *The Public Historian*, 6.4 (autumn 1984), pp. 17–36; A. W. Coats, 'Political Economy and the Tariff Reform Campaign of 1903', *Journal of Law and Economics*, 11.1 (April 1968), pp. 181–229.

40. Bernard Semmel, 'Sir Halford Mackinder: Theorist of Imperialism', *The Canadian Journal of Economics and Political Science/Revue canadienne d'Economique et de Science politique* 24 (1958), pp. 554–61.

41. Clarisse Berthezène, *Training Minds for the War of Ideas: Ashridge College, the Conservative Party and the Cultural Politics of Britain, 1929–54* (Manchester, 2015).

42. Gary Love, 'The Periodical Press and the Intellectual Culture of Conservatism in Interwar Britain', *The Historical Journal* 57 (2014), pp. 1027–56; Berthezène, *Training Minds for the War of Ideas*.

43. Junius (Arthur Bryant and John Drummond Wolff), *Britain Awake!* (London, 1940), published by Union and Reconstruction, a hard-right organization set up by the authors.

44. Sir Oswald Mosley, *House of Commons Debates*, 28 May 1930, cols. 1355–6.

45. *A National Policy: An Account of the Emergency Programme Advanced by Sir Oswald Mosley MP*. It was drafted by Allan Young, John Strachey MP, W. L. Brown MP and Aneurin Bevan MP.

46. See the work of the key ideologue, Jorian Jenks, and the pioneering historical work of Patrick Wright on British fascism and the land in the 1930s, *The Village That Died for England: The Strange Story of Tyneham* (London, 1995).

47. Sir Oswald Mosley, *Tomorrow we Live* (London, 1938).

48. Sir Oswald Mosley, *Greater Britain* (London, 1934), p. 128.

49. See Skidelsky, *Oswald Mosley*, p. 309.

50. See William Joyce, *Twilight over England* (Berlin, 1940).

51. Mandler, *English National Character*, pp. 184–95, which correctly notes this is, like Priestley's, a left version, made to seem more important by the later victory of the left.

52. This is usually missed, for example, in the interesting piece by John Baxendale, ' "I had seen a lot of Englands": J. B. Priestley, Englishness and the People', *History Workshop Journal* 51 (2001), pp. 87–111, who insists on the nationalism.

53. Mandler, *English National Character*, pp. 184–95, sees the images of England associated with wartime writings of Priestley and Orwell as being late versions of commonplaces from the interwar years.

54. Julia Stapledon, *Sir Arthur Bryant and National History in Twentieth Century Britain* (Lanham, Maryland, 2005), pp. 166–7.

55. George Orwell, 'The Lion and the Unicorn: Socialism and the English Genius' (1941), in Sonia Orwell and Ian Angus (eds.), *The Collected Essays, Journalism and Letters of George Orwell*, vol 2: *My Country Right or Left* (London, Penguin). Yet it is interesting how little comment on these lines there is in the historical literature. Robert Holland is an exception, when he notes of the 'alone' period that the fight against Hitler jelled with 'an essentially Edwardian idyll of an integrated and disciplined nation' (Robert Holland, *The Pursuit of Greatness: Britain and the World Role, 1900–1970* (London, 1991), p. 177). Harold Nicolson's diaries provide an example from the centre right of a Churchill enthusiast celebrating Britain with new fervour, contemplating, on 31 July 1940, the possibility of fighting on and winning: 'I have always loved England. But now I am in love with England. What a people! What a chance!' Harold Nicolson, *Diaries and Letters, 1939–1945* (1967) (London, 1970), p. 101.

56. Geoffrey G. Field, *Blood, Sweat, and Toil: Remaking the British Working Class, 1939–1945* (Oxford, 2011), chapter 8: 'Wartime Radi-

cals Envision a New Order, 1940–2', provides ample evidence for this point, though he does not make it himself.

57. Edgerton, *Britain's War Machine,* pp. 147–54 and passim; James Hinton, 'Coventry Communism: A Study of Factory Politics in the Second World War', *History Workshop Journal* 10 (1980), pp. 90–118.

58. Ivor Montagu, *Traitor Class* (London, 1940). Montagu was the nephew of Edwin Montagu and the son of Lord Swaythling of the Montagu banking family.

59. J. T. Murphy, *Victory Production!* (London, 1942), p. 11.

60. Eton was the school of writers, among them: Aldous Huxley (b. 1894) George Orwell (b. 1903), Cyril Connolly (b. 1903), Anthony Powell (b. 1905), Henry Green (b. 1905), Peter Fleming (b. 1907) and his brother Ian (b. 1908). See http://www.etoncollege.com/Writers.aspx. Winchester produced two noted left lawyers, D. N. Pritt (b. 1887) and Stafford Cripps (b. 1889), as well as other Labour politicians, including Hugh Gaitskell (b. 1906), Douglas Jay (b. 1907), Richard Crossman (b. 1907) and Kenneth Younger (b. 1908).

61. For details see Edgerton, *Warfare State*, chapter 5, and Guy Ortolano, *Two Cultures Controversy: Science, Literature and Cultural Politics in Postwar Britain* (Cambridge, 2009).

62. Mathew Thomson, *Psychological Subjects: Identity, Culture, and Health in Twentieth-Century Britain* (Oxford, 2006); Erik Linstrum, *Ruling Minds: Psychology in the British Empire* (Boston, Massachusetts, 2016); Geraint Thomas, 'Political Modernity and "Government" in the Construction of Inter-war Democracy: Local and National Encounters', in Laura Beers and Geraint Thomas (eds.), *Brave New World: Imperial and Democratic Nation-building in Britain Between the Wars* (London, 2011).

63. Paul Readman, 'The Edwardian Land Question' in *The Land Question in Britain, 1750–1950* (Basingstoke, 2010), pp. 181–200.

64. Donald MacKenzie, 'Eugenics in Britain', *Social Studies of Science 6* (1976), pp. 499–532.

65. Richard Overy, *The Morbid Age: Britain between the Wars* (London, 2009), chapter 3. Desmond King and Randall Hansen, 'Experts at Work: State Autonomy, Social Learning and Eugenic Sterilization in 1930s Britain', *British Journal of Political Science* 29 (1999), pp. 77–107.

CHAPTER 7: TOMORROW, PERHAPS THE FUTURE

1. This is beginning to happen. See, for example, Robert Crowcroft, 'Peering into the Future: British Conservative Leaders and the Problem of National Renewal, 1942–5', *Historical Research*, early access.

2. Alexandra Harris, *Romantic Moderns: English Writers, Artists and the Imagination from Virginia Woolf to John Piper* (London, 2010).

3. Richard Humphreys, *Tate Britain Companion to British Art* (London, 2007).

4. See Oscar Faber in www.engineering–timelines.com.

5. On interwar warlike R&D see Edgerton, *Warfare State*, chapter 3.

6. See ibid., chapter 4.

7. Elsbeth A. Heaman, *St Mary's: The History of a London Teaching Hospital* (Montreal, 2003); Jonathan Liebenau, 'The British Success with Penicillin', *Social Studies of Science* 17 (1987), pp. 69–86.

8. Margaret Gowing, *Britain and Atomic Energy, 1939–1945* (London, 1964).

9. On all this see Edgerton, *Britain's War Machine*, chapter 8.

10. B. R. Mitchell, *Abstract of British Historical Statistics* (Cambridge, 1962), pp. 25, 27.

11. Charlotte Wildman, 'Urban Transformation in Liverpool and Manchester, 1918–1939', *The Historical Journal* 55 (2012), pp. 119–43.

12. B. R. Mitchell, *Abstract of British Historical Statistics* (Cambridge, 1962), pp. 25, 27.

13. See M. J. Law, *The Experience of Suburban Modernity: How Private Transport Changed interwar London* (Manchester, 2014), chapter 5.

14. For a funny version see this newsreel of Lloyd George talking at his own farm: British Movietone News, 'Lloyd George Talks to Surrey Farmers, story no: 2013 (1932), available at http://www.movietone.com/assets/BMN0511/wmv/BMN_2013_3.wmv.

15. Robert Olby, 'Social Imperialism and State Support for Agricultural Research in Edwardian Britain', *Annals of Science* 48.6 (1991), pp. 509–26; Paolo Palladino, 'The Political Economy of Applied Research: Plant Breeding in Great Britain, 1910–1940', *Minerva* 28.4 (1990), pp. 446–68; Paolo Palladino, 'Between Craft and Science: Plant Breeding, Mendelian Genetics and British Universities, 1900–1920', *Technology and Culture* 34 (1993), pp. 300–323.

16. Keith Vernon, 'Science for the Farmer? Agricultural Research in England 1909–36', *Twentieth Century British History* 8 (1997), pp. 310–33.

17. *Report of the Royal Commission on the Coal Industry (1925)*, p. 40.

18. Ibid., p. 237.

19. Ibid., p. 26.

20. Ibid., chapter 4; *Department of Scientific and Industrial Research. Report for the Year 1933–34*, Cmd. 5013.

21. Anthony Stranges, 'From Birmingham to Billingham: High-Pressure Coal Hydrogenation in Great Britain', *Technology and Culture* 26 (1985), pp. 726–57. See also 'Presidential Address of Sir Richard A. S. Redmayne, President 1935', *Proceedings of the Institution of Civil Engineers* 239 (1935), pp. 1–35.

22. Robert Self, 'Treasury Control and the Empire Marketing Board: The Rise and Fall of Non-Tariff Preference in Britain, 1924–1933', *Twentieth Century British History* 5 (1994), pp. 153–82.

23. See, for example, *Department of Scientific and Industrial Research. Report for the Year 1933–34*.

24. *The Advertiser* (Adelaide), 10 June 1935, p. 16.

25. Sabine Clarke, 'A Technocratic Imperial State? The Colonial Office and Scientific Research, 1940–1960', *Twentieth Century British History* 18 (2007), pp. 453–80.

26. Joseph Morgan Hodge, *Triumph of the Expert: Agrarian Doctrines of Development and the Legacies of British Colonialism* (Columbus, Ohio, 2007); Peder Anker, *Imperial Ecology: Environmental Order in the British Empire, 1895–1945* (Cambridge, Massachusetts, 2009); Helen Tilley, *Africa as a Living Laboratory: Empire, Development, and the Problem of Scientific Knowledge, 1870–1950* (Chicago, Illinois, 2011); D. Graham Burnett, *The Sounding of the Whale: Science and Cetaceans in the Twentieth Century* (Chicago, Illinois, 2012).

27. Sally M. Horrocks, 'Enthusiasm Constrained? British Industrial R&D and the Transition from War to Peace, 1942–51', *Business History* 41 (1999), pp. 42–63.

28. Hermione Giffard, *Making Jet Engines in World War II: Britain, Germany and the United States* (Chicago, Illinois, 2016).

29. Sophie Forgan, 'Festivals of Science and the Two Cultures: Science, Design and Display in the Festival of Britain, 1951', *The British Journal for the History of Science* 31 (1998), pp. 217–40.

30. Paolo Palladino, 'The Political Economy of Applied Research: Plant Breeding in Great Britain, 1910–1940', *Minerva* 4.28 (December 1990), pp. 446–68; Paolo Palladino, 'Science, Technology, and the Economy: Plant Breeding in Great Britain, 1920–1970', *The Economic History Review* 49 (1996), pp. 116–36.

31. J. G. Bennett, *Witness: The Story of a Search* (London, 1962), pp. 159–60, 162–4, 174–5.

32. Herbert Morrison, *The Peaceful Revolution: Speeches by Herbert Morrison* (London, 1949), p. 99.

33. Hence the title of Margaret Gowing's brilliantly clear *Independence and Deterrence: Britain and Atomic Energy, 1945–1952*, 2 vols. (London, 1974).

34. Ibid., vol. 2: *Policy Making*, p. 189.

35. Ibid., p. 449.

36. Ibid., pp. 172–85.

37. Communist Party of Great Britain, *For Soviet Britain*.

38. S. Sturdy and R. Cooter, 'Science, Scientific Management, and the Transformation of Medicine in Britain c. 1870–1950', *History of Science* 36 (1998), pp. 421–66; Charles Webster, 'Conflict and Consensus: Explaining the British Health Service', *Twentieth Century British History* 1.2 (1990), pp. 115–51. Daniel M. Fox, *Health Policies, Health Politics: The British and American Experience, 1911–1965* (Princeton New Jersey, 2014).

39. *Mr. Churchill's Declaration of Policy to the Electors*, 1945 Conservative Party manifesto, available at http://www.politicsresources.net/area/uk/man/con45.htm, accessed 12 January 2018.

40. 'Sir John Russell Presidential Address BAAS 1949', p. 182.

41. Nevil Shute, *The Far Country* (London, 1952) and *In the Wet* (London, 1953). See Philip Hensher, 'Nevil Shute – Profile', *Daily Telegraph*, 4 December 2009. L. T. C. Rolt, *Winterstoke* (London, 1954), reprinted 2015.

42. I am relying on Ralph Desmarais, forthcoming.

43. *Let Us Face the Future: A Declaration of Labour Policy for the Consideration of the Nation*, 1945 Labour Party manifesto, available at http://www.politicsresources.net/area/uk/man/lab45.htm, accessed 12 January 2018.

CHAPTER 8: A MIRROR OF THE NATION AT WORK

1. The phrase was coined by Morgan Phillips, *Labour in the Sixties* (London, 1960), p. 13, referring to the Labour Party in claiming it was at its greatest strength in the past.

2. Michael Stewart, *Life and Labour* (London, 1980), p. 75.

3. Bevan's resignation speech, 23 April 1951.

4. Some lives are obsessively documented – notably those of a handful of writers and politicians.

5. John Hilton, *Rich Man Poor Man* (London, 1944).

6. 'Unidentified Factory Gate Exit in Lancashire 1900' (film by Mitchell and Kenyon no. 238), available at https://player.bfi.org.uk/free/film/watch-unidentified-factory-gate-exit-in-lancashire-c1900-1900-online, accessed 12 January 2018.

7. Board of Trade, *Statistical Abstract for the United Kingdom for Each of the Fifteen Years 1924 to 1938*, pp. 332–3, 336.

8. Jonathan Rose, *The Intellectual Life of the British Working Classes* (London, 2001).

9. Arthur McIvor, 'Employers, the Government, and Industrial Fatigue in Britain, 1890–1918', *British Journal of Industrial Medicine* 44 (1987), pp. 724–32.

10. Bowley, *Economic Consequences*, pp. 149–50.

11. Ina Zweiniger-Bargielowska, *Austerity in Britain: Rationing, Controls, and Consumption, 1939–1955* (Oxford, 2000), chapter 3.

12. On housewifery, see Ina Zweiniger–Bargielowska (ed.), *Women in Twentieth-Century Britain: Social, Cultural and Political Change* (London, 2014).

13. Board of Trade, *Statistical Abstract for the United Kingdom for Each of the Fifteen Years 1924 to 1938*, p. 127.

14. E. M. Sigsworth, *Montague Burton: The Tailor of Taste* (Manchester, 1990), p. 56. Laura Ugolini, *Men and Menswear: Sartorial Consumption in Britain 1880–1939* (London, 2007); Katrina Honeyman, *Well Suited: A History of the Leeds Clothing Industry, 1850–1990* (Edinburgh, 2000).

15. See Raphael Samuel, 'Class Politics: The Lost World of British Communism, Part III', *New Left Review* 1.165 (September–October 1987), pp. 52–91.

16. Bernard Elbaum, 'Why Apprenticeship Persisted in Britain but Not in the United States', *The Journal of Economic History* 49.2 (1989), pp. 337–49.

17. *Portrait of an Engineer*, Merton Park Productions, 1954, follows the work of a production engineer at the Vulcan Foundry, Newton-le-Willows, making locomotives, available at https://www.youtube.com/watch?v=XpB7hkZl2No, accessed 30 January 2018.

18. Crown Film Unit, *The Railwaymen* (1946), available at www.bfi.org.uk/inview/title/6300 (restricted access).

19. George Sturt, *The Wheelwright's Shop* (1923) (Cambridge, 1934), pp. 201–2.

20. Michael R. Weatherburn, 'Scientific Management at Work: The Bedaux System, Management Consulting, and Worker Efficiency in British Industry, 1914–48' (PhD Dissertation, Imperial College London, 2014), p. 79. Christopher McKenna, *The World's Newest Profession: Management Consulting in the Twentieth Century* (Cambridge, 2006).

21. Weatherburn, 'Scientific Management at Work', provides the only reliable biography.

22. The Tavistock Institute of Human Relations, for example, did a lot of work on technology and work organization in the 1940s. E. L. Trist and K. W. Bamforth, 'Some Social and Psychological Consequences of the Longwall Method of Coal-getting: An Examination of the Psychological Situation and Defences of a Work Group in Relation to the Social Structure and Technological Content of the Work System', *Human Relations* 4 (1951), pp. 3–38. Bamworth was a former miner with eighteen years of experience who went on with a scholarship to Leeds University.

23. Herbert Tracey, 'Makers of the Labour Movement: The Brigade of Guards of Trade Unionism', *Labour Magazine* 3 (1924), pp. 3–5.

24. See 'Labour Representation Committee Members of the British Parliament Elected in 1906', in the *Oxford Dictionary of National Biography*, available at http://www.oxforddnb.com/search?q=Labour+Representation+Committee+Members+of+the+British+Parliament+Elected+in+1906&searchBtn=Search&isQuickSearch=true, accessed 12 January 2018.

25. Ross M. Martin, *The Lancashire Giant: David Shackleton, Labour Leader and Civil Servant* (Liverpool, 2000).

26. Bowley, *Economic Consequences*, pp. 160–65.

27. Keith Middlemas, *Politics in Industrial Society: The Experience of the British System since 1911* (London, 1979).

28. Ross McKibbin, *Parties and People, England 1914–1951* (Oxford, 2010), p. 28, says, 'the [Labour] Party did not split'. A rare case of a historian noting the Labour split is the Conservative W. N. Medlicott, *Contemporary England 1914–1964* (London, 1967), pp. 118–19. Andrew Thorpe, *A History of the Labour Party* (London, 2015), p. 43, is another, as, less clearly, is A. J. P. Taylor, *English History*, pp. 171–2. Surprisingly, since it is strong confirmation of his argument, Ralph Miliband did not note it in his *Parliamentary Socialism: A Study in the Politics of Labour* (London 1961), a pioneering critical history of the party.

29. The first PS was David Shackleton, a former Labour MP and cotton TU and chairman of the TUC Parliamentary Committee, the appropriate

name for its ruling body (later the General Council). Ross M. Martin, *The Lancashire Giant: David Shackleton, Labour Leader and Civil Servant* (Liverpool, 2000).

30. Roy Douglas, 'The National Democratic Party and the British Workers' League', *The Historical Journal* 15 (1972), pp. 533–52; J. O. Stubbs, 'Lord Milner and Patriotic Labour, 1914–1918', *The English Historical Review* 87.345 (1972), pp. 717–54. Brock Millman, *Managing Domestic Dissent in First World War Britain* (London, 2000), pp. 110–18, puts it into the context of patriotic anti-socialist groups organized with government backing but does not make enough of the split in the Labour Party in 1918.

31. *Labour's Call to the People.*

32. Stefan Berger, ' "Organising Talent and Disciplined Steadiness": The German SPD as a Model for the British Labour Party in the 1920s?', *Contemporary European History* 5 (1996), pp. 171–90.

33. The others were William Adamson, J. H. Thomas, J. R. Clynes, Arthur Henderson and Tom Shaw.

34. Ken Warpole, *Dockers and Detectives: Popular Reading, Popular Writing* (London, 1983); Jonathan Rose, *The Intellectual Life of the British Working Classes* (London, 2001); Christopher Hilliard, 'The Twopenny Library: The Book Trade, Working-Class Readers, and "Middlebrow" Novels in Britain, 1930–42', *Twentieth Century British History* 25 (2013), pp. 199–220.

35. *Trades Union Congress Annual Report, 1931*, pp. 86–7, available at http://www.unionhistory.info/reports/index.php.

36. Six Labour MPs left to form the New Party, led by Oswald Mosley. They included his wife, Cynthia, daughter of Lord Curzon; Oliver Baldwin, gay eldest son of the Conservative Leader; John Strachey (soon to become a communist); W. J. Brown; and Dr Robert Forgan. Brown returned to parliament as an independent in 1942. Baldwin returned for Labour in 1945.

37. *Statistics Relating to the War Effort of the United Kingdom*, p. 34.

38. Ministry of Information, *Clyde Built.*

39. Analysis of opposition from within the Labour Party to the party's role in the government is rare. For the telling and important example of the Labour left's key intellectual see Isaac Kranmick and Barry Sheerman, *Harold Laski: A Life on the Left* (London, 1993), chapter 17.

40. George Orwell, 'The British Crisis', London letter to *Partisan Review*, 8 May 1942, in Sonia Orwell and Ian Angus (eds.), *The Collected Essays, Journalism and Letters of George Orwell*, vol. 2: *My Country*

Right or Left (London, 1970); Wartime Diary, 19/5/42; George Orwell, *All Propaganda Is Lies, 1941–1942*, ed. Peter Davison (London, 1998), p. 331.

41. For example, Paul Addison, *The Road to 1945* (London, 1975); and Ross McKibbin, *Parties and People* (Oxford, 2010).

42. Steven Fielding, 'What Did "The People" Want?: The Meaning of the 1945 General Election', *The Historical Journal* 35 (1992), p. 628. For an example, see Orwell, 'The British Crisis'.

43. Fielding, 'What Did "The People" Want?'.

44. Martin Pugh, *Speak for Britain! A New History of the Labour Party* (London, 2010).

45. Fielding, 'What Did "The People" Want?'.

46. For example, Ross McKibbin, *Classes and Cultures: England, 1918–1951* (Oxford, 1998), Conclusion.

47. Pollitt, *Looking Ahead*, p. 91.

48. John Saville, *The Politics of Continuity: British Foreign Policy and the Labour Government, 1945–46* (London, 1993).

49. Alan Booth, 'How Long Are Light Years in British Politics? The Labour Party's Economic Ideas in the 1930s', *Twentieth Century British History* 7.1 (1996), pp. 1–26; D. E. H. Edgerton, 'State Intervention in British Manufacturing Industry, 1931–51: A Comparative Study of State Policy for the Military Aircraft and Cotton Textile Industries' (PhD, University of London, 1986).

50. One of the few works to note this is James Hinton, *Protests and Visions: Peace Politics in Twentieth Century Britain* (London, 1989), chapter 11. For a strong case for Labour's success in 1945 being the result of a combination of patriotism and socialism more successfully presented than by some Labour candidates in 1918, see Pugh, *Speak for Britain!*, p. 280; for the nationalism of Labour in 1945, see also David Edgerton, 'War, Reconstruction, and the Nationalization of Britain, 1939–1951', *Past & Present* 210.6 (January 2011), pp. 29–46.

51. *Let Us Face the Future*.

52. Aneurin Bevan, Speech at Manchester, 4 July 1948, *Manchester Guardian*, 5 July 1948.

53. *Let Us Win Through Together*.

54. Tom Nairn, 'The Left Against Europe?', *New Left Review* 1.75 (September–October 1972), p. 43.

CHAPTER 9: FROM CLASS TO NATION

1. Aneurin Bevan, 'National Health Service Bill', second reading, *House of Commons Debates,* 30 April 1946, vol. 422, c. 43.

2. Richard Titmuss, *Essays on 'The Welfare State'* (London, 1958), p. 22.

3. Ibid., pp. 80–84.

4. For example, Derek Fraser, *The Evolution of the British Welfare State: A History of Social Policy since the Industrial Revolution* (London, many editions), and more nuanced in Bernard Harris, *The Origins of the British Welfare State: Society, State and Social Welfare in England and Wales, 1800–1945* (London, 2004).

5. Roy Church, *The History of the British Coal Industry*, vol. 3: *1830–1913: Victorian Pre-eminence* (Oxford, 1986), pp. 598–9.

6. Bernard Harris, 'Health and Welfare', in R. Floud, J. Humphries and P. Johnson (eds.), *The Cambridge Economic History of Modern Britain: Growth and Decline, 1870 to the Present*, vol. 2 (Cambridge, 2014), pp. 122–50.

7. ONS, *Mortality in England and Wales: Average Life Span, 2010* (London, 2012), available at https://www.ons.gov.uk/peoplepopulationandcommunity/birthsdeathsandmarriages/deaths/articles/mortalityinenglandandwales/2012-12-17, accessed 12 January 2018.

8. Adrian Gregory, *The Last Great War: British Society and the First World War* (Cambridge, 2013), pp. 285–6.

9. Clare Griffiths and Anita Brock, 'Twentieth Century Mortality Trends in England and Wales', *Health Statistics Quarterly* 18 (Summer 2003), pp. 5–17.

10. Pat Thane, *Old Age in English History: Past Experiences, Present Issues* (Oxford, 2000), pp. 216–35.

11. Michael Heller, 'The National Insurance Acts 1911–1947, the Approved Societies and the Prudential Assurance Company', *Twentieth Century British History* 19 (2007), pp. 1–28.

12. Deborah Dwork, *War Is Good for Babies and Other Young Children: A History of the Infant and Child Welfare Movement in England, 1898–1918* (London, 1987).

13. John Clapham, *An Economic History of Modern Britain*, vol. 3: *Machines and National Rivalries (1887–1914) with an Epilogue (1914–1929)* (Cambridge, 1938), p. 425.

14. *Report of the Committee on National Debt and Taxation* 1927, Cmd. 2800, p. 226.

15. Bowley, *Economic Consequences*, p. 159.

16. Susan Pedersen, *Family, Dependence, and the Origins of the Welfare State: Britain and France, 1914–1945* (Cambridge, 1993).

17. Deborah Cohen, *The War Come Home: Disabled Veterans in Britain and Germany, 1914–1939* (Berkeley, 2001).

18. Janis Lomas, ' "Delicate Duties": Issues of Class and Respectability in Government Policy towards the Wives and Widows of British Soldiers in the Era of the Great War', *Women's History Review* 9.1 (2000), pp. 123–47; Susan Pedersen, 'Gender, Welfare, and Citizenship in Britain during the Great War', *The American Historical Review* 95.4 (1990), pp. 983–1006.

19. W. R. Garside, *British Unemployment, 1919–1939: A Study in Public Policy* (Cambridge, 1990), p. 41.

20. John Macnicol, *The Politics of Retirement in Britain, 1878–1948* (Cambridge, 1998).

21. Ibid., pp. 181–224; Thane, *Old Age in English History*, pp. 308–32.

22. Macnicol, *Politics of Retirement*; Pedersen, 'Gender, Welfare, and Citizenship'.

23. Garside, *British Unemployment*, appendix 3.1.

24. Charles Mowat, *Britain between the Wars 1918–1940* (London, 1955), p. 483.

25. As John Pickstone commented, 'We tend to forget the sheer size of the Poor Law facilities as we concentrate on novel developments in welfare or in the development of clinical medicine' (John Pickstone, *Medicine and Industrial Society: A History of Hospital Development in Manchester and Its Region, 1752–1946* (Manchester, 1985), p. 213).

26. Ibid., p. 7.

27. Peter Scott, *The Making of the British Home: The Suburban Semi and Family Life Between the Wars* (Oxford, 2013).

28. Taylor, *English History*, pp. 726–7.

29. Angus Calder, *The People's War* (London, 1969), p. 17.

30. For example, see Paul Addison, *The Road to 1945: British Politics and the Second World War* (London, 1975).

31. Kevin Jefferys, 'British Politics and Social Policy during the Second World War', *The Historical Journal* 30 (1987), pp. 123–44; Harold Smith, *War and Social Change, British Society in the Second World War* (Manchester, 1986).

32. For example, see Sidney Pollard, *The Development of the British Economy 1914–1980*, 3rd edn (London, 1983), p. 272; Jose Harris, 'War and Social History: Britain and the Home Front during the

Second World War', *Contemporary European History* 1 (1992), pp. 17–35; John Welshman, 'Evacuation and Social Policy during the Second World War: Myth and Reality', *Twentieth Century British History* 9 (1998), pp. 28–53.

33. Edgerton, *Britain's War Machine*, p. 35.

34. Mowat, *Britain between the Wars*, p. 595.

35. Institute for Fiscal Studies, 'Fiscal Facts: Tax and Benefits', http://www. ifs.org.uk/tools_and_resources/fiscal_facts/, accessed 25 April 2017.

36. Edgerton, *Britain's War Machine*, pp. 169–75.

37. Diana Davenport, 'The War against Bacteria: How Were Sulphonamide Drugs Used by Britain during World War II?' *Medical Humanities* 38.1 (2012), pp. 55–8.

38. Tony Lane, *The Merchant Seamen's War* (Manchester, 1990).

39. Richard Titmuss, *Problems of Social Policy* (London, 1950), p. 501.

40. Ibid., p. 486.

41. Ibid., p. 489.

42. Ibid., p. 530.

43. Ibid., p. 531.

44. John Macnicol, 'The Evacuation of Schoolchildren', in H. L. Smith, *War and Social Change: British Society in the Second World War*, pp. 3–31; John Welshman, 'School Meals and Milk in England and Wales, 1906–45', *Medical History* 41 (1997), pp. 6–29.

45. Alan Deacon, 'An End to the Means Test? Social Security and the Attlee Government', *Journal of Social Policy* 11 (1982), pp. 289–306.

46. Deacon, 'An End to the Means Test?'; Macnicol, *Politics of Retirement*, pp. 340–41.

47. Macnicol, *Politics of Retirement*, p. 344.

48. Ibid., p. 350.

49. Peter Baldwin, *The Politics of Social Solidarity: Class Bases of the European Welfare State, 1875–1975* (Cambridge, 1990), p. 108.

50. Sir William Beveridge, BBC Home Service, 2 December 1942, available at http://www.bbc.co.uk/archive/nhs/5139.shtml, accessed 23 April 2010. The Atlantic Charter was also mentioned by Attlee in a rich broadcast on the eve of the joint inauguration of the National Health Service, National Insurance, National Assistance and Industrial Injuries provision, BBC Home Service, 4 July 1948, available at http:// www.bbc.co.uk/archive/nhs/5147.shtml, accessed 23 April 2010.

51. *Social Insurance and Allied Services, Report by Sir William Beveridge*, 1942, Cmd. 6404, para. 17.

52. Ibid., para. 9.

53. Ibid., paras 17, 19.
54. Macnicol, *Politics of Retirement*, p. 354.
55. Ibid., pp. 347–84.
56. Ibid., p. 354.
57. Ibid., pp. 371–9.
58. Ibid., p. 391.
59. Pedersen, *Family, Dependence, and the Origins of the Welfare State*, pp. 316–36.
60. N. Hayes, 'Did We Really Want a National Health Service? Hospitals, Patients and Public Opinions before 1948', *English Historical Review* 128 (2012), pp. 625–61.
61. Jim Tomlinson, *Democratic Socialism and Economic Policy: The Attlee Years, 1945–1951* (Cambridge, 1997), p. 249.
62. Hayes, 'Did we Really Want a National Health Service?'.
63. Pickstone, *Medicine and Industrial* Society, p. 6.
64. Jim Tomlinson, 'Why So Austere? The British Welfare State of the 1940s', *Journal of Social Policy* 27 (1998), pp. 63–77, p. 74.
65. J. Stirling, 'Social Services Expenditure during the Last 100 Years', *Advancement of Science* 8 (1952), pp. 379–92, Appendix.
66. Roger Middleton, *Government and Market: The Growth of the Public Sector, Economic Management and British Economic Performance, c. 1890–1979* (Cheltenham, 1996).
67. Pollard, *Development of the British Economy*, p. 272.
68. Charles Webster, *Health Services since the War* (London, 1988), pp. 12–13.
69. T. J. Hatton and R. E. Bailey, 'Seebohm Rowntree and the Postwar Poverty Puzzle', *Economic History Review* 53 (2000), pp. 544–64.
70. Edgerton, *Warfare State*; Sir Alex Cairncross in Nicholas Timmins, *The Five Giants: A Biography of the Welfare State* (London, 2001), p. 6.
71. Harry Pollitt, J. R. Campbell and R. P. Dutt, *Welfare State or Warfare State? An Appeal to Every Sincere Labour Man and Woman* (London, 1950), p. 15.
72. Tom Clark and Andrew Dilnot, 'British Fiscal Policy since 1939', *The Cambridge Economic History of Modern Britain*, vol. 3: *Structural Change and Growth, 1939–2000* (2004).
73. Jose Harris, 'Society and the State in Twentieth-century Britain', in F. M. L. Thompson (ed.), *The Cambridge Social History of Britain, 1750–1950*, vol. 3: *Social Agencies and Institutions* (Cambridge, 1990).
74. Ibid.

CHAPTER 10: A NATION IN THE WORLD

1. Margaret Thatcher, '1950 General Election Address', 3 February 1950, http://www.margaretthatcher.org/document/100858, accessed 29 August 2017.

2. *Britain Belongs to You: The Labour Party's Policy for Consideration by the British People,* 1959 Labour Party manifesto, available at http://www.politicsresources.net/area/uk/man/lab59.htm, accessed 12 January 2018.

3. *The United Kingdom and the European Communities* (1971), Cmnd. 4715.

4. For the involvement of Stalin see John Callaghan, *Rajani Palme Dutt: A Study in British Stalinism* (London, 1993), pp. 239–42, 275–6.

5. Churchill Archives Centre, Powell Papers, POLL 3/2/1/1 'The Church', p. 6.

6. See Philip Murphy, *Monarchy and the End of Empire: The House of Windsor, the British Government and the Postwar Commonwealth* (Oxford, 2013) for the background, and the earlier arguments as to whether the crown was already divided.

7. She therefore erred in her first Christmas broadcast as monarch when she intoned: 'We belong, all of us, to the British Commonwealth and Empire, that immense union of nations, with their homes set in all the four corners of the earth.' First Christmas broadcast by HMQ, 1952, available at https://www.royal.uk/queens-first-christmas-broadcast-1952, accessed 12 January 2018.

8. For example her Coronation Day speech, 2 June 1953, available at https://www.royal.uk/coronation-oath-2-june-1953, accessed 29 August 2017.

9. Murphy, *Monarchy and the End of Empire*, chapter 6.

10. Stephen Constantine, 'Waving Goodbye? Australia, Assisted Passages, and the Empire and Commonwealth Settlement Acts, 1945–72', *The Journal of Imperial and Commonwealth History* 26 (1998), pp. 176–95; Stephen Constantine, 'British Emigration to the Empire-Commonwealth since 1880: From Overseas Settlement to Diaspora?', *The Journal of Imperial and Commonwealth History* 31.2 (2003), pp. 16–35.

11. Constantine, 'Waving Goodbye?', pp. 176–95; Constantine, 'British Emigration to the Empire-Commonwealth', pp. 16–35.

12. I owe this to Matthew Johnes' paper presented at the Modern British Studies conference, Birmingham, July 2017.

13. Alan Thornett, *Militant Years: Car Workers' Struggles in Britain in the 60s and 70s* (London, 2011), p. 129.

14. From IHR seminar paper by Jon Davis, 31 October 2013.

15. Enoch Powell, speech to The Royal Society of St George in London on St George's Day, 23 April 1961; available at https://alterorbisworld.word press.com/2017/02/15/enoch-powell-st-georges-day-speech/, accessed 12 January 2018. Peter Brooke, 'India, Post-imperialism and the Origins of Enoch Powell's "Rivers of Blood" Speech', *Historical Journal* 50 (2007), pp. 669–87, points out that he was a racist, while still not an imperialist, which was surely correct.

16. Andrew Roberts, 'Churchill, Race and the "Magpie Society"', in *Eminent Churchillians* (London, 1994), is an instance. Ben Pimlott, *The Queen: A Biography of Elizabeth II* (London, 1996), pp. 508–14.

17. Geoffrey Jones, *The Evolution of International Business: An Introduction* (London, 1996), p. 211.

18. See data in R. C. O. Matthews, C. H. Feinstein and J. Odling-Smee, *British Economic Growth 1856–1973: The Post-war Period in Historical Perspective* (Oxford, 1982), tables 14.2, 14.3; Nicholas Crafts and Stephen Broadberry, 'Openness, Protectionism and Britain's Productivity Performance over the Long-run', Department of Economics, University of Warwick (CAGE Online Working Paper Series, no. 36/2010); Catherine Schenk, *The Decline of Sterling: Managing the Retreat of an International Currency 1945–1992* (Cambridge, 2010), figure 1.2, p. 16.

19. Leandro Prados de la Escosura, 'Economic Freedom in the Long Run: Evidence from OECD Countries (1850–2007)', *Economic History Review* 69 (2016), pp. 435–68.

20. For example, Andrew Gamble, *Britain in Decline: Economic Policy, Political Strategy and the British State* (London, 1994), pp. 168–9.

21. Alan S. Milward and George Brennan, *Britain's Place in the World: A Historical Inquiry into Import Controls 1945–60* (London, 1996), pp. 2–3.

22. Schenk, *The Decline of Sterling*, pp. 97–9.

23. Jim Tomlinson, *Democratic Socialism and Economic Policy* (Cambridge, 1997), pp. 58–61.

24. Catherine Schenk, *Britain and the Sterling Area: From Devaluation to Convertibility in the 1950s* (London, 1994).

25. Winston Churchill, 1951 Conservative Party manifesto 1951, available at http://www.conservativemanifesto.com/1951/1951-conservative-manifesto.shtml, accessed 12 January 2018.

26. *United for Peace and Progress: The Conservative and Unionist Party's Policy*, 1955 Conservative Party manifesto, available at http://www.

conservativemanifesto.com/1955/1955-conservative-manifesto.shtml, accessed 12 January 2018.

27. *The Next Five Years*, 1959 Conservative Party manifesto, available at http://www.conservativemanifesto.com/1959/1959-conservative-man ifesto.shtml, accessed 12 January 2018.

28. For a critique of the missing the boat historiography see Oliver Dad-dow (ed.), *Harold Wilson and the European Integration: Britain's Second Application to Join the EEC* (London, 2003).

29. Schenk, *The Decline of Sterling*.

30. M. Taylor, 'English Football and "the Continent" Reconsidered', in P. Vonnard, G. Quin and N. Bancel (eds.), *Building Europe with the Ball: Turning Points in the Europeanization of Football, 1905–1995* (Oxford, 2016), pp. 75–97.

31. *Membership of the European Communities* (May 1967), Cmnd. 3269.

32. Benjamin Grob-Fitzgibbon, *Continental Drift: Britain and Europe from the End of Empire to the Rise of Euroscepticism* (Cambridge, 2016).

33. Felix Klos, *Churchill on Europe* (London, 2016).

34. Ibid., pp. 43–4.

35. Alan S. Milward, *The UK and the European Community*, vol. 1: *The Rise and Fall of a National Strategy* (London, 2002).

36. By 1977 tariffs were eliminated between EFTA and the EEC, by which time the United Kingdom and Denmark were in the EEC. Portugal joined in 1986, and Austria, Sweden and Finland in 1995.

37. Neil Rollings, *Business in the Formative Years of European Integration, 1945–1973* (Cambridge, 2007).

38. Ibid.

39. Mark Abrams, 'British Elite Attitudes and the European Common Market', *Public Opinion Quarterly* 29.2 (1965), pp. 236–46.

40. Rollings, *Business in the Formative Years of European Integration*.

41. Mathias Haeussler, 'The Popular Press and Ideas of Europe: The *Daily Mirror*, the *Daily Express*, and Britain's First Application to Join the EEC, 1961–63', *Twentieth Century Brit History* 25 (2014), pp. 108–31.

42. Speech by Hugh Gaitskell, Labour Party Conference, 3 October 1962, available at https://www.cvce.eu/en/obj/speech_by_hugh_gaitskell_against_uk_membership_of_the_common_market_3_october_1962-en-05f2996b-000b-4576-8b42-8069033a16f9.html, accessed 29 August 2017.

43. Ted Ainley, *Say 'No' to the Common Market*, Communist Party Conference, 1962, p. 16, available at https://www.cvce.eu/content/

publication/2005/4/7/fecf964d-77e0-4639-af79-6941bbcfeb28/publish able_en.pdf, accessed 29 August 2017.

44. Nairn, 'The Left against Europe?', p. 5.

45. Speech by Harold Wilson, 'Labour's Plan for Science', Labour Party Conference, 1 October 1963, available at http://nottspolitics.org/wp-content/uploads/2013/06/Labours-Plan-for-science.pdf, accessed 12 January 2018.

46. J. B. Priestley, *New Statesman*, 26 May 1967, reprinted 10–16 April 2015.

47. Nairn, 'The Left against Europe?', p. 5.

48. Extract from speech by the Rt Hon. J. Enoch Powell MP at a public meeting at the Technical College, Brunswick Road, Gloucester at 7.45 p.m., Friday, 29 October 1976, available at http://enochpowell.info/Resources/Oct-Dec%201976.pdf, accessed 29 August 2017.

49. See the debate on the *Panorama* programme between the two key Labour figures in the debate, Roy Jenkins and Tony Benn, broadcast just before the referendum, available at https://www.bing.com/videos/search?q=yout ube+panoram+Benn+Jenkins&view=detail&mid=5BA82B5F5B5BD985 1E8D5BA82B5F5B5BD9851E8D&FORM=VIRE, accessed 12 January 2018.

50. Richard Vinen, *Thatcher's Britain: The Politics and Social Upheaval of the Thatcher Era* (London, 2009), chapter 2. Another nationalist anti-American and anti-EEC figure of the right was Alan Clark, though he was a protectionist.

51. Ronald Hyam, *Britain's Declining Empire: The Road to Decolonisation, 1918–1968* (Cambridge, 2007) has a rich brief analysis.

52. Aneurin Bevan speech, Trafalgar Square, 4 November 1956, recording available at https://www.youtube.com/watch?v=XZmw8XIoZeY, accessed 12 January 2018.

53. Nigel Ashton, *Kennedy, Macmillan and the Cold War: The Irony of Interdependence* (London, 2002).

54. John Campbell, *Edward Heath: A Biography* (London, 2013).

55. Thomas Robb, 'The Power of Oil: Edward Heath, the "Year of Europe" and the Anglo-American "Special Relationship"', *Contemporary British History* 26 (2012), pp. 73–96.

56. Harold Macmillan, 'Wind of Change' speech, 3 Feburary 1960, recording available at http://www.bbc.co.uk/archive/apartheid/7203.shtml, accessed 29 August 2017.

CHAPTER 11: BUILDING THE FUTURE

1. *The Macmillan Diaries*, vol. 1: *The Cabinet Years 1950–1957*, ed. Peter Catterall (London, 2003), 4 May 1953.

2. This was quoted against him by Konni Zilliacus MP, in *House of Commons Debates*, 8 March 1966, vol. 725, c. 1988.

3. Speech to the House of Commons by Herbert Morrison, July 1947, *The Peaceful Revolution: Speeches by Herbert Morrison* (London, 1949), pp. 133–4.

4. Crown Film Unit, *From the Ground Up* (1950), online ID: 1315093. BFI, available at https://www.bfi.org.uk/inview/title/6362, restricted access.

5. *Living in Britain Results from the 2000/01 General Household Survey* (London, 2001).

6. H. H. Liesner, *The Import Dependence of Britain and Western Germany: A Comparative Study*, Princeton Studies in International Finance 7 (Princeton, New Jersey, 1957).

7. R. E. Rowthorn and J. R. Wells, *De-Industrialization and Foreign Trade* (Cambridge, 1987), p. 97. For the same years, raw materials (net) went from 5.1 to 0.8 per cent of GDP.

8. 'Statistical Data Set: Overseas Trade in Food, Feed and Drink', https://www.gov.uk/government/statistical–data–sets/overseas–trade–in–food–feed–and–drink, accessed 29 August 2017.

9. Andrew Pettigrew, *The Awakening Giant: Continuity and Change in ICI* (London, 1985), pp. 134–5.

10. Palladino, 'Science, Technology and the Economy'.

11. Paul Brassley, 'Silage in Britain, 1880–1990: The Delayed Adoption of an Innovation', *The Agricultural History Review* (1996), pp. 63–87.

12. S. P. Cauvain and L. S. Young, *The Chorleywood Bread Process* (London, 2006).

13. DEFRA, 'UK Food Production to Supply Ratio (Commonly Referred to as the "Self-Sufficiency" Ratio)', available at https://www.gov.uk/government/uploads/system/uploads/attachment_data/file/316223/trade-selfsuff-02jun14.xls, accessed 30 January 2018.

14. John Martin, 'The International Crisis of 1972–7: The Neglected Agrarian Dimension', in A. T. Brown, Andy Burn and Rob Doherty (eds.), *Crises in Economic and Social History: A Comparative Perspective* (Martlesham, 2015).

15. *Food from Our Own Resources* (1975), Cmnd. 6020.

16. Rowthorn and Wells, *De-industrialization*, table 6.2, p. 106.

17. Ibid., p. 103.
18. *House of Commons Debates*, 17 December 1973, vol. 866, col. 1035.
19. See http://beefandlamb.ahdb.org.uk for statistics on meat imports and exports.
20. They were the *Darro, Drina, Durango* and *Deseado*, which like the Highland ships were built at Harland & Wolff.
21. Robert E. Forrester, *British Mail Steamers to South America* (London, 2014), http://www.timetableimages.com/maritime/images/rml.htm. The by then closely related Houlder Line also had two passenger meat ships built in 1959–60, the *Hardwicke Grange* and the *Royston Grange*, which remained on the route a little longer. The latter suffered a devastating fire following a crash into a tanker in the River Plate in 1972, the last British naval disaster in which all on board, crew and passengers, were lost.
22. Colin Ross, *Death of the Docks* (Milton Keynes, 2010), p. 58. See also A. E. Smith, *London's Royal Docks in the 1950s: A Memoir of the Docks at Work*, kindle edn (London, 2011), loc. 3200.
23. Thanks to Callum Petty for this insight.
24. Joe Moran, *Armchair Nation: An Intimate History of Britain in Front of the TV* (London, 2013).
25. *A Programme of Nuclear Power* (1955), Cmd. 9389, para. 2.
26. Ibid.
27. Roger Williams, *The Nuclear Power Decisions: British Policies, 1953–78* (London, 1980), pp. 64–5.
28. Ibid., pp. 157–62.
29. P. D. Henderson, 'Two British Errors: Their Probable Size and Some Possible Lessons', *Oxford Economic Papers* 29 (1977), pp. 159–205.
30. Chris Harlow, *Innovation and Productivity under Nationalisation: The First Thirty Years* (London, 1977).
31. William Ashworth, *History of the British Coal Industry*, vol. 5: *1946–1982: The Nationalized Industry* (Oxford, 1986), pp. 82–8.
32. Ibid., p. 40.
33. Rowthorn and Wells, *De-industrialization*, p. 99.
34. Department for Business, Energy and Industrial Strategy, 'Historical Gas Data: Gas Production and Consumption 1882 to 2014', available at https://www.gov.uk/government/statistical-data-sets/historical-gas-data-gas-production-and-consumption-and-fuel-input-1882-to-2011#history, accessed 2 September 2017.
35. *Digest of UK Energy Statistics (DUKES): 60th Anniversary* (London, 2009), available at https://www.gov.uk/government/statistics/digest-of-uk-energy-statistics-dukes-60th-anniversary, accessed 12 January 2018.

36. Alex Kemp, *The Official History of North Sea Oil and Gas*, vol. 2: *Moderating the State's Role* (London, 2013), p. 384.

37. *Digest of UK Energy Statistics (DUKES): 60th Anniversary*, chart 1, p. 5, plus 1913 coal production converted to toe (tons of oil equivalent) by dividing by 1.43.

38. Christopher Harvie, *Fool's Gold: The Story of North Sea Oil* (London, 1994), p. 219.

39. Kemp, *Official History*, p. xii.

40. Harvie, *Fool's Gold*, pp. 81, 144–5.

41. Ibid., p. 73.

42. See the wonderful Joe Moran, *On Roads: A Hidden History* (London, 2009).

43. Paul Barker, *The Freedoms of Suburbia* (London, 2009).

44. Patrick Dunleavy, *The Politics of Mass Housing 1945–75* (Oxford, 1981). I remember the tiny and smelly lifts in the freezing and largely empty tower block I lived in briefly in Everton, Liverpool in 1984.

45. Guy Ortolano, 'Planning the Urban Future in 1960s Britain', *The Historical Journal* 54 (2011), pp. 477–507.

46. Peter Sutton, 'Technological Change and Industrial Relations in the British Postal Service, 1969–1975' (unpublished PhD thesis, King's College London, 2013).

47. Lise Butler, 'Michael Young, the Institute of Community Studies, and the Politics of Kinship', *Twentieth Century British History* 26 (2015), p. 224.

48. Andrew Seaton, 'Against the "Sacred Cow": NHS Opposition and the Fellowship for Freedom in Medicine, 1948–72', *Twentieth Century British History* 26 (2015), pp. 424–49; Joan Keating, 'Faith and Community Threatened? Roman Catholic Responses to the Welfare State, Materialism and Social Mobility, 1945–62', *Twentieth Century British History* 9 (1998), pp. 86–108, on the formerly socialist, but now Catholic and liberal, economist Colin Clark on the post-war welfare state.

49. Morgan Philips, *Labour in the Sixties* (London, 1960), p. 8.

50. Paul Bridgen, 'A Straitjacket with Wriggle Room: The Beveridge Report, the Treasury and the Exchequer's Pension Liability, 1942–59', *Twentieth Century British History* 17 (2006), pp. 1–25.

51. Richard Titmuss, *Essays on 'The Welfare State'* (London, 1958), p. 51.

52. Ibid, p. 25.

53. Hugh Pemberton, 'The Failure of "Nationalization by Attraction": Britain's Cross-Class Alliance against Earnings-Related Pensions in the 1950s', *The Economic History Review* 65 (2012), pp. 1428–49.

54. Frank Field, Molly Meacher and Chris Pond, *To Him Who Hath: A Study of Poverty and Taxation* (London, 1977).

55. Jon Agar, *The Government Machine: A Revolutionary History of the Computer* (Cambridge, Massachussets, 2003), p. 368.

56. D. Wincott, 'Images of Welfare in Law and Society: The British Welfare State in Comparative Perspective', *Journal of Law and Society* 38 (2011), pp. 343–75.

57. Tom Rutherford, 'Historical Rates of Social Security Benefits', House of Commons Library Briefing, SN/SG 6762 (November 2013), available at http://researchbriefings.files.parliament.uk/documents/SN06762/SN06762.pdf, accessed 2 September 2017.

58. Peter Mandler, 'Educating the Nation III: Social Mobility', *Transactions of the Royal Historical Society* 26 (2016), pp. 1–23.

59. As did Bristol Cathedral School, where I was at the time of the change. See Jane Collard, David Ogden and Roger Burgess, *'Where the Fat Black Canons Dined': A History of Bristol Cathedral School 1140 to 1992* (Bristol, 1992).

60. David Marquand, *Britain since 1918: The Strange Career of British Democracy* (London, 2008), p. 154.

61. For example, Perry Anderson, 'The Figures of Descent', *New Left Review* 1.161 (1987).

62. See Simon Gunn, 'Ring Road: Birmingham and the Collapse of the Motor City Ideal in 1970s Britain', *The Historical Journal* (2017).

CHAPTER 12: NATIONAL CAPITALISM

1. Margaret Thatcher, 'Speech to Conservative Party Conference', 10 October 1975, http://www.margaretthatcher.org/document/102777, accessed 29 August 2017. Thanks to Thomas Kelsey.

2. C. J. F. Brown and T. D. Sheriff, 'De-industrialisation: A Background Paper', in F. Blackaby (ed.), *De-industrialisation* (London, 1979), pp. 239–40.

3. Ibid., p. 241.

4. For examples, see Michael Barratt-Brown, 'The Controllers II', *Universities and Left Review* 6 (spring 1959), available at http://banmarchive.org.uk/collections/ulr/06_38.pdf, accessed 5 February 2018; Sam Aaronovitch, *The Ruling Class* (London, 1961).

5. Raphael Samuel, 'The Boss as Hero', *Universities and Left Review* 7 (autumn 1959), p. 28.

6. Ralph Miliband, 'Who Governs Britain?', *Universities and Left Review* 3 (winter 1958).

7. Lord Hives 1950; Sir Clive Baillieu (Dunlop) 1953; Lord Bennett (Lucas and politics) 1953; Lord Strathalmond (BP) 1955; Lord Heyworth (ICI and Unilever) 1955; Lord Godber (Shell) 1956; Lord Rank (Rank Organization) 1957; Lord Rootes (Rootes Motors) 1959; Lord Nelson (English Electric) 1960; Lord Fleck (ICI) 1961; Lord Beeching (ICI) 1965; Lord Marks (M&S) 1961; Lord Mills (W. T. Avery and politics) 1962; Lord Sinclair (Imperial Tobacco) 1957; Lord Sainsbury (Sainsbury) 1962; Lord Renwick (TV) 1964; Lord McFadzean (BICC) 1966; Lord Pilkington (Pilikington) 1968; Lord Stokes (BMC) 1969; Lord Kearton (Courtaulds) 1970.

8. Michael Moran, *The End of British Politics?* (Basingstoke, 2017).

9. Benwell Community Project, *The Making of a Ruling Class: Two Centuries of Capital Development on Tyneside* (Newcastle-upon-Tyne, 1978). In the 1980s this was noted for the case of Liverpool by the then environment secretary, Michael Heseltine. In Manchester in the late 1980s the last *bourgeoise* on Manchester City council, Dame Kathleen Ollerenshaw, lamented she was the last of the line, and for one delicious moment, assuming I was an Egerton, rather than an Edgerton, exclaimed: 'Once upon a time one had to be either an Egerton or a Mosley,' referring to the lords of the manor of Manchester, from which Oswald Mosley was descended, and the dukes of Bridgewater, and their descendents, including Earl Egerton, chairman of, among other things, the Manchester Ship Canal Company.

10. Benwell Community Project, *The Making of a Ruling Class*.

11. See Andrew Pickering, *The Cybernetic Brain: Sketches of Another Future* (Chicago, Illinois, 2010), chapter 6. Beer was later a very successful management consultant; he dropped out in the 1970s and was involved in an extraordinary experiment in economic planning in Allende's Chile, on which see also Eden Medina, *Cybernetic Revolutionaries: Technology and Politics in Allende's Chile* (Cambridge, Massachusetts, 2011).

12. L. Nasbeth and G. F. Ray, *The Diffusion of New Industrial Processes. An International Study* (Cambridge, 1974).

13. Foreword to the 3rd edition of *This Is Our Concern* (1955) by Alexander Fleck, chairman of ICI.

14. Ibid., p. 1.

15. Ibid., p. 50.

16. Imperial Chemical Industries, *ICI Wilton Works* (1970).

17. Alan S. Milward and George Brennan, *Britain's Place in the World: A Historical Inquiry into Import Controls 1945–60* (London, 1996), p. 245.

18. *Goulburn Evening Post* (NSW), 18 May 1951, p. 7.

19. Kersten T. Hall, *The Man in the Monkeynut Coat: William Astbury and the Forgotten Road to the Double-Helix* (Oxford, 2014).

20. *The Charleville Times* (Brisbane), 22 November 1951.

21. *The Argus* (Melbourne), 5 April 1951.

22. Art Buchwald, 'It Might Serve as a Sackcloth', *Detroit Free Press*, 3 November 1957 (syndicated).

23. Nicholas J. White, 'Government and Business Divided: Malaya, 1945–57', *The Journal of Imperial and Commonwealth History* 22 (1994), pp. 251–74.

24. Edmund Dell, *Political Responsibility and Industry* (London, 1973), p. 120.

25. For a very clear inside story in a book of general interest see ibid., pp. 103–21.

26. *The Inverness Smelter*, film, 1972, http://movingimage.nls.uk/film/2216, accessed 30 August 2017.

27. Geoffrey Owen, *From Empire to Europe: The Decline and Revival of British Industry since the Second World War* (London, 2000), p. 83 and passim.

28. Virinder Kalra, *From Textile Mills to Taxi Ranks: Experiences of Migration, Labour and Social Change* (Aldershot, 2000).

29. *British Motor Corporation Story*, film, Kings Rose Archives, https://www.youtube.com/watch?v=QJ6wgLqwDYY, accessed 30 August 2017.

30. Ian Henry, 'Industrial Dispersal in Britain in the 1960s: An analysis of How the Government's Policy and Approach to the Motor Industry Influenced the Development of Ford and Vauxhall and Changed in Response to Evolving Corporate Business Strategies' (unpublished MA Dissertation, King's College London, 2015).

31. Richard Whipp, 'Crisis and Continuity: Innovation in the British Automobile Industry 1896–1986', in Peter Mathias and John A. Davis (eds.), *Innovation and Technology in Europe: From the Eighteenth Century to the Present Day* (London, 1991), table 4, p. 130.

32. A. K. Cairncross and J. R. Parkinson, 'The Shipbuilding Industry', in Duncan Burn (ed.), *The Structure of British Industry*, vol. 2 (Cambridge, 1958), p. 101.

33. Ibid., p. 102.

34. *Full Ahead* (1965), made for the shipbuilding firm Austin & Pickersgill, showing new equipment and facilities; bulk carrier ships built in

months using prefabrication, available at https://player.bfi.org.uk/free/film/watch-full-ahead-1965-online, accessed 30 January 2018.

35. Alan Booth, *The Management of Technical Change: Automation in Britain and the USA since 1950* (Basingstoke, 2007); H. Melling and A. Booth (eds.), *Managing the Modern Workplace: Productivity, Politics and Workplace Culture in Postwar Britain* (Aldershot, 2008); Nasbeth and Ray, *Diffusion*; G. F. Ray, *The Diffusion of Mature Technologies* (Cambridge, 1984).

36. *TUC General Council, Report, 1960*, available at http://www.unionhistory.info/reports/index.php.

37. Keith Middlemas, *Politics in Industrial Society: The Experience of the British System since 1911* (London, 1979).

38. *The Macmillan Diaries*, vol. 2: *Prime Minister and After, 1957–1966*, ed. Peter Catterall (London, 2011), 15 March 1957.

39. Richard Hyman, *Strikes* (London, 1972), pp. 25–34.

40. Jack Saunders, 'The Untraditional Worker: Class Re-formation in Britain 1945–65', *Twentieth Century British History* 26 (2015), pp. 225–48.

41. Stephen Broadberry, *The Productivity Race: British Manufacturing in International Perspective, 1850–1990* (Cambridge, 2005).

42. Theo Nichols, *The British Worker Question: A New Look at Workers and Productivity in Manufacturing* (London, 1986).

43. British Steel Corporation Development Plan, *House of Lords Debates*, 21 December 1972, vol. 337, cc. 1261–4.

44. Alan Wood, *The Groundnut Affair* (London, 1950), p. 126.

45. Sir Dennis Robertson, *Britain in the World Economy* (London, 1954), p. 29.

46. Quoted in Mathias Haeussler, 'The Popular Press and Ideas of Europe: The *Daily Mirror*, the *Daily Express*, and Britain's First Application to Join the EEC, 1961–63', *Twentieth Century British History* 25 (2014), pp. 108–31.

47. Harold Wilson, *Memoirs* (London, 1986), p. 123.

48. Andrew Pierre, *Nuclear Politics: British Experience with an Independent Strategic Force, 1939–70* (London, 1972), p. 143; and Lorna Arnold, *Britain and the H-Bomb* (London, 2001), p. 197.

49. *Challenge to Britain* (1953), part of series 'Labour Party Political Broadcasts', available at www.bfi.org.uk/inview/title/6391 (restricted access).

50. Matthew Eisler, ' "A Modern Philosopher's Stone'": Techno-Analogy and the Bacon Cell', *Technology and Culture* 50 (2009), pp. 345–65.

51. S. Waqar and H. Zaidi, 'The Janus-face of Techno-nationalism: Barnes Wallis and the "Strength of England" ', *Technology and Culture* 49 (2008), pp. 62–88.

52. Ibid.

53. P. D. Henderson, 'Two British Errors: Their Probable Size and Some Possible Lessons', *Oxford Economic Papers* 29 (1977), pp. 159–205.

54. John W. Young, 'Technological Cooperation in Wilson's Strategy', in Oliver Daddow (ed.), *Harold Wilson and the European Integration: Britain's Second Application to Join the EEC* (London, 2003), pp. 95–114.

55. David Edgerton, *Warfare State: Britain, 1920–1970* (Cambridge, 2005), p. 257.

56. *A Framework for Government Research and Development* (contains Rothschild and Dainton Reports) 1971–2, Cmnd. 4814, para. 8, http://www.nuffieldtrust.org.uk/, accessed 30 August 2017. For basic research, he endorsed the existing research councils (and even allowed three to continue to do applied research, but now commissioned from outside). Crucially, by far the largest SRC was doing basic only, the old DSIR having long lost its applied elements to departments. The point was that the nation, Rothschild echoed, was not doing enough directed medical or agricultural research. The Rothschild report is routinely misconstrued in the science policy literature.

57. *This Is Our Concern* (ICI, 1955), pp. 75–81.

58. See, for example, J. S. Metcalfe and John V. Pickstone, 'Replacing Hips and Lenses: Surgery, Industry and Innovation in Post-War Britain', in Andrew Webster and Sally Wyatt (eds.), *Innovative Health Technologies: New Perspectives, Challenge and Change* (Basingstoke, 2006).

59. Dominic Sandbrook, *The Great British Dream Factory: The Strange History of Our National Imagination* (London, 2015), pp. 57–8.

60. Bob Rowthorn, 'Imperialism in the Seventies – Unity or Rivalry?', *New Left Review* 1 (September–October 1971).

61. Nairn, 'The Left against Europe?', p. 35.

62. Ibid., pp. 18–19.

63. Alan Booth, 'The Manufacturing Failure Hypothesis and the Performance of British Industry during the Long Boom', *The Economic History Review* 56.1 (2003), pp. 1–33.

64. Owen, *From Empire to Europe*, pp. 339–442.

65. Nasbeth and Ray, *Diffusion*; David Edgerton, *Science, Technology and the British Industrial 'Decline' 1870–1970* (Cambridge, 1996).

66. For post-war R&D see Sally M. Horrocks, 'Enthusiasm Constrained? British Industrial R&D and the Transition from War to Peace, 1942–51', *Business History* 41 (1999), pp. 42–64.

CHAPTER 13: WARFARE STATE

1. On the 1950s and religion see Callum Brown, *The Death of Christian Britain: Understanding Secularisation 1800–2000* (London, 2001).

2. *Spithead Review 1953* (1954), film, ID 2259.03, available at https://www.britishpathe.com/video/spithead-review-1953, accessed 30 August 2017; https://www.youtube.com/watch?v=F2SNJ627-ps, accessed 30 August 2017.

3. *RAF Coronation Review 1953*, film, ID 106.11, available at https://www.britishpathe.com/video/raf-coronation-review, accessed 30 August 2017. This film downplays the existence of some non-British aircraft in the RAF, notably the Washington. For a fuller, partly colour film, see http://www.forces.net/news/raf/our-archive-raf-coronation-review-1953, accessed 30 August 2017.

4. Edgerton, *Warfare State*, p. 179.

5. Margaret Gowing, *Britain and Atomic Energy* (London, 1965); Margaret Gowing, *Independence and Deterrence* (London, 1974); Peter Morton, *Fire across the Desert: Woomera and the Anglo-Australian Joint Project 1946–1980* (Canberra: Department of Defence, 1989); S. R. Twigge, *The Early Development of Guided Weapons in the United Kingdom 1940–1960* (Amsterdam, 1993); Brian Balmer, *Britain and Biological Warfare: Expert Advice and Science Policy, 1930–1965* (London, 2001); Lorna Arnold, *Britain and the H-Bomb* (London, 2001).

6. Robert Bud, *The Uses of Life: A History of Biotechnology* (Cambridge, 1994).

7. See 'Defence Expenditure', *NIESR* (July 1960).

8. Alexandros Oikonomou, 'The Hidden Persuaders: Government Scientists and Defence in Post-war Britain' (unpublished PhD thesis, Imperial College London, 2011).

9. *The Macmillan Diaries*, vol. 2: *Prime Minister and After, 1957–1966*, 5 April 1957.

10. Duncan Redford, 'The "Hallmark of a First-Class Navy": The Nuclear-Powered Submarine in the Royal Navy 1960–77', *Contemporary British History* 23 (2009), pp. 181–97.

11. Aneurin Bevan, resignation speech, 23 April 1951, *House of Commons Debates*, vol. 487, cols. 34–43.

12. An earlier use of the term and concept of a 'paradox' – in this case that there was a peculiarly *British* problem of lack of correlation between R&D spend and growth, due among other things to too much defence

R&D – is attributable to the declinist Michael Shanks, writing in 1970. Michael Shanks, 'Setting the Scene Five: The United Kingdom', in Maurice Goldsmith (ed.), *Technological Innovation and the Economy* (London, 1970), pp. 55–61.

13. David James Gill, 'The Ambiguities of Opposition: Economic Decline, International Cooperation, and Political Rivalry in the Nuclear Policies of the Labour Party, 1963–1964', *Contemporary British History* 5 (2011), pp. 251–76, stresses the role of defence in the election of 1964 and underplays the role of economics in this one too.

14. He was by the standards of C. P. Snow or Jacob Bronowski a truth-teller. Guy Ortolano, *The Two Cultures Controversy: Science, Literature and Cultural Politics in Postwar Britain* (Cambridge, 2009); Ralph Desmarais, 'Jacob Bronowski: A Humanist Intellectual for an Atomic Age, 1946–1956', *The British Journal for the History of Science* 45 (2012), pp. 573–89.

15. *House of Commons Debates,* 15 July 1964, vol. 698, cols. 1382–94.

16. Ronald Hyam, *Britain's Declining Empire: The Road to Decolonisation, 1918–1968* (Cambridge, 2007), pp. 334–40.

17. See, in particular, Neil Cooper, *The Business of Death: Britain's Arms Trade at Home and Abroad* (London, 1997), chapter 6.

18. *Defence: Outline of Future Policy* (1957), Cmnd. 124, para. 6.

19. Matthew Jones, 'Great Britain, the United States, and Consultation over Use of the Atomic Bomb, 1950–1954', *The Historical Journal* 54 (2011), pp. 797–828.

20. John Simpson, 'British Nuclear Weapon Stockpiles, 1953–78: A Commentary on Technical and Political Drivers', *The RUSI Journal* 156.5 (2011), pp. 74–83; John R. Walker, 'British Nuclear Weapon Stockpiles, 1953–78', *The RUSI Journal* 156 (2011), pp. 66–72; Robert S. Norris and Hans M. Kristensen, 'The British Nuclear Stockpile, 1953–2013', *Bulletin of the Atomic Scientists* 69 (2013), pp. 69–75.

21. Gowing, *Independence and Deterrence*, pp. 406–7. See also pp. 448–9 for Churchill's continued hope for a US supply of bombs to Britain, and Cherwell's continued role in educating Churchill as to the realities of the US position, and insistence that a British nuclear programme was essential to British national survival. Britain could not be reduced to the non-nuclear European nations.

22. *The Macmillan Diaries*, vol. 2: *Prime Minister and After, 1957–1966*, 12 August 1957.

23. Gowing, *Independence and Deterrence*, pp. 234–5.

24. Katherine Pyne, 'The Nuclear Dimension – the Development of the Warheads for the Royal Air Force "Special Weapons"', *Royal Air Force Historical Society Journal* 62 (2016), pp. 9–30.

25. Pyne, 'The Nuclear Dimension', p. 25.

26. *Agreement between the Government of the United Kingdom of Great Britain and Northern Ireland and the Government of the United States of America for Cooperation on the uses of atomic energy for mutual defense purposes, signed in Washington, 3 July 1958* (1958), Cmnd. 537.

27. Richard Moore, 'Bad Strategy and Bomber Dreams: A New View of the Blue Streak Cancellation', *Contemporary British History* 27 (2013), pp. 145–166.

28. Nigel Ashton, *Kennedy, Macmillan and the Cold War: the irony of Interdependence* (London, 2002); *The Macmillan Diaries*, vol. 2: *Prime Minister and After, 1957–1966*, 5 November 1957.

29. Harold Macmillan, 'Commencement address', June 1958 at DePauw University in Greencastle, Indiana, available at https://www.youtube.com/watch?v=_owteARcSnI, accessed 12 January 2018.

30. Macmillan, quoted in Ashton, *Kennedy, Macmillan and the Cold War*, pp. 161–3.

31. Ibid., chapter 8.

32. Emphasis in original. *The Macmillan Diaries*, vol. 2: *Prime Minister and After, 1957–1966*, 23 December 1962.

33. *The New Britain*, 1964 Labour Party manifesto, available at http://www.politicsresources.net/area/uk/man/lab64.htm, accessed 12 January 2018; David James Gill, 'The Ambiguities of Opposition: Economic Decline, International Cooperation, and Political Rivalry in the Nuclear Policies of the Labour Party, 1963–1964', *Contemporary British History* 25.2 (2011), pp. 251–76.

34. See the Liberal manifestos for 1955, 1959 and 1964, all available at http://www.politicsresources.net/area/uk/man.htm, accessed 12 January 2018.

35. Peter Hennessy and James Jinks, *The Silent Deep: The Royal Navy Submarine Service since 1945* (London, 2015), pp. 236–47.

36. *A Better Tomorrow*, 1970 Conservative Party manifesto, available at http://www.conservativemanifesto.com/1970/1970-conservative-manifesto.shtml, accessed 12 January 2018.

37. See Simon Heffer, *Like the Roman: The Life of Enoch Powell* (London, 1998), pp. 403–4, 423, 432–4, 548–9.

38. Enoch Powell, review of Sir Solly Zuckerman, *Scientists at War*, *Sunday Telegraph*, 24 July 1966.

39. Enoch Powell, review of Verrier, *An Army for the Sixties*, *Sunday Telegraph*, 17 July 1966.

40. Caroline Elkins, *Britain's Gulag: The Brutal End of Empire in Kenya* (London, 2005); David Anderson, *Histories of the Hanged: The Dirty War in Kenya and the End of Empire* (London, 2005).

41. Ministry of Defence, 'UK Armed Forces Operational Deaths Post World War II' (4 November 2014), taken from www.gov.uk, accessed 30 August 2017, no longer available.

42. This was the argument of Enoch Powell at a Monday Club dinner speech on 7 December 1967 (while opposition spokesman on Defence), reproduced in Lord Howard of Rising (ed.), *Enoch at 100* (London, 2012).

43. See Steve Marsh, 'Churchill, SACLANT and the Politics of Opposition', *Contemporary British History* 27 (2013), pp. 445–65.

44. David French, *Army, Empire, and Cold War: The British Army and Military Policy, 1945–1971* (Oxford, 2012).

45. Andrea Benvenuti, 'The Heath Government and British Defence Policy in Southeast Asia at the End of Empire (1970–71)', *Twentieth Century British History* 20 (2009), pp. 53–73.

46. *Now Britain's Strong: Let's Make It Great to Live In*, 1970 Labour Party manifesto, available at http://www.politicsresources.net/area/uk/man/lab70.htm, accessed 12 January 2018.

47. In the autumn of 1973 the USA had 145 F4 fighters (excluding reconnaissance versions) and 78 F-111s – compared with a total RAF force, many stationed overseas, of 140 Lightning fighters, 130 F4s, 60 Vulcan bombers and 40 Buccaneers. For comparison, the numbers of offensive RAF aircraft in RAF bases in the UK were 71 Lightnings, 42 F4s, 32 Vulcans and 12 Buccaneers. Thus there were more US fighters and bombers in the UK than UK fighters and bombers. Calculated from the Appendix to Malcolm Fife, *British Military Aviation in the 1970s* (Stroud, 2016).

CHAPTER 14: TWO CLASSES, TWO PARTIES, ONE NATION

1. Neil Rollings, 'Cracks in the Post–War Keynesian Settlement? The Role of Organised Business in Britain in the Rise of Neoliberalism before Margaret Thatcher', *Twentieth Century British History* 24

(2013), pp. 637–59. See also Ben Jackson, 'Currents of Neo-Liberalism: British Political Ideologies and the New Right, *c.*1955–1979', *The English Historical Review* 131 (2016), pp. 823–50.

2. Keith Middlemas, *Politics in Industrial Society: The Experience of the British System since 1911* (London, 1979).

3. Robin Blackburn, 'The Unequal Society', in John Urry and John Wakeford (eds.), *Power in Britain* (London, 1973), p. 19.

4. E. Gwen Jones and Edward Nevin, 'The British National Debt', *Economica* 24 (1957), pp. 307–14.

5. In 1900 it got 42 per cent excluding the Liberal Unionists, an allied but separate party. Together they got 50 per cent.

6. Richard Keen and Vyara Apostolova, 'Membership of UK Political Parties', House of Commons Library, Briefing Paper Number SN05125, 16 January 2018, p. 6, available at http://researchbriefings.parliament.uk/ResearchBriefing/Summary/SN05125#fullreport, accessed 6 February 2018.

7. *The Macmillan Diaries*, vol. 2: *Prime Minister and After, 1957–1966*, 5 October 1957.

8. From Zweiniger-Bargielowska, *Austerity in Britain*, pp. 250–55.

9. W. L. Guttsman, 'The British Political Elite', in John Urry and John Wakeford (eds.), *Power in Britain* (London, 1973), p. 206.

10. Wing Commander Ernest Millington DFC was elected for Common Wealth at a by-election in 1945 and won in the general election. He switched to Labour and lost in 1950.

11. *The Macmillan Diaries*, vol. 1: *The Cabinet Years 1950–1957*, 7 May 1953.

12. Andrew Roth, 'The Business Backgrounds of MPs' in John Urry and John Wakeford (eds.), *Power in Britain* (London, 1973), p. 132.

13. Ibid., pp. 134–5.

14. William Waldegrave, *A Different Kind of Weather: A Memoir* (London, 2015) provides a rich account. See also Kenneth Rose, *Elusive Rothschild: The Life of Victor, Third Baron* (London, 2003). Rose (on pp. 183–4) compares Rothschild to another scientist in high advisory positions, Solly Zuckerman.

15. Harvie, *Fool's Gold*, p. 181.

16. The exception is Geoffrey Robinson, who went from the IRC to Leyland and was a Labour MP from 1976.

17. Jose Harris, 'Labour's Political and Social Thought', in Duncan Tanner, Pat Thane and Nick Tiratsoo (eds.), *Labour's First Century* (Cambridge, 2000).

18. Stuart Middleton, '"Affluence" and the Left in Britain, *c.*1958–1974', *English Historical Review* 134 (2014), pp. 107–38.

19. 'The Insiders', *Universities and Left Review* 3 (winter 1958).

20. *Britain Belongs to You: The Labour Party's Policy for Consideration by the British People*, 1959 Labour Party manifesto.

21. Steven Fielding, 'Rethinking Labour's 1964 Campaign', *Contemporary British History* 21 (2007), pp. 309–24.

22. Anthony Seldon, *Churchill's Indian Summer: The Conservative government 1951–55* (London, 1981), pp. 61–5.

23. Ben Pimlott, Dennis Kavanagh and Peter Morris, 'Is the "Postwar Consensus" a Myth?', *Contemporary British History* 2 (1989), pp. 12–15. See Pimlott here rightly dismissing it as an invented 1970s concept, anachronistic and misleading.

24. Robert Holland, *The Pursuit of Greatness: Britain and the World Role, 1900–1970* (Toronto, 1991), p. 19.

25. E. H. H. Green, 'The Treasury Resignations of 1958: A Reconsideration', *Twentieth Century British History* 11 (2000), pp. 409–30.

26. Klaus Journal of European Social Policy, p. 45; Edgerton, *Warfare State*, pp. 59–60.

27. Klaus Petersen and Jørn Henrik Petersen, 'Confusion and Divergence': Origins and Meaning of the Term "Welfare State" in Germany and Britain, 1840–1940, *Journal of European Social Policy* 23 (2013), pp. 45–7.

28. Jose Harris, 'Enterprise and Welfare States: A Comparative Perspective', *Transactions of the Royal Historical Society* 40 (1990), p. 180.

29. *Forward with Labour: Labour's Policy for the Consideration of the Nation*, 1955 Labour Party manifesto, available at http://www.politicsresources.net/area/uk/man/lab55.htm, accessed 12 January 2018.

30. *United for Peace and Progress: The Conservative and Unionist Party's Policy*, 1955 Conservative Party manifesto, available at http://www.conservativemanifesto.com/1955/1955-conservative-manifesto.shtml, accessed 12 January 2018.

31. Neil Rollings, 'Poor Mr Butskell: A Short Life, Wrecked by Schizophrenia?', *Twentieth Century British History* 5 (1994), pp. 183–205.

32. Edmund Dell, *Political Responsibility and Industry* (London, 1973), p. 20. He uses the term 'consensus' – interestingly (p. 28), he sees the break as a move to the right by both Labour and the Tories; Labour towards intervention rather than nationalization; the Tories from intervention to non-intervention.

33. Frances Stonor Saunders, *Who Paid the Piper?: CIA and the Cultural Cold War* (London, 1999); Hugh Wilford, '"Unwitting Assets?":

British Intellectuals and the Congress for Cultural Freedom', *Twentieth Century British History* 11 (2000), pp. 42–60. For Natopolitan culture see E. P. Thompson, 'Outside the Whale', in E. P. Thompson (ed.), *Out of Apathy* (London, 1960) and revised in E. P. Thompson, *The Poverty of Theory and Other Essays* (London, 1978).

34. David Henderson, 'Innocence and Design: Reith Lectures 1985' are available as recordings and transcripts on http://www.bbc.co.uk/programmes/p00gq1cr. Also published as *Innocence and Design* (Oxford, 1985).

35. June Morris, *The Life and Times of Thomas Balogh: A Macaw among Mandarins* (Eastbourne, 2007), chapter 9.

CHAPTER 15: SOCIAL DEMOCRACY, NATIONALISM AND DECLINISM

1. Tom Nairn, 'The Nature of the Labour Party, Part II', *New Left Review* 1.28 (November–December 1964), pp. 51–2.

2. E. P. Thompson, 'Socialist Humanism: An Epistle to the Philistines', *The New Reasoner* 1 (summer 1957), pp. 105–43.

3. *Now Britain's Strong – Let's Make It Great to Live In*, 1970 Labour Party manifesto, available at http://www.politicsresources.net/area/uk/man/lab70.htm, accessed 12 January 2018.

4. Henry Fairlie, *Spectator*, 23 September 1955, p. 5.

5. For a rich recent case see Patrick Joyce, *The State of Freedom: A Social History of the British State Since 1800* (Cambridge, 2013), pp. 322ff, passim.

6. Noel Thompson, 'Socialist Political Economy in an Age of Affluence: The Reception of J. K. Galbraith by the British Social-Democratic Left in the 1950s and 1960s', *Twentieth Century British History* 21 (2010), pp. 50–79. For the limits of the New Left response to revisionist accounts of capitalism see Madeleine Davis, 'Arguing Affluence: New Left Contributions to the Socialist Debate 1957–63', *Twentieth Century British History* 23 (2012), pp. 496–528. Kenny's New Left political economy is an exception, *First New Left*, pp. 119–64.

7. Morris, *The Life and Times of Thomas Balogh*.

8. Jim Tomlinson, *The Unequal Struggle: British Socialism and the Capitalist Enterprise* (London, 1982), chapter 5.

9. Peter Worsley, 'New Reasoner', *The New Reasoner* 5 (summer 1958), p. 64.

10. Alec Nove, *Efficiency Criteria for Nationalised Industries* (London, 1973).

11. For example, see Sally Sheard, *The Passionate Economist: How Brian Abel-Smith shaped Global Health and Social Welfare* (Bristol, 2013).

12. Seaton, 'Against the "Sacred Cow"'.

13. Stephen M. Davies, 'Promoting Productivity in the National Health Service, 1950 to 1966', *Contemporary British History* 31 (2017), pp. 47–68.

14. The thesis of Harold Perkin, *The Rise of Professional Society: England since 1880* (London, 1989).

15. See, for example, David Marquand's discussion of Tory nationalism in *Britain since 1918: The Strange Career of British Democracy* (London, 2008), p. 44.

16. Jimmi Østergaard Nielsen and Stuart Ward, '"Cramped and Restricted at Home"? Scottish Separatism at Empire's End', *Transactions of the Royal Historical Society* (sixth series) 25, pp. 159–85. They argue that Scottish nationalism was not rhetorically the product of the end of empire in the 1960s but needs to be seen in the context of the new nationalisms of the 1960s and 1970s across the former British world, but they do see that one of these post-imperial nationalisms was British nationalism. 'Britain' could and indeed did exist without empire. Priya Satia suggests the importance of Indian nationalism to the left nationalism of E. P. Thompson. Priya Satia, 'Byron, Gandhi and the Thompsons: The Making of British Social History and Unmaking of Indian History', *History Workshop Journal* 81 (2016), pp. 135–70. I would add to this analysis the need to take account of the Communist Party inheritance of E. P. Thompson, which, as I note above, was itself deeply nationalist while also encased in an internationalist frame. These rich papers are remarkable testimony to the invisibility of British nationalism.

17. Nairn, 'The Left against Europe?'. Nairn sees the war as a triumph of working-class (but not labour) mobilization, and also a conservative one; Labour reaped where it had not sowed. What it enacted in 1945 was a liberal welfare state the liberals would have enacted had they continued. But this ignores 1) other possible readings of the war and 2) that after 1945 there was a distinctly national political economy in play, unlike before 1914.

18. Nairn, 'Left against Europe', notes the centrality of 1940 in this context but not the lack of attention to 1945. See, for example, Paul Addison, *The Road to 1945* (London, 1975); Ross McKibbin, *People and Parties: England, 1914–1951* (Oxford, 2010); and also, despite its title, Ken Loach's film *The Spirit of '45* (2013).

19. Eric Hobsbawm, *Industry and Empire: From 1750 to the Present Day* (London, 1999), p. 245.

20. Example in P. J. Cain and Antony G. Hopkins, *British Imperialism, 1688–2000* (London, 2002).

21. Ashley Jackson, *The British Empire and the Second World War* (London, 2006); Edgerton, *Britain's War Machine*.

22. Niall Ferguson has defended the nineteenth-century empire on liberal grounds. To my knowledge there is no imperialist-protectionist-realist history of empire in or of the twentieth century.

23. See John Charmley, *Churchill: The End of Glory, A Political Biography* (London, 1993), p. 649 for quotation; see also pp. 2–3, 422–3. See also Maurice Cowling, *The Impact of Hitler: British Politics and British Policy 1933–1940* (Cambridge, 1975), who also saw the war as disastrous for the United Kingdom, in that it brought Labour to power and ended the empire. The Churchillians and Labour were able to tell history as they wished; they blackened Chamberlain and overlooked the extent to which Labour, some Liberals and Conservatives pushed Chamberlain into war, despite not having a reasoned alternative policy.

24. Tom Nairn, *The Enchanted Glass* (London, 1988).

25. Correlli Barnett, *The Audit of War: The Illusion and Reality of Britain as a Great Nation* (London, 1986).

26. Angus Calder, *The Myth of the Blitz* (London, 1992).

27. Blaming empire and imperialism for the problems of the UK had a long history on the left, and continues to be important. Stephen Howe, 'Internal Decolonization? British Politics since Thatcher as Post-colonial Trauma', *Twentieth Century British History* 14 (2003), pp. 286–304.

28. The economic nationalism of most declinist arguments is noted by Donald Winch in his contribution to Peter Clarke and Clive Trebilcock, *Understanding Decline: Perceptions and Realities of British Economic Performance* (Cambridge, 1997) and in my review in *The Historical Journal* 42 (1999), pp. 313–14. To describe Eric Hobsbawm as a nationalist may seem bizzare, but it will not surprise the careful reader of *Industry and Empire*. In any case the British Communist Party was deeply nationalist, as even a cursory reading of the Communist Party of Great Britain, *The British Road to Socialism Programme Adopted by the Executive Committee of the Communist Party* (January 1951), will make clear. Karl Miller's memoir of Hobsbawm has some telling details on Hobsbawm's relations with nationalism: *London Review of Books* 34 (25 October 2012), p. 12.

29. Robert Tombs, *The English and Their History* (London, 2014), pp. 789, 795, 799–800.

30. See Jim Tomlinson, 'The Empire/Commonwealth in British Economic Thinking and Policy', in Andrew Thompson (ed.), *Britain's Experience of Empire in the Twentieth Century* (Oxford, 2012), pp. 211–50.

31. Hobsbawm, *Industry and Empire*, p. 178.

32. Ibid., pp. 207, 213.

33. Nairn, 'The Nature of the Labour Party, Part II', p. 51.

34. Tom Nairn, 'The British Political Elite', *New Left Review* 23 (1964).

35. Nairn, 'The Nature of the Labour Party, Part II', p. 60.

36. Perry Anderson, 'Components of the National Culture', *New Left Review* 50 (July–August 1968), p. 11.

37. Perry Anderson, 'The Origins of the Present Crisis', *New Left Review* 23 (January–February 1964).

38. Christopher Harvie, *A Floating Commonwealth: Politics, Culture, and Technology on Britain's Atlantic Coast, 1860–1930* (Oxford, 2008) is a rich instance.

39. Thompson contended that political economy and science are central to English ideology in the nineteenth century and beyond. In close relation with these points he contended that Anderson (and Nairn) also ignored the Protestant and bourgeois democratic inheritance, and that they confused the British empirical idiom with an empiricist ideology; E. P. Thompson, 'The Peculiarities of the English' (1965), reprinted in *The Poverty of Theory* (London, 1978), p. 57.

40. Ibid., p. 56.

41. 'There was only one firm – ICI – capable of taking an entrepreneurial role in the construction of a single atomic plant ... the firm devoted nearly all its capital development in the 1930s not to the revolutionary new chemicals but to a plant with imperial purpose, one designed to saturate the British Empire with fertilizers it did not want.' Margaret Gowing, 'Science, Technology and Education: England in 1870: The Wilkins Lecture, 1976', *Notes and Records of the Royal Society of London* 32 (1977), pp. 86–7.

42. Extract from speech by Rt Hon. J. Enoch Powell, at the Institute of Petroleum (London) Luncheon, 29 November 1976, available at http://enochpowell.info/Resources/Oct-Dec%201976.pdf, accessed 31 August 2017. Vinen, *Thatcher's Britain*, pp. 34–5; D. N. McCloskey, *Economic Maturity and Entrepreneurial Decline: British Iron and Steel, 1870–1913* (Cambridge, Massachusetts, 1973), and *Enterprise and Trade in Victorian Britain: Essays in Historical Economics* (London, 1981).

43. Sir James Hamilton, see obituary in the *Independent*, 10 July 2012.
44. Edgerton, *Warfare State*, pp. 188–9.
45. Noel Annan, *Our Age: Portrait of a Generation* (London, 1990).
46. Sir Roy Fedden, *Britain's Air Survival* (London, 1957), p. 10.
47. Ibid., p. 15.
48. Ibid., p. 71.
49. Sam Brewitt-Taylor, 'The Invention of a "Secular Society"? Christianity and the Sudden Appearance of Secularization Discourses in the British National Media, 1961–4', *Twentieth Century British History* 24 (2013), pp. 327–50.

CHAPTER 16: POSSIBILITIES

1. *House of Commons Debates*, 28 March 1979, vol. 965, c. 582. These were among the very last words ever spoken by Old Labour from the government benches.
2. http://www.margaretthatcher.org/, accessed 2 September 2017.
3. Huw Beynon and Hilary Wainwright, *The Workers' Report on Vickers: The Vickers Shop Stewards Combine Committee Report on Work, Wages, Rationalisation, Closure and Rank-and-File Organisation in a Multinational Company* (London, 1979), p. 140.
4. For a vigorous argument to this effect see John Medhurst, *That Option No Longer Exists: Britain, 1974–76* (Winchester, 2014).
5. See 'A Blueprint for Survival', *The Ecologist* 2 (January 1972), and Edward Goldsmith, 'De-industrialising Society', *The Ecologist* 7 (May 1977).
6. *The Economist*, 2 June 1979.
7. M. Artis, D. Cobham and M. Wickham-Jones, 'Social Democracy in Hard Times: The Economic Record of the Labour Government 1974–1979', *Twentieth Century British History* 3 (1992), pp. 32–58.
8. For reflections see Eric Hobsbawm, 'The 1970s: Syndicalism without Syndicalists', *New Society* (5 April 1979), and *Worlds of Labour: Further Studies in the History of Labour* (London, 1984).
9. Colin Hay, 'Chronicles of a Death Foretold: The Winter of Discontent and Construction of the Crisis of British Keynesianism', *Parliamentary Affairs* 63 (2010), pp. 446–70.
10. P. Edwards, 'The Local Organisation of a National Dispute: The British 1979 Engineering Strike', *Industrial Relations Journal* 13 (1982), pp. 57–63. Other strikes running at the time were the two very long-running ones at Times newspapers and ITV.

11. ONS, Labour Market Statistics time series dataset (LMS) release of 16 August 2017, available at www.ons.gov.uk, accessed 4 September 2017.
12. Carol Ackroyd et al., *The Technology of Political Control* (Harmondsworth, 1977) is a typical work. See also Hilary Rose and Steven Rose (eds.), *The Radicalisation of Science* (London, 1976).
13. Stuart Holland, 'Alternative European and Economic Strategies', in Lawrence Black, Hugh Pemberton and Pat Thane (eds.), *Reassessing 1970s Britain* (Manchester, 2013).
14. BBC2 *Horizon* 1977–8, 'Now the Chips Are Down' (March 1978), Edward Goldwyn (writer and producer) (BBC Four Collection), http://www.bbc.co.uk/iplayer/, accessed 2 September 2017.
15. M. McLean and T. Rowland, *The INMOS Saga – a Triumph of National Enterprise* (London, 1985).
16. Tom Lean, *Electronic Dreams: How 1980s Britain Learned to Love the Computer* (London, 2016).
17. On which see Andy Roberts, *Albion Dreaming: A Popular History of LSD in Britain* (London, 2012).
18. Raymond Williams (ed.), *The May Day Manifesto, 1968*, available at https://www.lwbooks.co.uk/sites/default/files/free-book/Mayday.pdf, accessed 2 September 2017.
19. Harvie, *Fool's Gold*, chapter 6.
20. For example, C. P. Snow and many of the trade union cabinet ministers in the 1960s Labour governments.
21. *The New Hope for Britain*, Labour Party manifesto, available at http://www.politicsresources.net/area/uk/man/lab83.htm, accessed 12 January 2018.
22. Harvie, *Fool's Gold*, 213.
23. Richard Jobson, 'A New Hope for an Old Britain? Nostalgia and The British Labour Party's Alternative Economic Strategy, 1970–83', *Journal of Policy History* 27 (2015), pp. 670–94, gets only part of the story, the defence of old industries, of British parliamentary freedoms and the memory to some extent of 1940s import controls.
24. Frank Field, Molly Meacher and Chris Pond, *To Him Who Hath: A Study of Poverty and Taxation* (Harmondsworth, 1977); Mary Kaldor, Dan Smith and Steve Vines (eds.), *Democratic Socialism and the Cost of Defence: The Report and Papers of the Labour Party Defence Study Group* (London, 1979); Stuart Holland, *The Socialist Challenge* (London, 1976); Stuart Holland (ed.), *Out of Crisis: A Project for European Recovery* (London, 1983); Jim Tomlinson, *The Unequal Struggle?: British Socialism and the Capitalist Enterprise* (London, 1982).

25. The Tory MP William Waldegrave, *A Different Kind of Weather: A Memoir* (London, 2015) notably reports encounters with one at GEC in Leicester (p. 156), and a long friendship with another (implicitly non-CP) from the aerospace complex in Filton, Bristol (1961).

26. Tony Cliff and Ted Grant were both of Jewish heritage and grew up in the empire, in Palestine and South Africa respectively. Gerry Healy was Irish.

27. Dave Nellist and Terry Fields were MPs from 1983 and were expelled from Labour in 1991, losing their seats in 1992. Pat Wall was elected in 1987 and died in 1990.

28. Ted Grant, *History of British Trotskyism* (London, 2002), pp. 220–21.

29. Ted Grant, 'British Capitalism Faces Catastrophe', *Militant International Review*, 21 (winter 1980–81), available at http://www.tedgrant.org/archive/grant/1980/07/catastrophe.htm, accessed 2 September 2017.

30. Daisy Payling, ' "Socialist Republic of South Yorkshire": Grassroots Activism and Left-Wing Solidarity in 1980s Sheffield', *Twentieth Century British History* 25 (2014), pp. 602–27.

31. A. H. Halsey, *Trends in British Society since 1900: A Guide to the Changing Social Structure of Britain* (London, 1972), table 4.7.

32. Jonathan Moss, ' "We Didn't Realise How Brave We Were at the Time": The 1968 Ford Sewing Machinists' Strike in Public and Personal Memory', *Oral History* 43 (spring 2015). Also Sheila Cohen, *Notoriously Militant: The Story of a Union Branch at Ford Dagenham* (Pontypool, 2014).

33. Evan Smith and Daryl Leeworthy, 'Before *Pride*: The Struggle for the Recognition of Gay Rights in the British Communist Movement, 1973–85', *Twentieth Century British History* 27 (2016), pp. 621–42.

34. David Feldman, 'Why the English Like Turbans: Multicultural Politics in British History', in David Feldman and Jon Lawrence (eds.), *Structures and Transformations in Modern British History* (Cambridge, 2011), pp. 281–302.

35. Iain Sinclair, *Hackney, That Rose-Red Empire: A Confidential Report* (London, 2009).

36. The play, now a Methuen Classic, was not revived till 2006.

CHAPTER 17: DEFENDING THE NATION

1. Edward Thompson, 'Notes on Exterminism, the Last Stage of Civilization', *New Left Review* 1 (May–June 1980).

2. Margaret Thatcher, speech to Conservative rally at Cheltenham, 3 July 1982, ID 104989, available at http://www.margaretthatcher.org/document/104989, accessed 12 January 2018.

3. Ian Cobain, 'Last Man Sentenced to Death in UK Has Conviction Quashed', *Guardian*, 21 June 2012.

4. E. P. Thompson, *Writing by Candlelight* (London, 1980); *Zero Option* (London, 1982).

5. As a child, *c*.1968, I went aboard HMS *Endurance* in Montevideo. The moment I heard of the invasion of the Falklands by Argentina, I knew this was not a post-imperial joke, but deadly serious for both sides.

6. Borges was the child of a Uruguayan mother and a half–English father, a bilingual boy educated in Geneva, well used to traversing the Atlantic. He had relatives near Fray Bentos, which he visited, and which is the setting for his story 'Funes the Memory Man', about an unfortunate who could remember everything but make sense of nothing.

7. Michael Foot, *House of Commons Debates*, 3 April 1982, vol. 21, cc. 633–68.

8. The danger of having nuclear weapons is illustrated by the fact that it appears that Margaret Thatcher did consider the possible use of nuclear bombs against Argentina in extreme circumstances. Peter Hennessy and James Jinks, *The Silent Deep: The Royal Navy Submarine Service since 1945* (London, 2015), p. 457.

9. See Anthony Barnett, *Iron Britannia: Time to Take the Great Out of Britain* (London, 1982).

10. Dane Kennedy, 'Imperial History and Post-Colonial Theory', *The Journal of Imperial and Commonwealth History* 24 (1996), pp. 345–63; Stephen Howe, 'Internal Decolonization? British Politics since Thatcher as Post-colonial Trauma', *Twentieth Century British History* 14 (2003), pp. 286–304.

11. Mark Phythian, *The Politics of British Arms Sales Since 1964: 'To Secure Our Rightful Share'* (London, 2000).

12. Lawrence Freedman, *The Official History of the Falklands Campaign*, vol. 1: *The Origins of the Falklands War* (London, 2005), pp. 149–50.

13. Matthew Jones, *The Official History of the UK Strategic Nuclear Deterrent*, vol. 1: *From the V-Bomber Era to the Arrival of Polaris, 1945–64* (London, 2017) and *The Official History of the UK Strategic Nuclear Deterrent*, vol. 2: *The Labour Government and the Polaris Programme, 1964–70* (London, 2017), both published by Routledge in 2017.

14. See John Baylis and Kristian Stoddart, *The British Nuclear Experience: The Role of Beliefs, Culture and Identity* (Oxford, 2015), chapter 7.

15. Ibid., p. 161.

16. Matthew Pawson, 'The United Kingdom, Intermediate Nuclear Forces and the 1983 Invasion of Grenada' (unpublished undergraduate dissertation, University of London, 2016).

17. Nicholas Henderson, *Old Friends and Modern Instances* (London, 2000), p. 161.

18. Brendan Simms, *Britain's Europe: A Thousand Years of Conflict and Cooperation* (London, 2016), p. 193.

19. 'A Speech by the Queen to Parliament on Her Silver Jubilee', 4 May 1977, available at https://www.royal.uk/silver-jubilee-address-parliament-4-may-1977, accessed 1 September 2017.

20. During the Scottish independence referendum the queen, and the government, made sure her unionist views were known in a deniable way.

21. In the 'ABC' trial, there were two lots of ABCs: the defendants, Crispin Aubrey, John Berry and Duncan Campbell, and the unnamed prosecution witnesses, Colonel A, Colonel B and Mr C. Col. B was outed by *The Leveller* and Mr C by Lance Price, in *The Orwellian*, October 1978, p. 2.

22. Resulting in, for example, Stephen Dorril and Robin Ramsay, *Smear! Wilson and the Secret State* (London, 1991).

23. Peter Johnson, *Neutrality: A Policy for Britain* (London, 1985).

CHAPTER 18: RULERS' REVOLT

1. See for an internal Conservative discussion on this, Vinen, *Thatcher's Britain*, pp. 85–6.

2. Ibid., pp. 29, 81–92, 292–5.

3. By the Tory MP and wit Julian Critchley. See Jonathan Aitken, *Margaret Thatcher: Power and Personality* (London, 2013), pp. 158–60.

4. Dennis Skinner, *Sailing Close to the Wind: Reminiscences* (London, 2014), pp. 244–6.

5. Margaret Thatcher, Speech to Conservative rally at Cheltenham, 3 July 1982.

6. Vinen, *Thatcher's Britain*, pp. 187–9.

7. See, for an example of robust anti-nationalism, Tim Congdon, *Against Import Controls* (London, 1981), which argued that import controls would do for the United Kingdom what they had done between the 1930s and the 1970s for Chile and Argentina.

8. Ben Jackson, 'The Think-Tank Archipelago: Thatcherism and Neo-Liberalism', in Ben Jackson and Robert Saunders (eds.), *Making Thatcher's Britain* (Cambridge, 2012).

9. Seaton, 'Against the "Sacred Cow"'.

10. Nicholas Ridley, *Industry and the Civil Service* (London, 1973); John Jewkes, 'Government and High Technology', *Institute of Economic Affairs Occasional Paper* 37 (1972); Duncan Burn, *Nuclear Power and the Energy Crisis: Politics and the Atomic Industry* (London, 1978). P. D. Henderson, 'Two British Errors: Their Probable Size and Some Possible Lessons', *Oxford Economic Papers* 29 (1977), pp. 159–205. It is also worth noting the importance of economists in British environmentalism – for example, Barbara Ward, E. F. Schumacher and E. J. Mishan.

11. On this see David Edgerton and Kirsty Hughes, 'The Poverty of Science: A Critical Analysis of Scientific and Industrial Policy under Mrs Thatcher', *Public Administration* 67 (1989), pp. 419–33.

12. On Polanyi, see McGucken, *Scientists, Society and State*; Frances Stonor Saunders, *Who Paid the Piper?: The CIA and the Cultural Cold War* (London, 1999).

13. John Jewkes et al., *The Sources of Invention* (London, 1958, 1969).

14. See also Adrian Johns, *Piracy: The Intellectual Property Wars from Gutenberg to Gates* (Chicago, Illinois, 2010).

15. Thatcherite scientists were rare – an exceptional neo-liberal account of science met with howls of rage: Terence Kealey, *The Economic Laws of Scientific Research* (London, 1996).

16. Andrew Roberts, *Eminent Churchillians* (London, 1994).

17. Maurice Cowling, *The Impact of Hitler: British Politics and British Policy 1933–1940* (Cambridge, 1975); Charmley, *Churchill: The End of Glory*. See also the pro-Nazi David Irving, who said Churchill was convinced 'he was protecting his country and its Empire from its greatest enemy. Yet in reality he had allied himself with that Empire's profoundest enemies, and presided over its dissolution.' David Irving, *Churchill's War*, vol. 1: *The Struggle for Power* (London, 1989), p. xix.

18. Martin Wiener, *English Culture and the Decline of the Industrial Spirit, 1850–1980* (Cambridge, 1981).

19. See my analysis of the academic reviews in David Edgerton, 'The Prophet Militant and Industrial: The Peculiarities of Correlli Barnett', *Twentieth Century British History* 2 (1991), pp. 360–79. It is worth noting, too, the success of another military historian of the 1960s, Alan Clark, later a very right-wing MP, who was notably nationalist-protectionist and anti-American.

20. Vinen, *Thatcher's Britain*, pp. 284–7.

21. Ibid., p. 190.

22. Notably John Hoskyns, formerly of IBM, who had set up and sold his own IT services company, and Norman Strauss, formerly of Unilever.

23. M. J. Oliver, 'Whatever Happened to Monetarism?: A Review of British Exchange Rate Policy in the 1980s', *Twentieth Century British History* 8 (1997), pp. 49–73.

24. Andrew Pettigrew, *The Awakening Giant: Continuity and Change in ICI* (London, 1985), pp. 75–6.

25. Owen Jones, *Chavs: The Demonization of the Working Class* (London, 2011).

26. It is a crucial insight due to R. E. Rowthorn and J. R. Wells, *De-Industrialization and Foreign Trade* (Cambridge, 1987), pp. 100–101.

27. It is a myth that the Conservative manifesto of 1979 did not mention privatization – it did, but not the big ones which happened after 1983. What they promised was: 'We will offer to sell back to private ownership the recently nationalised aerospace and shipbuilding concerns, giving their employees the opportunity to purchase shares. We aim to sell shares in the National Freight Corporation to the general public in order to achieve substantial private investment in it. We will also relax the Traffic Commissioner licensing regulations to enable new bus and other services to develop – particularly in rural areas – and we will encourage new private operators.' It also proposed the sale of council housing and the review of BNOC.

28. BP had had a government shareholding since 1914. Burmah Oil, disastrously managed (among the directors was Denis Thatcher, husband of Margaret), was nationalized in 1975, and its holdings in BP passed to the state. In 1977 the government had nearly 70 per cent of the shares; it sold a chunk that year, leaving it with 51 per cent.

29. Dieter Helm, *Energy, the State, and the Market: British Energy Policy since 1979* (Oxford, 2003), p. 61; research briefing, 20 November 2014, available at http://researchbriefings.files.parliament.uk/documents/RP14–61/RP14–61.pdf, accessed 2 September 2017.

30. Freedom of Information request 2013–1822, https://www.gov.uk/government/uploads/system/uploads/attachment_data/file/203389/2013–1822.pdf. accessed 1 September 2017.

31. Dieter Helm, *Energy, the State and the Market: British Energy Policy since 1979* (Oxford, 2004), pp. 75–6.

32. See ibid., p. 85.

33. I owe this estimate to Ben Taylor.

34. Vinen, *Thatcher's Britain*, pp. 176–7.
35. 'We must retain the child's readiness to forgive, with which we are all born and which it is all too easy to lose as we grow older. Without it, divisions between families, communities and nations remain unbridgeable. We owe it to our children and grandchildren to live up to the standards of behaviour and tolerance which we are so eager to teach them . . . The enemies of 1944, against whom so many of our countrymen fought and died on those beaches in Normandy, are now our steadfast friends and allies. But friendship, whether we are talking of continents or next door neighbours, should not need strife as its forerunner.' The Queen's Christmas Broadcast, 1984, available at: http://www.royal.gov.uk/ImagesandBroadcasts/TheQueensChristmasBroadcasts/ChristmasBroadcasts/ChristmasBroadcast1984.aspx, accessed 2 September 2017.
36. *Guardian*, 3 October 2000.
37. Wincott, 'Images of Welfare'.
38. Ibid.
39. Mike Savage, *Social Class in the 21st Century* (London, 2015).
40. I owe this last point to Neil Rollings, in a contribution to the Rethinking British Neoliberalism conference, 11–12 September, 2017. See also his 'The Twilight World of British Business Politics: The Spring Sunningdale conferences since the 1960s', *Business History* 56 (2014), pp. 915–35.
41. Ben Pimlott, *The Queen: A Biography of Elizabeth II* (London, 1996), pp. 508–14.

CHAPTER 19: A NATION LOST

1. *House of Commons Debates,* 22 November 1990, vol. 181, cc. 448.
2. Margaret Thatcher, 'Europe's Political Architecture', speech in The Hague, 15 May 1992, available at http://www.margaretthatcher.org/document/108296, accessed 2 September 2017.
3. I am alluding to Dani Rodrik's trilemma. He argues that only two of the three can be maintained at the same time. Dani Rodrik, *The Globalization Paradox: Democracy and the Future of the World Economy* (New York, 2011).
4. The concept of neo-liberalism is deeply flawed. Firstly, it is a term used only by critics in recent decades; secondly, its meanings are not clear, and it is usually too concerned with ideas rather than practices and assumes coherence between different ideas and practices; there is also a

distinct lack of clarity as to what is neo or new about neo-liberalism as compared to liberalism. It also posits a radical rupture with a pre-neo-liberal world which is itself misconstrued as 'social democracy'.

5. Geoffrey Owen, *From Empire to Europe: The Decline and Revival of British Industry since the Second World War* (London, 2000), afterword, July 2000 (original 1999).

6. *The Heroin Epidemic of the 1980s and 1990s and Its Effect on Crime Trends – Then and Now*, Home Office Research Report 79 (2014), available at https://www.gov.uk/government/publications/the-heroin-epidemic-of-the-1980s-and-1990s-and-its-effect-on-crime-trends-then-and-now, accessed 12 January 2018.

7. See Aled Davies, *The City of London and Social Democracy: The Political Economy of Finance in Britain, 1959–1979* (Oxford, 2017).

8. Andrew Bowman, Julie Froud, Sukhdev Johal, Michael Moran and Karel Williams, *Business Elites and Undemocracy in Britain: A Work in Progress*, CRESC Working Paper Series, no. 125, July 2013.

9. ONS, *Ownership of UK Quoted Shares: 2010* (2012), figure 4, available at https://www.ons.gov.uk/economy/investmentspensionsand trusts/bulletins/ownershipofukquotedshares/2012-02-28, accessed 12 January 2018.

10. *FA Chairman's England Commission Report*, May 2014, p. 22, exhibit 1.

11. Nicholas Henderson, *Old Friends and Modern Instances* (London, 2000), p. 165.

12. DEFRA, *Food Statistics Pocketbook* (2008), available at http://webarchive.nationalarchives.gov.uk/20130124042733/, http://www.defra.gov.uk/statistics/files/defra-stats-foodfarm-food-pocketbook-2008.pdf, accessed 2 September 2017, accessed 12 January 2018.

13. Rowena Crawford, Carl Emmerson and Gemma Tetlow, 'A Survey of Public Spending in the UK', Institute for Fiscal Studies Briefing Note BN43, September 2009, updated version at https://www.ifs.org.uk/publications/1791, accessed 2 September 2017.

14. IFS, 'Social Security Spending' (updated September 2015), https://www.ifs.org.uk/tools_and_resources/fiscal_facts/public_spending_survey/social_security, accessed 1 September 2017.

15. *Historical Pet Ownership 1965–2004*, Pet Food Manufacturers' Association data, available at http://www.pfma.org.uk/historical-pet-ownership-statistics, accessed 2 September 2017.

16. House of Commons Library, *Privatisation* (Research Paper 14/61), 20 November 2014, available at http://researchbriefings.files.parliament.

uk/documents/RP14-61/RP14-61.pdf, accessed 2 September 2017; Helm, *Energy, the State, and the Market*, p. 61.

17. Helm, *Energy, the State, and the Market*, p. 15.

18. Department of Transport, *Maritime Statistics 2006*, table 4.1(a), no longer available online.

19. Helm, *Energy, the State, and the Market*, pp. 157–61.

20. Ibid., pp. 194–5.

21. The Magnox reactors and their vast liabilities for clean-up remained public.

22. Helm, *Energy, the State, and the Market*, pp. 104–7.

23. *Engineering Our Future: Report of the Committee of Inquiry into the Engineering Profession* (Chm Sir Montague Finniston, FRS), Cmnd. 7794, January 1980, p. 76.

24. 'Austin Metro: A British Car to Beat THE WORLD', available at https://www.youtube.com/watch?v=E4-8LgXjQbc, accessed 2 September 2017.

25. David Henderson, *Innocence and Design: The Influence of Economic Ideas on Policy* (London, 1986).

26. Kenneth Baker, *The Turbulent Years: My Life in Politics* (London, 1993), pp. 59–63; Baker had a business background and had been an adviser to the leading software house Logica.

27. Department for Transport Statistics, *Port Freight Statistics*, table PORT0211, 'UK major port traffic, import/export trade motor vehicles by port, annually: 1999–2016', available at https://www.gov.uk/government/statistical-data-sets/port02-freight, accessed 6 February 2018.

28. See his fascinating memoirs, Alan Sugar, *What You See Is What You Get: My Autobiography* (London, 2010).

29. Michael M. Hopkins and Geoffrey Owen, *Science, the State and the City: Britain's Struggle to Success in Biotechnology* (Oxford, 2016). On the NEB see Daniel Kramer, *State Capital and Private Enterprise: The Case of the UK National Enterprise Board* (London, 1988).

30. Rachel Griffith and Rupert Harrison, *Understanding the UK's Poor Technological Performance* (London, 2003), available at https://www.ifs.org.uk/bns/bn37.pdf, accessed 2 September 2017.

31. David Edgerton, 'Research, Development and Competitiveness', in K. Hughes (ed.), *The Future of UK Industrial Competitiveness and the Role of Industrial Policy* (London, 1994).

32. Anthony Seldon, *Major: A Political Life* (London, 1997), p. 744.

33. Referendum Party election broadcast, 15 April 1997, available at https://www.youtube.com/watch?v=-dxZ1MoyXNA, accessed 5 February 2018. See also Referendum Party 1997 election video, available at https://www.youtube.com/watch?v=SSXdE8M-9Y4, accessed 5 February 2018, a slick video which was mailed out rather than broadcast. The theme was a conspiracy to create a federal superstate, hidden by British politicians and Eurocrats.

34. In the 1992 general election the Natural Law Party, supporting transcendental meditation, fielded 309 candidates. In 1997 Sir James Goldsmith funded 547 candidates through his Referendum Party, compared to 193 for UKIP, just slightly behind the Natural Law Party with 197.

CHAPTER 20: NEW TIMES, NEW LABOUR

1. David Owen, *In Sickness and in Power: Illness in Heads of Government during the Last 100 Years* (London, 2008), p. 276.

2. Speaking in private while cabinet secretary to David Goodhart, quoted in David Goodhart, *The Road to Somewhere: The Populist Revolt and the Future of Politics* (London, 2017), p. 15.

3. *Manifesto for New Times: A Communist Party Strategy for the 1990s*, Communist Party manifesto, 1989, pp. 4, 6, 7.

4. See his contribution to *Marxism Today* (October, 1991).

5. Robin Murray, 'Life after Henry (Ford)', *Marxism Today* (October 1988) and in Stuart Hall and Martin Jacques (eds.), *New Times: The Changing Face of Politics in the 1990s* (London, 1989). See also the critiques by Michael Rustin and Paul Hirst in this same volume.

6. *Manifesto for New Times*.

7. My undergraduate thesis was written on a golfball typewriter (1981); my PhD thesis was word-processed (1986).

8. *Britain United – The Time has Come*, the SDP/Liberal Alliance programme for government, 1987, available at http://www.politicsresources.net/area/uk/man/lib87.htm, accessed 12 January 2018.

9. Labour Party, *Meet the Challenge – Make the Change: A New Agenda for Britain. Final Report of Labour's Policy Review for the 1990s* (London, 1989), p. 12.

10. Jim Tomlinson, 'De-industrialization Not Decline: A New Meta-narrative for Post-war British History', *Twentieth Century British History* 27 (2016), pp. 76–99.

11. James Achur, *Trade Union Membership* 2010 (BIS/ONS), available at https://www.gov.uk/government/uploads/system/uploads/attachment_data/file/32191/11-p77-trade-union-membership-2010.pdf, accessed 2 September 2017.

12. They were described by one left journalist, Richard Gott, as the Welsh windbag and the Yorkshire gasbag, 'Tony [Benn] and Ken [Livingstone], the Natural Leaders that Labour Needs but Can't Have', *Guardian,* 17 June 1983.

13. Alan Watkins, 'Suet Pudding v. the Welsh Windbag', *Observer,* 26 June 1983.

14. A key figure was Brian Gould, a Eurosceptic, but a believer in the idea that the problem with British capitalism was that it was financial rather than industrial, that devaluation was needed. What it most needed to prosper was a strong, exporting, manufacturing industry, and R&D investment at home rather than abroad.

15. Ralph Miliband, *Capitalist Democracy in Britain* (Oxford, 1982).

16. Ibid., p. 69.

17. *Britain United – The Time Has Come.*

18. *Changing Britain for Good,* 1992 Liberal Democrat manifesto, available at http://www.politicsresources.net/area/uk/man/libdem92.htm, accessed 12 January 2018.

19. Colin Hughes and Patrick Wintour, *Labour Rebuilt: The New Model Party* (London, 1990), chapter 5.

20. Labour Party, *Looking to the Future: A Dynamic Economy, A Decent Society, Strong in Europe,* Labour Party, 1989/90; *Meet the Challenge – Make the Change: A New agenda for Britain: Final Report of the Labour's Policy Review for the 1990s* (London, 1989).

21. Labour Party, *It's Time to Get Britain Working Again,* 1992 Labour Party manifesto, p. 12, available at http://www.politicsresources.net/area/uk/man/lab92.htm, accessed 12 January 2018.

22. Paul Anderson and Nyta Mann, *Safety First: The Making of New Labour* (London, 1997), p. 73.

23. John Smith, leader's speech at the Labour Party conference, 1992, available at http://www.britishpoliticalspeech.org/speech–archive.htm?speech=198, accessed 2 September 2017.

24. John Smith, leader's speech at the Labour Party conference, 1993, available at http://www.britishpoliticalspeech.org/speech–archive.htm?speech=199, accessed online 2 September 2017.

25. James E. Cronin, *New Labour's Pasts: The Labour Party and Its Discontents* (London, 2004).

26. See Richard Brooks and Solomon Hughes, 'Public Servants, Public Paydays' [Revolving Doors Special], *Private Eye* 1426 (15 September 2016), pp. 19–24.

27. Speech as chancellor, Labour Party conference, 1997, available at http://www.britishpoliticalspeech.org/speech–archive.htm?speech=268, accessed 2 September 2017.

28. *New Labour Because Britain Deserves Better*, 1997 Labour Party manifesto, available at http://www.politicsresources.net/area/uk/man/lab97.htm.

29. Ibid.

30. Noted powerfully by David Marquand, *Britain since 1918: The Strange Career of British Democracy* (London, 2008), chapter 11. He notes that what was claimed as new was characteristic of the Edwardian years. On the theme see also James Cronin, *New Labour's Pasts* (London, 2004), note 25.

31. Especially Eric Hobsbawm, 'The Death Of Neo-Liberalism', and Stuart Hall, 'The Great Moving Nowhere Show', *Marxism Today Special Issue* (November/December 1998), available at http://banmarchive.org.uk/collections/mt/index_frame.htm, accessed 2 February 2018.

32. Hobsbawm, 'The Death of Neo-Liberalism', p. 14.

33. Alan Clark MP, *House of Commons Debates*, 21 October 1998, c. 1205.

34. Larry Elliott and Dan Atkinson, *Fantasy Island: Waking up to the Incredible Economic, Political and Social Illusions of the Blair Legacy* (London, 2007), in particular the chapter on creative industries, 'Bullshit Britain'.

35. R. M. May, 'The Scientific Wealth of Nations', *Science* 275 (1997), pp. 793–6. Robert May was then the chief scientific adviser to the British government. His arguments echoed those of Terence Kealey.

36. Luke Blaxill and Kaspar Beelen, 'A Feminized Language of Democracy? The Representation of Women at Westminster since 1945', *Twentieth Century British History* 27 (2016), pp. 412–49.

37. Peter Oborne, *The Rise of Political Lying* (London, 2005), pp. 3–5, 235.

38. Allyson Pollock, *NHS plc: The Privatisation of Our Healthcare* (London, 2004), p. 179.

39. 'Chart That Tells a Story – Pensions and Earnings', *Financial Times*, 10 April 2015.

40. Pollock, *NHS plc*, pp. 59–60.

41. Simon Lee, *Best for Britain? The Politics and Legacy of Gordon Brown* (Oxford, 2007).

42. For other bodies Westminster legislated for all sorts of systems. The Additional Member system was adopted for the Scottish Parliament, the National Assembly for Wales and the London Assembly in 1998 and 2000. The London Mayor was elected by Supplementary Vote (2000). The Single Transferable Vote was used for electing the Northern Ireland Assembly, local elections in Scotland and Northern Ireland and European Parliament elections in Northern Ireland. In the first European Parliament election of 1979 there was first-past-the-post for all except Northern Ireland, which had STV. From 1999 the Party List system was used, except in Northern Ireland. The House of Lords was not reformed until 1999, when most of the hereditary peers were forced out.

43. Here I am drawing on David Edgerton, 'Tony Blair's Warfare State', *New Left Review*, 1.230 (July–August 1998), pp. 123–30.

44. Neil Cooper, *The Business of Death: Britain's Arms Trade at Home and Abroad* (London, 1997), p. 135.

45. *The Report of the Iraq Inquiry*, HC 264 (Chilcot Report), Executive Summary, para 309, available at http://www.iraqinquiry.org.uk, accessed 12 January 2018.

46. Ibid., Executive Summary, para. 324.

47. Ibid., vol. 6, section 6.3, para. 362, and other sections of this volume.

48. Interview with Sir John Chilcot, BBC, 6 July 2017, available at http://www.bbc.co.uk/news/uk-politics-40510539, accessed 12 January 2018.

49. Gordon Brown, speech to the Fabian New Year Conference, London 2006. The speech, on Britishness, barely mentioned Europe. Lee, *Best for Britain?*, chapter 5.

50. Andy Beckett, *Pinochet in Piccadilly: Britain and Chile's Secret History* (London, 2002). As Thatcher put it, 'the small minority of communists who once nearly wrecked the country under Allende will now be encouraged to overturn the prosperous, democratic order that Pinochet and his successors built ... Senator Pinochet is in truth on trial, not for anything contained in Judge Garzon's indictment, but for defeating communism. What the Left can't forgive is that Pinochet undoubtedly saved Chile and helped save South America.' Margaret Thatcher, speech to the Conservative Party conference, 6 October 1999, available at http://www.margaretthatcher.org/document/108383, accessed 2 September 2017.

51. As it was called at the time. See 'The National Gladstone Memorial', *Manchester Guardian*, 4 November 1905; 'Gladstone Memorial: Speeches at the Unveiling Ceremony . . .', *Observer*, 5 November 1905.
52. Francis Beckett, David Hencke and Nick Kochan, *Blair Inc.: The Man Behind the Mask* (London, 2015).

Further Reading

Writing in the journal *Twentieth Century British History* the historian Susan Pedersen said that while we don't 'need a canon, exactly', we 'could really use (and our students still more would benefit from) a set of competing, strong, partial, integrative frameworks for our field' (*Twentieth Century British History*, vol. 21 (2010), p. 395). Readers may be surprised that analyses of such frameworks are not already standard, but Professor Pedersen is right. Guides to further reading in books and course outlines usually proceed by period and topic, not argument, conclusion or theme. If there is a sense of difference and development it tends to be in the form of the naive progressivist claim that the methods of academic history have advanced stage by historical stage, from dry and unproductive 'political' history, via something called 'social history' to 'cultural history', and through a series of 'turns' – including the cultural, imperial and material turns – and have in addition explored new historical territory. This innovation-centric, method-centric and ahistorical story tells us something important about changes in method and subject, but overall it caricatures the past and flatters the present. It underplays the continuing diversity of method, and of subject matters, and perhaps most importantly does not address development in substantive historical claims, key concepts or debates about them.

There are many different ways in which the history of the twentieth-century United Kingdom has been written, and is being written. The frameworks underlying these histories have proved hard to detect, harder to break out of, and it is harder still to see the far-reaching implications of so doing. Histories are freighted with concepts, such as 'welfare state', 'people's war', 'post-war settlement' or indeed 'empire', which are much less innocent and straightforward than they have appeared to be. Furthermore, much British national history has focused on very particular elements standing for the whole without this being explicit (for example, the welfare state for the state) and as a consequence has implicitly left much out. For example, empire was long left out of the history of the nation. Conversely studies putting in empire can remain trapped in old assumptions about the state as welfare state and write out everything from the working class to politics. Interpretative, integrative frameworks are deeply embedded in our histories: the problem is they are rarely explicit or recognized as such.

What follows is an attempt to make some sense of these frameworks to help the reader to read further and indeed to help put this book into what I take to be its historiographical context. It is not an annotated list, even a very select one, of the works that have informed this book, nor a listing of the most important for its writing, for not all significant works have proposed bold interpretation frameworks through which to think about our national past. For example, I don't discuss biography, a genre central to twentieth-century British history, but one particularly prone to promoting authorial judiciousness over historical analysis. Nor do I discuss the huge amount of academic historical work on the twentieth-century United Kingdom on everything from diplomacy to popular culture which has no reason to claim a connection to a broader national story, the concern of this book. My aim is to point to the richness and variety of argumentation which exists on the topics this book is most concerned with.

The dominant mode of writing of national histories, as opposed to histories of some topic within British history, is still something often called, misleadingly, 'political history' of a national entity, usually called 'Britain'. This should not be taken to mean they are histories of politics, for they are not generally histories of political debates, ideas or parties, but rather the history of the policies (domestic and foreign) of one administration after the other, focused on the politicians in office. This is the key organizing principle of such works as R. C. K. Ensor's contribution to the *Oxford History of England*, his *England, 1870–1914* (Oxford, 1936), as well as A. J. P. Taylor's work in this series *English History 1914–1945* (Oxford, 1965). Such administration-focused national histories did not end with the 1960s; they remain the norm for national histories to this day, as may be seen in very many works including Peter Clarke, *Hope and Glory: Britain 1900–2000* (London, 1996), David Marquand, *Britain since 1918: The Strange Career of British Democracy* (London, 2008) and Robert Tombs, *The English and Their History* (London, 2015), as well as many, many others. Such works have their own particular orientations and arguments, and are saturated with assumptions taken from other histories and from current politics. They have been written by academics, by journalists (often but not only political journalists) and by a significant group who were both (including both Ensor and Taylor).

A second genre of national history is the history of British society, a form with even less politics than the 'political history', and a much more domestic focus. The focus is the people, notably the working class, and the central idea is the rise, and fall, of the 'welfare state'. This was and is history without capitalists, the military, the state (except the welfare state), and one driven by progressive forces, though these are held back. Among the earliest were the works of Arthur Marwick, such as *The Explosion of British Society, 1914–1970* (London, 1963, 1971), *Britain in the Century of Total War: War, Peace and Social Change 1900–1967* (London, 1968) and *British Society since 1945* (London, 1982). The Second World War was particularly important for this approach, as in the work of Angus Calder, *The People's War* (London, 1969), and Paul Addison, *The Road to 1945* (London, 1975), which promoted a very national, social democratic account of the war focused on an emergent welfare state and on the people. This approach is still very much alive in, for example, Paul Addison, *No Turning Back: The Peacetime Revolutions of Post-War Britain* (Oxford, 2010), R. McKibbin, *Classes and Cultures: England 1918–1951* (Oxford, 1998) and Selina Todd, *The People: The Rise and Fall of the Working Class, 1910–2010* (London, 2014). It is perhaps largely through this literature that the idea of the British state as welfare state acquired its centrality. The welfare state remains as the unspoken core of the great majority of recent university textbooks.

The economy is remarkably absent from most national histories, whether the 'political' or those focused on 'society'. A separate economic history did produce its own national histories, perhaps most richly in the case of Sidney Pollard, *The Development of the British Economy* (London, many expanding editions 1962–), but no 'economic history' has stood in for national history in the way that 'political' and 'social' histories have. Much economic history and reflection on economic history used to distinguish between a pre-Keynesian and Keynesian economic era, a dichotomy which profoundly shaped writing on both periods. Economic history has become rather distant from history because many economic historians have embraced economic thinking over historical thinking and have focused on the application of neo-classical econometrics. As a result it is nearly silent on production, firms, entrepreneurs, labour and has become a dematerialized, abstract commentary on economic statistics. This development can be seen by comparing the successive editions of relevant volumes of the *Cambridge Economic History of Modern Britain* (Cambridge, 1981, 1994, 2004, 2014). However, this approach has been very productive, not least in being an element in undermining what declinism thought needed explaining – a serious long-standing failure or decline of the economy, a feature of many economic histories from the 1960s to the 1990s.

Declinism was always very much more than a position in economic history refuted by later economic history. From the 1960s to the 1990s and beyond declinism has been one of the central features of writing on the history of the United Kingdom of many different kinds, though this has not always been clear because many key declinist arguments are not recognized as such. Declinism has been very much more significant than being merely a misguided analysis of economic development. The focus was on explaining the supposed decline of the economy, but the key to declinism is not its account of that failure – which is often rudimentary – but its explanations of failure, which take the form of particular analyses of British history, often cultural historical ones. Indeed, much discussion of the British state, the administrative elite, business and the military is still in the grip of unrecognized declinist explanations. Declinism came in many forms. Eric Hobsbawm's *Industry and Empire* (London, 1968) represents a declinism of the nationalist left, Corelli Barnett, *The Collapse of British Power* (London, 1972) and *The Audit of War: The Illusion and Reality of Britain as a Great Nation* (London, 1986), of the nationalist right. Declinism was always closely linked to notions of British exceptionalism, as is very clear in the essays of the 1960s and beyond by Tom Nairn and Perry Anderson (key instances are Anderson's 'The Origins of the Present Crisis', *New Left Review* 23 (January–February 1964), pp. 26–53 and his 'The Figures of Descent', *New Left Review* 161 (1987), pp. 20–77). Nairn and Anderson emphasized the imperial and global nature of British capitalism, and the British elite, and its liberalism, and a deep continuity in that orientation lasting into the present. The liberal continuity thesis, not also necessarily declinist, is still used to not only explain economic decline, but the weakness of social democracy and socialism, by for example, Patrick Joyce, *The State of Freedom: A Social History of the British State since 1800* (Cambridge, 2013) and indeed many others.

Peter Cain and Anthony Hopkins, *British Imperialism 1688–2000* (Harlow, 2002), is one of a number of other works that set out important, broad-ranging arguments about British history by looking at particular aspects. It is probably the closest we have to a history of British capitalism, but for all its richness it is a version of the declinist, nationalist, critique of global, cosmopolitan British capitalism echoed in most left accounts of the United Kingdom. It is essentially financial rather than material and posits a gentlemanly financial capitalism oriented towards empire formal and informal as an explanation of the history of empire, and the failure of a national industrial strategy. This has been one of the most powerful analytical frameworks deployed, and its assumptions are to be found in many different literatures. For much of the left, the key to understanding twentieth-century British history has been the failure to throw off a liberal imperialist order because of the failure to develop a true democratic British or English nationalism. Like Indian nationalists before them, they criticized the liberal empire for restraining national industrial development, claiming a British imperial and global elite put its interests above those of not only the Indian, but the British people too.

Ralph Miliband's *Parliamentary Socialism: A Study in the Politics of Labour* (London, 1961) was the classic left analysis of a party which could not be effectively reformist because of its deep parliamentarism, ignoring where real power lay, one in which socialists were always weak. It helped shape a whole literature about Labour, discussing what it was not, rather than what it actually was. In an extraordinary rethinking Keith Middlemas, *Politics in Industrial Society: The Experience of the British System since 1911* (London, 1979) shifted attention from open parliamentary politics to behind-the-scenes secret orchestration of the interests of capital and labour by the state: it was here that one needed to understand real politics, and the real nature of the state. Harold Perkin, *The Rise of Professional Society: England since 1880* (London, 1989) is a national history around the rise of public sector (thought of as the welfare state) professionals gaining power in mid-century, until the private sector once more got the upper hand under Margaret Thatcher. My own *England and the Aeroplane* (London, 1991, 2013) and *Warfare State: Britain 1920–1970* (Cambridge, 2005) challenged the ingrained welfarism, and declinism, in histories of the United Kingdom and its elite, by arguing for the existence and importance of a technocratic warfare state, showing also how its existence was written out of historical narratives by intellectuals, including historians. It did not argue for the warfare state as opposed to the welfare state, but rather for taking the former seriously, and indeed for moving away from histories by the left of the left. Jim Tomlinson, *The Politics of Decline: Understanding Post-war Britain* (Abingdon, 2000) put the politics of decline at the centre of the politics of the post-war period. Some histories of the welfare state have pursued much bigger arguments. Two important books put the Great War and the 1920s, and not the 1940s, at the centre of the history of welfare: Susan Pedersen, *Family, Dependence, and the Origins of the Welfare State in Britain and France, 1914–1945* (Cambridge, 1995) argued for the centrality of gender in shaping the structure of the interwar and later welfare state, while John Macnicol, *The Politics of Retirement in Britain, 1878–1948* (Cambridge, 1998) focused on the political economy of compulsory flat-rate insurance systems, arguments which open up the whole history of welfare. Chris Renwick's *Bread for All: The Origins of the Welfare State* (London, 2017), appeared too late to influence this book. Susan

Kingsley Kent, *Gender and Power in Britain 1640–1990* (Abingdon, 1999) and Ina Zweiniger-Bargielowska (ed.), *Women in Twentieth Century Britain* (New York, 2001) both put gender at the centre of national history.

The British Empire and what has come to be called the British world was left out of most post-war national histories, but has become very much more important in recent decades. John Darwin, *The Empire Project: The rise and fall of the British world-system, 1830–1970* (Cambridge, 2009) tells the story of empire as a programme of maintaining a British system of world power which was highly variegated – and not to be too easily thought of as empire in that it included many different kinds of relations, though there was an attempt to imperialize more. James Belich, *Replenishing the Earth: The Settler Revolution and the Rise of the Anglo-World, 1783–1939* (Oxford, 2009), which mostly covers an earlier period, argues for a distinctive world of Anglo, white, horse-intensive agricultural settlement around the world, which was central to the United Kingdom's history. More recently, the claim that empire, understood as racism, has been central to ideology in the metropole, long after the end of empire, has developed into a distinctive broad thesis. Bill Schwarz, *The White Man's World* (Oxford, 2011) is primarily a very rich study of the place of notions of whiteness, specifically a British whiteness, in the work of imperialist intellectuals (themselves rarely studied critically) mainly of the first half of the twentieth century, showing *inter alia* the importance of imperialist thought into the Second World War. It seeks to argue for the political salience of a repressed racist memory of empire as central to the politics of the new right from the late 1960s, an example of the long-standing tendency to blame empire for national ills. Emphasis on the race-empire nexus and its importance for domestic UK history has been especially prominent in British history textbooks written in the USA.

The imperial project overlapped with, but was distinct from and sometimes in competition with, doctrines of free trade, which have themselves been put back into British history, though the relation with empire, in its many variants, is not always very clear. Rarely have these been connected to foreign policy, but there is a powerful set of literatures which does just this. Robert Boyce, *British*

Capitalism at the Crossroads, 1919–1932: A Study in Politics, Economics, and International Relations (Cambridge, 1987) and *The Great Interwar Crisis and the Collapse of Globalization* (London, 2009) deserve to be far better known for just this reason. The issue of trade largely disappears from most British histories after 1932, yet should be central to national history as George Brennan and Alan Milward, *Britain's Place in the World: Import Controls 1945–60* (London, 1996) made clear. Alan S. Milward, *The UK and the European Community*, vol. 1: *The Rise and Fall of a National Strategy* (London, 2002) went on to transform our understanding of the entry of the United Kingdom into the EEC, by focusing on British aspirations for, and the reality of, free trade after the Second World War. Milward is one of the few historians of the United Kingdom to make clear that trade and other relations with Europe were always central, and that the politics and policies of Europe mattered too. Recent histories and textbooks have, in emphasizing some aspects of empire, made it seem as if imperialism was the only overseas connection that mattered. Indeed, it is striking how little reference there has been in histories to the European connection – a notable exception which makes the point is Brendan Simms, *Britain's Europe: A Thousand Years of Conflict and Cooperation* (London, 2016).

The political economy of war has proved a rich site for making arguments about the nature of the United Kingdom, perhaps partly because while war has been central to national histories it tended to be discussed there in high political or (more commonly) in welfare-state oriented accounts. Avner Offer, *The First World War: An Agrarian Interpretation* (Oxford, 1989), David French, *The British Way in Warfare 1688–2000* (London, 1990), David Edgerton, *England and the Aeroplane* (London, 1991, 2013) and *Warfare State: Britain 1920–1970* (Cambridge, 2006) and George Peden, *Arms, Economics and British Strategy: From Dreadnoughts to Hydrogen Bombs* (Cambridge, 2007) all adumbrated a distinctive, powerful liberal militarism which said much about the United Kingdom's place in the world, its economic strength and its political and ideological culture. The significance of the claims can be seen by looking at the issue from the German perspective, as has been done by Adam Tooze, *The Wages of Destruction: The Making and Breaking of the Nazi*

Economy (London, 2006) and noting the symmetry with David Edgerton, *Britain's War Machine: Weapons, Resources and Experts in the Second World War* (London, 2011), which is an account of the politics and economics of the war very different from those within the 'people's war' framework.

There was a time when the novel was a prominent feature of national histories when they sketched out the life of the mind, but science and social science, and much else, were not. This is one of the few ways C. P. Snow's 'two cultures' thesis rings true. Today, many more ideas are in play in historical studies, including very bad ones, such as Snow's. Stefan Collini, *Absent Minds: Intellectuals in Britain* (Oxford, 2006) makes the essential historical point that British intellectuals have been responsible for the belief that the United Kingdom has no intellectuals. Many more kinds of ideas are now being explored. David Long and Peter Wilson (eds.), *Thinkers of the Twenty Years' Crisis: Inter-War Idealism Reassessed* (Oxford, 1995) argued strongly against the view that liberal internationalists were merely deluded pacifists. Frank Trentmann, *Free Trade Nation: Commerce, Consumption and Civil Society in Modern Britain* (London, 2008) looked at the deep commitment to liberal free trade. Bill Schwarz, *The White Man's World* (Oxford 2011) is essentially a history of racist ideas among imperialist intellectuals, notable also because it stands for, in effect, a rebalancing of accounts of British thought away from an earlier over-emphasis on liberals and the left. Tom Nairn, *The Enchanted Glass: Britain and Its monarchy* (London 1988) points to a complex of ideas and delusions around the monarchy, a topic thought beneath consideration in a supposedly liberal and social democratic nation, but central to Nairn's argument about the antique nature of the United Kingdom.

Sources

This book is not primarily a synthesis of existing historical literature, since it argues both with and against it. Indeed it cannot be synthetic, for a key point is to note huge absences in the literature and to attempt to make good that created deficiency. It also engages with old, non-historical accounts in two distinct ways. Firstly, it develops historical arguments in part from contemporary writings, for example about the revaluation of sterling in the early 1920s, arguments which might well not be in the historical literature. Secondly, it takes note of the way in which particular arguments from the past have been the common sense of histories, in order to tell a different story. Thirdly, it has often been necessary to turn to primary sources or raw historical data to make a point. The book thus relies on many disparate primary sources, as indicated in footnotes, including some archival sources. The abbreviations Cd., Cmd., and Cmnd., refer to series of Command Papers, which can be found in the published volumes of Parliamentary Papers, in libraries in the original bound editions and in a digital searchable version. Hansard – much but not all is available online – remains invaluable, as do party manifestos, also available online, which I have used repeatedly as a rich way of getting to policies and programmes that histories have not emphasized. I have also made use of many visual sources, including Britain from Above, BritishPathé, Imperial War Museum, BFI Screenonline, BFI Player, BFI InView and the British Movietone News archive, which provide a quite astonishing range of material almost all of which was, until recently, in practice inaccessible. Some, although online, is alas behind firewalls. Statistical sources online, often very detailed ones, have proved invaluable, for example the use of monthly strike statistics to make a crucial point about the so-called Winter of Discontent. I have also found very useful the work of compilers and creators of websites, often self-funding and outside the commerce of the academy, for example the creators of archives of manifestos, the lists of ships by shipping company and the marvellous enterprise Grace's Guide to British Industrial History, when I last looked containing 125,590 pages of information and 195,766 images. (https://www.gracesguide.co.uk).

Text and image are not the only surviving records of the past. There is no museum of twentieth-century British history, alas, but there are many covering different aspects. No other land is so rich in preserved machines and structures – in, for example, the RAF Museum, Hendon and Cosford. No historian could fail to learn from visiting HMS *Belfast* in London, a warship in service from the late 1930s into the Cold War, or the SS *John Brown*, a US-built Liberty ship docked in Baltimore, of British design of the sort which sailed the seven seas from the beginning of the century into the 1960s. The historian will get some sense of what British production was like by going down into the Big Pit in Blaenavon, the Leeds Industrial Museum, or the Dock Museum, Barrow-in-Furness. Best of all is the Museum of the Industrial Revolution, in Fray Bentos, Uruguay, the huge old Frigorifico Anglo and before that the Liebig Extract of Meat Company works, dating from the 1860s. It is surely the best-preserved British factory of the 1920s and before to be found anywhere in the world, the United Kingdom included. It in itself tells a once-familiar and now largely forgotten story of what the British world was.

Bibliography

Aaronovitch, Sam, *The Ruling Class* (London, 1961).

Abrams, Mark, 'British Elite Attitudes and the European Common Market', *Public Opinion Quarterly* 29.2 (1965), pp. 236–46.

Ackroyd, Carol et al., *The Technology of Political Control* (Harmondsworth, 1977).

Addison, Paul, *The Road to 1945* (London, 1975).

—, *No Turning Back: The Peacetime Revolutions of Post-War Britain* (Oxford, 2010).

Agar, Jon, *The Government Machine: A Revolutionary History of the Computer* (Cambridge, Massachusetts, 2003).

Aitken, Jonathan, *Margaret Thatcher: Power and Personality* (London, 2013).

Aldrich, Richard J., *GCHQ* (London, 2010).

Alibhai-Brown, Yasmin, *Exotic England* (London, 2015).

Allport, Alan, *Demobbed: Coming Home after the Second World War* (London, 2009).

Anderson, David, *Histories of the Hanged: The Dirty War in Kenya and the End of Empire* (London, 2005).

Anderson Paul and Nyta Mann, *Safety First: The Making of New Labour* (London, 1997).

Anderson, Perry, 'The Origins of the Present Crisis', *New Left Review* 1.23 (January–February 1964), pp. 26–53.

—, 'Components of the National Culture', *New Left Review* 1.50 (July–August 1968), pp. 3–57.

—, 'The Figures of Descent', *New Left Review*, 1.161 (January–February 1987), pp. 20–77.

Andrews, Maggie and Janis Lomas (eds.), *The Home Front in Britain: Images, Myths and Forgotten Experiences since 1914* (London, 2014).

Angell, Norman, *If Britain Is to Live* (London, 1923).

Anker, Peder, *Imperial Ecology: Environmental Order in the British Empire, 1895–1945* (Cambridge, Massachusetts, 2009).

Annan, Noel, *Our Age: Portrait of a Generation* (London, 1990).

Arnold, Lorna, *Britain and the H-Bomb* (London, 2001).

Artis, M., D. Cobham and M. Wickham-Jones, 'Social Democracy in Hard Times: The Economic Record of the Labour Government 1974–1979', *Twentieth Century British History* 3 (1992), pp. 32–58.

Ashton, Nigel, *Kennedy, Macmillan and the Cold War: The Irony of Inter-dependence* (London, 2002).

Ashworth, William, *The History of the British Coal Industry*, vol. 5 (Oxford, 1986).

Assael, Brenda, 'Gastro-cosmopolitanism and the Restaurant in Late Victorian and Edwardian London', *The Historical Journal* 56.3 (2013), pp. 681–706.

Bailkin, Jordanna, *The Afterlife of Empire* (London, 2012).

Baker, Kenneth, *The Turbulent Years: My Life in Politics* (London, 1993).

Baldwin, Peter, *The Politics of Social Solidarity: Class Bases of the European Welfare State 1875–1975* (Cambridge, 1990).

Ball, Simon, 'The German Octopus: The British Metal Corporation and the Next War, 1914–1939', *Enterprise & Society* 5 (2004), pp. 451–89.

Ball, Stuart, *Portrait of a Party: The Conservative Party in Britain, 1918–1945* (Oxford, 2013).

Bamberg, J. H., *The History of the British Petroleum Company*, vol. 2: *The Anglo-Iranian Years 1928–1954* (Cambridge, 1994).

Barker, Paul, *The Freedoms of Suburbia* (London, 2009).

Barnett, Anthony, *Iron Britannia: Time to Take the Great Out of Britain* (London, 1982).

—, *The Lure of Greatness: England's Brexit and America's Trump* (London, 2017).

Baxendale, John, ' "I Had Seen a Lot of Englands": J. B. Priestley, English-ness and the People', *History Workshop Journal* 51 (2001), pp. 87–111.

Baylis, John and Kristian Stoddart, *The British Nuclear Experience: The Role of Beliefs, Culture and Identity* (Oxford, 2015).

Bayly, Christopher and Tim Harper, *Forgotten Wars: The End of Britain's Asian Empire* (London, 2008).

Beckett, Andy, *Pinochet in Piccadilly* (London, 2002).

Beckett, Francis, David Hencke and Nick Kochan, *Blair Inc.: The Man Behind the Mask* (London, 2015).

Belich, James, *Replenishing the Earth: The Settler Revolution and the Rise of the Anglo-World, 1783–1939* (Oxford, 2009).

Bell, Duncan, *The Idea of Greater Britain: Empire and the Future of World Order, 1860–1900* (Princeton, New Jersey, 2007).

Bennett, J. G., *Witness: The Story of a Search* (London, 1962).

Benvenuti, Andrea, 'The Heath Government and British Defence Policy in Southeast Asia at the End of Empire (1970–71)', *Twentieth Century British History* 20 (2009), pp. 53–73.

Benwell Community Project, *The Making of a Ruling Class: Two Centuries of Capital Development on Tyneside* (Newcastle-upon-Tyne, 1978).

Berger, Stefan, ' "Organising Talent and Disciplined Steadiness": The German SPD as a Model for the British Labour Party in the 1920s?', *Contemporary European History* 5 (1996), pp. 171–90.

Berridge, Virginia, *Health and Society in Britain since 1939* (Cambridge, 1999).

Berthezène, Clarisse, *Training Minds for the War of Ideas: Ashridge College, the Conservative Party and the Cultural Politics of Britain, 1929–54* (Manchester, 2015).

Beveridge, Sir William, *Social Insurance and Allied Services* (London, 1942).

Beynon, Huw and Hilary Wainwright, *The Workers' Report on Vickers: The Vickers Shop Stewards Combined Committee Report on Work, Wages, Rationalisation, Closure and Rank-and-File Organisation in a Multinational Company* (London, 1979).

Black, Lawrence, Hugh Pemberton and Pat Thane (eds.), *Reassessing 1970s Britain* (Manchester, 2016).

Blackburn, Dean, 'Still the Stranger at the Feast? Ideology and the Study of Twentieth Century British Politics', *Journal of Political Ideologies* 22 (2017), pp. 1–15.

Blake, Robert, *The Decline of Power 1915–1964* (London, 1985).

Blaxill, Luke and Kaspar Beelen, 'A Feminized Language of Democracy? The Representation of Women at Westminster since 1945', *Twentieth Century British History* 27 (2016), pp. 412–49.

Booth, Alan, 'How Long Are Light Years in British Politics? The Labour Party's Economic Ideas in the 1930s', *Twentieth Century British History* 7 (1996), pp. 1–26.

—, *The British Economy in the Twentieth Century* (Basingstoke, 2001).

—, 'The Manufacturing Failure Hypothesis and the Performance of British Industry during the Long Boom', *The Economic History Review* 56 (2003), pp. 1–33.

—, *The Management of Technical Change* (Basingstoke, 2007).

Bosco, Andrea, *June 1940: Great Britain and the First Attempt to Build a European Union* (Cambridge, 2016).

Boswell, Jonathan and James Peters, *Capitalism in Contention: Business Leaders and Political Economy in Modern Britain* (Cambridge, 1997).

Bowley, Arthur, *Some Economic Consequences of the Great War* (London, 1930).

Bowman, Andrew, Julie Froud, Ismael Ertürk, Sukhdev Johal, John Law, Adam Leaver, Michael Moran and Karel Williams, *The End of the Experiment: From Competition to the Foundational Economy* (Manchester, 2014).

Bowman, Andrew, Julie Froud, Sukhdev Johal, Michael Moran and Karel Williams, *Business Elites and Undemocracy in Britain: A Work in Progress*, CRESC Working Paper Series, no. 125 (July 2013).

Boyce, Gordon and Simon Ville, *The Development of Modern Business* (Basingstoke, 2002).

Boyce, Robert W. D., *British Capitalism at the Crossroads 1919–1932: A Study in Politics, Economics, and International Relations* (Cambridge, 1987).

—, *The Great Interwar Crisis and the Collapse of Globalization* (London, 2009).

Bradley, Simon, *The Railways: Nation, Network and People* (London, 2015).

Brassley, Paul, 'Silage in Britain, 1880–1990: The Delayed Adoption of an Innovation', *The Agricultural History Review* (1996), pp. 63–87.

Brennan, George and Alan Milward, *Britain's Place in the World: Import Controls 1945–60* (London, 1996).

Brewitt-Taylor, Sam, 'The Invention of a "Secular Society"? Christianity and the Sudden Appearance of Secularization Discourses in the British National Media, 1961–4', *Twentieth Century British History* 24 (2013), pp. 327–50.

Bridgen, Paul, 'A Straitjacket with Wriggle Room: The Beveridge Report, the Treasury and the Exchequer's Pension Liability, 1942–59', *Twentieth Century British History* 17 (2006), pp. 1–5.

Broadberry, S. N., *The Productivity Race: British Manufacturing in International Perspective, 1850–1990* (Cambridge, 1997).

Brooke, Peter, 'India, Post-Imperialism and the Origins of Enoch Powell's "Rivers of Blood" Speech', *Historical Journal* 50 (2007), pp. 669–87.

Brooks, Richard and Solomon Hughes, 'Public Servants, Public Paydays' (Revolving Doors Special), *Private Eye* 1426 (15 September 2016), pp. 19–24.

Brown, Callum, *The Death of Christian Britain: Understanding Secularisation 1800–2000* (London, 2001).

Brown C. J. F. and T. D. Sheriff, 'De-industrialisation: A Background Paper', in F. Blackaby (ed.), *De-industrialisation* (London, 1979), pp. 239–40.

Brown, Judith M. and William Roger Louis, *The Oxford History of the British Empire*, vol. 4: *The Twentieth Century* (Oxford, 1999).

Burgess, Keith, *The Challenge of Labour* (London, 1980).

Burn, Duncan (ed.), *The Structure of British Industry*, 2 vols. (Cambridge, 1958).

Burnett, D. Graham, *The Sounding of the Whale: Science and Cetaceans in the Twentieth Century* (Chicago, Illinois, 2012).

Burns, Arthur, 'Beyond the "Red Vicar": Community and Christian Socialism in Thaxted, Essex, 1910–84', *History Workshop Journal* 75 (2013), pp. 101–24.

Butler, Lise, 'Michael Young, the Institute of Community Studies, and the Politics of Kinship', *Twentieth Century British History* 26 (2015), pp. 203–24.

Cain, Peter and A. Hopkins, *British Imperialism 1688–2000* (London, 1993, Harlow, 2002).

Calder, Angus, *The People's War: Britain 1939–45* (London, 1969).

—, *The Myth of the Blitz* (London, 1991).

Callaghan, John, *Rajani Palme Dutt: A Study in British Stalinism* (London, 1993).

Callaghan, John, et al. (eds.), *Interpreting the Labour Party: Approaches to Labour Politics and History* (Manchester, 2003).

Cammarosano, Joseph R., *John Maynard Keynes: Free Trader or Protectionist?* (Plymouth, 2013).

Campbell, John, *Edward Heath: A Biography* (London, 2013).

Cannadine, David, *The Decline and Fall of the British Aristocracy* (London, 1990).

Capie, Forrest and Michael Collins, *The Inter-war British Economy: A Statistical Abstract* (Manchester, 1983).

Carnevali, Francesca and Julie-Marie Strange, *20th Century Britain: Economic, Cultural and Social Change*, 2nd edn (London, 2007).

Cassis, Youssef and Margaret Rocques, *City Bankers 1890–1914* (Cambridge, 1994).

Catterall, Peter (ed.), *The Macmillan Diaries*, vol. 1: *The Cabinet Years 1950–1957* (London, 2003).

Chapman, James, *The British at War: Cinema, State and Propaganda 1939–1945* (London, 1998).

Charmley, John, *Churchill: The End of Glory: A Political Biography* (London, 1993).

Chatterjee, B., 'Business and Politics in the 1930s: Lancashire and the Making of the Indo-British Trade Agreement', *Modern Asian Studies* 15 (1981), pp. 527–73.

Chick, Martin, *Industrial Policy in Britain 1945–1951: Economic Planning, Nationalisation and the Labour Governments* (Cambridge, 1998).

Childs, David, *Britain since 1945: A Political History* (London, many editions).

Church, Roy, *The History of the British Coal Industry*, vol. 3: *1830–1913: Victorian Pre-eminence* (Oxford, 1986).

Clapham, J. H., *An Economic History of Modern Britain: Machines and National Rivalries (1887–1914) with an Epilogue (1914–1929)* (Cambridge, 1938).

Clark, Tom and Andrew Dilnot, 'British Fiscal Policy since 1939', in Roderick Floud and Paul Johnson (eds.), *The Cambridge Economic History of Modern Britain*, vol. 3: *Structural Change and Growth, 1939–2000* (Cambridge, 2004).

Clarke, Peter, *Hope and Glory: Britain 1900–1990* (London, 1996).

—, *The Cripps Version: The Life of Sir Stafford Cripps, 1889–1952* (London, 2002).

Clarke, Peter and Clive Trebilcock, *Understanding Decline: Perceptions and Realities of British Economic Performance* (Cambridge, 1997).

Clarke, Sabine, 'A Technocratic Imperial State? The Colonial Office and Scientific Research, 1940–1960', *Twentieth Century British History* 18 (2007), pp. 453–80.

—, 'Pure Science with a Practical Aim: The Meanings of Fundamental Research in Britain, circa 1916–1950', *Isis* 101 (2010), pp. 285–311.

Coates, David, *The Labour Party and the Struggle for Socialism* (Cambridge, 1975).

—, *The Question of UK Decline: The Economy, State and Society* (London, 1994).

—, (ed.), *Industrial Policy in Britain* (London, 1996).

Coats, A. W., 'Political Economy and the Tariff Reform Campaign of 1903', *Journal of Law and Economics*, 11 (1968), pp. 181–229.

Cohen, Deborah, *The War Come Home: Disabled Veterans in Britain and Germany, 1914–1939* (Berkeley, California, 2001).

Cohen, Sheila, *Notoriously Militant: The Story of a Union Branch* (London, 2013).

Collard, Jane, David Ogden and Roger Burgess, '*Where the Fat Black Canons Dined': A History of Bristol Cathedral School 1140 to 1992* (Bristol, 1992).

Colley, Linda, *Britons: Forging the Nation 1707–1837* (New Haven, Connecticut, 1992).

Collini, Stefan, *Public Moralists: Political Thought and Intellectual Life in Britain 1850–1930* (Oxford, 1991).

—, *Absent Minds: Intellectuals in Britain* (Oxford, 2006).

—, *Common Reading: Critics, Historians, Publics* (Oxford, 2008).

Colls, Robert, *The Identity of England* (Oxford, 2002).

Comfort, Nicholas, *The Slow Death of British Industry: A Sixty-Year Suicide 1952–2012* (London, 2012).

Conekin, Becky E., *'The Autobiography of a Nation': The 1951 Festival of Britain* (Manchester, 2003).

Constantine, Stephen, 'Waving Goodbye? Australia, Assisted Passages, and the Empire and Commonwealth Settlement Acts, 1945–72', *The Journal of Imperial and Commonwealth History* 26 (1998), pp. 176–95.

—, 'British Emigration to the Empire-Commonwealth since 1880: From Overseas Settlement to Diaspora?', *The Journal of Imperial and Commonwealth History* 31 (2003), pp. 16–35.

Cook, Hera, *The Long Sexual Revolution: English Women, Sex, and Contraception 1800–1975* (Oxford, 2004).

Cooper, Frederick, *Colonialism in Question: Theory, Knowledge, History* (Oakland, California, 2005).

Cooper, Neil, *The Business of Death: Britain's Arms Trade at Home and Abroad* (London, 1997).

Cooter, R., *Surgery and Society in Peace and War: Orthopaedics and the Organization of Modern Medicine, 1880–1948* (London, 1993).

Cooter, R., M. Harrison and S. Sturdy (eds.), *Medicine and Modern Warfare* (Amsterdam, 1999).

Cowling, Maurice, *The Impact of Labour, 1920–1924. The Beginning of Modern British Politics* (Cambridge, 1971).

—, *The Impact of Hitler: British Politics and British Policy 1933–1940* (Cambridge, 1975).

Cox, Andrew, Simon Lee and Joe Sanderson, *The Political Economy of Modern Britain* (Cheltenham, 1997).

Cox, Howard, *The Global Cigarette: Origins and Evolution of British American Tobacco, 1880–1945* (New York, 2000).

Crafts, Nicholas and Stephen Broadberry, 'Openness, Protectionism and Britain's Productivity Performance over the Long-Run', CAGE Online Working Paper Series, Number 36/2010, Department of Economics, University of Warwick, Coventry.

Cragoe, Matthew and Paul Readman (eds.), *The Land Question in Britain, 1750–1950* (London, 2010).

Cronin, James E., *The Politics of State Expansion: War, State, and Society in Twentieth-Century Britain* (London, 1991).

—, *New Labour's Pasts: The Labour Party and Its Discontents* (London, 2004).

—, 'Britain in the World: Implications for the Study of British Politics', *British Politics* 7 (2012), pp. 55–8.

Crouch, Colin, *The Politics of Industrial Relations* (Harmondsworth, 1979).

Croucher, Richard, *Engineers at War 1939–1945* (London, 1982).

Crowcroft, Robert, 'Peering into the Future: British Conservative Leaders and the Problem of National Renewal, 1942–5', *Historical Research* (forthcoming).

Daddow, Oliver (ed.), *Harold Wilson and the European Integration: Britain's Second Application to Join the EEC* (London, 2003).

Dangerfield, George, *The Strange Death of Liberal England* (London, 1935).

Darling, Elizabeth, *Re-forming Britain: Narratives of Modernity before Reconstruction* (London, 2006).

Darwin, John, *The Empire Project: The Rise and Fall of the British World-System, 1830–1970* (Cambridge, 2009).

Daunton, Martin, *Just Taxes. The Politics of Taxation in Britain, 1914–1979* (Cambridge, 2002).

Daunton, Martin, 'Britain and Globalisation since 1850: II. The Rise of Insular Capitalism, 1914–1939', *Transactions of the Royal Historical Society* 17 (2007), pp. 1–3.

—, *Wealth and Welfare: An Economic and Social History of Britain 1851–1951* (Oxford, 2007).

Davenport-Hines, Richard, *Dudley Docker: The Life and Times of a Trade Warrior* (Cambridge, 1984).

—, *Titanic Lives: Migrants and Millionaires, Conmen and Crew* (London, 2012).

Davies, Aled, *The City of London and Social Democracy: The Political Economy of Finance in Britain, 1959–1979* (Oxford, 2017).

Davies, Stephen M., 'Promoting Productivity in the National Health Service, 1950 to 1966', *Contemporary British History* 31 (2017), pp. 47–8.

Davis, John, *A History of Britain, 1885–1939* (London, 1999).

Davis, Madeleine, 'Arguing Affluence: New Left Contributions to the Socialist Debate 1957–63', *Twentieth Century British History* 23 (2012), pp. 496–528.

Deacon, Alan, 'An End to the Means Test? Social Security and the Attlee Government', *Journal of Social Policy*, 11 (1982), pp. 289–306.

Delap, Lucy, *Knowing Their Place: Domestic Service in Twentieth Century Britain* (Oxford, 2011).

Dell, Edmund, *Political Responsibility and Industry* (London, 1973).

Desmarais, Ralph, 'Science, Scientific Intellectuals, and British Culture in the Early Atomic Age: A Case Study of George Orwell, Jacob Bronowski, P. M. S. Blackett and J. G. Crowther' (PhD thesis, Imperial College London, 2010).

—, 'Jacob Bronowski: A Humanist Intellectual for an Atomic Age, 1946–1956', *The British Journal for the History of Science* 45 (2012), pp. 573–89.

Devine, Thomas Martin, *The Scottish Nation: A History, 1700–2000* (London, 1999).

Dintenfass, Michael, 'The Voice of Industry and the Ethos of Decline', in Jean-Pierre Dormois and Michael Dintenfass (eds.), *British Industrial Decline* (London, 1999).

Dorril, Stephen and Robin Ramsay, *Smear! Wilson and the Secret State* (London, 1991).

Douglas, Roy, 'The National Democratic Party and the British Workers' League', *The Historical Journal* 15 (1972), pp. 533–52.

Dumett, Raymond (ed.), *Gentlemanly Capitalism and British Imperialism: The New Debate on Empire* (London, 2014).

Dunleavy, Patrick, *The Politics of Mass Housing 1945–75* (Oxford, 1981).

Dwork, Deborah, *War Is Good for Babies and Other Young Children: A History of the Infant and Child Welfare Movement in England, 1898–1918* (London, 1987).

Dworkin, Dennis. *Cultural Marxism in Postwar Britain: History, the New Left, and the Origins of Cultural Studies* (Durham, North Carolina, 1997).

Eaton, Jack and Colin Gill, *The Trade Union Directory: A Guide to All TUC Unions* (London, 1981).

Edgerton, David, 'Liberal Militarism and the British State', *New Left Review* 1.135 (January–February 1991), pp. 138–69.

—, *England and the Aeroplane* (London, 1991, 2013).

—, 'The Prophet Militant and Industrial: The Peculiarities of Correlli Barnett', *Twentieth Century British History* 2 (1991), pp. 360–79.

—, *Science, Technology and the British Industrial 'Decline'* (Cambridge, 1996).

—, 'Tony Blair's Warfare State', *New Left Review* 1.230 (July–August 1998), pp. 123–30.

—, *Warfare State: Britain 1920–1970* (Cambridge, 2005).

—, *Britain's War Machine: Weapons, Resources and Experts in the Second World War* (London, 2011).

—, 'War, Reconstruction, and the Nationalization of Britain, 1939–1951', in *Post-war Reconstruction in Europe: International Perspectives, 1945–1949*, *Past & Present* 210 (2011), suppl. 6, pp. 29–6.

Edgerton, D. E. H. and S. M. Horrocks, 'British Industrial Research and Development before 1945', *Economic History Review* 47 (1994), pp. 213–38.

Edgerton, David and Kirsty Hughes, 'The Poverty of Science: A Critical Analysis of Scientific and Industrial Policy under Mrs Thatcher', *Public Administration* 67 (1989), pp. 419–33.

Edgerton, David and J. V. Pickstone, 'The United Kingdom, 1750–2000', in H. Slotten (ed.), *The Cambridge History of Science*, vol. 8: *Modern Science in National, Transnational, and Global Context* (Cambridge, 2018).

Edwards, P., 'The Local Organisation of a National Dispute: The British 1979 Engineering Strike', *Industrial Relations Journal* 13 (1982), pp. 57–63.

Eisler, Matthew, 'A Modern "Philosopher's Stone": Techno-Analogy and the Bacon Cell', *Technology and Culture* 50 (2009), pp. 345–65.

Elbaum, Bernard, 'Why Apprenticeship Persisted in Britain but Not in the United States', *The Journal of Economic History* 49 (1989), pp. 337–49.

Elbaum, Bernard and W. Lazonick (eds.), *The Decline of the British Economy* (Oxford, 1986).

Elkins, Caroline, *Britain's Gulag* (London, 2005).

Elliott, Larry and Dan Atkinson, *Fantasy Island: Waking up to the Incredible Economic, Political and Social Illusions of the Blair Legacy* (London, 2007).

Ertsen, Maurits W., *Improvising Planned Development on the Gezira Plain, Sudan, 1900–1980* (London, 2015).

Falkus, Malcolm, *The Blue Funnel Legend* (London, 1990).

Fawcett, H. and R. Lowe (eds.), *Welfare Policy in Britain: The Road from 1945* (London, 1999).

Fawcett, Millicent Garrett, *Women's Suffrage: A Short History of a Great Movement* (London, 1912).

Feldman, David and Jon Lawrence (eds.), *Structures and Transformations in Modern British History* (Cambridge, 2011).

Field, Frank, Molly Meacher and Chris Pond, *To Him Who Hath: A Study of Poverty and Taxation* (Harmondsworth, 1977).

Field, Geoffrey G., *Blood, Sweat, and Toil: Remaking the British Working Class, 1939–1945* (Oxford, 2011).

Fielding, Steven, 'What Did "The People" Want?: The Meaning of the 1945 General Election', *The Historical Journal* 35 (1992), p. 628.

Fine, Ben and Laurence Harris, *The Peculiarities of the British Economy* (London, 1985).

Fine, Ben, Michael Heasman and Judith Wright, *Consumption in the Age of Affluence: The World of Food* (London, 1996).

Floud, Roderick and Paul Johnson (eds.), *The Cambridge Economic History of Modern Britain*, 3 vols. (Cambridge, 2004).

Floud, Roderick, J. Humphries and P. Johnson (eds.), *The Cambridge Economic History of Modern Britain*, 2 vols. (Cambridge, 2014).

Foot, Paul, *The Politics of Harold Wilson* (Harmondsworth, 1968).

Forgan, Sophie, 'Festivals of Science and the Two Cultures: Science, Design and Display in the Festival of Britain, 1951', *The British Journal for the History of Science*, 31 (1998), pp. 217–40.

Forrester, Robert E., *British Mail Steamers to South America* (London, 2014).

Fox, Daniel M., *Health Policies, Health Politics: The British and American Experience, 1911–1965* (Princeton, New Jersey, 2014).

Francis, Martin, *The Flyer: British Culture and the Royal Air Force 1939–1945* (Oxford, 2008).

Francis, Martin and I. Zweiniger-Bargielowska (eds.), *The Conservatives and British Society, 1880–1990* (Chicago, Illinois, 1996).

Fraser, Derek, *The Evolution of the British Welfare State: A History of Social Policy since the Industrial Revolution* (London, many editions).

Freedman, Lawrence, *The Official History of the Falklands Campaign*, vol. 1: *The Origins of the Falklands War* (London, 2005).

French, David, *The British Way in Warfare 1688–2000* (London, 1990, 2014).

—, *Raising Churchill's Army: The British Army and the War against Germany, 1919–1945* (Oxford, 2000).

—, *Military Identities: The Regimental System, the British Army, and the British People c. 1870–2000* (Oxford, 2005).

—, *The British Way in Counter-insurgency, 1945–1967* (Oxford, 2011).

—, *Army, Empire and Cold War: The British Army and Military Policy 1945–1971* (Oxford, 2012).

Friedberg, Aaron L., *The Weary Titan* (Princeton, New Jersey, 1988).

Fryer, Peter, *Staying Power: The History of Black People in Britain* (London, 1984).

Gamble, Andrew, *Britain in Decline* (various editions from 1981).

—, *The Free Economy and the Strong State: The Politics of Thatcherism* (London, 1988).

Garside, W. R., *British Unemployment, 1919–1939: A Study in Public Policy* (Cambridge, 1990).

Giffard, Hermione, *Making Jet Engines in World War II: Britain, Germany and the United States* (Chicago, Illinois, 2016).

Gill, David James, 'The Ambiguities of Opposition: Economic Decline, International Cooperation, and Political Rivalry in the Nuclear Policies of the Labour Party, 1963–1964', *Contemporary British History* 25 (2011), pp. 251–76.

Gilroy, Paul, *There Ain't No Black in the Union Jack* (London, 1987).

Glennerster, Howard, *British Social Policy since 1945* (Oxford, 1995, 2000).

Goodhart, David, *The Road to Somewhere: The Populist Revolt and the Future of Politics* (London, 2017).

Gorsky, Martin, J. Mohan and T. Willis, 'Hospital Contributory Schemes and the NHS Debates 1937–46: The Rejection of Social Insurance in the British Welfare State?' *Twentieth Century British History* 16 (2005), pp. 170–92.

—, 'The British National Health Service 1948–2008: A Review of the Historiography', *Social History of Medicine* 21 (2008), pp. 437–60.

Gottlieb, Julie V. and Richard Toye (eds.), *The Aftermath of Suffrage: Women, Gender, and Politics in Britain, 1918–1945* (London, 2013).

Gowan, Peter, 'The Origins of the Administrative Elite', *New Left Review*, 1.62 (March–April 1987), pp. 4–34.

Gowing, Margaret, *Britain and Atomic Energy, 1939–1945* (London, 1964).

—, 'Science, Technology and Education: England in 1870: The Wilkins Lecture, 1976', *Notes and Records of the Royal Society of London* 32 (1977), pp. 86–7.

Gowing, Margaret, with Lorna Arnold, *Independence and Deterrence: Britain and Atomic Energy, 1945–1952*, 2 vols. (London, 1974).

Grainger, J. H., *Patriotisms: Britain 1900–1939* (London, 1986).

Grant, Matthew, *After the Bomb: Civil Defence and Nuclear War in Britain, 1945–68* (Basingstoke, 2010).

Grant, Ted, *History of British Trotskyism* (London, 2002).

Green, E. H. H., *Ideologies of Conservatism: Conservative Political Ideas in the Twentieth Century* (Oxford, 2004).

Greenleaf, W. H., *The British Political Tradition*, 3 vols. (London, 1983–7).

Gregory, Andrew, *The Last Great War: British Society and the First World War* (Cambridge, 2008).

Griffiths, Clare and Anita Brock, 'Twentieth Century Mortality Trends in England and Wales', *Health Statistics Quarterly* 18 (Summer 2003).

Griffiths, Clare V. J., James J. Nott and William Whyte (eds.), *Classes, Cultures, and Politics* (Oxford, 2011).

Grob-Fitzgibbon, Benjamin, *Continental Drift: Britain and Europe from the End of Empire to the Rise of Euroscepticism* (Cambridge, 2016).

Gunn, Simon, 'The Buchanan Report, Environment and the Problem of Traffic in 1960s Britain', *Twentieth Century British History* 22 (2011), pp. 521–42.

—, 'Ring Road: Birmingham and the Collapse of the Motor City Ideal in 1970s Britain', *The Historical Journal* (2017). Available at https://lra.le.ac.uk/bitstream/2381/38703/2/Ring%2bRoad%2boct%2b16.pdf, accessed 16 January 2018.

Gunn, Simon and James Vernon (eds.), *The Peculiarities of Liberal Modernity in Imperial Britain* (Berkeley, California, 2011).

Haeussler, Mathias, 'The Popular Press and Ideas of Europe: The *Daily Mirror*, the *Daily Express*, and Britain's First Application to Join the EEC, 1961–63', *Twentieth Century British History* 25 (2014), pp. 108–31.

Hall, Kersten T. *The Man in the Monkeynut Coat: William Astbury and the Forgotten Road to the Double-Helix* (Oxford, 2014).

Hall, L. A., *Sex, Gender and Social Change in Britain since 1880* (London, 2000).

Hall, Stuart and Martin Jacques (eds.), *New Times: The Changing Face of Politics in the 1990s* (London, 1989).

Halsey, A. H., *Trends in British Society since 1900* (London, 1972).

Hammond Perry, Kennetta, *London Is the Place for Me: Black Britons, Citizenship and the Politics of Race* (London, 2016).

Hancock, William Keith and Margaret Gowing, *British War Economy* (London, 1949).

Hannah, Leslie, *The Rise of the Corporate Economy* (London, 1976, 1983).

—, 'Pioneering Modern Corporate Governance: A View from London in 1900', *Enterprise & Society* 8 (2007), pp. 642–86.

—, 'Logistics, Market Size, and Giant Plants in the Early Twentieth Century: A Global View', *The Journal of Economic History* 68 (2008), pp. 46–9.

Hansen, R., *Citizenship and Immigration in Post-War Britain: The Institutional Origins of a Multicultural Nation* (London, 2000).

Harling, Philip, *The Modern British State: A Historical Introduction* (Malden, 2001).

Harlow, Chris, *Innovation and Productivity under Nationalisation: The First Thirty Years* (London, 1977).

Harris, Alexandra, *Romantic Moderns: English Writers, Artists and the Imagination from Virginia Woolf to John Piper* (London, 2010).

Harris, Bernard, *The Origins of the British Welfare State: Society, State and Social Welfare in England and Wales, 1800–1945* (London, 2004).

Harris, Jose, 'Enterprise and Welfare States: A Comparative Perspective', *Transactions of the Royal Historical Society* 40 (1990), pp. 175–95.

—, 'War and Social History: Britain and the Home Front during the Second World War', *Contemporary European History* 1 (1992), pp. 17–35.

—, *Private Lives, Public Spirit: A Social History of Britain 1870–1914* (Oxford, 1993).

—, 'Labour's Political and Social Thought', in Duncan Tanner, Pat Thane and Nick Tiratsoo (eds.), *Labour's First Century* (Cambridge, 2000).

Harris, Nigel, *Competition and the Corporate Society: British Conservatives, the State and Industry 1945–1964* (London, 1972).

Harrison, Brian, 'Women in a Men's House: The Women MPs, 1919–1945', *Historical Journal* 29 (1986), pp. 623–54.

—, *Seeking a Role: The United Kingdom, 1951–1970* (Oxford, 2009).

—, *Finding a Role? The United Kingdom, 1970–1990* (Oxford, 2010).

Harvie, Christopher, *No Gods and Precious Few Heroes: Scotland, 1914–80* (London, 1981).

—, *Fool's Gold: The Story of North Sea Oil* (London, 1994).

—, *A Floating Commonwealth: Politics, Culture, and Technology on Britain's Atlantic Coast, 1860–1930* (Oxford, 2008).

Hatherley, Owen, *A Guide to the New Ruins of Great Britain* (London, 1981).

—, *The Ministry of Nostalgia* (London, 2016).

Hatton, T. J. and R. E. Bailey, 'Seebohm Rowntree and the Postwar Poverty Puzzle', *Economic History Review* 53 (2000), pp. 544–64.

Haxey, Simon, *Tory M.P.* (London, 1939).

Hay, Colin, 'Chronicles of a Death Foretold: The Winter of Discontent and Construction of the Crisis of British Keynesianism', *Parliamentary Affairs* 63 (2010), pp. 446–70.

Hayek, Friedrich, *The Road to Serfdom* (London, 1944).

Hayes, N., 'Did We Really Want a National Health Service? Hospitals, Patients and Public Opinions before 1948', *English Historical Review*, 128 (2012), pp. 625–61.

Heaman, Elsbeth A., *St Mary's: The History of a London Teaching Hospital* (Montreal, 2003).

Heffer, Simon, *Like the Roman* (London, 1998).

Heinemann, Margot, *Wages Front* (London, 1947).

Heller, M., 'The National Insurance Acts 1911–1947, the Approved Societies and the Prudential Assurance Company', *Twentieth Century British History* 19 (2008), pp. 1–8.

Helm, Dieter, *Energy, the State, and the Market: British Energy Policy since 1979* (Oxford, 2003).

Henderson, David, *Innocence and Design* (London, 1985).

Henderson, Nicholas, *Old Friends and Modern Instances* (London, 2000).

Henderson, P. D., 'Two British Errors: Their Probable Size and Some Possible Lessons', *Oxford Economic Papers* 29 (1977), pp. 159–205.

Hennessy, Peter and James Jinks, *The Silent Deep: The Royal Navy Submarine Service since 1945* (London, 2015).

Henry, Ian, 'Industrial Dispersal in Britain in the 1960s: An Analysis of How the Government's Policy and Approach to the Motor Industry Influenced the Development of Ford and Vauxhall and Changed in Response to Evolving Corporate Business Strategies' (unpublished MA dissertation, King's College London, 2015).

Hewison, Robert, *In Anger: British Culture in the Cold War 1945–1960* (London, 1981).

Hilliard, Christopher, *English as a Vocation: The Scrutiny Movement* (Oxford, 2012).

—, 'The Twopenny Library: The Book Trade, Working-Class Readers, and "Middlebrow" Novels in Britain, 1930–42', *Twentieth Century British History* 25 (2013), pp. 199–220.

Hills, John, Francesca Bastagli, Frank Cowell, Howard Glennerster, Eleni Karagiannaki and Abigail McKnight, *Wealth in the UK* (Oxford, 2013).

Hills, John, John Ditch and Howard Glennerster (eds.), *Beveridge and Social Security: An International Retrospective* (Oxford, 1994).

Hilton, John, *Rich Man Poor Man* (London, 1944).

Hilton, Matthew, *Consumerism in Twentieth-Century Britain: The Search for a Historical Movement* (Cambridge, 2003).

Hinton, James, 'Coventry Communism: A Study of Factory Politics in the Second World War', *History Workshop* 10 (autumn 1980), pp. 90–118.

—, *Protests and Visions: Peace Politics in Twentieth Century Britain* (London, 1989).

Hoare, Philip, *Wilde's Last Stand: Decadence, Conspiracy and the First World War* (London, 1997).

Hobsbawm, Eric, *Industry and Empire 1750–1968* (Harmondsworth, 1968).

—, 'The 1970s: Syndicalism without Syndicalists', *New Society* (5 April 1979), and in Eric Hobsbawm, *Worlds of Labour: Further Studies in the History of Labour* (London, 1984).

Hodge, Joseph Morgan, *Triumph of the Expert: Agrarian Doctrines of Development and the Legacies of British Colonialism* (Columbus, Ohio, 2007).

Holland, James, *The War in the West: A New History*, 2 vols. (London, 2016–17).

Holland, R. F., *The Pursuit of Greatness: Britain and the World Role, 1900–1970* (London, 1991).

Holland, Stuart, *The Socialist Challenge* (London, 1976).

—, (ed.), *Out of Crisis: A Project for European Recovery* (London, 1983).

—, 'Alternative European and Economic Strategies', in Lawrence Black, Hugh Pemberton and Pat Thane (eds.), *Reassessing 1970s Britain* (Manchester, 2013).

Honeyman, Katrina, *Well Suited: A History of the Leeds Clothing Industry, 1850–1990* (Edinburgh, 2000).

Hopkins, Michael M. and Geoffrey Owen, *Science, the State and the City: Britain's Struggle to Success in Biotechnology* (Oxford, 2016).

Horrocks, Sally M., 'Enthusiasm Constrained? British Industrial R&D and the Transition from War to Peace, 1942–51', *Business History* 41 (1999), pp. 42–4.

—, 'The Internationalization of Science in a Commercial Context: Research and Development by Overseas Multinationals in Britain before the Mid-1970s', *The British Journal for the History of Science* 40 (2007), pp. 227–50.

House of Commons, *A Century of Change: Trends in UK Statistics since 1900* (London, 1999).

Howe, Anthony, *Free Trade and Liberal England, 1846–1946* (Oxford, 1997).

Howe, Stephen, 'Internal Decolonization? British Politics since Thatcher as Post-colonial Trauma', *Twentieth Century British History* 14 (2003), pp. 286–304.

Howell, David, *British Social Democracy: A Study in Development and Decay* (London 1976).

—, *British Workers and the Independent Labour Party 1888–1906* (Manchester, 1983).

Hughes, Colin and Patrick Wintour, *Labour Rebuilt: The New Model Party* (London, 1990).

Humphreys, Richard, *Tate Britain Companion to British Art* (London, 2007).

Hutton, Alexander, 'Literature, Criticism, and Politics in the Early New Left, 1956–62', *Twentieth Century British History*, 26 (2016), pp. 51–75.

Hyam, Ronald, *Britain's Declining Empire: The Road to Decolonisation, 1918–1968* (Cambridge, 2007).

Hyman, Richard, *Strikes* (London, 1972).

Jack, Ian, *The Country Formerly Known as Great Britain* (London, 2009).

Jackson, Ashley, *The British Empire and the Second World War* (London, 2006).

Jackson, Ben, 'Currents of Neo-Liberalism: British Political Ideologies and the New Right, c.1955–1979', *The English Historical Review* 131 (2016), pp. 823–50.

—, 'The Think-tank Archipelago: Thatcherism and Neo-liberalism', in Ben Jackson and Robert Saunders (eds.), *Making Thatcher's Britain* (Cambridge, 2012).

Jefferys, Kevin, 'British Politics and Social Policy during the Second World War', *The Historical Journal* 30 (1987), pp. 123–44.

Jeremy, David J., 'The Hundred Largest Employers in the United Kingdom, in Manufacturing and Non-Manufacturing Industries, in 1907, 1935 and 1955', *Business History* 33 (1991), pp. 93–111.

—, *A Business History of Britain, 1900–1990s* (Oxford, 1998).

Jevons, H. Stanley, *The British Coal Trade* (London, 1915).

Jewkes, John et al., *The Sources of Invention* (London, 1958, 1969).

Jobson, Richard, 'A New Hope for an Old Britain? Nostalgia and The British Labour Party's Alternative Economic Strategy, 1970–83', *Journal of Policy History* 27 (2015), pp. 670–94.

Johns, Adrian, *Piracy: The Intellectual Property Wars from Gutenberg to Gates* (Chicago, Illinois, 2010).

—, *Death of a Pirate: British Radio and the Making of the Information Age* (London, 2011).

Johnson, Peter, *Neutrality: A Policy for Britain* (London, 1985).

Jones, Charles, *International Business in the Nineteenth Century: The Rise and Fall of a Cosmopolitan Bourgeoisie* (Brighton, 1987).

Jones, Geoffrey, *The Evolution of International Business* (London, 1996).

—, *Merchants to Multinationals: British Trading Companies in the 19th and 20th Centuries* (London, 2000).

Jones, Matthew, 'Great Britain, the United States, and Consultation Over Use of the Atomic Bomb, 1950–1954', *The Historical Journal* 54 (2011), pp. 797–828.

—, *The Official History of the UK Strategic Nuclear Deterrent*, 2 vols. (London, 2017).

Jones, Owen, *Chavs: The Demonization of the Working Class* (London, 2011).

Joyce, Patrick, *The State of Freedom: A Social History of the British State since 1800* (Cambridge, 2013).

Joyce, William, *Twilight over England* (Berlin, 1940).

Junius (Arthur Bryant and John Drummond Wolff), *Britain Awake!* (London, 1940).

Kahn, Yasmin, *The Raj at War: A People's History of India's Second World War* (London, 2015).

Kaldor, Mary, Dan Smith and Steve Vines (eds.), *Democratic Socialism and the Cost of Defence: The Report and Papers of the Labour Party Defence Study Group* (London, 1979).

Kalra, Virinder, *From Textile Mills to Taxi Ranks: Experiences of Migration, Labour and Social Change* (Aldershot, 2000).

Keating, Joan, 'Faith and Community Threatened? Roman Catholic Responses to the Welfare State, Materialism and Social Mobility, 1945–62', *Twentieth Century British History* 9 (1998), pp. 86–108.

Kennedy, Dane, 'Imperial History and Post-colonial Theory', *The Journal of Imperial and Commonwealth History* 24 (1996), pp. 345–63.

Kenny, Michael, *The First New Left: British Intellectuals after Stalin* (London, 1995).

Keynes, J. M., *Essays in Persuasion* (London, 1931).

Kidd, Colin, *Union and Unionisms: Political Thought in Scotland, 1500–2000* (Cambridge, 2008).

King, Desmond and Randall Hansen, 'Experts at Work: State Autonomy, Social Learning and Eugenic Sterilization in 1930s Britain', *British Journal of Political Science* 29 (1999), pp. 77–107.

Kingsley Kent, Susan, *Gender and Power in Britain, 1640–1990* (Abingdon, 1999).

—, *A New History of Britain since 1688* (Oxford, 2017).

Kininmonth, Kirsten W., 'The Growth, Development and Management of J. & P. Coats Ltd, c.1890–1960: An Analysis of Strategy and Structure', *Business History* 48 (2006), pp. 551–79.

Klos, Felix, *Churchill on Europe* (London, 2016).

Kranmick, Isaac and Barry Sheerman, *Harold Laski: A Life on the Left* (London, 1993).

Kumar, Krishan, *The Making of English National Identity* (Cambridge, 2003).

Kynaston, David, *City of London* (London, 2011).

Lane, Tony, *The Merchant Seamen's War* (Manchester, 1990).

Langley, Kathleen, 'An Analysis of the Asset Structure of Estates', *Oxford Bulletin of Economics and Statistics* 13.10 (1951), pp. 339–56.

Law, M. J., *The Experience of Suburban Modernity: How Private Transport Changed Interwar London* (Manchester, 2014).

Lean, Tom, *Electronic Dreams: How 1980s Britain Learned to Love the Computer* (London, 2016).

Lee, Christopher, *Eight Bells and Top Masts: Diaries from a Tramp Steamer* (London, 2001).

Lee, Simon, *Best for Britain? The Politics and Legacy of Gordon Brown* (Oxford, 2007).

LeMahieu, D. L., *A Culture for Democracy* (Oxford, 1998).

Liesner, H. H., *The Import Dependence of Britain and Western Germany: A Comparative Study*, Princeton Studies in International Finance no. 7 (Princeton, New Jersey, 1957).

Light, Alison, *Forever England: Femininity, Literature, and Conservatism between the Wars* (London, 1991).

Linehan, Thomas, *Communism in Britain 1920–1939: From the Cradle to the Grave* (Manchester, 2007).

Linstrum, Erik, *Ruling Minds: Psychology in the British Empire* (Cambridge, Massachusetts, 2016).

Lomas, Janis, ' "Delicate Duties": Issues of Class and Respectability in Government Policy Towards the Wives and Widows of British Soldiers in the Era of the Great War', *Women's History Review* 9 (2000), pp. 123–47.

Long, David and Peter Wilson (eds.), *Thinkers of the Twenty Years' Crisis: Inter-war Idealism Reassessed* (Oxford, 1995).

Love, Gary, 'The Periodical Press and the Intellectual Culture of Conservatism in Interwar Britain', *The Historical Journal* 57 (2014), pp. 1027–56.

Lowe, Rodney, 'The Replanning of the Welfare State, 1957–1964', in M. Francis and I. Zweiniger-Bargielowska (eds.), *The Conservatives and British Society, 1880–1990* (London, 1996).

—, *The Welfare State in Britain since 1945* (London, 2005).

McCarthy, Helen, *The British People and the League of Nations: Democracy, Citizenship and Internationalism c. 1918–45* (Manchester, 2011).

—, Whose Democracy? Histories of British Political Culture between the Wars', *Historical Journal* 55 (2012), pp. 221–38.

McCarthy, W. E. J. (ed.), *Trade Unions* (Middlesex, 1972).

McCloskey, Deirdre, *If You're So Smart: The Narrative of Economic Expertise* (Chicago, Illinois, 1990).

McGucken, William, *Scientists, Society, and State: The Social Relations of Science Movement in Great Britain, 1931–1947* (Columbus, Ohio, 1984).

Macintyre, Stuart, *A Proletarian Science: Marxism in Britain, 1917–1933* (London, 1982).

McIvor, Arthur, 'Employers, the Government, and Industrial Fatigue in Britain, 1890–1918', *British Journal of Industrial Medicine* 44 (1987), pp. 724–32.

—, *A History of Work in Britain 1880–1950* (Basingstoke, 2001).

—, *Working Lives* (London, 2013).

McKenna, Christopher, *The World's Newest Profession: Management Consulting in the Twentieth Century* (Cambridge, 2006).

MacKenzie, Donald, 'Eugenics in Britain', *Social Studies of Science* 6 (1976), pp. 499–32.

McKibbin, Ross, *The Ideologies of Class: Social Relations in Britain 1880–1950* (Oxford, 1990).

—, *Classes and Cultures: England 1918–1951* (Oxford, 1998).

—, *Parties and People: England 1914–1951* (Oxford, 2010).

—, 'Political Sociology in the Guise of Economics: J. M. Keynes and the Rentier', *The English Historical Review*, 128 (2013), pp. 78–106.

Macnicol, J., 'The Evacuation of Schoolchildren', in H. L. Smith (ed.), *War and Social Change: British Society in the Second World War* (Manchester, 1986), pp. 3–31.

—, *The Politics of Retirement in Britain, 1878–1948* (Cambridge, 1998).

Magee, G. B. and A. S. Thompson, *Empire and Globalisation: Networks of People, Goods and Capital in the British World, c. 1850–1914* (Cambridge, 2010).

Maiolo, Joe, *Cry Havoc: The Arms Race and the Second World War, 1931–1941* (London, 2010).

Mandler, Peter, *The Fall and Rise of the Stately Home* (London, 1997).

—, *English National Character: The History of an Idea from Edmund Burke to Tony Blair* (London, 2007).

—, *Return from the Natives: How Margaret Mead Won the Second World War and Lost the Cold War* (London, 2013).

—, 'Educating the Nation III: Social Mobility', *Transactions of the Royal Historical Society* 26 (2016), pp. 1–3.

Manton, Kevin, 'Labour and the 1949 Parliament Act', *Contemporary British History* 26 (2012), pp. 149–72.

Marquand, David, *Britain since 1918: The Strange Career of British Democracy* (London, 2008).

Marquand, David and Anthony Seldon (eds.), *The Ideas that Shaped Post-War Britain* (London, 1996).

Marrison, Andrew J., 'Businessmen, Industries and Tariff Reform in Great Britain, 1903–1930', *Business History* 25 (1983), pp. 148–78.

Marsh, Steve, 'Churchill, SACLANT and the Politics of Opposition', *Contemporary British History* 27 (2013), pp. 445–65.

Martin, John, 'The International Crisis of 1972–: The Neglected Agrarian Dimension', in A. T. Brown, Andy Burn, Rob Doherty (eds.), *Crises in Economic and Social History: A Comparative Perspective* (Martlesham, 2015).

Martin, Ross M., *The Lancashire Giant: David Shackleton, Labour Leader and Civil Servant* (Liverpool, 2000).

Marwick, Arthur, *British Society since 1945* (Harmondsworth, 1990).

Matera, Marc, *Black London: The Imperial Metropole and Decolonization in the Twentieth Century* (London, 2015).

Matthews, R. C. O., Charles Feinstein and John Odling-Smee, *British Economic Growth, 1856–1973* (Oxford, 1982).

May, R. M. 'The Scientific Wealth of Nations', *Science* 275 (1997), pp. 793–96.

Mazower, Mark, *No Enchanted Palace: The End of Empire and the Ideological Origins of the United Nations* (Princeton, New Jersey, 2009).

Meades, Jonathan, *An Encyclopaedia of Myself* (London, 2014).

Medhurst, John, *That Option No Longer Exists: Britain, 1974–6* (Winchester, 2014).

Medlicott, W. N., *Contemporary England 1914–1964* (London, 1967).

Melling, H. and A. Booth (eds.), *Managing the Modern Workplace: Productivity, Politics and Workplace Culture in Postwar Britain* (Aldershot, 2008).

Mellors, Colin, *The British MP: A Socio-Economic Study of the House of Commons* (Farnborough, 1978).

Middlemas, Keith, *Politics in Industrial Society: The Experience of the British System since 1911* (London, 1979).

—, *Power, Competition and the State*, 3 vols. (London, 1986–91).

Middleton, Roger, *Government and Market: The Growth of the Public Sector, Economic Management and British Economic Performance, c. 1890–1979* (Cheltenham, 1996).

Middleton, Stuart, '"Affluence" and the Left in Britain, c.1958–1974', *English Historical Review* 124 (2014), pp. 107–38.

Miliband, Ralph, *Parliamentary Socialism: A Study in the Politics of Labour* (London, 1961).

—, *Capitalist Democracy in Britain* (Oxford, 1982).

Miller, Michael B., *Europe and the Maritime World: A Twentieth Century History* (Cambridge, 2012).

Millman, Brock, *Managing Domestic Dissent in First World War Britain* (London, 2000).

Milne, Seumas, *The Enemy Within* (London, 2014).

Milward, Alan, *The Economic Effects of the Two World Wars on Britain*, 2nd edn (London, 1984).

—, *The UK and the European Community*, vol. 1: *The Rise and Fall of a National Strategy* (London, 2002).

Mitchell, B. R. and Phyllis Deane, *Abstract of British Historical Statistics* (Cambridge, 1962).

Mitchell, Timothy, *The Rule of Experts: Egypt, Techno-Politics, Modernity* (Berkeley, California 2002).

—, *Carbon Democracy: Political Power in the Age of Oil* (London, 2011).

Moore, Richard, 'Bad Strategy and Bomber Dreams: A New View of the Blue Streak Cancellation', *Contemporary British History* 27 (2013), pp. 145–66.

Moran, Joe, *On Roads: A Hidden History* (London, 2009).

—, *Armchair Nation: An Intimate History of Britain in Front of the TV* (2013).

Moran, Michael, *The End of British Politics?* (Basingstoke, 2017).

Morgan, Kenneth O., *Rebirth of a Nation: Wales, 1880–1980* (Oxford, 1981).

—, *Labour in Power 1945–1951* (Oxford, 1984).

—, *The People's Peace: British History 1945–1989* (Oxford, 1990).

Morris, June, *The Life and Times of Thomas Balogh: A Macaw among Mandarins* (Eastbourne, 2007).

Mosley, Sir Oswald, *Greater Britain* (London, 1934).

—, *Tomorrow We Live* (London, 1938).

Moss, Jonathan, ' "We Didn't Realise How Brave We Were at the Time": The 1968 Ford Sewing Machinists' Strike in Public and Personal Memory', *Oral History* 43 (spring 2015), pp. 40–51.

Mowat, Charles Loch, *Britain between the Wars: 1918–1940* (London, 1955).

Muldoon, Andrew, *Empire, Politics and the Creation of the 1935 India Act: Last Act of the Raj* (London, 2016).

Mulhern, Francis, *The Moment of 'Scrutiny'* (London, 1979).

Mulligan, William and Brendan Simms, *The Primacy of Foreign Policy in British History, 1660–2000: How Strategic Concerns Shaped Modern Britain* (London, 2010).

Murphy, Philip, *Monarchy and the End of Empire: The House of Windsor, the British Government and the Postwar Commonwealth* (Oxford, 2013).

Nairn, Tom, 'The Nature of the Labour Party (Part II)', *New Left Review* 1.28 (November–December 1964), pp. 51–2.

—, 'The Left against Europe?', *New Left Review* 1.75 (September–October 1972).

—, *The Break-up of Britain: Crisis and Neonationalism* (London, 1982).

—, *The Enchanted Glass: Britain and Its Monarchy* (London 1988).

Nasbeth, L. and G. F. Ray, *The Diffusion of New Industrial Processes. An International Study* (Cambridge, 1974).

National Institute of Economic and Social Research, *Trade Regulations and Commercial Policy of the United Kingdom* (Cambridge, 1943).

Navias, Martin S., *Nuclear Weapons and British Strategic Planning, 1955–1958* (Oxford, 1991).

Nehru, Jawaharlal, *An Autobiography* (1936) (New Delhi, 2004).

—, *The Discovery of India* (1946) (New Delhi, 2004).

Newsinger, John, *British Counterinsurgency: From Palestine to Northern Ireland* (London, 2002).

—, *The Blood Never Dried: A People's History of the British Empire* (London, 2006).

Newton, Scott and Dilwyn Porter, *Modernization Frustrated: The Politics of Industrial Decline in Britain since 1900* (London, 1988).

Nicholas, Sian, *The Echo of War* (Manchester, 1996).

Nicholas, Tom, 'Wealth Making in Nineteenth- and Early Twentieth-Century Britain: Industry v. Commerce and Finance', *Business History* 41 (1999).

Nichols, Theo, *The British Worker Question* (London, 1986).

Nicolson, Harold, *Diaries and Letters, 1939–1945* (London, 1970).

Norris, Robert S., and Hans M. Kristensen, 'The British Nuclear Stockpile, 1953–2013', *Bulletin of the Atomic Scientists* 69 (2013), pp. 69–75.

Nove, Alec, *Efficiency Criteria for Nationalised Industries* (London, 1973).

O'Hara, Glen, *Britain and the Sea since 1600* (London, 2010).

—, *Governing Post-War Britain: The Paradoxes of Progress* (Basingstoke, 2012).

Oborne, Peter, *The Rise of Political Lying* (London, 2005).

Offer, Avner, 'Using the Past in Britain: Retrospect and Prospect', *The Public Historian* 6.4 (autumn 1984).

—, *The First World War: An Agrarian Interpretation* (Oxford, 1989).

—, *The Challenge of Affluence: Self-Control and Well-Being in the United States and Britain since 1950* (Oxford, 2005).

Oikonomou, Alexandros, 'The Hidden Persuaders: Government Scientists and Defence in Post-war Britain' (unpublished PhD thesis, Imperial College London, 2011).

Olby, Robert, 'Social Imperialism and State Support for Agricultural Research in Edwardian Britain', *Annals of Science* 48.6 (1991), pp. 509–26.

Oliver, M. J., 'Whatever Happened to Monetarism?: A Review of British Exchange Rate Policy in the 1980s', *Twentieth Century British History* 8 (1997), pp. 49–73.

Ortolano, Guy, *Two Cultures Controversy: Science, Literature and Cultural Politics in Postwar Britain* (Cambridge, 2009).

—, 'Planning the Urban Future in 1960s Britain', *The Historical Journal* 54 (2011), pp. 477–507.

Orwell, Sonia and Ian Angus (eds.), *The Collected Essays, Journalism and Letters of George Orwell*, vol. 2: *My Country Right or Left* (London, 1970).

Østergaard, Nielsen Thorsheim and Stuart Ward, 'Cramped and Restricted at Home? Scottish Separatism at Empire's End', *Transactions of the Royal Historical Society* (6th series) 25 (2015), pp. 159–85.

Overy, Richard, *The Morbid Age: Britain between the Wars* (London, 2009).

Owen, Geoffrey, *From Empire to Europe: The Decline and Revival of British Industry since the Second World War* (London, 2000).

Oxford University Socialist Discussion Group (ed.), *Out of Apathy* (London, 1989).

Palladino, Paolo, 'Science, Technology and the Economy: Plant Breeding in Great Britain, 1920–1970', *Economic History Review* 49 (1996), pp. 137–53.

Parker, R. A. C., 'The Pound Sterling, the American Treasury and British Preparations for War, 1938–1939', *The English Historical Review*, 98 (1983), pp. 261–79.

Payling, Daisy, ' "Socialist Republic of South Yorkshire": Grassroots Activism and Left-Wing Solidarity in 1980s Sheffield', *Twentieth Century British History* 25 (2014), pp. 602–27.

Peden, G. C., *The Treasury and British Public Policy 1906–1959* (Oxford, 2000).

Peden, George, *Arms, Economics and British Strategy: From Dreadnoughts to Hydrogen Bombs* (Cambridge, 2007).

Pedersen, Susan, 'Gender, Welfare, and Citizenship in Britain during the Great War', *The American Historical Review* 95.4 (1990), pp. 983–1006.

—, *Family, Dependence and the Origins of the Welfare State: Britain and France 1914–1945* (Cambridge, 1993).

Peele, Gillian, 'St. George's and the Empire Crusade', in Chris Cook and John Ramsden (eds.), *By-elections in British Politics* (London, 1973).

Pelling, Henry, *A History of British Trade Unionism* (Harmondsworth, 1963).

Pemberton, Hugh, 'The Failure of "Nationalization by Attraction": Britain's Cross-Class Alliance Against Earnings-Related Pensions in the 1950s', *The Economic History Review* 65 (2012), pp. 1428–49.

—, *Policy Learning and British Governance in the 1960s* (London, 2004).

Perkin, Harold, *The Rise of Professional Society: England since 1880* (London, 1989).

Perren, Richard, *Taste, Trade and Technology: The Development of the International Meat Industry since 1840* (London, 2006).

Petersen, Klaus Jørn and Henrik Petersen, 'Confusion and Divergence: Origins and Meanings of the Term "Welfare State" in Germany and Britain, 1840–1940', *Journal of European Social Policy* 23 (2013), pp. 37–51.

Pettigrew, Andrew, *The Awakening Giant: Continuity and Change in ICI* (London, 1985).

Phythian, Mark, *The Politics of British Arms Sales Since 1964: 'To Secure Our Rightful Share'* (London, 2000).

Pickering, Andrew, *The Cybernetic Brain: Sketches of Another Future* (Chicago, Illinois, 2010).

Pickstone, John, *Medicine in Industrial Society* (Manchester, 1985).

Pierre, Andrew J., *Nuclear Politics: The British Experience with an Independent Strategic Force, 1939–1970* (London, 1972).

Pimlott, Ben, *The Queen: A Biography of Elizabeth II* (London, 1996).

Pimlott, Ben, Dennis Kavanagh and Peter Morris, 'Is the "Postwar Consensus" a Myth?', *Contemporary British History* 2 (1989), pp. 12–15.

Platt, D. C. M. (ed.), *Business Imperialism 1840–1930: An Inquiry Based on British Experience in Latin America* (Oxford, 1977).

Pollard, Sidney, *The Development of the British Economy 1914–1950* (London, 1962 and many others).

—, *Britain's Prime and Britain's Decline* (London, 1989).

Pollock, Allyson, *NHS plc: The Privatisation of Our Healthcare* (London, 2004).

Porter, Bernard, *The Absent-Minded Imperialists: Empire, Society, and Culture in Britain* (Oxford, 2004).

Powell, Martin, 'An Expanding Service: Municipal Acute Medicine in the 1930s', *Twentieth Century British History* 8 (1997), pp. 334–57.

Prados de la Escosura, Leandro, 'Economic Freedom in the Long Run: Evidence from OECD Countries (1850–2007)', *Economic History Review* 69 (2016), pp. 435–68.

Pugh, Martin, *The Making of Modern British Politics, 1867–1945* (London, 1982 and subsequent).

—, *State and Society: A Social and Political History of Britain Since 1870* (London, 1999 and subsequent).

—, 'Lancashire, Cotton, and Indian Reform: Conservative Controversies in the 1930s', *Twentieth Century British History* 15 (2004), pp. 143–51.

—, *Speak for Britain! A New History of the Labour Party* (London, 2010).

Pyne, Katherine, 'The Nuclear Dimension – the Development of the Warheads for the Royal Air Force "Special Weapons"', *Royal Air Force Historical Society Journal* 62 (2016), pp. 9–30.

Raghavan, Srinath, *India's War: The Making of Modern South Asia 1939–1945* (London, 2016).

Ramnath, Aparajith, *The Birth of an Indian Profession: Engineers, Industry, and the State, 1900–47* (New Delhi, 2017).

Redford, Duncan, 'The "Hallmark of a First-Class Navy": The Nuclear-Powered Submarine in the Royal Navy 1960–77', *Contemporary British History* 23 (2009), pp. 181–97.

Rée, Jonathan, *Proletarian Philosophers: Problems in Socialist Culture in Britain, 1900–1940* (London, 1984).

Reid, Alastair J., *United We Stand: A History of Britain's Trade Unions* (London, 2004).

Reynolds, David, *Britannia Overruled: British Policy and World Power in the 20th Century* (London, 1991).

—, *In Command of History* (London, 2004).

Rhodes James, Robert (ed.), *Winston S. Churchill: His Complete Speeches, 1897–1963*, 8 vols. (London, 1974).

Rivett, Geoffrey, *From Cradle to Grave: Fifty Years of the NHS* (London, 1997).

Robb, Thomas, 'The Power of Oil: Edward Heath, the "Year of Europe" and the Anglo-American "Special Relationship"', *Contemporary British History* 26 (2012), pp. 73–6.

Roberts, Andrew, *Eminent Churchillians* (London, 1994).

Roberts, Andy, *Albion Dreaming: A Popular History of LSD in Britain* (London, 2012).

Roberts, Edwin A., *The Anglo-Marxists: A Study in Ideology and Culture* (Lanham, Maryland, 1997).

Robinson, Emily, *The Language of Progressive Politics in Modern Britain* (London, 2017).

Rollings, Neil, 'The Twilight World of British Business Politics: The Spring Sunningdale Conferences since the 1960s', *Business History* 56 (2014), pp. 915–35.

—, 'Cracks in the Post-War Keynesian Settlement? The Role of Organised Business in Britain in the Rise of Neoliberalism before Margaret Thatcher', *Twentieth Century British History* 24 (2013), pp. 637–59.

—, 'Poor Mr Butskell: A Short Life, Wrecked by Schizophrenia?', *Twentieth Century British History* 5 (1994), pp. 183–205.

—, *Business in the Formative Years of European Integration, 1945–1973* (Cambridge, 2007).

Rolt, L. T. C., *Winterstoke* (London, 1954, reprinted 2015).

Rooth, Tim, *British Protectionism and the International Economy: Overseas Commercial Policy in the 1930s* (Cambridge, 1993).

Rose, Hilary and Steven Rose (eds.), *The Radicalisation of Science* (London, 1976).

Rose, Jonathan, *The Intellectual Life of the British Working Classes* (London, 2001).

Rose, Kenneth, *Elusive Rothschild: The Life of Victor, Third Baron* (London, 2003).

Rose, Richard, 'Class and Party Divisions: Britain as a Test Case', *Sociology* 2.2 (1968), pp. 129–62.

Rose, Sonya O., *Which People's War?: National Identity and Citizenship in Wartime Britain 1939–1945* (Oxford, 2003).

Ross, Colin, *Death of the Docks* (Milton Keynes, 2010).

Rowthorn, Bob, 'Imperialism in the Seventies – Unity or Rivalry?', *New Left Review* 1 (September–October 1971).

Rowthorn, R. E. and J. R. Wells, *De-industrialization and Foreign Trade* (Cambridge, 1987).

Rozina, Visram, *Ayahs, Lascars and Princes: The Story of Indians in Britain 1700–1947* (London: Routledge, 2015).

Ruane, Kevin, *Churchill and the Bomb in War and Cold War* (London, 2016).

Rubinstein, William, *Capitalism, Culture, and Decline in Britain 1750–1990* (London, 1993).

—, *Twentieth-century Britain: A Political History* (London, 2003).

Samuel, Raphael (ed.), *Patriotism: The Making and Unmaking of British National Identity*, 3 vols. (London 1989).

—, *Island Stories: Unravelling Britain* (London, 1998).

—, 'Class Politics: The Lost World of British Communism, Part III', *New Left Review* 1.165 (September–October 1987).

Satia, Priya, *Spies in Arabia: The Great War and the Cultural Foundations of Britain's Covert Empire in the Middle East* (Oxford, 2008).

—, 'Byron, Gandhi and the Thompsons: The Making of British Social History and Unmaking of Indian History', *History Workshop Journal* 81 (2016), pp. 135–70.

Saunders, Frances Stonor, *Who Paid the Piper?: CIA and the Cultural Cold War* (London, 1999).

Saunders, Jack, 'The Untraditional Worker: Class Re-formation in Britain 1945–65', *Twentieth Century British History* 26 (2015), pp. 225–48.

Savage, Mike, *Identities and Social Change in Britain since 1940: The Politics of Method* (Oxford, 2010).

—, *Social Class in the 21st Century* (London, 2015).

Saville, John, *The Politics of Continuity: British Foreign Policy and the Labour Government, 1945–46* (London, 1993).

Schenk, Catherine, *Britain and the Sterling Area: From Devaluation to Convertibility in the 1950s* (London, 1994).

—, *The Decline of Sterling: Managing the Retreat of an International Currency 1945–1992* (Cambridge, 2010).

Schofield, Camilla, *Enoch Powell and the Making of Postcolonial Britain* (Cambridge, 2013).

Schwarz, Bill, *The White Man's World* (Oxford, 2011).

—, 'An Unsentimental Education. John Darwin's Empire', *The Journal of Imperial and Commonwealth History* 43 (2015), pp. 125–44.

Schwerin, Alan (ed.), *Bertrand Russell on Nuclear War, Peace, and Language: Critical and Historical Essays* (Westport, Connecticut, 2002).

Scott, L. V., *Conscription and the Attlee Governments: The Politics and Policy of National Service, 1945–1951* (Oxford, 1993).

Scott, Peter, *The Making of the British Home: The Suburban Semi and Family Life Between the Wars* (Oxford, 2013).

—, *Triumph of the South: A Regional Economic History of Early Twentieth Century Britain* (Farnham, 2007).

Searle, G. R., *The Liberal Party: Triumph and Disintegration, 1886–1929* (Basingstoke, 1992).

—, *A New England? Peace and War 1886–1918* (Oxford, 2005).

Seaton, Andrew, 'Against the "Sacred Cow": NHS Opposition and the Fellowship for Freedom in Medicine, 1948–72', *Twentieth Century British History* 26 (2015), pp. 424–49.

Seldon, Anthony, *Major: A Political Life* (London, 1997).

—, *Churchill's Indian Summer: The Conservative Government 1951–55* (London, 1981).

Self, Robert, 'Treasury Control and the Empire Marketing Board: The Rise and Fall of Non-Tariff Preference in Britain, 1924–1933', *Twentieth Century British History* 5 (1994), pp. 153–82.

Seligman, Matthew, 'The Anglo-German Naval Race, 1898–1914', in Thomas Mahnken, Joseph Maiolo and David Stevenson (eds.), *Arms*

Races in International Politics: From the Nineteenth to the Twenty-first Century (Oxford, 2016), pp. 21–40.

Semmel, Bernard, 'Sir William Ashley as "Socialist of the Chair"', *Economica* (1957), pp. 343–53.

—, 'Sir Halford Mackinder: Theorist of Imperialism', *The Canadian Journal of Economics and Political Science/Revue canadienne d'Economique et de Science politique* 24 (1958), pp. 554–61.

Shaw, Maureen and Helen D. Millgate, *War's Forgotten Women* (Gloucestershire, 2011).

Shaxson, Nicholas, *Treasure Islands* (London, 2011).

Sheard, Sally, *The Passionate Economist: How Brian Abel-Smith Shaped Global Health and Social Welfare* (Bristol, 2013).

Shenk, Timothy, *Maurice Dobb, Political Economist* (London, 2013).

Shute, Nevil, *The Far Country* (London, 1952).

—, *In the Wet* (London, 1953).

Sigsworth, E. M., *Montague Burton: The Tailor of Taste* (Manchester, 1990).

Simpson, John, 'British Nuclear Weapon Stockpiles, 1953–78: A Commentary on Technical and Political Drivers', *The RUSI Journal* 156.5 (2011), pp. 74–83.

Sinclair, Iain, *Hackney, that Rose-Red Empire: A Confidential Report* (London, 2009).

Sked, Alan and Chris Cook, *Post-War Britain: A Political History* (London, many editions from 1979).

Skidelsky, Robert, *Oswald Mosley* (London, 1975).

—, *Britain since 1900 – a Success Story?* (London, 2014).

Skinner, Dennis, *Sailing Close to the Wind: Reminiscences* (London, 2014).

Sloman, Peter, 'Partners in Progress? British Liberals and the Labour Party since 1918', *Political Studies Review* 12 (2014), pp. 41–50.

Sluga, Glenda, *Internationalism in the Age of Nationalism* (Philadelphia, 2013).

Smith, A. E., *London's Royal Docks in the 1950s: A Memoir of the Docks at Work*, Kindle edn (London, 2011), loc. 3200.

Smith, Evan and Daryl Leeworthy, 'Before *Pride*: The Struggle for the Recognition of Gay Rights in the British Communist Movement, 1973–85', *Twentieth Century British History* 27 (2016), pp. 621–42.

Smith, Harold (ed.), *War and Social Change: Britain in the Second World War* (Manchester, 1986).

—, *Britain in the Second World War: A Social History* (Manchester, 1996).

Smith, Malcolm, *Britain and 1940: History, Myth and Popular Memory* (Abingdon, 2000).

Stapleton, Julia, *Political Intellectuals and Public Identities in Britain since 1850* (Manchester, 2001).

Stewart, Iain, *Don Heriberto: Knight of the Argentine: The Life of Sir Herbert Gibson, Bart. KBE (1863–1934)* (Ely, 2008).

Stirling J., 'Social Services Expenditure during the Last 100 Years', *Advancement of Science*, 8.32 (1952), pp. 379–92.

Stockwell, Sarah (ed.), *The British Empire: Themes and Perspectives* (London, 2008).

Stoney, Barbara, *Twentieth Century Maverick* (East Grinstead, 2004).

Strachan, Hew, *The Politics of the British Army* (Oxford, 1997).

Stranges, Anthony, 'From Birmingham to Billingham: High-Pressure Coal Hydrogenation in Great Britain', *Technology and Culture* 26 (1985), pp. 726–57.

Stubbs, J. O., 'Lord Milner and Patriotic Labour, 1914–1918', *The English Historical Review* 87.345 (1972), pp. 717–54.

Sturdy, S. and Cooter, R., 'Science, Scientific Management, and the Transformation of Medicine in Britain *c*. 1870–1950', *History of Science* 36 (1998), pp. 421–66.

Summerfield, Penny, *Reconstructing Women's Wartime Lives: Discourse and Subjectivity in Oral Histories of the Second World War* (Manchester, 1998).

Supple, Barry (ed.), *Essays In British Business History* (Oxford, 1977).

—, 'Fear of Failing: Economic History and the Decline of Britain', *The Economic History Review* 47 (1994), pp. 441–58.

—, *The History of the British Coal Industry*, vol. 4 (Oxford, 1987).

Sutcliffe-Braithwaite, Florence, 'Neo-Liberalism and Morality in the Making of Thatcherite Social Policy', *The Historical Journal* 55 (2012), pp. 497–520.

—, 'Discourses of "Class" in Britain in "New Times"', *Contemporary British History* 31 (2017), pp. 294–17.

Sutton, Alex, *The Political Economy of Imperial Relations: Britain, the Sterling Area, and Malaya 1945–1960* (London, 2015).

Sutton, Peter, 'Technological Change and Industrial Relations in the British Postal Service, 1969–1975' (unpublished PhD thesis, King's College London, 2013).

Szreter, S. and K. Fisher, *Sex before the Sexual Revolution. Intimate Life in England 1918–63* (Cambridge, 2010).

Tanner, Duncan, Pat Thane and Nick Tiratsoo (eds.), *Labour's First Century* (Cambridge, 2000).

Taylor, A. J. P., *English History 1914–1945* (Oxford, 1965).

Taylor, Ben, 'Science and the British Police Service: Surveillance, Intelligence and the Rise of the Professional Police Officer, 1930–2000' (PhD thesis, King's College London, 2015).

Taylor, M., 'English Football and "the Continent" Reconsidered', in P. Vonnard, G. Quin and N. Bancel (eds.), *Building Europe with the Ball: Turning Points in the Europeanization of Football, 1905–1995* (Oxford, 2016), pp. 75–7.

Taylor, Robert, *The Trade Union Question in British Politics* (Oxford, 1993).

Thane, Pat, *Foundations of the Welfare State* (London, 1982, 1996).

—, *Old Age in English History: Past Experiences, Present Issues* (Oxford, 2000).

—, 'What Difference Did the Vote Make?', in A. Vickery (ed.), *Women, Privilege and Power* (London, 2001).

Thomas, Geraint, 'Political Modernity and "Government" in the Construction of Inter-war Democracy: Local and National Encounters', in Laura Beers and Geraint Thomas (eds.), *Brave New World: Imperial and Democratic Nation-building in Britain between the Wars* (London, 2011).

Thomas, Martin, *Violence and Colonial Order: Police, Workers and Protest in the European Colonial Empires, 1918–1940* (Cambridge, 2012).

—, *Fight or Flight: Britain, France, and Their Roads from Empire* (Oxford, 2014).

Thomas, William, *Rational Action: The Sciences of Policy in Britain and America, 1940–1960* (Cambridge, Massachusetts, 2015).

Thompson, Andrew (ed.), *Britain's Experience of Empire in the Twentieth Century* (Oxford, 2012).

Thompson, E. P., 'The Peculiarities of the English', *Socialist Register* (1965), reprinted in *The Poverty of Theory* (London, 1978).

—, 'Notes on Exterminism: The Last Stage of Civilization', *New Left Review* 1 (May–June 1980).

Thompson F. M. L. (ed.), *The Cambridge Social History of Britain, 1750–1950*, 3 vols. (Cambridge, 1990).

—, 'Presidential Address: English Landed Society in the Twentieth Century: I, Property: Collapse and Survival', *Transactions of the Royal Historical Society* 40 (1990), pp. 1–4.

—, *Gentrification and the Enterprise Culture: Britain 1780–1980* (Oxford, 2001).

Thompson, Noel, 'Socialist Political Economy in an Age of Affluence: The Reception of J. K. Galbraith by the British Social-Democratic Left in the 1950s and 1960s', *Twentieth Century British History* 21 (2010), pp. 50–79.

Thomson, M., *The Problem of Mental Deficiency: Eugenics, Democracy and Social Policy in Britain, c.1870–1959* (Oxford, 1998).

—, *Psychological Subjects: Identity, Culture, and Health in Twentieth-Century Britain* (Oxford, 2006).

Thornett, Alan, *Militant Years* (London, 2011).

Thorpe, Andrew, *A History of the British Labour Party* (London, 2015).

—, *Parties at War: Political Organization in Second World War Britain* (Oxford, 2009).

Tilley, Helen, *Africa as a Living Laboratory: Empire, Development, and the Problem of Scientific Knowledge, 1870–1950* (Chicago, 2011).

Timmins, Nicholas, *The Five Giants: A Biography of the Welfare State* (London, 1995, 2001).

Tiratsoo, Nick et al. (eds.), *From Blitz to Blair: A New History of Britain since 1939* (London, 1997).

Titmuss, Richard, *Problems of Social Policy* (London, 1950).

—, *Essays on 'the Welfare State'* (London, 1958 and 1963).

Todd, Selina, *Young Women, Work, and Family in England 1918–1950* (London, 2005).

—, *The People: The Rise and Fall of the Working Class, 1910–2010* (London, 2014).

Todman, Daniel, *Britain's War: I: Into Battle, 1937–1941* (London, 2016).

—, *Britain's War: II: A New World, 1942–1947* (London, 2018).

Tolliday, Steven, *Business, Banking and Politics: The Case of British Steel, 1918–1939* (Cambridge, Massachusetts, 1987).

Tombs, Robert, *The English and Their History* (London, 2014).

Tomlinson, Jim, *The Unequal Struggle: British Socialism and the Capitalist Enterprise* (London, 1982).

—, *Public Policy and the Economy since 1900* (Oxford, 1990).

—, *Democratic Socialism and Economic Policy: The Attlee Years, 1945–1951* (Cambridge, 1997).

—, 'Why So Austere? The British Welfare State of the 1940s', *Journal of Social Policy* 27 (1998), pp. 63–7.

—, *The Politics of Decline: Understanding Post-War Britain* (Abingdon, 2000).

—, 'Marshall Aid and the "Shortage Economy" in Britain in the 1940s', *Contemporary European History* 9 (2000), pp. 137–55.

—, 'The Deglobalisation of Dundee, c. 1900–2000', *Journal of Scottish Historical Studies* 29 (2009), pp. 123–40.

—, 'De-globalization and Its Significance: From the Particular to the General', *Contemporary British History* 26 (2012), pp. 213–30.

—, 'The Empire/Commonwealth in British Economic Thinking and Policy', in Andrew Thompson (ed.), *Britain's Experience of Empire in the Twentieth Century* (Oxford, 2012), pp. 211–50.

—, *Dundee and the Empire: 'Juteopolis' 1850–1939* (Edinburgh, 2014).

—, 'De-industrialization Not Decline: A New Meta-narrative for Postwar British History', *Twentieth Century British History* 27 (2016), pp. 76–9.

Tooze, Adam, *The Wages of Destruction: The Making and Breaking of the Nazi Economy* (London, 2006).

—, *The Deluge: The Great War, America and the Remaking of the Global Order, 1916–1931* (London, 2014).

Toye, Richard, 'The Attlee Government, the Imperial Preference System and the Creation of the GATT', *The English Historical Review* 118 (2003), pp. 912–39.

—, 'From "Consensus" to "Common Ground": The Rhetoric of the Postwar Settlement and Its Collapse', *Journal of Contemporary History* 48.1 (January 2013), pp. 3–23.

—, *The Roar of the Lion: The Untold Story of Churchill's World War II Speeches* (Oxford, 2013).

Trentmann, Frank, *Free Trade Nation: Commerce, Consumption and Civil Society in Modern Britain* (Oxford, 2008).

Trevor-Roper, Hugh, *Hermit of Peking: The Hidden Life of Sir Edmund Backhouse* (Harmondsworth, 1978).

Tribe, Keith, 'Liberalism and Neoliberalism in Britain, 1930–1980', in Philip Mirowski and Dieter Plehwe (eds.), *The Road from Mont Pèlerin: The Making of the Neoliberal Thought Collective* (Cambridge, Massachusetts, 2009), pp. 68–7.

Turner, John (ed.), *Businessmen and Politics* (London, 1984).

Twigge, S. R., *The Early Development of Guided Weapons in the United Kingdom 1940–1960* (Amsterdam, 1993).

Ugolini, Laura, *Men and Menswear: Sartorial Consumption in Britain 1880–1939* (London, 2007).

Urry, John and John Wakeford (eds.), *Power in Britain* (London, 1973).

Vernon, James, *Hunger: A Modern History* (Cambridge, Massachusetts, 2007).

Vernon, Keith, 'Science for the Farmer? Agricultural Research in England 1909–36', *Twentieth Century British History* 8 (1997), pp. 310–33.

Vinen, Richard, *Thatcher's Britain: The Politics and Social Upheaval of the Thatcher Era* (London, 2013).

—, *National Service: Conscription in Britain 1945–1963* (London, 2014).

Waldegrave, William, *A Different Kind of Weather: A Memoir* (London, 2015).

Walker, John R., 'British Nuclear Weapon Stockpiles, 1953–78', *The RUSI Journal* 156 (2011), pp. 66–72.

Ward, Paul, *Britishness since 1870* (London, 2004).

Wardley, Peter, 'The Emergence of Big Business: The Largest Corporate Employers of Labour in the United Kingdom, Germany and the United States *c.*1907', *Business History* 41 (1999), pp. 88–116.

Warpole, Ken, *Dockers and Detectives: Popular Reading, Popular Writing* (London, 1983).

Wasserstein, Bernard, *The Secret Lives of Trebitsch Lincoln* (London, 1988).

Weatherburn, Michael R., 'Scientific Management at Work: The Bedaux System, Management Consulting, and Worker Efficiency in British Industry, 1914–48' (PhD thesis, Imperial College London, 2014), p. 79.

Webb, Sidney and Beatrice, *A Constitution for the Socialist Commonwealth of Great Britain* (London, 1920).

Webster, Charles, *Health Services since the War* (London, 1988).

—, 'Conflict and Consensus: Explaining the British Health Service', *Twentieth Century British History* 1 (1990), pp. 115–51.

Webster, Wendy, *Englishness and Empire 1939–1965* (Oxford, 2005).

Weight, Richard, *Patriots* (London, 2002).

Weight, Richard and A. Beach (eds.), *The Right to Belong: Citizenship and National Identity in Britain, 1930–1960* (London, 1998).

Welshman, John, 'School Meals and Milk in England and Wales, 1906–45', *Medical History* 41 (1997), pp. 6–29.

—, 'Evacuation and Social Policy during the Second World War: Myth and Reality', *Twentieth Century British History* 9 (1998), pp. 28–3.

—, *Underclass A History of the Excluded 1880–2000* (London, 2006).

Werskey, Gary, *The Visible College: A Collective Biography of British Socialists and Scientists in the 1930s* (London, 1978).

Wheatcroft, Geoffrey, *Yo, Blair!* (London, 2007).

Whipp, Richard, 'Crisis and Continuity: Innovation in the British Automobile Industry 1896–1986', in Peter Mathias and John A. Davis (eds.), *Innovation and Technology in Europe: From the Eighteenth Century to the Present Day* (London, 1991).

White, Jerry, *London in the 20th Century* (London, 2001).

White, Nicholas J., 'Government and Business Divided: Malaya, 1945–57', *The Journal of Imperial and Commonwealth History* 22 (1994), pp. 251–74.

Wickham-Jones, M., *Economic Strategy and the Labour Party* (London, 1996).

Wiener, Martin, *English Culture and the Decline of the Industrial Spirit, 1850–1980* (Cambridge, 1981).

Wigham Richardson, John, *Memoirs of John Wigham Richardson 1937–1908* (privately printed, Glasgow, 1911).

Wildman, Charlotte, 'Urban Transformation in Liverpool and Manchester, 1918–1939', *The Historical Journal* 55 (2012), pp. 119–43.

Wilford, Hugh, ' "Unwitting Assets?": British Intellectuals and the Congress for Cultural Freedom', *Twentieth Century British History* 11 (2000), pp. 42–60.

Wilkinson, Ellen, *The Town That Was Murdered* (London, 1939).

Williams, Gavin, 'Marketing without and with Marketing Boards: The Origins of State Marketing Boards in Nigeria', *Review of African Political Economy* 12 (1985), pp. 4–5.

Williams, Philip, *Hugh Gaitskell: A Political Biography* (Oxford, 1982).

Williams, Raymond, *Culture and Society, 1780–1950* (London, 1958).

—, *The Long Revolution* (London, 1961).

— (ed.), *The May Day Manifesto, 1968*, available at https://www.lwbooks. co.uk/sites/default/files/free-book/Mayday.pdf, accessed 2 September 2017.

Williams, Roger, *The Nuclear Power Decisions: British Policies, 1953–78* (London, 1980).

Williamson, Philip, *Stanley Baldwin* (Cambridge, 1999).

Wilson, Harold, *Memoirs* (London, 1986).

Wilson, John E., *British Business History, 1720–1994* (Manchester, 1995).

Wilson, Jon, *India Conquered: Britain's Raj and the Chaos of Empire* (London, 2016).

Wimmer, Andreas and Nina Glick Schiller, 'Methodological Nationalism, the Social Sciences, and the Study of Migration: An Essay in Historical Epistemology', *The International Migration Review* 37.3 (2003), pp. 576–610.

Wincott, D., 'Images of Welfare in Law and Society: The British Welfare State in Comparative Perspective', *Journal of Law and Society* 38 (2011), pp. 343–75.

Winder, Robert, *Bloody Foreigners: The Story of Immigration to Britain* (London, 2005).

Wood, Alan, *Groundnut Affair* (London, 1950).

Wright, Patrick, *On Living in an Old Country* (London, 1985).

—, *The Village That Died for England: The Strange Story of Tyneham* (London, 1995).

Zaidi, Waqar A., 'The Janus-face of Techno-nationalism: Barnes Wallis and the "Strength of England" ', *Technology and Culture* 49 (2008), pp. 62–88.

—, '"A Blessing in Disguise": Reconstructing International Relations through Atomic Energy, 1945–1948', *Past and Present*, Supplement 6 (2011), pp. 309–31.

—, '"Aviation Will Either Destroy or Save Our Civilization": Proposals for the International Control of Aviation, 1920–1945', *Journal of Contemporary History* 46 (2011), pp. 150–78.

Zweig, Stefan, *The World of Yesterday*, trans. Anthea Bell (London, 2009).

Zweiniger-Bargielowska, Ina, *Women in Twentieth-Century Britain* (New York, 2001).

—, *Austerity in Britain: Rationing, Controls and Consumption, 1939–1955* (Oxford, 2002).

Acknowledgements

I arrived in the United Kingdom, out of time, as if a leftover from an older order of things, in 1970. I came by a ship built in Barrow-in-Furness in the 1940s, which carried refrigerated meat and fruit on what was one of its last voyages to the Royal Docks in London, not long for sea-going trade either. Until then, I had lived in Montevideo and Buenos Aires, places formed by British capital, largely before 1914. Without realizing it, I knew the land of my father (born 1903) from the design of railway stations, visiting Royal Navy warships, Senior Service cigarettes, the airmail edition of the *New Statesman,* Lily Bolero on the BBC World Service, Christmas pudding, Scottish dancing at St Andrew's School and Christmas card images of snowy landscapes. The real national United Kingdom of 1970 was unexpectedly and extraordinarily green, cold, damp and (then still) foggy rather than snowy. Food – baked beans, bread with the taste and consistency of cotton wool and inedible meat – was a matter of business, not pleasure. But there was so much to admire and to be amazed at, for example the welfare state, on which we would soon depend, the *Gingerbread* newsletter, the Giro, the double-decker bus and many other mysteries.

I was not especially interested in British history until my eyes were opened by Keith Middlemas' revelatory 1979 book, so very different from what I harshly thought of as the cosy sentimentalities and mindless archive compacting of so much of what stood for twentieth-century British history in the 1980s. Middlemas' book stimulated me into thinking about that history comparatively and indeed to teach British history as part of European history for many years. This book consolidates some arguments I put forward from the early 1990s, but it develops many new ones and takes the story right up to the present and back to 1900 and covers a very much wider range of topics. Its immediate source is my book on the Second World War, which argued for an imperial-internationalist war effort, and saw nationalism as a post-war phenomenon. This book is in some ways a working-out of the import of that analysis of the seminal moment in twentieth-century British history.

A book like this relies on the work of others in ways which make it impossible to acknowledge the source of every idea. It depends on years of reflection and discussion with friends and colleagues, remarks made at seminars and conferences, reviews of books rather than the books themselves and so on. I would like to record my thanks to friends and colleagues at the University of Manchester, and especially the late John Pickstone; my colleagues at the Centre for the History of Science, Technology and Medicine at Imperial College and then at King's College London, especially Jean-Baptiste Fressoz, Rob Iliffe, Andrew Mendelsohn, Andrew Warwick and Abigail Woods. I am grateful to King's College, where I and colleagues relocated in 2013, for their warm welcome, especially Paul Readman and Adam Sutcliffe. I am grateful to two cohorts of students in a special subject on twentieth-century British history for their input, and their interest in once sidelined issues such as trade. New colleagues, especially but certainly not only Joe Maiolo, Richard Vinen and Jon Wilson, have been a constant stimulus, as has my participation in the Sir Michael Howard Centre for the History of War, King's Contemporary British History and the Modern British History Seminar at the Institute for Historical Research. This book is also part of a long and enjoyable conversation with Adam Tooze not least about how new material histories of militarism and capitalism might be written. I am grateful to have been a member of the English Heritage Blue Plaque panel, under Sir David Cannadine, a superbly learned and entertaining body, in which we were educated by experts about now obscure British pugilists, comics, bandleaders, painters and composers, and the odd businessman and historian too. I would also like to thank those PhD students at Imperial College and King's College who took part in a twentieth-century British history reading group and my own students who have also in other ways contributed so much to my understanding of British history, including Thomas Bottelier, Sabine Clarke, Ralph Desmarais, Hermione Giffard, Thomas Kelsey, Stephen Marsh, Emily Mayhew, Alex Oikononou, Galina Shyndriayeva, Ben Taylor, Waqar Zaidi and Michael Weatherburn. Francesca Edgerton shared some reflections on studying British history at university. My old friend Jim Rennie read early drafts carefully and saved me from much grief. Tom Kelsey, Maggie Scull, Richard Vinen and Jon Wilson made many perceptive and helpful comments on the text, as did many PhD students in the Centre for the History of Science, Technology and Medicine. The encouragement and interest of Jim Cronin, Deborah Cohen, Patrick Joyce, Chris Mitchell and Guy Ortolano has been energizing.

I am most grateful to the following for the opportunity to develop elements of my argument in seminar and conference presentations in recent years. I had the pleasure and benefit of speaking at the Deutsches Museum Colloquium; the Department of History, McGill University, Montreal; the Modern British History Seminar, and Reading Group, at the Institute of Historical Research; the Science, Technology and Innovation Seminar, University of Edinburgh; the Department of History, Northwestern University; the Institute of Contemporary British History Summer Conference, King's College London; the War and the Fatherland Conference, Brussels; the Cultural Legacies of WWI Conference at King's College; the Public and Private Workshop, Department of Economic and Social History, University of Glasgow; the Seeley Society, Christ's College, Cambridge; the Foucault: Political Life and History group; and the Rethinking British Neoliberalism Conference at UCL. I am particularly grateful to Helmut Trischler, Elsbeth Heaman, Steve Sturdy, Deborah Cohen, Pat Thane, Kenneth Bertrams, Max Saunders, Neil Rollings, Jim Tomlinson, Colin Gordon, Patrick Joyce and Florence Sutcliffe-Braithwaite for these opportunities. I also benefited from a wonderfully stimulating discussion in Adam Tooze's reading group at Columbia. I am most grateful to Herbert Obinger and Klaus Petersen for inviting me to contribute to their conferences and the comparative project on War and Welfare in the Twentieth Century, which proved invaluable in the writing of this book.

I would like to thank Joanna Richardson, Stephen Wigham

Richardson and Kevin Karney for arranging access to the memoirs of John Wigham Richardson and Sir Philip Wigham Richardson MP. Thomas Gibson kindly sent me a copy of a biography of his grandfather, Sir Herbert Gibson. I am grateful to the Churchill Archives Centre for access to papers in their care. Mrinmoyee Roy helped find illustrations. I am deeply appreciative of the generosity of Linton Kwesi Johnson and Tom Robinson in giving permission to reproduce part of the lyrics of, respectively, 'Inglan Is a Bitch' and 'Glad to Be Gay'. I am grateful to Maggie Scull, Rosemary Rich and Lucía Edgerton for assistance with the text, and to Paolo Edgerton-Bachmann for some calculations and obtaining data. This book would not have existed but for Simon Winder's suggestion I should write it and for his understanding of many challenges of doing so – I owe him a great debt. I would also like to thank David Watson, Ellen Davies and Richard Duguid at Penguin, and my wonderful, and hospitable, agent, Clare Alexander.

Finally, special thanks must go to Claire and our children, Francesca, Lucía, and Andrew. This book is dedicated to my mother, Alicia Edgerton, in her ninetieth year, in the hope it will help her better understand her adopted country.

David Edgerton
January 2018

PERMISSIONS

Index

cruise missiles 434, 441
Cunard (shipping line) 53, 61, 137, 320
Cunliffe-Owen, Hugo 112
Cunningham, George 438–9
Cyprus 355

Daldry, Stephen 458
Dalton, Hugh 119, 161, 212, 214, 215, 218
Dams
  Aswan 136
  Jebel Aulia 100, 136
  Sennar 136
Dangerfield, George 30, 153, 173
Darwin, Charles 155, 162, 169
Davenport, Lord see Kearley, Hudson Ewbanke
Davies, David 109, 109–11
  as advocate of international air police 159
Davies, Donald 331
Davies, John 366
De Gaulle, Charles 270, 272
De L'Isle, Viscount 365, 425
death penalty 420, 427
death rates, changes in 225
Debenhams (firm) 48
decimalization 301
declinism 389–94
  1970s 406
  1980s 450–51
  anti-declinists 392–3, 394
  as anti-history 393, 394, 395–6
  defined 389
  and developmental state 307
  end of under New Labour 508–9
  comparisons to Germany 393, 406

as anti-imperialist, anti-liberal nationalism 389
  as jingoist delusion 390–91
  Hobsbawn as declinist 391
  of the left 391–92
  replaced by revivalism 466–9
  Harold Wilson and 371, 398
  see also Communist Party of Great Britain; technocracy
defence conversion 411
defence expenditures 49, 50, 122, 123, 190, 339, 344, 358, 390, 414, 433–4, 443, 513–14
deflation 121–3, 218, 452
Dell, Edmund 367
demand management 373–5
Department of Economic Affairs 367
Department of Employment 366
Department of Scientific and Industrial Research 143, 185
dependency theory, applied to UK 392
Deptford cattle market 91
Derby, Earl of 105
Development and Road Improvement Act, 1909 184
Development Commission 184
Development Councils 322
developmental state 307–8
  successes of Thatcherism relied on 454–5
Devlin, Bernadette 422
devolution 438–9
Devonshire, Dukes of 106, 115
Dewar, Lord 105
Diego Garcia (islands) 356
direct works, much reduced 461
Dirk Bogarde 332, 333
Distillers (firm) 451

Divorce Reform Act, 1969 420
Dobb, Maurice 163
dockers 84, 200, 205, 290, 324,
458, 498, 519
Docklands Development
Corporation (London) 23, 369
domestic service 199
Dorman Long (firm) 314
Douglas, Keith 45
dreadnoughts *see* warships
drugs 471
dry docks 50, 60–61, 132
Drysdale, Charles 169
Dublin 31
Dunlop Rubber (firm) 313, 317
Democratic Unionist Party 494
Durbin, Evan 161
Durham Miners' Federation 205
Durham Miners' Relief Society
224
Dyson, Sir James 488

Eagle Oil Company 86
East of Suez
withdrawal from 355–7
return to 494, 515
Easter Rising 31
Ebbw Vale steelworks 145, 411
economic nationalism *see*
nationalism, economic
economics 448
see also political economy
economists
advisers 383
health 485
of the left 415–16
Economist 489
Eden, Anthony 254, 275, 277, 279,
364
compared to Blair 516–17

education 76, 196, 202, 223, 306,
339, 365, 196, 365, 172, 306,
407, 433, 461
Conservatives and 306
Education Act, 1902 196
Education Act, 1944 172
elementary schools 42, 196, 223,
306, 365
and eugenics 172
grammar schools 155, 172, 202,
306, 365, 368
Labour and 42, 218, 306, 365
national curriculum 461–2
secondary 42, 172, 196, 306,
365, 461
see also universities
Edward VIII 118, 204
EEC *see* Common Market
EFTA 265, 269, 317, 493
Egerton, Sir Alfred 170
Egypt
Canal Zone bases 77, 276, 355
invasion of, 1956 275–7
revolt, 1919 56
Eisenhower, Dwight 275, 328, 345,
353
Elders & Fyffes (firm) 140
electoral system 36–9, 513, 362
electricity generation 292–4
new coal powered stations
1960s/70s 294
electrification 181–3
privatization 481–2
see also nuclear power
elementary schools *see* education:
elementary schools
Elgar, Edward 176
Eliot, T. S. 155, 381
elite, takes power again
464–5